A Companion to the
Philosophy of Education

Blackwell Companions to Philosophy

This outstanding student reference series offers a comprehensive and authoritative survey of philosophy as a whole. Written by today's leading philosophers, each volume provides lucid and engaging coverage of the key figures, terms, topics, and problems of the field. Taken together, the volumes provide the ideal basis for course use, representing an unparalleled work of reference for students and specialists alike.

A Companion to the Philosophy of Education

Edited by

Randall Curren

Blackwell
Publishing

350 Main Street, Malden, MA 02148-5018, USA
108 Cowley Road, Oxford OX4 1JF, UK
550 Swanston Street, Carlton South, Melbourne, Victoria 3053, Australia
Kurfürstendamm 57, 10707 Berlin, Germany

First published 2003 by Blackwell Publishing Ltd

Library of Congress Cataloging-in-Publication Data

A companion to the philosophy of education / edited by Randall Curren.
        p. cm. — (Blackwell companions to philosophy; 27)
Includes bibliographical references and index.
    ISBN 0-631-22837-3 (alk. paper)
    1. Education—Philosophy. I. Curren, Randall R. II. Series.
    LB17·C64 2003
    370′·1—dc21
                                        2002007777

A catalogue record for this title is available from the British Library.

Set in 10/12.5pt Photina
by Kolam Information Services Pvt. Ltd, Pondicherry, India
Printed and bound in the United Kingdom
by TJ International, Padstow, Cornwall

For further information on
Blackwell Publishing, visit our website:
http://www.blackwellpublishing.com

Contents

Notes on Contributors

Jonathan E. Adler is Professor of Philosophy at Brooklyn College and the Graduate School, City University of New York. He is an epistemologist whose areas of research and publication also include ethics, informal logic, philosophy of psychology, and philosophy of education. His publications include the book *Belief's Own Ethics* (2002).

David Archard is Reader in the Department of Moral Philosophy at the University of St Andrews, UK. He has published *Children: Rights and Childhood* (1993), and numerous articles and chapters in social, political, moral, and applied legal philosophy. His most recent book is *Sexual Consent* (1998).

Hanan A. Alexander is Associate Professor in the Faculty of Education and head of the Center for Jewish Education and the Ethics and Education Project at the University of Haifa, Israel, and a former Vice President for Academic Affairs and Dean of the Fingerhut School of Education at the University of Judaism in Los Angeles. He was Editor-in-Chief of the journal *Religious Education* from 1991 to 2000, and is the author of *Reclaiming Goodness: Education and the Spiritual Quest* (2001).

Minda Rae Amiran is Emerita Professor of English at the State University of New York, Fredonia. She chaired the English departments there and at Tel Aviv University, Israel, served nine years as an academic dean, was a consultant to the Department of Research and Evaluation of the Chicago Board of Education, served on college accreditation teams for two regional accrediting associations, and has presented and published widely on the assessment of general education.

Ronald Barnett is Professor of Higher Education and Dean of Professional Development at the Institute of Education, University of London, UK. He has published extensively in the theory and conceptual analysis of the university and higher education, his latest book being *Realizing the University in an Age of Supercomplexity* (1999).

Christian Barry is the commissioning editor of *Ethics and International Affairs*, and a consultant for the United Nations Development Program. He was a co-author of *Human Development Report 2000: Human Rights and Human Development*. His work focuses on the theory and measurement of human rights.

Frederick C. Beiser is Professor of Philosophy at Syracuse University and has taught previously at Yale, Indiana University, and the Universities of Wisconsin, Pennsylvania, and Colorado. His publications include *Fate of Reason* (1987), *Enlightenment, Revolution and Romanticism* (1992), and *Early Political Writings of the German Romantics* (1996).

Norman E. Bowie is the Elmer L. Andersen Chair in Corporate Responsibility at the University of Minnesota, where he holds a joint appointment in the Department of Philosophy and the Carlson School of Management. His most recent book is *Business Ethics: A Kantian Perspective* (1999).

Bernard Boxill is Professor of Philosophy at the University of North Carolina at Chapel Hill. He is the author of *Blacks and Social Justice* (1984, 1991) and the editor of *Race and Racism* (1991). His article "The Morality of Reparations" appeared in 1972 and has been widely reprinted.

Harry Brighouse is Professor of Philosophy at the University of Wisconsin at Madison, and was for two years Professor of Philosophy of Education at the London Institute of Education. He is the author of *School Choice and Social Justice* (2000) and other works in political philosophy and philosophy of education, and is co-editor of the journal *Theory and Research in Education*.

Noël Carroll is Monroe C. Beardsley Professor of Philosophy at the University of Wisconsin at Madison. His special research areas include aesthetics and the philosophy of history. His most recent books are *Philosophy of Mass Art* (1998) and *Philosophy of Art: A Contemporary Introduction* (1999).

David E. Cooper is Professor of Philosophy at the University of Durham. His many books include *Authenticity and Learning: Nietzsche's Educational Philosophy* (1992), *Existentialism: A Reconstruction* (1999), *World Philosophies: An Historical Introduction* (1995), and *Humanism, Humility and Mystery* (2002).

Randall Curren is Associate Professor, jointly appointed in the Department of Philosophy and the Margaret Warner Graduate School of Education and Human Development, at the University of Rochester. He is the author of *Aristotle on the Necessity of Public Education* (2000) and other works in moral, political, legal, and educational philosophy, and is co-editor of the journal *Theory and Research in Education*.

Andrew Davis is Senior Lecturer in Education at Durham University, UK, where he directs the Primary Mathematics provision and the PGCE Primary Course. For many years he taught children aged from four to eleven. His contributions to the theory of educational assessment include *The Limits of Educational Assessment* (1998) and *Educational Assessment: A Critique of Current Policy* (1999).

Michael Davis is Senior Fellow at the Center for the Study of Ethics in the Professions and Professor of Philosophy at the Illinois Institute of Technology. He is the author of over 120 articles and four books, including *Thinking Like an Engineer* (1998) and *Ethics and the University* (1999), and co-editor of three books, including *Conflict of Interest in the Professions* (2001).

Wendy Donner is Professor of Philosophy at Carleton University in Ottawa, Ontario. She is the author of *The Liberal Self: John Stuart Mill's Moral and Political Philosophy* (1991) and other works on Mill's utilitarianism, feminism, and political philosophy.

James Dwyer is Associate Professor in the Marshall Wythe School of Law at the College of William and Mary. He is the author of *Religious Schools v. Children's Rights* (1998) and *Vouchers within Reason: A Child-centered Approach to Education Reform* (2002).

Robert K. Fullinwider is Senior Research Scholar at the Institute for Philosophy and Public Policy, University of Maryland, and during 1996–8 was research director for the National Commission on Civic Renewal, whose report, *A Nation of Spectators*, appeared in 1998. He is the author of *The Reverse Discrimination Controversy* (1980) and other works in moral, social, and educational philosophy, editor of *Public Education in a Multicultural Society* (1995) and *Civil Society, Democracy, and Civic Renewal* (1999), and is presently co-authoring a book on college admissions.

William Galston is Director of the Institute for Philosophy and Public Policy, and Professor in the School of Public Affairs at the University of Maryland at College Park. He is the author of *Liberal Purposes: Goods, Virtues, and Diversity in the Liberal State* (1991), *Justice and the Human Good* (1980), and many other works in political and social philosophy, American politics, and public policy. He served as Deputy Assistant to President Clinton for Domestic Policy (1993–5) and is Executive Director for the National Commission on Civic Renewal (USA).

Christopher Gill is Professor of Ancient Thought at the University of Exeter, UK. His books include *Greek Thought* (1995) and *Personality in Greek Epic, Tragedy, and Philosophy* (1996). He has edited several collections of essays, including *The Person and the Human Mind: Issues in Ancient and Modern Philosophy* (1990), and *Form and Argument in Late Plato* (1996). He is completing a book on Hellenistic and Roman psychology and ethics.

Shmuel Glick is Director of the Schocken Institute of the Jewish Theological Seminary of America and teaches Education and Rabbinic Literature at the Schechter Institute of Jewish Studies. He is author of *Education in Light of Israeli Law and Halakhic Literature*, two volumes (1999, 2000), and editor of *Simcha Assafs' Mekorot le-toldot ha-Hinukh be-Yisrael (A Source-Book for the History of Jewish Education from the Beginning of the Middle Ages to the Period of the Hasklah* [nineteenth century]), two volumes (2001).

Amy Gutmann is Provost and Laurance S. Rockefeller University Professor of Politics at Princeton University, and was the founding Director of the Princeton University Center for Human Values. She is author, most recently, of a new edition of *Democratic Education* (1999), (with Dennis Thompson) *Democracy and Disagreement* (1998), and (with Anthony Appiah) *Color Conscious* (1996), and editor of *Freedom of Association* (1998).

Paul Hager is Professor of Education at the University of Technology, Sydney, Australia. His research interests include philosophy of education, critical thinking, informal learning at work, and Bertrand Russell's philosophy. His publications include *Continuity and Change in the Development of Russell's Philosophy* (1994) and *Life, Work and Learning: Practice in Postmodernity* (2002).

Graham Haydon is Lecturer in Philosophy of Education, and Course Leader of the MA in Values in Education, at the Institute of Education, University of London, and a former Lecturer in Moral Philosophy at the University of Glasgow, UK. He is author of *Teaching about Values* (1997) and *Values, Virtues and Violence: Education and the Public Understanding of Morality* (2000).

Craig Kallendorf is Professor of English and Classics at Texas A&M University. His most recent books are *Virgil and the Myth of Venice: Books and Readers in the Italian Renaissance* (1999), and an edition and translation of the works of four Italian Renaissance humanists for I Tatti Studies.

Douglas Kellner is George Kneller Chair in the Philosophy of Education at UCLA, and is author of many books on social theory, politics, history, and culture, including *Herbert Marcuse and the Crisis of Marxism* (1984), *Critical Theory, Marxism, and Modernity* (1989), *Jean Baudrillard: From Marxism to Postmodernism and Beyond* (1989), *Television and the Crisis of Democracy* (1990), *Media Culture* (1995), and (with Steven Best) *Postmodern Theory: Critical Interrogations* (1991) and *The Postmodern Turn* (1997).

Robert F. Ladenson is Professor of Philosophy in the Department of Humanities, and Faculty Associate in the Center for the Study of Ethics in the Professions, at the Illinois Institute of Technology. He specializes in practical and professional ethics, the philosophy of law, and political and moral philosophy. He is also a special education hearing officer for the State of Illinois.

Wolfgang Mann is Associate Professor of Philosophy at Columbia University. He works principally on Greek philosophy, and is the author of *Aristotle's Categories and Their Context* (2000) and other works in the history of philosophy.

Peter J. Markie is Professor of Philosophy and Vice Provost for Undergraduate Studies at the University of Missouri at Columbia. He is the author of *Descartes's Gambit* (1986), *A Professor's Duties* (1995), and articles in the history of modern philosophy, ethics, and logic. He is the editor with Steven M. Cahn of the anthology *Ethics* (1999).

Jane Roland Martin is Professor of Philosophy Emerita at the University of Massachusetts, Boston, and a past president of the Philosophy of Education Society. Her most recent book, *Coming of Age in Academe*, was published in 2000. Her earlier works include *Reclaiming a Conversation* (1985), *The Schoolhome* (1992), and *Changing the Educational Landscape* (1993).

Gareth B. Matthews is Professor of Philosophy at the University of Massachusetts, Amherst. He is the author of *Socratic Perplexity and the Nature of Philosophy* (1999), *The Philosophy of Childhood* (1996), and *Thought's Ego in Augustine and Descartes* (1992), and the editor of *The Augustinian Tradition* (1998).

Michael R. Matthews is Associate Professor of Education at the University of New South Wales, Sydney, Australia. He has degrees in geology, psychology, philosophy, philosophy of education, and the history and philosophy of science. He is the author of four books, editor of four books, and editor of the journal *Science and Education*. His most recent book is *Time for Science Education* (2000).

Gabriel Moran is Professor in the Philosophy of Education Program at New York University, and for the past twenty years has been an active member in the International Seminar on Religious Education and Values. He is the author of more than a dozen books on religious education, most recently *Reshaping Religious Education* (1998) and *Both Sides: The Story of Revelation* (2001).

G. Felicitas Munzel is Associate Professor in the Program of Liberal Studies at the University of Notre Dame. She is the author of *Kant's Conception of Moral Character* (1999), articles on Kant, moral and political philosophy, and aesthetics, and translator of Kant's 1775/6 Friedlaender Lectures on anthropology. With a grant from the Earhart Foundation she is currently working on *Immanuel Kant: Philosopher-Educator*, on the relation of Kant's critical philosophy to the eighteenth-century education reform debates.

D. C. Phillips is Professor of Education and, by courtesy, Professor of Philosophy at Stanford University, where he has also served as Interim Dean of the School of Education. A Past-President of the Philosophy of Education Society, he is author, co-author, or editor of ten books and has published more than a hundred essays in philosophy of education and philosophy of social science. His most recent work is on constructivism and philosophical issues in educational research.

C. D. C. Reeve is Professor of Philosophy at the University of North Carolina at Chapel Hill. He is the author of *Philosopher-Kings* (1988), *Socrates in the Apology* (1989), *Practices of Reason* (1992), and *Substantial Knowledge* (2000). He has translated Plato's *Republic* and *Cratylus* and Aristotle's *Politics*.

Rob Reich is Assistant Professor of Political Science, Ethics in Society, and, by courtesy, Education, at Stanford University, where he also directs the Stanford University Summer Philosophy Discovery Institute for high school students. His publications include *Bridging Liberalism and Multiculturalism in American Education* (2002) and other works in political and educational theory.

Patrick Riley is Oakeshott Professor of Political and Moral Philosophy at the University of Wisconsin-Madison. His books include *The General Will Before Rousseau* (1986), *Leibniz' Universal Jurisprudence* (1996), and *Kant's Political Philosophy* (2002/3). He is the editor of the *Cambridge Companion To Rousseau* (2001), and translator of the works of Bossuet, Fenélon, Malebranche, and Leibniz.

Emily Robertson is dual Associate Professor of Cultural Foundations of Education and Philosophy at Syracuse University, and a past president of the Philosophy of Education Society. Her published scholarship includes works on rationality and education, moral education, the ethics of teaching, and social philosophy.

Richard M. Ryan is Professor of Psychology and Psychiatry at the University of Rochester. He has published over 150 scholarly pieces, including, with Edward Deci, *Intrinsic Motivation and Self-determination in Human Behavior* (1985), and developed with Deci a widely tested theory of motivation, development, and education, known as Self-determination Theory. He has been a visiting scientist at the Max Planck Institute, a Cattell Fellow, and has won awards for both his teaching and his contributions to educational research. He is joined in his chapter in this volume by Martin Lynch, a collaborator in the Human Motivation Research Group at the University of Rochester.

Amy M. Schmitter is Associate Professor of Philosophy at the University of New Mexico. Her main areas of research are the history of early modern philosophy and the philosophy of art. She has published articles on several aspects of Descartes's philosophy and is working on a book on his notion of representation.

Harvey Siegel is Professor of Philosophy at the University of Miami. He is the author of *Relativism Refuted: A Critique of Contemporary Epistemological Relativism* (1987), *Educating Reason: Rationality, Critical Thinking and Education* (1988), *Rationality Redeemed? Further Dialogues on an Educational Ideal* (1997), and many papers in epistemology, philosophy of science, and philosophy of education. He also edited *Reason and Education: Essays in Honor of Israel Scheffler* (1997).

Robert L. Simon is Professor of Philosophy at Hamilton College. He writes in the fields of political and social philosophy, and ethics and sport. He is the author of *Fair Play* (1991), *Neutrality and the Academic Ethic* (1994), and (with Norman E. Bowie) *The Individual and the Political Order* (1998), and is editor of *The Blackwell Guide to Social and Political Philosophy* (2001).

Richard Smith is Professor of Education and Director of Combined Social Sciences at the University of Durham, UK. He was for ten years editor of the *Journal of Philosophy of Education*. He is (with Nigel Blake, Paul Smeyers, and Paul Standish) author of *Thinking Again: Education after Postmodernism* (1998) and *Education in an Age of Nihilism* (2000), and editor of the *Blackwell Guide to the Philosophy of Education* (2002).

Paul Standish is Senior Lecturer in Education at the University of Dundee, UK, and Editor of the *Journal of Philosophy of Education*. His recent books include (with Nigel Blake, Paul Smeyers, and Richard Smith) *Education in an Age of Nihilism* (2000), (edited with Nigel Blake) *Education at the Interface: Philosophical Questions Concerning Education Online* (2000), (edited with Pradeep Dhillon) *Lyotard: Just Education* (2000), and (edited with Francis Crawley and Paul Smeyers) *Universities Remembering Europe* (2000).

Mark Steiner is Professor of Philosophy at the Hebrew University of Jerusalem. He is author of *Mathematical Knowledge* (1975) and *The Applicability of Mathematics as a Philosophical Problem* (1998).

Kenneth A. Strike is Professor and Chair of Educational Policy and Leadership at the University of Maryland, and Professor Emeritus at Cornell. He is a past president of the

Philosophy of Education Society and was elected to the National Academy of Education in 1993. His many works on educational ethics and policy include (with Jonas Soltis) *The Ethics of Teaching* (1992), (with Jonas Soltis and Emil Haller) *The Ethics of School Administration* (1988), *Liberal Justice and the Marxist Critique of Schooling* (1989), and (with Pamela Moss) *Ethics and College Student Life* (1996).

Yael Tamir is Professor of Philosophy and Education at Tel Aviv University, Israel. Her books include *Liberal Nationalism* (1993), *Democratic Education in a Multicultural State* (editor) (1995), and, with Stephen Macedo, *Nomos XLIII: Moral and Politcal Education* (editor) (2002).

Nathan Tarcov is Professor in the Committee on Social Thought, the Department of Political Science, and the College, and Director of the John M. Olin Center for Inquiry into the Theory and Practice of Democracy at the University of Chicago. He is the author of *Locke's Education for Liberty* (1984, 1997) and articles on European and American political thought and American foreign policy. He is editor and translator with Harvey C. Mansfield of *Machiavelli's Discourses on Livy* (1996), editor with Ruth Grant of *Locke's Some Thoughts Concerning Education and Of the Conduct of the Understanding* (1996), and editor with Clifford Orwin of *The Legacy of Rousseau* (1997).

Jennifer Welchman is Associate Professor of Philosophy at the University of Alberta. She is the author of *Dewey's Ethical Thought* (1996) and works in the fields of ethics, applied ethics, and the history of philosophy.

Carol T. Wren is Associate Professor in the Department of Reading and Learning Disabilities of the School of Education at DePaul University in Chicago. Her publications include *Hanging by a Twig: Understanding and Counseling Adults with Learning Disabilities and ADD* (2000), *Learning Disabilities: Diagnosis and Remediation* (1983), and various chapters and articles on education and learning disabilities.

Thomas E. Wren is Professor of Philosophy at Loyola University in Chicago. His publications include *Caring about Morality: Philosophical Perspectives in Moral Psychology* (1991), *Philosophy of Development* (1997), *Moral Sensibilities and Education*, two volumes (1999, 2000), and numerous articles and book chapters. In addition to a doctorate in philosophy he holds masters degrees in education and English.

Preface

This *Companion* would not have existed without the initiative and assistance of Jeff Dean, and the encouragement and advice of Steve Cahn and Eamonn Callan. Their recognition of the need for a volume of this kind was essential to getting the project off the ground. As the plan for the volume took shape in the spring of 2000, Jeff, Eamonn, David Cooper, Harry Brighouse, and Ken Westphal all provided helpful suggestions. Others who offered valuable formative advice in the months that followed include Ronald Barnett, Steve Cahn, Jane Roland Martin, Michael Matthews, Emily Robertson, Amelié Rorty, Francis Schrag, Harvey Siegel, Paul Standish, Patricia White, and an anonymous referee for the press.

Like earlier volumes in the *Blackwell Companions to Philosophy* series, this *Companion* aims to provide in one volume a comprehensive and authoritative overview of its field. Every effort has been made to produce a work of the highest philosophical quality, and one that is accessible to undergraduates and the interested lay public; one that guides readers through the terrain in a way that is not only informative and accurate, but also philosophically fresh and engaging; one that brings together in a coherent manner work of philosophical significance spanning several disciplines, several continents, and several intellectual styles; and one that brings readers face-to-face, as much as possible, with the very thinkers who have shaped the debates and literature of their topics. In an enterprise of this complexity, not every dream can be fulfilled – more than one chapter that was planned did not materialize – but a format that makes space for genuinely creative contributions yields more than enough compensation in the form of unexpected gifts. The 53 contributors to this volume not only provide an unparalleled guide to the philosophy of education as it is, they move the field forward. In accomplishing this, they persevered through more than the normal distractions of academic life, and I am grateful to them for their excellent work, their fortitude, and their patience with my countless queries and requests.

Many others provided suggestions, corrections, bibliographical assistance, and other forms of help. I have probably forgotten as many of them as I can now remember, but they certainly include Julia Annas, Myles Burnyeat, Ann Cudd, Walter Feinberg, Thomas Groome, Paul Hirst, Steve Macedo, Wolfgang Mann, Kathleen McGowan, Ralf Meerbote, Martha Nussbaum, Shirley Ricker, Amartya Sen, Ken Strike, Harold Wechsler, Ed Wierenga, Nicholas Wolterstorff, and Tom Wren. Gabriel

Uzquiano read and provided comments on a draft of chapter 12, and Paul Collins and Margie Shaw read and commented on drafts of several chapters. In her capacity as my research assistant, Margie also provided welcome assistance with proofreading, word processing, and other aspects of production. The Spencer Foundation made it immeasurably easier for me to keep the project on schedule by providing assistance in the form of a generous grant, which provided funds for a research assistant, release from teaching responsibilities, and other expenses.

The format for this work does not give contributors space within their chapters to thank those who have provided them with assistance, so it is fitting that acknowledgment of such assistance be made here. For bibliographical assistance, Amy Schmitter would like to thank Patricia Easton (chapter 6). For their personal recollections of the early years of analytical philosophy of education, the authors of chapter 12 owe thanks to Tom Green and Mike Oliker. For comments on drafts, Jonathan Adler would like to thank Catherine Z. Elgin and Randall Curren (chapter 20). Mark Steiner would like to thank Carl Posy for pointing out errors, Stanley Ocken for corrections and help with the section on "logical applications," and Shmuel Weinberger for help with applications of topology (chapter 25). Amy Gutmann thanks Robert Fullinwider, who suggested the trilogy of aims possessed by educational authorities invoked at the opening of chapter 28. Christian Barry would like to thank Randall Curren, Joanna Piciotto, and Kate Raworth for comments on drafts, and Sidney Morgenbesser, Thomas Pogge, and Amartya Sen for instructive conversations on the themes of chapter 32. Jeff Spiner-Halev deserves thanks for supplying references and material on multiculturalism in recent political philosophy, for chapter 34. Robert Ladenson would like to thank, for their "generous and valuable" comments on drafts, Randall Curren, Michael Davis, Richard Eldridge, Bernard Gert, Roger Gilman, Owen Goldin, Austin Lewis, Martin Malin, Stephen Nathanson, Fay Sawier, Francis Schrag, and Ujjval Vyas. He also wishes to thank the Illinois Institute of Technology for a sabbatical leave in the fall of 2000, when his work leading to chapter 37 began, and the Department of Philosophy at Marquette University, which provided a stimulating and warmly collegial setting for the work. Minda Rae Amiran and I owe thanks to Amelié Rorty for formative advice and comments on the plan for chapter 39. Finally, Michael Davis would like to thank Louis Lombardi, Warren Schmaus, and Vivian Weil, as well as the audiences which responded to presentations of earlier versions of chapter 42.

Randall Curren
Rochester, New York

Introduction

The philosophy of education has enjoyed a notable resurgence in recent years, a resurgence fueled in part by developments in related branches of practical philosophy, or philosophy that is concerned with the conduct and guidance of human affairs. Philosophy of education is a field that is nourished by and largely ancillary to political philosophy and ethics, and much of what is most admirable in philosophy of education pertains to the politics and ethics of education. This is only part of the truth, however. Public debates have been an important stimulus to philosophical examination of educational issues, other philosophical sub-disciplines provide vital foundations for philosophy of education, and the wealth of recent work on the history of philosophy – work that is both philosophically significant and seriously historical – has been salutary in documenting the wealth of attention to educational questions through much of the history of philosophy, and in retrieving forgotten but valuable ways of thinking about education. From the time of Socrates onward, philosophy's claim to be a worthwhile enterprise has rested largely on its educative functions, and to flesh out this defense of philosophy (as Plato does in his dialogue the *Gorgias*, for instance) is *inter alia* to engage in philosophy of education.

Like other forms of *normative* inquiry concerned with distinct domains of practice, philosophy of education is shaped not only by the philosophical problems and resources it brings to its domain, but by the practical problems and perplexities intrinsic to that domain. Issues of authority, liberty, responsibility, justice, equality, and professional ethics are common to the various branches of practical philosophy, but philosophy of education must grapple with normatively significant features of and developments in the world of education, just as bioethics must grapple with normatively significant features of and developments in the world of medicine and biomedical research. The shortcomings and strengths of educational practices, policies, proposals, and theories are grist for the philosopher of education's mill. So while it is true that philosophy of education has benefited from the fact that political philosophy has recently begun to address questions about *children* that had been long neglected, philosophy of education has also benefited from the fact that some of the prominent public debates about education in recent years, including debates about parental choice in education, public support for religious schools, and the accomodation of students with disabilities, have been good candidates for philosophical inquiry.

Philosophy of education is also like other branches of practical philosophy in requiring serious engagement with the facts about its domain. Progress depends, as it does in any field of practical philosophy, on getting the facts right and developing conceptual frameworks adequate to the specific phenomena and institutional contexts in question. As it happens, the facts about education are dauntingly complex and elusive, and are also in some respects the concern of other philosophical sub-disciplines. Hence, although philosophy of education was integral to moral and political philosophy through much of the history of philosophy (the point of ethics being, in the view of Aristotle and others, not just to know what virtue is, but to possess and exercise it), it has also been associated with epistemology, the philosophy of mind, and the philosophy of language. This should not be surprising. Knowledge is a goal of education and the primary object of epistemological inquiry. Learning, understanding, remembering, thinking, and reasoning are mental phenomena that epistemology, the philosophy of mind, and the philosophy of psychology have been concerned with. Teaching is, among other things, a form of communication that relies upon language and shapes the language acquisition and language patterns of learners. It is thus not far removed from phenomena that philosophy of language and cognitive science are legitimately concerned with.

The present situation is admittedly quite different from that faced by Plato, Aristotle, Locke, or Rousseau, however. Philosophical accounts of human nature and the mind have been significantly displaced by scientific inquiry – displaced enough that one cannot pretend to have a serious philosophical account of such things without thoroughly mastering and in some way accommodating, contributing to, or cogently critiquing the relevant science. The demands inherent in this, especially in the decades since the displacement of behaviorist psychology by cognitive science, no doubt explain the decline in recent years of philosophy of education that is directly engaged with learning theory and topics associated with it. Nevertheless, some legitimate philosophical tasks remain even here. Cognitive science is an interdisciplinary enterprise to which philosophers have made substantial contributions, and it is certainly possible that they might do so in a way that sheds light on learning and instruction. Quite apart from this, however, there are conceptual and synthetic aspects of educational theory that fall within the purview of philosophy. Educational theory aspires to provide a systematic body of principles generated, tested, and justified by practical success as much as through research in the disciplines, and philosophy can play several roles in this enterprise.

Because educational theories are necessarily transdisciplinary, any approximation to a systematic theory of education will outstrip the resources of any one discipline. However, philosophy seems to be better equipped than other disciplines to undertake the conceptual and synthetic work necessary to the construction of a transdisciplinary practical theory. Philosophy is unlike other disciplines in engaging in rigorous normative inquiry, and in concerning itself with the nature and structure of theories as such. Inasmuch as a theory of education is a practical theory, aiming to guide educational practice, it has essential normative components: what are the educational aims to which the lessons of empirical investigation and educational experience will be harnessed, and what are the normative constraints on the manner, content, circumstances, and distribution of education? Philosophy is uniquely equipped to secure these normative components of educational theory, and it is important that it do so. It is also well suited to theoretical synthesis and critique. The role of philosophical synthesis is illustrated by *constructivism*, the currently reigning example of a unifed theory of education, which grew out of psychological theories of learning and instruction, but is rich in philosophical content and inferences. The examination of the philosophical content and inferences in such theories is a more manageable task than the construction of better theories, but these critical and constructive tasks are both feasible and desirable philosophical enterprises. Educational theory is no more empirical than normative – no more the province of science than philosophy – and a well trained philosopher is at least as well attuned to the architecture and adequacy of action-guiding theories as a well trained scientist is. On a smaller scale, there are more specific aspects of educational practice that are only marginally informed by the sciences and can be usefully informed by philosophical analysis. For instance, there are aspects of educational measurement, such as the testing of critical thinking, to which philosophers are making substantial contributions.

A final vital task for philosophy of education in evidence in this volume is to bring a philosophical grasp of the disciplines and arts to bear on the teaching of those disciplines and arts. The philosophies of science, mathematics, and other disciplines are concerned with the nature and structure of science, mathematics, and other disciplines as forms of inquiry and bodies of knowledge. In order to teach a subject with sensitivity to its epistemic structure, teachers must grasp and be guided by the same kind of understanding that philosophers seek – a secure, if nontechnical, sense of the methods of discovery and investigation, of the methods and logic of confirmation, and of the forms of explanation and theory that define their subject as a mode of inquiry. Moreover, they must attend to these aspects of their subjects both in teaching and in evaluating their students. Teachers of the arts would benefit similarly from a philosophical grasp of the communicative and educative capacities of the arts.

This volume is organized into four parts: Historical and Contemporary Movements, Teaching and Learning, The Politics and Ethics of Schooling, and Higher Education. The intent of the first of these parts is not to provide an exhaustive survey of philosophers of education and philosophical treatments of educational questions, which would be impossible in a single volume of this size. The aim, rather, is to provide a historically accurate and philosophically engaging introduction to the major movements and traditions that have most shaped and continue to shape educational thought. The remaining parts aim to provide a similarly accurate and engaging introduction to the major topics in educational theory, policy, and practice that are amenable to philosophical investigation. They divide the field in the way that seems most natural, given the foregoing observations and the distinctness of many issues pertaining to higher education. Other organizational structures might have served equally well, however, and there are many points of contact between topics in different parts. It should be noted in particular that the chapters on teaching and learning are not exclusively concerned with primary and secondary education; the topics addressed in them generally cut across all levels of education.

The resurgence of work in philosophy of education in recent years has not been confined to philosophers working in departments of philosophy and schools and departments of education. It has also been the product of philosophers and other scholars working in political science departments, law schools, humanities programs, and elsewhere. This volume is the first of its kind in attempting to bring together the best of all of this work, and in doing so it should serve to make the field of philosophy of education more transparent to its disparate and scattered practitioners, and thereby more easy to teach, to learn, and to advance. It also brings this work together in a way that is both retrospective and forward looking. Some of the topics addressed here have been widely discussed for years, but others, though ripe for philosophical investigation, have received relatively little attention. A synthesis of this kind will have fulfilled its function if it not only provides a serviceable resource and handbook of its field, but also serves as a stimulus to further work.

Part I

HISTORICAL AND CONTEMPORARY MOVEMENTS

1

The Socratic Movement

C. D. C. Reeve

Education in Classical Athens

Slave or free? Citizen or foreign? Rich or poor? Male or female? These questions largely determined the course of one's education (*paideia*) – as of one's life – in ancient Athens. Slaves, whether the children of slaves or war captives, were excluded from the gymnasia and wrestling schools (*palaistrai*) which prepared young males for future citizenship. The only training they received was in their domestic duties, which might include attending something like a cooking school, or in the art or craft (*technē*) of their master or someone else, or in what we now refer to as the sex industry – prostitution was legal in Athens. Unless their art or craft required it or they were *paidagōgoi*, who accompanied their master's sons to school and sat with them through the lessons, slaves did not learn to read or write.

Crafts were not the exclusive prerogatives of slaves, however. Poorer citizens as well as free foreigners worked as craftsmen. And their sons typically received an elementary education in *mousikē* and *gymnastikē* (described below) before being apprenticed in their father's workshop. Though training in a craft was not thought of as education in the strict sense, some knowledge of crafts such as medicine was considered – at least by some theorists – to be part of the repertoire of a well educated citizen.

After the creation of the Athenian *polis* (city, city-state) in the late seventh century BCE, free women spent their time at home. There they learned to spin, cook, take care of children, and manage the household. No schools were provided for women and, even in the Hellenistic period, illiteracy rates were higher among them than among men. Nonetheless, some women were well educated. Aspasia, the Milesian-born mistress of Pericles, is said to have taught rhetoric and to have had discussions with Socrates, and both Plato and Epicurus, as well as earlier Pythagoreans, are known to have admitted women into their schools.

For the first few years a boy was looked after by his mother or nurse (usually a slave). He played games and listened to stories based on traditional myths. Later he received elementary education, typically at the hands of three different teachers. The *paidotribēs* taught gymnastics, games, and general physical fitness, usually in the palestra. The *kitharistēs* taught music, lyric poetry, and song. The *grammatistēs* taught reading, writing, mathematics, and literature. Here a boy learned Homer and Hesiod by heart, not just for their beauty and cultural importance, but as a way of acquiring Greek moral values. Frequent public competitions in athletics, dance, music, recitation – often coinciding with religious festivals – provided an opportunity for both the exhibition of skill and its evaluation by adults.

By the mid-fourth century BCE, and probably earlier, Athens required the legitimate sons of Athenian citizens of all classes to undergo two years of compulsory, state-sponsored, military training (*ephēbeia*), beginning at age eighteen (see Plato, *Republic*). This was supervised by a *kosmētēs* and by ten (later twelve) *sōphronistai*, one from each Athenian tribe. In the first year, it consisted of physical training and technical weapons instruction conducted in a barracks in Piraeus. In the second year, *ephēboi* served at the frontier posts of Attica. From the third century BCE, with the decreased significance of citizen militia, intellectual training in philosophy, literature, rhetoric, and music came to play an increasing role in the *ephēbeia*.

From puberty (which probably occurred quite late in the ancient world) until he grew a full beard, an adolescent Athenian male was sexually pursued by older males. This *paiderasteia*, as it was called, was supposed to provide sexual pleasure for the older male (*erastēs*) and an education in male virtue, but no sexual pleasure, for his "boy" (*pais, erōmenos*). When the boy grew to manhood, he was supposed to become an *erastēs* in turn and cease to play the role of an *erōmenos*. The *symposium*, or drinking party, was a locus both for the transmission of traditional values and for male homosexual bonding. Its political and educational significance – somewhat strange to us – is manifest in the attention paid to it by Plato in his *Protagoras* and *Laws*.

By the late fifth century BCE, it was possible for Athenians to acquire further education by attending the lectures, or listening to the conversations, of a group of itinerant "professors," the sophists. Though not organizationally, doctrinally, or methodologically a school of any sort, the sophists tended to be pragmatic, naturalistic, humanistic, agnostic in religious matters, and relativistic (in some sense) in ethical ones. The sophists popularized Ionian natural philosophy (Thales, Anaximander, Anaximenes, Heraclitus), taught history, geography, and anthropology, and pioneered the systematic study of language, including techniques of argument and persuasion, grammar, literary criticism, and semantics. As a consequence, they were seen as potentially subversive of traditional values, especially by more conservative citizens.

Socrates (470/69–399 BCE)

Socrates was the son of Phaenarete, a midwife, and Sophroniscus, a stone-carver. In Plato's *Euthyphro* (11b), he traces his ancestry to the mythical sculptor Daedalus, so it may be that he too practiced his father's craft early in life. He served as a hoplite (heavily armored infantryman) in the Athenian army during the Peloponnesian War with Sparta, where he gained attention for his courage, his capacity to tolerate hunger, thirst, and cold, and powers of concentration that could keep him rooted to the spot for hours on end. Since hoplites had to own property and provide their own weapons, Socrates cannot have been very poor. Still, he seems to have been exceptionally frugal in his habits. He often went barefoot, seldom bathed, and wore the same thin cloak winter and summer. In a society that worshipped male beauty, he was noteworthy for his ugliness. He had a snub-nose, bulging eyes, thick lips, and a pot belly. Yet his personal magnetism was such that many of the best looking young men avidly sought out his company. In Plato's *Symposium*, indeed, he characterizes himself as a master of the art of erotic attraction (*ta erōtika*), though that characterization no doubt involves some ironic punning, since the verb *erōtan* means to ask questions.

In 406 BCE, Socrates served on the steering committee (*prytaneis*) of the Athenian Assembly, where he alone voted against an illegal motion to try as a group the generals who had failed to pick up the bodies of the dead after the sea battle at Arginusae. Later, at the risk of his own life, he disobeyed the unjust order of the Thirty Tyrants to bring in Leon of Salamis for execution.

In 423 BCE, he was made the subject of Aristophanes' comedy, *Clouds*, as he was of other non-extant comedies by other authors, including Amipsias and Eupolis. In *Clouds*, he appears: first, as the head of the *phrontistērion*, a school where, for a small fee, one can learn the just logic, which represents traditional aristocratic values, and also the unjust logic, which represents the new values of the sophists; second, as the ascetic high priest of a mystery religion, who teaches a variety of sciences, including a mechanistic theory of the cosmos, on the basis of which he denies the existence of Zeus and the other gods of tradition, worshipping in their place the various forms of Air, including the eponymous Clouds. It is not much of a reach to conclude that Socrates must have looked enough like other sophists to lend popular credibility to Aristophanes' portrait.

In any case, he was brought to trial in 399 BCE on a charge of corrupting the youth by teaching them not to believe in the gods, found guilty (in large part, he claims, because of the prejudice against him fanned by Aristophanes), and condemned by a close vote to death by hemlock poisoning. Central, it seems, to the prosecution's case was one of the most puzzling aspects of Socrates: his *daimonion* or spiritual voice, which held him back whenever he was about to do something wrong. Though this may, in fact, have been no different from other acceptable forms of religious practice, in someone already suspected of being an atheistic sophist, it no doubt seemed – or could be made to seem – much more sinister and subversive.

Socrates' personal characteristics played, and continue to play, a very significant role in attracting devotees to him. He demonstrates – what every teacher knows – that charisma can be as important as content. If Socrates hadn't been *erōtikos*, if he hadn't had that certain compelling something, who would have listened to what he had to say? As it is, however, many listened. And since Socrates himself wrote nothing, it is to those who did that we must turn for information. The problem is that some of the writings of those who knew him – Antisthenes, Phaedo of Elis, Eucleides of Megara, Aristippus of Cyrene, Aeschines of Sphettos – have disappeared or exist only in very fragmentary form, while others that we do possess – those of Aristophanes, Plato, and Xenophon – present us with very different portraits. Moreover, Plato's own portrait is a double one, at least: the Socrates of his early dialogues (*Apology, Charmides, Crito, Euthyphro, Hippias Minor, Hippias Major, Ion, Laches, Lysis, Menexenus*) is thought to be based to some extent on the historical figure (they are often called "Socratic" dialogues for this reason). The Socrates who appears in his transitional (*Euthydemus, Gorgias, Meno, Protagoras*), middle (*Cratylus, Parmenides, Phaedo, Phaedrus, Republic, Symposium, Theaetetus*), and some of his late (*Critias, Philebus, Sophist, Statesman, Timaeus, Laws, Seventh Letter*) dialogues, however, seems to be increasingly a mouth-piece for his own developing doctrines. When we look at Socrates, therefore, we are perforce looking at many potentially different figures. For some were influenced by the historical Socrates, some by portrayals of him only some of which we know, some more by the man and his character, and some more by his specific doctrines.

Nonetheless, a few significant ideas come close to being the common property of these different figures: (1) knowledge or theory (*logos*) is important for virtue; (2) virtue is important for happiness; (3) the sort of self-mastery (*enkrateia*), self-sufficiency (*autarkeia*), and moral toughness (*karteria*) exhibited by Socrates with regard to pleasures and pains is important for happiness; (4) the use of questioning based on *epagōgē* (induction, arguing from parallel cases) is important with regard to the possession of knowledge, and so of virtue; (5) *erōs* and friendship have important roles to play in philosophy, and philosophy in life; (6) the traditional teachers of virtue (the poets), as well as the alleged embodiments of wisdom (the politicians), are deficient in various ways that questioning reveals.

These ideas are vague, of course, and so can be understood in various ways. Socrates could hardly have influenced Cynics, Cyrenaics, Stoics, Epicureans, and Skeptics had it been otherwise. Important as these developments are, however, they are overshadowed by the decisive role Socrates played in Plato's thought and, via it, in Aristotle's.

Plato (428–347/8 BCE)

While Plato was still a boy, his father, Ariston, died and his mother, Perictione, married a friend of the great Athenian statesman Pericles. Plato was thus familiar with Athenian politics from childhood and was expected to take up a political career himself. Horrified by actual political events, however, especially the execution of Socrates in 399 BCE, he turned instead to philosophy, thinking that only education in it could rescue mankind from civil war and political upheaval, and provide a sound foundation for ethics and politics (*Seventh Letter*, 324b–326b). It was with Socrates, then, that our Plato began.

As represented in the early dialogues, Socratic philosophy consists almost exclusively in questioning people about the conventionally recognized ethical virtues. "What is justice?" he asks, "Or piety? Or courage? Or wisdom?" Moreover, he takes for granted that there are correct answers to these questions, that each virtue is some definite characteristic or form (*eidos, idea*). And though he does not discuss the nature of these forms, or develop any explicit theory of them or our knowledge of them, he does claim that only they can serve as reliable standards for judging whether any given type of action is an instance of a virtue, and that they can be captured in explicit definitions (*Euthyphro*, 6d–e; *Charmides*, 158e–159a).

Socrates' interest in definitions of the virtues, Aristotle tells us, resulted from thinking of them as ethical first principles (*Metaphysics*, 1078b12–32). That is why, if one does not know *them*, one cannot know anything else of any consequence about ethics (*Hippias Major*, 286c–d, 304-e; *Laches*, 190b–c; *Lysis*, 212a, 223b; *Protagoras*, 361c; *Republic*, 354c). Claiming not to know them himself, Socrates also claims to have little or no other ethical knowledge (*Apology*, 20c, 21b). These disclaimers of knowledge are often characterized as false or ironical, but Aristotle took them at face value (*Sophistical Refutations*, 183b6–8).

Socrates' characteristic way of questioning people is now called an *elenchus* (from the Greek verb *elegchein*, to examine or refute): Socrates asks what some virtue is; the interlocutor gives a definition he sincerely believes to be correct; Socrates then refutes this definition by showing that it conflicts with other beliefs the interlocutor sincerely holds and is unwilling to abandon (often a consideration of parallel or analogous cases plays an important role in eliciting these beliefs). In the ideal situation, which is never actually portrayed in the Socratic dialogues, this process continues until a satisfactory definition emerges, one that is not inconsistent with other sincerely held beliefs, and so can withstand elenctic scrutiny. Since consistency with false beliefs is no guarantee of truth, and untrue definitions are no basis for knowledge, Socrates' use of the *elenchus* seems to presuppose that some sincerely held beliefs are in fact true.

The definitions Socrates encounters in his elenctic examinations of others always prove unsatisfactory. But through these examinations, which are always at the same time self-examinations (*Charmides*, 166c–d; *Hippias Major*, 298b–c; *Protagoras*, 348c–d), he comes to accept some positive theses which have resisted refutation. Among these are the following three famous Socratic "paradoxes": (1) The conventionally distinguished virtues are all identical to wisdom or knowledge (*Charmides*, 174b–c; *Euthydemus*, 281d–e; *Protagoras*, 329b–334c, 349a–361d); (2) this knowledge is necessary and sufficient for happiness or perhaps even identical to it (*Crito*, 48b; *Gorgias*, 471e); (3) no one ever acts contrary to what he knows or believes to be best, so that weakness of will is impossible (*Protagoras*, 352a–358d). Together these three doctrines constitute a very strict kind of ethical intellectualism: they imply that all we need in order to be virtuous and happy is knowledge.

The goal of an *elenchus*, however, is not just to reach adequate definitions of the virtues, or seemingly paradoxical doctrines about weakness of will and virtue, but *moral reform*. For Socrates believes that regular elenctic philosophizing – leading the examined life – makes people happier and more virtuous than anything else can by curing them of the hubris of thinking they know when they don't (*Apology*, 30a, 36c–e, 38a, 41b–c). Philosophizing is so important for human welfare, indeed, that he is willing to accept execution rather than give it up (*Apology*, 29b–d).

In the transitional dialogues, as well as in some earlier ones, Socrates, as the embodiment of true philosophy, is contrasted prejudicially with the sophists. *They* are unscrupulous moral relativists, who think that virtue is different for different people and societies and undertake to teach it for a fee; *he* is an honest moral absolutist, who thinks that virtue is the same for everyone everywhere, claims not to know or teach it, and so accepts no fees. The problem latent in this contrast is that if moral beliefs do vary from culture to culture, it is not clear how the *elenchus*, which seems to rely wholly on them, could reach knowledge of the objective or non-culture-relative moral truth Socrates seeks.

11

In a number of the middle and late dialogues, Plato connects the relativist doctrines he attributes to the sophists with the metaphysical theory of Heraclitus (c.500 BCE), according to which perceptible things or characteristics are in constant flux or change, always *becoming*, never *being*. In the *Theaetetus*, he argues that Protagoras' claim that "man is the measure of all things" presupposes that the world is in flux; in the *Cratylus*, he suggests that the theory of flux may itself be the result of projecting Protagorean relativism onto the world (411b–c). Nonetheless, Plato seems to accept some version of this theory himself, as Aristotle claims (*Metaphysics*, 987a32–34). In *Republic* V, perceptible things and characteristics are characterized as "rolling around as intermediates between what is not and what purely is" (478a–479d; see also *Timaeus*, 52a).

The theory of flux clearly exacerbates the earlier problem with the Socratic *elenchus*. If perceptible things and characteristics are always in flux, how can justice and the other virtues be stable forms? How can there be stable definitions of them to serve as correct answers to Socrates' questions? And if there are no stable definitions, how can there be ethical *knowledge*? More generally, if perceptible things and characteristics are always in flux, always *becoming*, how can anything *be* something definite or determinate? How can one know or say what anything *is*? Aristotle tells us that it was reflection on these fundamental questions that led Plato to "separate" the forms from perceptible things and characteristics, as Socrates did not (*Metaphysics*, 987a29–b1, 1086b2–5). The allegories of the Sun and Line in the *Republic* (507a–511e), which divide reality into the intelligible part and the visible or perceptible part, seem to embody this separation.

Conceived of in this way, forms seemed to offer solutions to the metaphysical and epistemological problems to which the *elenchus* and flux give rise. As intelligible objects, set apart from the perceptible world, they are above the sway of flux, and therefore available as stable objects of knowledge, stable meanings or referents for words. As real mind-independent entities, they provide the definitions of the virtues with the non-conventional subject matter Socratic ethics needs. No surprise, then, that Platonic education culminates in access to them.

Like many putative solutions to philosophical problems, however, Plato's raises new problems of its own. If forms really are separate from the world of flux our senses reveal to us, how can we know them? How can our words connect with them? If items in the perceptible world really are separate from forms, how can they owe whatever determinate being they have to forms? In the *Meno*, *Phaedo*, and *Phaedrus*, Plato answers the first of these questions by appeal to the doctrine of recollection (*anamnēsis*). We have knowledge of forms through prenatal direct contact with them; we forget this knowledge when our souls become embodied at birth; then we "recollect" it in this life when our memories are appropriately jogged (for example, when we undergo elenctic examination). He answers the second question by saying that items in the world of flux "participate" in forms by resembling them. Thus perceptible objects possess the characteristic of beauty because they resemble the form of beauty, which is itself something beautiful (*Phaedo*, 100c; *Symposium*, 210b–211e).

The doctrine of recollection is problematic, however. Among other things, it presupposes the immortality of the soul (*Phaedo*, 69e–88b; *Republic*, 608c–611a; *Phaedrus*, 245c–e). Aware of this, Plato seems to have sought an alternative to it:

recollection is not mentioned in the *Republic* or in the late dialogues. This supposed alternative is dialectic, which is, or is significantly related to, the method of collection and division (*Phaedrus*, 265cff).

Dialectic is introduced in the *Republic* as having a special bearing on first principles – a feature it continues to possess in Aristotle (*Topics*, 101a37–b4) – particularly on those of the mathematical sciences. The importance of these sciences in Plato's thought is twofold. First, they provided a compelling example of a rich body of precise knowledge organized into a deductive system of axioms, definitions, and theorems – a model of what philosophy itself and formal instruction in it might aspire to be. Second, the brilliant mathematical treatment of harmony (musical beauty), developed by Pythagoras of Samos and his followers, suggested a role for mathematics within philosophy itself. It opened up the possibility of giving precise definitions in wholly mathematical terms of all characteristics, including such apparently vague and evaluative ones as beauty and ugliness, justice and injustice, good and evil, and the other things on which Socrates focused (*Republic*, 530d–533e; *Philebus*, 66a). This explains why philosophers, who must come to know forms, must study mathematics intensively from childhood until their thirtieth year (*Republic*, 526cff).

Though mathematics is crucial to philosophy, it does not itself provide us with scientific or expert knowledge (*epistēmē*), because mathematicians treat their first principles in a cavalier way. First, they give no argument for them, but take them simply as hypotheses (*Republic*, 510c–d). And, second, the accounts or definitions they provide for them are conceptually inadequate (527a–b). Yet if the first principles are false or defective, the entire system based on them is threatened. It is here that dialectic comes in. It renders these first principles "unhypothetical," not by deriving them from something yet more primitive (which is impossible), but by defending them against all objections (534b–c, 437a). In the process, they undergo conceptual revamping, so that their consistency with one another – and hence their immunity to an *elenchus* – is revealed and assured. This enables the dialectician to knit them all together into a single unified theory of everything. It is this unified, holistic theory that is now supposed to provide the philosopher with genuine knowledge (533d–534a). Dialectic, then, which philosophers, who have completed their mathematical training, must study for five years, is another major component of the education that leads to the forms – one that brings in the notion of a synthetic or holistic vision that has remained an ideal of liberal education ever since.

What one grasps by means of the unified and universal theory that dialectic makes possible is the form of the good, which seems to be an ideal of rational order or unity expressed in mathematical terms. This somewhat mysterious object provides the philosopher with the kind of knowledge he needs to design a genuinely good or happy city (the ideal city described in the *Republic*). On a larger scale, it also provides the maker of the cosmos, the Demiurge, with the knowledge he needs to perform his cosmic task (*Timaeus*, 29d–30b). For even the gods are bound by the objective truths and values embodied in the forms (*Euthyphro*, 10a–11b).

The emergence to prominence of mathematical science may seem like a major departure from the early dialogues in which ethical and political education are the near exclusive focus. In fact, as we have seen, it is a deeper probing of the problems raised in those dialogues. Ethics and politics remain central, but Plato has become aware that they need to be treated as component parts of a much wider and deeper philosophical theory.

The *Republic*, which is Plato's greatest and most synthetic work, offers us a brilliant attempt to articulate that theory in all its complexity. In Book I, Thrasymachus argues that those who are stronger in any society, the rulers, control education and socialization through legislation and enforcement. But, like everyone else, the rulers are self-interested. Hence they make laws and adopt conventions, including linguistic ones, that are in their own best interests, not those of their weaker subjects. It is these conventions that largely determine their subjects' conceptions of justice and the other virtues. Thus by being trained to follow or obey them, subjects are unwittingly adopting an ideology, a code of values and behavior, that serves not their own but their ruler's interests. That is why Thrasymachus defines justice not as what social-ized subjects, like Socrates, think it is (something genuinely noble and valuable that promotes their own happiness), but as what it really is: the interest of the stronger. Because this argument raises the problem for the *elenchus* we looked at earlier, by representing the beliefs the *elenchus* must rely on as false or untrustworthy, it cannot be fully answered by elenctic argument. That is why Plato abandons the *elenchus* and tries to answer Thrasymachus by developing a positive defense of justice of his own in Books II–X.

At the center of this defense is the concept of the philosopher-king, who unites political power and authority with philosophical knowledge of values based on mathematical science and dialectic – knowledge that is unmediated by conventionally controlled concepts and so is free from the distorting influence of power or ideology. What the philosopher-king does is to construct a political system, including primarily a system of socialization and education, that will distribute the benefits of this specialized knowledge among the citizens at large. For there is no question of the knowledge itself being so disseminated; like much expert knowledge in our own society, it is far too complex and difficult for that. Thus the examined life, which Socrates thought best for all human beings, is now led only by mature adults with extensive scientific and dialectical training.

The nature of the system the philosopher-kings design is based on Plato's psychology or theory of the soul (*psychē*). According to it, there are three fundamentally different kinds of desires within us: *appetitive* ones for food, drink, sex, and the money with which to acquire them; *spirited* ones for honor, victory, and good reputation; and *rational* ones for knowledge and truth (*Republic*, 437b–441c, 580d–581c). Each of these types of desire "rules" in the soul of a different type of person, determining his values. For people most value what they most desire, and so people ruled by different desires have very different conceptions of what is valuable, of their good or happiness. But just which desire "rules" an individual's soul depends on the relative strengths of his desires and the kind of education and socialization he receives. It is scarcely surprising, in light of these views, that Plato believes that the fundamental goal of ethical or political education isn't to put knowledge into people's souls but to train or socialize their desires, turning them around (to the degree possible) from the pursuit of what they falsely believe to be happiness to the pursuit of true happiness (518b–519d).

The famous allegory of the cave illustrates the effects of such education (514a). Uneducated people, tethered (or ruled) by their untrained or unsocialized appetites, see only images of models of the good (shadows cast by puppets on the walls of the cave). They are not virtuous to any degree, since they act simply on their whims. When their appetites are moderated through training in a traditional craft or through physical education and that mix of reading and writing, dance and song that the Greeks called *mousikē*, they are released from these bonds and are now ruled by their necessary or socialized appetites. They have at least that level of virtue required to act prudently and postpone gratification. Plato refers to them as *money-lovers*, since they pursue money as the best means of reliably satisfying their appetitive desires for food, drink, and sex in the long term. They see models of the good (the puppets that cast the shadows). For stable satisfaction of appetitive desires *is* a sort of good.

Further education, now in the mathematical sciences, leaves these people ruled by their spirited desires. They are *honor-lovers*, who seek success in difficult endeavors and the honor and approval it brings. They have true beliefs about virtue and hence that greater level of it which Plato calls "civic" virtue (430c).

Finally, yet further education in dialectic and practical city management results in people who are bound only by their rational desires. They are free from illusion, and see not mere images of the good, but the good itself. They are *wisdom-lovers* or philosophers, who have knowledge rather than mere true belief about virtue, and so are fully virtuous.

Not everyone is able to benefit, however, from all these types of education; there are some at each stage whose desires are too strong for education to break. That is why there are producers, guardians, and philosopher-kings in the ideal city. That is why, as the citizens of the ideal city, they can cooperate with one another in a just system, where the money-loving producers trade their products for the protection provided by the honor-loving guardians and the knowledge provided by the wisdom-loving kings, rather than competing with one another for the very same goods. Nonetheless, everyone in this ideal system is enabled to travel as far out of the cave of unsocialized desires as education can take him given the innate strength of those desires. Thus everyone comes as close to being fully virtuous and to pursuing and achieving genuine happiness as he can. It is this that makes Plato's city both an ethical and a prudential ideal, both maximally just and maximally happy.

This conception of the soul and of the education needed to make a person both virtuous and happy clearly involves significant revisions of Plato's Socratic inheritance. Since appetite may not be adequately socialized or habitutated it can sometimes overpower reason, resulting in weak-willed action (439e–440b). Hence intellectual knowledge of what virtue is and what it requires of us is not sufficient, as Socrates believed, to ensure virtuous action or the happiness it brings; our *desires* must also be appropriately habituated through education and training. Strict intellectualism must therefore be rejected. Moreover, virtue is no longer an all or nothing affair, as knowledge is. True, only the philosopher-kings have the knowledge of the good required for full virtue, but the other citizens, too, have levels of virtue that are by no means to be despised. These differences notwithstanding, Plato, like Socrates, never doubts that philosophical knowledge holds the key to virtue and so to happiness (*Republic*, 473c–e, 499a–c).

Perhaps because of his sense of the depth of the ethical problems Socrates raised, and because mathematical science seemed to offer a new, culturally uncontaminated

15

perspective on them, Plato was able in the *Republic* to think about a host of issues in a wholly fresh and revolutionary way. He argues, for example, that in a just society men and women with the same natural abilities should receive the same education, be eligible for the same social positions, and receive the same social rewards. Somewhat less attractively, he also argues that such a society would have to deny family life and private property at least to its ruling classes (philosophers and guardians), and rigorously censor artistic expression. It isn't a totalitarian urge that underlies these prohibitions, however, but a vivid sense of the power of desire and the need to keep it in bounds by reducing temptation.

Besides writing his dialogues, Plato contributed to philosophy by founding the Academy (385 BCE). This was a center of research and teaching both in theoretical subjects and also in more practical ones. For example, various cities invited its members to help them develop new political constitutions. Though we know little about the organization or curriculum of the early Academy, we can see in it the beginnings of the university. Plato's writings are so extraordinary and captivating that they easily cause us to overlook this other enormous and formative contribution to the philosophy of education. It was Plato's Academy, indeed, that brought his greatest student, Aristotle, to Athens.

Aristotle (384–322 BCE)

Aristotle was born in the small Macedonian town of Stagira in northern Greece. His father, Nicomachus, who died while Aristotle was still quite young, was physician to King Amyntas of Macedon. When Aristotle was seventeen, his uncle, Proxenus, sent him to study at the Academy, where he remained for twenty years, initially as a student, eventually as a researcher and teacher.

On Plato's death in 347 BCE, Aristotle left Athens for Assos in Asia Minor. Three years later he moved to Mytilene on the island of Lesbos, and two years after that he became tutor to the thirteen-year-old Alexander of Macedon – later the Great. In 335, Aristotle returned to Athens and founded his own school, the Lyceum. Alexander died in 323, with the result that anti-Macedonian feeling in Athens grew in strength. Perhaps for that reason, Aristotle left for Chalcis in Euboea, where he died twelve months later at the age of sixty-two.

A list of Aristotle's papers, probably made in the third century BCE, seems to describe most of his extant writings, as well as a number of works, some in dialogue form, that are now lost. When Sulla captured Athens in 87 BCE, these papers were taken to Rome, where they were edited, organized into different treatises, and arranged in a logical sequence by Andronicus of Rhodes in around 30 BCE. Most of the writings he thought to be genuinely Aristotelian have been transmitted to us via manuscript copies produced between the ninth and sixteenth centuries CE. These writings may be classified as follows:

- Logic, dialectic, metaphysics: *Categories, on Interpretation, Prior Analytics, Topics, on Sophistical Refutations, Metaphysics.*

- Science and philosophy of science: *Posterior Analytics, Physics, On the Heavens, On Generation and Corruption, Meteorology, History of Animals, Parts of Animals, Movement of Animals, Progression of Animals, Generation of Animals.*
- Psychology and philosophy of mind: *De Anima, Sense and Sensibilia, On Memory, On Sleep, On Dreams, On Divination in Sleep, On Length and Shortness of Life, On Youth, Old Age, Life and Death, and Respiration.*
- Ethics, politics, philosophy of art: *Nicomachean Ethics, Magna Moralia, Eudemian Ethics, Politics, Rhetoric, Constitution of Athens, Poetics.*

Most of these works are lecture notes written or dictated by Aristotle himself and not intended for publication. Their organization into treatises and the internal division of the treatises into books and chapters may, however, not be his. Nonetheless, that organization reveals immediately – what would in any case become obvious to an attentive reader – that "knowledge" is organized in them into fields that have retained much of their epistemological viability and continue to shape our curricula.

Of the various things in the world described in Aristotle's writings, some have a nature, an internal source of movement, growth, and alteration (*Physics*, 192b8–9, 13–15). Thus, for example, a feline embryo has within it a causal nexus that explains why it grows into a cat, why that cat moves and alters in the ways it does, and why it eventually decays and dies. A house or any other artifact, by contrast, has no such source within it. This nature is the same as the thing's essence (*to ti ēn einai*) or function (*ergon*), which is the same as its end (*telos*). Indeed, its end just is to actualize its nature by performing its function. Aristotle's view of natural things is therefore teleological: he sees them as being defined by an end for which they are striving, and as needing to have their behavior explained by reference to it. It is this end, essence, or function that fixes what the good for that being consists in, and what its perfections or virtues are (*Nicomachean Ethics*, 1098a7–20, *Physics*, 195a23–25).

Many natural things, as well as the products of art or craft, are hylomorphic compounds, compounds of matter (*hulē*) and form (*morphē*). Statues are examples: their matter is the stone or metal from which they are made; their form is their shape. Human beings are also examples: their matter is (roughly speaking) their body; their soul is their form. Thus a human soul is not something separable from a human body, but is more like the structural organization responsible for the body's being alive and functioning appropriately.

This soul consists of distinct, hierarchically organized constituents (*Nicomachean Ethics*, I.13). The lowest rung in the hierarchy is vegetative soul, which is responsible for nutrition and growth, and which is also found in plants and other animals. At the next rung up, we find appetitive soul, which is responsible for perception, imagination, and movement, and so is present in other animals too, but not in plants. This sort of soul lacks reason but, unlike the vegetative, can be influenced by it. The third element in the human soul is reason, which is further divided into the scientific element, which enables us to contemplate or engage in theoretical activity, and the calculative or deliberative element, which enables us to engage in practical or political activity.

Because a human soul contains these different elements, the human good might be defined by properties exemplified by all three of them or by properties exemplified by only some of them. In the famous function argument, Aristotle argues for the latter alternative: the human good is happiness, which is "an active life of the element that has a rational principle" (*Nicomachean Ethics*, 1098a3–4). The problem is that the scientific and the deliberative elements both fit this description. Human happiness might, therefore, consist in practical political activity, or in contemplative theorizing, or in a mixture of both. Even a brief glance at *Nicomachean Ethics* X.6–8 will reveal how hard it is to determine which of these Aristotle has in mind.

The various sciences Aristotle recognizes are what provide us with knowledge of the world, how to live successfully in it, and how to produce what we need to do so. Hence they fall into three distinct types:

- *Theoretical sciences*: theology, philosophy, mathematics, natural sciences.
- *Practical sciences*: ethics, household management, statesmanship, which is divided into legislation and politics, with politics being further divided into deliberative science and judicial science
- *Productive sciences* (crafts, arts): medicine, building, etc.

Of these, the theoretical ones are the Aristotelian paradigm, since they provide us with knowledge of universal necessary truths. The extent to which ethics or statesmanship fits the paradigm, however, is less clear. For a huge part of them has to do not with universal principles of the sort one finds in physics, but with particular cases, whose near infinite variety is not easy to sum up in a formula (*Nicomachean Ethics*, 1109b21; *Rhetoric*, 1374a18–b23). The knowledge of what justice is may well be scientific knowledge, but to know what justice requires in a particular case one also needs equity, which is a combination of virtue and a trained eye (*Nicomachean Ethics*, V. 10). Perhaps, then, we should think of practical sciences as having something like a theoretically scientific core, but as not being reducible to it.

Each Aristotelian theoretical science deals with a genus or natural class of beings having forms or essences. When appropriately regimented, it may be set out as a structure of demonstrations, the indemonstrable first principles of which are definitions of those essences. More precisely, the first principles special to a science are like this. Others that are common to all sciences, such as the principle of non-contradiction and other logical principles, have a somewhat different character. Since all these first principles are necessary truths, and demonstration is necessity-preserving syllogistic deduction, scientific theorems are also necessary.

Though we cannot grasp a *first* principle by demonstrating it from yet more primitive principles, it must, if we are to have any unqualified scientific knowledge at all, be "better known" to us than any of the science's other theorems. This better knowledge is provided by intuition (*nous*) and the process by which principles come within intuition's ken is induction (*Nicomachean Ethics*, 1139b28–9, 1141a7–8).

Induction begins with perception of particulars, which gives rise to retention of perceptual contents, or memories. And from a unified set of such memories experience arises, "when, from many notions gained by experience, one universal supposition about similar objects is produced" (*Metaphysics*, 981a1–7). Getting from particulars to universals, therefore, is a largely non-inferential process. If we simply attend to particular cases – perhaps to all, perhaps to just one – and have some acumen, we will get

18

there (*Prior Analytics*, 68b15–29; *Posterior Analytics*, 88a12–17, 89b10–13). When these universals are appropriately analyzed into their elements and first principles, they become intrinsically clear and unqualifiedly known (*Physics*, 184a16–21).

The inductive path to first principles and scientific knowledge begins with perception of particulars and of perceptually accessible, unanalyzed universals, and leads eventually to analyzed universal essences (first principles) and definitions of them. At this point, induction gives way to deduction, as we descend from these essences to other principles. Perception alone cannot reach the end of this journey, therefore, but without perception it cannot so much as begin. Perception, elaborated in theory, is the window on the Aristotelian world (*Prior Analytics*, 46a17–18; *De Anima*, 432a7–9). This marks that world's major difference from the Platonic alternative. Plato's first principles, the forms, are separate from the perceptible world and are accessible to disembodied souls that lack sense organs altogether. Aristotelian first principles are immanent in the world and are accessible only to souls that have the sense organs needed to make contact with them. As is often noticed, Plato's imagination is dominated by mathematics, Aristotle's by biology.

The first principles proper to a science cannot, of course, be demonstrated within that science: if they could, they would not be genuine *first* principles. They can, however, be defended by dialectic. For, since it "examines," and does so by appeal not to scientific principles but to common or generally accepted opinions (*endoxa*), "dialectic is a process of criticism wherein lies the path to the first principles of all inquiries" (*Topics*, 101a36–b4).

Now opinions are *endoxa* when they are accepted without demurral "by every one or by the majority or by the wise, either by all of them, or by most or by the most notable and illustrious of them," so that the majority do not disagree with the wise about them, nor does either group disagree internally (*Topics*, 100b21–3, 104a8–11). Generally accepted opinions, therefore, are beliefs to which there is simply no worthwhile opposition. Apparent *endoxa*, by contrast, are beliefs that mistakenly appear to have this uncontested status.

Defending first principles on the basis of *endoxa* is a matter of going through the difficulties (*aporiai*) on both sides of a subject until they are solved (*Topics*, 101a35). Suppose, then, that the topic to be dialectically investigated is: is being one and unchanging, or not? A competent dialectician will, first, follow out the consequences of each alternative to see what difficulties they face. Second, he will go through the difficulties he has uncovered to determine which can be solved and which cannot. As a result, he will be well placed to attack or defend either alternative in the strongest possible way.

Aporematic, which is the part of philosophy that deals with such difficulties, is like dialectic in its methods, but differs from it in important respects. In a dialectical argument, for example, the opponent may refuse to accept a proposition that a philosopher would accept, since he can see too readily that he will be defeated if he does (*Topics*, 155b10–16). Since the truth may well hinge on propositions whose status is just like these premises, there is no guarantee that what a dialectician considers most defensible will be true.

Drawing on this new class of *endoxa*, then, the philosopher examines both the claim that being is one and unchanging, and the claim that it is not, in just the way that the dialectician does. As a result, he determines, let us suppose, that the most defensible, or least problematic, conclusion is that in some senses of the terms being is one and unchanging, in others not. To reach this conclusion, however, he will have to disambiguate and reformulate *endoxa* on both sides, partly accepting and partly rejecting them. Others he may well have to reject outright, so that beliefs that initially seemed to be *endoxa* – that seemed to be unproblematic – will have emerged as only apparently such. These he will have to explain away: "we should state not only the truth, but also the cause of error – for this contributes towards producing conviction, since when a reasonable explanation is given of why the false view appears true, this tends to produce belief in the true view" (*Nicomachean Ethics*, 1154a22–5). If, at the end of this process the difficulties are solved and most of the most authoritative of *endoxa* are left, that will be a sufficient proof of the philosopher's conclusion, Aristotle claims (1145b6–7).

But in that claim lies a problem. For while dialectic treats things "only with an eye to general opinion," philosophy must treat them "according to their truth" (*Topics*, 105b30–1). *Endoxa*, however, are just generally accepted and unobjectionable opinions. Since even such unopposed opinions may nevertheless be false, how can an argument that relies on them be guaranteed to reach the truth? The answer lies in aporematic philosophy's dialectical capacity to criticize or examine.

Because he is a generally educated person, an aporematic philosopher knows what is essential to a genuine science of whatever sort (*Parts of Animals*, 639a1–8). Using his dialectical capacity to examine, therefore, a philosopher can, for example, determine whether a person, A, has any sort of mathematical knowledge or is simply a charlatan. If A passes the examination, the philosopher can use his own knowledge of what a mathematical science must be like to determine whether A's mathematical knowledge is genuinely scientific. If he finds that it is, he knows that the undemonstrated mathematical first principles which A accepts are true. If, in particular, A accepts as such a principle that magnitudes are divisible without limit, the philosopher knows that it is true.

When he uses his dialectical skill to draw out the consequences of this principle and of its negation, however, he sees difficulties and supporting arguments based on *endoxa* on both sides. Since he knows the principle is true, however, his goal will be to resolve the difficulties it faces and undo the arguments that seem to support its negation. If he is successful, he will have refuted all the objections to it, and so will have provided a negative demonstration, or demonstration by refutation, of it (*Metaphysics*, 1006a12). Such a demonstration is aporematic philosophy's way to a scientific first principle, and constitutes the sufficient proof of it to which Aristotle refers.

What aporematic philosophy offers us with regard to the first principles of the sciences, then, is to free our understanding from knots, or eliminate the impediments to a clear and exact intuitive grasp. And with such a grasp comes scientific knowledge of the most excellent and unqualified kind, knowledge that manifests the virtue of theoretical wisdom (*Nicomachean Ethics*, 1141a16–17).

How, then, are we to acquire knowledge of these various Aristotelian sciences, and who, exactly, is supposed to acquire it? Like Plato and Socrates, Aristotle thinks that education is of enormous ethical and political importance (*Politics*, 1310a12–14, 1332b10–11). People are unified and made into a community by means of education, he says, and a community could not really be a political one, a *polis* or city, if it did not educate its citizens in virtue (1263b36, 1280b1–8). Although it is extremely difficult to get clear even about the education that Aristotle himself recommends, in part because the *Politics* is incomplete, a rough picture can nonetheless be reconstructed.

The treatment of infants is largely a matter of diet (lots of milk, no wine), exercise (as much movement as possible), and habituation (especially to the cold, since babies are naturally hot). Once infancy is passed, a pre-five-year-old should play the sorts of games, and listen to the sorts of stories, that will fit it for later pursuits, and for life as a free individual (1336a3–b35).

From age five to seven, children should continue to be educated in the household as "observers of the lessons they themselves will eventually have to learn" (1336b35–7). They should spend their leisure time in ways that prevent them from picking up any "taint of servility." They shouldn't play with slaves, be exposed to the sort of obscene or abusive art or language that slavish people enjoy, or, indeed, to anything bad or vulgar, "particularly if it involves vice or malice." For "what we encounter first we like better" (1336a39–b35).

From age seven to 14 (puberty), children should do "lighter gymnastic exercises, but a strict diet and strenuous exertions should be forbidden, so that nothing impedes their growth" (1338b40–2).

From age 17 to 21 arduous physical training should be combined with a strict diet. From age 14 to 17, adolescents should engage in three years of what are referred to only as "other studies." These studies could consist in reading, writing, music, and drawing. But then the only thing that children are taught between the ages of seven and 14 is light gymnastics. This is sufficiently implausible in its own terms and a sufficiently large departure from common Greek practice and Plato's recommendations that we would expect Aristotle to acknowledge it as an innovation and defend it carefully. The fact that he does neither of these things suggests that he is in fact intending to follow tradition and begin reading, writing, drawing, and music at age seven (or age five if serving as observers is included).

If the "other studies" are not reading and the rest, however, what are they? In various places, Aristotle refers to a generally educated person (*pepaideumenos*) as someone who studies practically all subjects, not to acquire expert scientific knowledge (which would be impossible), but in order to become a good judge (*Parts of Animals*, 639a1–6; *Nicomachean Ethics*, 1094b28–1095a2). Generally educated in medicine, for example, he is capable of judging whether someone has treated a disease correctly (*Politics*, 1282a3–7). Acquainted with many subjects, methodologies, and areas of study, he knows "what we should and should not seek to have demonstrated" and "seeks exactness in each area to the extent that the subject-matter allows" (*Metaphysics*, 1106a5–11; *Nicomachean Ethics*, 1094b23–7).

Because he is able to judge the works and advice of experts, a generally educated person is free from the sort of intellectual enslavement to them that would otherwise be his lot. He knows who is and who isn't worth listening to on any matter, and so can get good expert advice when he needs it. But he is also free from the inner enslavement that is all too often the lot of the narrow expert, whose imagination is straitjacketed by the one thing he knows too well. For, while he has indeed studied all the "civilized sciences," he has done so only "up to a point," and not so assiduously or pedantically as "to debase the mind and deprive it of leisure" (*Politics*, 1337b14–17). Presumably, then, the citizens of Aristotle's best city, which is an aristocracy of virtue, must be trained in these subjects at some point. If not from age 14, then later in their lives.

In *Politics* VIII.3, we are promised a discussion of a kind of education "that sons must be given not because it is useful or necessary but because it is noble and suitable for a free person" (1338a30–4). This promise is unfortunately not fulfilled, but we do have some clues as to the nature of this education. We know, for example, that music and drawing are both to be taught in part because they are noble and free and contribute to leisure. But we also know that many other subjects, particularly philosophy and other theoretical sciences, are crucial to spending one's leisure time well and achieving happiness (1263b29–40, 1267a10–12, 1334a23). Since the goal of a city is to enable its citizens to lead the good life and achieve happiness, it must surely educate them in these subjects and sciences too.

Ethics and politics are practical sciences, not theoretical ones: their aim is good action (*praxis*), not contemplation of the truth (*theoria*). Hence habituation, the proper training of the appetites, desires, and emotions that cause actions, is crucial to them (*Nicomachean Ethics*, 1103b23–31). Much of the education provided prior to age 21, aimed as it is at shaping character, is therefore ethical in nature. When it has been carried out successfully, those who have received it will feel fear, anger, pity, pleasure, pain, and the rest "at the right times, about the right things, towards the right people, for the right end, and in the right way" (1106b21–3). And, as a result, their feelings will be in a mean between excess and deficiency, between feeling rage at a trivial slight and indifference at a serious injury, and they will have the various virtues of character. For these virtues – courage, moderation, generosity, justice – are largely a matter of having the sorts of desires that are in tune with what prudence or practical wisdom (*phronēsis*) decides on as best. When our desires are not so in tune, we are either weak-willed (if they cause us to act imprudently) or self-controlled (if in acting prudently we frustrate them).

Though much of education in ethics and politics is for these reasons aimed at our desires and emotions, we cannot become prudent or practically wise without more formal education in ethics and statesmanship of the sort that might be gained by listening to Aristotle's own lectures on ethics and politics in the Lyceum. For a practically wise person, a *phronimos*, must know what happiness is and, in his capacity as a citizen, what laws, constitutions, and so on will best promote it in the actual circumstances in which he finds himself (*Nicomachean Ethics*, I.1–7, X. 6–8; *Politics*, IV. 1). And without formal instruction such knowledge cannot be guaranteed to be available to him. Moreover, we know that training in rhetoric is crucial for political success, and that it too is part of general education (*Rhetoric*, 1356a7–9). It seems reasonable to conclude, therefore, that some training in the theoretical sciences must be included for the under-21s and that some further education in ethics, rhetoric, and perhaps in these sciences too must occur subsequently.

At 21, a young man becomes an adult citizen allowed to "recline at the communal table and drink wine" with the other adults (*Politics*, 1336b21–2). But here, too, his education continues. For communal meals, ideally provided free by cities to all citizens, are intended to serve many functions besides that of feeding them. For example, they enable the citizens to learn to know one another and to develop bonds of friendship and mutual trust – which is one reason tyrants outlaw them (1313a41–b6). Without this knowledge, the election of officials is bound, Aristotle thinks, to be largely arbitrary. Public meals also give young men the opportunity to observe virtuous older ones, and to see at close quarters and over long periods how they act and talk. But equally importantly, they are also the occasion for that peculiarly Greek institution, the *symposium*, at which poetry was sung, music played, and important topics, including ethical and political ones, discussed.

Just as important as the content of the education Aristotle advocates is the fact that he explicitly conceives of it not in the traditional Greek way as privately provided, but as *public* education suited to the particular political system or constitution and provided to citizens by it (*Politics*, 1260b15, 1337a14–26). As a result, most of his remarks about the education provided in the best city concern the education of future citizens, all of whom are, of course, males. It seems certain, nonetheless, that he thinks that public education should also be provided to girls and women (1260b13–20, 1269b12–24, 1335b11–12). But since he thinks that male and female virtues are different, it is bound to differ substantially from that of men.

Conclusion

We have come a long way from the strange and unique figure of Socrates alone in the Athenian agora buttonholing ordinary people, questioning them about virtue, and minimalist in his own claims to wisdom. Education, still conceived as primarily ethical, has become institutionalized in a school, and aspires, in Platonic theory anyway, to usurp the place of politics and rule the world. Nonetheless, dialectic, the successor of the *elenchus*, retains something like pride of place in that education, though now science, rather than ordinary untutored beliefs, is needed to provide the grist for its mill.

The effect of that reconception of the *elenchus* on Plato's overall picture is, nonetheless, profound. Ethical inquiry, like scientific inquiry of other sorts, has become a matter for experts: what started as a democratic process open to anyone has become an "academic" one. And whatever untutored capacities fitted people like Themistocles and Pericles for political leadership have been replaced by a complex mix of trained affective responses and esoteric theoretical knowledge.

Revolutionary in its "post-secondary" stages, Platonic education is traditional in its foundations: physical training, *mousikē*, craft apprenticeship, and what we can recognize as something like national military service are cultural borrowings. Professional training in mathematical science, dialectic, and practical city-management are Platonic innovations. So, too, is the cast the entire system of education is given. For the goal, as in the case of the Socratic *elenchus*, is to reform people's moral characters, so that they can live in harmony together and, in light of knowledge of the good, achieve happiness. Expertise for its own sake is no part of the picture. However, rule by experts, and with it the alienation of non-experts from control of their own lives, has decisively appeared on the scene for the first – though not, of course, the last – time.

In Aristotle, too, dialectic is the deepest of his Socratic and Platonic inheritances. But while the Socratic *elenchus* is every person's ticket to the ethically examined life and Platonic dialectic is the philosopher's ticket to scientific knowledge of ethics and politics, Aristotelian dialectic is in between: it is the generally educated, the liberally educated, citizen's ticket to reliable sources of expert scientific knowledge, and so to the liberating benefits of a socially and politically mediated division of epistemic labor. Aristotelian aporematic, on the other hand, remains, as in Plato, the philosopher's route to the first principles of the very best and highest science. Just how that science is related to ethics, politics, and the examined life, however, is unclear. Theory and practice are left, therefore, in the uncertain relationship – morally, epistemologically, and pedagogically – in which, to some extent, they have remained.

See also 2 STOICISM; 4 THE EDUCATIONAL THOUGHT OF AUGUSTINE; 9 ROMANTICISM; 10 HELLENISM, THE *GYMNASIUM*, AND *ALTERTUMSWISSENSCHAFT*

References

References in this chapter to the works of Plato and Aristotle use the system of pagination established by the editors of the Greek texts upon which various editions are based. These page and line numbers appear in the margins of most English editions. The translations provided here coincide for the most part with those found in these English editions.

Barnes, J. (ed.) (1984) *The Complete Works of Aristotle*. Princeton, NJ: Princeton University Press.

Cooper, J. M. (ed.) (1997) *Plato: Complete Works*. Indianapolis: Hackett.

Further Reading

Beck, F. A. G. (1964) *Greek Education*. London: Methuen.

Curren, R. (2000) *Aristotle on the Necessity of Public Education*. Lanham, MD: Rowman and Littlefield.

Gutherie, W. K. C. (1969–78) *A History of Greek Philosophy, Volumes 3–5*. Cambridge: Cambridge University Press.

Hornblower, S. and Spawforth, A. (1996) *The Oxford Classical Dictionary*. Oxford: Oxford University Press.

Kraut, R. (1998) *Aristotle: Politics Books VII and VIII*. Oxford: Oxford University Press.

Reeve, C. D. C. (1988) *Philosopher-kings: The Argument of Plato's Republic*. Princeton, NJ: Princeton University Press.

Reeve, C. D. C. (1989) *Socrates in the Apology*. Indianapolis: Hackett.

Reeve, C. D. C. (1992) *Practices of Reason: Aristotle's Nicomachean Ethics*. Oxford: Clarendon Press.

Rorty, A. (ed.) (1998) *Philosophers on Education: New Historical Perspectives*. London: Routledge.

Vlastos, G. (1991) *Socrates: Ironist and Moral Philosopher*. Cambridge: Cambridge University Press.

2

Stoicism

Christopher Gill

Introduction

Stoicism, like the other Greek philosophies discussed in chapter 1, can be seen as a continuation of the Socratic movement. There is no single, distinct branch of Stoic theory that we can identify as their "philosophy of education." But the Stoics produced an original and powerful set of ideas on human development, the acquisition of knowledge (especially knowledge of the good), and types of value, and these ideas are of continuing significance for modern students of the philosophy of education. Also important in this connection are their views about the need for an integrated philosophical curriculum, the teaching of practical ethics, and the relationship between philosophical theory and conventional beliefs and practices.

Context and History

Stoicism, like its great rival, Epicureanism, emerged in Athens at the start of the third century BCE. Through the activities of Socrates, Plato, and Aristotle, Athens had become by this date the main center of philosophy in Greece, indeed in the ancient Mediterranean world. Two major "schools" of philosophy had been established, in the Academy (by Plato and his successors) and in the Lyceum (by Aristotle and his successors). Two more schools emerged, that of Epicurus (based in his house and garden outside the city) and that of Zeno, based in the Painted Stoa in Athens. Though intellectually sophisticated and covering complex fields of knowledge, these schools were highly informal as institutions. They functioned as research groups for like-minded independent scholars and provided public lectures and more sustained courses of teaching for interested young people and adults. The philosophical schools, alongside the rhetorical schools (their more successful and more "mainstream" rivals) offered what could be considered as higher or university-level education. The teachers and students were predominantly (though not entirely) males; the students were mostly (though not invariably) from the upper classes in the Greek-speaking world. Stoicism and Epicureanism, together with other, still more informal, groups such as the Cynics, also represented a distinct set of ethical attitudes, way of life and world view.

Zeno (*c*.334–262 BCE), the founder of the Stoic school, was strongly influenced, in ideas and approach, by Socrates; his decision to teach in a public colonnade near the city center represented a renewal of the Socratic style of teaching by argument with all comers. During his lifetime, Zeno was strongly challenged by others, notably Aristo, who claimed, like Zeno, to be capturing the heart of the Socratic ethical message. After his death, Zeno was regarded as the clear leader of a new philosophical movement, and his ideas were developed and systematized by subsequent leaders of the school, notably Chrysippus, the greatest Stoic theorist (280–207 BCE). However, debate about the core doctrines and their implications continued thoughout the third and second centuries BCE; Stoicism also developed through argument with other schools, notably the Academic (Platonic) school. In the early first century BCE, Athens ceased to be the main center of philosophy, and Stoicism, like other philosophies, was taught and studied throughout the main cities of the Eastern (Greek-speaking) Mediterranean, now dominated by Rome, and at Rome itself. Stoicism, in this more widespread and diffused form, became the most influential of Greek philosophies during the first and second centuries CE. Subsequently, Stoicism was eclipsed in antiquity by revived forms of Platonism and Aristotelianism and by Christianity, though Stoic thought continued to influence all three traditions.

Stoic Theory as a System

As formulated by Chrysippus, Stoicism is highly systematic in its teachings. The philosophical curriculum, in its full form, consists of a combination of ethics, logic (in effect, philosophical method, including epistemology), and physics (study of nature) (Long and Sedley, 1987, section 26). Wisdom, the Stoic ideal – an ideal that no Stoic teacher claimed to have attained – depends on the complete integration of these branches of inquiry. The full understanding of core notions in Stoicism, such as reason, order, and the good (notions whose meaning is closely interconnected), depends on this combination and integration of branches of philosophy. In broad terms, the world view offered by Stoicism is both naturalistic and idealistic. It is naturalistic in rejecting the Platonic contrasts between soul and body, or forms and particulars, and in insisting that there is one (material) world that is the object of both perception and knowledge. It is idealistic in maintaining (in sharp contrast to Epicureanism) that this world is shaped by purposive, divine rationality and order (Long and Sedley, 1987, ss. 44–5, 53–5).

Ethics: Values and Development

Since Stoicism has this strongly unified character, "education" depends on understanding and integrating all three branches of philosophy and on putting this understanding into practice. Ethics may be the best point of access to Stoic thinking about education, though it needs to be taken with related aspects of logic and physics. Ethics was itself seen as a highly integrated set of topics, including categories of value and a theory of development (Long and Sedley, 1987, s. 56). A core ethical claim, going back to Zeno and taken to stem, ultimately, from Socrates (Long, 1996, chapter 1), is that virtue is the only good, and that other so-called goods (such as health, wealth, and beauty) are, by contrast, "matters of indifference" which have no effect on happiness. For Aristo, this seems to have been both the beginning and the end of Stoic ethics. But Zeno, followed by the main line of Stoic thinking, maintained that things such as health are, at least, "preferable indifferents," and that we are naturally inclined to "select" such preferable things rather than their opposites (Long and Sedley, 1987, s. 58). This process of "selection" forms a key part of the way we develop as rational human beings. But a crucial part of this process lies in coming to recognize that what matters, ultimately, is not obtaining preferable things but selecting them in the right way – that is, virtuously – and, to that degree, coming to know and express the good.

Stoic concepts of value are closely bound up with their thinking about development, a distinctive feature of their theory that is clearly relevant to the subject of education. Development is analysed by them as *oikeiōsis*, "familiarization" or "appropriation"; it consists in making the world "one's own" (*oikeios*) and in enabling the world (understood as a providential and rational system) to make one "its own." This process has several different aspects and stages. At a basic level, all animals, including humans, are seen as instinctively motivated to seek those things that maintain and nurture their own distinctive character or "constitution" (Long and Sedley, 1987, s. 57A). (There is a sharp and deliberate contrast with the Epicurean view that animals, including humans, naturally pursue pleasure (Long and Sedley, 1987, s. 21A). For human beings, who are fundamentally rational, this process comes to take the form of (rationally) "selecting" such things as being "preferable" to their alternatives. If human development takes its proper course, such selection becomes progressively more internally coherent, based on rational considerations and (in principle) open to rational justification. Also, selection is increasingly based on proper norms for "appropriate actions" (or "proper functions," *kathēkonta*). In this respect, selection comes increasingly to exhibit the features (consistency, order, rationality) that constitute "the good" for Stoicism. But a crucial further dimension is the realization, noted above, that what matters, ultimately, for human happiness is not obtaining the "preferable" things but selecting them in a rational and ordered (that is to say, virtuous) way. One comes to realize that "virtue is the only good" and the only thing that should be chosen for its own sake (Long and Sedley, 1987, s. 59D). This can also be expressed by saying that the ultimate goal of human life is living "according to virtue (or reason)," which can also be characterized as living "according to nature" (as the Stoics understand "nature") (Long and Sedley, 1987, s. 63).

A second dimension of development, which is also presented as a profoundly "natural" one, is the social one. Common to all animals, and built into their physical and psychological constitution, is the capacity for reproduction and (more crucially) the motivation to care for, and nurture, their offspring. This motivation is the most obvious manifestation of a more pervasive desire to "familiarize" oneself to others by bonding with them and benefiting them. For adult human beings, this process normally takes the form of full engagement in family and communal life or in other forms of positive social relationship, such as that of teaching philosophy. Another side of this process is the progressive extension of our concern to those outside our immediate family and community and the recognition that, as fellow rational human beings, we are also "familiarized" to them (Long and Sedley, 1987, s. 57D–H).

The relationship between these two aspects of development is not as fully explained in our sources as we would wish. But it seems clear that both are taken as key features of a developmental process that contributes toward, and includes, a more theoretical understanding of the good. Social engagement, both within and outside our immediate community, provides a context through which we can learn to select "appropriately" between preferable things and, thus, learn how to act virtuously and to recognize that this is, ultimately, all that matters in human life. Also, both the processes of rational discrimination and of appropriate bonding can be understood as ways of actualizing the order, rationality, and benefit that are the salient marks of the good. To that degree, both aspects of development are interconnected facets of learning to live the life "according to nature/reason/virtue" which is human happiness, as the Stoics understand this. (See further Inwood, 1985, chapter 5; Annas, 1993, chapters 5 and 12.2; Striker, 1996, chapters 12 and 13; Algra et al., 1999, chapter 21, especially pp. 677–82.)

Knowing the Good

Making sense of Stoic thought about coming to know the good involves consideration of several related aspects of Stoic thought. One of these is the Stoic theory of knowledge. From a modern perspective, the Stoic theory seems to combine aspects that are characteristic of both empiricist and idealist approaches and of both "correspondence" and "coherence" theories of knowledge. On the one hand, they see knowledge as based on perceptions (not innate ideas), which enable us to form concepts and beliefs. In their terms, we "assent" to an "impression" (*phantasia*) and thus produce "cognition" (*katalēpsis*), which may constitute either belief/opinion or knowledge. They also maintain that a certain kind of perception (a "cognitive impression") necessarily yields a true cognition, a claim defended through sustained argument with skeptics in the Platonic Academy during the third and second centuries BCE. On the other hand, they also maintain that we are naturally capable of forming (by inference from perception) "preconceptions" or "natural/common notions," such as those of the good or of god. Knowledge is based on a combination of cognitive impressions and preconceptions. True propositions correspond to actual states of affair in the world but also constitute an internally consistent set of ideas (Long and Sedley, 1987, ss. 39–41; Everson, 1990, chapter 9; Algra et al., 1999, chapter 9).

Coming to know the good, therefore, involves both inference from perceptions and the formation of a preconception. But it is a process of a very special kind because "good" represents both the highest kind of value and one that is applicable in widely different contexts. Stoics lay special stress on the role of analogy in enabling us to recognize connections between the forms of goodness found in these different contexts. Virtue – what we might call "ethical" or "moral" goodness – is one aspect of this notion. The recognition of our own developing virtue (if we develop as we should) and that of other people constitutes an important dimension of the process of coming to know the good. But Stoics emphasize that what we are recognizing is not just a moral notion (human virtue) but is one aspect of a broader concept. The salient marks of goodness are order, structure, harmony, and rationality. The development of virtue involves recognizing virtue as something good – that is, as manifesting order and rationality. But goodness also exists elsewhere, above all, in the universe, understood as an ordered and rational structure. Structure and rationality also, necessarily, confer "benefit," which is another of the salient marks of goodness. So coming to know the good, in the fullest sense of the word, is a matter of understanding how goodness manifests itself in these various sectors (which can be summed up as the spheres of ethics, physics, and logic) and also a matter of expressing this in your own life and character (Long and Sedley, 1987, ss. 60; cf. Ieradiakonou, 1999, chapter 3).

Interpreting Stoic ideas about the relationship between ethical goodness and goodness in other contexts (in particular, in the universe as a whole) is a difficult matter. (For contrasting interpretations see Annas, 1993, chapter 5; Striker, 1996, chapter 12, especially pp. 221–31.) But there is no doubt that wisdom, the Stoic ideal state, includes knowledge of goodness in all these areas and of their interconnection. The goodness of the universe is displayed in the visible order and harmony of the heavenly bodies and in the regular cycles of day and night and of the seasons. It is also manifested in the way that each species is naturally adapted (in its physical and psychological capacities) to function as a unified organism and to do so within the world, which itself functions as a coherent system. These manifestations of organic system and coherence are taken as evidence of divine providence – an aspect of Stoic thought that is strongly influenced by Plato's vision of the world in the *Timaeus*. But, unlike Plato's craftsman god, who is distinct from the world he creates, the Stoic god is an immanent force, at once a physical entity ("designing fire") and the active cause, a principle of order and rationality working within nature (Long and Sedley, 1987, s. 54, based especially on Cicero, *On the Nature of the Gods*, Book 2; also Long and Sedley, 1987, ss. 44, 46). Hence, recognizing the divinity of the world (its immanent structure and coherence) is another key aspect of coming to know the good (cf. Rousseau, 1979, pp. 313–14ff).

A related subject is Stoic thinking on determinism and agency, which involves recognizing in a different way the goodness of the universe. The Stoics are usually seen as "compatibilists," who try to reconcile universal causal determinism with the idea that human beings are responsible for their actions. This reconciliation is brought about, in part, by explaining human (and other) actions by reference to two kinds of cause: internal and external causes. The fact that (adult) human actions depend on a specific kind of internal cause (namely, assent to a rational impression) entitles us to hold human beings responsible for the actions that result from this assent. (This kind of compatibilism does not involve the idea of "indeterminist" freedom of choice, an idea that was developed in Epicurean theories.) But there is a different, and arguably more profound, way of understanding Stoic compatibilism. Universal causal determinism (the "seamless web" of causes) and adult human rationality are both manifestations of the order, rationality, and goodness that are fundamental to nature, as the Stoics understand this (Bobzien, 1998; also Long and Sedley, 1987, ss. 55, 62). This point helps to explain why accepting the fated outcome of events (even in cases where this seems, on the face of it, strongly disadvantageous to us as individuals or to our community or humankind) is seen as a key mark of a virtuous attitude or character. In doing so, we recognize that the universe, in the relevant respects, is good (despite apparent indications to the contrary) and we are thus expressing (at least some measure of) goodness in ourselves. This topic is another that exemplifies the importance of integrating physics, ethics, and logic, since the proper understanding of determinism embraces aspects of all three studies.

Practical Ethics and Conventional Thought

A further aspect of Stoicism relevant to their thinking about education centers on practical ethics. This aspect needs to be linked with their thought about the relationship between conventional beliefs and theory and about the best forms of political and social organization.

The idea that ethical philosophy should have a direct bearing on one's life goes back to Socrates. For Socrates, there was no distinction between theoretical and practical ethics: searching for the truth through dialectic was the only way to find the best way of life. In Hellenistic philosophy, we find a distinction between ethical theory (centered on claims about the nature of the human good) and the application of the outcome of theoretical inquiry to working out how to lead a good life in practice. There were different ways of classifying the main genres of practical ethics. For instance, Philo of Larisa, of the Academic school (158–84 BCE) classified these as "protreptic" (encouragement to engage in philosophy), therapy, and advice (both based on philosophy). Comparable systems of classification can also be found in Stoic authors. Seneca (1 BCE to 65 CE) outlines a three-fold system based on (1) assessing the value of each thing, (2) adopting an appropriate "impulse" or motivation toward things pursued, and (3) achieving consistency between impulse and action. In Epictetus (c.50–130 CE) the pattern is this: (1) focusing our desires on what is "up to us" (aiming at becoming virtuous), not at "indifferents" which are not "up to us," (2) converting our desires into correct "impulses" toward "appropriate actions" that match our social situation, and (3) working toward complete consistency in our belief-system and (accordingly) the way we respond to each situation that arises (Long and Sedley, 1987, s. 56, also s. 66). The *Meditations* of Marcus Aurelius (Roman emperor, 121–80 CE) adopt a version of Epictetus' pattern that includes a focus on the need to adopt a cosmic perspective toward oneself as a key part of applying these techniques.

How, exactly, do these methods of practical ethics relate to the core ideas of Stoic theory? It is sometimes suggested that the threefold typology in Epictetus is a practical version of the Stoic three-part philosophical curriculum (physics, ethics, logic) (see, for instance, Hadot, 1995, pp. 193–5). However, it is more plausible to see these techniques as falling within ethics, and as directed at helping people work out the practical implications of adopting Stoic ethical principles. These principles are taken to be supported by physics and logic; and writers of practical ethics, such as Marcus Aurelius, emphasize that the Stoic world view underpins ethical principles and the way of life that follows from these principles. None the less, the project of bringing out these implications for living a good life falls within the scope of ethics.

What is the relationship between Stoic theory and conventional ethical and social beliefs? On the one hand, the Stoics maintain that many of the errors that stop most people from completing the process of ethical development derive from their family and communal environment. The most common type of error is that of mistaking things that are "matters of indifference," which we should only prefer or not prefer to have, for things that are good or bad absolutely. It is this error that generates emotions or "passions," reactions that the Stoics regard as "sicknesses of the soul" (Long and Sedley, 1987, s. 65; cf. Inwood, 1985, chapter 5). On the other hand, Stoics stress that "all human beings have by nature the starting-points of virtue" (Long and Sedley, 1987, s. 61L). They also believe that conventional beliefs and practices in any given society contain some degree of ethical truth. What is needed is for us to "examine our impressions" (as Epictetus puts it) and to sift our belief-systems until we recognize the true core of beliefs that are latent within them. (As is brought out by Long, 2002, chapter 3, this is close to Socrates' view of the function of philosophical discourse.) To put it differently, one of the projects of Stoic practical ethics is to help us to recognize the underlying logic or rationale that is embodied within communal belief-systems. This point explains one of the more intriguing features of Stoic thought: their interest in allegorizing interpretations of myth, religious beliefs, and language (e.g. Cicero, *On the Nature of the Gods* 2.63–9). What this reflects is the idea that, if properly decoded, conventional beliefs contain (in at least partial form) aspects of the rational and systematized principles that Stoic theory seeks to convey.

A related point underlies Stoic political ideas. Early Stoic political thought seems to have centered on a Cynic-style rejection of conventional political structures in favor of a "natural" community, that of the wise, characterized above all by internal unity and harmony. In later Stoic thinking, we find, instead, ideals such as "natural law" and "the brotherhood of humankind" functioning as universal norms underpinning legal codes and political structures in conventional societies. Stoic "natural law" (unlike modern codes of "human rights") does not set out specific rules or entitlements. As Cicero brings out, in his *Republic* and *On Duties*, "natural law" and "brotherhood of humankind" signify the idea of a core of objective ethical principles underlying best practice within a conventional society such as the Roman republic (Long and Sedley, 1987, s. 67; cf. Annas, 1993, chapter 13.3; Algra et al., 1999, pp. 756–68). In this context too, then, we find the idea that philosophically guided examination of conventional beliefs and practices can disclose part at least of the ordered structure and rationality that Stoics identify as what is "good" absolutely.

Stoic ideas on practical ethics, conventional beliefs, and politics serve to illustrate further the richness and coherence of their philosophical system. Although not formulated as part of the "philosophy of education," these ideas can offer powerful insights for modern study of this area.

See also 1 THE SOCRATIC MOVEMENT; 6 ENLIGHTENMENT LIBERALISM; 7 ROUSSEAU, DEWEY, AND DEMOCRACY; 9 ROMANTICISM; 10 HELLENISM, THE *GYMNASIUM*, AND *ALTERTUMS-WISSENSCHAFT*

References

Algra, K., Barnes, J., Mansfeld, J., and Schofield, M. (eds) (1999) *The Cambridge History of Hellenistic Philosophy*. Cambridge: Cambridge University Press.

Annas, J. (1993) *The Morality of Happiness*. Oxford: Clarendon Press.

Bobzien, S. (1998) *Determinism and Freedom in Stoic Philosophy*. Oxford: Clarendon Press.

Everson, S. (ed.) (1990) *Epistemology. Companions to Ancient Thought, volume 1*. Cambridge: Cambridge University Press.

Hadot, P. (1995). *Philosophy as a Way of Life*, trans. M. Chase. Oxford: Blackwell.

Ieradiakonou, K. (ed.) (1999) *Topics in Stoic Philosophy*. Oxford: Clarendon Press.

Inwood, B. (1985) *Ethics and Human Action in Early Stoicism*. Oxford: Clarendon Press.

Long, A. A. (1996) *Stoic Studies*. Cambridge: Cambridge University Press.

Long, A. A. (2002) *Epictetus: A Stoic and Socratic Guide to Life*. Oxford: Clarendon Press.

Long, A. A. and Sedley, D. N. (1987) *The Presocratic Philosophers* (two volumes). Cambridge: Cambridge University Press.

Rousseau, J.-J. (1979) *Émile*, trans. A. Bloom. New York: Basic Books (original work published 1762).

Striker, G. (1996) *Essays on Hellenistic Epistemology and Ethics*. Cambridge: Cambridge University Press.

Further reading

Gill, C. (ed.) (1995) *Epictetus: The Discourses, Handbook, Fragments*, trans. R. Hard. London: Dent.

Gill, C. (ed.) (1997) *Marcus Aurelius: Meditations*, trans. R. Hard. Ware: Wordsworth.

Inwood, B. (ed.) (2002) *Cambridge Companion to Stoicism*. Cambridge: Cambridge University Press.

Inwood, B. and Gerson, L. P. (trans.) (1997) *Hellenistic Philosophy: Introductory Readings*. Indianapolis: Hackett.

Nussbaum, M. C. (1994) *The Therapy of Desire: Theory and Practice in Hellenistic Ethics*. Princeton, NJ: Princeton University Press.

Reydam-Schils, G. (1999) *Demiurge and Providence: Stoic and Platonic Readings of Plato's Timaeus*. Turnhout: Brepols.

Sorabji, R. (2000) *Emotion and Peace of Mind: From Stoic Agitation to Christian Temptation*. Oxford: Clarendon Press.

Zeyl, D. (ed.) (1997) *Encyclopedia of Classical Philosophy*. Westport, CT: Greenwood.

3

The Judaic Tradition

Hanan A. Alexander and Shmuel Glick

This chapter considers some of the contributions of Judaic – biblical and rabbinic – tradition to educational thought and practice. This tradition does not contain a uniform theory of education. Judaism is a religious civilization, not a philosophical tradition. It developed over time and is subject to a variety of interpretations (Kaplan, 1957; Neusner, 1970b; Kadushin, 1972). There are theories of Jewish education based on theological or philosophical traditions (Cohen, 1964; Chazan, 1978; Rosenak, 1987; Alexander, 2001b), but the task of this chapter is not to offer an account of how Jewish tradition ought to be transmitted across the generations.

Our task can be understood in light of Lee Shulman's conception of the "wisdom of practice." Shulman (1986) argues that research on teaching ought to consider the maxims and norms remembered in the precedents and parables of concrete pedagogic cases. These are to be found in the past as well as in the present, and in religious and cultural as well as educational traditions. History and tradition are important resources for building a case literature of pedagogic practice that can enrich our understanding of education. To the extent that educational philosophy is conceived in terms of the clarification of educational concepts (Peters, 1967; Scheffler, 1973), the interpretation of pedagogic practice, past and present, is a close ally of philosophical analysis (Winch, 1965). The Jewish tradition represents a vast repository of educational thought and practice accumulated and refined over centuries. Illumination of educational concepts and cases from this tradition has an important contribution to make to our understanding of educational concepts and practices.

The chapter is divided into three parts. First, we briefly describe the sources in which these educational traditions are recorded. Second, we survey the major educational ideas of the tradition. Finally, we consider an extended example of how these cases illumine educational thought and practice.

Sources of Jewish Tradition

The rabbinic tradition asserts that Moses received two divine communications on Mount Sinai, one written and the other oral (Neusner, 1970b). Both revelations are referred to by the Hebrew word "Torah," which literally means teaching or instruction.

Biblical sources

The Written Torah consists of the Hebrew Bible, known in Hebrew by the acronym "Tanakh," drawn from the first letter of each of its three parts – **T**orah (Pentateuch), **N**eviim (Prophets), and **K**etuvim (Writings). Jewish tradition does not consider the Hebrew Bible to be an Old Testament because it does not accept the Christian view that Jesus of Nazareth delivered a New Testament. Jews refer to the latter, therefore, as the Christian Bible.

In its narrowest sense, Torah refers to the Pentateuch or the Five Books of Moses (*Genesis, Exodus, Leviticus, Numbers*, and *Deuteronomy*), edited around the time of King David during the eleventh and twelfth centuries BCE. Neviim or Prophets contains former prophets (*Joshua, Judges, Samuel I* and *II, Kings I* and *II*) and latter prophets (*Jeremiah, Isaiah, Ezekiel*, and the so-called 12 minor prophets), composed during the first Jewish commonwealth from the eleventh until the sixth centuries. Finally, the Ketuvim or Writings are comprised of books composed during the second Jewish commonwealth between the fifth and first centuries BCE (*Psalms, Proverbs, Job, Song of Songs, Ruth, Lamentations, Ecclessiastes, Esther, Daniel, Ezra, Nehemia*, and *Chronicles I* and *II*). Many of these texts reflect Hellenistic influence and are consequently called "the wisdom tradition." Some relevant texts from this tradition, such as *Ecclessiasticus* or the Wisdom of Ben Sirah, did not find their way into the Hebrew canon but are preserved in the Christian Bible.

Rabbinic sources

The Oral Torah consists of legal and homiletic commentaries on the books of the Tanakh with a special emphasis on the Pentateuch (Ginzberg, 1955; Kadushin, 1972; Neusner, 1993). It also contains apodictic laws organized by the third century Rabbi Judah the Patriarch into the six orders of the Mishnah (Neusner, 1981; Halivni, 1986). The meaning of the term "Mishnah" is usually derived from the Hebrew "shinun" or repeat. However, the tenth-century Italian rabbi Nathan Ben Yehiel held that it follows from the Hebrew "sheini" or second, implying that the Rabbi Judah's Mishnah is a second rendition of the Torah (Ben Yehiel, 1926, p. 278).

Two compendiums of case deliberations on this Mishnah were compiled in the lands of Israel and Babylonia (modern Iraq) between the third and seventh centuries (Neusner, 1970a, 1984). They are known by the Aramaic for learning, "Gemara," referring to what we learn from tradition (Levine, 1972, pp. 48–9). Together with the Mishnah they comprise the Jerusalem and the Babylonian Talmuds. The term "Talmud" is taken from the Hebrew "lomed" or learn, which refers to what we learn through textual reasoning (Albeck, 1969, pp. 576–7; *Hebrew Encyclopedia*, 1993, 32, p. 861).

From the seventh century Jewish tradition developed in three directions: (1) textual criticism and commentary on the Tanakh; (2) legal codes, Talmud commentaries, and rabbinic responsa; and (3) homiletic, mystical, and philosophical tracts (Halivni, 1991). These texts were composed under the influences of Islamic culture in the Middle East, North Africa, and southern Spain, and of Christianity in Europe. North African and Middle Eastern traditions are called Sephardic, from the Hebrew name for

Spain. Central and Eastern European traditions are known as "Ashkenazic," from a medieval name for Northern France and Germany. Sephardic legal scholarship was dominant until around the fifteenth century. Ashkenazic scholarship matured somewhat later, during the medieval and early modern periods. Systematic philosophical and mystical tracts developed much earlier under Islamic than Christian influence, due in part to the flowering of Islamic intellectual life in the tenth to the twelfth centuries (Zimmels, 1958).

Education in Biblical and Rabbinic Thought

Aims and ideals

Classical Jewish tradition contains no specific book or chapter dedicated explicitly to educational philosophy or practice. Nor does it speak of a systematic or uniform philosophy or theory of education. A careful reading of relevant biblical texts, however, reveals two basic educational aims. First, children should be taught to revere God; for example, "The beginning of wisdom is the fear of God" (Ps. 111:10). Second, they should be instructed to observe the commandments, as in, "Keep the way of God by doing what is right and just" (Gen. 18:19). Indeed, according to Ben Sira reverence for God and observing His commandments are intrinsic goods. "The fear of the Lord gladdens the heart: it brings cheerfulness and joy and long life" (Ecclus. 1:12). Similarly, "Nothing is better than fear of the Lord, and nothing sweeter than obeying His commandments" (23:27).

After the destruction of the second Temple in 70 CE, the sacrificial cult was replaced with "service in the heart," which included reflection, repentance, and righteousness (Kadushin, 1964; Hoffman, 1979). Educational emphasis shifted from the central sanctuary in Jerusalem to the study and practice of the Torah. When the second-century Rabbi Akiva was asked whether study or practice of Torah was to be preferred, he answered that "study takes precedence, because it leads to practice" (BT *Kiddushin*, p. 40b). This attitude enabled the rabbis to place an extraordinary emphasis on Torah study for its own sake, because it leads to the practice of Torah, which further deepened its understanding (Alexander, 2001c). These goals became embedded in a Jewish Paideia or vision of the good life symbolized in the image of the "talmid haham" or learned sage, as opposed to the priest and the prophet. The sage became the model of religious, intellectual, and moral excellence (Moore, 1954; Finkelstein, 1962; Urbach, 1975). In the words of *Mishnah Avot* (3:2), "when two sages study Torah together, God's presence can be felt."

During the medieval period the pious sage steeped in the study and practice of Torah was transformed into the ideal of universal Jewish education. Devotion to Torah as a way of life was a primary tool against oppression (Baron, 1937, 2, p. 32; Graetz, 1955, p. 407). Thus, Rabbi Israel Elnekaveh, a fourteenth-century martyr from Toledo, commented that the verse "a gentle tongue can break bones" (Prov. 25:15) refers to the children in the house of study. Their Torah is gentle while they are young, but it breaks the back of persecution when they mature (Elnekaveh, 1929, p. 139).

An influential expression of this ideal is found in the educational writings of Maimonides, the twelfth-century Aristotelian philosopher and legalist. "Every Israelite," he wrote, "is under an obligation to study Torah, whether he is poor or rich, in sound health or ailing, in the vigor of youth or very old and feeble. Even a man so poor that he is maintained by charity or goes begging from door to door, as also a man with a wife and children to support, is under the obligation to set aside a definite period during day and night for the study of Torah" (*Mishneh Torah*, Laws Concerning the Study of Torah 1:8, Twersky, 1972, pp. 64–5). Moreover, each sage is obliged to teach every willing student, "for those who are obliged to study are also obligated to teach" (*Mishneh Torah*, 1:2). Nor is this obligation one for which one may receive remuneration. "It is forbidden to teach Oral Torah for a salary," for God gave us the Torah freely, and we are expected to do the same (*Mishneh Torah*, 5:7; also Glick, 1999, p. 9).

Pedagogic personnel

The education of children was initially placed in the hands of parents. The biblical tradition is replete with exhortations to parents concerning their obligation to transmit Torah across the generations (*Biblical Encyclopedia*, 1988, 3, p. 117):

Take utmost care...that you do not forget the things you saw with your own eyes.... Make them known to your children and to your children's children. The day you stood before the Lord your God at Horeb, when the Lord said... "Gather the people to Me that I may let them hear My words, in order that they may learn to revere Me as long as they live on earth, and may so teach their children." (Deut. 4:9–10)

You must love the Lord your God with all your heart, with all your soul, and with all your might. Take to heart these words with which I charge you this day. Impress them upon your children. (Deut. 6:4–5)

Impress these My words upon your very heart: bind them as a sign on your hand and let them serve as a symbol on your forehead, and teach them to your children, reciting them when you stay at home and when you are away, when you lie down and when you get up. (Deut. 11:18–20)

Take to heart all these words with which I have warned you this day. Enjoin them upon your children that they may observe faithfully all the terms of this Teaching. (Deut. 32:46)

The Torah places a particular obligation on the father to initiate his sons into the observance of the commandments; for example, "Ask your father and he will inform you" (Deut. 32:7; see Baumgarten, 1999, p. 35). Having said this, the responsibility for educating children was shared by both parents. We find an indication of this in the case of the disloyal and defiant son:

If a man has a disloyal and defiant son, who does not heed his father or mother and does not obey them even after they discipline him, his father and mother shall take hold of him and bring him out to the elders of his town at the public place of his community. They shall say to the elders of his town, "this son of ours is disloyal and defiant; he doe not heed us. (Deut. 21:18–20)

The sages asked why the text uses both the words "disloyal" and "defiant" when one of these terms would have sufficed. "Disloyal to his father" was the answer, and "defiant to his mother" (Finkelstein, 1969, p. 251). From this the sages concluded that "If the father desired [to declare him disloyal and defiant] but the mother did not, or the father did not desire [to declare him disloyal and defiant] but the mother did, he is not considered a disloyal and defiant son until both parents desire [to declare him as such]" (*Mishnah Sanhedrin* 8:4). In other words, both parents share equal responsibility for the education of sons (and by extension daughters).

Because of this joint responsibility, the earliest and most basic form of Torah education can be found in the enjoinder to respect one's parents: "Honor your father and your mother" (Exod. 20:1, Deut. 5:16), and "You shall each revere his mother and his father" (Lev. 19:3). The wisdom tradition also emphasizes the educational role of the mother as equal to that of the father: "My son, heed the discipline of your father, and do not forsake the instruction of your mother" (Prov. 1:8; see also 6:20, 23:22).

In time, elders, priests, prophets, scribes, and teachers supplemented the educational role of parents. The place of the tribal elders in the case of the disloyal and defiant son is perhaps the earliest supplement to the parent's role (see Exod. 21:17). Thus the passage quoted above, "Ask your father and he will inform you," concludes "your elders, they will tell you" (Deut. 32:7). The priests of the bamot (altars; before the unification of the cult under King David) and of Jerusalem also supplemented parental instruction. In some instances, fathers even served as or were identified with priests (Judg. 17:10, Prov. 6:20). Prophets also played a role in educating the young. In prophetic circles we find the first instances of relations between masters and disciples that later became prominent among the rabbis (2 Kings 3:11).

In the fifth century BCE, Ezra and Nehemia placed the Pentateuch at the center of the curriculum by institutionalizing its public reading on Mondays and Thursdays, and on the Sabbath. They prepared scribes to preserve the text, and learned Levites to interpret its meaning. It was out of this circle of the learned scribes and Levites that the rabbis emerged as teachers of Torah *par excellence*. The Torah, joined by other books of the canon, became their textbook (Alexander, 2001a).

The position of the teacher emerged during the rabbinic period, the first to seventh centuries in the lands of Israel and Babylonia. "Makrei dardekai" or "makrei yanukei" (BT, *Bava Batra*, p. 20b; *Shabbat*, p. 119b) taught reading – "makrei" is Aramaic for reader – liturgy, and Pentateuch to children until age ten. Adolescents learned Mishnah from a "Mashneh," or, in Aramaic, "Matnei," whose status was higher than that of the teacher of children but lower than that of the sage who excelled in and taught the intricacies of Talmud to adults (Glick, 2000, pp. 388–9).

The sages none the less heaped praise on the qualities of a good teacher. Good pedagogy was conceived as the work of the Creator (Rawidowicz, 1986, pp. 135–6; Alexander, 1999, 2001b; Glick, 2000, p. 390), and God was said to teach the children of rabbinic academies – Rabbi Haim Beyad understood this to mean martyred children (Pallaggi, 1873, s. 126) – during the fourth hour of every day. God is greater than any human ruler, therefore, since the latter only wages war and does not teach children, while the Holy One excels at both. Teachers of children were viewed as "seekers of heaven" who were even allowed to pursue their educational activities on the Sabbath (BT, *Shabbat*, p. 150a). Additionally, some important sages, such as Rabbi Hiyyah Ben Abba and Levi Bar Sisi, third-century students of Rabbi Judah the Patriarch, were even known for teaching children (Glick, 2000, p. 390–2).

Maimonides went as far as to determine that although children should be taught Torah from the time they begin to speak, there is an obligation to pay a teacher when they reach the age of six or seven. Indeed, residents of a city that has no schools in which children study Torah are to be excommunicated unless they hire teachers, as "the world exists only for the sake of the sound of children studying Torah" (*Mishneh Torah*, Laws Concerning the Study of Torah, 2:1). Nevertheless, a gap has existed throughout Jewish history between the importance attached to the teaching of Torah to children and adolescents on the one hand, and the material status teachers were afforded in terms of salaries on the other (Gafni, 1999, pp. 72–3). This was true even for the learned sage after the rabbinate was institutionalized as a salaried communal position.

Educational institutions

As in other ancient Near Eastern cultures, the earliest formal learning outside the home probably developed alongside altars in such places as Shilo. It may be in these study groups that the tradition emerged for children to begin the study of Torah with Leviticus, which contains the Priestly Code. It is probably here too that Psalms, which were an important part of the liturgies at these sites, became significant texts for instructing the young. There are also allusions to "bands of the prophets" (I Sam. 10:5). It may be in these bands that the concept of moral instruction independent from the commandments began to emerge as a key educational concept (Jer. 2:30, 7:28, 17:23, 32:33).

Give ear, my people, to my teaching, turn your ear to what I say. I will expound a theme, hold forth on lessons of the past, things we have heard and known that our fathers have told us. We will not withhold them from their children, telling the coming generation the praises of the Lord and His might, and the wonders He performed. (Ps. 78:1–4; see also Ps. 15, 19, 119)

In the first century, the high priest Yehoshua Ben Gamla reformed and reorganized the educational system. Prior to the destruction of the Temple by the Romans, the Talmud explains, "Whoever has a father studies Torah with him, whoever has no father does not study Torah" (BT, *Bava Batra*, p. 21a). By the end of the first century, teachers of children were appointed first in Jerusalem and later in every province and town (Shepansky, 1951, p. 15; Baumgarten, 1999, p. 35).

This does not mean that there were no schools prior to this time, but Yehoshua Ben Gamla formalized a system of educational institutions that existed in Jerusalem under Hellenistic influence. He also expanded this system of public schools to the whole of the land of Israel. Institutions of this kind eventually took hold among the Jews of Babylonia as well (Glick, 1999, pp. 34–47). Schools in Israel were attached to synagogues, which emerged after the destruction of the Temple as the communal center for Jewish worship. In Babylonia they were adjacent to community centers that were not houses of worship, as it was against local custom to teach children in the synagogue (Gafni, 1999, p. 108).

Curriculum content

The Torah was considered the source of wisdom, its "wonders" to be discovered through serious study. Ben Sira (180 BCE) wrote, for example, that true wisdom is to be found in Torah, which existed with God before creation. The student of this legacy "preserves the sayings of the famous and penetrates the subtleties of parables. He explores the hidden meaning of proverbs and knows his way among enigmatic parables" (Ecclus. 39:2–3).

Secular wisdom existed alongside tradition, but it was viewed with suspicion because it does not lead to the moral life associated with Torah study. Until the destruction of the Temple, the prevailing view of educational content was articulated by Shimon the son of Raban Gamliel the Elder when he said that righteous deeds are more essential than needless interpretation (*Mishnah Avot* 1:17).

Under the influence of Hellenism, wisdom texts such as Proverbs, Job, Ecclessiastes, and Ecclessiasticus (Ben Sirah) were composed as textbooks by and for wisdom teachers (Melchert, 1998). Especially among the upper classes, they taught that intellectual and ethical enlightenment would awaken a fear of God and a desire to fulfill His commandments (Prov. 9:10; Job 28:28). Some of these texts were written on tablets, so their use in pedagogy corresponds to the emergence of literacy as a goal of instruction. This was accompanied by oral recitation of laws and narratives that preceded it and that continued well into the third century CE (Lieberman, 1942).

The classical curriculum emerged with the formalization of instruction: "At five years one is fit for Torah, at ten for Mishnah, at thirteen for the commandments, at fifteen for Talmud" (*Mishnah Avot* 5:21). This triumvirate of Torah, Mishnah, and Talmud became a curriculum for lifelong learning. "A man should divide his years into thirds, one third for Torah, one third for Mishnah, and one third for Talmud" (BT, *Kiddushin*, p. 30a). Medieval authorities differed as to the meaning of this division, for younger as well as more mature students.

According to Maimonides, one-third of the curriculum should be devoted to Written Torah, one-third to Oral Torah (presumably his code discussed below), and one-third to "Gemara." This includes all forms of rational reflection on Torah, from the derivation of the laws in the oral tradition to the philosophical reflection of God (*Mishneh Torah*, Laws Concerning the Study of Torah, 1:11–12, Twersky, 1972, p. 65). In his commentary on Maimonides, the fifteenth-century legalist Rabbi Joseph Caro followed the view of Rabbi Jacob Ben Meir Tam, grandson of Rashi, which held that less time should be allocated to Bible and Mishnah since they are already included in the study of Talmud. The curriculum should include Talmud text, therefore, not the abstract forms of reasoning advocated by Maimonides. This usually meant the Babylonian rather than the Jerusalem Talmud, because more extensive editing rendered it easier to decipher.

Instructional methods

The tradition was transmitted by doing and listening. Jewish tradition has historically embraced rote learning – what some philosophers of education call training (Green, 1971; Alexander, 1999). The Deuteronomist enjoins: "Take to heart these words with which I charge you this day. Impress them upon your children. Recite them when you stay at home, and when you are away, when you lie down and when you get up" (Deut. 6:6–7). The Hebrew *shinantem*, translated here as "impress them," comes from a root that means to repeat by rote. The import is to commit these words to memory, whether or not they are understood.

It is not surprising that memory would be important in a tradition that emphasizes oral transmission. The Deuteronomist also admonishes to "take utmost care and watch yourselves scrupulously so that you do not forget the things that you saw with your own eyes and so that they do not fade from your mind as long as you live" (Deut. 4:9). And the Talmudic sages debated whether "one who forgets something he has learned" commits one or two transgressions (BT, *Menahot*, p. 99b). In this spirit, the eleventh-century scholar Rabbi Shimon Yitzhaki (Rashi) interprets the verse "If you faithfully keep all this instruction" (Deut. 11:22) as a warning to "guard one's learning carefully lest it be forgotten."

This emphasis on rote learning and memory has led many to misinterpret the famous response of the Israelites to the revelation at Sinai, "All that the Lord God has spoken – *naaseh venishma* – we will faithfully do" (literally "we will do and we will hear") (Exod. 24:7). This does not mean, as many would have it, that following God's commandments is important to the exclusion of understanding them. Instead, the word *venishema* – "we will hear" – implies a deep sense of listening from which we acquire understanding. It is through fulfilling the commandments that they become meaningful. Thus, the sages stated, *mitokh shlo lishma ba lishma* – we understand the intrinsic meaning of Torah through its consistent practice (BT, *Pesahim*, p. 50b). Rote learning is a prerequisite to religious understanding.

That which is to be learned by rote, according to the text, is also to be loved. "You must love the Lord Your God with all your heart and with all your soul and with all your might" (Deut. 6:5). Even the alphabet was taught with attention to the moral context of the Torah written with these letters (BT, *Shabbat*, p. 104a). Maimonides admonishes that the teacher should reward students with sweets, so that they associate learning with that which they love (*Commentary on Perek Helek*, Twersky, 1972, p. 404). Training, in other words, should lead to teaching, which requires a deeper understanding and appreciation of concepts and practices (Alexander, 2001c, pp. 142–5).

This love and understanding was transmitted in the context of stories central to collective identity, such as the Exodus from Egypt, ritual re-enactments of these stories, such as the sacrificial rites of the pilgrimage festivals, and discussions between parents and children concerning both. Children witnessed rituals, inquired about their meaning, and were told stories in response (Alexander, 1999, 2001b). Dialogue rooted in observation of communal practice, therefore, stood at the heart of this pedagogic tradition.

Thus, following what became the watchword of Jewish faith, "Hear, O Israel! The Lord is our God, the Lord Alone," *Deuteronomy* (6:20–5) states:

When, in time to come, your son asks you, "What mean these exhortations, laws, and norms which the Lord our God has enjoined upon you?" You shall say to your son, "We were slaves to Pharaoh in Egypt and the Lord freed us from there with a mighty hand.... The Lord commanded us to observe all these laws, with reverence.... It will be therefore to our merit before the Lord our God to observe faithfully this whole instruction as he commanded us."

Similarly, concerning the Passover sacrifice: "When your children ask you, 'What do you mean by this rite?' you shall say, 'It is the Pascal sacrifice to the Lord, because He passed over the households of the Israelites in Egypt when He smote the Egyptians, but saved our houses'" (Exod. 12:26–7). So too, in relation to eating Matzoth – the unleavened bread of the Passover holiday – the text states, "And you shall explain to your son on that day, 'It is because of that which the Lord did for me when I went free from Egypt'" (Exod. 13:8).

Finally, in reference to the redemption of first-born males, the Torah relates:

And when, in time to come, your son asks you saying, "What does this mean?" you shall say to him, "It was with a mighty hand that the Lord brought us forth from Egypt, the house of bondage. When the Pharaoh stubbornly refused to let us go, the Lord slew every first-born in the land of Egypt, the first-born man and beast. Therefore I sacrifice to the Lord every first male issue of the womb, but redeem every first born among my sons." (Exod. 13:14–15)

This dialogical pedagogy was so essential to the tradition – God first spoke to Adam with a question, "where are you?" (Gen. 3:9) – that the sages constructed a typology of questions and questioners based on these passages (*Mikhilta* Bo, parasha 18; JT *Pesahim*, 10:4; *Yalkut Shimoni*, 226) that became part of the traditional Passover liturgy (Rabinowicz, 1982, pp. 12–14). This attitude was built into the Passover evening liturgy that centers on four mandatory questions to be asked even if all present know the answers (*Mishnah Pesahim*, 10:4; BT *Pesahim*, p. 116a). The rabbinic tradition that emerged took the "give and take" of this dialogical pedagogy to heart (Halivni, 1986, 1991; Glick, 1999, pp. 81–2). Thus Rashi could assume in his classical Bible commentary that the questions inherent in the biblical texts were already understood, and it was his job to supply answers (Melamed, 1978, pp. 353–448; Pearl, 1988, pp. 24–62).

Parents – and later elders, priests, prophets, and scribes – served as role models that youngsters were to imitate and with whom they were to identify. It is no accident that the Hebrew root for "teacher" is the same as that for "parent." Their task was to transmit the legacy of Torah from one generation to the next with sensitivity to the needs of the child. Thus, the wisdom tradition enjoins that children should be taught according to their abilities (Prov. 22:6), and the *Mishnah Pesahim* (10:4) explains that if children do not know how to ask the Passover questions, parents are to teach them, with answers given according to their capacity to understand. It has become customary, therefore, for fathers to examine their sons each Shabbat on what they learned the previous week.

Discipline and development

To the extent that the Bible has a conception of childhood (Aries, 1962), it is viewed as a morally treacherous period in human development, "since the divinings of a man's mind are evil from his youth" (Gen. 8:21). The educational task, according to this view, is to prepare youngsters for a moral life by conquering their evil inclinations, not by extreme asceticism that disdains worldly pleasures, but by following a "golden mean" that eschews extremism (see Maimonides, *Eight Chapters*, chapter IV; Twersky, 1972, p. 369).

Hence, it is necessary to be diligent with children lest they become defiant. To this end, physical punishment was considered a legitimate form of instruction. "A father who spares the rod hates his son, but one who loves his son brings him up strictly" (Prov. 13:24). "Have you sons? Discipline and break them in from their earliest years. Have you daughters? Keep a close watch over them and do not look on them with indulgence" (Ecclus. 7:23–4). "Rod and reprimand impart wisdom, but an uncontrolled youth brings shame on his mother.... Correct your son, and he will be a comfort to you" (Prov. 29:15, 17).

As the tradition evolved so did recognition of the developmental needs of the child. The sages taught that specific commandments would become obligatory upon children in accordance with their physical and intellectual growth. A minor who knows how to wave the lulav – the ritual palm branch waved on Sukkot festival – is obliged to do so. A youngster who can wrap himself in a talit – a garment recalling the commandments – is obliged to wear the fringes traditionally tied to its corners. If he knows how to put on the tefilin – phylacteries worn in prayer – his father should provide them, and if he knows how to talk, his father should teach him to recite the "Shema Yisrael" – watchword of the Jewish faith (BT, *Sukkah*, p. 52a). Rabbi Judah even permits a minor to read from the Torah and other scrolls in the synagogue (*Mishnah Megilah*, 2:4). When it comes to the Atonement fast, the minor should fast for a few hours by the ages of nine or ten and for the entire 24 hours by the age of 12 or 13 (BT *Yoma*, p. 62a; Glick, 1999, p. 51).

Higher education and adult learning

From the very earliest periods of Jewish history, it was understood that Torah was not only to be transmitted to the young, but to be studied by adults as well. "Let not this book of the teaching cease from your lips, but recite it day and night" (Josh. 1:8). There is a close link between the roles of the judge and the teacher, since both transmit and interpret Divine instruction. Perhaps the earliest form of adult learning, therefore, was found in the biblical system of courts and appeals that required interpretation and application of Torah. "You shall appoint magistrates and clerks for your tribes, in all the settlements that the Lord your God is giving you" (Deut 16:18).

If a case is too baffling for you to decide ... you shall promptly repair to the place which the Lord your God has chosen and appear before the levitical priests, or the magistrate in charge at that time, and present your problem. When they have announced to you the verdict ... you shall carry [it] out, observing scrupulously all their instructions to you. (Deut. 17:8–10)

Early on families also came together to hear public recitations of the Torah on the Sukkot festival (Deut. 31:12) and other public feasts, such as covenant renewal ceremonies (Exod. 24:7). The national and religious heritage was recited and reenacted during these ceremonies, reminding people "to love the stranger . . . because you were strangers in the land of Egypt" (Exod. 12:26–7; Lev. 23:43).

The traditions of public court proceedings (Deut. 21:18–19) and communal recitation of the law were combined during the sixth century BCE when Ezra the Priest began public readings of the Pentateuch.

On the first day of the seventh month, Ezra the priest brought the Teaching before the congregation, men and women and all who could listen with understanding. He read from it, facing the square before the water Gate, from the first light until midday, to men and women and those who could understand, the ears of the people were given to the scroll of the Teaching. (Neh. 8:2–3)

By the Hellenistic period, synagogues – a Babylonian development – emerged in the land of Israel. They complemented household instruction and public reading of the Torah on Monday and Thursday with longer recitations on the Sabbath, festivals, and other occasions. These readings were accompanied by liturgical re-enactments and meditations, and by public homilies.

During this period, the position of the scribe was fortified. He became recognized for learned deliberations concerning the written and oral traditions that were formalized in the institution of the Sanhedrin, or court of 70 elders, that met on the steps of the Temple mount. Adult students would attend these discussions and associate themselves with leading figures of the court who were eventually identified in pairs, such as Hillel and Shammai. These learned conversations would continue in private homes, and students were admonished to "make their homes a house of meeting for sages." The dialogues that emerged became the earliest "yeshivot" or Talmudic academies (*Mishnah Avot*, 1:4).

The role of the "talmid haham" or rabbinic sage emerged out of the scribe as the quintessential educational, academic, and religious leader of the Jewish people. This was accompanied by the establishment of the first Talmudic academy in Yavneh by Yohanan ben Zakkai in 70 CE, which led to the flowering of such academies in the Galilee and Babylon. From these academies new texts emerged, including the Mishnah of Rabbi Judah the Patriarch, the Jerusalem and Babylonian Talmuds, collections of legal and literary commentaries on books of the Hebrew Bible, compendia of rabbinic homilies, and eventually responsa, legal codes, and theological tracts.

During the sixth and seventh centuries Babylonian Jews took advantage of late winter and summer lulls in the agrarian economy between the Tigris and Euphrates. Students of all ages would gather twice each year for month-long study retreats known as "yarhei kallah" (Neusner, 1965). The curriculum consisted of a single tractate for the month-long term selected by the "Gaon" or head of the Yeshiva. Seating was determined according to level of textual mastery, and students were called upon to recite according to their place in this hierarchy (Assaf 2001, pp. 31–2).

In the twelfth century, Maimonides reorganized the Oral Torah into a new code so that the students could study the written law and then learn this complex tradition from a single text (Introduction to the *Mishneh Torah*, Twersky, 1972, pp. 35–41). He called it the *Mishneh Torah* – taken from Moses' repetition of the Torah in the last book of the Pentateuch (Deut. 17:18). Once the oral tradition was mastered through study of Maimonides' new code, the learned student could devote himself to *pardes*. According to the mystics this referred to the hidden truths of creation and unification with the deity, but in Maimonides' view it meant the study of natural science and mathematics (*Mishneh Torah*, Laws Concerning the Study of Torah, 1:12, Twersky, 1972, p. 65; *Guide to the Perplexed*, part III, chapter 51, Twersky, pp. 241–349). This formed an early precedent for later arguments to combine Torah with secular learning (Wiezel, 1826), to achieve the Maimonidean ideal of the "wise and good person." Wisdom, in this view, is found in philosophy and secular learning, while goodness grows from the study, practice, and celebration of Torah (Alexander, 2001c, pp. 183–98).

Yeshivot developed in Ashkenaz in the twelfth and thirteenth centuries in which interactions between students and rabbis were more spontaneous than those found in Babylonia. Study was more independent and the curriculum was enlarged to include legal and homiletic interpretation of biblical as well as rabbinic material (Gafni, 1999, pp. 83ff; Grossman, 2001, pp. 166–7). Pedagogy was characterized by the method of study known as "pilpul." According to this method, contradictions among the vast array of rabbinic opinions were resolved by limiting statements attributed to a sage to particular cases and not others. The acumen and mastery required to apply this method energized the academies of Europe, inspiring generations to place the study of Talmud at the pinnacle of Jewish intellectual and spiritual life (Assaf, 2002, p. 115).

This method turned many scholars inward, leading to criticism of Maimonides' openness to philosophical truths. Such criticism was found more frequently among the Ashkenazic rabbis of Europe than the Sephardic sages of North Africa and the Middle East. Thus Rabbi Joseph Ibn Casspi of fourteenth-century Venice urged his son not to rush into the study of Maimonides' *Guide to the Perplexed* or Aristotle's *Metaphysics*. Better to attend to ethical traditions found in *Proverbs*, *Ecclessiastes*, and *Mishnah Avot*, although he was also prepared to endorse Aristotle's *Nichomachean Ethics* and Maimonides' "laws concerning knowledge" in the *Mishneh Torah* (Abrahams, 1976, 1, pp. 143–5). The "pilpul" movement was ultimately deposed in the sixteenth century by such luminaries as Rabbi Judah Loewy, known as the "Maharal of Prague," who emphasized the plain meaning of biblical and rabbinic texts (Reiner, 1993, pp. 5–80).

The Study of Sacred Texts

Until this point we have considered major trends in biblical and rabbinic educational thought and practice. But what relevance do these themes have to contemporary pedagogy? Consider the Mishnah in *Avot* (5:21), which states that a child should begin studying the Bible at the age of five. There are four interpretations of this Mishnah. Each reflects a different aspect of what it means to teach a child to study a sacred text. One claims that our Mishnah deals with the age at which Bible study should begin. A second approach considers what should count as the study of the Bible. The third position concerns the number of years that ought to be devoted to this subject matter. A fourth attitude reflects the impact of available instructional materials on Bible pedagogy.

The fifteenth-century Italian scholar Don Isaac Abravanel objected to the Ashkenazic practice of teaching children Bible before the age of five. This was not the custom in Spain and Portugal, where he was raised. Sepharadim did not begin teaching the Bible to children before the age of five. In his commentary to *Avot*, *Nahlat Avot*, he writes:

It is fitting for you to know that the times mentioned here [in *Avot*] pertain to the commencement and not to the conclusion of study. For it does not say that until five years of age one should be involved in studying the Bible, nor as the practice still followed by the Ashkenazim. Rather, at the age of five, he will begin to study the Bible. (Assaf, 2001, pp. 116–17)

At stake in this dispute is the very nature of Bible study, and the level of maturity it demands. The Sephardic tradition was deeply influenced by the Islamic intellectual renaissance of the tenth to the twelfth centuries, which prized the precision of the Arabic language and the reasoning of Islamic philosophers. The Sephardic vision of religious identity, therefore, emphasized the precise reading of Hebrew verses and a rational understanding of biblical texts. Ashkenazic education did not emphasize accentuation or correct reading. Nor did it focus on rational understanding. Instead, it stressed the religious meaning of the Bible as interpreted in rabbinic lore.

A minimum level of development is required to teach youngsters the linguistic and thinking skills required for Sephardic exegesis. Additionally, an extended period of growth is required to attain a mature understanding of the text. Hence, Abravanel states that our Mishnah "pertains to the commencement and not the concluding time of study." It was assumed that this study would continue for the duration necessary to attain such an understanding. However, the biblical and rabbinic stories associated with Ashkenazic eisegesis can be more readily shared with very young children.

This debate goes to the very heart of what it means to learn a sacred text. Is the meaning of the text grounded in linguistic and rational criteria, as believed by many Sephardic scholars, or is it found in the context of traditional narratives and stories, as evidenced in Ashkenaz? Is this text written in human language, as held by the second-century sage Rabbi Ishmael, and as such subject to treatment according to the rules of human language? Or is it written in a special Divine tongue that has its own hermeneutic rules, as held by Rabbi Akiba (BT, *Berakhot*, p. 32b)? And, whether human or Divine, to what degree ought language, reason, and tradition to play key roles in deciphering the meaning into which students are to be initiated in studying that text?

These issues are sharpened when we consider the interpretation of Rabbi David Hanagid, Maimonides' grandson. He wrote that our Mishnah teaches that, at the age of five, great emphasis must be placed on the technical side of reading, with the appropriate vowels, signs, and accent marks.

The saying "scripture at five" means that one is minimally required to study each verse of the entire Bible correctly because it provides a strong foundation. For one finds many people studying the Talmud in depth but not reading a verse properly. And to this the Rav [Maimonides] instructed people: "First read the verse precisely, then turn to the Talmud." (Hanagid, 1993)

According to this view, learning the Bible means that students are able to correctly pronounce the words and punctuate the sentences. More importantly, the ultimate end of acquiring these skills, and the knowledge that accompanies them, is not to facilitate biblical understanding for its own sake, but to enable students to study "Talmud." Bible study is prerequisite to learning Gemara, or to its method of reasoning, which derives practical instruction from the interpretation of biblical and mishnaic passages.

At stake here is the ultimate purpose of Bible study. Is the Bible curriculum merely an instrumental value leading to higher learning – Talmud? If so, what skills and information are required? Rabbi David's view conforms to Abravanel's approach to Bible study as rooted in linguistic precision and Aristotelian logic, and diverges from the less rigorous and more literary attitude prevalent among Ashkenazim.

The third interpretation of our Mishnah deals with the time to be allotted to this subject matter in the curriculum. In his *Commentary on Avot*, Provençal scholar Rabbi Abraham Fritzul states:

This saying comes to teach us the commencement period of study . . . it is fitting for one to read [properly] from the Bible at the age of five. For at the age of four the child begins with the consonants and vowels and in the [basic] manner of reading. By five, he will read perfectly. Let him continue with Bible for five consecutive years until the age of ten, like the students who mainly study one discipline for five years. From here, [the dictum of our sages:] "If a student does not see results in his studies within five years, he never will." (Fritzul, 1964, p. 68)

According to this view, the technical aspects of reading emphasized by the previous interpretations are prerequisite to, but not part of, studying the Bible. This begins only once one has mastered basic linguistic skills – before the age of five – and continues for five years to enable mastery of the biblical text itself, presumably not as a means to some other form of learning, but as an educational value in its own right.

Although it did not necessarily embrace the theological consequences of Aristotelian rationalism, the "pilpul" movement of nineteenth-century Eastern Europe did inherit a love for textual reasoning. It thus preferred the Sephardic emphasis on the rigors of Talmud study to biblical and rabbinic lore. In this spirit, the Lithuanian Rabbi Yehiel Epstein explained why many scholars did not mention the requirement to learn the Bible by the age of five in their legal decisions.

It would seem that in those times all of Scripture was written without vowels like our scrolls of the law. Therefore, students had to be proficient by heart in vocalization, accentuation, plene and defective spelling. For all these skills they required five years of study. . . . This is not the case in our times.

They also required five years to become proficient in the study of Mishnah. According to Epstein, this too "is not the case these days. We can see that it is almost impossible to be occupied with the Bible for five years and with Mishnah for five years. Moreover, the Babylonian Talmud contains them all" (Epstein, 1970; *Yoreh De'a*, 245).

There is no need to invest five years in Bible study, according to Epstein, because books were readily available in nineteenth-century Poland and Lithuania (Assaf, 2001, p. 4). By contrast, a lack of books in nineteenth-century Yemen prompted teachers to encourage students to learn the Bible by heart. This required a greater investment of time. Jacob Sapir (1930) describes this reality in his lively and engaging diary, *Even Sapir*.

46

These comments on our Mishnah do not deal with the meaning of the text alone. They also reflect the educational realities of their times. They constitute not only a significant source of educational history, but also a rich body of pedagogic experience. Analysis of these cases can highlight key conceptual issues and contribute to grounded theories of textual instruction. Such analysis sheds light on the teaching of Jewish, Christian, and Muslim sources, and on contemporary literature, history, theology, and law. They address such questions as: What does it mean to read a text? What skills and modes of interpretation are required to do so? What is its purpose? At what ages should students begin? What is the relative priority of one text over another? How much time ought to be devoted in the curriculum to this task? What instructional materials and technologies are required, and how do the materials and technologies available influence the pedagogies we choose to employ?

Biblical and rabbinic sources, therefore, have a significant contribution to make to the philosophical analysis of educational concepts, such as the very meaning of text study, and to the practical analysis of teaching methods, such as the impact of age and instructional materials on pedagogy.

See also 4 THE AUGUSTINIAN TRADITION; 23 RELIGIOUS EDUCATION

References

Abrahams, I. (1976) *Wills of the Geonim of Israel*. Philadelphia: The Jewish Publication Society (in Hebrew).

Albeck, H. (1969) *Introduction to the Talmuds*. Tel Aviv: Devir (in Hebrew).

Alexander, H. (1999) A Jewish view of human learning. *International Journal of Children's Spirituality*, 4(2), 155–64.

Alexander, H. (2001a) Education. In D. Lieber (ed.), *Etz Hayim: Torah and Commentary*. New York: The Rabbinical Assembly, pp. 1365–9.

Alexander, H. (2001b) God as teacher: Jewish reflections on a theology of pedagogy. *Journal of Beliefs and Values*, 22(1), 5–17.

Alexander, H. (2001c) *Reclaiming Goodness: Education and the Spiritual Quest*. Notre Dame, IN: University of Notre Dame Press.

Aries, P. (1962) *Centuries of Childhood: A Social History of Family Life*. New York: Random House.

Assaf, S. (2001) *A Source Book for the History of Jewish Education from the Middle Ages to the Enlightenment, volume 2*, ed. S. Glick. New York: The Jewish Theological Seminary of America (in Hebrew).

Assaf, S. (2002) *A Source Book for the History of Jewish Education from the Middle Ages to the Enlightenment, volume 1*, ed. S. Glick. New York: The Jewish Theological Seminary of America (in Hebrew).

Baron, S. (1937) *A Social Religious History of the Jews*. New York: Columbia University Press.

Baumgarten, A. (1999) Knowledge of reading and writing and the polemics surrounding interpretation of the Bible. In R. Peledhai and I. Etkes (eds), *Education and History*. Jerusalem: Shazar Center (in Hebrew).

Ben Yehiel, Y. (1926) *Arukh hashalem* [*Talmudic Lexicon*], ed. H. Kohath. Vilna: Menorah (in Hebrew).

Biblical Encyclopedia (1988) Jerusalem: Mossad Bialik (in Hebrew).

Chazan, B. (1978) *The Language of Jewish Education*. New York: Hartmore House.

Cohen, J. (1964) *Jewish Education in Democratic Society*. New York: Reconstructionist Press.

Elnekaveh, I. (1929) *Menorat hameor*, ed. D. Immanuel. New York: Bloch (in Hebrew).

Epstein, Y. (1970) *Arukh hashulhan*. Jerusalem: Talmud Press (in Hebrew).

Finkelstein, L. (1962) *Akiba: Scholar, Saint, and Martyr*. Cleveland, OH: World Publishing.

Finkelstein, L. (1969) *Sifre on Deuteronomy*. New York: The Jewish Theological Seminary of America (in Hebrew).

Fritzul, A. (1964) *Commentary on Avot*. Jerusalem: Mahon Torah Shleima (in Hebrew).

Gafni, I. (1999) Education of minors in the Talmudic period: tradition and reality. In R. Peledhai and I. Etkes (eds), *Education and History*. Jerusalem: Shazar Center (in Hebrew).

Ginzberg, L. (1955) *On Jewish Law and Lore*. Philadelphia: The Jewish Publication Society.

Glick, S. (1999) *Education in Light of Israeli Law and Halakhic Literature, volume 1*. Jerusalem: The Schechter Institute of Jewish Studies (in Hebrew).

Glick, S. (2000) *Education in Light of Israeli Law and Halakhic Literature, volume 2*. Jerusalem: The Schechter Institute of Jewish Studies (in Hebrew).

Graetz, H. (1955) *A History of the Jews*. Tel Aviv: Yizrael (in Hebrew).

Green, T. (1971) *The Activities of Teaching*. New York: McGraw-Hill.

Grossman, A. (2001) *The Sages of France and Ashkenaz*. Jerusalem: Magnes (in Hebrew).

Halivni, D. (1986) *Midrash, Mishnah, and Gemara: The Jewish Predilection for Justified Law*. Cambridge, MA: Harvard University Press.

Halivni, D. (1991) *Peshat and Derash: Plain and Applied Meaning in Rabbinic Exegesis*. New York: Oxford University Press.

Hanagid, D. (1993) *Commentary on Mishnah Avot*. Jerusalem: Mahon Hakhtav (in Hebrew).

Hebrew Encyclopedia (1993) Jerusalem: The Encyclopedia Company (in Hebrew).

Hoffman, L. (1979) *The Canonization of the Synagogue Service*. Notre Dame, IN: University of Notre Dame Press.

Kadushin, M. (1964) *Worship and Ethics: A Study in Rabbinic Judaism*. Evanston, IL: Northwestern University Press.

Kadushin, M. (1972) *The Rabbinic Mind*. New York: Bloch.

Kaplan, M. (1957) *Judaism as a Civilization*. New York: Reconstructionist Press.

Levine, B. (ed.) (1972) *Letter of Rabbi Shirira Gaon*. Jerusalem: Makor (in Hebrew).

Lieberman, S. (1942) *Greek in Jewish Palestine*. New York: The Jewish Theological Seminary of America.

Maimonides, M. (1956) *Guide to the Perplexed*, trans. M. Friedlander. New York: Dover.

Melamed, E. (1978) *Bible Commentaries*. Jerusalem: Magnes (in Hebrew).

Melchert, C. (1998) *Wise Teaching: Biblical Wisdom and Educational Ministry*. Harrisburg, PA: Trinity.

Moore, G. (1954) *Judaism in the First Centuries of the Christian Era*. Cambridge, MA: Harvard University Press.

Neusner, J. (1965) *A History of the Jews in Babylonia*. Leiden: Brill.

Neusner, J. (ed.) (1970a) *The Formation of the Babylonian Talmud*. Leiden: Brill.

Neusner, J. (1970b) *The Way of Torah*. Belmont: Dickenson.

Neusner, J. (1981) *Judaism: The Evidence of the Mishnah*. Chicago: University of Chicago Press.

Neusner, J. (1984) *Invitation to the Talmud*. San Francisco: Harper and Row.

Neusner, J. (ed.) (1993) *Classical Judaism*. Frankfort: Lang.

Pallaggi, H. (1873) *Response of Hayyim Beyad*. IZMIR: Raditi (in Hebrew).

Pearl, C. (1988) *Rashi*. New York: Grove Press.

Peters, R. (1967) *The Concept of Education*. London: Routledge and Kegan Paul.

Rabinowicz, R. (ed.) (1982) *Passover Haggadah: The Feast of Freedom*. New York: The Rabbinical Assembly.

Rawidowicz, S. (1986) *Jews the Ever Dying People and Other Essays*. Rutherford, NJ: Farliegh Dickinson University.

Reiner, E. (1993) The contribution of sixteenth and seventeenth century Polish yeshivot to the "pilpul" controversy. In Y. Bartal (ed.), *Studies in Jewish Culture in Honor of Chone Shmeruk*. Jerusalem: Shazar Center, pp. 5–80 (in Hebrew).

Rosenak, M. (1987) *Commandments and Concerns*. Philadelphia: The Jewish Publication Society.

Sapir, J. (1930) *Even Sapir*. Jerusalem: Sifriat Mekorot (Hebrew).

Shepansky, I. (1951) *Hatakanot beyisrael* [*The Takkanot of Israel*]. Jerusalem: Mossad Harav Kook (in Hebrew).

Scheffler, I. (1973) *Reason and Teaching*. London: Routledge and Kegan Paul.

Shulman, L. (1986) Those who understand: knowledge growth in teaching. *Educational Researcher*, 15(2), 4–16.

Twersky, I. (ed.) (1972) *A Maimonides Reader*. New York: Behrman House.

Urbach, E. (1975) *The Sages: Their Concepts and Beliefs*. Jerusalem: Magnes.

Wiezel, N. (1826) *Words of Peace and Truth*. Vienna: A. Schmidt (in Hebrew).

Winch, P. (1965) *The Idea of Social Science and Its Relation to Philosophy*. London: Routledge and Kegan Paul.

Zimmels, H. (1958) *Ashkenazim and Sepharadim: Their Relations, Differences and Problems as Reflected in the Rabbinical Responsa*. London: Oxford University Press.

4

The Educational Thought of Augustine

Gareth B. Matthews

St Augustine, Bishop of Hippo, was a teacher of rhetoric before he became a Christian priest. It is therefore not surprising that he should have been interested in education. Nor is it surprising that, as one of the great "Fathers" of the Christian Church, he should have taught later generations how to use the language and techniques of classical rhetoric to interpret Christian Scriptures.

What is much more surprising, given Augustine's heavily Ciceronian education, is how remarkably introspective a person he was. His interest in his own introspectively revealed motivation and in a search for "inner" understanding strikes a reader today as amazingly "modern." What follows is a discussion of some of the most interesting topics relevant to learning and teaching that Augustine addresses in his vast and varied corpus.

Prelinguistic Learning

Learning how to talk is normally one of the first things a child does. But even before a child acquires a language, there is much else to learn. In a remarkable passage from the first book of Augustine's autobiography we find this vivid description of the frustrations that face a prelinguistic infant in learning how to get its desires satisfied:

Little by little I began to realize where I was and to want to make my wishes known to others, who might satisfy them. But this I could not do, because my wishes were inside me, while other people were outside, and they had no faculty which could penetrate my mind. So I would toss my arms and legs about and make noises, hoping that such few sighs as I could make would show my meaning, though they were quite unlike what they were meant to mime. And if my wishes were not carried out, either because they had not been understood or because what I wanted would have harmed me, I would get cross with my elders, who were not at my beck and call, and with people who were not my servants, simply because they did not attend to my wishes; and I would take my revenge by bursting into tears. (*Confessions*, 1.6.8; Augustine, 1961, pp. 25–6)

Earlier writers had described, *from the outside*, how babies behave. But this is the first attempt to say *from the inside* what it is like to be an infant, indeed, what it is like to be an infant without language. Augustine is, in fact, the first philosopher in our Western tradition to assign significant value to the first-person point of view in philosophy. As we can see in this passage, Augustine views even a baby as having desires it wishes to express to others, and well before it has effective means for doing so.

Language Acquisition

There is no unanimity among experts on language acquisition today as to how infants first learn to talk. Noam Chomsky is generally thought to have discredited B. F. Skinner's attempt to understand language acquisition as a form of operant conditioning (Chomsky, 1959). But there is no agreement about whether we should think of an infant as already capable of "talking to itself" in "mentalese" as it tries to figure out what words of English, or Russian, or Swahili mean. As the passage above suggests, and as the passage below makes explicit, Augustine was in no doubt that a prelinguistic infant could form thoughts and use gestures to express those thoughts in an effort to figure out the meanings of the words.

Here, then, is a second relevant passage from Book 1 of Augustine's *Confessions*. This, in fact, is the passage Wittgenstein uses to begin his *Philosophical Investigations* (Wittgenstein, 1958, para. 1):

It was not my elders who showed me the words by some set system of instruction, in the way that they taught me to read long afterwards; but, instead, I taught myself by using the intelligence you, my God, gave to me. For when I tried to express my meaning by crying out and making various sounds and movements, so that my wishes should be obeyed, I found that I could not convey all that I meant or make myself understood by everyone whom I wanted to understand me. So my memory prompted me. I noticed that people would name some object and then turn towards whatever it was they had named. I watched them and understood that the sound they made when they wanted to indicate that particular thing was the name they gave to it, and their actions clearly showed what they meant, for there is a kind of universal language, consisting of expressions of the face and eyes, gestures and tones of voice, which can show whether a person means to ask for something and get it, or to refuse it and have nothing to do with it. So by hearing words arranged in various phrases and constantly repeated, I gradually pieced together what they stood for; and when my tongue had mastered the pronunciation, I began to express my wishes by means of them. In this way I made my wants known to my family and they made theirs known to me. (*Confessions*, 1.8.13; Augustine, 1961, p. 29)

The Ambiguity of Ostension

Wittgenstein criticizes the view of meaning he finds implicit in Augustine's brief account above of how he learned to talk. But it is interesting that one of Wittgenstein's criticisms of the Augustinian picture of language-learning is anticipated by Augustine himself. Thus, Wittgenstein thinks the view presented in the passage above offers only an inadequate account of language-learning, since each ostensive definition is, by itself, incurably ambiguous. Thus, Wittgenstein tells us, the learner "might equally well take the name of a person, of which I give an ostensive definition, as that of a colour, of a race, or even of a point of the compass . . . an ostensive definition can be variously interpreted in *every* case" (Wittgenstein, 1958, para. 28).

Augustine, however, is on to the same point when, in his dialogue on language, *Concerning the Teacher (De magistro)*, he records this exchange with his son, Adeodatus:

Augustine:	Now do this: tell me – if I were completely ignorant of the meaning of the word ["walking"] and were to ask you what walking is while you were walking, how would you teach me?
Adeodatus:	I would do it a little bit more quickly, so that after your question you would be prompted by something novel [in my behavior], and yet nothing would take place other than what was to be shown. (*De magistro*, 3.6; Augustine, 1995, pp. 101–2)

Wittgenstein's own response to the problem of the ambiguity of ostension is to try to understand our various uses of language as each parts of some "language game" we play with other speakers. The meanings of words, according to him, should not be thought of as mental images. Instead we should think of the meanings words have as their uses in particular language games. "For a *large* class of cases – though not for all – in which we employ the word 'meaning' it can be defined thus: the meaning of a word is its use in the language" (Wittgenstein, 1958, para. 43). Ultimately, word usage rests on rules, which, in turn, rest on "forms of life" (ibid., paras 239–41).

The Doctrine of Illumination

Augustine responds to the problem of the ambiguity of ostension in quite a different way from Wittgenstein. In *Concerning the Teacher* Augustine proposes the radical conclusion that no human teacher ever really teaches anyone anything by pointing to examples, or even by using words. According to him, what a human teacher can do is, at most, to put us, individually, in a situation in which we can learn or come to understand something for ourselves. Coming to know what a word means is an inner "illumination" that enables us to link a word or phrase either with something we have seen or otherwise perceived with our senses, or with something abstract that we have natural access to through our intelligence. This inner illumination by which we come to understand what it is that a word picks out is something he also describes as learning from Christ, our "Inner Teacher" (*De magistro*, 11.38; Augustine, 1995, p. 139).

Historically, the major competitor to Augustine's illumination theory of learning is "abstraction theory," which is often linked with Aristotle, Aquinas, and the British Empiricists. According to the abstraction theory, I learn what, say, red is by being shown, perhaps, a red ball, a red dress, and a red pencil. I then abstract what these three objects have in common, namely, their redness, and hold that in my mind as the meaning of the word "red." Many people find the abstraction theory immediately appealing, even though it seems vulnerable to criticism from the problem of the ambiguity of ostension. How does one ever learn which of the various features common to any collection of objects being pointed to is the feature that should be abstracted from them?

The British Empiricists, who tended to think of the meanings of words as mental images, found difficulty with a closely related problem. My mental image of a triangle, it seems, must be an image of either an equilateral triangle or a non-equilateral triangle. But if the image I have to give the word "triangle" its meaning is an image of an equilateral triangle, how can it help me pick out isosceles and scalene triangles as triangles as well? And if my image is an image of a scalene triangle, how can it help me to understand that an equilateral triangle is a triangle? Yet I can hardly have an image of a triangle that is "neutral" with respect to these various possibilities.

One might criticize the Wittgensteinian approach to language learning and meaning on the ground that it seems to make meaning merely conventional; it rests, ultimately, on a shared form of life. Yet, even if color distinctions, say, are in this way culturally relative, numbers and geometrical shapes and many other things are neither purely conventional nor culturally relative, the critic will insist.

Augustinian illumination theory has an answer to all these criticisms; but perhaps it leaves itself open to the criticism that it has not explained very much. Even if true illumination will lead us to classify things correctly, we may surely be led to think we have had an illumination when what we have "seen" is only an illusion or a falsity.

Or suppose I say, in keeping with the idea of illumination, that I understand a proof in mathematics, not just when I have checked all the steps and convinced myself that each step is legitimate but because "a light has gone on" and I now "see" why the proof works. This description of what has happened may be phenomenologically correct, but one could still wonder whether it explains in any helpful way what has happened, let alone how I can be sure that my "illumination" is genuine.

The Computational View of Mind

There is, however, an important way in which Augustine's doctrine of illumination addresses directly an important twentieth-century controversy on the nature of mind, as well as the nature of teaching and learning. The most dramatic way to appreciate the relevance of Augustine to this controversy is to consider a thought experiment John Searle has made famous (see King, 1998). Searle invites us to suppose that he, knowing no Chinese, is locked in a room with a "large batch of Chinese writing" (Searle, 1980). Suppose the batch of writing correlates specific Chinese characters with other specific Chinese characters.

Now suppose that slips of paper with Chinese characters written on them are slipped through a slit in the door into the room in which Searle is locked up. Suppose that Searle takes each slip he receives through the slit in the door, correlates the shapes of the characters on the slip with characters on the "correlation pages" he has in the room, finds in each case another slip of paper on which is written the characters correlated with the characters on the slip that just came through the door. Suppose Searle then passes back through the slit in the door the slip of paper on which appear the correlated characters.

53

We can imagine that this whole practice of passing slips of paper with Chinese characters on them through the slit in the door and getting back other slips of paper with other Chinese characters on them can be understood by a reader of Chinese as asking questions on the slips that go through the slit and receiving answers on the slips that come back. All this question-and-answer exchange could go on without the intermediary, John Searle, understanding anything of what was being asked on the slips that came into his room and without his understanding anything of what he "said" in response by passing the correlated characters into the world outside.

The moral Searle draws is that human minds cannot be simply computers – machines able to recognize written questions by their shape (or spoken questions by their sound) and then able to respond with appropriate written (or spoken) answers. For, as the Chinese room thought experiment shows, a person with a good set of correlation rules connecting questions with answers might successfully respond to each question with an appropriate answer without understanding either the question or the answer – indeed, without even understanding that a question had been posed and answered.

Augustine's doctrine of illumination seems to back up Searle's point. Understanding a question and giving a good answer cannot be simply a matter of "computation," such as a computer might be capable of, or even of "rule-following." A computer can be programmed to answer a wide variety of "questions" it is asked in a "reasonable" way without really understanding either the question or the answer. What is missing for the computer, as well as for Searle locked in his room, is an understanding both of what it is being asked and of what answer it is giving. That missing understanding, Augustine would tell us, is an appropriate episode of "illumination."

Illumination and Platonic Recollection

We can go further. Consider Plato's example in his dialogue *Meno* of the slave boy coming to understand how to construct a square with an area twice that of a given square. What is important here, one could say, is not that the slave boy comes to "store" the rule that a square constructed on the diagonal of a given square will have an area twice that of the given square. What is important is that the slave boy comes to "see" why this is so and, because of having "seen" why it is so, is able to construct a proof that it is so. Just learning the rule without achieving any understanding of why it is so would be like having the right correlation rule in Searle's Chinese room without understanding what correlates with what.

Plato, in *Meno*, construes the illumination that the slave boy achieves as recollecting the abstract geometrical objects the soul has already known from a previous life. Augustine criticizes Plato's Theory of Recollection as excessive. In his great work, *On the Trinity*, Augustine chides Plato for suggesting that a randomly chosen individual could be brought to recollect a geometrical truth. Not everyone would have been a geometrician in a previous life, he insists, "since there are so few of them in the human race that one can hardly be found" (12.15.24). We ought instead to believe, Augustine writes, that the nature of the intellectual mind is so formed as to see those things which, according to the disposition of the Creator, are subjoined to intelligible things in the natural order, in a sort of inrorporeal light of its own kind, as the eye of the flesh sees the things that lie about it in this corporeal light, of which light it is made to be receptive and to which it is adapted (*On the Trinity*, 12.15.24; Augustine, 2002).

Truth and Meaning

Augustine, of course, takes the Christian Bible, both Old Testament and New Testament, to be the divinely revealed word of God. Indeed, he supposes that every statement in this Bible is true. However, what biblical statements mean, he thinks, is often quite unclear. Having been himself a professor of rhetoric, he was well aware of the various ways in which language can be used non-literally. So it was natural that, among his most important writings, there are some that focus especially on allegorical and other non-literal language in the Bible. Most of Book 3 of his treatise *On Christian Doctrine*, for example, concerns the multiple senses of words in the Bible, as well as biblical use of allegory.

The most important philosophical point that arises from Augustine's biblical hermeneutics, however, is his clear distinction between truth and meaning, as in this passage from his *Confessions*:

I realize that when a message is delivered to us in words, truthful though the messenger be, two sorts of disagreement may arise. We may disagree either as to the truth of the message itself or as to the messenger's meaning. It is one thing to ask what is true about the manner of creation, and another to ask what [the messenger] Moses, who was so good a servant to the family of your faithful, meant those who read or heard his words to understand by them. (*Confessions*, 12.23.32, Augustine, 1961, p. 300)

The biblical sentence Augustine is discussing at this point in his *Confessions* is *Genesis* 1:1: "In the beginning God made heaven and earth." Augustine discusses what this sentence could mean in at least five of his works. The sentence inspires him to reflect, often very philosophically, on time and creation. It inspires him to formulate at least three different theories of time. Even in a single discussion he may allow several different ways of understanding this one sentence.

What Augustine never doubts, apparently, is that, on some appropriate interpretation, "In the beginning God made heaven and earth" is true. Right after the passage quoted above, Augustine considers two different interpretations of this one sentence and concludes, "Nevertheless, whether this great man [Moses] had one of these two meanings in mind when he wrote those words, or was thinking of some other meaning which I have not set down here, I am quite sure that he saw the truth and expressed it accordingly" (*Confessions*, 12.24.33, Augustine, 1961, p. 301).

The role Augustine allows himself here is similar to that taken by many "logical positivists," as well as many "common-sense" and "ordinary-language" philosophers, in the twentieth century. The positivists supposed that scientists could tell them the most important truths about reality, but they, the philosophers, could analyze and say what the true statements of science actually mean. Similarly, "ordinary-language" and "common-sense" philosophers supposed that ordinary language and common sense encapsulate many truths about reality. Their role as philosophers was to say what these truths of common sense and ordinary language mean.

The freedom Augustine allows himself, and others, in the interpretation of Scripture is structured by the principles of classical rhetoric he took over, principally from Cicero. Thus Augustine's *On Christian Doctrine*, Books 2 and 3, are a manual for biblical exegesis, and Book 4 is a manual for Christian oratory – that is, homilectics. At the end of Book 2, at 2.40.60, Augustine admonishes his readers to draw on "heathen" learning, even philosophy – especially that of the Platonists – as long as it is in harmony with Christian truth (Augustine, 1963, p. 75). That admonition, plus the classical references scattered throughout Augustine's writings, gave a qualified stamp of approval to the later study of the classical texts of Greece and Rome.

Science and Religion

With the interpretive freedom Augustine thinks he enjoys as a steadfast Christian believer comes a remarkable openness to the discoveries of science, an openness that Galileo appealed to in his battle with the Catholic Church (see Galileo, 1989). Here are two passages, both from his *Literal Meaning of Genesis*, in which Augustine displays this openness:

When they are able, from reliable evidence, to prove some fact of physical science, we shall show that it is not contrary to our Scripture. But when they produce from any of their books a theory contrary to Scripture, and therefore contrary to the Catholic faith, either we shall have some ability to demonstrate that it is absolutely false, or at least we ourselves will hold it so without any shadow of doubt. (*Literal Meaning of Genesis*, 1.21.41, Augustine, 1982, p. 45)

But someone may ask: "Is not Scripture opposed to those who hold that heaven is spherical, when it says, *who stretches out heaven like a skin?*" [*Psalms* 103:2] Let it be opposed indeed if their statement is false. The truth is rather in what God reveals than in what groping men surmise. But if they are able to establish their doctrine with proofs that cannot be denied, we must show that this statement of Scripture about the skin is not opposed to the truth of their conclusions. If it were, it would be opposed also to Sacred Scripture itself in another passage where it says that heaven is suspended like a vault. ...But if it is necessary, as it surely is, to interpret these two passages so that they are shown not to be contradictory but to be reconcilable, it is also necessary that both of these passages should not contradict the theories that may be supported by true evidence. (*Literal Meaning of Genesis*, 2.9.21, Augustine, 1982, p. 59)

Socratic Puzzlement

This distinction between truth and meaning also seems to give additional scope to Augustine's proclivity for seeing philosophical perplexity in what many others would view as mundane truth. Take Augustine's marvelously philosophical discussion of time in Book 11 of his *Confessions*. To the question "What, then, is time?" he answers, in one of his most famous lines, "I know well enough what it is, provided that nobody asks me; but if I am asked what it is and try to explain, I am baffled" (*Confessions*, 11.14.17, Augustine, 1961, p. 264).

Augustine's puzzlement, it turns out, rests on these common-sense assumptions:

1   Some times are long, some are short.
2   If (1), then (3).
3   There are times that can be measured.
4   If (3), then (5).
5   There are times that
    (a)   are present and
    (b)   have duration.
6   All that is ever present is a durationless "now."
7   If (6), then not (5).
8   If not (5), then not (3).
9   If not (3), then not (1).

But surely, as common sense tells us,

1 Some times are long, some are short.

In the face of the puzzlement that this reasoning generates, Augustine makes a distinction between periods of time *in the mind* (as, say, recalled, or anticipated in the imagination) and periods of time *outside the mind*. Although, he continues to insist, nothing with temporal spread or duration exists outside the mind, we can spread out events and also hold them together in the mind. And so he concludes that time is the measure of something mental.

This famous passage shows Augustine perplexed in a genuinely Socratic manner about the nature of time. Although he does seek to preserve the truths of common sense (and of the Bible, which certainly includes common-sense talk about time), he is free to respond creatively to a philosophical puzzle in a way that reinterprets the truths of common sense. Moreover, the respect Augustine shows for Socrates has important implications for the philosophy of education. If one follows Augustine's example one can remain open to the perplexities that philosophically problematic notions generate without needing to make the truths of science, common sense, or even religious faith hostage to one's ability to resolve the perplexity. Thus, for example, a science teacher today may go on insisting that time is, as Einstein's theory has it, the fourth dimension, even if that teacher does not know how to deal with a question like this from a student: "If time is really a fourth dimension, why can't I turn myself around in these dimensions so that my height, say, can become my lifespan?"

Our "Fallen" State

In the Platonic dialogue *Protagoras*, Socrates is made to suggest that having knowledge of what is good and bad would be sufficient to make one do the morally good thing (352c). Augustine, by contrast, clearly rejects the idea that to have such knowledge is automatically to be virtuous. In the famous story he tells about stealing pears as a 16-year-old, he makes clear that it was not ignorance of the wrongfulness of his act that explained his behavior. He knew full well that what he was doing was morally wrong. In fact, he says he had no motive for his wickedness but the wickedness itself (*Confessions*, 2.4.9, Augustine, 1961, pp. 49–50).

Wrong-doing, according to Augustine, is sin, and sin is a product of a depraved and fallen nature, which, in turn, comes from the sin of Adam. In embracing the doctrine of human depravity Augustine rejects the contention of his contemporary, Pelagius, that it is possible for a human being to live without sinning. He defines "Pelagianism" as a Christian heresy and, in so doing, rejects the doctrine modern philosophers tend to associate with Kant, that "Ought implies can."

Augustine also rejects the notion of a fully divided self, which seems to be proposed in this famous passage from St Paul's *Epistle to the Romans* (7:15–17):

I do not understand my own actions. For I do not do what I want, but I do the very thing I hate. Now if I do what I do not want, I agree that the law is good. So then it is no longer I that do it, but sin that dwells within me.

In the place of a fully divided self, Augustine suggests that what we have is a "dissociated" self, where such dissociation, or alienation, is, of course, taken to be the standard human condition:

When I was trying to reach a decision about serving the Lord my God, as I had long intended to do, it was I who willed to take this course and again it was I who willed not to take it. It was I and I alone. But I neither willed to do it nor refused to do it with my full will. So I was at odds with myself. I was throwing myself into confusion. All this happened to me although I did not want it, but it did not prove that there was some second mind in me besides my own. (*Confessions*, 8.10.22, Augustine, 1961, p. 173)

Intentionalism

Wrong-doing, according to Augustine, requires consent of the will to some suggestion that one's will should not consent to. In his *Commentary on the Lord's Sermon on the Mount* (1.12.34, Augustine, 1963, pp. 33–4) Augustine identifies the necessary and sufficient conditions for committing a sin as (1) entertaining mentally an evil suggestion, (2) taking pleasure in contemplating the evil thought or action suggested, and (3) consenting to accept the thought or undertake the action. Whether any "bodily action" actually follows from this consent of the will he thought irrelevant to whether there was a sin. And even when some action does follow, it is the intention, he thought, rather than any consequences that result, that gives the action its sinful character.

It follows from all this that simply learning what is morally good or morally right will be ineffectual in making people good, or even making them morally better than they were. What is required is a conversion of the will, which cannot happen apart from the grace of God.

Virtue

One might think from all this evidence of the ineffectualness of what we might otherwise consider moral education that Augustine has no account of virtue, or the virtues. In fact, he does have an account. He follows St Ambrose in adding the four cardinal virtues of classical Greek thought to the distinctively Christian virtues – faith, hope, and love – mentioned in St Paul (I *Corinthians* 13). Augustine follows Paul in assigning primacy to love. He even suggests an interpretation of the four Greek virtues that makes them expressions of love too, in particular, expressions of the love of God. Thus temperance, he says, is "love keeping itself whole and incorrupt for God"; courage (fortitude) is "love bearing everything readily for the sake of God"; justice is "love in serving God alone and therefore ruling everything else well"; and prudence (wisdom) is "love making the right distinction between what helps one toward God and what hinders one" (*On the Morals of the Catholic Church*, 15.25, Augustine, 1966, pp. 22–3). In this way Augustine can maintain that virtue is nothing other than the perfect love of God. And in this way he offers a Christian analogue to the old Platonic idea of the "unity of the virtues" (cf. *Protagoras*, 329cd).

One implication of this idea that the virtues are one is that there can be no such thing as genuine bravery in the service of an evil deed. And one implication of Augustine's Christian version of this idea is that, for example, there can be no true temperance apart from the love of God.

Teachers and Learners

What can one say, in summary, about the picture Augustine gives us of teachers and learners? As for learners, the most striking feature of Augustine's discussion of learning is that it proceeds from a first-person point of view. In a way this should not be surprising. After all, it was Augustine who anticipated Descartes by 1,200 years in listing his very own existence as the first thing he could not be deceived about (see *On Free Choice of the Will*, 2.3.20, Augustine, 1993, p. 33; and *City of God*, 11.26, Augustine, 1972, p. 460). Although Augustine does not go on, in the fashion of Descartes, to provide a full reconstruction, from a first-person perspective, of everything he knows (see Matthews, 1992, chapter 3), he is the first philosopher in our Western tradition to privilege the first-person perspective in learning and knowing. Learning, according to Augustine, is an inner illumination. It is Divine in origin, and not reducible to simply following rules. We may come to know eternal truths, not by recollecting our vision of Platonic Forms from a previous life, but because God has made our intellect in such a way that it is naturally suited to see such truths in the Divine light.

Morality is also an inward matter in that what counts as sin is an inner consent to turn away from God and flout His commandments. There is no prospect of producing moral education by getting people simply to learn what God has commanded. Fallen creatures that we are, we may consent to what we know to be evil, just for the pleasure of doing evil. There really is no such thing, on Augustine's view, as cognitively based moral development. Only efforts at moral self-improvement or the moral improvement of others that are blessed by the grace of God and that produce a genuine change of heart and will can succeed. And thus Socratic or Kohlbergian efforts to understand moral development as a cognitive process are, in principle, misconceived.

Augustine's Influence on the Philosophy of Education

The most obvious way in which Augustine has influenced later philosophy of education is that, with important qualifications, he put a Christian stamp on classical learning. Thus, for example, in Book 9 of his *Confessions* Augustine tells the story of his ascent, with his mother, to a mystical union with God, an ascent which echoes Plato's ascent of love in the dialogue, *Symposium*. Moreover, in his *De ordine*, at 2.12.35–2.16.44 (Augustine, 1948, pp. 313–21), Augustine actually gives a curricular structure to the ascent of love. His curricular ascent proceeds through the study of the "trivium" (grammar, rhetoric, and dialectic or logic) to the "quadrivium" (arithmetic, geometry, astronomy, and music), after which one is prepared to contemplate the eternal Forms and God Himself. No doubt Augustine's theological and philosophical endorsement of these subjects has had a significant effect on Christian instruction in subsequent centuries.

Perhaps Augustine's most pervasive legacy in the philosophy of education, however, has been his idea that true understanding rests on insight, "illumination," and cannot be adequately understood in purely operational or computational terms. Thus drill that does not lead to insight is unsuccessful teaching. This idea is, of course, also Platonic and Neoplatonic in origin. But its Augustinian credentials have also been important to its influence on later Western thought.

See also 1 THE SOCRATIC MOVEMENT; 6 ENLIGHTENMENT LIBERALISM; 12 THE ANALYTICAL MOVEMENT; 16 THEORIES OF TEACHING AND LEARNING; 22 MORAL EDUCATION; 23 RELIGIOUS EDUCATION

References

Augustine (1948) *Divine Providence and the Problem of Evil (De ordine)*. In R. P. Russell (trans.), *The Fathers of the Church, volume 5*. New York: Cima Publishing Co., pp. 227–332.

Augustine (1958) *On Christian Doctrine*, trans. D. W. Robertson. New York: Macmillan.

Augustine (1961) *Confessions*, trans. R. S. Pine-Coffin. London: Penguin.

Augustine (1963) *Commentary on the Lord's Sermon on the Mount*, trans. D. J. Kavanagh. Washington, DC: Catholic University of America Press.

Augustine (1966) *The Catholic and Manichaean Ways of Life*, trans. D. A. and I. J. Gallagher. Washington, DC: Catholic University of America Press.

Augustine (1972) *City of God*, trans J. O'Meara. London: Penguin.

Augustine (1982) *The Literal Meaning of Genesis, volume 1*, trans. J. H. Taylor. New York: Newman.

Augustine (1993) *On Free Choice of the Will*, trans. T. Williams. Indianapolis: Hackett.

Augustine (1995) *Against the Academicians* and *The Teacher*, trans. P. King. Indianapolis: Hackett.

Augustine (2002) *The Trinity 8–15*, trans. S. McKenna. Cambridge: Cambridge University Press.

Chomsky, N. (1959) Review of B. F. Skinner, *Verbal behavior*. *Language*, 35, 26–58.

Galileo (1989) Letter to the Grand Duchess Christina (1615). In M. A. Finocchiaro, *The Galileo Affair: A Documentary History*. Berkeley: University of California Press, pp. 87–118.

King, P. (1998) Augustine on the impossibility of teaching. *Metaphilosophy*, 29, 179–95.

Matthews, G. B. (1992) *Thought's Ego in Augustine and Descartes*. Ithaca, NY: Cornell University Press.

Searle, J. (1980) Minds, brains, and programs. *Behavioral and Brain Sciences*, 3, 417–24.

Wittgenstein, L. (1958) *Philosophical Investigations*, 2nd edn. Oxford: Blackwell.

5

Humanism

Craig Kallendorf

In one sense it is easy to define humanism: on one level, it is the basic educational philosophy of the Renaissance. To clarify what that educational philosophy is, however, turns into a surprisingly difficult endeavor, in which fundamental terms and concepts remain disputed and even broad transformations resist generalization. The discussion that follows begins where the movement itself began, in Italy, and first identifies the educational practices of the Middle Ages against which humanism reacted, then surveys the most influential recent definitions of humanism and their ramifications for the educational philosophy of the Renaissance. The second major section attempts to delineate this educational philosophy as precisely as possible, beginning with a survey of the major works in which it is developed, moving to general conclusions about the theory and practice of education at this time, and ending with a consideration of the strengths and weaknesses of humanism as a distinct period in the history of education. The discussion concludes by tracing the spread of the new educational philosophy from Italy into the rest of Europe, during which distinct Catholic and Protestant traditions emerge as the basis for later developments in European education.

Italy

Medieval education

Beginning in the early Middle Ages, education unfolded within the liberal arts, divided into the *trivium* (grammar, rhetoric, and logic) and the *quadrivium* (arithmetic, geometry, music, and astronomy). Late medieval education rested on a common group of textbooks often called *auctores* (authors), with the man who taught them called an *auctorista*. Instruction began with elementary grammars like the *Ars minor* attributed to Donatus and various morally edifying texts like the distichs of Cato, Aesop's fables, and the eclogue of Theodulus. The next group of books included a series of more advanced grammars and glossaries like the *Doctrinale* of Alexander de Villedieu, the *Elementarium doctrinae rudimentum* once attributed to Papias, the *Derivationes* of Hugutio of Pisa, the *Graecismus* of Évrard de Bethune, and the *Catholicon* of

Giovanni Balbi. Instruction in Latin continued through books like the *Dittochaeum*, a Christian morality poem attributed to Prudentius, and the extracts from Augustine collected by Prosper of Aquitaine, along with a smattering of Roman poets like Virgil and Ovid. As organized by medieval teachers, the *auctores* amounted to an undifferentiated collection of classical and medieval, pagan and Christian, imaginative literature, grammar book, and dictionary, all valued equally and seen as part of one continuous cultural tradition. Those who wanted further education could study the *ars dictaminis*, or the art of letter-writing. The *dictatores* who developed this art relied on a highly codified preceptive method that correlated in turn with the speculative grammar of the day, which elevated logical consistency over actual usage (Grendler, 1989, pp. 111–17). The medieval system of education culminated in a university experience that rested on two contradictory impulses. On the one hand, instruction was dominated by abstract, syllogistically structured systems and formal disputations that moved further and further from everyday life. But, on the other hand, the goals of the medieval university were overwhelmingly practical, preprofessional, and scientific, with approved textbooks in logic, natural philosophy, medicine, law, and theology designed to produce doctors, lawyers, and theologians.

The humanist challenge

At the turn of the fourteenth century, late medieval scholastic culture and the educational system that perpetuated it came under attack from individuals like Albertino Mussato (1261–1329) who lived around Padua and are now referred to as prehumanists. Their work was continued, refined, and disseminated by Francesco Petrarca (1304–74), who self-consciously withdrew himself from the culture of his day in an effort to effect a rebirth of the classical past. The intellectual underpinnings of this work have come to be known as humanism, a term that has proved notoriously difficult to define. Three definitions have proved especially influential in recent decades, with each definition having distinctly different implications for our understanding of the theory and practice of education in this period.

The first approach is that developed by Paul Oskar Kristeller, who discovered that texts of the fourteenth and fifteenth centuries record a change in the words used to describe teachers, and that this verbal change marks a change in curriculum as well. The medieval *auctorista* gradually gave way to the Renaissance *umanista*, who taught a fixed cycle of subjects focused on human interactions: grammar and rhetoric, which facilitate human communication; moral philosophy, or what people should do; history, the record of human action in the past; and poetry, the product of a uniquely human aesthetic sensibility. Kristeller also discovered that the *dictatores* were replaced by men with a humanist education during this period, so that official correspondence reflects the change in educational philosophy. The models for these letters, as well as for the study of the five disciplines at the center of the new educational philosophy, were to be found in Greece and Rome, for the ancients had perfected the study of what it meant to be human.

The approach of Eugenio Garin is broadly compatible with that of Kristeller, but it shifts the focus from institutional settings to the values and assumptions about reality that humanists shared. Garin argues that humanism was marked in particular by a new sense of history and a new emphasis on individual experience over abstract speculation. The medieval mind, one might argue, tended to see the past through the prism of the present; Renaissance humanism insisted on seeing the past as a series of distinct cultures, different from one another and from the present vantage point from which they are being observed. Medieval scholasticism in turn relied on systems of thought that gave meaning to events and ideas by positioning them in relation to other events and ideas, while humanists tended to interpret events and ideas through personal experience and perspectives.

The third approach to humanism that has proved influential in recent decades is that of Hans Baron, who devoted special attention to the origins and development of the movement, which he pursued to a specific moment in Florentine history. At the close of the fourteenth century, one group of Florentine intellectuals gravitated toward Niccolò Niccoli (1364–1437), who was interested in the new classical learning but scorned participation in contemporary political life; the other group is represented by Cino Rinuccini, who stressed the importance of traditional Florentine values and civic service. When Florence was invaded by the Milanese under Giangaleazzo Visconti, who ultimately died outside the city walls in 1402, the pressures of defending the city brought classical studies into the service of the state in a phenomenon Baron calls civic humanism (Wilcox, 1975, pp. 74–84).

Each of these approaches offers a different series of implications for the educational theory and practice of the early Renaissance. Kristeller's findings sharpen our focus on curriculum, where disciplines like history, moral philosophy, and poetry received greater emphasis at the expense of disciplines in the *quadrivium*, and on what we might call today job placement: the typical product of a medieval scholastic education was a doctor, lawyer, or theologian, while the product of a humanist school was either a well educated noble trained to take his role in society or a government employee who could speak and write in the new style. Humanism as Garin interprets it also predicates educational change, for distinguishing past from present requires that the medieval canon of *auctores* be expanded and reorganized chronologically, and emphasizing individual experience over abstract speculation requires a new approach to the language by which this experience is communicated. Medieval grammar approached language as a logical structure with affinities to the structures of reality, so that rules overrode practice and there was little if any need to consider the historical evolution of language. For the humanists, however, reality is known through individual experience rather than abstract systems, so that advocates of the new approach to grammar elevated usage over precept and approached grammar as a tool, not as a way of understanding the world. This did not, however, lead to linguistic idiosyncraticism, for as texts like the *Rudimenta grammatices* of Niccolò Perotti (1429–80) show, there was a standard for determining proper usage: classical antiquity, the practice of the best writers of the past. And, finally, civic humanism as Baron defines it also requires a different kind of education than the medieval school could produce, for if the classics were to help educated people respond to contemporary events, then knowledge of the classics would have to be both broader and deeper than it was in the typical medieval schoolroom. When the humanist chancellor of Florence, Leonardo Bruni (1370–1444), wrote his panegyric of Florence (*Laudatio Florentiae urbis*, 1403/4), he turned to a work that was almost unknown in the

Middle Ages, Aristides' panegyric of Athens, in a language (ancient Greek) that few people in the Middle Ages could read, to show how the Florence of his day defended her liberty just as Athens had once done. Thus humanist scholars turned up works like Cicero's *On the Orator* and Quintilian's *Education of the Orator* that were little known or used in the Middle Ages but that in turn helped to guide the educational philosophy of the Renaissance.

The new system established itself throughout northern and north-central Italy in the 1430s, 1440s, and 1450s, and as communes and individual parents hired humanist schoolmasters, the contracts they drew up (*condotte*) reflected these changes. The terminology of the medieval system – *auctores*, *ars dictaminis*, speculative grammar, *Doctrinale* – gave way to the terminology of the new system – *Rudimenta grammatices*, *umanista* – and the contracts specify that teaching was supposed to be concentrated in the five humanistic disciplines and to rely on a growing number of ancient texts (Grendler, 1989, pp. 133–41).

Humanism as an Educational Philosophy

Survey of the major texts

Like the term "humanism" itself, humanism as an educational philosophy also resists easy definition. Fortunately there are a number of treatises from the period that present in detail the educational theory of the day. A brief survey of their contents should allow some general conclusions to emerge.

From the Italian environment, the following constitute the major theoretical treatments of humanist education: Piero Paolo Vergerio (1370–1444), *The Character and Studies Befitting a Free-Born Youth* (c.1402–3); Leonardo Bruni, *The Study of Literature* (written between 1422 and 1429); Maffeo Vegio (1407–58), *On Education and Excellence of Character in Children* (1444); Aeneas Sylvius Piccolomini (1405–64), who became Pope Pius II, *The Education of Boys* (1450); and Battista Guarino (1434–1505), *A Program of Teaching and Learning* (1459). Relevant material may also be found in treatises devoted to other concerns (for example, Francesco Barbaro (1390–1454), *The Education of Boys*, a chapter (2.9) of his *On Marriage* (1428)). There were other books about education (e.g. *A Treatise on the Education and Learning of Children* of Gregorio Correr (1411–64)), but they had only a limited circulation in their own day. It is also worth noting that a number of other prominent humanists (e.g. Giannozzo Manetti (1396–1459), Sicco Polenton (1375/6–1447), Niccolò Perotti, and Pier Candido Decembrio (1392–1477)) also wrote treatises on education that now appear to be lost (Woodward, 1996, pp. 180–1).

For Vergerio, as for the other major Italian theorists, education involved both character and learning, so he begins his treatise with an analysis of what kind of student will be most receptive to education and how the character of the student can be improved. Typical as well is Vergerio's acknowledgment that the program he is setting out is designed for the general education of princes and aristocrats, men with civic obligations whose lives are guided and enriched by books but not limited to them. The disciplines to be studied are the ones appropriate to a free man who, like his

65

ancestors in Greece and Rome, needs to be skilled in both arms and letters. Vergerio's treatise, however, also develops some ideas that are not prominent in the other works under consideration here. He briefly mentions, for example, a fourfold approach to education that goes back to the Greeks and rests on letters, gymnastics, music, and drawing, and he is unusually sympathetic to the different needs of different students.

Bruni's treatise stresses the need for an education that is wide and varied, with both the ability to express one's self and factual knowledge as goals. Learning to express one's self well in Latin requires careful study of the best authors from the classical canon, and factual knowledge requires broad reading in moral philosophy, rhetoric, history, and poetry. Several distinctive themes are sounded here: one should not devote too much time to rhetoric, for example, and ancient literature, particularly poetry, should be carefully corrected in accordance with the precepts of religion and moral philosophy. The fact that Bruni's treatise is addressed to a woman may well account for both of these points, since the society of his day did not allow women opportunities to express themselves publicly and placed a special emphasis on the preservation of female virtue.

The first three books of Vegio's treatise deal with the obligations of parents and teachers toward children. Book One deals with children before they go to school, while Book Two focuses on the responsibilities of the first schoolmaster and Book Three runs through the various subjects the youth should study and the need to cultivate morality as well as the intellect. The last three books in turn consider the obligations of children toward their parents and teachers. Book Four takes up the ways in which a youth should deal with the different classes of people he encounters, and Book Five treats the modesty that should inform a young man's speech and movements, with Book Six extending this discussion to modes of modest behavior at home and in public places. The ideal involved the education of the individual from the broadest possible perspective, aimed at a sound mind in a sound body, with the intellectual in harmony with the spiritual.

Piccolomini also notes that education must train both the body and the mind. The former is treated first, with a discussion of how proper character can be formed by regulating games, sleep, and food and drink. The training of the mind, however, is more difficult and is treated at greater length. Self-expression requires exacting attention to grammar, defined according to the best humanist practice as knowing how to speak correctly, to interpret literature, and to compose written texts on one's own. Within this discussion, we find the usual treatment of the key humanist disciplines, but it is worth noting that grammar is presented here as the master discipline and developed at sufficient length to suggest how much effort went into cultivating good Latin style in the humanist schoolroom. Here again we also find warnings against morally questionable authors and reminders that education should improve character at the same time as it deepens knowledge.

As the son of one of the most famous schoolmasters of Renaissance Italy, Battista Guarino focuses on the elementary grammar instruction that Bruni downplays and outlines the method that prevailed in the humanist classroom. As Guarino explains it, "there are two parts to grammar: the first is called 'methodical,' which lays out the paradigms of all the parts of speech; the other is called 'historical,' which gives a detailed treatment of historical knowledge and past achievements" (Kallendorf,

2002). "Methodical" studies include syntax and prosody, while "historical" studies include books about the past as well as poetry and rhetoric, in both Greek and Latin.

General conclusions

From these summaries it should be clear that humanism cannot be reduced to a systematic educational philosophy. Indeed, in the end it is even impossible to associate humanism with any particular philosphical school, mode of life, or political system. It has often been said that Renaissance humanism stimulated a Platonic revival that supplanted the Aristotelianism on which medieval scholasticism was based, but this is simply not true: Platonism had never died out during the Middle Ages, and interest in Aristotle among humanists like Bruni was actually stimulated by the desire to edit and translate his texts so that this Greek philosopher could be separated from his medieval commentators (Wilcox, 1975, p. 76). Some modern scholars have also claimed that humanism favored the active life over the contemplative one, which might seem to follow from the discussion of civic humanism above, but again we must be careful not to overgeneralize; in developing his commentary to Virgil's *Aeneid* according to Neoplatonic principles, Cristoforo Landino (1424–98), a Florentine professor whose humanist credentials are beyond question, allegorized the heroic journey of Aeneas as a movement from the lower plane of the active life to the higher one of contemplation. Again it might seem to follow that Florentine civic humanism might favor the republican ideology dominant in that city over the tyrannical form of government represented by the defeated Milanese – a predilection undoubtedly fostered by Baron's vantage point as an exile from Nazi tyranny – but we should not forget that Petrarca, the figure who in essence launched the humanist trajectory throughout Europe, served tyrannies and republics with equal enthusiasm. Finally, given that humanism emphasizes the quality of earthly life as we experience it, we might be tempted to see it as a secularizing phenomenon. There is clearly an element of truth here, but we must be careful not to make early modern people for whom Christianity was a given into modern atheists. As Charles Trinkaus (1995) has noted, the humanists developed a new interest in man as an image of God and in the humanity of Christ, but they did not forget that God was the creator and Jesus was his son.

If, however, humanism cannot be reduced to a systematic educational philosophy, it does present several characteristic features along with a distinctive method in the history of education. A number of these features have already been identified: a predilection for grammar, rhetoric, history, moral philosophy, and poetry; an insistence on the value of concrete human experience over abstract philosophical systems; an emphasis on speaking and writing in accordance with classical norms as the surest means of communicating that concrete human experience; and the importance of a broad knowledge of ancient literature in its cultural uniqueness as the best model for human thought and action. Two other more specific methodological points, however, also require comment.

Like the philosophy of education, reading, too, has a history, and modern scholars working in this field have discovered that people in the Renaissance read in three different ways: first, by focusing not on the story as a whole, but on episodes that were detached and analyzed separately; second, by mining the text for easily memorized formulas, proverbs, maxims, and ready-made expressions; and third, by attempting to grasp the text in its totality. The third option is most common today, of course, but the first two, particularly the second, are the direct result of humanist pedagogy. Tens of thousands of books from this period survive in which students and teachers have made marginal notations next to memorable phrases. This procedure led to the next step in the humanist educational method: transferring the maxims, proverbs, and moralizing tags from the texts in which they originally appeared to notebooks kept by the reader, which were first divided into sections focused on rhetorical form or manner of expression (Battista Guarino's "methodical") and moral content ("historical"), then into further subsections ("simile" or "anaphora," "munificence" or "courage"). When called upon to write something himself, anyone who had benefited from a humanist education therefore had to hand a ready-made supply of elegant, thought-provoking quotations that anchored the newly created Renaissance text in the ancient sources from which the quotations were taken (Moss, 1996). Indeed, it is worth noting that the five treatises discussed above which present the educational philosophy of humanism were themselves composed according to this method, echoing Quintilian's *Education of the Orator*, pseudo-Plutarch's *On the Education of Children*, and St Basil's *Letter to Young Men on Reading Pagan Literature*, along with both well known ancient authors like Cicero, Seneca, and Plutarch and lesser known ones like Aulus Gellius, Vegetius, and Valerius Maximus.

The humanist gesture toward the past often took a characteristic form: imitation. As Thomas Greene notes, when imitation essentially rewrites a classical model ("reproductive" or "sacramental" imitation), it betrays its roots in quotation, and even when allusions and echoes from a large number of authors exist side-by-side in a Renaissance work ("eclectic" or "exploitative" imitation), the creative voice is in danger of being stifled by the burden of the past. But when imitation becomes "heuristic," it distances itself from its subtexts at the same time as it advertises its origins in them, eventually shading into a fourth type of imitation ("dialectical") in which there is a conflict between two signifying systems that each comment upon the other (Greene, 1982, pp. 38–48). To a post-romantic sensibility, imitation often suggests copying, but in the theory and practice of humanist education, it meant competition (*aemulatio*) as well: what a humanist wrote acknowledges its origins with respect but also seeks to improve upon its model.

Strengths and weaknesses

As the educational philosophy that underlay Renaissance Europe, humanism produced many positive results. Generations of students lived lives that were at least a little richer and fuller for their contact with the literature of Greece and Rome. They shared a common culture with all those who had been educated similarly, and most of them seemed to have benefited at least somewhat from an education that rested not in abstract systems far removed from daily life, but in the lived experiences of the human spirit. As writers and artists sought to imitate the ancients, the best of them produced literary works like Castiglione's *Courtier* which are still read with pleasure today. For every work like this, to be sure, there are thousands of mediocre compositions, but even in these cases we should note that the humanist method made it possible for many people of modest talent to write with a modicum of insight and elegance.

Several of the greatest teachers in the history of education – e.g. Gasparino Barzizza (1360–1430), Guarino da Verona (1374–1460), and Vittorino da Feltre (1373 or 1378 to 1446/7) – were humanists, but a number of scholars have recently begun to postulate a disjunction between the lofty goals set out in the humanist educational treatises and what actually went on in a humanist classroom. The goals, of course, focused on imparting a broad education that would refine the student's character and prepare him to take his place as a free citizen in his community. But these goals were to be reached through painstaking attention to the details of linguistic expression and through brief discussions that would illuminate small problems in the text: explanations of etymologies, identifications of mythological references, locations of place names, and so forth. Lecture notes from even great teachers like Guarino record what may well look to us to be a stultifying environment of regimented note-taking, memorization, repetition, and close imitation, and in the hands of a lesser master it must have been even more difficult to make the transition from classroom work to the broader vision behind it. Anthony Grafton and Lisa Jardine (1986, pp. 1–28) have also suggested that this environment not only failed to nurture intellectual curiosity, but actually fostered a passive docility that was in the best interests of the despots who would eventually employ the products of the humanist educational system. There may well be an element of exaggeration here, but it is undoubtedly true that, as is usually the case, the reality of humanist educational practice seldom coincided with the ideal.

A second problem also emerged in the efforts to make classical Latin the stylistic norm in Renaissance schools. Grammar texts like Perotti's *Rudimenta grammatices* explicitly rejected medieval words and constructions, but these same words and constructions crept back into later editions and into the grammatical compendia in which much humanist language instruction was based. Education is by nature a conservative process – teachers tend to teach what they were taught, publishers want to sell everything they have printed even after it is out of date, and parents often hesitate to entrust their children to those in the avant-garde – so that in fact, the language instruction on which humanist pedagogy relied remained problematic. Because fourteenth- and fifteenth-century Latin was still a living language bound to the medieval culture from which it had emerged, only a handful of the most highly skilled humanists ever succeeded in writing a Latin that could not be distinguished from that of Cicero (Jensen, 1996, pp. 69–71).

The Spread of Humanism

By the 1480s and 1490s, students from northern Europe were studying in Italy, and they took home with them what they learned of the new educational philosophy, so that we can begin to speak of a northern humanism by the beginning of the sixteenth century. Some names and dates will help to chronicle the spread of educational reform from Italy. Greek, neglected for centuries in the medieval West but now considered essential for the recovery of classical culture, was first regularly taught in the University of Paris in 1508. In 1516 both the *Utopia* of Thomas More (1477–1535) and the Greek New Testament of Desiderius Erasmus (1466–1536) were published, and the humanist colleges of Corpus Christi, Oxford, and Christ's and St John's, Cambridge, were established in the same year. In 1520 the great Greek scholar Guillaume Budé (1467–1540) persuaded the humanist King Francis I (1494–1547; reigned 1515–47) to found the Bibliothèque Royale, with the Collège de France following in 1530. French humanism centered on Jacques Lefèvre d'Étaples (1461–1536); German, on Luther's right-hand man Philipp Melanchthon (1497–1560), the *praeceptor Germaniae* (teacher of Germany), and Johannes Sturm (1507–89), who founded a famous humanist school in Strasbourg in 1537; Spanish, on Cardinal Francisco Ximenes de Cisneros (1436–1517), who founded the humanist university at Alcalá and funded the triumph of Christian humanist scholarship, the Complutensian polyglot Bible; and English, on Elizabeth I and St Paul's school, founded in London in 1512 by John Colet (1467?–1519) (Bullock, 1985, pp. 25–6, 34). Significant treatises in which the ideas of Italian humanist educational philosophy were spread throughout Europe include *On Educational Method* (1523) by Juan Luis Vives (1492–1540), *The Scholemaster* (1570) by Roger Ascham (1515–68), Desiderius Erasmus's *On the Rationale of Studies* (1511) and *On the Education of Children* (1529), and Johannes Sturm's *On Rightly Initiating the Study of Letters* (1538).

As humanism spread geographically northward and chronologically into the sixteenth century, it remained true to its roots in the early Italian Renaissance but also developed a couple of distinctive features. First, beginning around 1510, increased emphasis was placed on the classroom aids, like textbooks and teaching drills, that would help to systematize the new approach and make it widely transferable. The key figures in this movement include Rudolph Agricola (1444–85), Desiderius Erasmus, Philipp Melanchthon, and Johann Sturm, and the method developed was initially rhetorical – that is, it utilized *topoi* (or commonplaces) as a way of organizing what one knew and *copia* (or abundant variation) as a way of writing and talking about that knowledge (Grafton and Jardine, 1986, pp. 122–60). The schools of this period picked up techniques developed earlier by the Brethren of the Common Life, in which students were organized into a fixed sequence of graduated classes (*ordines*), competition was fostered among smaller groups, and the educational environment was closely controlled (Scaglione, 1986, pp. 12–13). By the third quarter of the sixteenth century, the standardized curriculum and the best-selling textbook had prevailed, as seen in the practice of Peter Ramus (1515–72), who put forth a "one and only method" that was applicable to any subject, and Gabriel Harvey (*c.*1545–1630), briefly professor of rhetoric at Cambridge (1573–75) (Grafton and Jardine, 1986, pp. 161–200).

In both Protestant and Catholic countries, humanist education in the sixteenth century became intertwined with the religious developments of the day. Melanchthon's Latin school at Eisleben, the first Lutheran school (established in 1526), set out specifically to combine religion and the classics to produce good citizens and effective preachers: rhetoric, for example, was required both for interpreting Scripture and for communicating its truth to others. Sturm's school in Strasbourg was widely imitated in Protestant cities: striving for *pietas litterata* (an educated piety), it presented a typical series of readings from classical authors in a highly structured environment. In time Protestants like Calvin began to doubt the efficacy of classical studies, but the Jesuit college system embraced the humanist program enthusiastically. The Jesuits placed special emphasis on rhetoric, used to develop both character and intellect, with an original emphasis on a graduated, progressively ordered psychology of learning, beginning in Messina (1548) and Rome (1551) and reaching 33 colleges at Loyola's death (1556), 293 in 1607, and 669 in 1750. The colleges began as seminaries for Jesuit novices, but quickly developed into a major public school system that helped transfer the original humanist program into the Italian *liceo*, the French *lycée*, and the German *Gymnasium* of later centuries (Scaglione, 1986, pp. 33–74).

Conclusion

As Allen Bullock (1985, p. 47) has observed, "Renaissance humanism was neither a creed nor a philosophical system; it represented no interest group and made no attempt to organize itself as a movement." It did, however, present a central theme: *humanitas*, the cultivation to the fullest possible extent of human creativity, modeled on the achievements of ancient Greece and Rome. This creativity, however, could only come into being if it was nurtured and developed (Bullock, 1985, p. 35). That is, people could only reach their full potential through education, and it is this belief that makes the values and methods of humanism one of the key moments in the history of education.

See also 1 THE SOCRATIC MOVEMENT; 2 STOICISM; 6 ENLIGHTENMENT LIBERAL-ISM; 10 HELLENISM, THE GYMNASIUM AND ALTERTUMSWISSENSCHAFT

References

Bullock, A. (1985) *The Humanist Tradition in the West*. New York and London: W. W. Norton.

Grafton, A. and Jardine, L. (1986) *From Humanism to the Humanities*. Cambridge, MA: Harvard University Press.

Greene, T. M. (1982) *The Light in Troy: Imitation and Discovery in Renaissance Poetry*. New Haven, CT and London: Yale University Press.

Grendler, P. F. (1989) *Schooling in Renaissance Italy: Literacy and Learning, 1300–1600*. Baltimore and London: Johns Hopkins University Press.

Jensen, K. (1996) The humanist reform of Latin and Latin teaching. In J. Kraye (ed.), *The Cambridge Companion to Renaissance Humanism*. Cambridge: Cambridge University Press, pp. 63–81.

Kallendorf, C. W. (ed. and trans) (2002) *Humanist Educational Treatises*. Cambridge, MA: Harvard University Press.

Moss, A. (1996) *Printed Commonplace-books and the Structuring of Renaissance Thought*. Oxford: Clarendon Press.

Scaglione, A. (1986) *The Liberal Arts and the Jesuit College System*. Amsterdam and Philadelphia: John Benjamins.

Trinkaus, C. (1995) *In Our Image and Likeness: Humanity and Divinity in Italian Humanist Thought*. Notre Dame, IN: University of Notre Dame Press. (Original work published in 1970.)

Wilcox, D. J. (1975) *In Search of God and Self: Renaissance and Reformation Thought*. Boston: Houghton Mifflin.

Woodward, W. H. (1996) *Vittorino da Feltre and Other Humanist Educators*. Toronto: University of Toronto Press. (Original work published in 1897.)

Further reading

Bolgar, R. R. (1954) *The Classical Heritage and Its Beneficiaries*. Cambridge: Cambridge University Press.

Bushnell, R. W. (1996) *A Culture of Teaching: Early Modern Humanism in Theory and Practice*. Ithaca, NY and London: Cornell University Press.

Cassirer, E., Kristeller, P. O., and Randall, H. H., Jr (trans.) (1948) *The Renaissance Philosophy of Man*. Chicago: University of Chicago Press.

Garin, E. (1957) *L'educazione in Europa (1400–1600)* [*Education in Europe (1400–1600)*]. Bari: Laterza.

Garin, E. (ed.) (1958) *Il pensiero pedagogico dello Umanesimo* [*The Pedagogical Thought of Humanism*]. Florence: Giuntine/Sansoni.

Kristeller, P. O. (1961, 1965) *Renaissance Thought*, two volumes. New York: Harper and Row.

Proctor, R. E. (1988) *Education's Great Amnesia: Reconsidering the Humanities from Petrarch to Freud, with a Curriculum for Today's Students*. Bloomington and Indianapolis: Indiana University Press.

Rabil, A. (ed.) (1988) *Renaissance Humanism: Foundations, Forms, and Legacy*, three volumes. Philadelphia: University of Pennsylvania Press.

Woodward, W. H. (1967) *Studies in Education During the Age of the Renaissance 1450–1600*. New York: Columbia University Press. (Original work published in 1906.)

6

Enlightenment Liberalism

Amy M. Schmitter, Nathan Tarcov, and Wendy Donner

> *[T]here is no need for minds to be confined at all within limits...*
> **René Descartes, *Rules*, rule one**

Editor's Prologue

The Enlightenment was both a movement – philosophical, political, social, and educational – and a historical period, roughly coinciding with the eighteenth century, in which that movement flourished. Considered as a philosophical movement, it celebrated the autonomy of individual reason and rational self-governance as a human birthright, and embraced various revolutionary and egalitarian consequences of these commitments. These consequences included notions of rule by popular consent, freedom of conscience, and religious tolerance as a solution to the seemingly interminable Reformation wars, and the advancement of reason and science as at least the equal partners, if not successors, of revelation and ecclesiastical authority. Hence the naturalness of speaking of "Enlightenment liberalism": political liberalism and the epistemic egalitarianism on which it rested were the philosophical core of Enlightenment thought.

From Descartes to Kant, Enlightenment thinkers erected "natural religion" – religion "within the bounds of reason alone" – as a challenge to "revealed religion," daring to imagine that God's existence, his moral law, and the rewards of virtue in the afterlife would be evident to the "natural reason" of anyone freed of prejudice and emboldened to think for himself or herself. By imagining that this much faith would suffice for salvation, they were able to argue that Europe could emancipate itself from wars fought over "matters indifferent" – theological disputes or points of scriptural interpretation that were without consequence for salvation and beyond rational adjudication – without collapsing into faithless moral skepticism and anarchy (see, for instance, the Author's Letter to Descartes's *Principles of Philosophy*). Would not the common possession of natural religion, the moral faith arguably at the heart of Christianity, suffice to enable "men" – now citizens rather than subjects, Christians but not bound to any church or religious tradition except by their own choice – to live in peace and mutual tolerance?

The compatibility of religion and peace was thus one of the central preoccupations of Enlightenment philosophy. The compatibility of scientific and moral knowledge was another, albeit related: if the new science embodied knowledge, what did this reveal of the nature of knowledge in general, and thus of anything that could qualify as moral knowledge? Whether the scientific revolution left any epistemic room for morality and religion was a question of ongoing concern in such venues as the Royal Society of London, and an apparent concern of Locke's in writing his *Essay on Human Understanding* (see Woolhouse, 1983).

Locke's account of knowledge, including moral knowledge, derives directly from the methodological and epistemological views of Descartes, and it is arguably in those views that we find the origin of the revolutionary tendencies in Locke's thought (see Schouls, 1992). If the "clarity and distinctness" of the ideas grasped in thought is essential to knowledge, if clarity and distinctness can only be achieved through *one's own* activity of analysis, and if natural reason is the *common* possession of human beings, then a kind of epistemic individualism or atomism follows. From there, Locke argues (at the beginning of his *Conduct of the Understanding*) that human beings *act* from their ideas, and act *freely* to the extent that they take individual epistemic responsibility for what they believe. It is characteristic of Enlightenment liberal thought that this link between the exercise of *reason* and *freedom* is embedded in a larger cluster of ideas, to the effect that an education that exercises reason and enables people to be rational – to achieve *mastery*, including self-mastery – is consistent with human nature and its *perfectibility*, and in a regime of political *liberty* is conducive to *progress*.

There are many Enlightenment and liberal figures whose thought might have been surveyed in this chapter (besides Kant, who appears in a later chapter), and much that might have been said about the educational thought of important precursors of Enlightenment thought, such as Hobbes, who advocated illiberal models of the relationship between civil, ecclesiastical, and educational authority (see Lloyd, 1992). Locke appears here as the central educational philosopher of the Enlightenment liberal movement, in a section authored by Professor Nathan Tarcov, but preceded by Descartes, whose epistemic egalitarianism was arguably foundational to Locke's views and the Enlightenment generally, in a section authored by Professor Amy Schmitter. Among later liberals who retain commitments characteristic of the Enlightenment (even while also moving beyond it in some ways), John Stuart Mill stands out for the importance of his educational thought and its influence on later thinkers, such as (importantly) John Dewey. A section on Mill, authored by Professor Wendy Donner, closes the chapter.

Descartes

In *An Essay Concerning Human Understanding*, John Locke argues against innatism about knowledge and ideas on the grounds that it can make no sense of the labor and time of learning difficult truths. Were we born with the knowledge of such truths as the principle of non-contradiction, we would need only to consult the already formed contents of our minds to avail ourselves of them. In reply, Gottfried Wilhelm Leibniz's

New Essays describes our possession of such truths as merely implicit, enabling knowledge – a view Leibniz could defend on what he took to be the priority of logical order and on the hypothesis of *petites perceptions* that fail to reach consciousness. But those are not responses readily available to earlier advocates of innatism, such as René Descartes (1596–1650). Descartes, in fact, explicitly rejected the importance of any formal logical order for reasoning, and he was notoriously opposed to relying on experience or authority, favoring instead the autonomous use of the reason that "is naturally equal in all of us" (Descartes, 1996, VI, p. 2; 1984–91, I, p. 111). On the other hand, he also showed a longstanding concern with methods for discovering new knowledge, and had reforming ambitions for education. What are we to make of these seeming conflicts?

Descartes's training

Descartes discussed his own education in Part I of the *Discourse on Method* (1637), referring specifically to his eight years spent at the Jesuit school of La Flèche. (He also studied civil and canon law at the University of Poitiers, finishing in 1616.) Languages occupied the largest part of the curriculum at La Flèche, with only the last three years devoted to natural science (particularly "novelties," unusual and spectacular phenomena), pure and applied mathematics, ethics, and metaphysics. The texts used for these subjects were largely Scholastic-Aristotelian, but works of Renaissance and early modern authors far outnumbered those of Aristotle himself. Although declaring himself "glad [to have received] a scholastic education of this sort" (Descartes, 1996, X, p. 364; 1984–91, I, p. 11), Descartes expressed dissatisfaction with its content for providing little knowledge that was certain and "evident." The one exception he allowed was mathematics. Descartes's praise for mathematics was no mere platitude, for the early seventeenth century saw a raging debate on "the question of the certainty of mathematics." The main culprit stirring controversy, and drawing widespread attention to issues of method, was a then current Scholastic model of scientific demonstration that required syllogistic reasoning from universal premises and causes (thereby eliminating many important and time-honored mathematical proofs).

Much of Descartes's interest in mathematics, however, developed after his formal schooling, through collaboration with Isaac Beekman, whom Descartes met in 1618. Beekman was keenly interested in physical science, with a novel approach to understanding macroscopic phenomena in terms of the dynamics of microscopic parts. Under Beekman's tutelage, Descartes worked on problems in "physico-mathematics," applying mathematical models to explain ordinary physical phenomena. Shaky though some of his first explanations were, Descartes learned a mathematical and mechanical approach from Beekman very different from what was taught at La Flèche.

The method

In 1619 Descartes had a vision of a new science (described in the *Discourse*), and seems to have embarked on his first major philosophical work, the unfinished and undated *Rules for the Direction of our Native Intelligence* [*Ingenium*]. Like the later *Discourse*, the topic was the proper "method" for the discovery of new knowledge.

Although some commentators see these works as proposing general procedures for discovery, it is not easy to tease out anything very specific. Instead, the first few rules heap scorn on *formal* accounts of reasoning, particularly on the "chains [of syllogisms]" with which "dialecticians suppose they regulate human reason" (Descartes, 1996, X, p. 365; 1984–91, I, p. 12). Such regulation is unnecessary, Descartes maintained, for the acts of thought that provide certain knowledge [*scientia*] are "not something a man can perform wrongly" (Descartes, 1996, X, p. 368; 1984–91, I, p. 14), although one may fail to perform them. Such demands may even cause harm, by preventing the discovery of attainable knowledge, and promoting obscure definitions and tangled reasoning. Even the syllogistic presentation of a demonstration offers little benefit: at best, it rehashes results otherwise obtained, compelling agreement with the conclusion, but not explaining it. Descartes wanted a method that would be genuinely explanatory, as he claimed the analysis of the ancient geometers was, and as the "outlandish art of algebra" (Descartes 1996, X, p. 377; 1984–91, I, p. 19), which "treats the unknown as if it were known," might be. The keys are "order" and "measure." But despite many examples illustrating varieties of order and measure, Descartes offered no general account of their nature. But he did provide a theory of error – caused, he maintained, by carelessness and failures of memory. We can avoid these pitfalls by practicing mental discipline, developed by exercises ranging from working on proportional series to examining embroidery.

Rules 12–18, however, describe specific techniques for solving "perfectly understood problems," problems where the solution can be determined by the relations among various givens, which may thus be susceptible to mathematical expression. These techniques were designed to make full use of our bodily faculties of sense, imagination and memory, faculties Descartes described in Rule 12. (Note that *ingenium* does not refer to the intellect alone, but to its interaction with imagination and other *embodied* faculties.) Particularly important were proper representations of a problem and their transformations into different media – sensory, imaginative, figurative, and symbolic. Such transformations allowed an increasingly fine focus on the salient relations of the problem, those by which the unknown can be determined by what is known. Descartes's own mathematics illustrated many of these techniques, although the solution to Pappus's problem in the *Geometry* (*c.*1636) takes some algebraic shortcuts. Several features of Descartes's practice deserve mention: (1) its reliance on simple pictorial (and mechanical) constructions that illustrate the relations involved at each step *ad oculos*; (2) the restriction to the simplest mathematical operations and the dearth of theorems and axioms; (3) the premium placed on techniques fruitful for finding solutions to other problems. Descartes thereby aimed to produce a solution recognizable as explanatory and certain by any attentive mind. But *finding* such a solution is another matter. Rejecting formal constraints, Descartes favored a kind of free play with pictorial and symbolic expressions. But this play requires considerable ingenuity to be successful, and nothing in the *Rules* suggests that there is any mechanical substitute for ingenuity. Although the work proved influential for such later authors as Antoine Arnauld and Leibniz (for his "geometrical" and "universal characteristics"), few shared Descartes's extreme anti-formalism. None the less, the intuitive explanatory appeal of Descartes's work did win him an audience and helped to broaden the conception of acceptable mathematical practices.

In contrast, the *Discourse on Method* treats mathematics somewhat perfunctorily and offers only four very general rules for approaching problems. Descartes, in fact, denied teaching the method in the *Discourse*, leaving it to the companion essays to exemplify particular achievements (e.g. the solution of Pappus's problem in the *Geometry*, Snell's law in the *Dioptrics*, and the explanation of rainbows in the *Meteorology*). But if he elaborated little on the method, Descartes expanded his discussion in other ways: written in vernacular French, the *Discourse* contains a short autobiography, an account of explanation in natural philosophy, guides for practical reasoning under the pressures of time and uncertainty, and a metaphysical sketch. Part V also presents his mature conception of mind, a conception that abandons the faculty psychology of the Scholastics – which located different mental acts in separate faculties – and clears the way for the theory of innate ideas, further developed in the *Meditations on First Philosophy* (1641).

Innate ideas, error and experience

To appreciate what motivated this theory, we should bear in mind that Descartes rejected not only Scholasticism's formal models of demonstration, but also its empiricist and abstractionist account of concept-formation. These are closely connected moves, for Scholastic empiricism (unlike the later British version) held that the very *structure* of thought is borrowed from the world – received by processes of abstraction that refine materials introduced through sense-perception. In contrast, the *Meditations* argues that various crucial ideas – notably those of body, of mind, and of God – cannot be derived from experience, but are required to interpret experience. Yet that leaves a pressing worry: why should we think that the explanatory force these ideas provide (however hard won) signals anything other than the tendencies of our own thinking? Innatism provides the solution by proposing a correspondence relation between our thought and the world, grounded in their common source in God. Just as God has created those eternal truths and essences that constitute the fundamental outlines of the objective world, so too has God created the basic shape of our thinking, imprinting our nature with innate ideas of those truths and essences.

The authority God has conferred on our innate ideas does not make us immune to error. Yet there must be some discernible difference between our mistaken and our reliable thoughts, or the entire theory becomes useless. To this end, Descartes devoted the Fourth Meditation to the nature of judgment, whereby we affirm or deny a thought and so commit ourselves to a belief. As a commitment, judgment requires an act of volition. That does not, however, make judgment either arbitrary or under our immediate control. Our commitments cannot be exchanged like a suit of clothes, and so we should undertake them only on the basis of reasons. Committing ourselves without good reason, we err. Of course, we would not do so unless we *thought* we had good reason. But thinking we have good reason when we don't must mean that we have been careless in some way, at least by jumping to conclusions without sufficient justification. The good news is that this makes our errors corrigible: we can always suspend our judgment. Even better, we can often achieve certain knowledge through recourse to our innate ideas. Innate ideas provide perceptions of the nature of things that are clear and distinct and thus compel assent. Because we cannot think otherwise, they constitute the court of ultimate appeal, the reliability of which is guaranteed by God. Descartes invokes this appeal in, for example, the "distinct conceivability" argument for mind – body dualism. Since we cannot help but think that the natures of mind and body are clearly very different, they must be judged distinct substances, separable by God, however closely intertwined in human experience.

We may now see how Descartes would answer Locke's puzzle. We have innate ideas, but not immediate access to them. Not only do we need to constrain our will to avoid over-hasty, careless commitments, but teasing out the contents of our innate ideas requires good method (and a great deal of ingenuity besides) to discover what genuinely compels assent. It is true that Descartes hoped to set philosophy and natural science on a footing that would eliminate traditional errors, and thus spare us some of the work involved in overcoming Scholastic "prejudices" (for which he developed a specific "method of doubt"). Indeed, Descartes hoped to replace Scholastic textbooks with his own *Principles of Philosophy* (1644). None the less, there are certain kinds of error and carelessness to which we are "naturally" prone; the Sixth Meditation depicts Scholastic empiricism as a natural (if not inevitable) extension of commonsense beliefs. Because sensory ideas are particularly vivid and (seem to) appear first in our experience, "nature itself" seems to teach that sensations resemble external bodies, and that there is "nothing at all in the intellect . . . not previously had in sensation" (Descartes, 1996, VII, p. 75; 1984–91, II, p. 52).

Descartes, however, held no animus towards sense-experience as such. Later experience itself provides grounds for doubting the lessons of "nature." Moreover, empirical observations (*expériences*) are crucial to proper scientific practice, as the Sixth Part of the *Discourse* explains. While our innate ideas of body and considerations of the simplicity of God give us framing laws for the physical world, only particular observations can determine which possible configurations of matter in motion hold in fact. The need to accumulate observations mandates a pooling of efforts, for which Descartes envisioned a division of labor between the natural philosopher and various assistants (although the explanatory work of natural philosophy still seems a solitary enterprise). In short, Descartes acknowledged that advancing knowledge requires a great deal of work, both individual and collective, critical and empirical. Indeed he praised God for making us *perfectible*, rather than gifted with perfect knowledge from the start (Descartes, 1996, VII, pp. 62–3; 1984–91, II, p. 43).

The education of the passions

Perhaps Descartes's most interesting remarks on education concern the "passions," those emotions originating in the body, and the topic of his last work, *The Passions of the Soul* (1649). Descartes maintained that the passions – like our appetites, feelings of pleasure and pain, and sensations – serve as a rough yet ready guide to how differences in the physical world affect us for good or ill. The perceptions they provide are thus functional in achieving our ends, particularly that of preserving the union of mind and body. But the passions are generated by mechanical impacts on and within our bodies, and so they can also be dysfunctional, conflicting with the properly considered evaluations of our reason. For instance, the disposition to feel fear when confronted with grizzly bears is usually functional, but not when felt in the face of tame or dead or caged grizzlies (especially if we are zookeepers or bear researchers). Descartes dubbed the remedy for such conflicts the "discipline of virtue." It transforms our dispositions through our bodies, using imaginative constructions to rouse the passions we deem reasonable in various situations, which in turn prompts bodily changes. The long-term goal is to reshape our physiologies, so as to feel the right passion on the right occasion (a process comparable to training hunting dogs, except that we are both trainer and trainee, and the choice of ends is our own). But in no way did Descartes think we should abandon our passions: perceptions originating in our bodies are indispensable sources of information, and the passions in particular provide crucial guides to our well-being. They are also motivating, among our most effective spurs to action. What the discipline of virtue ensures is that our passions constitute genuine *reasons* for actions. Although Descartes held that there are also purely intellectual emotions that can sometimes conflict with our passions, the force the passions exert on embodied humans makes it particularly important to educate them properly.

Disciplining the passions also serves the search for knowledge, as shown by the passion of wonder. Unlike the other passions, wonder involves no perception of its object as good or bad, simply taking it as unusual and worthy of our regard. But it produces striking physiological changes: wonder brings all the resources of our bodies into play to fix our attention, stir up the investigative juices and stimulate our memory. To be sure, the disposition to wonder can also be dysfunctional if it becomes excessive or wrongly directed. But it is educable, and properly trained wonder becomes our rational response to those features of the world that deserve investigation, motivating its own resolution in intellectual achievement. The benefits of wonder, however, are only possible because we are embodied creatures. Embodiment itself, then, seems a real boon to the search for knowledge. And, indeed, much of Descartes's educational program – whether a matter of the method to direct our *ingenium* or of the discipline of virtue – is directed at teaching the best use of our bodily resources.

Descartes's influence

Descartes's works were placed on the Index of Prohibited Books in 1663. None the less, his metaphysics, natural philosophy, and parts of his method became widely disseminated (without, however, establishing the educational standard he had hoped). Cartesianism of various stripes took hold in a number of Dutch universities. But Descartes's most important influence in the history of education may lie in changing the conception of its clientele. Descartes himself had been the beneficiary of educational expansion for the secular middle classes. Later Cartesianism widened educational opportunities yet further, particularly for (privileged) women. A notable example in this respect is the work of François Poulain de la Barre advocating sexual equality. But Descartes deserves personal credit too. He was a dedicated and respectful correspondent with women such as Elizabeth of Bohemia, and his views on the nature of mind have markedly egalitarian tendencies. If one can speak a natural language and make mistakes – fairly widespread abilities – one surely has a mind. Nor do minds come in degrees. Then too, Descartes's method denied any need for specialized knowledge or institutionalized training. Although his emphasis on educating the body might have been put to exclusionary uses, it was largely ignored. In any case, he never suggested that sex-based bodily differences make any difference at all.

John Locke

John Locke (1632–1704) was the most influential educational thinker of Enlightenment liberalism. He spent much of his life as an educator and was always a careful observer of children. He received a scholastic education at Westminster and Oxford, where he pursued an academic career (1658–65), teaching Latin, Greek, philosophy, ethics, and religion, but focusing his own research on medicine and the new natural science. He then served as secretary to the Whig leader, the first Earl of Shaftesbury, and tutor to his son and later his grandchildren, while continuing his medical and scientific activities and beginning his great philosophical works. Locke later received his medical degree and held a post as teacher of medicine at Oxford, but spent his time traveling in France, partly as tutor to a wealthy merchant's son. After political exile in Holland (1683–9), he served on the Board of Trade and advised leading Whig statesmen. His major works include *Two Treatises of Government* (1689), *A Letter Concerning Toleration* (1689), *An Essay Concerning Human Understanding* (1689), *Some Thoughts Concerning Education* (1693), *The Reasonableness of Christianity* (1695), and *Of the Conduct of the Understanding* (1706).

Education in Locke's political thought

Education played a narrowly circumscribed role in the political theory of Locke's *Two Treatises*. Government is based on the free consent of individuals as they come of age, and acts only to preserve their lives, liberties, and properties because all normal adults are presumed to be rational and therefore by nature free and equal. In opposition to the claim of his patriarchalist predecessor Sir Robert Filmer, that fathers by nature have a right to permanent absolute political power over their children, reaching to life and death, Locke argued that parents – that is, mothers and fathers equally – have not so much a right as a duty to preserve, nourish, and educate their children lasting until they reach maturity, which being a duty to preserve excludes a power of life and death. The educative component of this duty informs children's minds and governs their actions to give strength and health to their bodies and vigor and rectitude to their minds so that they will be most useful to themselves and others. Locke thus separates the power of education, which he assigns to parents, from the power of life and death, which he assigns to government, a separation of powers fundamental to Lockean liberalism. Because government exists to preserve its subjects' rights to life, liberty, and property rather than to teach them the truth or improve or save their souls, it is obligated, according to the *Letter Concerning Toleration*, to tolerate all opinions and practices that do not threaten those rights. Lockean government is emphatically not educative or paternalistic, though it protects a private sphere of society in which parents, churches, and writers such as Locke can educate in their different ways.

There is, however, an important ambiguity about the role of education in Locke's political theory. Locke writes at times as if reason simply comes with age, as seems consonant with the presumption that every normal adult is rational, and at times as if reason is a result also of education, as seems consonant with the parental duty to educate. A parallel ambiguity emerges in Locke's *Letter Concerning Toleration*, where religion is treated as freely chosen by individuals but parents bring up their children in the parents' religion. Perhaps only in a society whose members follow the recommendations in Locke's educational works would adults be truly rational and freely choose their religion.

Locke on the education of children

Locke, unlike Descartes, extensively discussed the education of children, although he did so in *Some Thoughts Concerning Education* rather than in political works, unlike Plato and Aristotle, for whom government was essentially educative. Hobbes too attributed to his sovereign the duty to instruct his people, performed through appointing their teachers and examining the doctrines they taught. He expressed the hope in *Leviathan* that a sovereign would protect the public teaching of its doctrine in the universities, since most people derived their opinions from the clergy and the learned among the gentry, who in turn derived theirs from the universities or from books by university faculty. Locke, in contrast, addressed his *Thoughts* to parents rather than to professional teachers, let alone to the sovereign, not only because he distrusted the clergy who dominated the teaching profession and because he denied an educative role to government, but also because he regarded early childhood moral education as crucial. He indeed favored home schooling, since schools paid more attention to Greek and Latin than to moral virtue, innocent schoolboys were likely to be corrupted by their unruly peers, and even the best schoolmaster could not form the morals of 50 to 100 pupils with the proper attention to their individual tempers, as parents or tutors could at home. Locke took this position when the alternatives for country gentry were home schooling or boarding school, but he thought ways might be found to avoid the disadvantages of both, perhaps including our common combination of moral education at home with learning at day school.

Locke addressed the *Thoughts* primarily to the gentry, expecting that if they were set right by their education they would "quickly bring all the rest into order," but he described the moral virtues he recommends as necessary for a man or gentleman and the intellectual virtues as suitable for a gentleman or "anyone who pretends to be a rational creature" (Locke, 1996, pp. 8, 140). He noted that he used the masculine pronoun for the pupil since his principal aim was the education of gentlemen, but he thought the nearer girls came to the hardships of their brothers in their education the better, and boys could well be brought up with the bashfulness of their sisters and be spared the roughness and boisterousness that distinguished men from women.

Locke stressed the difference between his "method" of education and the ordinary method of schools. By this he meant above all that instead of relying on rules and duties enforced by corporal punishments and material rewards, he relied on example, habit, freedom, and play, supported by rewards and punishments of praise and blame. The usual method, he argued, only reinforced our propensity to be moved by immediate physical pleasure and pain and produced an aversion to the studies and virtues it enforced. Useful studies and virtues should instead be pursued freely, not from fear of corporal punishment but from desire for praise; freedom for Locke, unlike Rousseau, was compatible with concern for the esteem of others. Learning should therefore be made into play, since play is distinguished only by its freedom. Locke's method was meant to be consistent with his view that neither knowledge nor virtue is innate, and that human beings are innately concerned only with bodily pleasure and pain but are capable of developing their reasoning, an acute sensitivity toward their reputation, and a love of freedom closely connected to pride in their rationality. It also took account of the natural individuality of temperaments, since children have to be motivated by what appeals to them. Parents were to establish their authority early by denying the child's demands for the satisfaction of wants of fancy, as distinguished from natural wants, thereby also developing the child's capacity to deny his desires at the behest of his own reason. But they were to exercise their authority rarely and relax it gradually until the child became their rational, free, and equal friend rather than their obedient subject. Locke's method thus educated children to become neither slavish nor domineering but good citizens of a liberal polity.

This method was to be applied to develop virtues that would make the pupil useful to himself and others, adjusted to the limitations of the individual's temperament. In addition to the capacity to deny one's desires, or self-mastery, these virtues included civility, liberality, justice, hardiness, courage, compassion, thrift, curiosity, industry, and truthfulness. Civility was meant to overcome the love of power and dominion over others by transforming it into a desire, even a contest, for the love, respect, and esteem of others, gained by showing love, respect, and esteem for them. Civility excludes censoriousness, contradiction, and interruption, but allows opposing the opinions of others with due caution, since "the greatest advantage of society" is the light gotten from the opposite arguments of able men (Locke, 1996, p. 111). Civility thus allows for mutual adult education in a liberal society tolerating diverse opinions and encouraging free discussion. Liberality and justice mitigate the love of property by making it compatible with the needs and rights of others. Hardiness and courage enable one to withstand the pains and dangers of life in general as well as to bear arms and face death in battle, which a gentleman ought to be bred to be fit for. Compassion and thrift in opposition to cruelty and waste are required for the preservation of all mankind, which is "everyone's duty and the true principle to regulate our religion, politics, and morality by" (Locke, 1996, p. 91). Curiosity is the motive for intellectual labor, as desire in general is the spur of industry, without which men cannot be useful or happy. Above all, children should be encouraged to reason: "For when all is done, this, as the highest and most important faculty of our minds, deserves the greatest care and attention in cultivating it: the right improvement and exercise of our reason being the highest perfection that a man can attain to in this life" (Locke, 1996, p. 95). Virtue itself is valued only as conducing to our happiness, which consists in pleasure.

Lockean moral education rests partly on the child's concern for reputation and partly on religion, which is eventually the belief that to follow one's own God-given reason is to obey one's Maker with hope of reward. Children were therefore to be taught early "a true notion of God, as of the independent Supreme Being, Author and Maker of all things, from whom we receive all our good, who loves us and gives us all things"

(Locke, 1996, pp. 102–3). They should love and revere this benevolent Being, and be content with this simple and positive notion of Him; Locke said nothing in this context about fear or punishment and excluded any teaching about terrifying spirits. He added that it would be better for adults too if they were not "too curious in their notions about a Being which all must acknowledge incomprehensible," so as to avoid both superstition and atheism (Locke, 1996, p. 103). Children should learn the Lord's Prayer, the Creed, and the Ten Commandments by heart, but instead of reading the whole Bible, the worst basis for religion and altogether very disproportionate to their understandings, they should learn principles drawn from it suited to their understandings, stories such as Joseph and his brothers, David and Goliath, and David and Jonathan, and plain moral rules such as the golden rule. Older children should read a history drawn from the Bible. Locke preferred to start a child's reading rather with Aesop's fables, "the only book almost that I know fit for children" (Locke, 1996, pp. 116–17, 141). This religious education was meant to be supportive of morality, regulated by the principle of the preservation of all mankind, and consistent with human reason.

Locke subordinated learning to moral virtue, wisdom (knowledge of the social world and ability to manage one's affairs in it), and breeding (civility and manners), and selected the subjects to be learned according to his standard of utility for actual life. This led him to demote the scholastic and humanist curriculum of classical languages, grammar, rhetoric, logic, metaphysics, and poetry, and to promote instead drawing, shorthand, French, accounting, geography, arithmetic, astronomy, geometry, chronology, classical history, modern natural law (Grotius and Pufendorf), English law and history, letterwriting, and the new natural science of his friend Isaac Newton. In these studies Locke emphasized learning things rather than words, practice rather than rules (e.g. in learning languages), and play rather than compulsion. He criticized scholastic composition of Latin themes, orations, and verses as useless to gentlemen who needed to be proficient in speaking and writing English in ordinary life and he decried scholastic disputation as making its practitioners opinionated wranglers or pursuers of victory rather than truth. He denounced scholastic education generally as fitting us rather for the university than the world. Locke's emphasis on utility also led him to downplay aesthetic education and imagination (in sharp contrast to Plato, Rousseau, and the Romantics), recommending learning to draw only because pictures record buildings, machines, and costumes better than can words, urging parents of a son with a poetic vein to try to stifle it, and warning that music was, like painting, a waste of time and led to odd company. The only exception was dancing, which "I know not how" gives children manly thoughts through graceful motion (Locke, 1996, pp. 43, 150). This utilitarian strand culminated in Locke's concluding proposals that the sons of gentlemen be taught manual trades such as agriculture, carpentry, metalwork, jewelry, and lens crafting, as well as accounting, and that they travel abroad to acquire languages and learn about different ways of life, customs, manners, laws, and governments.

Locke on adult self-education

Locke's *Conduct of the Understanding* is a self-help book designed to assist adults in re-educating themselves and freeing themselves from intellectual slavery. Although published separately and posthumously, it was originally intended as the last chapter of the *Essay Concerning Human Understanding*. The *Essay* argued against the doctrine of innate ideas, which Locke regarded as a justification for subservience to prejudice, superstition, and intellectual tyranny. Knowledge instead was to be gained by careful examination of one's ideas and their origins in sensation and reflection, the acquisition of clear and distinct ideas, the consideration and intellectual perception of their relations, the use of words clearly signifying such ideas, and the careful weighing of probabilities. The *Essay* laid out Locke's theory of the association of ideas, which underlay both his emphasis on habituation and his warning against the aversion to study produced by the usual method of education in the *Thoughts*. The *Essay* encouraged its readers, under Locke's gentle guidance, to question the opinions church or party leaders imposed on them by authority, refrain from imposing their own opinions on others, and think for themselves.

The *Conduct* is a detailed manual of self-education, diagnosing intellectual pathologies and prescribing a diverse set of remedies for them. These pathologies include prejudices, unexamined first principles, reliance on authority, belief in infallibility, partiality, passion, interest, obscure and insignificant words, triviality, book learning, imagination, and the association of ideas. Most of these are the results of intellectual laziness and defective childhood education. Accepting the prejudices, first principles, authority, or infallibility of one's parents, neighbors, party, or sect saves one the pains of thinking for oneself and prevents one from developing one's reason through exercise. The peculiar faults of scholars include pursuing trivial and purely logical inquiries, looking in books for arguments for one side while neglecting those favoring the other or collecting arguments pro and con so as to talk on either side, and improperly transferring methods from one science to another, such as applying mathematical methods or laboratory science to theology or politics. Imagination seeks the pleasant rather than the true, resting content with simile and metaphor. Association of ideas subjects us to the empire of habit by making unnatural connections between ideas seem natural. Locke portrays all these conditions as forms of mental slavery, a greater evil than corporal chains, reinforced by social condemnation and political persecution of free inquiry and dissent.

Locke's countervailing prescriptions in the *Conduct* emphasize the need for intellectual labor to exercise our reason and so strengthen our minds, enlarge our capacities, and improve our faculties. On the analogy of bodily exercise, Locke argues our minds are improved by the practice and habit of reasoning rather than by learning the supposed rules of reasoning of scholastic logic:

would you have a man reason well...exercise his mind in observing the connection of ideas and following them in train. Nothing does this better than mathematics, which therefore I think should be taught all those who have the time and opportunity, not so much to make them mathematicians as to make them reasonable creatures;...we are born to be, if we please, rational creatures, but it is use and exercise that makes us so. (Locke, 1996, p. 178)

He claims that most apparent inequalities of natural intellectual endowments among different cultures, races, and classes are only the product of exercise and the lucky chance of education.

His account of knowledge rests in the doctrine of natural reason:

Every man carries about him a touchstone, if he will make use of it, to distinguish substantial gold from superficial glitterings, truth from appearances. And indeed the use and benefit of this touchstone, which is natural reason, is spoiled and lost only by assumed prejudices, overweening presumption, and narrowing our minds. (Locke, 1996, p. 171)

The proper use of this natural reason is to occupy one's mind only with clear and determined ideas, preferably stripped of words or at least expressed in words of settled signification, and to judge things for oneself by tracing "the dependence of any truth in a long train of consequences to its remote principles" (Locke, 1996, pp. 173, 175, p. 177):

For in all sorts of reasoning, every single argument should be managed as a mathematical demonstration, the connection and dependence of ideas should be followed until the mind is brought to the source on which it bottoms and observes the coherence all along. (Locke, 1996, p. 180)

Where knowledge "bottoms" out, then, is – for Locke as it was for Descartes – in the perception or "intuition" of relationships between clearly and distinctly or "determined" ideas, items of knowledge being themselves "relations of ideas."

For the partiality all of us show, Locke prescribes talking with different sorts of men and reading different sorts of books and offers the countervailing ideal of what he calls indifferency. By this he means that we should not wish any opinion to be true but should examine all opinions impartially, moved only by the evidence, an attitude he realizes will be criticized especially as regards religion. In opposition to scholarly trifling, he insists that we seek fundamental truths, such as Newton's discovery of gravitation, the basis of natural philosophy, or the golden rule or natural equality, fundamental truths for regulating human society. As to book learning, he admits reading is of great help to the understanding but says knowledge is gained from it by examining the coherence and foundations of the author's arguments, not by repeating them or taking them on trust. To counter the ill effects of the association of ideas, we need to examine whether ideas are linked together in our minds from their real agreement or only from habitual custom. To preserve the freedom of our minds from the tyranny of passion, we must allay the dominating passion or counterbalance it with another. This program for self-education and liberation from authority and prejudice is the heart of the liberal Enlightenment.

John Stuart Mill

John Stuart Mill's philosophy of education is an exemplar of Enlightenment liberalism rooted in the utilitarian philosophy and art of life of Jeremy Bentham and James Mill. The principle of utility, which is the foundation of John Stuart Mill's ethical theory, "holds that actions are right in proportion as they tend to promote happiness, wrong as they tend to produce the reverse of happiness. By happiness is intended pleasure, and the absence of pain" (Mill, 1969, p. 210). Mill explains that this theory of morality is grounded on a "theory of life . . . namely, that pleasure, and freedom from pain, are the only things desirable as ends" (Mill, 1969, p. 210). Despite this initial formulation, Mill actually propounds a sophisticated form of qualitative hedonism in which those things that are desirable as ends are certain kinds of complex, satisfying mental states (see Donner, 1991). The principle of utility, which is concerned with "utility in the largest sense, grounded on the permanent interests of man as a progressive being," is a principle of the good or value, one that governs morality, but that also governs all of the practical arts and all practical reasoning (Mill, 1977b, p. 224).

Mill's philosophy of education can be approached fruitfully by exploring his claim in the *Logic* that education is one of the primary practical arts. In Book VI of the *Logic*, Mill explores the practical or (as he here calls them) the moral arts and their companion sciences. The purpose of a moral or practical art is to define or set down the ends that are desirable or that promote utility, and thus ought to be aimed at. Each practical art is coupled or linked with a practical or moral science that investigates the "course of nature" in order to formulate effective means to promote the ends of the art. Mill says

The art proposes to itself an end to be attained, defines the end, and hands it over to the science. The science receives it, considers it as a phenomenon to be studied, and having investigated its causes and conditions, sends it back to art with a theorem of the combinations of circumstances by which it could be produced. (Mill, 1973, p. 944)

Education is explored in this context as one of the more important particular practical arts. Significantly for Mill's Enlightenment liberalism, he pairs the practical art of education with the moral science of what he calls ethology. This science of ethology is the science of character formation. Seen in this light, Mill construes education very broadly, as the art of character formation guided by its corresponding science. If the goal of education is interpreted broadly, as the appropriate socialization or character formation to encourage the development of certain character traits and the nurturing and development of certain human capacities, then the goals and principles of Enlightenment liberalism are promoted and advanced (Mill, 1973, pp. 869–70). These goals are to educate and socialize autonomous persons of individuality and responsible democratic citizens. While it is beyond the scope of this chapter to pursue in detail the content of Mill's approach, his conception of education is radically democratic and egalitarian, and he advocates kinds of education that are concerned not just with a narrow form of freedom, but with social, economic and political emancipation (see Gutmann, 1980; Donner, 1991; Morales, 1996; Ashcroft, 1999; Baum, 2000).

Mill's utilitarianism and Enlightenment liberalism are ultimately grounded in the principle of utility as set out above. But if the principle of utility, which governs all of the practical arts including education, calls for the promotion of utility, much will depend upon the conception of utility at its core. In Mill's view, utility is analyzed in terms of a conception of the good or value that is appropriate for human beings with a certain human nature. The most valuable kinds of happiness for humans consist in the development and self-development of our higher human capacities. C. B. Macpherson discusses Mill's philosophy as an example of developmental democracy, one of the major models of liberal democracy. Macpherson says that according to Mill's model, "man [sic] is a being capable of developing his powers or capacities. The human essence is to exert and develop them . . . . The good society is one which permits and encourages everyone to act as exerter, developer, and enjoyer of the exertion and development, of his or her own capacities" (see Macpherson, 1977, p. 48). Mill's philosophy of education sets down a program in which humans are educated in childhood to develop their generic human cognitive, affective, and moral capacities. In adulthood, this process continues as one of self-development, in which the person herself develops the higher-order capacities of autonomy, individuality, and sociality. For this process to continue, the support of and participation in various social and political institutions are prerequisites.

For many liberals, the cultivation of the cognitive and rational capacities is the most fundamental aspect of education. Mill places great stress upon training the intellect in childhood, and returns often to his claim that intellectual training requires active exercise of the mind, to develop habits of critical awareness (e.g. Mill, 1981, pp. 33–7). Indeed, the promotion of active use of our capacities, instead of passive receptivity and conformity, is a key principle governing all forms of education. The use of any sort of rote learning, such as memorization of facts without critical understanding, does not promote the development of critical cognitive ability. Unlike some other Enlightenment liberals, Mill places equal stress upon affective development or the development of feelings, and reacts against his own excessively rationalistic education, which produced a "mental crisis" in early adulthood (Mill, 1981, pp. 137–63). After this crisis, he recognized acutely the need for the "internal culture" of the feelings, and argues that the educative process is incomplete without attention to affective cultivation (Mill, 1981, pp. 147–57). Appreciation of poetry and encounters with natural beauty are but two recommended methods for promoting this cultivation. The process of moral development, which develops sympathy with others and feelings of benevolence and connection, is equally central to childhood education. In adulthood, the process continues with the cultivation of autonomy, the ability to reflect upon, choose, and revise our conception of the good as well as our character, relationships, projects, and life plans. Individuality encourages our ability to explore the range of these goods most in harmony with our abilities and particularities (Mill, 1977b, pp. 260–75). Equally important are the higher-order social capacities, those that draw us into community and cooperative enterprises to work with others in the public domain for the common good.

Mill's *Inaugural Address Delivered to the University of St Andrews* provided an opportunity and occasion for him to lay out his views about university education. This address casts further light on the content as well as the principles that Mill sees as guiding this significant moral art. In this document, Mill distinguishes two senses of education, the first broader than the second.

The larger sense refers back to the broad meaning of education elucidated in the *Logic*. In his *Inaugural Address*, Mill says of education that

Not only does it include whatever we do for ourselves, and whatever is done for us by others, for the express purpose of bringing us somewhat nearer to the perfection of our nature; it does

87

more: in its largest acceptation, it comprehends even the indirect effects produced on character and on the human faculties, by things of which the direct purposes are quite different; by laws, by forms of government, by the industrial arts, by modes of social life. (Mill, 1984b, p. 217)

This first broad sense of education is the predominant one in Mill's writings and the major focus of his concerns. In his *Inaugural Address*, however, he separates out this broadly characterized form from the narrower sense, the sense most often used in connection with education in our culture. It is the broader definition, however, which most distinctively marks Mill out as a representative of Enlightenment liberalism, the sense that education is applicable to every domain of life and is not restricted to schooling.

The broader view is that "whatever helps to shape the human being; to make the individual what he is, or to hinder him from being what he is not – is part of his education" (Mill, 1984b, p. 217). But even Mill's characterization of what he calls the narrower sense of education – that provided primarily by educational systems of schools and universities – is in keeping with the tradition of Enlightenment liberalism and is clearly weighted in favor of a liberal education in the arts and sciences. He defines the narrower sense as "the culture which each generation purposely gives to those who are to be its successors, in order to qualify them for at least keeping up, and if possible for raising, the level of improvement which has been attained" (Mill, 1984b, p. 218). Mill specifically has in mind a liberal education including arts and sciences, and he specifically repudiates and sets aside the view that universities should include professional schools and faculties. A university "is not a place of professional education. Universities are not intended to teach the knowledge required to fit men for some special mode of gaining their livelihood. Their object is not to make skilful lawyers, or physicians, or engineers, but capable and cultivated human beings" (Mill, 1984b, p. 218). Other public institutions should take on this task of training and educating for work or the professions. "But these things are no part of what every generation owes the next, as that on which its civilization and worth will principally depend" (Mill, 1984b, p. 218). Specialized education is needed by a small number only. If professionals do also acquire a university education, it should be to "bring the light of general culture to illuminate the technicalities of a special pursuit" (Mill, 1984b, p. 218). University public education, although narrower in its scope than the general sense of education, is still distinct from professional or work and business training, and it still has as its goals to promote both intellectual education and, to a lesser extent, moral education, which are "the two main ingredients of human culture" (Mill, 1984b, p. 251).

In returning to an examination of Mill's perspective on the first, broader characterization of education, I revisit his claim that many forms of social institutions can shape and be affected by the qualities that this form of education is intended to promote as part of its utilitarian commitments.

The goal of the art of education, as of all the practical arts, is to promote utility, conceived of as the development of desirable human characteristics, specifically as the development and nurturing of certain human capacities and excellences. But because Mill conceives of humans as both social beings and autonomous agents whose good consists in exploring and developing their individuality, the educative process must promote these interrelated goals of bringing to fruition the progressive view of human nature and promoting a conception of the good for humans that is at its core concerned with self-development.

Contemporary liberal John Rawls claims that Mill's utilitarianism is what he calls a comprehensive doctrine, meaning that "the principle of utility ... is usually said to hold for all kinds of subjects ranging from the conduct of individuals and personal relations to the organization of society as a whole" (Rawls, 1993, p. 13). As a representative of the lineage and tradition of Enlightenment liberalism, Mill holds the view that the heart of the educative and developmental process is the creation and sustenance of autonomous individuals who are prepared to participate in the public democratic arena or forum. The unified nature of the educative process comes into play because the same educative process that produces participatory democratic citizens also prepares people to lead fulfilling, meaningful and autonomous lives. A precondition of this latter is, according to a tenet of contemporary liberalism with which Mill would agree, that people are "free to form, revise, and act on our plans of life" (Kymlicka, 1990, p. 209). So Mill argues for a unified view of the educative and developmental process, which serves to promote both of the above goals and ends by developing capacities and character traits that allow agents autonomously to form conceptions of and choose meaningful and fulfilling lives while also cooperating with other citizens to promote the common good in the public domain.

While Mill is concerned to promote life-long education and development in the first, broad sense, he does not neglect the second, narrower sense of education for children. He was a political and social activist, and distinguished himself by fighting, not just for universal suffrage, but also for the universal right to schooling and education in the era before universal rights to education were widely recognized. In *On Liberty*, as well as in other writings, Mill argues that the human capacities for autonomy should be developed by groundwork laid in childhood education, and so children have a right to an education. He says

Is it not almost a self-evident axiom, that the state should require and compel the education, up to a certain standard, of every human being who is born its citizen .... It still remains unrecognized, that to bring a child into existence without a fair prospect of being able, not only to provide food for its body, but instruction and training for its mind, is a moral crime, both against the unfortunate offspring and against society. (Mill, 1977b, pp. 301–2)

Mill argues that the state ought to enforce this right, and so there is a "duty of enforcing universal education" (Mill, 1977b, p. 302). However, Mill goes on to argue that, while the state has a duty to enforce the universal right to education, up to certain standards, the state should not itself provide universal public education. Parents should have the right to determine the means of education for their children, and the state should subsidize the fees of poor children to ensure they receive an education. "All that has been said of the importance of individuality of character, and diversity in opinions and modes of conduct, involves, as of the same unspeakable importance, diversity of education" (Mill, 1977b, p. 302). According to Mill, universal state education would run the risk of undermining diversity and individuality and of "moulding people to be exactly like one another" (Mill, 1977b, p. 302). This is the sort of conformity that Mill abhors as leading to a "despotism over the mind" (Mill, 1977b, p. 302). State education should be one alternative among several. Public examinations would ensure that the diverse educational experiences live up to certain standards, although Mill does not tackle the obvious question of how to balance diversity of experiences with uniformity of standards as tested by public examinations. The aim is to make "the universal acquisition, and what is more, retention of a certain minimum of general knowledge, virtually compulsory" (Mill, 1977b, p. 303). Complicating his claims further, he says that to prevent inappropriate influence by the state over opinions, these exams should be "confined to facts and positive science exclusively" (Mill, 1977b, p. 303). He advocates the establishment of teachers' colleges to train and examine teachers, an advocacy also ahead of its time (Mill, 1984a, pp. 207–14).

While Mill's perspective on the universal right to education was ahead of its time, his views were undoubtedly affected by his own remarkable education by his father, received outside of any school system, and by the fact that he never attended or taught at any university. In the *Autobiography*, Mill recollects and reflects upon his own education, describing in detail its content, scrutinizing the principles that guided it, exploring those aspects that he endorses from the perspective of adulthood as well as those elements that he rejects and revises (Mill, 1981, pp. 3–191; see also Donner, 1991, pp. 92–117). The elements he most strongly rejects are the excessive rationalism, which, he later comments, had threatened to turn him into "a mere reasoning machine" (Mill, 1981, p. 111). The imbalance is addressed by giving a central place to affective and moral cultivation.

But it is not just formal and informal schooling that is the source of education in Mill's view. According to Stefan Collini,

Mill's conception of society is an exceptionally and pervasively educative one . . . he makes their effect on the shaping of character the ultimate test of all institutions and policies, and one could without strain regard his whole notion of political activity itself as an extended and strenuous adult-education course. (Collini, 1984, p. xlviii)

The educative effect of social institutions cannot be underestimated. All institutions can be used to promote the radically progressive, egalitarian, and democratic ends of Mill's Enlightenment liberalism. Mill's philosophy of education, then, cannot be understood simply by examining those writings whose announced purpose is to discuss this theme. As Collini and others have argued at length, Mill's exploration of social, political and economic institutions is guided by his conviction that one of their major purposes is educative. Thus democratic political institutions are deemed to be agents of "national education" and one key criterion of a good government is "the degree in which it tends to increase the sum of good qualities in the governed, collectively and individually" (Mill, 1977a, p. 390). In his later writings on economics, Mill argues for participatory and democratic workplace partnerships and associations and hoped that this would bring about "the conversion of each human being's daily occupation into a school of the social sympathies and the practical intelligence" (Mill, 1965, p. 792). In *The Subjection of Women*, Mill advances a classic feminist argument for equality of relations and power between women and men, and argues that the moral principle regarding gender relations, especially within the family, should be "a principle of perfect equality, admitting no power or privilege on one side" (Mill, 1984c, p. 261; see also Morales, 1996). The family should be "a school of sympathy in equality, of living together in love, without power on one side or obedience on the other" (Mill, 1984c, p. 295). The family is the early major sphere of moral education (Mill, 1984b, p. 248).

John Stuart Mill's extensive writings on education, rooted in his utilitarianism and emancipatory and egalitarian liberalism, argue that not just formal educational institutions, but also a wide range of social, political, and economic institutions, can offer opportunities for life-long education and human self-development.

See also 4 THE EDUCATIONAL THOUGHT OF AUGUSTINE; 5 HUMANISM; 7 ROUSSEAU, DEWEY AND DEMOCRACY; 8 KANT, HEGEL, AND THE RISE OF PEDAGOGICAL SCIENCE; 9 ROMANTICISM; 21 CULTIVATING REASON; 28 THE AUTHORITY AND RESPONSIBILITY TO EDUCATE; 29 CHURCH, STATE, AND EDUCATION; 31 CHILDREN'S RIGHTS

References

Ashcroft, R. (1999) John Stuart Mill and the theoretical foundations of democratic socialism. In E. J. Eisenach (ed.), *Mill and the Moral Character of Liberalism*. University Park, PA: Penn State University Press.

Baum, B. (2000) *Rereading Power and Freedom in J. S. Mill*. Toronto: University of Toronto Press.

Collini, S. (1984) Introduction. In J. M. Robson (ed.), *The Collected Works of John Stuart Mill, volume XXI*. Toronto: University of Toronto Press.

Descartes, R. (1996) *Oeuvres de Descartes*, 11 volumes, ed. C. Adam and P. Tannery. Paris: J. Vrin.

Descartes, R. (1984–91). *The Philosophical Writings of Descartes, volumes I and II*, trans. J. Cottingham, R. Stoothoff, and D. Murdoch, and *volume III*, trans. J. Cottingham, R. Stoothoff, D. Murdoch, and A. Kenny. Cambridge: Cambridge University Press.

Donner, W. (1991) *The Liberal Self: John Stuart Mill's Moral and Political Philosophy*. Ithaca, NY: Cornell University Press.

Gutmann, A. (1980) *Liberal Equality*. Cambridge: Cambridge University Press.

Hobbes, T. (1994) *Leviathan*, ed. E. Curley. Indianapolis: Hackett Publishing.

Holmes, S. (1993) *The Anatomy of Antiliberalism*. Cambridge, MA: Harvard University Press.

Kymlicka, W. (1990) *Contemporary Political Philosophy: An Introduction*. Oxford: Clarendon Press.

Lloyd, S. A. (1992) *Ideals as Interests in Hobbes's Leviathan*. Cambridge: Cambridge University Press.

Locke, J. (1983) *A Letter Concerning Toleration*, ed. J. H. Tully. Indianapolis: Hackett Publishing.

Locke, J. (1988) *Two Treatises of Government*, ed. P. Laslett. Cambridge: Cambridge University Press.

Locke, J. (1989) *An Essay Concerning Human Understanding*, ed. P. H. Nidditch. Oxford: Oxford University Press.

Locke, J. (1990) *The Reasonableness of Christianity*, ed. G. W. Ewing. Chicago: Henry Regnery Co.

Locke, J. (1996) *Some Thoughts Concerning Education and Of the Conduct of the Understanding*, eds R. W. Grant and N. Tarcov. Indianapolis: Hackett Publishing.

Macpherson, C. B. (1977) *The Life and Times of Liberal Democracy*. Oxford: Oxford University Press.

Mill, J. S. (1965) Principles of political economy. In J. M. Robson (ed.), *The Collected Works of John Stuart Mill, volumes II and III*. Toronto: University of Toronto Press. (Originally published in 1848.)

Mill, J. S. (1969) Utilitarianism. In J. M. Robson (ed.), *The Collected Works of John Stuart Mill, volume X*. Toronto: University of Toronto Press. (Originally published in 1861.)

Mill, J. S. (1973) A system of logic. In J. M. Robson (ed.), *The Collected Works of John Stuart Mill, volumes VII and VIII*. Toronto: University of Toronto Press. (Originally published in 1843.)

Mill, J. S. (1977a) Considerations on representative government. In J. M. Robson (ed.), *The Collected Works of John Stuart Mill, volume XIX*. Toronto: University of Toronto Press. (Originally published in 1861.)

Mill, J. S. (1977b) On liberty. In J. M. Robson (ed.), *The Collected Works of John Stuart Mill, volume XVIII*. Toronto: University of Toronto Press. (Originally published in 1859.)

Mill, J. S. (1981) Autobiography. In J. M. Robson (ed.), *The Collected Works of John Stuart Mill, volume I*. Toronto: University of Toronto Press. (Originally published in 1873.)

Mill, J. S. (1984a) Educational endowments. In J. M. Robson (ed.), *The Collected Works of John Stuart Mill, volume XXI*. Toronto: University of Toronto Press. (Originally published in 1866.)

Mill, J. S. (1984b) Inaugural address. In J. M. Robson (ed.), *The Collected Works of John Stuart Mill, volume XXI*. Toronto: University of Toronto Press. (Originally published in 1867.)

Mill, J. S. (1984c) The subjection of women. In J. M. Robson (ed.), *The Collected Works of John Stuart Mill, volume XXI*. Toronto: University of Toronto Press. (Originally published in 1869.)

Morales, M. (1996) *Perfect Equality: John Stuart Mill on Well-constituted Communities*. Lanham, MD: Rowman & Littlefield.

Rawls, J. (1993) *Political Liberalism*. New York: Columbia University Press.

Schouls, P. A. (1992) *Reasoned Freedom: John Locke and Enlightenment*. Ithaca, NY: Cornell University Press.

Woolhouse, R. S. (1983) *Locke*. Minneapolis: University of Minnesota Press.

Further reading

Ariew, R., Cottingham, J., and Sorrell, T. (eds) (1998) *Background Source Materials: Descartes' Meditations*. New York: Cambridge University Press.

Broughton, J. (2001) *Descartes's Method of Doubt*. Princeton, NJ: Princeton University Press.

Carriero, J. (1990) *Descartes and the Autonomy of the Human Understanding*. New York: Garland Publications.

Garber, D. (2001) *Descartes Embodied: Reading Cartesian Philosophy through Cartesian Science*. Cambridge: Cambridge University Press.

Gaukroger, S. (1995) *Descartes: An Intellectual Biography*. New York: Oxford University Press.

Gaukroger, S. (1980) *Descartes: Philosophy, Mathematics and Physics*. Brighton: Harvester Press.

Hatfield, G. (1986) The senses and the fleshless eye. In A. Rorty (ed.), *Essays on Descartes' Meditations*. Berkeley: University of California Press.

Poulain de la Barre, F. (1674) *De l'éducation des dames pour la conduite de l'esprit dans les sciences et dans les moeurs, entretiens* [*On the Education of Women for the Direction of the Mind in Science and Morality*]. Paris: Chez A. Dezallier, reprinted 1679.

Poulain de la Barre, F. (1990) *The Equality of the Two Sexes*, trans. D. Clarke. Manchester: Manchester University Press. Translation of *Discours physique et moral de l'egalité des deux sexes*. Paris: Chez J. Du Puis, 1673.

Rorty, A. (1996) Descartes and Spinoza on epistemological egalitarianism. *History of Philosophy Quarterly*, 13, 35–53.

Schmitter, A. M. (2000) Mind and sign: method and the interpretation of mathematics in Descartes's early work. *Canadian Journal of Philosophy* 30, 371–411.

Shapiro, L. (1999) Princess Elizabeth and Descartes: the union of mind and soul and the practice of philosophy. *British Journal for the History of Philosophy*, 7, 503–20.

Shea, W. (1991) *The Magic of Numbers and Motion: The Scientific Career of René Descartes*. Canton, MA: Science History Publications.

Tarcov, N. (1999) *Locke's Education for Liberty*. Lanham, MD: Rowman & Littlefield. (Originally published in 1984 by the University of Chicago Press.)

Yolton, J. W. (1971) *John Locke and Education*. New York: Random House.

7

Rousseau, Dewey, and Democracy

Patrick Riley and Jennifer Welchman

Editor's Prologue

In the twentieth century "democracy" came to be synonymous with political respectability, and the question of what would constitute "democratic education" became an important one for philosophy of education. Answers to this question have proliferated. Some focus on the *content* of education: that it should cultivate the virtues suitable to citizenship in a democracy; that it should promote or enable individual autonomy; that it should be tolerant or respectful of legitimate religious and cultural diversity and not homogenize a population in seeking to create a cohesive national political culture. The cultivation of virtues suitable to citizenship in a democracy, or democratic *civic education*, has at one time or another been thought to embrace the virtues of voluntary obedience to law (Kaestle, 1983, pp. 34–9, 97; Curren, 2002), economic productivity and self-sufficiency (economic independence being essential to political independence and full citizenship; see Shklar, 1991), social cohesion or integration (see Osler, 2000; Blum, 2002; Galston, 2002), loyalty to community and country (cultivated more or less intensively through symbols of national unity, "civic religion," and other means) or cosmopolitan attitudes that qualify or transcend such loyalty (see Nussbaum, 1996; Callan, 1997, pp. 100–31; Gutmann, 2002), and readiness to participate constructively in civic life and political processes (see Gutmann, 1987; Barber, 1992). Other answers focus on *equity* and *commonality*: that democratic education entails schooling all children *together* and in the same things (see Pangle and Pangle, 1993, p. 92); that it provides all children with the same curriculum or experiences (see Adler, 1982); that it provides children with educational resources of equal value or equal value *to them* (see Bastian, 1986). Still other answers focus on the *control* of education: that in a democracy it should be collectively controlled by democratically constituted governing bodies, such as local school boards (see Gutmann, 1987); that control should rest with individual families whose liberties must be respected by liberal democracies (McConnell, 2002); that classrooms should be constituted as democratic communities with significant control over their internal affairs, such as their curricula and rules of conduct (see Apple and Beane, 1995, p. 9).

Matters were quite different through most of recorded history, inasmuch as "democracy" was not an honorific term, but instead was generally understood to signify one of the worst possible forms of social and political organization. The literal meaning of "democracy," in its Greek origins, was rule by the *demos*, the *poor* who were numerous, uneducated, and without the leisure to acquire much experience or knowledge of public affairs. Aristotle understood it to be a form of rule by force in which the poor dominate and exploit the rich, much as oligarchy was understood to be a form of rule by force in which the rich dominate and exploit the poor. Both involved economic and social polarization, an absence of power sharing, and rule in the interests of the rulers that was exercised beyond the restraint of law or constitutional limits (*Politics*, III.3, III.6).

So although *we* would call Aristotle's best possible constitution and best constitution that is practical for most city-states *democracies*, he did not. In his terms, the first was an ideal aristocracy, a form of shared rule by a citizen class whose virtue, excellent judgment, and mutual goodwill are the product of universally moderate wealth and advantage, good laws, and publicly operated common schools and other institutions that nurture civic friendship, good judgment, and the fulfillment of human rational potential. The best generally attainable system, which he calls a *polity*, is a *mixed* constitution in the sense that it provides institutional roles or offices for both rich and poor, and a *middle* constitution in the sense that it is dominated by a large middle class, rather than socially and politically polarized into rich and poor factions. What is educationally best in such a system is no different from what is essential to an ideal aristocracy. (See Curren, 2000, pp. 65–75, 100–1, 118–23, 131–9.) In modern terms a mixed regime of this sort is a *constitutional democracy*, designed to protect the interests of rich and poor alike, and it rests in arguments that eventually came to be regarded as potent arguments in favor of constitutional democracy. It rests, first of all, in the fundamental premise that the possession of normal deliberative capacities and a share of virtue or practical wisdom entitles a person to rule himself or herself and entitles a citizen to *participate* in collective self-rule, a premise reflecting an underlying ethic of respect for persons as rational agents (see Curren, 2000, pp. 20–65). It also rests in associated arguments from the collective wisdom of the many:

the many...when they meet together may be better than the few good, if regarded not individually but collectively.... For each individual among the many has a share of virtue and practical wisdom, and when they meet together...some understand one part, and some another, and among them they understand the whole. (*Politics*, III.11, 1281a42–b9)

There are some arts whose products are not judged of solely, or best, by the artists themselves.... The master of the house will actually be a better judge [of it] than the builder, just as...the guest will judge better of a feast than the cook. (*Politics*, III.11, 1282a18–23)

Aristotle thus regards good judgment in public affairs as incremental and as requiring the perspective of those who must live with the consequences of a government's acts. The latter consideration would in time be adduced in support of democracy by John Dewey, one of the central protagonists in this chapter.

Jean-Jacques Rousseau (1712–78) and John Dewey (1859–1952) stand out among the great philosophers of education for their egalitarian and democratic

95

sympathies. They share a central concern with collective rationality, predicated on what would now be called participatory democracy. Rousseau described his preferred form of constitution as "republicanism," but he envisioned it as a system in which ordinary citizens retain direct legislative sovereignty and exercise it through a legislative assembly of the whole. The central problem in his political and educational thought, addressed by Patrick Riley in the section that follows, is how this legislative sovereignty and the freedom associated with it can be reconciled with the demands of citizenship: the demand that citizens will the common good, and not love themselves in a way that is socially stratifying and predicated on an "inversion" of the natural value of different kinds of work. Education must not only preserve freedom and preclude any form of dependency, including economic dependency, but must induce citizens to adopt the "general will" as their own. Dewey, whose educational thought is surveyed by Jennifer Welchman in the second section of this chapter, regarded democracy as the only social and political form of life in which human beings can continue to "grow" and fully flourish, and he envisioned a democratic public as properly engaged in collective problem solving, modeled on the activity of an open scientific community. On this account, the citizen virtues essential to a democratic community include the intellectual, social, and communicative virtues essential to collective, cooperative *inquiry*.

Rousseau and Dewey also shared the view that learning is a natural imperative of human beings associated with the demands of survival, and should be allowed to follow its natural course to the greatest extent possible. They also held the related view that the social patterns of youth must conform to the social patterns of adulthood. Rousseau held, *contra* Locke, that children once accustomed to obeying others will not grow into free adults. Dewey held, in opposition to traditional schooling, that children accustomed to competing against each other in completing the same tasks at school, rather than making distinctive and valued contributions to common projects, will not grow into a public able to cooperate in solving its problems.

Rousseau's Philosophy of Transformative, "Denaturing" Education

Jean-Jacques Rousseau is widely, and correctly, viewed as the greatest political philosopher of the French Enlightenment; he is also widely, and correctly, viewed as the most important philosopher of education in the *Siècle des Lumières*. For Rousseau politics and education are strongly connected: he gives education the task of transforming naturally self-loving egoists animated only by their own "particular wills" into polis-loving citizens with a civic "general will" ("the general will is the will one has as a citizen"). For Rousseau the "Great Legislator" (more accurately the great civic educator) must, over educative time, "change the nature of man" by turning self-lovers into "Spartan mothers" (who ask not whether their own sons have survived battles but whether the "general good" of the city still lives). Rousseau, then, gives an absolute primacy to radically *transformative* education (which makes people "what they ought to be") – a primacy accorded to education by only one earlier social philosopher of comparable stature, namely Plato. But Rousseau also insists that education, however transformative, however "denaturing," must finally produce autonomous adults who can ultimately say to their teachers (with Émile), "I have decided to be what you made me" (Rousseau, 1910, p. 435). How far Rousseau succeeds in finding a stable equilibrium between denaturing education and final adult autonomy is the central difficulty of his social thought – as the following pages will try to show.

Had Rousseau not been centrally concerned with freedom – above all with the voluntariness of morally legitimate human actions – some of the structural features of his political thought would be (literally) unaccountable. Above all, the notion of the *volonté générale* or *general will* would not have become the core idea of his political philosophy: he would just have spoken, *à la* Plato, of achieving perfect *généralité* through civic education, as in *Republic* 462b ("do we know of any greater evil for a state than the thing that distracts it and makes it many instead of one, or a greater good than that which binds it together and makes it one?"), or would have settled for Montesquieu's republican *esprit général* (Montesquieu, 1949, pp. 1134, 1144); he would never have spoken of generalizing the *will* as something central but as difficult as squaring the circle – difficult because one must "denature" particularistic beings without destroying their (ultimate) autonomy. But one must (for Rousseau) have *volonté générale*, not a mere *esprit général*: for "to deprive your will of all freedom is to deprive your actions of all morality," and "civil association is the most voluntary act in the world" (Rousseau, 1962b, pp. 105, 28). That voluntarist side of Rousseau is brought out best by Judith Shklar, who has argued persuasively that the notion of general will "conveys everything he most wanted to say" precisely because it is "a transposition of the most essential individual moral faculty [volition] to the realm of public experience" (Shklar, 1969, p. 184; see also Shklar, 1973).

Moreover, were not generalized will – a will of a very particular kind – essential in Rousseau, the Great Legislator would not have to achieve his civic results (in *The Social Contract*, II, 7) by such tortured means – such as "compelling without violence" and "persuading without convincing." Plato didn't worry about this kind of difficulty because the philosopher-king simply knew the eternal verities, such as "absolute goodness" (*Phaedo*, 7d) which even the gods know and love (*Euthyphro*, 10d–e), and therefore deserved to educate and rule (*Republic*, 1V). For Rousseau what is needed for perfect politics (*The Social Contract*, II, 6) is "a *union* of will and understanding," so that the Great Legislator's civic knowledge is finally, at the end of civic time, *absorbed* into an (originally ignorant) popular general will which is ultimately as "enlightened" as it was always "right."

Here the history of "the general will" before Rousseau is illuminating. In Rousseau, the general will is non-natural: it is artificially produced (over time) through the "denaturing," counter-egoistic educative ministrations of Lycurgus or Moses – though at the end of education informed, independent choice must finally be possible. But in the thought of the seventeenth-century inventors of *volonté générale* – Arnauld, Pascal, Malebranche, Fénelon, Bayle, Leibniz – the general will of God (to "save all men" after the Fall; see Riley, 1986, pp. 4ff) is *naturally* general: how could one "denature" or transform the will of a perfect being, make him "become" over time what he "naturally" was not? Rousseau – who knew intimately the entire seventeenth-century controversy over "general will" (see Riley, 1986, chapter 5) – knew too that a non-divinity must be (to revise a phrase) "forced to be general." But that

97

non-divinity's freedom must finally arrive, as a child (in *Émile*) finally becomes what it was not. Indeed, the central problem of all Rousseau's thought is to find a form of non-authoritarian educative authority which will "make men what they ought to be" (*Économie politique*; Rousseau, 1950b, p. 297), without (permanently) depriving them of the freedom without which "neither virtues, nor vices, nor merit, nor demerit, nor morality in human actions" is conceivable (*Lettre à M. de Franquières*, 1769; Rousseau, 1974a, pp. 180–1).

None the less, even if Rousseau's aim is to "generalize" will over time without destroying freedom – which makes it crucial that he find a non-authoritarian authority that can "compel without violence" – one can say that Rousseau has a more difficult time in *reconciling* freedom and "what men ought to be" than (most notably) Kant; and here a comparison with Hegel will also be helpful. Rousseau, Kant, and Hegel – separated by whole universes as they are – are all voluntarists who make "will" ethically weighty (in the shape of "general will," "good will," and [so-called] "real will"; see Riley, 1982). All three are in search of a non-willful will; all are in full flight from capricious *volonté particulière*, from what Shakespeare calls "hydra-headed will-fulness" (*Henry V*, I, i). But for Rousseau the flight from egoism and *amour-propre* (self-love of a comparative, invidious kind) ends at the border of Sparta (with the "Spartan mother" on the opening page of *Émile*), while for Kant one "ought" to move on to a universal Kingdom of Ends or (failing that) at least to universal republicanism and eternal peace (Kant, 1922, pp. 161–2; see also Riley, 1983, pp. 167ff). But Kant more easily preserves freedom or autonomy than Rousseau – or Hegel, who wants our "real" will to be "recognition" of the state as rational freedom concretely *realized* (Hegel, 1942, p. 105; see also Kelly, 1978, pp. 113–14; Oakeshott, 1975, p. 160) – because what "generalizes" (or rather universalizes) will is reason-ordained "objective ends," *not* Lycurgus (or *Bildung*). Rousseau doubted that there could be a reason-ordained *morale universelle* (universal morality); for him the crucial line should be drawn *between* the "general" and the "universal," the *polis* and the *cosmopolis*. Doubting (in advance of Kant) that a "Kantian" *kind* of autonomy was possible, Rousseau set himself the daunting task of generalizing will without recourse to "objective ends" – but *with* recourse to educative authority whose highest ambition is to wither away after injecting its (civic, "politan") knowledge into beings who become free in the course of time.

What follows is an examination of the (particular) way in which Rousseau generalizes *volonté*, leaving it (he hopes) free but not willful.

Rousseau's reasons for using "general will" as his central political concept were essentially philosophical – however ready-made for his purposes the seventeenth-century theological notion may have been. (Does not the Spartan mother have a *volonté générale* to "save" the city, as God has a general will to save "all men"?) After all, the two terms of *volonté générale* – "will" and "generality" – represent two main strands in Rousseau's thought. "Generality" stands, *inter alia*, for the rule of law, for civic education that draws us out of ourselves and toward the general (or common) good, for the non-particularist citizen-virtues of Sparta and republican Rome (see especially Rousseau, 1962c, pp. 424ff). "Will" stands, again, for Rousseau's conviction that civil association is "the most voluntary act in the world," that "to deprive your will of all freedom is to deprive your actions of all morality" (Rousseau, 1962b, pp. 105, 28). And if one could "generalize" the will, so that it "elects" only law, citizenship, and the common good, and avoids willful self-love, then one would have a general will in Rousseau's particular sense. The (originally divine) *volonté générale* of Pascal, Malebranche, Fénelon, and Leibniz corresponded closely to these moral aims: hence why not employ a term already rendered politically usable by Bayle in the *Pensées diverses sur la comète* (Bayle, 1704, pp. 452ff)?

It is scarcely open to doubt, indeed, that the notions of *will* and *generality* are equally essential in Rousseau's moral and political philosophy. Without will there is no freedom, no self-determination, no "moral causality" (*First Version of the Social Contract*; Rousseau, 1962e, p. 499), no obligation; without generality the will may be capricious, egoistic, self-obsessed, willful.

Rousseau shared with modern individualist thinkers (notably Hobbes and Locke) the conviction that all political life is conventional, that it can be made obligatory only through voluntary, individual consent. Despite the fact that he sometimes treats moral ideas as if they simply "arise" in a developmental process, in the course of socialization (*Lettre à M. de Beaumont*; Rousseau, 1971c), he often – particularly in his contractarian vein – falls back on the view that the wills of free men are the "causes" of duties and of legitimate authority. Thus, in an argument against slavery in *The Social Contract*, Rousseau urges that "to deprive your will of all freedom" is to deprive your actions of "all morality," that the reason one can derive no notion of right or morality from mere force is that "to yield to force is an act of necessity, not of will" (Rousseau, 1962b, p. 26). (This shows in advance how carefully one must interpret the *deliberately* paradoxical phrase "forced to be free.") In *The Origins of Inequality*, in a passage that almost prefigures Kant, he insists on the importance of free agency, arguing that while "physics" (natural science) might explain the "mechanism of the senses," it could never make intelligible "the power of willing or rather of choosing" – a power in which "nothing is to be found but acts which are purely spiritual and wholly inexplicable by the laws of mechanism" (Rousseau, 1950a, p. 208). It is this power of freely willing, rather than reason, that distinguishes men from beasts. In the (unpublished) *First Version of the Social Contract* he had even said that "every free action has two causes which concur to produce it: the first a moral cause, namely the will which determines the act; the other physical, namely the power which executes it" (Rousseau, 1962e, p. 499). Rousseau, then, not only requires the Kant-anticipating idea of will as "moral causality," he actually uses that term.

All of this is confirmed by what Rousseau says about will in *Émile*, in which he argues (through a speech put into the mouth of the Savoyard Vicar) that "the motive power of all action is in the will of a free creature," that "it is not the word freedom that is meaningless, but the word necessity." The will is "independent of my senses": I "consent or resist, I yield or I win the victory, and I know very well in myself when I have done what I wanted and when I have merely given way to my passions." Man, he concludes, is "free to act," and he "acts of his own accord" (Rousseau, 1910, pp. 243–4). Moreover, human free will does not derogate from Providence, but magnifies it, since God has "made man of so excellent a nature, that he has endowed his actions with that morality by which they are ennobled." Rousseau cannot agree with those theologians (for example, Hobbes) who argue that human freedom would diminish God by robbing him of his omnipotence:

Providence has made man free that he may choose the good and refuse the evil...what more could divine power itself have done on our behalf? Could it have made our nature a contradiction and have given the prize of well-doing to one who was incapable of evil? To prevent a man from wickedness, should Providence have restricted him to instinct and made him a fool? (Rousseau, 1910, pp. 243–4)

To be sure, the pre-Kantian voluntarism of *Émile* and of *The Origins of Inequality* is not the whole story; even in the *Lettres morales* (1757), which were used as a quarry in writing *Émile*, the relation of free will to morality is complicated and problematical. The opening of the fifth *Lettre* – "the whole morality of human life is in the intention of man" (Rousseau, 1958, pp. 1106ff; on the importance of the *Lettres* see Shklar, 1969, pp. 229–30) – seems at first to be a voluntarist claim, almost prefiguring Kant's notion in the *Grundlegung* that a "good will" is the only "unqualifiedly" good thing on earth (Kant, 1949, p. 11). But this *intention* refers not to the "will" of Émile, but to "conscience" – which is a "divine instinct" and an "immortal and heavenly voice." Rousseau, after a striking passage on moral feelings ("if one sees...some act of violence or injustice, a movement of anger and indignation arises at once in our heart"), goes on to speak of feelings of "remorse" that "punish hidden crimes in secret"; and this "importunate voice" he calls an involuntary feeling (*sentiment involontaire*) which "torments" us. That the phrase *sentiment involontaire* is not a mere slip of the pen (or of the mind) is proven by Rousseau's deliberate repetition of "involuntary":

Thus there is, at the bottom of all souls, an innate principle of justice and of moral truth [that is] prior to all national prejudices, to all maxims of education. This principle is the involuntary rule [*la règle involontaire*] by which, despite our own maxim, we judge our actions, and those of others, as good or bad; and it is to this principle that I give the name conscience.

Conscience, then, is an involuntary moral feeling – not surprisingly, given Rousseau's view that "our feeling is incontestably prior to our reason itself" (Rousseau, 1971c, pp. 1111, 1107, 1108, 1109). And so, while the fifth *Lettre morale* opens with an apparent anticipation of Émile's voluntarism, this is only an appearance that proves that it is not straightforwardly right to "find" in Rousseau a predecessor of Kant. Rousseau's *morale sensitive* (one strand of his thought) is not easy to reconcile with rational self-determination (another, equally authentic, strand) – for if Rousseau says that "to deprive your will of all freedom is to deprive your actions of all morality," he also says that conscience is a *sentiment* which is *involontaire*.

The fact remains, however, that while *Émile* was published, the *Lettres morale* were held back. And in *Émile* Rousseau insists on the moral centrality of free will. Hence he can understand "will" as an independent moral causality with the power to produce moral effects. He definitely thought that he had derived political obligation and rightful political authority from this "power" of willing: "Civil association is the most voluntary act in the world; since every individual is born free and his own master, no one is able, on any pretext whatsoever, to subject him without his consent" (Rousseau, 1962b, p. 105). Indeed, the first four chapters of *The Social Contract* are devoted to refutations of erroneous theories of obligation and right – paternal authority, the "right of the strongest," and obligations derived from slavery.

"Since no man," Rousseau concludes, "has natural authority over his fellow men, and since might in no sense makes right, [voluntary] convention remains as the basis of legitimate authority among men" (Rousseau, 1962b, pp. 105, 27).

Even if "will" is plainly a central moral, political, and theological notion in Rousseau's thought, this does not mean that he was willing to settle for just any will – such as a particular will or a "willful" will. His constant aim, indeed, is to "generalize" will (Rousseau, 1962e, pp. 472–3) – either through civic education, as in the *Government of Poland*, or through private education, as in *Émile*. In his view, ancient societies such as Sparta and Rome had been particularly adept at generalizing human will. Through their simplicity, their morality of the common good, their civic religion, their moral use of fine and military arts, and their lack of extreme individualism and private interest, the city-states of antiquity had been political societies in the proper sense. In them man had been part of a greater whole from which he "in a sense receives his life and being" (Rousseau, 1962b, p. 52); on the other hand, modern "prejudices," "base philosophy," and "passions of petty self-interest" assure that "we moderns can no longer find in ourselves anything of that spiritual vigor which was inspired in the ancients by everything they did" (Rousseau, 1962c, p. 430). And that "spiritual vigor" may be taken to mean the avoidance – through identity with a greater whole – of self-love, "that dangerous disposition which gives rise to all our vices." Political education in an extremely unified ("generalized") state will "lead us out of ourselves" and provide us with a general will before the human ego "has acquired that contemptible activity which absorbs all virtue and constitutes the life and being of little minds" (Rousseau, 1950b, p. 308). It follows that the best social institutions "are those best able to denature man, to take away his absolute existence and to give him a relative one, and to carry the *moi* into the common unity" (*Émile*; Rousseau, 1962a, volume 2, p. 145).

If these reflections on the pernicious character of self-love and particularism are reminiscent of Malebranche – who had urged that "to act by *volontés particulières* shows a limited intelligence" (Malebranche, 1958, pp. 147–66), and whose love for divine *généralité* had led Rousseau to rank the great Oratorian Father with Plato and Locke (Rousseau, 1971b, p. 1111) – it is in contrasting Rousseau with Malebranche that an important difficulty arises. In Malebranche, God's will is essentially and naturally general; in Rousseau, men's will must be *made* general – a problem which he likens (in the correspondence with Malesherbes) to that of squaring the circle (Rousseau, 1974b). But one can reasonably ask: is will still "will" (*qua* independent "moral cause") if it must be denatured, transformed? Do Rousseau's notions of education – private and civic – leave will as the autonomous producer of moral "effects" that he seems to want? One is tempted to say that this is the question for one who wants *volonté* and *généralité* to fuse – so that (at the end of time) a perfect "*union* of will and understanding" will synthesize (Lockean) "voluntary agreement" and (Platonic) generalizing education, will blend antiquity ("Sparta") and modernity ("contract") in this "modern who has an ancient soul" (Rousseau, 1962d, p. 421).

To retain the moral attributes of free will while doing away with will's particularity and selfishness and "willfulness" – to generalize this moral "cause" without causing its destruction – is perhaps the central problem in Rousseau's political, moral, and educational thought, and one that reflects the difficulty Rousseau found in making free will and rational, educative authority coexist in his practical thought. Freedom of

101

the will is as important to the morality of actions for Rousseau as for any voluntarist coming after Augustine's insistence that *bona voluntas* (good will) alone is good (*On Free Choice of the Will*, Book I, chapter 12); but Rousseau was suspicious of the very "faculty" – the only faculty – that could moralize. Thus he urges in the *Discourse on Political Economy* that "the most absolute authority is that which penetrates into a man's inmost being, and concerns itself with his will no less than with his actions" (Rousseau, 1950b, p. 297). Can the will be both an autonomous "moral cause" and subject to the rationalizing, generalizing effect of educative authority? This is Rousseau's constant difficulty. Even Émile, the best educated of men, chooses to continue to accept the guidance of his teachers: "Advise and control us; we shall be easily led; as long as I live I shall need you" (Rousseau, 1910, p. 444). How much more, then, do ordinary men need the guidance of a "great legislator" – the Numa or Moses or Lycurgus of whom Rousseau speaks so often (Rousseau, 1962c, pp. 427–30; 1971a, pp. 118–20) – when they embark on the setting up of a system which will not only aid and defend but also moralize them. The general will is dependent on "a union of understanding and will within the social body" (Rousseau, 1962b, p. 51); but that understanding, which is provided (at least initially) by educative authority – rather than by a Kantian "fact of reason" giving (timeless) "objective ends" – is difficult to make perfectly congruent with "will" as an autonomous "moral cause."

This notion of the relation of educative authority to will appears not just in Rousseau's theories of public or civic education (particularly in the *Économie politique* and the *Gouvernement de Pologne*; Rousseau, 1962c, pp. 437–43), but also in his theory of private education in *Émile*. In educating a child, Rousseau advises the tutor, "let him think he is master while you are really master." And then: "there is no subjection so complete as that which preserves the forms of freedom; it is thus that the will itself is taken captive" (Rousseau, 1910, p. 84). One can hardly help asking what has became of "will" when it has been "taken captive," and whether it is enough to preserve the mere "forms" of freedom. On this point Rousseau appears to have been of two minds: the poor who "agree" to a social contract that merely legitimizes the holdings of the rich "preserve the forms of freedom," but Rousseau (in *Origins of Inequality*) dismisses this contract as a fraud (Rousseau, 1950a, pp. 180–2). Thus it cannot be straightforwardly the case – as John Charvet argues in his remarkable Rousseau study – that Rousseau, the *citoyen de Génève*, simply was not "worried by the gap which opens up between the appearance and the reality of freedom" (Charvet, 1974, p. 58). Yet Charvet has something of a point, since will is "taken captive" in *Émile* and "penetrated" by authority in the *Discourse on Political Economy*; and neither that captivity nor that penetration is criticized by Rousseau – despite his *dictum* about depriving one's actions "of all morality" if one deprives his will of "freedom." So one sees again why a *general* will would appeal to him: capricious willfulness would be "canceled," will rationalized by authority, "preserved" (Hegel, 1967, p. 234).

If will in Rousseau is generalized primarily through an educative authority, so that volition as "moral cause" is not quite as free as he would sometimes prefer, it is at least arguable that any tension between "will" and the authority that "generalizes" it is only a *provisional* problem. Rousseau seems to have hoped that at the end of political time (so to speak) men would finally be citizens and would will only the common good in virtue of what they had learned *over* time; at the end of civic time, they might actually be free, and not just "forced to be free" (Rousseau, 1962b, p. 36). At the end of its political education – no *more* "denaturing" or transformative than any true education – political society would finally be in a position to say what Émile says at the end of his "domestic" education: "I have decided to be what you have made me." At this point (of "decision") there would be a "union of understanding and will" in politics, but one in which "understanding" is no longer the private possession of a Numa or a Lycurgus. At this point, too, "agreement" and "contract" would finally have real meanings: the "general will," which is "always right," would be enlightened as well, and contract would go beyond being the mere rich man's confidence trick (legalizing unequal property) that it is in *Origins of Inequality*. At the end of political time, the "general will one has as a citizen" would have become a kind of second nature, approaching the true naturalness of *volonté généralé* in Malebranche's version of the divine *modus operandi*. "Approaching," however, is the strongest term one can use, and the relation of will to the educative authority that generalizes it remains a problem in Rousseau – the more so because he often denied (in his more Lockean moods) that there is any natural authority on earth (Rousseau, 1962b, p. 27).

One can still ask: how can one reconcile Rousseau's insistence on an all-shaping educative authority with his equal insistence on free choice and personal autonomy? A possible answer is: *through* his theory of education, which is the heart of his thought – the one thing that can make Rousseaueanism "work." At the end of civic time, when men have been denatured and transformed into citizens, they will finally have civic knowledge and general will – just as adults finally have the moral knowledge and the independence that they (necessarily) lacked as children. For Rousseau there are unavoidable stages in all education, whether private or public: the child, he says in *Émile*, must first learn necessity, then utility, and finally morality, in that inescapable order. If one says "ought" to an infant he simply reveals his own ignorance and folly. This notion of necessary educational time, of *becoming* what one was not, is revealed perfectly in Émile's utterance "I have decided to be what you made me." That is deliberately paradoxical (as many of Rousseau's central moral-political beliefs are cast in the form of paradoxes); but it shows that the capacity to "decide" is indeed "made." It is education that "forces one to be free" – by slowly "generalizing" the will. Similarly, Rousseau's "nations" are at first ignorant: "There is with nations, as with men, a time of youth, or, if you prefer, of maturity, for which we must *wait* before subjecting them to laws (Rousseau, 1962b, p. 56). Waiting, however, requires time; autonomy arrives at the end of a process, and the general will is *at last* as enlightened as it was (always) right. On the most favorable reasonable reading, then, Rousseau does not, as some critics allege, vibrate incoherently between "Platonic" education and "Lockean" voluntariness; if his notion of becoming-in-time works, then the *généralité* of antiquity and the *volonté* of modernity are truly fused by this "modern who has an ancient soul."

Dewey

As Rousseau stands apart from other Enlightenment thinkers in his treatment of education as a central issue for social philosophy, American philosopher John Dewey stands apart from his contemporaries in treating education as a central issue for philosophy generally, both theoretical and social. Although Rousseau and Dewey differed profoundly in their conceptions of human nature and understanding, they agreed that social freedom is more than the absence of external or legal impediments to action. A society that guarantees its citizens freedom of choice and makes opportunities open to talents is not necessarily free or democratic. Dewey (1988, p. 41) writes, "Freedom from restriction...is to be prized only as a means to a freedom which is power: power to frame purposes, to judge wisely, to evaluate desires by the consequences which will result [and] to select and order means to carry chosen ends into operation."

Both men agreed that power over external resources and materials is meaningless unless the projects, values, and purposes for which we enlist those resources are truly our own. Likewise, social freedom is meaningless unless citizens are each their own persons in the relevant sense. So Dewey (1988, p. 43) argues, "It is a sound instinct which identifies freedom with the power to frame purposes and execute...purposes so formed. Such freedom is in turn identical with self-control." As it is through education that we develop self-control, i.e. critical and reflective skills and the habits of using them, education is the *sine qua non* of a free or democratic society. Dewey goes beyond Rousseau, however, in identifying education as the central problem not merely for social philosophy but for philosophy itself. To Dewey, philosophy is better understood as love of education than love of wisdom, i.e. love of inquiry for its own sake, not just its results.

Dewey's interest in education was lifelong. He worked briefly as a public school teacher before starting graduate work in philosophy. Thus his philosophical and professional interests in efforts to standardize curricula and professionalize education in the late nineteenth and twentieth centuries were supplemented by a certain practical appreciation of the challenges teachers faced. Because of his interest, he eagerly took a position as chair of the Departments of Philosophy and Pedagogy at the new University of Chicago, where he would found the University of Chicago's famous Laboratory School. During his ten years in Chicago (1894–1903), he developed the main lines of his theory of education. Dewey never considered his work on education to be mere "applied philosophy." On the contrary, he recommended *Democracy and Education* as the key to his philosophy (although a later work, *Experience and Education*, is perhaps an easier starting point).

Philosophical approach

Dewey's distinctive attitude arose in part from the pragmatic or "instrumentalist" view of human understanding he developed during the 1890s. Unlike contemporaneous philosophers (realist and idealist) for whom the problem of knowledge was deciding whether and how our ideas mirror the real world outside our individual minds, Dewey argued that the problem of knowledge is better conceived as the problem of determining why certain ideas work better in facilitating human activities and goals. If we insist upon treating ideas as mirrors of the world outside us, pragmatists argued, we make knowledge an insolvable problem. There simply is no way to step outside our minds to determine how well our ideas reflect external reality.

But if we recognize that what really matters to us about ideas is how they function as tools with which to model, predict, and interpret our experience, the problem of knowledge is no longer insolvable. We can check the instrumental value of our ideas by comparing the expected effects of adopting or acting upon particular models, theories, and interpretations with what we subsequently experience. The problem is how to determine the best methods of doing so. For Dewey, theoretical philosophy was in effect the study of new and better methods of *educating* ourselves about our ideas and their value.

As a pragmatist, Dewey saw ideas, interpretations, and theories as socially constructed instruments for managing human experience. But his constructivism was not limited to his understanding of our ideas. Because he came to pragmatism via neo-Hegelianism, he also saw personality as largely socially constructed. We are biological creatures born with physiological and psychological traits that are the basic stuff of our development as persons. But our development is given direction and purpose by social and cultural practices. Take everything from a person that her culture provides, Dewey argued – language, history, religion, art, politics – and she would no longer be a person, let alone the person she was. Development of a functional and well integrated personality out of the multiple and competing drives that constitute raw human nature is an achievement, not a given. If we are free, autonomous persons it is not because we were born so but because social life has taught us to reflect upon and to take control of ourselves and our actions.

Dewey's pragmatic view of ideas, theories, and explanations as more or less functional tools, and of education as the process by which we learn methods for constructing, testing, and applying them, meant that Dewey could not identify education, intellectual or moral, with "schooling" as it was conducted in American public schools. Most public schools devoted the elementary years (which were all many children received) to drilling in the basic skills of reading, writing, and mathematics, supplemented in higher grades by further drilling in an expanded range of subjects (history, geography, physical science) and/or manual (job) training. Dewey (1977, p. 236) considered this sort of schooling the reverse of education in every sense. Intellectually, the problem is that "acquiring takes the place of inquiring." Schools treated students as vessels to be filled with correct ideas rather than as active inquirers needing apprenticeship in techniques of discovery and interpretation. Consistent with this approach, schooling was "complete" when students could reproduce the information or basic literary and mathematical forms in which they were drilled, whether or not they were able to think critically or inquire for themselves.

If schools offered little training in the critical and reflective skills citizens of a democracy must have, this was still better than the training provided for moral and social life. Dewey (1988, p. 40) remarked, "the non-social character of the traditional school is seen in the fact that it erected silence into one of its prime virtues." Schools were authoritarian institutions that inculcated conformity and passivity, motivating acceptance of their rules and requirements by threats of social censure, while discouraging cooperation, self-control, and what Dewey confusingly called "social control," meaning appeal to a participant's desire to engage in a social practice to motivate acceptance of the rules that make it possible (as the desire to play chess motivates acceptance of its rules).

105

In earlier days, inadequacy of schooling was less significant because education was so readily available elsewhere. Intellectual and social education took place informally, through children's apprenticeships as members of families, trades, guilds, congregations, voluntary societies, and civic institutions. Pragmatic standards of inquiry were inculcated in a rough and ready way, since new ideas had to "work" to achieve acceptance and an ability to use one's knowledge to solve problems was a mark of intellectual competence. When the pace of technological and social change was slow, and opportunities to observe and participate were relatively unimpeded, education of this sort could prepare citizens for participation in democratic social life. But as Dewey (1976a, p. 259) noted, "in the urban and suburban life of the child of today this is simply a memory." Children no longer grew up in or regularly visited their families' workplaces. The inner workings of the new technology around them were not directly visible. Social services were provided by distant and impersonal social agencies. Informal education could no longer compensate for poor schools. And simply mandating attendance in traditional schools was not enough to satisfy a democracy's requirement for educated citizens. Dewey worried that expanding literary skills without also expanding critical skills might actually undermine democracy. He recognized that the new mass media were creating an era of "information-overload." In such an environment democratic decision-making faces a new threat, tyranny through propaganda. Social freedom, the freedom to frame and make authentic choices and to participate in public projects that reflect one's genuine interests and goals, is unrealizable if the citizenry is unable to resist the influence of mass media or to judge matters for itself.

Education as growth

If we needed further proof that education cannot be mere schooling in the inherited ideas and skills of older generations, we have but to consider that, as Dewey remarked (1972a, p. 86), "it is impossible to foretell definitely just what civilization will be twenty years from now. Hence it is impossible to prepare the child for any precise set of conditions." We must recognize that no subjects or technical skills we can hand down to our children are guaranteed to be necessary or sufficient to make them flourishing, independent people throughout their lives. If they are to become and remain functional autonomous persons, we must teach them to do by choice what in infancy they do by nature, which is to grow and adapt.

Dewey's identification of education with growth aligned him in the public view with progressive educators who argued for so-called "child-centered" curricula based upon the child's own "natural" development. These educators feared that schooling in opposition to the natural unfolding of the child's nature could permanently distort or stunt the child's ultimate development. Although Dewey welcomed the new focus on child development by progressive educators, he did not endorse their sometimes romantic notion of growth as the revelation of latent powers or dispositions. Like their traditionalist opponents, progressives of this ilk mistook "the fulfillment of growing [as] an accomplished growth: that is to say, an Ungrowth, something which is no longer growing" (Dewey, 1978a, p. 47). Thus education and growth are valuable solely as means to this end. Dewey's conception is, by contrast, one of continual adaptation. He writes, "translated into its education equivalents, this means (i) that the educational process had no end beyond itself; it is its own end; and that (ii) the educational process is one of continual reorganizing, reconstructing, transforming" (Dewey, 1978a, p. 54). Thus the value of education and growth are not *limited* to their instrumental value in helping us to achieve specific goals, for they are themselves intrinsically valuable. In keeping with his view, the University of Chicago's Laboratory School, during Dewey's tenure, adopted a "teacher-centered" approach to elementary education, leaving it to teachers to determine the curriculum best suited to help students develop the cooperative skills of inquiry that would enable them to take increasing responsibility for their own education in upper grades.

Dewey's conception of education as growth provided the basis for assessing educational schemes: a scheme is effective when or if students tend to increase their willingness and ability to educate themselves further. Educational schemes are ineffective or "miseducative" (Dewey, 1988, p. 11) if they discourage students from further education or fail to help them to increase their knowledge and skills. Traditional schools were often miseducative in the first sense since they persuaded students that learning was unpleasant in itself and largely irrelevant to the problems of their daily lives. Teachers resorted to "sugar-coating" lessons "with all manner of pretty devices and tricks in order that the child may absorb them unawares" (Dewey, 1972b, p. 257). But such tricks did not address the more fundamental problem of the irrelevance of schooling to life.

More than anything else, Dewey thought it was the separation of schooling from life that made contemporary schooling miseducative. To be genuinely educative, schooling must be continuous with living. It cannot be limited to a particular time or place or doled out at another's discretion. To be educative schooling must be available when and where it is wanted and in such a way as to make its further pursuit possible as well as desirable. One part of the solution is clearly to disperse schooling from its traditional institutional settings, so that it is accessible when and as it is required, during evenings and weekends, via correspondence as well as in classrooms, at educational centers and satellite locations, and so forth. To this extent, the remedy is within the scope of the administrative hierarchy. But the sort of education a person needs is largely determined by individual interests and circumstances. Thus, to be educative, schooling must also become more democratic.

Dewey remarks, "There is, I think, no point in the philosophy of progressive education which is sounder than its emphasis upon the importance of the participation of the learner in the formation of the purposes which direct his activities in the learning process, just as there is no defect in traditional education greater than its failure to secure the active cooperation of the pupil in construction of the purposes involved in his studying" (Dewey, 1988, p. 43). It is, for example, not "sugar-coating" to reform the curriculum of elementary grades to accommodate the normal interests of young children in the world around them, the occupations people pursue, the tools they use, and the ways they travel. Nor is it a "pretty device" to delay introduction of grammar, spelling, or arithmetic until after inquiry into other more immediately absorbing topics has presented problems that make learning abstract verbal or mathematical skills desirable to the students. And when students are old enough to identify interests for themselves, it is not a motivational "trick" to involve them in

107

determining the course of their further studies. When education serves students' interests, they are motivated to follow instructions, try experiments, and solicit advice because these are integral to the realization of their own interests. Education is not then an imposition but a cooperative activity and the discipline students develop is genuinely *self*-discipline.

Democracy as education

Dewey's recognition of the importance of decentralizing and democratizing public education to make it effective led him to develop a new and powerful argument for liberal democracy. Dewey notes:

> The devotion of democracy to education is a familiar fact. The superficial explanation is that a government resting upon popular suffrage cannot be successful unless those who elect and who obey their governors are educated ... but there is a deeper explanation. A democracy is more than a form of government; it is primarily a mode of associated living, of conjoint and communicated experience. (Dewey, 1978a, p. 93)

Enlightenment liberals had defended representative government as a means of protecting personal security and property against depredations of the governing elite. Dewey, by contrast, defended democracy as creating and sustaining personal autonomy against depredations of ignorance, prejudice, or hidebound custom.

If education is to enable us to flourish through the vicissitudes of personal and social fortune, Dewey argues, society must be arranged so that individuals can interact with whoever has expertise that they want and to work cooperatively with whoever is willing and able to develop expertise where none exists. Non-democratic societies, whether monarchies or theocracies, aristocracies, or dictatorships, all tend to divide society into classes whose interests become opposed. Association across class lines is curtailed and so also opportunities to engage in cooperative inquiry. The tendency to divide along class lines internally is replicated externally. It becomes a mark of loyalty to one's own class to deprecate the intelligence, civilization, judgment, or morals of those who live in societies differently organized, as well as those who live in different classes within one's own society. Minds become mistrustful of difference and closed to change, with the result that personal and social growth and adaptation are constrained. By contrast, democracy – by which Dewey understood mutual participation in the design of social institutions and the designation of public projects – enhances educational opportunities by encouraging interaction and shared interests across class lines. Intellectual and personal growth requires freedom to experiment, and liberal social democracy provides this to a greater degree than any other form of social life. Thus, if education is a life-long process of growth and adaptation, and if growth and adaptation have become essential to human flourishing, then liberal democracy is a form of education and as such essential to human flourishing.

Influence

Despite the considerable educational and social reforms that have occurred during and since Dewey's lifetime, Dewey's works still provide a critical perspective on education whose value has by no means been exhausted. Dewey developed his philosophy of education at a time of widespread discontent with public schools. His writings on education, such as *The School and Society*, *The Child and the Curriculum*, *How We Think*, *Democracy and Education*, and *Experience and Education*, were widely read and admired by American educators. Many of these writings were also influential internationally. He was more often read than understood, however. His refusal to propose "universal" principles of curricular design was often misinterpreted as simple neglect. Others began making him gifts of their own. "As his reputation grew," Herbert M. Kliebard notes, "Dewey's name was invoked in connection with curriculum and general school reforms of all sorts whether they reflected his ideas or not. At the same time, the educational theory Dewey so painstakingly developed...was either converted into caricature, such as 'learning by doing,' or neglected altogether" (Kliebard, 1995, p. 27). Meanwhile, the educational and social problems to which Dewey called attention were often overlooked by reforms introduced during his lifetime. "It is our American habit," Dewey (1978b, p. 183) lamented, "that if we find the foundations of our educational structure unsatisfactory to add another story or a wing." It is not enough to reform schools if the surrounding society is itself undemocratic, destructively competitive, and divided along class or racial divisions, as American (and not only American) society has been.

Dewey's use of his educational theory to critique American social institutions was also influential during his lifetime but afterwards fell from favor as social debate became polarized around the relation of capitalism and democracy. To Marxist and socialist critics, Dewey's approach lacked the apparent rigor and depth of economic critiques, while their libertarian and capitalist interlocutors found Dewey's conception of liberal democracy too "communitarian" for their purposes. As this debate has cooled and openness to more moderate positions increased, Dewey's account of democracy is again commanding attention. Thus, Dewey's philosophy of education continues to repay interest from within and beyond educational circles.

See also 1 THE SOCRATIC MOVEMENT; 2 STOICISM; 6 ENLIGHTENMENT LIBERALISM; 8 KANT, HEGEL, AND THE RISE OF PEDAGOGICAL SCIENCE; 9 ROMANTICISM; 16 THEORIES OF TEACHING AND LEARNING; 28 THE AUTHORITY AND RESPONSIBILITY TO EDUCATE; 29 CHURCH, STATE, AND EDUCATION

References

Adler, M. (1982) *The Paideia Proposal*. New York: Collier Books.
Apple, M. and Beane, J. A. (eds) (1995) *Democratic Schools*. Alexandria, VA: Association for Supervision and Curruculum Development.
Aristotle (1988) *The Politics*, trans. B. Jowett and J. Barnes. Cambridge: Cambridge University Press.
Barber, B. (1992) *An Aristocracy of Everyone: The Politics of Education and the Future of America*. Oxford: Oxford University Press.
Bastian, A. (1986) *Choosing Equality: The Case for Democratic Schooling*. Philadelphia: Temple University Press.

Bayle, P. (1704) *Pensées diverses, Ecrites à un docteur de Sorbonne* [*Diverse Thoughts, Writings of a Doctor of Sorbonne*], tome 2, 4th edn. Rotterdam: Chez Reinier Leers.

Blum, L. (2002). The promise of racial integration in a multicultural age. In S. Macedo and Y. Tamir (eds), *Moral and Political Education*. New York: New York University Press, pp. 383–424.

Callan, E. (1997) *Creating Citizens: Political Education and Liberal Democracy*. Oxford: Clarendon Press.

Charvet, J. (1974) *The Social Problem in the Philosophy of Rousseau*. Cambridge: Cambridge University Press.

Curren, R. (2000) *Aristotle on the Necessity of Public Education*. Lanham, MD: Rowman & Littlefield.

Curren, R. (2002) Moral education and juvenile crime. In S. Macedo and Y. Tamir (eds), *Moral and Political Education*. New York: New York University Press, pp. 359–80.

Dewey, J. (1972a) *My Pedagogical Creed*. In J. A. Boydston (ed.), *Early Works of John Dewey, 1882–1898, volume 5: 1895–1898*. Carbondale: Southern Illinois University Press, pp. 84–95 (originally published 1897).

Dewey, J. (1972b) *The Primary-education Fetich*. In J. A. Boydston (ed.), *Early Works of John Dewey, 1882–1898, volume 5: 1895–1898*. Carbondale: Southern Illinois University Press, pp. 254–69 (originally published 1898).

Dewey, J. (1976a) *The School and Society*. In J. A. Boydston (ed.), *The Middle Works, 1899–1924, volume 1: 1899–1901*. Carbondale: Southern Illinois University Press, pp. 1–109 (originally published 1899).

Dewey, J. (1976b) *The Child and the Curriculum*. In J. A. Boydston (ed.), *The Middle Works, 1899–1924, volume 2: 1902–1903*. Carbondale: Southern Illinois University Press, pp. 271–91 (originally published 1902).

Dewey, J. (1977) Democracy in education. In J. A. Boydston (ed.), *The Middle Works, 1899–1924, volume 3: 1903–1906*. Carbondale: Southern Illinois University Press, pp. 229–39 (originally published 1903).

Dewey, J. (1978a) *How We Think*. In J. A. Boydston (ed.), *The Middle Works, 1899–1924, volume 6: 1910–1911*. Carbondale: Southern Illinois University Press, pp. 177–355 (originally published 1910).

Dewey, J. (1978b) *Democracy and Education*. In J. A. Boydston (ed.), *The Middle Works, 1899–1924, volume 9: 1916*. Carbondale: Southern Illinois University Press (originally published 1916).

Dewey, J. (1978c) Universal service as education. In J. A. Boydston (ed.), *The Middle Works, 1899–1924, volume 10: 1916–1947*. Carbondale: Southern Illinois University Press, pp. 183–90 (originally published 1916).

Dewey, J. (1988) *Experience and Education*. In Jo Ann Boydston (ed.), *The Later Works, 1925–1953, volume 13: 1938–1939*. Carbondale: Southern Illinois University Press, pp. 1–62 (originally published 1938).

Galston, W. (2002) Individual experience and social policy: thinking practically about overcoming racial and ethnic prejudice. In S. Macedo and Y. Tamir (eds), *Moral and Political Education*. New York: New York University Press, pp. 425–33.

Gutmann, A. (1987) *Democratic Education*. Princeton, NJ: Princeton University Press.

Gutmann, A. (2002) Civic minimalism, cosmopolitanism, and patriotism: where does democratic education stand in relation to each? In S. Macedo and Y. Tamir (eds), *Moral and Political Education*. New York: New York University Press, pp. 23–57.

Hegel, G. (1942) *Philosophy of Right*, trans. T. M. Knox. Oxford: Clarendon Press.

Hegel, G. (1967) *Phenomenology of Mind*, ed. and trans. J. B. Baillie. New York: Harper & Row.

Kaestle, C. (1983) *Pillars of the Republic: Common Schools and American Society 1780–1860*. New York: Hill and Wang.

Kant, I. (1922) *Rechtslehre* [*The Doctrine of Right*]. In E. Cassirer (ed.), *Immanuel Kants Werke, volume 7*. Berlin: Bruno Cassirer Verlag, pp. 3–180.

Kant, I. (1949) *Grundlegung* [*Fundamental Principles of the Metaphysics of Morals*], trans. T. K. Abbott. Indianapolis: Library of Liberal Arts.

Kelly, G. A. (1978) *Hegel's Retreat from Eleusis*. Princeton, NJ: Princeton University Press.

Kliebard, H. M. (1995) *The Struggle for the American Curriculum, 1893–1958*, 2nd edn. New York: Routledge.

Macedo, S. and Tamir, Y. (eds) (2002) *Moral and Political Education*. New York: New York University Press.

McConnell, M. (2002) Educational disestablishment: why democratic values are ill-served by democratic control of schooling. In S. Macedo and Y. Tamir (eds), *Moral and Political Education*. New York: New York University Press, pp. 87–146.

Malebranche, N. (1958) *Traité de la nature et de la grace* [*Treatise on Nature and Grace*]. In A. Robinet (ed.), *Oeuvres Complètes, tome 5*. Paris: Vrin.

Montesquieu (1949) *Mes Pensées* [*My Thoughts*]. In R. Caillois (ed.), *Oeuvres Complètes, tome 1*. Paris: Pléiade, pp. 1134–44.

Nussbaum, M. (1996) Patriotism and cosmopolitanism. In J. Cohen (ed.), *For Love of Country: Debating the Limits of Patriotism*. Boston: Beacon Press.

Oakeshott, M. (1975). *On Human Conduct*. Oxford: Clarendon Press.

Osler, A. (2000) Citizenship, human rights and cultural diversity. In A. Osler (ed.), *Citizenship and Democracy in Schools*. Stoke on Trent: Trentham Books, pp. 3–17.

Pangle, L. S. and Pangle, T. (1993) *The Learning of Liberty: The Educational Ideas of the American Founders*. Lawrence: University of Kansas Press.

Plato (1961) *Republic*. In E. Hamilton and H. Cairns (eds), *Plato: The Collected Dialogues*. New York: Bollingen.

Riley, P. (1982) *Will and Political Legitimacy: A Critical Exposition of Social Contract Theory in Hobbes, Locke, Rousseau, Kant and Hegel*. Cambridge, MA: Harvard University Press.

Riley, P. (1983) *Kant's Political Philosophy*. Totowa, NJ: Rowman & Littlefield.

Riley, P. (1986) *The General Will before Rousseau*. Princeton, NJ: Princeton University Press.

Rousseau, J.-J. (1910) *Émile*. London: Dent.

Rousseau, J.-J. (1950a) *Discourse on the Origin of Inequality*. In G. D. H. Cole (trans.), *The Social Contract and Discourses*. New York: Everyman, pp. 175–282.

Rousseau, J.-J. (1950b) *A Discourse on Political Economy*. In G. D. H. Cole (trans.), *The Social Contract and Discourses*. New York: Everyman, pp. 283–330.

Rousseau, J.-J. (1958) *Lettres morales* [*Moral Letters*]. In B. Gagnébin and M. Raymond (eds), *Oeuvres Complètes, tome 4*. Paris: Gallimard.

Rousseau, J.-J. (1962a) *Political Writings*, ed. C. Vaughan. Oxford: Basil Blackwell.

Rousseau, J.-J. (1962b) *Du contrat social*. [*On the social contract*]. In C. Vaughan (ed.), *Political Writings, volume 2*. Oxford: Basil Blackwell, pp. 1–136.

Rousseau, J.-J. (1962c) *Gouvernement de Pologne* [*Government of Poland*]. In C. Vaughan (ed.), *Political Writings, volume 2*. Oxford: Basil Blackwell, pp. 369–516.

Rousseau, J.-J. (1962d) *Jugement sur las Polysynodie* [*Judgment on the Polysynodie*]. In C. Vaughan (ed.), *Political Writings, volume 1*. Oxford: Basil Blackwell, pp. 413–22.

Rousseau, J.-J. (1962e) *Première version du contrat social* [*First Version of the Social Contract*]. In C. Vaughan (ed.), *Political Writings, volume 1*. Oxford: Basil Blackwell, pp. 434–511.

Rousseau, J.-J. (1971a) Discours sur la vertu du heros [Discourse on the virtue of the hero]. In M. Launay (ed.), *Oeuvres Complètes, tome 3*. Paris: Editions de Seuil, pp. 1078–95.

Rousseau, J.-J. (1971b) *Le persifleur* [The banterer]. In *Oeuvres Complètes, tome 1*. Paris: Gallimard, pp. 1111–12.

Rousseau, J.-J. (1971c) *Lettre à M. de Beaumont*. In M. Launay (ed.), *Oeuvres Complètes de Rousseau, tome 3*. Paris: Editions du Seuil.

Rousseau, J.-J. (1974a) *Lettre à M. de Franquières*. In H. Gouhier (ed.), *Lettres philosophiques*. Paris: Vrin, pp. 180–1.

Rousseau, J.-J. (1974b) *Lettre à M. de Malesherbes*. In H. Gouhier (ed.), *Lettres philosophiques*. Paris: Vrin, pp. 77–80.

Shklar, J. (1969) *Men and Citizens: A Study of Rousseau's Social Theory*. Cambridge: Cambridge University Press.

Shklar, J. (1973) "General Will." In Wiener, P. (Ed.). *Dictionary of the history of ideas*. (Vol. 2). New York: Charles Scribner's Sons.

Shklar, J. (1991) *American citizenship: The quest for inclusion*. Cambridge, Mass.: Harvard University Press.

Further reading

Dewey, J. (1988) *Freedom and Culture*. In J. A. Boydston (ed.), *The Later Works, 1925–1953, volume 13: 1938–1939*. Carbondale: Southern Illinois University Press, pp. 63–188 (first published 1939).

Bernstein, R. J. (1967) *John Dewey*. New York: Washington Square Press.

Gouinlock, J. (1986) *Excellence in Public Discourse: John Stuart Mill, John Dewey, and Social Intelligence*. New York: Teachers College Press.

Mayhew, K. C. and Edwards, A. C. (1966) *The Dewey School*. New York: Atherton.

Parry, G. (2001) *Émile*: learning to be men, women, and citizens. In P. Riley (ed.), *The Cambridge Companion to Rousseau*. Cambridge: Cambridge University Press, pp. 247–71.

Ryan, A. (1995) *John Dewey and the High Tide of American Liberalism*, chapter 4, The Pedagogue as Prophet. New York: W. W. Norton, pp. 118–53.

Shell, S. M. (2001) *Émile*: nature and the education of Sophie. In P. Riley (ed.), *The Cambridge Companion to Rousseau*. Cambridge: Cambridge University Press, pp. 272–301.

Steiner, D. M. (1994) *Rethinking Democratic Education: The Politics of Reform*. Baltimore: Johns Hopkins University Press.

Westbrook, R. B. (1991) *John Dewey and American Democracy*. Ithaca, NY: Cornell University Press.

8

Kant, Hegel, and the Rise of Pedagogical Science

G. Felicitas Munzel

Three passages from Kant's lectures on pedagogy are repeatedly cited in the literature (especially European) on the nature and status of education, both as an institution and as a discipline: his call to transform the mechanism in the art of education into a science, his assertion that human beings can only become human beings through education, and his exhortation to educate, not for a present state of affairs, but for a future possible improved human condition, in accordance with the idea of humanity and its entire destiny (*Ak*, 9, pp. 447, 443). Yet the same literature, to this date, frequently expresses skepticism not only about the successful establishment thus far of such a "science of education" (*Erziehungswissenschaft*), but in general as to whether and in what sense pedagogy can even be understood as a science. Moreover, when one turns to the writings of Kant and Hegel, beyond the publication of Kant's lecture notes (*On Pedagogy*) just one year before his death, neither produced a philosophical treatise devoted explicitly to the topic of pedagogical science.

The first problematic, then, in exploring their relevance for the "rise of pedagogical science," is to locate Kant (1724–1804) and Hegel (1770–1831), both as historical figures and as philosophical thinkers making significant contributions to this subject, in relation to the emergence of a call for such a science in the course of the eighteenth-century pedagogical reform debates. The effort to do so in the discussion here proceeds through the following stages.

1   A brief philological and historical analysis of the terms "pedagogy" and "science" in the context of the effort in general in the eighteenth century to distinguish science (*Wissenschaft*) and art (*Kunst*).
2   An overview of the historical, philosophical, literary, and political development of education reform writings, debates, and institutions in the long eighteenth century.
3   A biographical snapshot of Kant and Hegel in relation to these pedagogical movements.
4   Analyses of Kant's and Hegel's respective philosophical writings to identify highlights of their contributions to pedagogical science.
5   A concluding summary of the influence of their thought on subsequent developments in the field.

"Pedagogy" and "Science"

The issues discussed under the rubric of "pedagogy" are widely recognized. As Wolfgang Brezinka summarizes them, they include the goals and desired outcome of education, the principles and techniques of effective teaching (which may include moral, judicial, and technical norms), the institutional and organizational frameworks as well as the related political dimensions, relevant value judgments and conceptions of the proper conduct of human life, and factual considerations such as the physical, psychological, social, and cultural conditions that effective educational practice must take into account (Brezinka, 1971, pp. 3–4). The very range of topics, together with the typical dependency on other sciences when engaging them (for example, psychology, moral philosophy, anthropology, and sociology), makes it difficult to define the distinct subject matter of pedagogical science. One can, as I do in the section that follows, treat pedagogy as being itself a distinctive human or cultural science whose object then consists in the texts on the subject. A traditional philosophical point of departure for inquiry, however, is the analysis of the central concepts involved. In this case, "pedagogy" or "*paideia*" is intrinsically bound up with the self-conception of philosophy in its Greek origins (see Jaeger, 1939–44). The propensity of eighteenth-century thinkers and educators to refer back to this ideal may be seen in (among other things) the important philosophical and rhetorical role the widespread appeal to the figure of Socrates serves in their discourse. For methodological and historical philosophical reasons, then, we begin with the etymological origins and history of "pedagogy."

From the outset it is clear that both an art and a science, a praxis and a theory or doctrine, are involved and that the pedagogical activity encompasses the full range of all that counts as rearing, upbringing, and educating. Concepts for the last trace their roots to terms for horticultural and agricultural activities of tending, raising, and cultivating. A *paidagogos*, the Greek or Roman slave who accompanied the child to school and acted as its tutor, was literally the "child's guide" (from *paidos* for child, and *agein*, to lead). The tasks falling to such a guide (from discipline, to manners and moral conduct, to schooling) themselves became the subject of theorizing, or the art and doctrine of education (*Erziehungskunst, Erziehungslehre*). As the question of *paideia* in its inception was increasingly refined, the quest to establish an appropriate canon of instruction led to the notion of an *enkyklios paideia*, a comprehensive system of instruction, or a complete circle of the arts and sciences. One of its most longstanding forms was the quadrivium and trivium of the seven liberal arts constituting the course of study of the medieval university. Collecting the materials of such comprehensive learning into books was undertaken long before the term "encyclopedia" was used for such books. The earliest effort is attributed to Speusippus, a fourth-century BCE disciple of Plato, with Varro's *The Disciplines* (30 BCE) held to be the first Roman effort. Notable contributions in the medieval period include the thirteenth-century *Speculum Majus* (*Great Mirror*), with the Renaissance *Encyclopaedia: seu, Orbis Disciplinarum, tam Sacrarum quam Prophanarum Epistemon* (entire circle of sciences, sacred and profane) seen as the first instance of the term "encyclopedia" in the title. With the Enlightenment, in particular with Diderot's *L'encyclopédie*, the familiar modern form (effectively an encyclopedic dictionary) and the effort to make such comprehensive learning universally available were ushered in.

The points to be made with regard to the eighteenth-century effort to articulate a conception of "pedagogical science" include the following. The concepts used by its authors are most fruitfully read, not in terms of the later nineteenth-century division of the human and natural sciences (as Wilhelm Dilthey articulated these), but in relation to the classical and medieval tradition from which the Enlightenment arises. Even its breaks with that tradition can be well illuminated in terms of the issues of pedagogy, for the Enlightenment as self-conceived was in its essence an enormous pedagogical project, of which the encyclopedia is but one, albeit important, component. The record of Kant's teaching assignments includes six semesters of a course in intellectual history called *Enzyklopädie*. Hegel wrote his own *Encyclopedia of the Philosophical Sciences*, consisting of three parts: logic, philosophy of nature, and philosophy of spirit. An earlier essay from his Nürnberg period, "Philosophical Encyclopedia," was an express response to considerations arising in relation to his work as an educator. Hence (in light of the backdrop of the tradition), were space to permit it, a complete scholarly account of Hegel's conception of pedagogical science would give an analysis of what his *Encyclopedia* reveals about it. A member of the Prussian ministry, Johannes Schulze, who was strongly influenced by Hegel's system, did devise and institute an encyclopedic form of education in the Prussian school system in the nineteenth century, thereby overturning previous reforms achieved in the movements of the age.

Over and above the philosophical writings, the period from 1750 to 1830 spawned some forty texts (doctrines of education), whose specific aim of articulating a scientific pedagogy (Lenhart, 1977, pp. 145, 148) made manifest a self-perception of engagement in developing such a science. However, this self-perception is generally set aside in relegating the movement and its works to the history of education (or pedagogy); the invention of a science of education is generally taken to be a twentieth-century phenomenon, with the nineteenth century credited for preliminary versions. This might be explained in at least two ways. First, the efforts of the long eighteenth century are assessed in retrospect by the criteria of the contemporary sense of "science," conceived through a distinction between human and natural science and defined in its procedures of inquiry and argumentation on the model of the physical and mathematical sciences. Second, the very effort to distinguish the concepts of "art" and "science," closely linked throughout the millennia of the evolving *enkyklios paideia*, was first explicitly taken up, but not yet fully worked out, in the eighteenth century. Their interchangeable use did leave open the controversy as to whether such technical sciences as medicine and others explicitly incorporated by Diderot were to remain excluded under the traditional rubric. As Christa Kersting has concluded, the reformers and authors recognized the nascent stage of pedagogy as a science in their day; for them it was a matter of blazing a trail and traveling down it all at once (Kersting, 1992, p. 16).

Dilthey himself acknowledges that a guiding idea of the pedagogical movements stretching from John Amos Comenius (1592–1670) to Johann Heinrich Pestalozzi (1746–1827) is that the scientific spirit must become dominant in education, that a work such as Rousseau's *Émile* presents an experiment in education which figures such as Johann B. Basedow and Christian G. Salzmann eagerly test out in practice, and that Kant's lectures on pedagogy express the theory of these pedagogical experiments (Dilthey, 1960, p. 170). The effort to separate pedagogy as a discipline distinct from the fields of philosophy, theology, morality, or politics (under which it had traditionally been subsumed) included the attempt to define the conceptual distinctions between the art and science of education. Just as "arts" in the seven liberal arts included the mathematical and physical sciences, so the use of art (*Kunst*) as interchangeable with knowledge (*Wissen*) or science (*Wissenschaft*) continued well into the eighteenth century. So, for example, "art" named scientific fields (logic as the "art of demonstration," or geometry as the "art of measurement") and to know how to perform these functions was an "art of reason" or "science." The general effort to distinguish more precisely the universal principles (constituting a scholarly discipline) from the skill in and principles of execution of the universals was carried into the attempts to distinguish the art, science, and doctrines of education. In the passage in which Kant calls for transforming the mechanism in the art of education into a science, it is proceeding in a mechanical fashion that he essentially challenges. As the development of our natural aptitudes, a development for which human beings are not endowed with an instinct, education is *de facto* an art. As an art, education must be based on a plan, on principles, aimed at developing human nature in such a way that human destiny (or vocation) is realized, instead of proceeding on purely contingent, experiential grounds, whereby we discover only accidentally what is useful or harmful (*Ak*, 9, pp. 447, 451).

The two concepts in terms of which the pedagogical discussion proceeded were education or rearing (*Erziehung*) and *Bildung* ("formation," but its range of meaning defies the naming of a good English equivalent). The latter's close connection with enlightenment (*Aufklärung*) and culture or cultivation (*Kultur*) is testified to by Moses Mendelssohn in his essay answering the question, "what is enlightenment?" Mendelssohn notes that the usage of the terms is new in the language and he too associates them with the goal of realizing human destiny (the *Bestimmung des Menschen*, a concept traceable to a 1748 essay by Johann Joachim Spalding). The concept of *Bildung* has a long history of evolving meanings stretching back to its fourteenth-century mystical use for the realization of the divine image. In Idealist thought it refers to the formation of the soul's innate powers (especially as Schiller uses it), and it is Kant's term for the formation of character. Thus it is closely allied with the notion of the beautiful soul. In the early nineteenth century, Hegel's critique of the latter and his reformulation of the conception of *Bildung* sets a different course for pedagogical theory and praxis.

The Educational Reform Movement of the Eighteenth Century

The players in this pedagogical drama of the age were active on all levels: philosophy, literature, education, and the political, social, and popular spheres. Especially given the interaction and influence of one on the other, a survey of the stage with its cast of characters is valuable for situating Kant and Hegel in relation to it. Moreover, the historical context supports the claim of early histories of the period, namely that Enlightenment philosophy was tightly and necessarily bound up with the striving for the reform of the entire system of education. The writings and speeches express a fundamental assumption informing the century-long debate: that the overall goal of pedagogy should be the production of a moral- and civic-minded citizenry. A central question of the age was thus how systems and institutions could best fulfill their function and responsibility in the moral development of their students.

The key philosophical and literary works began with John Locke's *Some Thoughts Concerning Education* (written between 1683 and 1689), a treatise recognized for the attention it brought to the physical, psychic, and moral development of children. Major works that followed include Rousseau's *Émile or On Education* (1762), J. M. R. Lenz's *The Tutor, or Advantages of Private Education* (1774), G. E. Lessing's *The Education of the Human Race* (1777), Schiller's *On the Aesthetic Education of Man* (1795), Goethe's *Wilhelm Meisters Lehrjahre* (1796), A. F. Knigge's *On Human Social Intercourse* (1796), and Fichte's *The Vocation of Man* (1800). Deserving particular mention for its significance for Kant is the tradition of logic, which from the seventeenth century forward was at the center of an effort to renew the liberal arts. The discipline of the mind as provided by studies in logic was no mere theoretical or academic exercise; instead, such discipline was deemed to be the *sine qua non* for the prudent and moral, just life. Georg Friedrich Meier's *Vernunftlehre*, the logic text used by Kant, continued in this tradition, giving expression to its basic premise that the training or cultivation of reason, through logic broadly conceived, was the point of departure for and foundation of the education of the human being for the whole of life.

The major educators both incorporated these philosophical writings in their thinking and produced their own works. In their self-conception, they were philosophers of education, but they found themselves at the heart of the struggle to establish pedagogy as a distinct discipline. Their contributions may be seen as beginning with Juan Luis Vives's *De disciplinis* in 1531, a treatise influential for the Czech reformer and religious leader Comenius. Included in Vives's ideas was the emphasis on the need for the pedagogical training of teachers, an emphasis repeated throughout the period and underscored by Kant. Comenius's most philosophical work is held to be his *Great Didactic* (conceived in 1628, but published in 1657). Principles shared with Comenius appear in the thought and writings of the German reformers Wolfgang Ratke (1571–1635) and August Hermann Francke (1663–1727). The Philanthropinismus reform movement (named after a school, the Philanthropin) dominates the mid eighteenth century, and the age closes with the prominent Swiss reformer Pestalozzi, whose many writings include the four-volume didactic novel *Leonard and Gertrude* (1781–5). Pestalozzi's legacy continued in the life and writings of (1) Friedrich Fröbel, who published *The Education of Man* in 1826, (2) Johann Friedrich Herbart, a critic of Kant, whose main writings span the period from 1806 (*General Theory of Education*) to 1825 (*Psychology as a Science*), and (3) Wilhelm von Humboldt (1767–1835), whose writings, reform of the Prussian school and university system, and founding of the university in Berlin forge a dynamic transition from the "pedagogical century" into the nineteenth.

The Philanthropinismus reformers warrant more detailed treatment because of Kant's particular relation with them. However inspiring Kant may otherwise have found Rousseau's *Émile*, with regard to the latter's actual pedagogical methodology he was disappointed. While he notes at one point that a Rousseauian education is the "only means" of improving society, the twenty years devoted by the tutor to raising a single individual to adulthood was simply impracticable and afforded no clear sense of how such instruction might be translated into a system of education for the schools. In the same period, however, in 1774, a new educational institute, the Philanthropin, was founded in Dessau. Kant's unequivocal, enthusiastic, and unwavering support for its program of education constituted his own earliest and most explicit public entry into the education reform debate. The "pedagogical purpose" of the school, as expressed by its first director, Johann Bernhard Basedow, was the "reform of the foundations of the educational system," to be effected through six steps: (1) providing prospective teachers with practical training, not just through lectures, but through supervised experience in the "difficult art of the instruction and education of young people"; (2) basing instruction on a well thought out curriculum; (3) eliminating all memorization and translation of terms (which by such means remain uncomprehended); (4) training governesses and tutors employed by the nobility so that "greater insight and virtue might be attained by the higher classes"; (5) separating civic and ecclesiastical instruction; (6) revising the method of teaching Latin so that this language, deemed so useful to all refined persons, might be acquired without ordeal. Depending on their own level of achievement, its students were intended to become teachers for the aristocracy and in the higher schools, schoolmasters in the country schools, and governors and governesses (Schmid, 1884–1902, pp. 204, 210).

The program of instruction in the Philanthropin followed the principles and curriculum developed in Basedow's writings, beginning with his 1758 *Practical Philosophy for All Walks of Life*, a work relying (by his own account) on Locke's book on education. By 1768 Basedow began to take Rousseau's *Émile* and its increasing influence in Germany into consideration; in the same year his *Presentation to Humanitarians* appeared, indicating a plan for producing a further work which initially appeared in two parts: the *Methodology* (1770, used by Kant in his first lectures on pedagogy) and the *Book of Elements*. The two together made up his *Elementarwerk*, which underwent further revisions and outlived the school in Dessau. Over fifty years after Basedow's death and almost eighty years after his initial publication of it, a third edition was produced in 1847. The introduction of this edition credited Basedow with being the one who provided the original inspiration for efforts everywhere to improve the schools and education of children. The Institute and Basedow were further credited with having brought the development of thinking about pedagogy itself to the level of a science.

Kant hailed the school as an "institution of education" whose founders were "dedicated to the well-being and improvement of humanity," whose pedagogy was genuinely "in keeping with nature as well as all civic purposes," and which could thus effect the "development of the natural aptitudes inherent in human nature" (*Ak*, 2, pp. 447–8). He called upon "all humanitarians" (literally, friends of humanity, *Menschenfreunde*) to give their support to and inform themselves about this new school and its "true method of education," which not only thus benefited its students, but also served to educate teachers in accordance with its ways (*Ak*, 2, pp. 449–50). In short, he was personally convinced that what was needed for the well-being of the human race was already at hand, that the seed (itself inherent in human nature) had flowered into the first exemplar of what promised to be, with the participatory supportof the entire European community, the advent of a new phase in humanity's progress toward perfection and completion (see Munzel, 1999, chapter 5). Kant maintained correspondence with the school's three directors, Basedow, followed by Joachim Heinrich Campe and Christian Heinrich Wolke, as well as with members of the second generation of Philanthropists, who established schools elsewhere and continued to contribute to the literature of the movement. In a 1778 letter to Wolke, Kant explicitly states what he regards as the chief role and importance of education: the only thing necessary is not theoretical learning (*Schulwissenschaft*), but the *Bildung* of human beings, with regard to both their talents and their character (*Ak*, 10, p. 221). A statement in the same spirit in his lectures on pedagogy underscores the difference between the mere instructor who informs and educates solely for school and the tutor who is a leader or guide and educates for life (*Ak*, 9, p. 452).

Campe went on to direct schools in Hamburg and Trittau, and from 1769 to 1773, and again in 1775, served as a private tutor in the Humboldt household. He was the author and editor of a 16–volume *Allgemeine Revision des gesammten Schul- und Erziehungswesen von einer Gesellschaft praktischer Erzieher* (*Universal Revision of the Entire School and Educational System by a Company of Practical Educators*), which appeared between 1785 and 1793. Kersting concludes that one can date the reform movement itself, which develops toward establishing pedagogy as an independent discipline (with the professionalization of its members and institutionalization of its knowledge), from Basedow's 1768 *Presentation* to the final year of the publication of the *Revision*, a work that Campe himself saw as a way to achieve disciplinary status for pedagogy (Kersting, 1992, pp. 10, 71). The *Revision* reprinted Locke's *Thoughts Concerning Education* and Rousseau's *Emile*. Its program consisted of an anthropologically–psychologically based concept of education that largely bracketed out politics and religion, its goal being to institutionalize the rearing and instruction of human beings, starting with earliest childhood, in accordance with rational principles (Kersting, 1992, pp. 76, 88). Other notable Philanthropist educator reformers included among the contributors to the *Revision* were (together with some of their own writings): Johann Stuve (1785: *Most Universal Principles of Education*), Ernst Christian Trapp (1780: *Attempt at a Pedagogy*), Peter Villaume (1784: *Education For Cultivating Love of Humanity*), and Christian Gotthilf Salzmann (1780: *Directives for a Methodical Education of Children*). In their self-conception, the Philanthropists saw pedagogical inquiry and its application as nothing less than a matter of self-enlightenment (Kersting, 1992, pp. 21–2). Isaac Iselin (1728–82), a member of the city hall in Basel and an avid supporter of the Philanthropist movement, summed up the spirit of pedagogical reform of the age as follows:

The task of the new education was to be the achievement of a happy human race; this striving lends the character of philanthropy to the Age of Enlightenment and makes it a pedagogical age. The happiness and dignity of human beings consists in their doing as much good and thinking as many great and beautiful things as their abilities and circumstances permit them; to lead them to this, to prepare them to conform to their great destiny, to teach them to be human beings – this is called educating them, and this is the greatest benefit which a human being can give to human beings. (Scherer, 1897, p. 485)

Iselin's testimony points to the active participation in the reform efforts at the popular, social, and political levels. Among the literate citizenry (especially in

Germany) there was a prevalent conviction that the improvements they desired in society, state, and church could only be achieved by means of a reform of the school systems. One of the media fostering this conviction was the moral weeklies; a widespread popular literature promoting the Enlightenment message of virtue, it flourished for about 50 years, from the early 1720s to the 1770s. The reform of the Prussian school system began during Kant's lifetime (with the 1794 Prussian legal code including an entire section on universities). Indeed, the king's personal interest in the matter is noteworthy. Reportedly Frederick the Great recommended *bien raisonner* as the "goal for all teachers" and affirmed "morality as society's strongest bond and source of public peace"; he further held that the "exemplary school would always be the one effecting the best influence on lived morality and making society more secure, benevolent, and virtuous" (Schmid, 1884–1902, p. 15). Kant here again had personal correspondence with the Prussian Minister in charge of education as of 1771, Karl Abraham von Zedlitz, himself an active advocate of education reforms, sympathetic to the Philanthropinismus movement, and personally influenced by Locke's treatise. Nevertheless, in his lectures on both pedagogy and anthropology, Kant is highly skeptical of looking to the government or upper classes for leadership in the matters of cultivating the human mind and spirit, affirming instead (as he also does in his essay "What Is Enlightement?" *Ak*, 8) the role of the private individual and of the public, of the spectator participating in humanity's well-being. In Hegel's account of the state, he identifies the pressures of the economic changes of modern society as giving rise to the necessity of the widespread question of *Bildung* and the changes in it. There were, of course, also forces of opposition. The philosophers of education found the universities very slow to recognize any need for a separate discipline, and on the societal level they also had to work on forging a consciousness of a need for a new, scientific pedagogy (Kersting, 1992, p. 18). On the whole, however, the climate of striving for change and a hoped for improvement of the human condition was at the very least in accord with Kant's call to educate for such a future state.

Some of the basic principles and elements of the self-described experiments in education of the age may be summed up as follows. It was axiomatic that instruction should proceed in accordance with nature (that is, in agreement with the capacities and aptitudes of human nature). Pedagogy was essentially teleological: its goal was the perfection of humanity. To make progress toward the realization of human destiny was at once to make progress in enlightenment. So the education called for enlightening human beings (not merely training or mechanically instructing them). Such cultivation and the production of morality, even if there was evil in human beings, was affirmed as the greatest and most difficult, but indispensable, task of humanity; hence too it was a task for generations into the future. A primary focus of the task was to train the teachers.

Kant, Hegel, and the Reform Movement

It was in the German universities that the great modern philosophers also first were themselves professional teachers of their field, with Kant and Hegel belonging to this select group. Kant's teaching career spans nearly half a century, from private tutor (1748–54), to magister and lecturer (1755–70), to professor of logic and metaphysics (1770–96), during which time he accumulated an astounding record in number and range of courses taught (from logic and metaphysics, to physical geography, anthropology, moral philosophy, jurisprudence, physics, encyclopedia, theology, and pedagogy). Hegel too began as a tutor (in Bern in 1793 and Frankfurt in 1796); he left for Jena in 1800, was headmaster of a school (*Gymnasium*) in Nürnberg from 1808 to 1816, received his appointment as Professor of Philosophy in Heidelberg in 1816, and moved on to Berlin in 1818.

In their own statements about their life's work and writings, in their affirmations about moral education, Kant and Hegel seem at first blush to have a number of affinities. Consonant with his remarks to Wolke, in his lectures on pedagogy, Kant asserts that the primary endeavor of moral education is to establish a character (*Ak*, 9, p. 481). In these, the anthropology lectures, and elsewhere, he further expresses his preoccupation with the problematic of educating the educator: how is one who is oneself in need of such education to be able to lead others? The answer is ultimately the classical one: the appeal to the philosopher. Kant's self-conception, as expressed in his letters to his former student Marcus Herz, is that the "main purpose of his academic life" is the cultivation of good character and the training of his students' talents, providing them with exercises in skill, prudence, and wisdom. The critical philosophy itself is accorded a role in keeping with the claim of the tradition of logic that discipline of the mind is essential for human moral life. In the Doctrine of Method of the *Critique of Practical Reason*, Kant's self-described purpose is to "point out the most general maxims of the doctrine of method of a moral education (*Bildung*) and exercise" (*Ak*, 5, p. 161). In conclusion he makes one of his most explicit claims for the pedagogical function of the critical philosophy as such, declaring the remedy for the "error of still crude, unpracticed judgment" to be the critical philosophy, as the science required for the cultivation of reason, a science to be mastered precisely by those who would take upon themselves a pedagogical role in relation to others, a "science (critically sought and methodically instituted), a narrow gate leading to a doctrine of wisdom, when by this is understood not merely what one ought to do, but what ought to serve teachers as a guideline in order that they may clearly and capably pave the path to wisdom that everyone should follow and keep others from straying from. Philosophy must at all times preserve this science" (*Ak*, 5, pp. 162–3).

From his Nürnberg writings to his philosophy of right, Hegel affirms that an essential part of education is instruction in moral concepts and principles, that "pedagogy is the art of making human beings ethical" (*Werke*, 4, p. 346; 7, p. 302, para. 151, addition). Out of context, Hegel's terminology strikes a reader of Kant as familiar: the appeal to *Bildung*, the formation of mind and character, the notions of freedom, maturity, union of nature and freedom. For example, in Hegel's 1810 account of rights, duties, and doctrine of religion for the junior class, he affirms that the "purpose of education is to make human beings independent, that is beings of a free will" (*Werke*, 4, p. 227). The differences in their respective philosophies, however, make all the difference and result, especially in the hands of their followers, in two fundamentally different pedagogical strategies, discussed in the education literature under the rubrics of "autonomy" and "control." The differences revolve around the

121

respective primacies of practical and theoretical reason in Kant's and Hegel's philosophies and the metaphysical reformulation of the concept of *Bildung* by Hegel. While
Hegel affirms that the stages of *Bildung* consist in pedagogical progress, it is essentially
a progress in the formation and self-actualization of world spirit, served by the *Bildung*
of the individual. Hence the concept of human destiny (the *Bestimmung des Menschen*)
too is reformulated and the relation of the individual to the activity of *Bildung* is
changed.

Kant

A full development of Kant's conception of pedagogy can take several approaches. On
the basis of the anthropological levels of skill, prudence, and wisdom, one can explore
what program of education may be gleaned from Kant's various writings, what the
stages are and how they fit together (a common approach in the literature; see also
Munzel, 1999, chapter 5). These stages are alternatively identified by Kant as consisting of discipline, civilization, cultivation, and moralization, or of a threefold
pedagogical task of nurturing, discipline, and instruction, in addition to *Bildung*.
Another way to proceed is on the basis of the historical context, showing how Kant's
conceptions link up with the pedagogical debates spanning the eighteenth century
and beyond (an angle found in the education literature). A related approach is to
focus on Kant's quarrel with the popular project of enlightenment and its modes of
instruction. His critical reformulation of the goal, of the nature of the good sought,
may be seen as central to that quarrel. As evident in Iselin's testimony, the pedagogical project of the age named human happiness as its purpose, a goal that Kant in
his moral philosophy reformulates as the worthiness to be happy. Kant also objects to
what he sees as the confusion of elements in popular teaching. Hence the philosophical work he sees as needed for the sake of the pedagogical project of enlightenment
consists of the articulation and clarification of distinctions he finds blurred in the
extant moral instruction. Kant seeks to define three levels, which may be technically
expressed as the objective, subjective, and empirical-pragmatic levels. These correspond to three distinct questions (which in turn may be seen as paralleling the
emerging distinctions of science, art, and doctrine in the pedagogical writings): (1)
what we ought to do, or the articulation of the objective moral principle and
identification of its transcendental ground of possibility, the fact of reason whose
defining act is to issue the moral law as an imperative to human rational and sensible
nature expected to carry it out in the world; (2) what we are able to do and how we
can be brought to do it, or the anthropological investigation into human nature to
ascertain its capability of fulfilling what is required of it, of ascertaining what human
beings, as freely acting beings, can and should make of themselves; (3) what we
actually do, as documented in the historical record and in such writings as biograph-
ies, thus acquiring the empirical information which can be used in moral education
both for taking advantage of certain human characteristics and for safeguarding
against others.

A fourth way to proceed is to examine what is at stake for Kant in his call to
transform the mechanism in the art of education into a science. Based on the

discussion thus far, in relation to the other established and emerging sciences, four are immediately relevant: logic (broadly conceived), morality, anthropology, and the critical philosophy as such. The last of these defines what "science" means for Kant, namely a systematic unity of manifold cognitions under one idea. The idea is a rational concept of the form of the whole and determines *a priori* both the domain of the manifold as well as the position of the parts with respect to one another (*Critique of Pure Reason*, A832/B860). The critical philosophy functions as an instructor and disciplinarian for reason, teaching us to treat the ideas of reason as concepts of perfection definitive of a task, of work we are to perform to bring about a concrete manifestation of reason's ideas in the world. Kant's call for education based on a plan, on principles, aimed at developing human nature in such a way that human destiny (or vocation) is realized, may be fruitfully read in light of the critical sense of science. In his lectures on pedagogy, Kant refers to a "theory of education" as a "splendid ideal" and observes that it "does not matter if we are not immediately in the position to realize it" (*Ak*, 9, p. 444). More specifically, "the idea of an education which develops all the human natural aptitudes must be admitted to be true"; as an idea it is a "concept of a perfection not yet found in experience," a concept of an education which in its own "form befits humanity" (*Ak*, 9, pp. 443–5). Its guiding principle is the "idea of human-ity and its entire vocation" (*Ak*, 9, p. 447). We are to work on such a plan of a more purposive education and pass the directive for it on to our progeny (*Ak*, 9, p. 445). Theory and praxis, as Kant explicates these in his 1793 essay, consist respectively in principles considered universally, and in effecting a purpose; the value of praxis is measured by the extent to which it is in keeping with its underlying theory, not by the empirical conditions of the execution of the principles (*Ak*, 8, pp. 276, 277).

In sum, what defines pedagogical science as a systematic unity is the idea defining the work to be performed, that work ultimately being the establishment of character and the training of human talents. The stages of discipline, cultivation, civilization, and moralization are to be understood in terms of what is required for effecting the relation of the idea of perfected humanity to the natural conditions in which it is to be concretely realized. There is empirical work to be done. For instance, in the Doctrine of Method of the second *Critique*, Kant recommends that examples of morally judging reason be analyzed in repeated experiments on common human understanding, in a manner similar to procedures in chemistry, separating the empirical from the rational components so that both can come to be known with regard to what they can each achieve (*Ak*, 5, p. 163). A number of latent issues, which cannot be examined here, are also involved. For example, Kant himself often enough speaks of the perfection to be realized in terms of the human race, while the realization of moral character is clearly an individual matter. Most important for the discussion here, however, is that the "*Paidagogos*" (so to speak) of pedagogical activity is effectively reason's idea (itself interpreted by critique). In a Kantian science of pedagogy, the idea (of an education that develops all the human natural aptitudes) gives direction to all empirical aspects. It is just this nature of an ideal normative concept that allows the pedagogical activity to surpass its own existing state and that of the human affairs around it.

The education called for results in enlightening the individual (*Ak*, 9, p. 450). For Kant, this means moral instruction in which the pedagogical question is how inher-ent moral insight can be raised into the students' clear consciousness, without confusing it with other motives, and allowing its own full force to be realized. Kant's basic premise (as stated in the *Groundwork*) is that the concept of the good will is inherent in the natural, sound human understanding, and does not so much need to be taught, but only brought to an enlightened state (*aufgeklärt*; Ak, 4, p. 397). Moral *Bildung* is based on principles into which individuals themselves have insight (*Ak*, 9, p. 455). The process of bringing students to the point of such insight, of securing access to the human mind and influence on its maxims for the laws of practical reason, is the essence of the pedagogical method Kant outlines in the Doctrine of Method of the *Critique of Practical Reason*. The method must foster and facilitate the consciousness of the law in the students and make them proficient in adopting it in their judgments as the subjective, guiding maxim that will orient them rightly in relation to the human vocation and the highest good. The wisdom to which the teacher is thereby to guide the students is well expressed in Kant's anthropology lectures: the "idea of a practical employment of reason that is perfectly in accord with law" (*Ak*, 7, p. 200). Where such wisdom is achieved, where the law is thus efficacious in an individual's consciousness and judgment, he or she hearkens to a perpetually present inner guide for the conduct of life, the law in essence as an internal pedagogical principle. Put in terms of Kant's 1784 essay ("What Is Enlightenment?"), the pedagogical method (necessarily Socratic) results in the student making the transition from immaturity (taking one's guidance from others) to maturity (employing one's own reason).

Kant as critical philosopher thus stands by his affirmation of the primacy of practical over theoretical learning in 1778 to Wolke and shifts the center of pedagogical instruction as it is captured in the encyclopedic project of the age. In his *Critique of Judgment*, Kant is clear that not only is the striving for knowledge not the supreme goal, but such "intellectual curiosity" in fact hinders the attainment of "true enlightenment," which is achieved far more easily by "those who only want to measure up to their essential purpose" (*Ak*, 5, p. 294fn). The complete account of Kant's conception of pedagogy involves a political dimension, specifically the republican constitution, the role of nature, the public employment of reason, the role of conscience, detailed analyses of particulars of the pedagogical method (such as the proper use of example), and, of course, the fundamental concept of freedom. The effect of the pedagogical method described is to lead the child to the realization of its own freedom; determination by another must be transformed into rational self-determination. The literature testifies to the tenacity of the resulting great problem of education, as Kant himself indicated it: reconciling subjection to lawful constraint with the capacity of availing oneself of one's own freedom. To this date, concludes a contemporary Basel educator and philosopher, the problem remains where Kant left it (Hügli, 1999, p. 47).

Hegel

The transcendence of the Idea in Hegel's philosophy and the associated reconceptions of such central notions as freedom and *Bildung* result in locating the primary pedagogical activity with the "universal individual, self-conscious Spirit"; its *Bildung* is what must be studied, writes Hegel in the preface to his *Phenomenology of Spirit*. This paragraph (para. 28) may be read as Hegel's own summary of the pedagogical process and the role that the "particular individual" who is "incomplete Spirit" has in it. In his or her development, an individual "must also pass through the contents of the universal Spirit's stages of *Bildung*, but as shapes which Spirit has already left behind, as stages on a way that has been prepared and levelled out." In the individual's "pedagogical progress," we "recognize the history of the *Bildung* of the world, traced, as it were, in a silhouette." The next paragraph articulates the Hegelian conception of science (that is, of philosophy): "science presents both this formative process [*bildende Bewegung*] in all its details and necessity, as well as what has already been assimilated as a moment and property of Spirit.... The goal is Spirit's insight into what knowledge is" (para. 29). Spirit's insight is gained by itself becoming genuine knowledge; it must work itself through a long process, that of the coming-to-be of science (para. 27). *Bildung* thus has a double meaning: (1) from the point of view of individuals, it consists of acquiring what is at hand, taking possession of the past existence that is already the property of universal Spirit and constitutes the substance of individuals, but appears to them as their inorganic nature; (2) the same process from the point of view of universal Spirit is nothing but its own acquisition of self-consciousness (para. 28). The Spinozistic cast to this relation of particular individual and universal spirit is confirmed by a statement Hegel makes in his philosophy of right: "Spirit has actuality [or reality], and individuals are its accidents" (*Werke*, 7, p. 305, para. 156, addition).

How does this metaphysical system with its inherent pedagogical process translate into pedagogical principles, praxis, and institutions in human life? What difference does it make to view education, not as the Kantian moral task defined by reason's idea of humanity, but as an immanent part of a metaphysical, systematic unfolding whose concrete forms (as articulated by Hegel in his *Philosophy of Right*) include family relations (of love), civil society (characterized by the concepts of work and needs), and the state (with its system of law and constituting the highest realization of objectified free will)? In this text Hegel claims that *Bildung*, in its "absolute determination" (or destiny, *Bestimmung*) "is liberation and the work of [still] higher liberation." That is to say, it is the "absolute transition to a no longer immediate and natural, but a spiritual ethical substantiality," one which is both "infinitely subjective" and "elevated to the form of universality" (*Werke*, 7, pp. 344–5, para. 187). For the individual, this liberation means "hard work against the mere subjectivity of behavior, against the immediacy of desire, as well as against the subjective vanity of feeling, and the arbitrariness of suiting oneself" (*Werke*, 7, p. 345, para. 187). How does the metaphysical context in which Hegel embeds such seemingly familiar descriptions of overcoming self-interest impact the pedagogical project?

Hegel's own translation of his philosophical framework into specific elements of pedagogical praxis in human life is prima facie more concrete than Kant's discussion. It is not possible to do justice here to the particulars of Hegel's account of the role and nature of family life, of the connection of *Bildung* with work and needs in the economic context of civil society and the resulting required forms *Bildung* must take, of the moral *Bildung* required for recognizing and accepting the laws of society (which limit private interest), and finally of the civic disposition of mind in which the individual's self-knowledge is identical with the universal as objectified in the state (see Krautkrämer, 1979, for a detailed analysis). The short answer to the questions posed focuses on Hegel's particular way of dealing with the issue of the reconciliation of nature and freedom. When Hegel says that "pedagogy is the art of making human beings ethical," he elaborates the point as follows. Pedagogy regards humans as natural beings and shows them the path to their rebirth, to transforming their first nature into a second spiritual one. In the latter, the opposition of natural and subjective willing (of immediate desire and ethical spirit) is eliminated, and the conflict of the subjects is over. The spiritual as a habit is proper to both ethical and philosophical thinking, for the Spirit demands that arbitrary notions be defeated and overcome (*Werke*, 7, p. 302, para. 151, addition). Three discernible pedagogical moments, in which such a transformation to ever higher objectifications of freedom occur, are thus the spheres of nature (family and love), of the state (spirit of a people, concretely manifest as the law permeating all relationships, as well as the mores and consciousness of its citizens), and of the ideal world (absolute knowing). In philosophical science the one truth found in these three complementary manifestations is freely comprehended (*Werke*, 7, p. 512, para. 360).

While Hegel may have understood his project as an effort to seek a balance between individual autonomy and the role of institutions that he took to be necessary for its achievement, his critics regarded his account of the objectification of freedom as a break with the project of enlightenment. For the ultimate subject of this *Bildung* is Spirit, whose objectivity entails negating individual particularities. In Kant's sense of subjectivity, the tension remains: judgment informed by the moral law is the universal exercised as a normative activity that, in the individual, always exists in a relation to the particular and contingent. In Hegel's elevation to universality, the goal is to eliminate contingency; *Bildung* is not for the sake of the particular individual (nor even humanity), but for the sake of Spirit coming to its own self-knowledge. Effectively, the Kantian problematic is dissolved, rather than resolved. The problem for education, of facilitating the transition from external guidance to internal rational self-determination, of transforming an object of *Bildung* into a subject of self-*Bildung*, is replaced with developing techniques for conducting the individual into the objective manifestations (of Spirit), into culture, religion, society, and state (see Hügli, 1999, pp. 40ff).

Conclusion

It should come as no surprise to find the philosophy of education literature speaking about the two strategies of autonomy and control. The description of the first pedagogy affirms that the Enlightenment appeal to the figure of Socrates was not at all an idle one. The pedagogy of autonomy is one where the educator supports, advises, and reflects upon what the students grapple with on the basis of their own will, effectively playing the role of midwife for the freedom of the one undergoing the process of self-education or self-*Bildung* (Hügli, 1999, p. 51). The ancient conception of the pedagogical task comes to the fore here. As spelled out in Plato's *Theaetetus* (167a), the educator must effect a change, much as a physician would, from one condition to a better or healthy one. The strategy of control assumes the pedagogical determinability of human persons, of external agency bringing about an outcome befitting the society and state into which the student is being initiated (Hügli, 1999,

p. 51). In the final analysis it fails, because one cannot ultimately control whether individuals will maintain what one has taught them (Hügli, 1999, p. 69).

The subsequent history of the efforts in the nineteenth and twentieth centuries to carry through a transcendental pedagogy, however, show that the question has yet to be satisfactorily answered as to how to make sense of a strategy of autonomy, how it can be pedagogically meaningfully executed, and wherein its pedagogical effect consists (Hügli, 1999, p. 69). The criticism in general is that neither a Spinozistic type of determinism of freedom by the laws of nature, nor a Kantian determinism of freedom by the moral law, leaves the requisite room for the individual development of freedom. Johann Friedrich Herbart (1776–1841), professor of philosophy in Königs-berg from 1809 to 1833 (i.e. holder of Kant's former chair), student of Fichte, but influenced by Pestalozzi's thought, articulated such criticism against philosophical systems that assumed either fatalism or transcendental freedom, claiming that both preclude pedagogical efficacy. His own pedagogical system rested on the two discip-lines of psychology (as the means of education) and ethics (as definitive of its aim). Herbart identified this aim as moral strength of character, a will with inner freedom and volitions in accord with the moral law, but in changing Kant's causality of freedom into a causality of nature, he fell into another version of the contradiction of asserting both that the task of education is such formation of character in which the students are led to find themselves, and that an educator cannot influence another's soul. The self-described neo-Kantian pedagogical school (whose adherents included Paul Natorp, Jonas Cohn, and Richard Hönigswald) was silenced in 1933. In his recent publication, Anton Hügli offers an outline of 17 premises toward an on-going project of developing a convincing theory and praxis of a pedagogy of auton-omy (Hügli, 1999, pp. 191–4).

Dilthey's influential response to and criticism of nineteenth-century pedagogical systems established on the basis of their seventeenth- and eighteenth-century forerun-ners dealt further blows to the Enlightenment project. Rejecting the idea that the goal and purpose of human life can be expressed in terms of universal concepts, he asserts that ethical principles arise on an historical basis and whatever can be said about human beings is historically conditioned (Dilthey, 1960, p. 171–4). The appeal to a universal ethic as a basis for pedagogy is thus eliminated. The subsequent develop-ments in the nineteenth and twentieth centuries based on principles of psychology and the epistemological norms of neopositivism brought the empirical procedures, statis-tical analyses, and modes of experimentation to bear on education. This enhanced its credibility as a science, but as Dietrich Benner concludes, it effectively changed it from a practical (moral) science to a technical discipline (Benner, 1994, p. 79). With that, the central question of character development was displaced and has only over the past decade regained its status as a fundamental concern for moral and psychological inquiry. As this inquiry takes up the pedagogical issues, its own development can only be aided by being armed with an understanding of their previous incarnation in the fervent debates of the pedagogical age of Enlightenment.

See also 6 ENLIGHTENMENT LIBERALISM; 7 ROUSSEAU, DEWEY, AND DEMOCRACY; 9 ROMAN-TICISM; 10 HELLENISM, THE GYMNASIUM, AND ALTERTUMSWISSENSCHAFT; 18 MOTIVATION AND CLASSROOM MANAGEMENT; 21 CULTIVATING REASON

References

Primary

Kant, I. (1900–) *Kants gesammelte Schriften*, ed. Preussischen Akademie der Wissenschaften. Berlin: Walter de Gruyter. References follow the Academy edition, with relevant volume and page number cited (e.g. *Ak*, 9, p. 447); for the *Critique of Pure Reason* the standard practice of citing A/B for the 1781 and 1787 editions is followed. For English translations, see the *Cambridge Edition of the Works of Immanuel Kant*; the volume and page numbers of the German text from the Academy edition are given in the margins of this translation. See also *Kant: Political Writings*, ed. H. Reiss, in the *Cambridge Texts in the History of Political Thought*, 1970, reprinted 1996.

Hegel, G. W. F. (1979) *Werke*, 20 volumes. Frankfurt am Main: Suhrkamp. For English translations see: *Hegel's Philosophy of Right*, trans. T. M. Knox. Oxford: Oxford University Press (1967); *Hegel's Phenomenology of Spirit*, trans. A. V. Miller. Oxford: Oxford University Press (1977).

Secondary

Beck, L. W. (1979) Kant on Education. In J. D. Browning (ed.), *Education in the 18th Century*. New York: Garland, pp. 10–24.

Benner, D. (1994) *Studien zur Theorie der Erziehungswissenschaften. Pädagogik als Wissenschaft, Handlungstheorie und Reformpraxis* [*Studies on the Theory of the Sciences of Education. Pedagogy as Science, Theory of Action and Praxis of Reform*]. Weinheim: Juventa Verlag.

Brezinka, W. (1971) *Von der Pädagogik zur Erziehungswissenschaft* [*From Pedagogy to the Science of Education*]. Weinheim: Beltz Verlag.

Dilthey, W. (1960) *Pädagogik: Geschichte und Grundlinien des Systems* [*Pedagogy: History and Main Features of the System*], volume 9 of *Gesammelte Schriften*. Göttingen: Vandenhoeck & Ruprecht (originally published 1934).

Hügli, A. (1999) *Philosophie und Pädagogik* [*Philosophy and Pedagogy*]. Darmstadt: Wissenschaftliche Buchgesellschaft.

Jaeger, W. W. (1939–44) *Paideia: The Ideal of Greek Culture*, trans. G. Highet, three volumes. New York: Oxford University Press.

Kersting, C. (1992) *Die Genese der Pädagogik im 18. Jahrhundert. Campes "Allgemeine Revision" im Kontext der neuzeitlichen Wissenschaft* [*The Genesis of Pedagogy in the Eighteenth Century. Campe's "Universal Revision" in the Context of Modern Science*]. Weinheim: Deutscher Studien Verlag.

Krautkrämer, U. (1979) *Staat und Erziehung. Begründung öffentlicher Erziehung bei Humboldt, Kant, Fichte, Hegel und Schleiermacher* [*The State and Education. The Founding of Public Education According to Humboldt, Kant, Fichte, Hegel and Schleiermacher*]. Munich: Johannes Berchmans Verlag.

Lenhart, V. (1977) Zur Wissenschaftsgeschichte der Erziehungswissenschaft: Erziehungskunst–Erziehungslehre–Erziehungswissenschaft. Die Entstehung des Programms einer wissenschaftlichen Pädagogik in Deutschland 1750–1830 [On the scientific history of the science of education: art of education–doctrine of education–science of education. The origin of a program of a scientific pedagogy in Germany 1750–1830]. In V. Lenhart (ed.). *Historische Pädagogik. Methodologische Probleme der Erziehungsgeschichte* [*Historical Pedagogy. Methodological Problems of the History of Education*]. Wiesbaden: Akademische Verlagsgesellschaft, pp. 145–73.

Munzel, G. F. (1999) *Kant's Conception of Moral Character. The "Critical" Link of Morality, Anthropology, and Reflective Judgment.* Chicago: The University of Chicago Press.

Scherer, H. (1897) *Die Pädagogik vor Pestalozzi in ihrer Entwicklung im Zusammenhange mit dem Kultur- und Geistesleben und ihrem Einfluß auf die Gestaltung des Erziehungs- und Bildungswesens dargestellt* [*Presenting the Development of Pedagogy Prior to Pestalozzi in Relation to the Cultural and Intellectual Life and Its Influence on the Organization of the Field of Education and Its System*]. Leipzig: Friedrich Brandstetter.

Schmid, K. A. (1884–1902) *Geschichte der Erziehung vom Anfang an bis auf unsere Zeit* [*History of Education from Its Inception to Our Times*], six volumes. Stuttgart: J. G. Cotta'schen Buchhandlung.

Further reading

Dietrich, T. (1992) *Zeit- und Grundfragen der Pädagogik. Eine Einführung in pädagogisches Denken* [*Current and Fundamental Issues of Pedagogy. An Introduction to Pedagogical Thinking*]. Bad Heilbrunn: Verlag Julius Klinkhardt.

Fischer, W. and Löwisch, D.-J. (eds) (1998) *Philosophen als Pädagogen. Wichtige Entwürfe klassischer Denker* [*Philosophers as Pedagogues. Important Essays by Classical Thinkers*]. Darmstadt: Wissenschaftliche Buchgesellschaft.

Kauder, P. and Fischer, W. (1999) *Immanuel Kant über Pädagogik* [*Immanuel Kant on Pedagogy*]. Hohengehren: Schneider Verlag.

Nohl, H. (1988) *Die Pädagogische Bewegung in Deutschland und ihre Theorie* [*The Pedagogical Movement in Germany and Its Theory*]. Frankfurt am Main: Vittorio Klostermann (first published 1935).

Winkels, T. (1984) *Kants Forderung nach Konstitution einer Erziehungswissenschaft* [*Kant's Call for the Constitution of a Science of Education*]. Munich: Profil Verlag.

9

Romanticism

Frederick C. Beiser

A Romantic Philosophy of Education?

Prima facie education was a topic of little importance to the romantics. If we carefully examine the writings of the founding figures of the German romantic school – Friedrich Schlegel (1772–1829), Ludwig Tieck (1773–1853), Friedrich von Hardenberg (Novalis) (1772–1801), Friedrich Hölderlin (1770–1843), F. D. Schleiermacher (1776–1834), and F. W. J. Schelling (1775–1845) – we find almost nothing about education. If we look for a detailed discussion of child-rearing, pedagogy, curricula, the structure of universities, or the purpose of schools, we are bound to come away disappointed. It is not that the romantics completely ignored the subject. Schlegel wrote about it now and then in his notebooks; Schelling gave a series of lectures ostensibly devoted to the method of education; and Schleiermacher wrote an influential tract on the role and structure of the university. But these writings were only a small fraction of their general output. There is nothing in the romantic corpus to compare with the writings on education of some of their notable contemporaries, say Fichte, Schiller, and Wilhelm von Humboldt. If we measure the importance of a subject by the number of pages explicitly devoted to it, then we have to conclude that the German romantics gave little importance to education. It is indeed not surprising that the subject has received little attention in studies of German Romanticism.

But such a conclusion would be a grave error. We have to reject its main premise. For, even if they write little about it, the romantics themselves tell us – repeatedly, explicitly, and emphatically – that there is nothing more important than education. Friedrich Schlegel once wrote: "The highest good, and the source of everything useful, is education [*Bildung*]." Novalis put forward a similar view about the end of life: "We are on a mission; we have been called upon for the education [*Bildung*] of the earth." Hölderlin once wrote to his brother that the ideal most dear to himself was "education, the improvement of the human race [*Bildung, Besserung des menschlichen Geschlechts*]." If this were not enough, the romantics swore the following oath in *Athenäum*, their common journal: "To fasten together all into one the rays of education [*Bildung*], to distinguish the sick from the healthy, to that we strive in a free bond."

We now face a puzzle. If the romantics gave such importance to education, why did they write so little about it? The source of the mystery lies in translation, more specifically in the notoriously rich and ambiguous German word *Bildung*, the term preferred by Schlegel, Novalis, and Hölderlin. *Bildung* is only one of many German terms for the English word "education." Education might be *Unterricht*, which usually means instruction; it might be *Erziehung*, which implies teaching; or it might be *Ausbildung*, which suggests training or apprenticeship. In some contexts the term *Bildung* simply means education; but it usually also has much richer connotations. It literally means "formation," suggesting an organic process whereby something potential, implicit, and inchoate becomes actual, explicit, and determinate. But in some contexts *Bildung* also means culture. These connotations sometimes coalesce in the idea of the process or product of acculturation. Sometimes they suggest the ethical idea of self-realization, the process by which someone becomes what they are.

If we keep in mind these connotations of *Bildung*, the mystery disappears. There is no longer a discrepancy between the importance the romantics gave to education and the amount of writing they devoted to it. Though the romantics had little to say about the *means* of education, they had a great deal to say about its *end*. Indeed, their central concern was the kind of person we become through education. This was the subject of their *Bildungsromanen*, of works like Hölderlin's *Hyperion*, Tieck's *Franz Sternbald's Wanderungen*, and Novalis's *Heinrich von Ofterdingen*. More significantly, the concept of *Bildung* plays a pivotal role in romantic aesthetics, ethics, and politics. The romantics saw the fundamental purpose of art, society, and the state as nothing less than *Bildung*, the self-realization of the individual.

Granted that education was a fundamental issue for the romantics, why should their views on it be of any concern to us? Why should someone today even bother with them? The short and simple answer to this question is that most of us today are romantics, even though we do not know it. We have subconsciously inherited many beliefs about education that are the legacy of the romantics. The value of individuality, the negative role of sexual stereotypes, the rights of both sexes to an education, the importance of educating the senses as well as the intellect, the central role of the experience of love in the development of the personality, and the fundamental importance of love in marriage: we virtually take all these ideas for granted today, but the romantics were among the very first to defend them. Hence to study the romantics is to know our own roots.

But this is not the end of the matter. The romantics reward study because they gave some interesting and original answers to some of the classical issues in the philosophy of education. What is the purpose of education? What is the role of the state in education? How is it possible to educate someone to be a responsible citizen yet to respect their freedom? What is the role of arts in education? In responding to these issues the romantics took issue with some of their famous forebears, especially Plato and Rousseau. Their views on education are best seen as continuing the conversation begun by them.

On some contemporary issues the romantics remain of crucial importance. They represent the main conceptual alternative to the technological and economic worldview which still dominates the contemporary life. The romantics were the first to protest against some of the more negative consequences of modernity, especially the technological domination of society and nature. If we live in a world of our creation, they argued, then that world must satisfy all aspects of our being, and not simply our immediate material needs; this means that we must create our world according to not only the demands of science but also those of art. As part of their rebellion against the hegemony of technology the romantics criticized the growing professionalization or vocationalization of education, which would reduce education down to learning technical skills. The romantics were among the first rebels against these trends, and their objections against them remain as valid today as they were in the late eighteenth century.

The Romantic Ideal of *Bildung*

The first and most basic question to ask about the romantic philosophy of education is "What was its ideal of *Bildung*? What was the romantics' ideal human being, which it was the purpose of education to develop?" No question goes more to the heart of German Romanticism; yet none is more difficult to answer.

If we view the romantic ideal of *Bildung* from a general philosophical perspective, it would be most accurate to describe it as an ethics of self-realization. The classical account of such an ethics is Aristotle's *Nicomachean Ethics*, where the highest good is defined in terms of human excellence, the development of characteristic human virtues. In fundamental respects, the romantics go back to the Aristotelian tradition. In the classical world the fundamental alternatives to Aristotle's ethics of self-realization were hedonism and stoicism. While the hedonists defined the highest good in terms of pleasure alone, the stoics saw the supreme end of life as the execution of duty and cultivation of virtue alone. It is noteworthy that the romantics rejected, for very Aristotelian reasons, the two eighteenth-century counterparts of hedonism and stoicism: the empiricist ethics of Bentham and Helvetius, and the rationalist ethics of Kant and Fichte. The romantics criticized Kant's and Fichte's ethics of duty for exaggerating the importance of duty, for giving no place to feeling, pleasure, and desire within the highest good; and they faulted Bentham and Helvetius for pushing feeling, pleasure, and desire too far, for failing to see that devotion to pleasure alone would neglect the development of our characteristic human powers.

The most crucial and conspicuous feature of the romantic ideal of *Bildung* is that it is holistic. There were two aspects to this holism. First, it stressed the development of *all* our characteristic human powers, rejecting any one-sidedness that would develop one aspect of our humanity at the expense of others. Second, it emphasized that all these powers should be formed into an integrated, harmonious and balanced whole. True to such holism, the romantics insisted that we should educate not only reason but also sensibility, not only the intellect but also feeling and sensation. They argued that sensibility – the power to sense, feel, and desire – is no less human than reason itself. How we sense and feel as human beings differs markedly from how any animal does these things.

This aspect of the romantic ideal seems to fit one of the most common views of Romanticism: that it was a rebellion against the narrow intellectualism of the Enlightenment, a defense of the rights of feeling against the hegemony of reason. While there is some truth to this interpretation, it is valid only with some qualification. In the realm of aesthetics, the romantics did affirm the role of emotion in artistic creation and perception against the narrow rationalism of neoclassicism; and in the field of ethics, they criticized Kant and Fichte for their emphasis on reason because it seemed to leave little place for feeling and desire. Yet it would be a mistake to assume that the romantics' defense of sensibility was their chief and characteristic contribution to ethics. The defense of the rights of feeling was a battle waged decades before them by the *Sturm und Drang* or *Empfindsamkeit* movement of the 1760s and 1770s. This was the campaign led by Hamann, Herder, Möser and Lenz, and popularized by the young Schiller and Goethe. By the time of the rise of *Frühromantik* in the late 1790s these *Sturmer und Dränger* had made their point, and it seemed necessary to temper their tempestuous claims by once again reinstating the role of rational restraint in ethics and aesthetics. This was indeed the role of the romantics: to correct both the sensibility of *Sturm und Drang* and the rationalism of the *Aufklärung* by emphasizing the equal importance of both reason and sensibility. The romantic commitment to a holistic ideal demanded nothing less: the rights of reason had to be affirmed and limited no less than those of sensibility.

The romantic ideal of *Bildung* was not only holistic but also individualistic. In other words, *Bildung* should consist in the development of not only our characteristic human powers, which we all share as human beings, but also our distinctive individual powers, which are unique to each of us. The romantics stressed that each individual had to realize his human powers in his own unique and individual fashion. No two persons were ever alike; each had characteristics that distinguished him from everyone else. Complete self-realization demanded realizing these distinctively individual characteristics no less than our universal ones. This ethic of individuality is especially marked in Friedrich Schlegel's and Schleiermacher's idea of "divine egoism," according to which the individual is sovereign over all the values of his life and should choose that which is most suitable to his personality. Inevitably, in stressing the importance of individuality, the romantics sometimes took issue with Kant's and Fichte's ethics of duty. They contended that Kant's emphasis on universal laws as the heart of morality left no place for individuality in ethics. Fichte had taken this aspect of Kant's ethics so far that he stated that the moral ideal should be for everyone to be completely alike and to dissolve into a single person. This was the romantic idea of hell, the *reductio ad absurdum* of the ethics of duty.

For the romantics, the secret to *Bildung*, and the source of self-realization, ultimately lay in the human heart. "The heart is the key to life and the world," Novalis once wrote, a perfect epitome of the romantic attitude toward life. We realize our common humanity, and we develop our unique individuality, the romantics often insisted, only through love. It is through love that we unify our opposing powers – that we reconcile our reason and sensibility – because in loving someone I act on the rational principles of duty from, rather than contrary to, inclination. It is also through love that I fulfill my individuality because love derives from my innermost self, from my unique passions and desires, and it consists in a unique bond between myself and another. It is noteworthy that the romantic ethic of love has more classical than Christian roots; it has more affinities with Plato's *eros* than Paul's *agape*. In their youth Hölderlin, Schlegel, Schleiermacher, and Novalis were enthusiastic students of Plato, especially his *Symposium* and *Phaedrus*.

133

The romantic ethic of love has been profoundly influential in modern culture. It is easy to overlook its importance today if only because we have become such romantics. We take it for granted, for example, that marriage should be based first and foremost on love. But that assumption derives from a long battle first waged by the romantics. In late eighteenth-century Germany, as in most countries in Europe, marriage was usually understood as an alliance based on economic interests, its main purpose being to procreate and protect children. True to these beliefs, Kant himself defined marriage as a contract for the mutual use of the genitals. In the most passionate and indignant tones the romantics protested against such a doctrine, disclaiming against laws and customs that perpetuated loveless marriages. In their view a loveless marriage was no better than concubinage, and there was nothing wrong with cohabitation or even a *ménage à quatre*. The romantics combatted sexual stereotypes no less than rigid divorce laws. They defended a woman's right to education, and stressed that men should develop their tenderness and passivity as much as women their independence and assertiveness.

In insisting upon the importance of love for self-realization the romantics were following in the footsteps of their great predecessor, Jean-Jacques Rousseau. No one more stressed the need to educate human sensibility, to free the human capacity to love and be loved, than Rousseau. There can be no doubt that, in this respect, as in so many others, the romantics were influenced by him. They shared Rousseau's doctrines about the importance of developing natural bonds of affection, about the need to cultivate the child's independence, about the value of respecting the intrinsic qualities of childhood. Yet some of their most important differences with Rousseau concern the topics of love and sexuality. For one thing, Rousseau wrote of loveless marriages as if they were natural and inevitable. In his *La nouvelle Héloise*, for example, Julie, the heroine, renounces her feelings and marries a man she does not love, while her lover has to content himself with Platonic affection. For another thing, in *Émile* Rousseau endorsed the traditional sexual stereotypes by arguing that women should follow the authority of man and have a different education from them (Rousseau, 1979, p. 377). In both respects the romantics took issue with their great predecessor, whom they saw as much too conventional and traditional, and whom they faulted for failing to take his principles of independence and equality to their natural conclusions.

The Enlightenment and Educational Reform

The romantic ideal of *Bildung* reveals its full meaning and purpose only in its social and political context. This ideal was first and foremost a protest against the educational reforms of the German Enlightenment or *Aufklärung*, reforms which took place in the second half of the eighteenth century. In fundamental respects the young romantics rebelled against the ideology of the *Aufklärung*; and in no other domain was this rebellion more passionate than in the field of education. To understand this rebellion, we must first have some idea of the policies that provoked it.

It is no exaggeration to say that the central goal of the *Aufklärung* was education. To enlighten the public essentially meant to educate it: to improve its taste, to cultivate its intellect, and to free it from the chains of tradition, superstition, and prejudice. The importance of education for the *Aufklärung* was expressed eloquently and clearly by the *Aufklärer* Issak Iselin: "The happiness and the dignity of man consist in his doing as much good, and in his thinking as many great and beautiful things, as his capacities and circumstances permit. To lead and prepare him for such a grand vocation, to teach him how to be human, is to educate him; this is the greatest deed which one person can perform for humanity" (Hettner, 1979, I, p. 555).

Given the importance of education for the *Aufklärung*, it was only natural that the *Aufklärer* would set about reforming German universities and schools, whose structure and purpose were still those of the Middle Ages. The educational reforms arose chiefly in reaction against the arid scholasticism and religious controversy which had dominated university life for centuries. In late eighteenth-century Germany most universities and schools still had a religious function. The universities were essentially training grounds for clerics. The goal of both university and school education was *"sapiens atque eloquens pietas."* A university education would teach a student how to excel in the arts of rhetoric and dialectic, so that he could demonstrate the truth of his religion against opponents. The *rabies theologorium*, the zealotry of religious controversy, was widely regarded as one of the chief plagues of university life. Fitting its religious needs, the curriculum in both schools and universities focused on Latin, the Bible, and catechism.

The educational reforms of the late eighteenth century might be summarized in a single word: *utility (Nutzen)*. The demand for utility meant that learning should be directly relevant to life, that it should be useful for human needs, showing people the means to happiness. Hence the avowed aim of the *Aufklärer* was to break down that barrier between theory and practice, that gulf between learning and life, which had infected the world of medieval learning. The medievals treated learning as if it were an end in itself, as if its sole purpose were contemplation; but in believing this, the *Aufklärer* protested, they had made learning irrelevant to life.

There were two aspects behind the call for utility, depending on whose purpose learning should serve. In the first place learning would have to be useful for the student himself, so that he could acquire the knowledge and skills necessary for life. Hence the demand for utility sometimes meant professional or vocational training. In the second place, learning would also have to serve society and the state, so that the student would be a useful citizen. This second aspect, which is often overlooked, was crucial to the reform movement. The reforms of the schools and universities in the eighteenth century took place under the direction of, and indeed for the sake of, the absolutist state, which was in desperate need of an educated elite to fill its bureaucracy and administer its laws. Hence the reforms were simply another respect in which the absolutist state consolidated and expanded its power. Thanks to the reforms, the German university of the late eighteenth century ceased to be an autonomous corporation with an elected head and professors; instead, it became essentially a state institution, whose professors were appointed, promoted, and dismissed by the state.

The reform of German universities began in Halle in the early eighteenth century, and by mid-century it had spread to Leipzig and Göttingen. The reforms in Halle were directed by A. H. Francke and Christian Thomasius, who were weary of the religious controversy and scholasticism of the past, and who were determined that learning should be useful to pupil and the state. Hence they installed a more practical curriculum. In addition to Latin, theology and the Bible, students would now learn modern languages, the natural sciences, geography, mathematics, and history. Neither Francke nor Thomasius was sympathetic to the humanist tradition of learning, which emphasized learning the Greek and Roman classics. In their view, the study of such texts could have no direct practical relevance.

Undoubtedly, the most notable educational reforms of the *Aufklärung* were those of Johann Bernhard Basedow, whose school *Philanthropin* became a model throughout Germany. Like all *Aufklärer*, Basedow stressed the practical function of education; its chief goal should be to make a person happy. Basedow's ideals were in many respects like Rousseau's, though they were articulated even before *Émile*. Basedow stressed that the child should learn from direct experience and example rather than from verbal formulas and general precepts, that he should speak and write a language rather than learning by rote memory, that he should learn the principles of natural religion and not the catechism of any specific religion. In one respect Basedow took the new spirit of utility a radical step further: he was one of the first to advocate business education, learning the skills necessary for successful entrepreneurship. After all, what could be more useful to the state than the creation of wealth? Although Basedow's school soon failed, his example still proved contagious. Many schools throughout the German-speaking world were based upon it; and Basedow's efforts won the acclaim of some of the most prominent *Aufklärer*, among them Kant, Mendelssohn, Iselin, Garve, Nicolai, and Sulzer.

The Romantic Revolt

By the late 1790s, when the romantics came of age, the reform movement had already begun to grow old and to show its limitations. The demand for utility, so apparently reasonable in the face of a moribund scholasticism, had been pushed to an extreme. If learning is to be useful to the life of the student, then it easily degenerates into professionalism or vocationalism, into what contemporaries called *Brotstudium*, studying only what is necessary for one's career. Rather than acquiring a liberal education, one more apt to develop all one's talents, the student became a narrow specialist, a technician, a *Fachidiot*. If, furthermore, learning is to serve the state, then it is in danger of becoming a mere means to its ends, so that the student turns into a "cog in a machine." Here indeed lay a deep tension within the ideology of the *Aufklärung*: it proclaimed the value of intellectual autonomy, of thinking for oneself; yet it also preached that the student should be a servant of the state. Utility and autonomy were odd bedfellows, to say the least.

These consequences of the reform movement did not escape the young romantics. Although they say little about them, there can be no doubt that they knew them, and indeed were deeply affected by them. It is certainly significant that some of the leading romantics – Friedrich and August Wilhelm Schlegel, Novalis, Tieck, and Schleiermacher – attended universities where the reform movement had been especially active: Halle, Leipzig, and Göttingen. It is indeed fair to say – dramatic though it sounds –

that they were *victims* of the reform program. True to its narrow utilitarian spirit, their parents and teachers expected them to study for a business, legal, or clerical career, when their aspirations were to be writers, and when their inclinations were to study the classics, philosophy, and literature. Not surprisingly, then, the young romantics rebelled against the utilitarian mentality, which they felt to be a direct threat to their deepest ambitions. If they did not throw off the utilitarian yoke, they submitted to it with the greatest distaste and reluctance. Wackenroder, Tieck, and Friedrich Schlegel abandoned their legal careers, while Schelling, Hegel and Hölderlin escaped the clerical fate. Although Schleiermacher eventually became a cleric, he too rebelled against the utilitarian spirit at Halle, where he studied literature and philosophy more than theology. Of all the romantics only Novalis seemed to accept and to profit from his vocational training as a mine inspector; but he had that rare talent of turning a necessity into a virtue.

The romantic rebellion against the reform movement is especially evident in their critique of utilitarianism. Without a doubt, there was no aspect of the ideology of the *Aufklärung* the romantics more despised than its utilitarianism. The idea that culture was only a means to an end – whether it was a profession or the needs of state – filled them with contempt and indignation. In protest against the utilitarian spirit they insisted that the entire realm of culture – philosophy, science, and the arts – is an end in itself, having a value which transcends any of the uses to which it can be put. It is noteworthy how they revived the classical Aristotelian idea of the purpose of learning: contemplation. The purpose of philosophy, science, and art was contemplation or speculation, the intuition or experience of truth, regardless of its specific purposes. Both Schelling and Schleiermacher self-consciously reaffirmed this idea in protest against the utilitarian mentality of the *Aufklärung*.

The utilitarian spirit of the reforms blatantly violated every aspect of the romantic ideal of *Bildung*. If the student learns only what is necessary for his vocation, there can be no hope for the all-rounded development of the personality. If, furthermore, the student becomes a mere servant of the state, there cannot be any hope for the realization of individuality. The first condition of individuality, the romantics argued, was nothing less than freedom, the right of the individual to explore all kinds of possibilities in life. The more the state had a vested interest in education, however, the more such freedom would be curtailed. The romantics were sharp critics of the "machine state" of the *Aufklärung*, of the enlightened absolutism of Friedrich II of Prussia and Joseph II of Austria. Their hatred of absolutism made their opposition to the reforms inevitable, for they were simply another means of increasing state control over all aspects of life. It is not surprising, then, that Schelling and Schleiermacher both defended the autonomy of the university, its right to direct its own affairs independent of the powers of the state.

To counteract these dangers of the reform program, some of the romantics made their own proposals for reform of university curricula. One of their most important proposals is their insistence that philosophy should be the core of a university education. The great value of philosophy, Schelling and Schleiermacher argued, is that it gives the student a conception of the whole of knowledge, the fundamental principles and presuppositions behind all the more specialized fields of learning. It was the study of philosophy that would surmount the dangerous specializations of the modern age, and that would be able to address the need for an all-round education. The romantics' ideas for the curriculum were essentially inspired by the humanist tradition of education – the very tradition slighted by Francke and Thomasius. They admired the Renaissance ideal of the humanist scholar, the cosmopolitan intellectual who knew the classics, whose scope was the whole field of learning, and who could think and write well about all kinds of subjects. They stressed the value of learning the classical languages, not only as a means of knowing the classics but also as a form of intellectual discipline. It is indeed not inaccurate to see the romantic ideal of *Bildung* as a reaffirmation of the Renaissance ideal against the utilitarianism of the *Aufklärung*.

Human versus Political Education

For all their problems, the educational reforms of the late eighteenth century raised a fundamental question which the romantics could not avoid: what is the social and political purpose of education? If education were only an end in itself, as the romantics so often insisted, then it would seem to have no redeeming social or political value. But this only seemed to license the worst kind of moral and political irresponsibility, to endorse the worst sort of cultural elitism.

The romantics too would not have approved of such consequences. They did not want to return to an ivory tower elitism, to escape from social and political responsibility. Still less did they yearn to go back to the dark ages of scholasticism, where learning had a merely religious significance. While the romantics reject the utilitarian dogma that learning has value *only* if it serves extrinsic ends, they did not want to defend the opposite extreme: that it is *only* an end in itself. Although they stress that culture has an intrinsic value, they also insist that it should serve social and political ends. In general, they saw no conflict between recognizing the independent value of culture and giving it a social and political significance. Indeed, they believed that the more we developed culture for its own sake, the more useful it would be for all kinds of specific ends.

The romantic belief in the social and political role of education had its roots deep in their general political philosophy, and more specifically in their communitarianism. In fundamental respects the early romantics, like Rousseau, went back to the classical communitarian tradition, to the communitarian values of Plato and Aristotle. Like Plato and Aristotle, they believed that the purpose of the state should be the pursuit of the good life, the promotion of the excellence or self-realization of all its citizens. The romantics saw their community as a republic, where the interests of the whole would be determined by the general will of all citizens. Their commitment to the communitarian tradition made them reject the modern liberal idea that the purpose of the state is simply to protect the freedom of the individual to pursue his own happiness. They disputed an apparent assumption behind this theory of the state: that the individual is self-sufficient, having fixed desires and needs in the state of nature. Here again the romantics go back to the Aristotelian tradition, reaffirming Aristotle's dictum that, apart from the *polis*, man is either a beast or a god.

Such communitarianism meant that, no less than Plato and Aristotle, the romantics had to give the first importance to social and political education. After all, it was only through education that a human being became human, a citizen rather than a beast or god. Furthermore, it was also through education that the citizen acquired the virtue and wisdom necessary for a republic; only if the citizen could acquire moral and intellectual excellence would he have the capacity to make the laws. Hence, for the romantics, it was simply unthinkable for education to have no social or political function. Indeed, the irony is that the romantics had to give education much more social and political significance than any *Aufklärer*, who were more loyal to the liberal and absolutist traditions.

But the romantics' communitarianism left them with a quandary. They were deeply committed to the ideal of a social and political education; but they also despised the educational reforms because they seemed to make every individual a servant of the state, a cog in the machine of enlightened absolutism. This raised a very difficult question: how is it possible to educate a citizen and not a subject? How is it possible for education to be social and political yet to respect freedom?

This was the very issue that Rousseau faced at the beginning of his *Émile*. He too was inspired by the classical republican ideal, and he too believed that the success of a republic depends chiefly upon the education of its citizens. But to educate a citizen was impossible in the world as it was, for the simple reason that "where there is no longer fatherland there is no longer citizen" (Rousseau, 1979, p. 40). How could one educate a citizen for a republic if the republic still does not exist? All that existed in Rousseau's France was the absolutist state, which was intent on making passive subjects rather than active citizens.

In the face of this quandary Rousseau elaborated interlocking educational and political visions in *Émile* and *On the Social Contract*. For the education of a man for himself to coincide with the education of a citizen for his state, the form of direct democracy he envisioned in *On the Social Contract* would already have to exist. Such a democracy, for its part, could only succeed with citizens who remained both free and good through the forms of natural learning and discovery of the elements of natural religion, the civic religion suitable to a republic, envisioned in *Émile*. In the world as it was, such an education would have to be conducted privately and beyond the reach of corrupting influences.

It is noteworthy that, in his *Ästhetische Briefe*, a seminal work for the romantic school, Schiller encountered a comparable dilemma. At the beginning of this work Schiller noted a vicious circle facing any attempt to educate the citizen: a republic exists only if it consists of citizens having the virtue and wisdom to make laws; but citizens can be educated only if there is already a republic. Like Rousseau, Schiller maintains that the purpose of education should be to stimulate and cultivate the general intellectual and sensitive faculties, though without molding them for any specific ends. Such a general or liberal education will later be useful for all kinds of ends, though it does not bow to the constraints of any specific end. With their emphasis upon a human education Rousseau and Schiller believed that they could have it both ways: they could avoid making the individual into a tool of the absolute state yet also recognize the social and political value of education.

Rousseau's *Émile* and Schiller's *Briefe* were crucial precedents for the romantic approach to the problem of political education. The romantics accepted the essentials of Rousseau's and Schiller's solution to this problem. They too believed that, in the corrupt modern world, the education of the man should precede the education of the citizen. They too affirmed that the purpose of education is to develop one's general human powers, which can later serve all kinds of social and political ends. But, on one fundamental score, the romantics sided with Schiller against Rousseau. The difference is crucial, and indeed the fundamental dividing line between Rousseau and the romantic generation.

The Role of the Arts in Education

The basic difference concerns the role of the arts in education. In his infamous 1758 *Lettre à M. d'Alembert* Rousseau attacked the proposition that the arts could play a useful role in public education. Rather than educating the citizen, the arts were at best a form of amusement and entertainment. If they had any moral benefit at all, that was only because the spectator was already well educated; he got out of a play or poem only what he had already put into it. If Rousseau did not go as far as Plato in banishing poets from the republic, he did not see any reason to support them by creating a public theater. In his *Ästhetische Briefe* Schiller explicitly took issue with Rousseau and the Platonic tradition. Rather than banishing the artist from the republic, Schiller enthroned him. The ideal specimen of humanity was the artist; and the ideal state was "the aesthetic state," a perfect work of art.

While Schiller conceded that the arts were of little value in the education of the citizen, he stressed that they were decisive in the education of the man. The arts were indeed a more effective instrument of a human education than philosophy or religion. While philosophy could instruct only through the general precepts of reason, the arts could appeal directly to the heart and imagination, which were a far more powerful spring of human action than reason alone. While religion too could inspire the heart and the imagination, it was steadily losing its credibility due to the rational criticism of the Enlightenment; the arts had the advantage over religion that they did not require belief or faith. Schiller held that Plato's criticism of the arts in the *Republic* had failed to distinguish between deception and self-conscious semblance; the arts could corrupt no one as long as they were understood to be art. He also held that Plato failed to do justice to the problem of *akrasia*, or weakness of will; that he assumed incorrectly that to know the good is to act on it, whereas the only way to bridge the gap between knowledge and action is to appeal to the heart and imagination through the arts.

Schiller's argument for the arts in the *Briefe* did not rest simply on stressing their possible beneficial effects. Indeed, this point played an almost negligible role, since Schiller readily admitted that the arts could sometimes have harmful effects on spectators. The brunt of Schiller's argument on behalf of aesthetic education is his contention that human excellence has to be understood in aesthetic terms. Human excellence consists of the harmonious balance of our sensitive and intellectual powers, in the unity of rational principle form and sensible experience; but such a harmony of the sensitive and intellectual, such a unity of form and content, are defining characteristics of beauty itself. Hence, for Schiller, aesthetic education consists not simply of having our character formed by works of art but of making our characters into works of art.

It was Schiller's argument on behalf of the arts that had such a powerful impact on the romantic generation. Early German Romanticism was first and foremost an aesthetic movement, one which believed in the redemptive powers of art in the creation of culture. It was fundamentally this belief in the power of the arts that separated them from Plato and Rousseau, with whom they otherwise shared so many values. The romantics accepted Schiller's contention that the arts, rather than religion and philosophy, should be the leading power behind the moral education of mankind. They also endorsed his argument that human excellence should be defined in aesthetic terms. Hence Schlegel, Tieck, and Novalis would often say that the best life is the beautiful life, one where the individual forms all his experiences into an organic whole, as if it were a novel. The ideal society and state would be the "poetic" society and state, where rulers were directors of a vast public play in which all citizens were actors.

See also 1 THE SOCRATIC MOVEMENT; 6 ENLIGHTENMENT LIBERALISM; 7 ROUSSEAU, DEWEY, AND DEMOCRACY; 8 KANT, HEGEL, AND THE RISE OF PEDAGOGICAL SCIENCE; 10 HELLENISM, THE *GYMNASIUM*, AND *ALTERTUMSWISSENSCHAFT*; 15 THE NATURE AND PURPOSES OF EDUCATION; 26 AESTHETICS AND THE EDUCATIVE POWERS OF ART

References

Hardenberg, F. von (1960–88) *Novalis Schriften, kritische Ausgabe* [*Novalis's Writings, Critical Edition*], ed. R. Samuel, H. J. Mähl, and G. Schulz. Stuttgart: Kohlhammer.

Hettner, H. (1979) *Geschichte der deutschen Literatur im Achtzehnjahrhundert* [*History of German Literature in the Eighteenth Century*], 8th edn. Berlin: Aufbau.

Hölderlin, F. (1961) *Sämtliche Werke, Grosse Stuttgarter Ausgabe* [*Collected Works, Large Stuttgart Edition*], ed. F. Beissner. Stuttgart: Kohlhammer.

Rousseau, J.-J. (1979) *Émile*, ed. A. Bloom. New York: Basic Books.

Rousseau, J.-J. (1988) *On the Social Contract*, trans. D. Cress. Indianapolis: Hackett.

Schelling, F. W. J. (1856–61) *Vorlesungen über die Methode des akademischen Studiums* [*Lectures on the Method of Academic Study*]. In K. F. A. Schelling (ed.), *Sämtliche Werke* [*Collected Works*], 14 volumes. Stuttgart: Cotta.

Schiller, F. (1962) *Über die Ästhetische Erziehung des Menschen in Einer Reihe von Briefen* [*On the Aesthetic Education of Man, in a Series of Letters*]. In *Schillers Werke (Nationalausgabe)* [*Schiller's Works (National Edition)*], volume 20. Weimer: Hermann Böhlausnachfolger.

Schleiermacher, F. D. (1846) *Gelegentliche Gedanken über Universitäten in deutschen Sinn* [*Occasional Thoughts on Universities in the German Sense*]. In *Friedrich Schleiermacher's Sämmtliche Werke* [*Friedrich Schliermacher's Collected Works*], Band 1, Dritte Abtheilung [*Volume 1, third part*]. Berlin: Reimer.

Tieck, L. (1963) *Werke in vier Bänden* [*Works in Four Volumes*], ed. M. Thalmann. Munich: Winkler.

Further reading

Bruford, W. H. (1978) *Germany in the Eighteenth Century*. Cambridge: Cambridge University Press.

Paulsen, F. (1896) *Geschichte des Gelehrten Unterrichts auf den deutschen Schulen und Universitäten* [*History of Scholarly Instruction in German Schools and Universities*]. Leipzig: Veit.

Sagarra, E. (1977) *A Social History of Germany, 1648–1914*. London: Methuen.

Ziolkowski, T. (1990) *German Romanticism and Its Institutions*. Princeton, NJ: Princeton University Press.

10

The Past as Future? Hellenism, the *Gymnasium*, and *Altertumswissenschaft*

Wolfgang Mann

During the past twenty-five or so years, interest has increased considerably in three distinct, albeit related, phenomena of the nineteenth century: (1) cultural Hellenism, (2) the place of Greek (and Latin) in secondary and university education, and (3) the reorientation of classical philology under the banner of *Altertumswissenschaft*, i.e. the systematic and comprehensive study of Greek (and Roman) antiquity. English speaking readers have been well served by works devoted to developments in Britain. (On 1, see Jenkyns, 1980; Turner, 1981; on 2, see Clarke, 1959; Stray, 1998; on 3, which is most importantly a German phenomenon, see Grafton, 1983. Briggs and Calder, 1990, contains short biographical and bibliographical entries on many key individuals who figure in 3.) The rise, or reconstitution, of the *Gymnasium* (the premier sort of secondary school) in Germany, especially Prussia, has, unsurprisingly, received less attention in the English-language literature (but see Albisetti, 1983).

Here, I focus on developments in Germany (with only occasional glances at Britain). I do so, in part, precisely because they are less familiar. But the discussions about the goals of the *Gymnasia* and about the role of Greek (and Latin) are also quite interesting in their own right. Moreover, the partial implementation of those goals documents the importance of Hellenism, which was invoked to legitimate those goals; and the institutionalization of the study of Greek contributed to the rapid advance of *Altertumswissenschaft*, just as *Altertumswissenschaft* in turn enhanced the status of Greek as a secondary school subject. It is somewhat ironic, then, that the course which *Altertumswissenschaft* took ended up *undermining* the "philosophical" foundations of the *Gymnasium*. By the end of the nineteenth century, in the light of the changed conception of *Altertumswissenschaft*, the *Gymnasium* can easily appear to be what its critics charged it always was, namely an institution for reinforcing or creating class distinctions, where a mere veneer of "classical" learning serves to separate the elite (conceiving of itself as, in the first instance, a cultural elite, on the basis of its learning) from the masses. (For an analogous point about the English public schools, see Bowen, 1989; Stray, 1998.)

In addition, by the end of the century, the teaching imparted by the (by then) traditional *Gymnasium* seemed to many irrelevant, given the needs of contemporary society. Emblematic of this sense of irrelevance is a remark by Kaiser Wilhelm II, made at a conference devoted to educational reform in 1890: he said that while the

Gymnasium may indeed be well suited for producing young Greeks and Romans, it ought to be oriented to producing young Germans. The pressures on the traditional *Gymnasium* continued. The ultimate result of a further conference on educational reform (in 1900) was that, by 1908, the traditional *Gymnasium* (now called a "humanistic" *Gymnasium*) lost its monopoly as the gatekeeper to the German universities. Successful graduation from other kinds of secondary schools (some not offering Greek, some offering neither Greek nor Latin) also made possible matriculating at any German university – even though certain subjects, e.g. theology, continued to require Greek (see Albisetti, 1983, pp. 208–91). Latin continued being required for a greater range of subjects, but, again, not for university admission *per se*. (Similarly, after 1920, Cambridge and Oxford no longer required Greek for admission; the Latin requirement was only eliminated in 1960; see Murray, 2000, a useful corrective to Stray, 1998.) Thus for all practical purposes, the privileged status of Greek had come to an end before the First World War, even though the humanistic *Gymnasia* continued to enjoy special prestige for a long time afterwards.

However, in what follows, I concentrate on the formative period, and the role of Hellenism within it. In the second part, I consider the change in self-conception that *Altertumswissenschaft* underwent during the nineteenth and early twentieth centuries, and its impact on the theoretical foundations of the *Gymnasium*.

The *Gymnasium* as a "School for Mankind"

In the early years of the nineteenth century, a number of writers in Germany discuss the goals of (secondary) school education, and the proper constitution of the *Gymnasium* and its curriculum. Ernst August Evers (1779–1822), Reinhold Bernhard Jachmann (1767–1843), Friedrich Immanuel Niethammer (1766–1848), Franz Ludwig Passow (1786–1833), and, most famously, Wilhelm von Humboldt (1767–1835) argue for a radical reorientation and revitalization of education (see, for example, Humboldt, 1793a, b; Jachmann, 1812a, b, c; Passow, 1812a, b). Their neohumanism, as it is frequently called, was profoundly influential. (Humboldt, for example, was also to play a key role in the foundation of the University of Berlin (see Muhlack, 1978); indeed, his conception of the relation between teaching and research defined the path which, subsequently, all serious universities were eventually to profess to follow (Humboldt, 1809–10; cf. Grafton, 1983).) Crucial to the Neohumanists' program for secondary education was an essential and paradigmatic role for ancient Greece, more particularly an absolutely central place for the study of Greek within the *Gymnasium*. This centrality demands, and deserves, our attention.

First, a quick caveat. I am mostly not concerned with the actual development of the *Gymnasium* in Germany, and thus not with two serious *historical* questions: how well, or how poorly, did the *Gymnasia* live up to the ideals promulgated; and what part did the state play in furthering, or hindering, the implementation of those ideals? (The *realia* are discussed extensively in Jeismann, 1974, 1996; Kraul, 1980; Albisetti, 1983.) My subject is instead those ideals themselves and the rationales offered for them.

The German Neohumanists hold that the goal of education is the formation (*Bildung*) of "the whole human being," rather than the inculcation of various specialized, task- or profession-specific skills – which are frequently written off as mere "training for immediate circumstances" (*Bedarfsdressur für die Gegenwart*; see Evers, 1807, p. 52). Jachmann provides a striking formulation of the overall objective:

It is the purpose and duty of mankind to treat every person, from his youth onwards, as an image of God, and to arrange any and all institutions which are established for his education, so that the humanity [*Menschheit*] within him is fully developed and formed [*gebildet*]. Now since only *one* path can be the correct one towards this goal, it follows that there can be only *one* School for Mankind, and that each individual is given his own goal, not through different sorts of schooling, but only through his capacities and earthly circumstances – and for attaining that goal, he should use this School of Mankind for his education [*Ausbildung*]. (Jachmann, 1812a, p. 71)

(*Note*: Although Jachmann speaks of every person, he (and his contemporaries) are actually thinking only about the education of boys and young men; the issue of education for girls and young women, which became increasingly contentious during the course of the nineteenth century, would require a separate investigation. But see already Humboldt, 1795, for some awareness of the matter.) Self-realization thus makes people become better human beings, in the sense of realizing the human potential within themselves more fully. Moreover (see Jachmann, 1812a), by becoming better human beings, people will become better Germans – here understood as having a better relation to their own language, culture, and traditions – and thus, finally, better citizens. But, and this is emphasized in different ways by different writers, the goal of schooling precisely must *not* be simply producing loyal subjects. Indeed, any schooling with that aim will only reduce people to wretched slavery (Evers, 1807, pp. 59ff), making them similar to "conditioned dogs" (ibid., pp. 71ff). Instead (or so these figures argue), developing and perfecting human capacities *for the sakes of the persons themselves* is what results in individuals who will prove better citizens. Thus the state has a self-interested motive for promoting a kind of education that has no immediate connection with its state interests.

Certain of our own contemporaries might agree with the basic outlook of these figures, even if they would express themselves less high-mindedly. But matters take an abrupt turn when we consider the question: what exactly is supposed to happen in a school that actively furthers this kind of human development? The answer of course is: learning about ancient Greece, i.e. studying Greek. But that invites two obvious rejoinders. Why Greek? And, given the historical importance of Latin throughout all of Europe, why Greek rather than Latin? To the second question, there is a short and simple answer – because of the French:

At the very same time when Frederick the Great used the sword of war to break the control the French had over our nation, Lessing, using the sword of the mind [*das Schwerdt des Geistes*], freed us from their literary despotism, freed us from the essentially Roman way of thinking [*wesentlich Römische Anschauungsweise*] which ... underlies the French [way of thinking], and turned us towards *das Griechische*, which is related to the spirit of Protestantism and [to the spirit] of our nation.... (So one H. Schmidt wrote in 1849; cited in Sochatzy, 1973, p. 41)

The invocation of Rome by revolutionary and Napoleonic France no doubt contributed to keeping the posteriority of Rome – and thus of Latin – alive. More complicated factors include the massive upsurge of interest in ancient Greece as exemplifying "the classical." This conception of "the classical," while going back to the Renaissance, and in important ways even to antiquity itself, is most immediately the legacy of the eighteenth century. Relevant moments in its emergence include the official excavations at Herculaneum (begun 1738) and Pompeii (begun 1748); the travels to Athens by the British artists James Stuart and Nicholas Revett (1751–5), which led to their multivolume work, *The Antiquities of Athens, Measured and Delineated* (1769–1830); and, most importantly, the publication and reception of Johann Joachim Winckelmann's works, especially his *Geschichte der Kunst des Altertums* (1764). To exaggerate only slightly: in Germany (and also in England; see Turner, 1989), the Romans came to be seen as standing between the Greeks and the modern world, and so as being, at best, imperfect mediators of the classical tradition, with no real cultural contributions of their own; thus if one was interested in antiquity insofar as it was classical, it was best to bypass Rome and turn instead to the source, ancient Greece.

This brings us back to the first question. It is especially important, since there are three *prima facie* objections to making the study of Greek the foundation of secondary schooling. (A) The avowed goal of the Neohumanists was to present a program for *national*, i.e. German, education. But what does Greece have to do with Germany? This is the question which, as mentioned, the German emperor will press in 1890. (B) Greek is actually rather difficult. Thus it seems that, right from the start, an elitist bias is built into the idea of the *Gymnasium*, such that it *cannot* function as a broadly based institution. And this, too, seems to conflict with the objective of a genuinely national education. (C) Greek seems esoteric and irrelevant – so much so, that even given the stated lack of interest in immediately relevant learning, one might have doubts about its benefit. But the Neohumanists hold that Greece is special and exemplary in a way that ought simply to silence concerns B and C. (I return to A below.) Franz Passow, for example, writes:

at the bright dawn of the great world-day, the Hellenes stood in pure, pastoral natural-simplicity [*Unbefangenheit*]: Since they did not know doubt, which only guilt brings into the mind, they always did what was right out of inner necessity, and spurned what was alien without arrogance, and developed themselves from out of themselves, pure and undisturbed – and so they became the exemplary people [*Mustervolk*], by means of which God wanted to show what was possible for human beings. Thus the foundation [*Bedingung*] of their life and being was also perfected [*vollendet*] by them: their language, their literature and art, [and] their constitution [*Verfassung*]. (Passow, 1812b, p. 338)

The Greeks thus are the beginning, not just in the sense of being the historical origin *of* the West, but in the sense of being an *Urbild*, a trans-historical model *for* the West. Yet there is a problem: the history of the world, for many thinkers and writers from the end of the eighteenth and beginning of the nineteenth centuries, represents an (only semi-secularized) account of the Fall of Man. (Abrams, 1971, provides an excellent discussion of this idea in English and German Romanticism.) Therefore, those regarding Greece as exemplary often also see it as having been, or representing, the world *before* the Fall. Thus their Hellenism, which has been called "romantic" or "idealizing," is essentially *nostalgic*, pervaded by a sense of loss. And the task for thinking can seem to be nothing less than healing the post-lapsarian world.

146

Friedrich Schiller's well known poem "Die Götter Griechenlands" (1788) gives expression to that loss and offers an essentially poetic cure for it. (For textual issues and for the reactions of Schiller's contemporaries, see Frühwald, 1969.) Schiller contrasts our modern world with the ancient one. There, the Gods were omnipresent and had actually animated the world; that world was one of light and happiness, joy and celebration, with the Gods actively participating in our human lives. But with the advent of Christianity and its *one* God, with the advent of modern science, which has the sun being a mere "ball of fire, turning soullessly" (rather than being Helios, a God, "steering his golden chariot") and which sees nature as "slavishly" governed by impersonal laws, like "the law of gravity" – indeed, with the advent of the Enlightenment more generally the Gods became *müßig*: superfluous for us, and tired of our world. Nature has been *entgöttert*: emptied of the Gods. Schiller, giving a twist to the story of the Fall, has the Gods leaving us and returning "home" to the "realm of the poets," rather than us falling from, or out of, paradise. But the effect is similar; the last stanza begins:

> Ja, sie kehrten heim, und alles Schöne,
> Alles Hohe, nahmen sie mit Fort,
> Alle Farben, alle Lebenstöne,
> Und uns blieb nur das entseelte Wort.

> (Yes, they [the Greek Gods] returned home; and everything beautiful,
> Everything lofty, they took away:
> All colors, all the tones of life;
> For us there remained only the lifeless Word.)

The elegiac tone in evidence here had already been set in the first stanza. But the poem's conclusion – as well as its consolation – is a poetological one: "Was unsterblich im Gesang soll leben, / Muß im Leben untergehen." In other words, while there can be no restoration *realiter* of the Greek world, and the unity of Gods and humans characteristic of it, poetry can celebrate that world, and recreate, or at least represent, it in art. But for such loss, how much recompense is that?

Several of Friedrich Hölderlin's poems modify and radicalize the picture of antiquity and modernity in two ways. First, in a bold melding of Greek myths and the accounts of the Gospels (combined, in fact, with an attendant thoroughgoing removal of Jesus from his Judaic world), Christ is seen not so much as the initiator of a new age, but rather as the final manifestation of the ancient (Greek) world: Heracles, Dionysus, and Christ are *all* sons of (the highest) God, but with Christ's "departure," with the end of the "day" that was antiquity, there no longer is on earth any divine presence. And so the modern world seems to be just as *entgöttert* (emptied of the Gods) as it is in Schiller's poem. Yet, as the penultimate stanza of "Brod und Wein" (1800/1) indicates, *traces* of that presence remain (I follow the text of Beissner, 1951):

> Nemlich, als vor einiger Zeit, uns dünket sie lange,
>   Aufwärts stiegen sie all, welche das Leben beglükt,
> Als der Vater gewandt sein Angesicht von den Menschen,
>   Und das Trauern mit Recht über der Erde begann,

Als erschienen zu letzt ein stiller Genius, himmlisch
   Tröstend, welcher des Tags Ende verkündet' und schwand,
Ließ zum Zeichen, daß er einst da gewesen und wieder
   Käme, der himmlische Chor einige Gaaben zurük,
Derer menschlich, wie sonst, wir uns zu freuen vermöchten[.]

(For when some time ago – to us it seems very long –
   Upwards they stepped all, who bless life,
When the Father turned his face from mankind,
   And rightly mourning began all over the earth,
When there appeared, lastly, a Quiet Spirit who, offering
   Heavenly consolation, proclaimed the End of the Day, and vanished –
As a sign, that once He had been here and would again
   Come, the Heavenly Choir left a few gifts behind,
In which we might, humanly, as elsewhere, take joy.) (Lines 125–33)

Second, those traces – in this poem, the gifts of Bread and Wine which the Gods have left behind – are *signs* not only of their past presence, but of their promised *future* return. (In Hölderlin's imagery, the night of divine absence precedes a new day of divine presence; and the task of the poets during this night, i.e. during his, viz. our own, times, is to keep alive the memory of those signs *as* signs, and so to prepare for the new day.) What Hölderlin seems to be looking forward to is not so much the actual restoration of the Greek world as the transformation of the modern world so that it will be harmonious and whole, beautiful and good. Indeed, the world to come will be *more so* than the ancient world had been; thus the transformed world will be able to endure, unlike the ancient one, which, for all its beauty and goodness, nonetheless had perished (cf. the fragment in Beissner, 1951, p. 228). Nostalgia or mourning for the lost ancient past thus is not the only available stance – that very past is a source of hope, an image for a better future.

One might well wonder what these poetic utterances have to do with anything so prosaic as secondary schooling. For surely Jachmann, Passow, and Humboldt are not thinking in terms of the departure (or return) of the Greek Gods. But they too see the Greek world as having been a unified one – where that is not understood as a matter of divine presence, but rather in terms of the relations people have to each other, to their own activities, and indeed to themselves. We saw that Passow thinks that the Greeks fully actualized human possibilities. What exactly does he have in mind? At this crucial juncture (or so I would suggest), Passow and the other Neohumanists, whether they openly invoke it or not, rely on something like the picture of Athens as presented in Pericles' "Funeral Oration" from Thucydides' *History of the Peloponnesian War*, i.e. they proceed as if that picture were literally true, rather being than a literary construction, in the service of Pericles' (or Thucydides') ideologically circumscribed agenda. The striking feature of the Athens of the "Funeral Oration" is the combination of the unhampered private cultivation of diverse intellectual and cultural pursuits with a public ethos of civic harmony and solidarity – a combination which, according to the ideology of the speech, is never threatened by a possible tension between the two. Each *citizen* (and this means that each child, woman, slave, and foreign male resident is not part of the story) is able, in private, to develop whatever interests he likes; but when it comes to public affairs, he joins in with the *polis* as a whole, having been enriched by those private pursuits and recreations. For its part, the *polis* builds monuments (e.g. the Parthenon) and holds festivals (e.g. the Panathenaea) to celebrate itself publicly; but in doing so, the *polis* also enriches its citizens' private lives. And Thucydides' Pericles wants the citizens to reflect on this greatness of Athens (which depends on the mutually supporting relationship between the private and the public) until they become *lovers* of the city, and so are prepared to die for Athens, precisely because they know how great and valuable a thing it is for which they are fighting. Greek – i.e. Athenian – civilization thus is an unfragmented world, but not one where that unity is somehow imposed from outside, nor one where the harmony and solidarity among people threatens to obliterate a person's individuality. On the contrary, this harmony and solidarity makes for the greatness of the Athenians, while that greatness is what allows for, and contributes to, each person's individuality. And that very plurality of individuals (somehow) makes for the unity of the whole. (The implied contrast is with Sparta, where – in the eyes of democratic Athens – each Spartiate's individuality *is* sacrificed for the homogeneity of the whole *polis*.)

Now even if we could bring ourselves to accept all this, why think that we should study the Greek *language* rather than Greek *culture*? First, Greek is supposed to be a perfect language – in the sense of showing us most fully the possibilities inherent in human language. So studying Greek will enhance our understanding of language more generally and thus allow us to return to our vernaculars with a more sophisticated sense of language *tout court*; this (supposedly) will refine our sense of our own languages and make us better at them. There is, then, an instrumental value to studying Greek, which could not be realized by learning about the Greeks in German (or English). But this cannot be the whole story: for, with the European discovery of Sanskrit, one might argue that *Sanskrit* is really the language to be studied; not surprisingly, this route was not taken. Second, and more importantly, the Neohumanists see a given language not just as a vehicle that the culture which uses it (so to speak) *happens* to employ; the language instead *expresses* that culture – so that what is *essential* to a culture (or a people) cannot be preserved independently of its (their) language. In short: mastering the Greek language is constitutively involved in any understanding of Greek culture and civilization worthy of the name.

Humboldt explicitly embraces the consequences of so privileging Greek and thus simply rejects objections B and C, mentioned above. Just as one would not say that it is useless for a scholar to have learned how to make tables, so one should not say that it is useless for a carpenter to have learned Greek (Humboldt, 1809, p. 278). As a matter of fact, if everyone actually were to study the language, it would not be a divisive, elite-forming force separating people into two classes, a higher one that had studied Greek, and a lower one that had not. On the contrary, the study of Greek would exert a unifying force, since it would be the foundation of all education. And as Humboldt's arguments make clear, he really does envision a single kind of secondary school for all (see his 1809, pp. 259–68, 274–81). Indeed, there must be one and the same basis for all education: "the most lowly day-worker [*der gemeinste Tagelöhner*] and the most finely educated person [*der am feinsten Ausgebildete*] must initially be made to have the same mindset [*müßen in [ihrem] Gemüt ursprünglich gleich gestimmt werden*], if the former is not to turn out crude to a degree that lies beneath human

149

dignity, and the latter...is not to turn out sentimental, chimerical, and merely eccentric" (ibid., p. 278).

It is also clear that the *Bildung* acquired is not primarily something we might call "cultural literacy" (although this is what the term will later come to connote). No doubt, cultural literacy will be a part of what the Neohumanists hold *Bildung* leads to. But the Neohumanists in effect embrace and avow an Enlightenment picture of autonomous thinking (familiar to us from works like Kant's essay "What is Enlightenment?") according to which the educated person (*der gebildete Mensch*), rather than deferring to the authority of others, will be able to think *soundly* for himself about, among other matters, religious and moral questions. This soundness of thinking and judging – as opposed to thinking just anything that might happen to enter one's mind – is actually the most important part of *Bildung*. And, ultimately, the point of studying Greek, and understanding and valuing the civilization of the Greeks, is (as suggested) that this will allow each student to become fully human, which we can now gloss as: will bring about the relevant kind of intellectual autonomy, where that will presumably include an autonomous judgment to the effect that Greek culture embodies the highest manifestation of human possibilities. (Whether there can be any effective, non-question-begging argument in favor of this assessment of antiquity is of course another matter.)

Still, there is concern A. Why think that Greek is especially suited for *German* education? The passage from H. Schmidt quoted above asserts, in passing, the relationship of *das Griechische* with the spirit (*Geist*) of "our nation." This idea persists. Indeed, it eventually becomes so widespread, commonplace, and utterly empty that even Adolf Hitler could go on about German indebtedness to antiquity (see Näf, 1986, p. 285, n41 for an illustrative citation). But why believe in such a special affinity between (ancient) Greece and (modern) Germany? The idea, one suspects, seemed especially congenial for two reasons. First, because the Greek nation achieved "greatness," despite *not* having been united into a pan-Hellenic nation-state. (Only considerably later in the nineteenth century, and then in the twentieth century, do German ancient historians come to regard the period of Alexander the Great as the highpoint of Greek civilization; for the Neohumanists, that highpoint is Periclean Athens, or perhaps Athens until its final conquest by Phillip of Macedon.) Thus the hoped-for and about-to-be-achieved German "greatness" also need not depend on the existence of any single pan-German nation-state – obviously an encouraging idea in the early decades of the nineteenth century (when no such state existed). Second, because there *is* of course a genuinely close relationship between Latin and French. Affirming a close relationship between Greek and German, and so making the Germans be the heirs of Hellas, thus is a way of counterbalancing the implicit French claim to being the heirs of Rome. Moreover, given the priority of Greece over Rome, this inheritance can be used to trump the French claim: Germany is related to the truly *classical* nation of antiquity, not its imitators. (The tenuousness of these thoughts perhaps needs no elaboration; still it is striking that similar ideas, *mutatis mutandis*, are put forward in Britain about the relationship between the English and ancient Greece.)

A potentially more promising line of thinking has the Germans *becoming* Germans *via* the Greeks. Very roughly, the idea here is that whole nations undergo developments analogous to those which individuals undergo (infancy, childhood, adolescence,

150

maturity, and so on), and that just as one can write a *Bildungsroman* (a novel depicting the progress and "growth" of an individual) about a single person, so too there is the analogue of the *Bildungsroman*, to be "written" about a whole nation or people. And just as the hero of a *Bildungsroman* (to oversimplify enormously) needs to travel, encounter others, and so on, in order to become truly himself, so a nation or a people must proceed similarly in order to become truly itself. Indeed, as Hölderlin's novel *Hyperion* shows, the *Bildung* of an individual can even stand in for the (hoped for) development of the nation or people as a whole. This essentially Romantic schema would need to be filled in with a great deal of detail before we could venture to assess its plausibility. But we can already note a problem. It seems that someone could perfectly well argue that an encounter with, say, ancient India could play the same functional role (in the *Bildung* of the nation), and that there thus need be no special role for ancient Greece. This route (once again, not surprisingly) was not taken. Yet it seems that it was not taken, not because the Neohumanists (and similar figures) had principled reasons for orienting their thinking *vis-à-vis* only the Greeks, but because they presupposed and assumed all along the special and exemplary status of ancient, viz. *classical*, Greece. In short, their classicism would seem most compelling to those who were already committed to it.

Altertumswissenschaft and the Fate of Classicism

The story of the reorientation of philology, associated with the names of Friedrich August Wolf (1759–1824) (a close friend of Wilhelm von Humboldt) and Christian Heyne (1729–1812), Wolf's teacher, is an oft-told tale (a succinct and enjoyable telling of it is provided by Grafton, 1983). What matters for us is not the question of just which innovations (if any) should be ascribed to Wolf or his close contemporaries, but the fact that there is in Wolf's own work, right from the start, a serious tension, perhaps even an outright contradiction. On the one hand, Wolf wants to replace the tradition of commentary on, and emendation of, Greek (and Latin) texts, a tradition of which he himself is part, with a genuinely *scientific* enterprise, aimed at a systematic understanding of antiquity. Indeed, he introduces the term *Altertumswissenschaft*, which literally means "science of antiquity," for precisely this reason. Later in the century, this notion is associated especially with August Boeckh (1785–1867), and his advocacy of a so-called *Sachphilologie* (a philology of objects), as opposed to the so-called *Wortphilologie* (philology of words) of his opponent, Gottfried Hermann (1772–1848) (see Horstmann, 1992, pp. 101–15). What Boeckh, following this strand of Wolf's program, is calling for, is the systematic study of the whole of antiquity, including the use of sub-literary texts (e.g. inscriptions) and non-literary *realia* (e.g. the artifacts uncovered by archeology) as evidence to be utilized in that study. And what Boeckh is seeking is a historical understanding of antiquity of a sort where we cannot assume *ab initio* that the "great" works will contribute more, or prove of greater value, than seemingly minor ones. Thus we may in fact learn more about fifth-century Athens by painstakingly collecting, organizing, and studying inscriptions than by reading all of Athenian literature. One consequence of this approach is that the very notion of a "great" work is called into question, or is at least rendered

151

largely irrelevant. Moreover, the "greatness" of the Greeks – in the sense of having somehow been aesthetically or morally exemplary – is also undercut. For the study of actual Greek history, in all its concrete details, shows that the ancient world was not one of "sweetness and light"(Matthew Arnold's expression, but equally apt for the Greeks of the Neohumanists). But this then leaves the whole enterprise of *Altertums-wissenschaft* needing to address the question: what exactly is the purpose and value of studying ancient Greece (or Rome) supposed to be? The kind of answer the Neohu-manists had so enthusiastically given, it seems, is ruled out as naively mistaken: for "the science of antiquity" itself shows that we can no longer take for granted that studying "classical" antiquity will be edifying in the ways in which the Neohumanists held that it was.

On the other hand, Wolf himself remains fully in the grip of a classicizing or idealizing picture of antiquity, so much so that he holds that really only ancient Greece – and not Rome – is a suitable object of study. And part of his motivation for producing the *Prolegomena ad Homerum* (1795) is to defend Homer against his modern detractors, who often are champions of Vergil, the quintessentially Roman poet. In short, it is because Homer and the Greeks of the "classical" period are "great" that they and their language merit the attention and effort devoted to them by people like Wolf. Thus it is after all the great works which matter, not the minor ones – to say nothing of sub-literary texts. And the Greeks prove to be a special people after all.

Wolf's reputation contributed to the rapid rise of *Altertumswissenschaft* as a prestige subject in the universities during the nineteenth century. The universities thus were able to provide teachers – in many cases, extremely well educated ones – for the *Gymnasia*, just as the *Gymnasia* provided the universities with students – in many cases, very well prepared ones – of *Altertumswissenschaft* (Grafton, 1983). And as long as the tension was not really focused on, the two sides of Wolf's conception could actually reinforce each other. Thus the *Gymnasia* implicitly relied on a classicistic conception of antiquity. In effect, the justification for studying Greek (and Latin) was simply that it was valuable to do so, because it made for *Bildung*. The universities, on the other hand, increasingly more committed to research (see Turner, 1980; Grafton, 1983), could operate more "positivistically" (an expression used in these contexts for an allegedly value-free concentration on historical details, detached from any ques-tions about "greatness," about the exemplary status of this or that work, and so on). In fact, by the end of the nineteenth century, many prominent philologists and ancient historians take great pains to distance themselves from a classicistic or humanistic conception of their enterprises, and they do so despite (or, perhaps, precisely because of) having first come to those enterprises via the *Gymnasium*, with its classicistic picture of antiquity. This distancing comes across most clearly in the work of the Roman historian Theodor Mommsen (1817–1903). (It would be a nice irony of history, if, as it is sometimes said, more German *Gymnasia* are named after Mommsen than after anyone else.)

Yet a (sometimes unacknowledged) commitment to classicism within classical studies lived on. Consider Ulrich von Wilamowitz-Moellendorf (1848–1931), the most accomplished scholar of ancient Greek of his era. Wilamowitz tells us that the object of philology (which he *refuses* to call "classical") is "the essence [*Wesen*] of Greco-Roman culture and all the manifestations of its life"; and he maintains that this culture is a unity (*Einheit*) and thus needs to be studied as such (Wilamowitz-Moellendorf, 1921, p. 1). In a paper on philology and school reform, he says:

> Because this culture...is a unity, each of its manifestations [*Erscheinungen*], in its own individual life, can be fully understood only with reference to the whole, just as each tiniest manifestation [*Erscheinung*] contributes its bit to the understanding of the whole whence it originated and in which it continues to live on. Philology forms a unity, because the object of philology is [a single] one. The [Greek] particle *"an"* and Aristotle's doctrine of actuality, the sacred groves of Apollo and the idol Besas, the song of Sappho and the sermon of St Thecla, the metrics of Pindar's poetry and the measuring table of Pompeii, the grotesque faces on the Dipylon vases and the baths of Caracalla, the official documents of the magistrates of Abdera and the *Res Gestae* of the divine Augustus, the conic sections of Apollonius and the astrology of Petosiris: all, all belong to philology, for they all belong to the object which it aims to understand; and it cannot do without even a single one of them. (Wilamowitz-Moellendorf, 1892, p. 105)

Confronted with this astonishing list, one might ask, first, what justifies the assumption of unity? Second, suppose one granted that Greco-Roman civilization is, in some meaningful sense, unified – still, why assume that the unity is so strong and so pervasive that we need to understand the whole of that civilization so as to understand any part of it? (After all, even in the case of the human body – which surely has a far better claim to being a thoroughly unified entity than does the whole of antiquity – it is not obvious that one needs to have mastered, say, orthopedic surgery in order to understand disorders of the retina.) Most important, however, is this. Wilamowitz-Moellendorf evidently takes for granted that this "one object" is supremely worthy of study; therefore the question, why bother, never arises and so is never confronted. Even in his 1902 *Griechisches Lesebuch* (a reader, in line with Wilamowitz-Moellendorf's conception of philology, for students in the *Gymnasium*), which, with its impressively diverse selections from a wide range of authors normally *not* studied in schools (because they are not "classical"), gives us a concrete picture of what this expanded study of antiquity would look like if implemented at the secondary school level – even here, Wilamowitz-Moellendorf offers no rationale for the study of Greek, besides saying that many current ideas, practices, and institutions ultimately derive from the Greeks. (On the *Lesebuch*, see Canfora, 1985.)

Now it has frequently been observed that Wilamowitz-Moellendorf, in his own practice, did rely on something like a classicizing or idealizing conception of the Greeks (Reinhardt, 1941, p. 348, refers to this as the "charming contradiction" in Wilamowitz-Moellendorf's work). Certainly his accomplishments in teaching and scholarship, not to mention the fervor, industry, and learning with which he pursued them, suggest that he saw *special value* (beyond the absolute value of truth, which he affirmed unquestioningly and dogmatically) in the study of antiquity, such that even if the same qualities of mind could be developed with respect to another object of study, say the Trobriand Islanders, he would not have pursued that object with the same intensity, nor urged others to do so.

But the charming contradiction did not hold up: Wilamowitz-Moellendorf's successors could not maintain his enthusiasm and "missionary zeal" (see Reinhardt, 1941, p. 347) for the sake only of *Wissenschaft* and truth themselves. There were two significantly different kinds of responses to this predicament with which they felt themselves confronted.

One response was to embrace what we can safely call a kind of *irrationalism*. Classicists and ancient historians of this stripe – in some cases, actually members of the "Circle" of the poet and would-be visionary Stefan George (1868–1933) (Goldsmith, 1985), more frequently, simply "inspired" by him – claimed for themselves special insights into the Greeks which were supposedly deeper and more authentic than any that positivistic research (*Forschung*) could provide. They thus sought to preserve the privileged character of antiquity by sacrificing methods of inquiry which built on intersubjectively accepted results and aimed for intersubjective agreement. The question of how much this tendency contributed, whether intentionally or unintentionally, to the legitimation of National Socialism's claims to privileged, transhistorical insights of *its* own has been much discussed (see Patzig, 1978; Näf, 1986, 1995; Stahlmann, 1995). What is clear is that such a necessarily elitist and exclusivistic conception of the relationship between the privileged individual and antiquity is wholly at odds with the kind of classicism the Neohumanists had advocated. For they had regarded the greatness of Greek antiquity as essentially *transparent*, such that everyone, at least in principle, could benefit by, and see for himself the benefit of, an education centered on Greek. Indeed, for the Neohumanists, the point was for us ourselves to read the great works and to be shaped (*gebildet*) by them, not to wait for a "visionary" interpreter to tell us, on the basis of his quasi-mystical insights, what was "truly" going on in them.

There is also a further point. The kind of nationalism advocated by the Neohumanists was not intended to preclude internationalism; on the contrary, it was somehow supposed to be compatible with internationalism. However, certain proponents of the irrationalistic direction were also susceptible to a profoundly anti-internationalist thought. Just as antiquity was to be the province of special individuals, who would not "betray" the ancients by making them available, in an inevitably debased and even defiled form, to just anyone (Wilamowitz-Moellendorf was charged with having provided "a Plato for house-maids" by one of Stefan George's followers), so it was the province of a special people, with its spiritual (*geistig*) or (as it came increasingly to be put in the 1920s and 1930s) *racial* closeness to the Greeks, to safeguard antiquity from those other peoples who, in virtue of lacking that closeness, could not hope to "see" the essential truths and values of the ancient world. (It thus comes as no surprise to learn that some found the "truths" of National Socialism anticipated in antiquity. H. F. Günther is an especially notorious example. His "work" on Plato is discussed in Patzig, 1978, pp. 207–8, his "activity" as an ancient historian, in Näf, 1986, pp. 122–6.)

Werner Jaeger (1888–1961), Wilamowitz-Moellendorf's successor at the University of Berlin, perhaps best represents the other prominent kind of response to the predicament mentioned. Jaeger sought to recover a conception of "the classical" from within *Altertumswissenschaft*. Thus the historical knowledge gained during the nineteenth century (and still to be gained in the future) was not to be set aside on account of a "deeper" understanding of the "essence" of the Greeks. Rather, that deeper understanding, which would vindicate a picture of the Greeks as "classical," was to be won on the basis of philology and ancient history (of the familiar sort). The positivism of the nineteenth century, however, was to be rejected as a self-imposed and falsifying limitation on genuinely *understanding* antiquity, as opposed to merely *knowing* about it.

Jaeger presented his ideas often, beginning with a lecture in 1914 (reprinted in Jaeger, 1960), and culminating in his multivolume work, *Paideia: Die Formung des griechischen Menschen* (volume 1, 1933). Bruno Snell's devastating review (Snell, 1935) showed not only that Jaeger's rhetoric of a "classical" politics was so vacuous that it could be made to serve almost any political ideology, including National Socialism (cf. Näf, 1992; White, 1992), but also that there was no reason to think that *paideia* (= *Formung* [Formation] = *Bildung*) really was as central a notion for the Greeks as Jaeger tried to maintain. More precisely, Jaeger was imposing onto the Greeks a modern conception of *Bildung*, but one which (see Snell) was incompatible with what an unbiased reading of the ancient evidence would suggest. By this sleight of hand (and that, really, is Snell's charge), Jaeger made it possible to recover that *Bildung* just by turning to the Greeks. Jaeger presumably was prompted to proceed as he did because he recognized that simply learning Greek and looking at the Greeks (as Jachmann, Passow, and Humboldt – or so it seemed – had urged) would *not* yield the hoped for *Bildung*: the formation of a *whole* person, including his values and, quite generally, his orientation in thinking.

In short, the "positivism" of the nineteenth century proved not so easy to overcome; nor was it clear what one ended up with if one rejected positivism. Simply asserting that it was "the classical" only raised (once again) the question of what it means to say that the Greeks were, or are, "classical."

Symptomatic of the unclarity of the conception of Jaeger and his contemporaries, I would suggest, are the following remarks by W. Schadewaldt, made in 1930 at a conference organized by Jaeger, devoted to "the problem of 'the classical' and antiquity":

I rely on a picture of the classical, which we all bear within ourselves and which collectively arises in our memory, quite irrespective of whether we are thinking about Sophoclean tragedy or the Parthenon frieze. Our eyes are seized and led by a liberating force [*eine befreiende Gewalt*], which I would like to call the power of the surface [*Gewalt der Oberfläche*]. Because no swirling coercion [*kein strudelnder Zwang*] demands that we dive into torturous depths, and because no enticing magic of the unfathomable approaches us all too humanly [(*da*) ... *keine verlockende Magie des Unergründlichen uns allzu menschlich nahetritt*], we remain ourselves in the apprehension of that form [*im Anschauen jener Gestalt*] which is wholly itself. Without asking anything more of us than our intellectual-and-spiritual involvement [*geistige Teilnahme*]..., it [that form], from its own simplicity [*Einfalt*], bestows a calm abundance of inner joy [*eine ruhige Fülle innern Glücks*]. A harmony of line that does not bewitch us; a greatness of structure that does not oppress us; a movement [*Bewegtheit*] of inner and outer life that does not sweep us away along with it; a celebratory solemnness that is not grave [*feierlicher Ernst ohne Gravität*]; a pleasing gracefulness [*Anmut*] that is not mere play. There rests upon all of these an intellectual-and-spiritual nobility [*geistige Noblesse*] – a nobility to which, without any prompting, we show respect, and which heeds us to respect ourselves [*die uns zur Selbstachtung mahnt*]. Confronted with these images [*Bilder*], we, being as we are, are slightly ashamed, somewhat at a loss, and yet not humbled [... *leicht beschämt, verlegen, doch nicht gedemütigt*]. No, on the contrary, a cheerful belief in ourselves arises; we feel ourselves enlivened by a certain lightness and ease of our inner being [*erquickt in einer gewissen Leichtigkeit und Lockerheit unseres inneren*

Daseins], which could, by raising us above ourselves, raise us to ourselves [*die uns über uns selbst erheben könnte zu uns selbst*]. This, roughly, is the effect of a classical work. (Schadewaldt, 1931, pp. 15–16)

Schadewaldt sent a copy of the article from which this passage is taken to Wilamowitz-Moellendorf, who sent a postcard in reply, observing that he had always found the expression "the classical" "a horror show" (*eine Greuel*), and that he had actually never been able to make any sense of the notion, and so very much doubted that anyone else could do so either (cited in Henrichs, 1995, p. 447). Our initial shock at finding one of the greatest classical scholars saying, near the end of his long life, that he had no use for "the classical," I believe, dissipates on reading Schadewaldt's words. Schadewaldt insists, far too strenuously, on something which may have been natural for Winckelmann, Goethe, and Humboldt, and their contemporaries, but which was decidedly not a part of the world of 1930, where classical studies, and the humanistic *Gymnasium* in which Greek was taught, had already become far more marginal. Hitler could utter platitudes about the German indebtedness to classical antiquity, but in fact the National Socialist regime viewed the humanistic *Gymnasia* as inherently too elitist, and it did so despite the fact that German *Altertumswissenschaft* was, for the most part, not only not hostile to National Socialism, but in many cases all too eager to embrace it (see, for example, Näf, 1986, 1995; Stahlmann, 1995; Wegeler, 1996).

That fateful embrace, we may be tempted to think, contributed to the further marginalization of the humanistic *Gymnasium* (and to the continued decline of their actual number) following the Second World War, but especially in the years after 1968. Having so thoroughly compromised themselves in the National Socialist era, classical studies did not look like a promising foundation for a pluralistic and democratic society. Tempting, but likely only one factor, and probably not the most important one. For the parallel decline of Greek and Latin in British secondary education suggests that factors not specific to Germany were very much also at work (cf. Stray, 1998; Murray, 2000). The sense of the central importance of mathematics and the sciences in modern life on the one hand, and a commitment to the more immediate relevance of modern languages on the other, made the study of the ancient languages seem increasingly less important – and left less time for them in the curriculum.

One very clear indication that such a sense of lessened importance is *ours* as well, is that we find the rationales (for the study of Greek) offered by the Neohumanists to be mostly "chimerical" – to appropriate Humboldt's term. Moreover, as we have seen in brief, classical studies, beginning already in the nineteenth century itself, evolved in ways which not only undermined those rationales, but also failed to replace them with more compelling ones.

One may thus want to write off the entire movement to give ancient Greek a central place in secondary education, and all the steps taken, during the course of the nineteenth century, to institutionalize it as a school subject, as hopelessly misguided. Only from the peculiar cultural perspective of the late eighteenth and early nineteenth centuries could this so much as seem like a promising idea. In fact, even at the time, the "arguments" in favor of Greek were hardly compelling; to us, they look like wishful thinking, at best. Nonetheless, in an era where the discussion of education is all too often narrowly focused on topics like the so-called "digital divide," "computer literacy," and "improving test-scores," or producing individuals with the "skills" needed for a "twenty-first-century workforce," it may be salutary to remember the warnings of the Neohumanists against a *Bedarfsdressur für die Gegenwart*, a mere training for immediate (economic) circumstances. The ideal of a *rein menschliche Bildung*, an education of the whole person and its potentially liberating effects, including the ability to step back from (and thus be able critically to reflect on) exactly those circumstances, is worth keeping in view, despite the undoubted difficulties involved in giving sufficient content to that ideal for it in any way to prove practicable. Still, one might hold that providing such content is a task for the philosophy of education. What role the thinking of the Neohumanists (and similar figures, like Matthew Arnold) specifically, or cultural Hellenism more generally, could play in carrying it out – besides reminding us that at one time intellectuals were very much alive to the perceived *necessity* of engaging with exactly such a task – is of course another matter.

See also 1 THE SOCRATIC MOVEMENT; 2 STOICISM; 5 HUMANISM; 8 KANT, HEGEL, AND THE RISE OF PEDAGOGICAL SCIENCE; 9 ROMANTICISM

References

Abrams, M. H. (1971) *Natural Supernaturalism: Tradition and Revolution in Romantic Literature*. New York: W. W. Norton.

Albisetti, J. C. (1983) *Secondary School Reform in Imperial Germany*. Princeton, NJ: Princeton University Press.

Beissner, F. (ed.) (1951) *Hölderlin. Sämtliche Werke, Band 2: Gedichte nach 1800*. [*Hölderlin. Complete Works, volume 2: Poems after 1800*]. Grosse Stuttgarter Ausgabe. Stuttgart: W. Kohlhammer Verlag.

Bowen, J. (1989) Education, ideology and the ruling class: Hellenism and English public schools in the nineteenth century. In G. W. Clarke (ed.), *Rediscovering Hellenism: The Hellenic Inheritance and the English Imagination*. Cambridge: Cambridge University Press, pp. 161–86.

Briggs, W. W. and W. M. Calder III (eds) (1990) *Classical Scholarship: A Biographical Encyclopedia*. New York and London: Garland.

Calder, W. M. III (ed.) (1992) *Werner Jaeger Reconsidered*. Illinois Studies in the History of Classical Scholarship, volume 3. Atlanta: Scholars Press.

Calder, W. M. III, H. Flashar, and T. Lindken (eds) (1985) *Wilamowitz Nach 50 Jahren* [*Wilamowitz after 50 Years*]. Darmstadt: Wissenschaftliche Buchgesellschaft.

Canfora, L. (1985) Wilamowitz und die Schulreform: das "Griechische Lesebuch" [Wilamowitz and educational reform: the "Greek Reader"]. In W. M. Calder III, H. Flashar, and T. Lindken (eds), *Wilamowitz Nach 50 Jahren*. Darmstadt: Wissenschaftliche Buchgesellschaft, pp. 613–31.

Clarke, G. W. (ed.) (1989) *Rediscovering Hellenism: The Hellenic Inheritance and the English Imagination*. Cambridge: Cambridge University Press.

Clarke, M. L. (1959) *Classical Education in Britain 1500–1900*. Cambridge: Cambridge University Press.

Evers, E. A. (1807) *Über die Schulbildung zur Bestialität*. Aarau. Reprinted in R. Joerden (ed.), *Dokumente des Neuhumanismus* [*On Schooling towards Mere Animality*], 2nd edn. Weinheim: J. Belz (1962), pp. 46–87.

Flashar, H. (ed.) (1995) *Altertumswissenschaft in den 20er Jahren: Neue Fragen und Impulse* [*Classical Studies in the 1920s: New Questions and New Directions*]. Stuttgart: Franz Steiner Verlag.

Frühwald, W. (1969) Die Auseinandersetzung um Schillers Gedicht Die Götter Griechenlands" [The debate about Schiller's poem "The gods of Greece"]. *Jahrbuch der Deutschen Schillergesellschaft*, 13, 251–71.

Goldsmith, U. K. (1985) Wilamowitz and the *Georgekreis*: New documents. In W. M. Calder III, H. Flashar, and T. Lindken (eds), *Wilamowitz Nach 50 Jahren*. Darmstadt: Wissenschaftliche Buchgesellschaft, pp. 583–612.

Grafton, A. (1983) Polyhistor into *Philolog*: Notes on the transformation of German classical scholarship, 1780–1850. *History of Universities*, 3, 159–92.

Henrichs, A. (1995) Philologie und Wissenschaftsgeschichte: Zur Krise eines Selbsverständnisses [Philology and the history of science: on the crisis in an academic discipline's self-understanding]. In H. Flashar (ed.), *Altertumswissenschaft in den 20er Jahren: Neue Fragen und Impulse*. Stuttgart: Franz Steiner Verlag, pp. 424–57.

Horstmann, A. (1992) *Antike Theoria und Moderne Wissenschaft: August Boeckhs Konzeption der Philologie* [*Ancient Theoria and Modern "Science": August Boeckh's Conception of Philology*]. Frankfurt: Peter Lang.

Humboldt, W. von (1793a) Theorie der Bildung des Menschen (Bruchstück) [A theory of human education (fragment)]. In A. Leitzmann (ed.), *Wilhelm von Humboldts Gesammelte Schriften, Band 1*. Herausgegeben von der Preussischen Akademie der Wissenschaften. Berlin: B. Behr's Verlag (1903), pp. 282–7.

Humboldt, W. von (1793b) Über das Studium des Altertums und des griechischen insbesondere [On the study of antiquity, especially Greek]. In A. Leitzmann (ed.) *Wilhelm von Humboldts Gesammelte Schriften, Band 1*. Herausgegeben von der Preussischen Akademie der Wissenschaften. Berlin: B. Behr's Verlag (1903), pp. 255–81.

Humboldt, W. von (1795) Über die männliche und weibliche Form [On the male and the female form]. In A. Leitzmann (ed.) *Wilhelm von Humboldts Gesammelte Schriften, Band 1*. Herausgegeben von der Preussischen Akademie der Wissenschaften. Berlin: B. Behr's Verlag (1903), pp. 335–69.

Humboldt, W. von (1809) Der königsberger und der litauische Schulplan [The school-curricula of Königsberg and Lithuania]. In A. Leitzmann (ed.) *Wilhelm von Humboldts Gesammelte Schriften, Band 13*. Herausgegeben von der Preussischen Akademie der Wissenschaften. Berlin: B. Behr's Verlag (1920), pp. 259–83.

Humboldt, W. von (1809–10) Über die innere und äussere Organisation der höheren Wissenschaften in Berlin [On the internal and external organization of the higher academic disciplines in Berlin]. In A. von Harnack (ed.) *Geschichte der königlich preussischen Akademie der Wissenschaften zu Berlin, Band 2*. Berlin: Reichsdruckerei (1900), pp. 361–7.

Jachmann, R. B. (1812a) Ideen zur National-Bildungslehre [Ideas for a theory of national education]. In R. B. Jachmann and F. L. Passow (eds), *Archiv Deutscher Nationalbildung*. Berlin. Reprinted, with an introduction by H.-J. Heydorn. Frankfurt: Sauer und Auvermann (1969), pp. 1–45.

Jachmann, R. B. (1812b) Die Nationalschule [The national school]. In R. B. Jachmann and F. L. Passow (eds), *Archiv Deutscher Nationalbildung*. Berlin. Reprinted, with an introduction by H.-J. Heydorn. Frankfurt: Sauer und Auvermann (1969), pp. 61–98.

Jachmann, R. B. (1812c) Die Berücksichtigung der Individualität bey der Erziehung, nach dem Prinzip einer idealischen Erziehungslehre geprüft [Taking account of individuality in education, tested in accord with the principles of an idealist theory of education]. In R. B. Jachmann and F. L. Passow (eds), *Archiv Deutscher Nationalbildung*. Berlin. Reprinted, with an introduction by H.-J. Heydorn. Frankfurt: Sauer und Auvermann (1969), pp. 202–47.

Jachmann, R. B. and F. L. Passow (eds) (1812) *Archiv Deutscher Nationalbildung* [*Archive of German National Education*]. Berlin. Reprinted, with an introduction by H.-J. Heydorn. Frankfurt: Sauer und Auvermann (1969).

Jaeger, W. (1960) *Humanistische Reden und Vorträge*, 2nd edn. [*Humanistic Lectures*]. Berlin: Walter de Grutyer (1st edn, Berlin, 1937).

Jaeger, W. (ed.) (1931) *Das Problem des Klassischen und die Antike. Acht Vorträge gehalten auf der Fachtagung der klassischen Altertumswissenschaft zu Naumburg 1930* [*The Problem of the Classical and Antiquity: Eight Lectures Held at the Conference of Classical Studies in Naumburg, 1930*]. Leipzig and Berlin: Teubner.

Jeismann, K.-E. (1974) *Das preußische Gymnasium in Staat und Gesellschaft: Die Entstehung des Gymnasiums als Schule des Staates und der Gebildeten, 1787–1817* [*The Prussian Gymnasium in State and Society: The Origins of the Gymnasium as the School of the State and the Educated Classes*]. Industrielle Welt: Schriftenreihe des Arbeitskreises für moderne Sozialgeschichte, Band 15. Stuttgart: Ernst Klett Verlag.

Jeismann, K.-E. (1996) *Das preußische Gymnasium in Staat und Gesellschaft, Band 2: Höhere Bildung zwischen Reform und Reaktion, 1817–1859.* [*The Prussian Gymnasium in State and Society, volume 2: Education between the Forces of Reform and Reaction, 1817–1859*]. Industrielle Welt: Schriftenreihe des Arbeitskreises für moderne Sozialgeschichte, Band 56. Stuttgart: Klett-Cotta Verlag.

Jenkyns, R. (1980) *The Victorians and Ancient Greece.* Oxford: Oxford University Press.

Kraul, M. (1980) *Gymnasium und Gesellschaft im Vormärz* [*The Gymnasium and Society in the Period from 1815 to 1848*]. Studien zum Wandel von Gesellschaft und Bildung im Neunzehnten Jahrhundert, Band 18. Göttingen: Vandenhoeck und Ruprecht.

Muhlack, U. (1978) Die Universitäten im Zeichen von Neuhumanismus und Idealismus: Berlin [The influence of Neohumanism and Idealism on the universities: the case of Berlin]. In P. Baumgart and N. Hammerstein (eds), *Beiträge zu Problemen deutscher Universitätsgründungen der frühen Neuzeit.* Nendeln, Liechtenstein: KTO Press, pp. 299–340.

Murray, O. (2000) Classics in England [Review of Stray, 1998]. *Classical Review,* 50, 256–9.

Näf, B. (1986) *Von Perikles zu Hitler? Die athenische Demokratie und die deutsche Althistorie bis 1945* [*From Pericles to Hitler? Athenian Democracy and the Study of Ancient History in Germany through 1945*]. Europäische Hochschulschriften: Reihe III, Geschichte und ihre Hilfswissenschaften, Band 308). Bern: Peter Lang.

Näf, B. (1992) Werner Jaegers *Paideia*: Entstehung, kulturpolitische Absichten und Rezeption [Werner Jaeger's *Paideia*: its origins, goals for educational policy, and its reception]. In W. M. Calder III (ed.), *Werner Jaeger Reconsidered.* Illinois Studies in the History of Classical Scholarship, volume 3. Atlanta: Scholars Press, pp. 125–46.

Näf, B. (1995) Deutungen und Interpretationen der Griechischen Geschichte in den zwanziger Jahren [Interpretations of Greek history during the 1920s]. In H. Flashar (ed.), *Altertumswissenschaft in den 20er Jahren: Neue Fragen und Impulse.* Stuttgart: Franz Steiner Verlag, pp. 275–301.

Passow, F. (1812a) Die griechische Sprache, nach ihrer Bedeutung in der Bildung deutscher Jugend [The Greek language, as regards its significance for the education of German youth]. In R. B. Jachmann and F. L. Passow (eds), *Archiv Deutscher Nationalbildung.* Berlin. Reprinted, with an introduction by H.-J. Heydorn. Frankfurt: Sauer und Auvermann (1969), pp. 99–140.

Passow, F. (1812b) Der Griechischen Sprache pädagogischer Vorrang vor der Lateinischen, von der Schattenseite betrachtet [The pedagogical priority of Greek over Latin, as viewed from the shadow-side]. In R. B. Jachmann and F. L. Passow (eds), *Archiv Deutscher Nationalbildung.* Berlin. Reprinted, with an introduction by H.-J. Heydorn. Frankfurt: Sauer und Auvermann (1969), pp. 324–67.

Patzig, G. (1978) "Furchtbare Abstraktionen": Zur irrationalistischen Interpretation der griechischen Philosophie im Deutschland der 20er Jahre ["Terrible abstractions": On the irrationalistic interpretation of Greek philosophy in Germany during the 1920s]. In R. von Thadden (ed.) *Die Krise des Liberalismus zwischen den Weltkriegen*. Göttingen: Vandenhoeck und Ruprecht, pp. 193–210.

Reinhardt, K. (1941) Die klassische Philologie und das Klassische [Classical philology and the classical]. Reprinted in K. Reinhardt, *Vermächtnis der Antike*, 2nd edn. Göttingen: Vandenhoeck und Ruprecht (1966), pp. 334–60.

Schadewaldt, W. (1931) Begriff und Wesen der antiken Klassik [The concept and the essence of classical antiquity]. In W. Jaeger (ed.), *Das Problem des Klassischen und die Antike. Acht Vorträge gehalten auf der Fachtagung der klassischen Altertumswissenschaft zu Naumburg 1930*. Leipzig and Berlin: Teubner, pp. 15–32.

Snell, B. (1935) Review of Werner Jaeger: *Paideia. Die Formung des griechishen Menschen*, Band 1. *Göttingsche Gelehrte Anzeigen*, 197, 329–53.

Sochatzy, K. (1973) *Das Neuhumanistische Gymnasium und die rein-menschliche Bildung: Zwei Schulreformversuche in ihrer weiterreichenden Bedeutung* [The Neohumanistic Gymnasium and Wholly Human Education: Two Attempts at Educational Reform and Their Further Influence]. Studien zum Wandel von Gesellschaft und Bildung im Neunzehnten Jahrhundert, Band 6. Göttingen: Vandenhoeck und Ruprecht.

Stahlmann, I. (1995) "Nebelschwaden eines geschichtswidrigen Mystizismus"? Deutungen der Römischen Geschichte in den zwanziger Jahren ["Foggy swathes of antihistorical mysticism"? Interpretations of Roman history during the 1920s]. In H. Flashar (ed.), *Altertumswissenschaft in den 20er Jahren: Neue Fragen und Impulse*. Stuttgart: Franz Steiner Verlag, pp. 303–28.

Stray, C. (1998) *Classics Transformed: Schools, Universities, and Society in England, 1830–1960*. Oxford: Oxford University Press.

Turner, F. M. (1981) *The Greek Heritage in Victorian Britain*. New Haven, CT: Yale University Press.

Turner, F. M. (1989) Why the Greeks and not the Romans in Victorian Britain? In G. W. Clarke (ed.), *Rediscovering Hellenism: The Hellenic Inheritance and the English Imagination*. Cambridge: Cambridge University Press, pp. 61–81.

Turner, R. S. (1980) The Prussian universities and the concept of research. *Internationales Archiv für Sozialgeschichte der deutschen Literatur*, 5, 68–93.

Wegeler, C. (1996) "... wir sagen ab der internationalen Gelehrtenrepublik": Altertumswissenschaft und Nationalsozialismus. Das Göttinger Institut für Altertumskunde 1921–1962 ["... we are withdrawing from the international republic of letters": Classical Studies and the Institute for the Study of Antiquity at Göttingen, 1921–1961]. Vienna: Böhlau Verlag.

White, D. O. (1992) Werner Jaeger's "Third Humanism" and the crisis of conservative cultural politics in Weimar Germany. In W. M. Calder III (ed.), *Werner Jaeger Reconsidered*. Illinois Studies in the History of Classical Scholarship, volume 3. Atlanta: Scholars Press, pp. 267–88.

Wilamowitz-Moellendorf, U. von (1892) Philologie und Schulreform [Philology and educational reform]. Reprinted in his *Reden und Vorträge*, 3rd edn. Berlin: Weidmann (1913), pp. 98–119.

Wilamowitz-Moellendorf, U. von (1902) *Griechisches Lesebuch* [A Greek Reader]. Berlin: Weidmannsche Buchhandlung.

Wilamowitz-Moellendorf, U. von (1921) *Geschichte der Philologie* [A History of Philology]. Stuttgart and Leipzig: Teubner (3rd edn 1998).

Wolf, F. A. (1795) *Prolegomena to Homer*. Translated, with introduction and notes, by A. Grafton, G. W. Most, and J. E. G. Zetzel. Princeton, NJ: Princeton University Press (1985).

11

Critical Theory

Douglas Kellner

The theory associated with Marxism was developed in mid-nineteenth-century Europe by Karl Marx and Friedrich Engels. Although Marx and Engels did not write widely about education, they developed theoretical perspectives on modern societies that have been used to highlight the social functions of education, and their concepts and methods have served to theorize and criticize education in the reproduction of capitalist societies and to support projects of alternative education. In this chapter, I first briefly sketch the classical perspectives of Marx and Engels, highlighting the place of education in their work. Then, I outline the way that Marxian perspectives on education were developed in the Frankfurt School of critical theory, in British cultural studies, and in the global critical pedagogy movement emanating from the work of Paulo Freire. I argue that Marxism provides influential and robust perspectives on education, still of use, but that classical Marxism has certain omissions and limitations that contemporary theories of society and education need to overcome.

Marx and Engels: The Classical Paradigm

The materialist doctrine that men are products of circumstances and upbringing, and that, therefore, changed men are products of other circumstances and changed upbringing, forgets that it is men who change cirumstances and that it is essential to educate the educator himself.

Karl Marx

Both Marx and Engels left comfortable bourgeois families to pursue a life of revolutionary scholarship and struggle (see McLellan, 1973; Carver, 1989; Wheen, 2000). Meeting in Paris with Engels in 1843, Marx began studying economics and associated himself with communist groups, writing that,

When communist *artisans* form associations, education and propaganda are their first aims. But the very act of associating creates a new need – the need for society – and what appeared to be a means has become an end . . . the brotherhood of man is no empty phrase but a reality, and the nobility of man shines forth upon us from their toil-worn bodies. (Marx and Engels, CW4 [1844], p. 313)

Marx's collaborator Engels grew up in the German capitalist town of Barmen, his family owned factories, and he experienced the industrial revolution and rise of the working class at first hand. In his early writings, Engels describes the lot of the new industrial working class as a miserable one:

Work in low rooms where people breathe in more coal fumes and dust than oxygen – and in the majority of cases beginning already at the age of six – is bound to deprive them of all strength and joy in life. The weavers, who have individual looms in their homes, sit bent over them from morning till night, and desiccate their spinal marrow in front of a hot stove. Those who do not fall prey to mysticism are ruined by drunkenness. (Engels in CW2 [1839], p. 9)

Likewise, the "local-born leather workers are ruined physically and mentally after three years of work: three out of five die of consumption." In sum,

terrible poverty prevails among the lower classes, particularly the factory workers in Wuppertal; syphilis and lung diseases are so widespread as to be barely credible; in Elberfeld alone, out of 2,500 children of school age 1,200 are deprived of education and grow up in the factories – merely so that the manufacturer need not pay the adults, whose place they take, twice the wage he pays a child. (Engels, CW2, p. 10)

The young Marx and Engels thus perceived that without education the working class was condemned to lives of drudgery and death, but that with education they had a chance to create a better life. In their famous 1848 "Communist Manifesto," Marx and Engels argued that growing economic crises would throw ever more segments of the middle classes, and the older peasant and artisan classes, into the impoverished situation of the proletariat and would thus produce a unified working class, or one with common interests at any rate. They declared that the bourgeois class is constantly battling against the older feudal powers, among its own segments, and against the foreign bourgeoisie, and thus enlists the proletariat as its ally. Consequently, the proletariat gains education and experience which it can use to fight the ruling class. As bourgeois society dissolves, a section of the bourgeoisie goes over to the proletariat, including a radical intelligentsia "who have raised themselves to the level of comprehending theoretically the historical movement as a whole" (CW6 [1848], p. 494).

In the *Manifesto*, expanded public education for the working class was one of the major demands, and henceforth both Marx and Engels saw themselves as providing education and theoretical guidance to the working class and socialist movement. Marx and Engels did not write much on educational institutions in bourgeois society, or develop models of education in socialist societies. Yet their historical materialist theory of history has been used to theorize and critique educational institutions within bourgeois society and to develop alternative conceptions of education that are in accord with Marxian socialist principles. As the "Thesis from Feuerbach" that opens this section suggests, changing social conditions create new forms of education, so that the rise of capitalist-bourgeois societies would produce educational institutions that reproduce dominant social relations, values, and practices. Likewise, transforming capitalist societies and creating socialist ones requires new modes of education and socialization.

The classical Marxian paradigm thus sees education as functioning within the hegemonic social system which is organized by and serves the interest of capital, while calling for alternative modes of education that would prepare students and citizens for more progressive socialist modes of social organization. Marx and Engels envisaged education and free time as essential to developing free individuals and creating many-sided human beings. The sketch of socialism in *The German Ideology* – where one would "hunt in the morning, fish in the afternoon, rear cattle in the evening, criticize after dinner, just as I have a mind, without ever becoming hunter, fisherman, shepherd or critic" (*CW*5, p. 47) – reflects the ideals of a non-alienated life in which education is a key part of the life process.

Marx argued in his 1857–8 notebooks, collected under the name of the *Grundrisse*, that increasing free time under socialism would allow for more education and development of a social individual who can then enter "in the direct production process as this different subject. This process is then both discipline, as regards the human being in the process of becoming; and, at the same time, practice [*Ausubung*], experimental science, materially creative and objectifying science, as regards the human being who has become, in whose head exists the accumulated knowledge of society" (Marx and Engels, 1978, p. 290). For Marx, transforming social relations would produce the basis for a new society of non-alienated labor in which individuals could utilize their free time to fully develop their human capacities and labor itself would be a process of experimentation, creativity, and progress. In the vision of a free society sketched out in the *Grundrisse*, the system of automation would produce most of society's goods, and individuals could thus enjoy leisure and the fruits of creative work, whereby education would become an essential part of the life-process.

Such a society would be a completely different social order from that of capitalist society, which is organized around work and the production of commodities. Marx acknowledges that the new society would have a totally "*changed* foundation of production, a new foundation first created by the process of history" (Marx and Engels, 1978, p. 293). In the third volume of *Capital*, Marx described this radically new social order in terms of a "realm of freedom," writing "Freedom in this field can only consist in socialized man, the associated producers, rationally regulating their interchange with Nature, bringing it under their common control, instead of being ruled by it as by the blind forces of Nature; and achieving this with the least expenditure of energy and under conditions most favourable to, and worthy of, their human nature" (Marx and Engels, 1978, p. 441).

Marx's most distinctive vision of socialism thus envisages socialism as constituting a break in history as dramatic as the rupture between pre-capitalist and capitalist societies that produced modernity. While capitalism is a commodity-producing society organized around work and production, socialism would be a social order aiming at the full development of individual human beings. Marx formulated this radical vision of a new society in his late text *Critique of the Gotha Program* (1875) as the product of a transition to a higher phase of communism. In the first stage, the "prolonged birth pangs from capitalist society" would limit the level of social and individual development, but:

> In a higher phase of communist society, after the enslaving subordination of the individual to the division of labor, and therewith also the antithesis between mental and physical labour, has vanished; after labour has become not only a means of life but life's prime want; after the productive forces have also increased with the all-round development of the individual, and all the springs of cooperative wealth flow more abundantly – only then can the narrow horizon of bourgeois right be crossed in its entirety and society inscribe on its banner: From each according to his ability, to each according to his needs! (Marx and Engels, 1978, p. 531)

Thus in Marx's utopian vision of communism, education would help to fully develop socialized individuals, create a cooperative and harmonious society, and unleash creativity in all its forms. In historical retrospect, however, the classical Marxian theory's lack of a more fully articulated theory of education and subjectivity, and of the subjective conditions of revolutionary transformation, vitiated its theory and practice. Marx seemed to think that class and revolutionary consciousness would develop naturally, as a result of the workers' position in the process of production. Subsequent Marxian theorists, however, engaged in a heated debate concerning whether class consciousness would develop spontaneously (as Rosa Luxembourg claimed), or would have to be brought to the workers from outside (as Kautsky and Lenin argued). And later generations of neo-Marxian theorists would develop more sophisticated theories of consciousness, communication, and education, whereby political subjectivities could be formed which would strive for socialist or democratic social change.

Succeeding generations of Marxists perceived that the classical paradigm over-emphasized the dimension of class, and overlooked the importance of gender, race, sexuality, and other key constituents of human experience, lacunae filled in by many neo-Marxian theories, as I note in the following sections. Moreover, many of Marx's texts also seem to place too heavy an emphasis on labor as the distinctly human activity, as the key to the development of the human being. Overemphasis on production is accompanied by an inadequate concept of intersubjectivity, lacking a fully developed theory of individual consciousness and its development in communication, symbolic action, and culture. Unlike later social theorists such as Émile Durkheim, George Herbert Mead, John Dewey, and Jürgen Habermas, Marx failed to perceive the importance of wider communication in the development of new forms of association and solidarity. He thus put too much emphasis on class struggle, on direct action, and not enough on communication and democracy.

Indeed, Marx never grasped the significance of the institutions of liberal democracy as an important heritage of modern societies that should be absorbed into socialism. Although he espoused a model of radical democratic self-government in his writings on the Paris Commune, and while he long championed democracy as an ideal, he never properly appreciated the separation of powers and system of rights, checks and balances, and democratic participation developed within bourgeois society. Thus, Marx had an inadequate theory of education and democracy, and failed to develop an institutional theory of democracy, its constraints under capitalism, and how socialism would make possible fuller and richer democracy. These lacunae in the classical Marxian theory would be filled by later generations of Marxist theorists.

Within the Marxian tradition, a tremendous variety and diversity of different schools, movements, and positions have evolved. In the following narrative, I will trace developments within key neo-Marxian traditions, including those of the Frankfurt School, British cultural studies, and a diverse grouping of neo-and post-Marxian positions covered by the label of "critical pedagogy." In these traditions, certain positions overlap and there are also divergences based, in part, on responses to different socio-historical conditions in the trajectory from state and organized capitalism in the 1930s to the resurgence of neo-liberalism and return to market capitalism in the 1980s. The dynamics of globalization and a variety of anti-globalization movements from the 1990s to the present have also generated a global proliferation of the various formations of neo-Marxian theory which has produced a dizzying diversity of Marxian discourse.

Other narratives of the trajectory of Marxism and education have traced the development of different positions within education through the prisms of Antonio Gramsci, Louis Althusser and structural Marxism, and reproduction theory, as well as the schools that I chart (see Morrow and Torres, 1995). There have also been studies of the role of Marxian ideas in curriculum and schooling in capitalist societies (see Pinar et. al., 1996, pp. 243ff), as well as presentations of contemporary debates within Marxian theory on a vast range of topics in the field of education (see Rikowski, 1996, 1997; Hill, 2001; *Cultural Logic*, 2001). I, however, focus on the development of perspectives on education within the tradition of critical social theory and pedagogy developed by Western Marxism.

The Frankfurt School, Culture, and Regimes of Capital

Frankfurt School theorists have rarely explicitly addressed problems of education and pedagogy, although I will suggest that their critique of the culture industries provides an important model of Marxian cultural studies and pedagogy that anticipates the Birmingham School and provides important contributions to educational philosophy today. The Frankfurt School's concern with consciousness, ideology, culture, and socialization highlights the importance of transforming individuals and societies through change of consciousness, culture, and the institutions of everyday life such as education.

In Weimar Germany in the early 1930s, the Frankfurt School were carrying out research into the family and authority, and were concluding that the family was declining as an agent of authority, giving way to the media, peer groups, schooling, and other institutions. In exile in the United States after 1934, the Frankfurt School focused on the role of the media in educating and socializing individuals. To a large extent, the Frankfurt School inaugurated critical studies of mass communication and culture, and thus produced an early model of cultural studies (see Kellner, 1989, 1995). In a wide-ranging set of studies and texts, the group developed a critical and transdisciplinary approach to cultural and communications studies, combining critique of political economy of the media, analysis of texts, and audience reception

165

studies of the social and ideological effects of mass culture and communications (see Jay, 1973; Arato and Gebhardt, 1982; Bronner and Kellner, 1989; Kellner, 1989; Wiggershaus, 1994).

The Frankfurt School theorists coined the term "culture industries" to signify the industrialization of mass-produced culture and its commercial imperatives. The group analyzed all mass-mediated cultural artifacts within the context of industrial production, in which the products of the culture industries exhibited the same features as other goods of mass production: commodification, standardization, and massification. They held, however, that the culture industries had the specific function of providing ideological legitimation of the existing capitalist societies and of integrating individuals into the framework of its social formation. Theodor Adorno's analyses of popular music (1932, 1941, 1982, 1989), Leo Lowenthal's studies of popular literature and magazines (1961), Herta Hertzog's studies of radio soap operas (1941), and the critiques of mass culture developed in Max Horkheimer and Adorno's famous study of the culture industries (1972; Adorno, 1991) provide many examples of the value of the critical theory approach. Moreover, in their theories of the culture industries and critiques of mass culture, they were the first to systematically analyze and criticize mass-mediated culture and communications within critical social theory. The critical theorists scrutinized the pedagogical and social functions of the culture industries in the reproduction of contemporary societies, and held that mass culture and communications stand at the center of leisure activity, are important agents of socialization and education, are mediators of political reality, and should thus be seen as major institutions of contemporary societies with a variety of economic, political, cultural, and social effects.

Furthermore, the critical theorists investigated the cultural industries in a political context as a form of the integration of the working class into capitalist societies. The group were among the first neo-Marxian theorists to examine the effects of mass culture and the rise of the consumer society on the working classes which were to be the instrument of revolution in the classical Marxian scenario. They also analyzed the ways that the culture industries and consumer society were performing new kinds of pedagogy and stabilizing contemporary capitalism. Accordingly, they sought novel strategies for political change, agencies of political transformation, and models for political emancipation that could serve as norms of social critique and goals for political struggle. This project required rethinking the Marxian project and produced many important contributions, as well as some problematical positions.

After the Second World War, the critical theorists examined how the state and public education produced a form of *Halb-Bildung* (half-education), and they called for education that fully developed individual subjectivities. Their form of "critical theory" emphasized the importance of critique, reflexivity, and the achievement of emancipatory consciousness, free from indoctrination and socialization. Although the Frankfurt School did not systematically explore the institutions of higher education, Adorno, Horkheimer, Herbert Marcuse, and Habermas wrote occasional critiques of the university and intervened frequently in educational debates.

In retrospect, one can see the Frankfurt group's critical theory as an articulation of a stage of capitalism that has been dubbed "Fordism," an era of mass production and consumption characterized by uniformity and homogeneity of needs, thought, and behavior producing a "mass society" and what the Frankfurt School described as "the end of the individual" (Kellner, 1989). The era corresponds to the staid, ascetic, conformist, and conservative world of corporate capitalism that was dominant in the 1950s, with its organization men and women, its mass consumption, and its mass culture. It was against this background that Herbert Marcuse criticized the ways that educational institutions, the media, and other forms of socialization were creating conformist modes of thought and behavior, producing what he called "one-dimensional man" (Marcuse, 1964).

Thus, the Frankfurt School theory of mass culture articulates a major historical shift to an era in which mass consumption and culture were indispensable to producing a consumer society based on homogeneous needs and desires for mass-produced products. In this context, the media and public education helped to generate a mass society based on social organization and homogeneity. It is culturally the period of highly controlled network radio and television, insipid top forty pop music, glossy Hollywood films, national magazines, and standardized public schooling.

Of course, media culture and schooling were never as massified and homogeneous as in the Frankfurt School model. Indeed, one could argue that the model was flawed even during its time of origin and influence and that other models were preferable, such as those of Walter Benjamin (1969), Siegfried Kracauer (1995), Ernst Bloch (1986), and others of the Weimar generation. Yet the original critical theory model of the culture industry and mass society did articulate the vital social roles of media culture and schooling during a specific regime of capital. It provided a model, still of use, of a highly commercial and technologically advanced culture that serves the needs of dominant corporate interests, and plays a major role in ideological reproduction and in enculturating individuals into the dominant system of needs, thought, and behavior. The Frankfurt School also influenced and helped to produce other neo-Marxian approaches to culture, society, and education as we see in what follows.

The Trajectories of Cultural Studies

It may be argued, then, that British cultural studies emerged in a later era of capital, on the cusp of what became known as "post-Fordism" and a more variegated and conflicted cultural formation. The forms of culture described by the earliest phase of British cultural studies in the 1950s and early 1960s articulated conditions in an era in which there were still significant tensions in England and much of Europe between an older working class-based culture and the newer mass-produced culture whose models and exemplars were the products of American culture industries. The initial project of cultural studies developed by Richard Hoggart, Raymond Williams, and E. P. Thompson attempted to preserve working-class culture against onslaughts of mass culture produced by the culture industries.

Thompson's (1963) historical inquiries into the history of British working-class institutions and struggles, the defenses of working-class culture and education by Hoggart (1957) and Williams (1961, 1962), and their attacks on mass culture were part of a socialist and working-class-oriented project that assumed that the industrial working class was a force of progressive social change and that it could be mobilized and organized to struggle against the inequalities of the existing capitalist societies and for a more egalitarian socialist one. Williams and Hoggart were deeply involved in projects of working-class education and oriented toward socialist working-class politics, seeing their form of cultural studies as an instrument of progressive social change.

The early critiques in the first wave of British cultural studies of Americanism and mass culture, in Hoggart, Williams, and others, thus paralleled to some extent the earlier critique of the Frankfurt School, yet valorized a working class that the critical theorists saw as defeated in Germany and much of Europe during the era of fascism, and in any event never a strong resource for emancipatory social change. The early work of the Birmingham school, as I will now argue, was continuous with the radicalism of the first wave of British cultural studies (the Hoggart–Thompson– Williams "culture and society" tradition) and, in important ways, with the Frankfurt. School. Yet, as I suggest below, the Birmingham project also paved the way for a postmodern populist turn in cultural studies, which responds to a later stage of capitalism.

It has not yet been widely recognized that the second stage of the development of British cultural studies – starting with the founding of the University of Birmingham Centre for Contemporary Cultural Studies in 1963/4 by Hoggart and Stuart Hall – shared many key perspectives with the Frankfurt School (Kellner, 1997). During this period, the Centre developed a variety of critical approaches for the analysis, inter- pretation, and criticism of cultural artifacts (see Hall, 1980b; Johnson, 1986/7; Grossberg et al., 1992; McGuigan, 1992; During, 1993; Kellner, 1995; Durham and Kellner, 2001).

Through a set of internal debates, and responding to social struggles and move- ments of the 1960s and the 1970s, the Birmingham group came to focus on the interplay of representations and ideologies of class, gender, race, ethnicity, and nationality in cultural texts, including media culture. Like the Frankfurt School, they analyzed critically the pedagogical effects of newspapers, radio, television, film, music, and other popular cultural forms on audiences, and they developed critiques of schooling in Britain. They also focused on how and why various audiences in various contexts interpreted and used media culture in different ways.

The now classical period of British cultural studies from the early 1960s to the early 1980s were marked by continued adoption of Marxian approaches to the study of culture, especially ones influenced by Althusser and Gramsci (see Hall, 1980a; Johnson, 1986/7). Yet although Hall and his colleagues usually omit the Frankfurt School from their narratives of their history and influences, some of the work done by the Birmingham group replicated certain classical positions of the Frankfurt School, in their social theory and methodological models for doing cultural studies, as well as in their political perspectives and strategies. Like the Frankfurt School, British cultural studies observed the integration of the working class and its decline of revolutionary consciousness, and studied the conditions of this catastrophe for the Marxian project of revolution. Like the Frankfurt School, British cultural studies concluded that mass culture was playing an important role in integrating the working class into existing capitalist societies and that a new consumer and media culture was forming a new mode of capitalist hegemony.

Both traditions focused on the intersections of culture and ideology and saw ideology critique as central to a critical cultural studies (CCCS, 1980a, b). Both viewed culture as a mode of ideological reproduction and hegemony, in which educational institutions and cultural forms help to shape the modes of thought and behavior that induce individuals to adapt to the social conditions of capitalist societies. Both also interpreted culture as a potential form of resistance to capitalist society and both the earlier forerunners of British cultural studies, especially Raymond Williams, and the theorists of the Frankfurt School perceived high culture as a force of resistance to capitalist modernity. Later, British cultural studies would celebrate resistant moments in media culture and audience interpretations and use of media artifacts, while the Frankfurt School tended, with some exceptions, to view mass culture as a homogeneous and potent form of ideological domination – a difference that would seriously divide the two traditions.

From the beginning, British cultural studies was highly political in nature and focused on the potentials for resistance to capitalist hegemony in oppositional subcultures, first working-class cultures, then youth subcultures. Unlike the classical Frankfurt School (but similar to Herbert Marcuse), British cultural studies turned to youth cultures as providing potentially new forms of opposition and social change. Through studies of youth subcultures, British cultural studies demonstrated how subcultural formations came to constitute distinct forms of identity and group membership, and appraised the oppositional potential of various youth subcultures (see Jefferson, 1976; Hebdige, 1979).

British cultural studies also investigated how schooling integrates youth into capitalist societies and the ways that working-class youth rebel and resist. Paul Willis's now classic *Learning to Labor* (1981) carried out ethnographic and critical studies of how working-class youth confront disciplinary schooling that tries to get them to conform to authority and middle-class values and mores. Willis documented modes of both disciplinary schooling and resistance, showing how working-class youth rebel and construct identities outside of schooling and middle-class norms.

Within the university, British cultural studies developed interdisciplinary programs to study the intersection of culture, society, and politics, and developed critiques of academic fragmentation and disciplinarity. British cultural studies insisted, as the Frankfurt School did, that culture must be studied within the social, political, and economic systems through which it is produced and consumed. British cultural studies and the Frankfurt School were thus both founded as fundamentally transdisciplinary enterprises which resisted established academic divisions of labor, denied the autonomy of culture and the various disciplines, and thereby implicitly revolutionized university education. Employing Gramsci's model of hegemony and counterhegemony, cultural studies sought to analyze "hegemonic," or ruling, social and cultural forces of domination and to seek "counterhegemonic" forces of resistance and struggle. The project was aimed at social transformation and attempted to specify forces of domination and resistance in order to aid the process of political struggle and emancipation from oppression and domination.

Some earlier authoritative presentations of British cultural studies stressed the importance of a transdisciplinary approach to the study of culture that analyzed its political economy, process of production and distribution, textual products, and reception by the audience – positions remarkably similar to the Frankfurt School. For instance, in his classic programmatic article, "Encoding/Decoding," Stuart Hall (1980b, pp. 128ff) began his analysis by using Marx's *Grundrisse* as a model to trace the articulations of "a continuous circuit," encompassing "production–distribution–consumption–production." Hall concretizes this model with focus on how media institutions produce meanings, how they circulate, and how audiences use or decode the texts to produce meaning. Moreover, in a 1983 lecture published in 1986/7, Richard Johnson provided a model of cultural studies, similar to Hall's earlier model, based on a diagram of the circuits of production, textuality, and reception, parallel to the circuits of capital stressed by Marx, illustrated by a diagram that stressed the importance of production and distribution. Although Johnson (1986/7, pp. 63ff) emphasized the importance of analysis of production in cultural studies and criticized the abandonment of this perspective in favor of more idealist and textualist approaches, much work in British and North American cultural studies has replicated the neglect of production and political economy.

In more recent cultural studies, however, there has been a turn, throughout the English-speaking world, to what might be called a "postmodern" problematic which emphasizes pleasure, consumption, and the individual construction of identities in what McGuigan (1992) has called a "cultural populism" and "new revisionism." Media culture from this perspective produces material for identities, pleasures, and empowerment, and thus audiences constitute the "popular" through their selective consumption of cultural products. During this phase, roughly from the mid-1980s to the present, cultural studies in Britain and North America has turned from the socialist and revolutionary politics of the previous stages to postmodern forms of identity politics and less critical (economic, historical, and political) perspectives on media and consumer culture. Emphasis has been placed more and more on the audience, consumption, and reception, and less and less on production and distribution of texts by the media industries. This revisionist cultural populism is associated in postmodernism theory with an abandonment of Marxism and its alleged reductionism, master narratives of liberation and domination, and historical teleology.

In context, the forms of cultural studies developed from the late 1970s to the present reflect a shift from the stage of state monopoly capitalism, or Fordism, rooted in mass production and consumption, to a new regime of capital and social order, sometimes described as "post-Fordism" (Harvey, 1989), or "postmodernism" (Jameson, 1991), to a global form of capital characterized by difference, multiplicity, eclecticism, populism, and intensified consumerism in a new information and entertainment society. From this perspective, the proliferating media culture, postmodern architecture, shopping malls, and culture of the postmodern spectacle become the promoters and palaces of a new stage of technocapitalism, purveying a postmodern image and culture of consumer choice (see Best and Kellner, 1997, 2001).

Critical Pedagogy from Freire to North America and Beyond

The pedagogy of the oppressed ... is a task for radicals; it cannot be carried out by sectarians. (Paulo Freire)

Alongside of the proliferation of neo-Marxian theories of culture and society and globalization of cultural studies, forms of an oppositional critical pedagogy emerged that explicitly criticized schooling in capitalist societies while calling for more emancipatory modes of education. In his now classic *The Pedagogy of the Oppressed* (1972), Brazilian educator and activist Paulo Freire criticized the "banking concept of education," while calling for more interactive, dialogical, and participatory forms of pedagogy that are similar in interesting ways to those of John Dewey. While Dewey wanted education to produce citizens for democracy, however, Freire sought, in the spirit of Marxist revolutionary praxis, to develop a pedagogy of the oppressed that would produce revolutionary subjects, empowered to overthrow oppression and to create a more democratic and just social order.

Freire's pedagogy of the oppressed seeks to transform individuals from being objects of educational processes to subjects of their own autonomy and emancipation. Freire suggests that classical Marxism had not adequately developed the subjective and pedagogical dimension and that the oppressed must be educated so that they can perform their own self-emancipation. Setting up schools that practiced his critical pedagogy in his native Brazil, Freire was expelled when a military dictatorship took over his country, but continued his work in Chile and throughout the world until his death.

Freire's work found resonance on a global scale and by the 1980s there were many schools of critical pedagogy. In North America, a series of books on Freire appeared and groups and individuals took up his ideas in a variety of contexts (see McLaren and Leonard, 1993). Theorists such as Henry Giroux, Donaldo Macedo, Carlos Torres, and Peter McLaren linked Freiren perspectives with those of Frankfurt School critical theory and other neo-Marxian approaches in works from the 1990s to the present. Cultural theorists and educators developed critical pedagogies of media and representation, and articulated neo-Marxian class perspectives with those of gender, race, and multiculturalism (see Luke and Gore, 1992; hooks, 1994; McLaren et al., 1995; Steinberg, 2001; the journal *Taboo*). Feminists, poststructuralists and others criticized what they saw as biases and limitations of critical pedagogy (e.g. Lather, 2001), and there were sharp debates over the value or limitations of the continuing role of Marxism within critical pedagogy.

Henry Giroux's early work was frequently linked to Michael Apple's attempts to link neo-Gramscian theories of hegemony to analyses of capitalist schooling as instruments of corporate power and domination, such as those of Samuel Bowles and Herbert Gintis (1976; on Giroux and Apple, see Morrow and Torres, 1995). Apple was more influenced by Althusserian structural Marxism and Bowles and Gintis's critique of schooling in capitalist society. Both Giroux and Apple, however, saw the need for theories of resistance, transforming education in the interests of radical democracy, and bringing in multiculturalist problematics that would address issues of gender and race, as well as class. These moves led Marxist critics to suggest that they were abandoning Marxism for democratic populism, although one could argue that they were reconstructing Marxism for the present age, in the spirit of a revisionist dialectic.

Giroux urged movement from a language of critique to a language of hope and possibility, combining critique of the dominant mode of schooling with advocacy of resistance and alternative conceptions of education. After publishing a series of books on contemporary education and critical pedagogy, Giroux turned to cultural studies in the late 1980s to enrich education with expanded conceptions of pedagogy and literacy (see Giroux, 1992, pp. 180ff). This cultural turn was animated by a desire to reconstruct schooling with critical perspectives that can help us to better understand and transform contemporary culture and society. Giroux's work provides cultural studies with a critical pedagogy missing in many versions and a sustained attempt to link critical pedagogy and cultural studies with the development of a more democratic culture and citizenry. The result is a fusion of critical pedagogy and cultural studies that enhances both enterprises, providing a cultural and transformative political dimension to critical pedagogy and a pedagogical dimension to cultural studies (see Giroux 2000a, b, 2001).

The recent work of Peter McLaren adopts a Marxist–humanist perspective, and advocates a return to classical Marxism as a strategy to transform educational practices within a larger project of social and cultural transformation. McLaren's most recent book, *Che Guevara, Paulo Freire, and the Pedagogy of Revolution* (2000), sets out to introduce educators to the life and politics of Che Guevara; to recover the legacy of Paulo Freire from the interpretive efforts of educational humanists who have for the most part depotentiated the revolutionary import of Freire's teachings and largely domesticated the Marxist trajectory of his politics; and to analyze the philosophical and political writings of these two figures in the context of their pedagogical theories and practices. In McLaren's view, the work of Marxist revolutionaries is too often overlooked in discussions of educational theory and pedagogical practice.

The many works of Carlos Torres also navigate through the Marxian tradition and advance the positions of Paulo Freire and critical pedagogy. In addition to producing much on Freire, Torres has published important books in the political sociology of education and comparative education from neo-Marxian perspectives on topics such as education, the state, and power; the role of schooling in social and cultural reproduction; the role of social theory in comprehending the nature and conflicts in contemporary education; the problematics of globalization; the interconnections between citizens, multiculturalism, and democracy; the ways that a democratic restructuring of schooling involve engaging the problematics of gender, race, and class in constructing pedagogies that promote agency, solidarity, and respect for difference, and ultimately create a more just and democratic society; and the contributions of critical pedagogy to transforming education and democratizing society (see Torres, 1998).

Concluding Comments

Recent discussions of globalization, education, and the potential imposition of business models on educational institutions throughout the world, point to the continuing relevance of Marxian perspectives for educational philosophy and practice today (see Burbules and Torres, 2000). Indeed, the continuing viability of Marxian perspectives today is bound up with the continuing expansion of capitalism in a global economy and the growing importance of the economy in every domain of life. Marxism has historically presented critical perspectives on capitalism and the ways that economic imperatives shape institutions like schooling to correspond to the interests of the ruling class. Neo-Marxist theories have sought to overcome a too-narrow focus on class and economics by stressing the importance of developing theories of agency and resistance and incorporating dimensions of gender, race, sexuality, and other subject positions into an expanded notion of multicultural education, democratization, and social justice. The type of structuralist Marxist theories of capital and schooling that began to circulate in the 1970s have been largely replaced by more poststructuralist versions of Marxism that articulate together gender, race, class, and other subject positions (see Morrow and Torres, 1995), although some Marxist critics of postmodern theories have called for a reassertion of the centrality of class and capital in a Marxist philosophy of education (see McLaren, 1998). Neo-Marxist theories have also developed a wide range of proposals for the reconstruction of education and development of alternative pedagogies and educational practices. These neo-Marxian positions are fiercely contested by conservative positions, however, and the field of education remains today a contested terrain where neo-Marxian positions are part of the force of opposition.

See also 14 POSTMODERNISM; 15 THE NATURE AND PURPOSES OF EDUCATION; 32 EDUCATION AND STANDARDS OF LIVING; 33 EDUCATIONAL EQUALITY AND JUSTICE; 35 EDUCATION AND THE POLITICS OF IDENTITY; 40 UNIVERSITIES IN A FLUID AGE

References

Adorno, T. W. (1932) On the social situation of music. Reprinted in *Telos*, 35 (Spring 1978), 129–65.

Adorno, T. W. (1941) On popular music (with G. Simpson). *Studies in Philosophy and Social Science*, 9(1), 17–48.

Adorno, T. W. (1982) On the fetish character of music and the regression of hearing. In A. Arato and E. Gebhardt (eds), *The Essential Frankfurt School Reader*. New York: Continuum, pp. 270–99.

Adorno, T. W. (1989) On jazz. In S. Bronner and D. Kellner (eds), *Critical Theory and Society: A Reader*. New York: Routledge, pp. 199–209.

Adorno, T. W. (1991) *The Culture Industry*. London: Routledge.

Arato, A. and Gebhardt, E. (eds) (1982) *The Essential Frankfurt School Reader*. New York: Continuum.

Benjamin, W. (1969) *Illuminations*. New York: Shocken.

Best, S. and Kellner, D. (1997) *The Postmodern Turn*. New York: Guilford Press.

Best, S. and Kellner, D. (2001) *The Postmodern Adventure*. New York: Guilford Press.

Bloch, E. (1986) *The Principle of Hope*. Cambridge, MA: MIT Press.

Bowles, S. and Gintis, H. (1976) *Schooling in Capitalist America*. New York: Basic Books.

Bronner, S. and Kellner, D. (eds) (1989) *Critical Theory and Society: A Reader*. New York: Routledge.

Burbules, N. and Torres, C. (eds) (2000) *Globalization and Education*. London and New York: Routledge.

Carver, T. (1989) *Friedrich Engels: His Life and Thought*. London: Macmillan.

Centre for Contemporary Cultural Studies (1980a) *On Ideology*. London: Hutchinson.

Centre for Contemporary Cultural Studies (1980b) *Culture, Media, Language*. London: Hutchinson.

Cultural Logic (2001) Special issue: Marxism and education. http://eserver.org/clogic/4–1/4/1.html

Durham, M. G. and Kellner, D. (2001) *Media and Cultural Studies: Key Works*. Malden, MA and Oxford: Blackwell.

During, S. (ed.) (1993) *The Cultural Studies Reader*. London and New York: Routledge.

Freire, P. (1972) *The Pedagogy of the Oppressed*. New York: Herder and Herder.

Giroux, H. (1992) *Border Crossings: Cultural Workers and the Politics of Education*. New York: Routledge.

Giroux, H. (2000a) *Stealing Innocence*. New York: St Martin's Press.

Giroux, H. (2000b) *Impure Acts: The Practical Politics of Cultural Studies*. New York and London: Routledge.

Giroux, H. (2001) *Public Spaces, Private Lives*. Lanham, MD: Rowman and Littlefield.

Grossberg, L., Nelson, C. and Treichler, P. (1992) *Cultural Studies*. New York: Routledge.

Hall, S. (1980a) Cultural studies and the centre: some problematics and problems. In S. Hall et al. (eds), *Culture, Media, Language*. London: Hutchinson, pp. 15–47.

Hall, S. (1980b) Encoding/decoding. In S. Hall et al. (eds), *Culture, Media, Language*. London: Hutchinson, pp. 128–38.

Hall, S. et al. (eds) (1980) *Culture, Media, Language*. London: Hutchinson.

Harvey, D. (1989) *The Condition of Postmodernity*. Cambridge: Polity Press.

Hebdige, D. (1979) *Subculture: The Meaning of Style*. London: Methuen.

Hertzog, H. (1941) On borrowed experience: an analysis of listening to daytime sketches. *Studies in Philosophy and Social Science*, 9(1), 65–95.

Hill, D. (2001) State theory and the neo-liberal reconstruction of schooling. *British Journal of Sociology of Education*, 22(1), 135–55.

Hoggart, R. (1957) *The Uses of Literacy*. New York: Oxford University Press.

hooks, b. (1994) *Teaching to Transgress*. London and New York: Routledge.

Horkheimer, M. and Adorno, T. W. (1972) *Dialectic of Enlightenment*. New York: Herder and Herder.

Jameson, F. (1991) *Postmodernism, or the Cultural Logic of Late Capitalism*. Durham, NC: Duke University Press.

Jay, M. (1973) *The Dialectical Imagination*. Boston: Little, Brown and Company.

Jefferson, T. (ed.) (1976) *Resistance through Rituals*. London: Hutchinson.

Johnson, R. (1986/7) What is cultural studies anyway? *Social Text*, 16, 38–80.

Kellner, D. (1989) *Critical Theory, Marxism, and Modernity*. Cambridge: Polity Press; Baltimore: Johns Hopkins University Press.

Kellner, D. (1995) *Media Culture: Cultural Studies, Identity, and Politics between the Modern and the Postmodern*. London and New York: Routledge.

Kellner, D. (1997) Critical theory and British cultural studies: the missed articulation. In J. McGuigan (ed.), *Cultural Methodologies*. London: Sage, pp. 12–41.

Kracauer, S. (1995) *The Mass Ornament*. Cambridge, MA: Harvard University Press.

Lather, P. (2001) Ten years later, yet again: critical pedagogy and its complicities. In K. Weiler (ed.), *Feminist Engagements*. London and New York: Routledge, pp. 183–95.

Lowenthal, L. (1961) *Literature, Popular Culture and Society*. Englewood Cliffs, NJ: Prentice Hall.

Luke, C. and Gore, J. (1992) *Feminisms and Critical Pedagogy*. London and New York: Routledge.

McGuigan, J. (1992) *Cultural Populism*. London and New York: Routledge.

McLaren, P. (1998) Revolutionary pedagogy in post-revolutionary times: rethinking the political economy of critical education. *Educational Theory*, 48(4), 431–62.

McLaren, P. (2000) *Che Guevara, Paulo Freire, and the Pedagogy of Revolution*. Boulder, CO: Rowman and Littlefield.

McLaren, P., Hammer, R., Reily, S. and Sholle, D. (1995) *Rethinking Media Literacy: A Critical Pedagogy of Representation*. New York: Peter Lang.

McLaren, P. and Leonard, P. (1993) *Paulo Friere: A Critical Encounter*. London and New York: Routledge.

McLellan, D. (1973) *Karl Marx: His Life and Thought*. New York: Harper and Row.

Marcuse, H. (1964) *One-dimensional Man*. Boston: Beacon Press (2nd edn, Beacon and Routledge, 1999).

Marx, K. and Engels, F. (1975–) *Collected Works*. New York and London: International Publishers and Lawrence & Wishart (referred to in text as *CW* with volume number, e.g. *CW*5).

Marx, K. and Engels, F. (1978) *The Marx–Engels Reader*, ed. R. Tucker. New York: Norton.

Morrow, R. A. and Torres, C. A. (1995) *Social Theory and Education*. Albany: State University of New York Press.

Pinar, W. F., Reynolds, W. M., Slattery, P. and Taubman, P. M. (1996) *Understanding Curriculum*. New York: Peter Lang.

Rikowski, G. (1996) Left alone: end time for Marxist educational theory? *British Journal of Sociology of Education*, 17(4), 415–37.

Rikowski, G. (1997) Scorched earth: prelude to rebuilding Marxist educational theory. *British Journal of Sociology of Education*, 18(4), 551–74.

Steinberg, S. R. (2001) *Multi/Intercultural Conversations*. New York: Peter Lang.

Thompson, E. P. (1963) *The Making of the English Working Class*. New York: Pantheon.

Torres, C. (1998) *Democracy, Education, and Multiculturalism: Dilemmas of Citizenship in a Global World*. London and New York: Routledge.

Wiggershaus, R. (1994) *The Frankfurt School*. Cambridge: Polity Press.

Wheen, F. (2000) *Karl Marx: A Life*. New York: Norton.

Williams, R. (1961) *The Long Revolution*. London: Chatto and Windus.

Williams, R. (1962) *Communications*. London: Penguin.

Willis, P. (1981) *Learning to Labor*. New York: Columbia University Press.

12

The Analytical Movement

Randall Curren, Emily Robertson, and Paul Hager

References to philosophical "analysis" have been common since the seventeenth century, but the terms "analytic philosophy" and "analytical philosophy" refer more specifically to the mid-twentieth-century confluence and descendants of the work of Gottlob Frege (1848–1925), G. E. Moore (1873–1958), Bertrand Russell (1872–1970), Ludwig Wittgenstein (1889–1951), Rudolph Carnap (1891–1970), Gilbert Ryle (1900–76), J. L. Austin (1911–60), W. V. O. Quine (1908–2000), Wilfred Sellars (1912–89), and others. Analytical philosophy is not a "school of thought" united by shared doctrines, but a loosely defined style of investigation employing a variety of logical, linguistic, and epistemological methods, predicated on the belief that such methods are useful in solving a variety of philosophical problems, or dissolving philosophical confusions. These methods include techniques of definition, articulating and evaluating arguments, and making explicit the structure of thoughts, bodies of thought, and normative relationships, including ones that obtain between persons, institutions, and the like. For the most part analytical philosophers have regarded these methods as useful and central to philosophical inquiry – though not the whole of it – because they are powerful aids to identifying an intelligible structure in what is complex and otherwise opaque or unclear. As analytical philosophy broadened its reach both geographically and topically through the late twentieth century, these methods also broadened to include such tools as game theory and computational modeling, and analytical philosophers deployed these methods in combination with others – exegetical, narrative, historical, empirical, etc. – in addressing an expanding array of philosophical topics. These diverse sub-domains of investigation have come to include analytical feminism, analytical Marxism, analytical history of philosophy (including analytical studies of such "continental" figures as Hegel and Heidegger), and diverse foci of normative inquiry, including analytical philosophy of education (see Baldwin, 1998; Stroll, 2000).

Our topic here is analytical philosophy of education, and we begin by indicating the nature and diversity of work in analytical philosophy in the decades when analytical methods were first brought to bear on educational topics. From there we turn to the history of analytical philosophy of education itself, the criticisms that have been leveled against it, and the contemporary practice of analytical philosophy of education.

176

The Early Decades of Analytical Philosophy

Although Frege must be credited with providing some of the tools and models of analysis most essential to the development of analytical philosophy, the movement is generally thought to have begun in England at the beginning of the twentieth century, in the work of Moore and Russell. It was Moore, an heir to the common sense tradition of Thomas Reid (1710–96), who first broke with the Hegelianism and other forms of idealism that dominated British philosophy in the late nineteenth century, inspiring Russell to do the same. Moore's talent for acute analysis was legendary and a celebrated model for later generations of analytic philosophers, including Ryle, Austin and C. D. Broad. His publication in 1903 of "The Refutation of Idealism" and *Principia Ethica*, the one a defense of epistemological realism (the view that we have knowledge of mind-independent entities) and the other a defense of moral realism (the view that there are mind-independent moral facts), had a profound impact on philosophy. The former precipitated the nearly complete collapse and disappearance of idealism (the view that reality is exclusively mental) through the century that followed. The latter set in motion debates about the nature of moral judgments that continue today, with logical positivists such as A. J. Ayer and others in the opposition (Ayer, 1948), and a revival of moral realism ensuing after the decline of positivism (see Sayre-McCord, 1988). In combination with the publication of Russell's book *The Principles of Mathematics* in the same year, the effect on philosophy was revolutionary (Stroll, 2000, p. 93). *The Principles of Mathematics* was an attempt to derive mathematics from logic, showing thereby that mathematics is a branch of logic, and it laid the groundwork for the more exacting effort that followed in Russell and Alfred North Whitehead's *Principia Mathematica*.

It was Russell who adapted the tools of mathematical (symbolic) logic and set-theory developed by Frege and the Italian mathematician Giuseppe Peano to wider philosophical purposes. Russell's 1905 article "On Denoting," arguably the most influential philosophical paper of the twentieth century, brought these tools to bear on a cluster of problems pertaining to reference and ontology. These concerned attributions to non-existents, as in "The present King of France is bald," which seemed to require that the nonexistent subjects exist in some sense in order to have or not have the attributes in question, and the problem (already addressed by Frege) of how identity statements, such as "The Morning Star is the Evening Star," can be informative; those that are true seem to say that a thing (in this case, Venus) *is itself*. The fundamental claim of "On Denoting" is that the grammatical forms of statements often do not coincide with their true logical forms, and that many philosophical problems can be solved by recognizing this and drawing one's metaphysical conclusions from statements analyzed into their true logical forms, rather than from the apparent logical forms suggested by their surface grammar. "On Denoting" offered the beginnings of what Russell hoped would be a "logically perfect" language in which grammatical form coincided with true logical form: it offered an analysis of denoting expressions as "incomplete symbols" that contribute to the meaning of statements, but not by standing for anything. On his analysis, the true logical form of the sentence "The present King of France is bald" is "There is an x, such that

177

(1) x is the King of France, (2) and for all x, if y is the King of France, then y is x, and (3) x is bald." Such analyzed forms contain quantifiers, free variables, and predicates, but no denoting phrases, hence no invitation to posit metaphysically suspect entities.

Nine years later in *Our Knowledge of the External World* (*OKEW*) (1914), Russell announced in more sweeping terms his conception of philosophical analysis and knowledge:

The following lectures are an attempt to show, by means of examples, the nature, capacity, and limitations of the logical-analytic method in philosophy. This method, of which the first complete example is to be found in the writings of Frege, has gradually, in the course of actual research, increasingly forced itself upon me as something perfectly definite, capable of embodiment in maxims, and adequate, in all branches of philosophy, to yield whatever objective scientific knowledge it is possible to obtain. (*OKEW*, p. 7)

The main example that he provides by way of illustration is the matter of whether "the existence of anything other than our own hard data [can] be inferred from the existence of those data" (*OKEW*, p. 80). He identified those "hard data" as "sense data," and held a view of meaning to the effect that, "if an expected sense-datum constitutes a verification, what was asserted must have been *about* sense-data" (*OKEW*, p. 89; italics added). It follows that "*in so far* as physics or common sense is verifiable, it must be capable of interpretation in terms of actual sense-data alone" (*OKEW*, pp. 88–9). But such scientific and common knowledge, though it may be doubted piecemeal, constitutes the very data which epistemology must do justice to:

While admitting that doubt is possible with regard to all our common knowledge, we must nevertheless accept that knowledge in the main if philosophy is to be possible at all. There is not any superfine brand of knowledge, obtainable by the philosopher, which can give us a standpoint from which to criticize the whole of the knowledge of daily life. (*OKEW*, p. 73; cf. pp. 214–15, where Russell defines the nature of "philosophic analysis")

Russell adopts in this passage a methodological stance that remains pervasive in analytical philosophy – in moral theory no less than epistemology, in recent decades – and it leads him to accept that there must be, by and large, adequate evidence or grounds for "our common knowledge." In combination with the discredited view of meaning noted above, this leads in turn to the radically empiricist conclusion that space, time and permanent objects in the "external world" are merely "constructions" or "purely logical constructions" (anticipating the psychological and pedagogical constructivism of Jean Piaget and Ernst von Glaserfeld; see Piaget, 1970; von Glaserfeld, 1995). Much as Russell reduces a number, n, to the class of all classes containing n members, he here defines particles, points, and instants as "series or classes of sense-data" (*OKEW*, p. 128). (Although various related doctrines to the effect that meaning is a function of verification – various forms of *verificationism* – would soon be espoused by the *logical positivists*, Russell himself seems to abandon this view of meaning in the course of *OKEW*. See especially p. 94, where he makes "a new start," and pp. 103–4, where he offers a non-reductive "reconciliation of psychology and physics.")

From these beginnings and the *Tractatus Logico-Philosophicus* (1922) of Russell's student and presumed successor, Wittgenstein, Russell's "scientific philosophy,

178

grounded in mathematical logic," flourished in the hands of Carnap, Moritz Schlick (founder of "The Vienna Circle" of logical positivists), Carl Hempel, Quine, and others (see Stroll, 2000, pp. 45ff). This "formal language" analytical philosophy (as it later came to be called) outlived, and continues to outlive, some of the controversial doctrinal commitments of its early exponents (e.g. that all meaningful statements are either "analytic" – that is, reducible to logical truths – or empirically verifiable, that metaphysical statements are thus meaningless, that propositions about mental phenomena are meaningless unless they are reducible to publicly verifiable state-ments about living bodies).

Sellars and Herbert Feigl, a founding member of The Vienna Circle, would write in the preface of their landmark 1949 collection, *Readings in Philosophical Analysis*, of the new approach to philosophy created by the confluence of "the Cambridge movement deriving from Moore and Russell, and the Logical Positivism of the Vienna Circle (Wittgenstein, Schlick, Carnap) together with the Scientific Empiricism of the Berlin group (led by [Hans] Reichenbach) . . . together with related developments in America stemming from Realism and Pragmatism, and the . . . contributions of Polish logicians" (Feigl and Sellars, 1949, p. vi). It is noteworthy that they detected no fundamental cleavage between pragmatism and analytical philosophy, and that Sell-ars, son of the American pragmatist Roy Wood Sellars, went on to become a major exponent of what has sometimes been called "social practice philosophy," and mounted an influential critique of the dominant empiricist conception of the founda-tions of knowledge (Sellars, 1963).

Yet by the mid-1920s Wittgenstein himself had already come to doubt the philo-sophical usefulness of symbolic logic, and by the 1930s he was developing alternative analytical methods (which remained unpublished however until after his death). Rejecting Russell's notion of logical form, he held that philosophical problems are confusions which philosophers themselves generate when they strip perfectly good ordinary language from its everyday contexts – when "language *goes on holiday*" (Wittgenstein, 1958, s. 38). The point of good philosophy, then, was essentially to undo bad philosophy, to diagnose the confusions philosophers ensnare themselves in, and the method was to return the words abused by philosophers to the everyday contexts that give them meaning – the "language games" or units of linguistic practice in which words can be seen at work, rather than at play. This *therapeutic* and deflationary conception of philosophy is balanced somewhat by the fact that it suggests and to some extent articulates a naturalistic conception of human linguistic practices, a novel refutation of skepticism resting in an account of "that which stands fast" (Wittgenstein, 1969, s. 116), and other substantive philosophical results. Beyond this, Wittgenstein may be credited with asking, if not answering, a wealth of philosophical questions that had not been asked before.

Ryle met Wittgenstein in 1929, and before the 1940s had run their course Ryle and his younger colleague Austin had both joined Wittgenstein in attracting inter-national attention to the new "informal philosophy" or "ordinary language" philoso-phy. Austin's critique of the sense-data empiricism of Russell, Ayer, and others provides a useful illustration of his methods, as well as the diversity of substantive views within the expanding analytic movement. Austin's lectures on "Sense and Sensibilia," delivered several times between 1947 and 1959, address the doctrine that "we never *directly* perceive or sense, material objects (or material things), but only sense-data (or our own ideas, impressions, sensa, sense-perceptions, percepts, &c.)" (Austin, 1962, p. 2). He argues that this doctrine is attributable "to an obsession with a few particular words, the uses of which are over-simplified, not really understood or carefully studied or correctly described; and second, to an obsession with a few (and nearly always the same) half-studied 'facts' " (p. 3). Ridding oneself of the illusions on which such doctrines are built "is a matter of unpicking, one by one, a mass of seductive (mainly verbal) fallacies" (pp. 4–5). In the present instance, the word "directly," among others, is "gradually stretched, without caution or definition or any limit, until it becomes, first perhaps obscurely metaphorical, but ultimately meaningless. One can't abuse ordinary language without paying for it" (p. 15).

Austin's remedy was to recover the meaning of "*directly* perceive" through examples of "indirectly" perceiving (through a periscope, for instance, but not a telescope), the meaning of "real" through the variety of terms we ordinarily contrast with "real" ("counterfeit," "imitation," "fake," and so on), the meaning of "free" through *its* variety of contrasting terms. He held that in these and other instances "the abnormal will throw light on the normal," and the *distinctions* that have come down through the language reveal enduring *features of the world* we have developed the language to talk about (Austin, 1970, p. 179; on his methodological assumptions, see Stroll, 2000, pp. 168–9). The distinctions that Austin brings to light in examining what we view "directly" reveal that directness of visual perception is associated in ordinary language with a straight line of sight, and thus that (unless some new meaning for the word "directly" is stipulated) it is nonsense to insist that people do not *directly* see what is right before their eyes.

As powerfully negative as Austin's painstaking approach was, his account of freedom and responsibility in "A Plea for Excuses" and his development through several works of a complex theory of speech acts – carried forward and refined by John Searle (1969, 1995) and others – demonstrated the constructive capacity of ordinary language analysis, and suggested its potential usefulness in addressing the normative dimensions of human practices.

Analytic Philosophy of Education

Analytic philosophy of education did not emerge all at once. It came to exist in a number of ways and settings, before taking on the dimensions and institutional aspects of a movement in the mid-1950s and 1960s. Its first documentary manifestation in North America was the publication in 1938 of B. Othanel Smith's book, *Logical Aspects of Educational Measurement*, which explores the "preconceptions of the nature of mind and learning" on which educational measurement rests, and how these ideas bear on the "preciseness" of such measurement (Smith, 1938, p. vi). Smith had learned his philosophy of science from Ernest Nagel at Columbia University and was influenced by Nagel's unpublished manuscript, "On the Logic of Measurement." He also acquired at Columbia an enduring interest in "critical thinking," the term itself having apparently originated there with the publication of James Harvey Robinson's book, *The Mind in the Making* (1921). From his professorship in education at the University of Illinois, Smith went on to train Robert Ennis, James McClellan, and Paul Komisar, who became prominent figures in American analytical philosophy of education. Ennis wrote a dissertation on the measurement of critical thinking under Smith and went on to play a pioneering role in the American critical thinking movement, which became both a theoretical enterprise and a national educational phenomenon (see Ennis, 1962, 1996).

These developments were rooted in the formal language wing of analytical philosophy, and it is worth noting in this regard that two of the original members of the Vienna Circle, Feigl and Otto Neurath, both devoted some attention to educational questions as an adjunct to their primary philosophical interests. In conjunction with the positivist Unity of Science movement, Neurath worked through the last twenty years of his life toward developing an International System of Typographic Picture Education (Isotype) (Neurath, 1951). Feigl contributed an essay to the 1995 *Yearbook of the National Society for the Study of Education*, "Aims of Education for Our Age of Science: Reflections of a Logical Empiricist" (Feigl, 1955).

The earliest analytic philosophers of education in Britain and Australia also displayed a logical empiricist orientation. C. D. Hardie's influential book *Truth and Fallacy in Educational Theory* (1942) developed critiques of the dominant educational theories of his time. Referring to the "Cambridge analytical school, led by Moore, Broad and Wittgenstein," his former teachers, Hardie prefaces his work with the suggestion that educational theory would benefit from a similar approach. Russell, however, is the philosopher he cites most often, and his logical empiricism is evident in the book's preoccupation with science and *meta-ethical emotivism* (the view that ethical statements express and aim to elicit emotions, but are devoid of propositional or "cognitive" content; Hardie, 1942, pp. 123ff), and its insistence that in the curriculum only mathematics, logic, and the sciences qualify as knowledge. The function of other subjects taught in schools must therefore be something else, and Hardie holds that the function of the humanities can only be to foster approved emotions, attitudes, and desires. In keeping with his emotivism, he views moral education as simply seeking to arouse feelings of approval and disapproval. Such "noncognitivism" with respect to normative judgments, combined with an *emotivism* that could not conceive of morality as *rationally grounded* or as providing *reasons* to act, meant that whatever analytical philosophy of education could do in the way of clarifying the nature and logical relationships among the various statements constituting a theory of education, it could *not* do what philosophy of education traditionally had done: offer *guidance* for the conduct of educational practice *grounded in rationally examined substantive moral principles* (so-called *normative ethics*). What it could do, according to Hardie, was assist empirical research by elucidating the educational concepts employed, and help to insure that knowledge claims about the practice of education are restricted to well founded empirical generalizations.

In 1953, shortly before analytical philosophy of education became a recognizable movement in the United States, the Philosophy of Education Society (PES) adopted a statement of "The Distinctive Nature of the Discipline of the Philosophy of Education" (Philosophy of Education Society, 1954). In its statement, PES accepted the existence of alternative philosophical schools of thought as frameworks for evaluating educational choices concerning goals, methods, curriculum, and so forth. (The major philosophic positions explicitly mentioned were realism, idealism, and experimental-ism.) The task of philosophers of education was to make explicit the underlying assumptions of educational choices and policies (whether they assumed a "realist" metaphysics, for example) and evaluate these assumptions for consistency with alternative philosophical frameworks that could justify the educational practices as "reasonable." The PES statement also recognized "the speculative task" of developing new frameworks for guiding and assessing educational practice. Thus this statement accepted the then current model of philosophical work in education that consisted in developing or extending various comprehensive frameworks and elaborating the "implications" of these frameworks for educational policy and practice. Although this feature is not explicit in the PES statement, the synthetic frameworks typically included normative principles that could justify the choice of particular educational ends in light of various conceptions of how individual and social life should be led, along with metaphysical and epistemic positions. In Abraham Edel's (1956, p. 140) vivid language, philosophy of education was conceived of as running "a speculative workshop equipped with logical machinery, to which theories in . . . [education] may be brought for processing."

Early analysts found this conception of philosophy of education problematic. First, the practice of *deriving* educational implications from philosophic theories of the kind in question was misguided because the relationship between the statements in the theories and educational policies was seldom very strong. Two people might accept the same philosophic positions and still reasonably disagree about how best to teach or what the curriculum should be. Conversely, two people might accept the same educational practices but justify these choices through different philosophic theories (see Hirst, 1963). An educator's choice of philosophical theory appeared to be of no consequence, then:

Except insofar as he acquires from a particular philosopher a new vocabulary in which to formulate his educational programmes, the educator can go on saying and doing exactly what he said and did before he decided to become, let us say, an idealist rather than a realist. (Passmore, 1980, p. 5)

Second, it was assumed, as John Passmore observed, "that to each 'philosophical school' there necessarily corresponds a philosophy of education" so that "to accept a particular metaphysics, a particular ontology, is at once to be, in principle, education-ally committed" (Passmore, 1980, p. 4). This assumption caused (and continues to cause) considerable mischief, inasmuch as it invites faulty derivations predicated on the unquestioned but erroneous conviction that *any* work of fundamental philosophy *must* have educational consequences.

In his 1954 *Harvard Educational Review* article, "Toward an Analytic Philosophy of Education," Israel Scheffler acknowledged that "philosophy of education" had been used to designate many different practices. While not wanting to "cast doubt" on any of these practices, Scheffler argued for a different conception of the field, namely "philosophy of education . . . as the rigorous logical analysis of key concepts related to the practice of education" (p. 333). In explaining his proposal, Scheffler noted that philosophical efforts to clarify meaning were as old as Socrates. But what he found

182

distinctive about the new analytic philosophy was its "greater sophistication" in semantic analysis, its appropriation of a scientific outlook (involving an "empirical spirit," "rigor," "attention to detail," "respect for alternatives," and "objectivity of method"), and the use of techniques of symbolic logic (p. 333). As an advantage of the new approach, Scheffler cited the prospect of a community of inquirers sharing common methods rather than "doctrines," an oblique (and none too flattering) reference to the various philosophical schools. Others concurred. At least now philosophers could understand each other and engage in mutual discussion, something that had been rare among members of the diverse schools (Archambault, 1972, p. 10).

Scheffler's plea for an analytic philosophy of education was reinforced by further developments taking place in Great Britain. D. J. O'Connor's *Introduction to the Philosophy of Education* was simultaneously published in England and the United States in 1957, and Hardie's 1942 book was republished in the United States in 1962, with an introduction by James McClellan. The American philosopher of education Reginald Archambault made a trip to England "to study the relations between philosophy and education" (funded by the Ford Foundation), resulting in the publication in the United States in 1972 of *Philosophical Analysis and Education*, a collection of essays written entirely by contributors from Great Britain.

Much as Hardie had, O'Connor argued that the task of philosophy of education is to ensure that theorizing and practice in education are conducted on a properly rigorous basis. Thus, philosophy of education should classify and evaluate the plethora of theories that shape and guide educational practice: "Educational theories are not all of the same kind and cannot be judged in the same way. It is one of the philosopher's jobs to try to elucidate such theories and assess their logical worth and their explanatory function" (O'Connor, 1957, p. 13). While subscribing to the view that the best kinds of theories are scientific ones, O'Connor accepted that the then primitive stage of development of the social sciences meant that, at that time, they had little assistance to offer the practice of education. So his view was that the role of philosophy of education was one of applying rational criticism and a scientific outlook to educational theorizing: "in the present condition of human knowledge we cannot hope for more from philosophy than occasional and fragmentary glimpses of enlightenment along with a reasonable confidence that its continuous practice will keep our minds free of nonsense" (p. 45).

With the passage of time, however, analytical philosophy of education came to be less influenced by the commitments of the formal language wing of the analytical movement, and more by the ordinary language wing. In the United States, Thomas Green brought to the movement a style of analysis consciously modeled on Wittgenstein's. Having taken up doctoral work at Cornell under Norman Malcolm and Max Black in the year, 1949, when Malcolm was hosting Wittgenstein, and later immersing himself in educational development and policy work, he joined Scheffler, McClellan, and others in the forefront of the movement. Pre-eminent in Great Britain, and also influential in the United States, was the work of Richard S. Peters and his collaborator, Paul Hirst (e.g. Peters, 1965, 1966, 1973; Hirst, 1974b, 1983; Hirst and Peters, 1971). Peters's interest in the philosophy of education had been reinforced by a term as Visiting Professor at the Harvard Graduate School of Education in 1961, and he exercised an immense formative influence on the development of analytic philosophy of education from his Chair of Philosophy of Education at the University of London, which he held from 1962 to 1983:

the scene was set for someone with the necessary philosophical expertise, the necessary insight into and understanding of education, and the necessary commitment to the enterprise, to give new life to the subject and to re-characterize philosophy of education as a major intellectual enterprise of practical significance....Richard Peters proved to be the right man in the right place at the right time....He...not only redefined British philosophy of education but set its programme for some twenty years and has been its dominating creative thinker throughout that period. (Hirst, 1986, p. 8)

Because educational issues raise both theoretical and practical questions, Peters understood the task of philosophy of education to involve both conceptual analysis and work in the theory of justification, guided by salient borrowings from moral and social philosophy, philosophical psychology (such as the theory of motivation), and epistemology. The agenda he set included, then, not only the analysis of educational concepts, but examination of what is desirable and justified in educational practice, and philosophical scrutiny of the foundations of psychological research on learning and educational processes. His analysis of education as initiation into the forms of knowledge, in order to develop the mind as well as transmit a valuable social heritage, was particularly influential (Peters, 1973), as was Hirst's related account of liberal education, which stimulated subsequent work on the forms of knowledge (Hirst, 1974a).

Although there was variation in the understanding of what constituted analysis, the initially dominant view in North America held that the goal of analysis was discovering the necessary and sufficient conditions for the proper use of concepts (although it was understood that this ideal would rarely be fully attained). Peters held a more Kantian conception of analysis as making explicit the presuppositions of linguistic and social practices for critical purposes, but this view had little currency in North America. Some analytical philosophers of education, but not all, adopted Austin's view that the distinctions of ordinary language reveal facts about the world that have been observed and enshrined in the language. Hirst and Peters (1970, p. 33), for example, write: "The point [of conceptual analysis] is to see *through* the words, to get a better grasp of the similarities and differences that it is possible to pick out." Despite some references to logic, the mathematical or symbolic logic deployed in formal language analysis was not a factor in analytical philosophy of education, which owed more to the ordinary language methods of Moore, Ryle, and Austin and the slogan stemming from the work of the later Wittgenstein that "meaning is use." Green, for example, declared in his introductory text that "The analysis of a concept is the description of its use" (Green, 1971, p. 11).

Among philosophers of education, the presumption was that the concepts that could be usefully analyzed were those that were implicated in educational theory and practice, concepts whose lack of clarity contributed to educational or philosophical problems. They did not seek clarity for its own sake. Through analysis philosophers of education hoped to uncover the logical structure of the language of education. Such analyses could clarify educational thought, prevent misconceptions, and forestall the development of conceptually or logically incoherent theories. Thus analytic work could be done both on everyday concepts that provide the background to educational thought (e.g. teaching) and on the theoretical concepts that were developed within specific educational theories (e.g. behavioral objectives).

In the developing practice of analytic philosophy of education, the analysis of concepts, or linguistic analysis, played a key role. Nevertheless, analytical practice was not wholly limited to analyzing concepts in the interest of clarifying philosophical or practical problems. Other roles claimed by analytical philosophers of education included attending to methodological issues in the construction of educational theory (Lucas, 1969, p. 13), criticizing the theories of other philosophers (O'Connor, 1957, p. 113), constructing theories that would "systematize and elucidate human experience" (O'Connor, 1957, p. 113), exploring criteria for the justification of knowledge claims made in educational discourse (Hirst and Peters, 1970), and unearthing and examining the presuppositions of educational discourse and practices (Hirst and Peters, 1970).

With the return of accounts of morality as rationally action-guiding in the late 1950s (Baier, 1958), the way was paved for a reconceptualization of analytical philosophy of education as a domain of practical or action-guiding philosophy grounded in normative ethics. William Frankena, whose style of moral philosophy was shaped by his work under Moore and Broad at Cambridge, defended such a view of philosophy of education and made significant contributions along those lines (Frankena, 1965a, b). Kurt Baier, a student of Austin and Ryle at Oxford, produced influential accounts of morality, reason, and the foundations and aims of moral education (Baier, 1958, 1973, 1995), and trained students whose contributions to analytical philosophy of education have also reflected a conception of it as a domain of practical philosophy (Pincoffs, 1986; Curren, 2000). Yet it would be some years before the liberalized conception of analytical methods implied by these developments would gain much acceptance beyond Peters's commitment to deploy "theories of justification" developed in ethics and social philosophy. The work of John Rawls was pivotal in this regard. Acknowledging the influence of Baier, Rawls published in 1971 A Theory of Justice, which fundamentally altered the landscape of political philosophy, and provided theoretical and analytical resources which found their way into philosophy of education through the work of Kenneth Strike and others (see Strike, 1989). The publication in 1993 of Rawls's Political Liberalism has had a similar extensive impact on analytical philosophy of education (see, for instance, Strike, 1994; Callan, 1997; Levinson, 1999).

Some analytical philosophers of education, such as Archambault (1972), continued to hold that philosophers could not provide answers to questions of educational practice or the normative guidance traditionally expected of philosophy. Instead, philosophers of education were to specialize in "second-order" questions of meaning and logic, though the clarification achieved through analysis was thought useful in establishing some claims about education and in making educational discourse more coherent.

Despite (or, perhaps, because of) these deflationary views of the philosopher's role, many analytic philosophers of education were clearly excited by the prospects of a way of philosophizing that promised an end to the standoff among the various philosophical schools. The new analytic philosophers emphasized the importance of "doing" philosophy rather than merely studying its history as embedded in the various systematic frameworks. Many embraced Scheffler's notion that what united the analysts was their *way* of philosophizing, their methods, manner, and ways of thinking, not shared substantive beliefs. As Scheffler and Archambault had noted, philosophers using the new methods could communicate with each other and make progress on common problems. Less attracted to systematic philosophy, the early analysts tended to focus more on discrete issues and problems (Soltis, 1981), and this focus led some to argue that analysis made philosophy of education less remote from practice (Soltis, 1978, p. 88).

By the late 1960s, centers of analytical philosophy of education had been established at over a dozen universities in North America, as well as in Great Britain and Australasia (Heslep, 1996, p. 22; Kaminsky, 1993). The movement was supported by journals such as *Educational Theory* (USA), *Studies in Philosophy and Education* (USA), *The Journal of Philosophy of Education* (UK), and *Educational Philosophy and Theory* (Australasia), as well as through professional organizations, such as PES and the Philosophy of Education Society of Great Britain. Texts such as Green's *The Activities of Teaching* (1971) and Jonas Soltis's *An Introduction to the Analysis of Educational Concepts* (1978) communicated the new practice of analysis to students of philosophy of education. Analytical papers published in journals and numerous anthologies analyzed key educational concepts, including: fundamental notions such as teaching, learning, education, and knowledge; others more directly connected with schooling such as curriculum content, student rights, teacher authority, school organization and administration, grading, competition; psychological concepts of needs, creativity, intelligence, critical thinking, interest, motivation, wants and desires; features of moral and civic education such as the logic of moral judgment; matters of educational policy such as equal educational opportunity and affirmative action; and aspects of educational theories and research such as values clarification.

Criticism

Limitations of the prevalent conception of analysis, and of limiting philosophy to analysis, were quickly apparent to critics, including critics within the analytical movement itself. A philosophy of education limited to second-order questions was "formalist" and too remote from educational policy and practice, as well as from wider social and political concerns (Greene, 2000). Abraham Edel (1973) argued that analytic methods had been poorly served by assumptions inherited from logical positivism. He urged that analysts reject positivism's strict separation of the analytic from the empirical and normative, dichotomies on which the then prevalent conception of analysis was based, Edel held. And, challenging the methodological assumption of Austin, Peters, and others that the distinctions embedded in ordinary language are *enduring* and reveal *real features of the world*, he held that ordinary language comes embedded in contexts that shape and reshape it for specific purposes within specific historical and cultural locations. Analytic philosophers must integrate "the empirical, the normative, and the contextual (especially the socio-cultural) *within* the analytic method," Edel (p. 41) argued.

When considering the practice of analysis, some have rejected what they see as an implicit "privileging" of ordinary language and its commonsense view of the world. Feminists and Marxists, for instance, see ordinary language as a repository of systematic misrepresentations of reality. Thus they will not accept ordinary language analyses as clarifying "misconceptions" or providing a structure for educational theory (Evers, 1993). Jane Roland Martin (1981), for example, argued that Peters's conception of education in fact articulated a conception of the educated man, ignoring the question of an educated woman.

Whose concepts, it was asked, are being analyzed? This question struck at the heart of the conception of analysis as providing *analytically* necessary conditions for the proper use of a concept. If meaning is socially constructed and thus potentially variable from context to context, as Edel claimed, then there will at best be *contingently* universal conditions for the proper use of a concept. More likely, conditions that are essential within one context may be unnecessary in another. According to this line of argument, the claims of the analysts to have discovered the distinctive features of teaching as opposed to indoctrination, for example, or the general conditions required for a genuinely educative process, were in fact unreflective expressions of the analysts' frequently shared contexts of gender, class, and culture. A full defense of their claims would require that they be set within a broader theoretical framework that defended the claims rather than taking them as given in the structure of language.

In fact, and even in explicit theory, the practice of the analysts sometimes acknowledged these points. For example, Soltis (1978, p. 90), in his introductory text, noted that "words have power" and that

[a] language system carries with it many unstated assumptions and beliefs about the world and our actions in it. The language of education shares these features of language in general. . . . [Thus] we must ask "To what assumptions, values, theories, procedures and strategies for teaching do these words commit us?"

Soltis, however, was less clear than Edel about whether the tacit presuppositions of educational discourse are relative to cultural and historical context. Evers (1993, p. 122) has suggested that some analysts sought *logical* presuppositions of educational discourse, claims that are "presupposed by *any* educational theorizing." Peters's initial analysis of the concept of education may be an instance of such work. On the other hand, Hirst and Peters (1970) held that uncovering presuppositions of thought is important because such presuppositions *can then be criticized and revised*, thus potentially liberating humans from the presuppositions of their age. In this comment they explicitly acknowledged the contingent nature of the presuppositions in question. Uncovering the presuppositions of a form of thought required understanding not only the ideas but also the "non-linguistic purposes that people have in their social life" (p. 32). Understanding the concept of authority, for example, requires understanding a form of social organization in which some people are legitimately entitled to issue commands to others. Becoming clearer about authority makes it possible to raise questions about the grounds for its exercise and the appropriate occasions for its use, as well as to consider alternative forms of social coordination.

Contemporary Practice

The initial hard line that confined analytic philosophy of education to semantic and logical analysis, rejecting synthetic work and normative ethics, gradually yielded as it had already done in general philosophy. Analytical philosophy now offers the full range of services available in Edel's philosophical workshop, and – as we noted at the outset – it does so in ways that integrate analysis with other forms of inquiry. Many analytical philosophers of education would accept the importance of locating meaning in context and acknowledging the social aspect of meaning; they agree that meaning is embedded in social practices. For this reason, some hold that current work in philosophy of education is "post-analytic." Some see analytical philosophy of education as having its heyday in the 1960s and 1970s (Heslep, 1996; Phillips, 2000). Paul Hirst and Patricia White (1998, p. 9), however, claim that

by 1980 analytic philosophy of education had become a robust discipline with its own momentum, constantly drawing life and energy from developments in academic philosophy and from demands for ever more rationally constructed educational theory and practice.

One could cite in support of this view much of the ongoing work brought together in this volume, on knowledge, reason, measurement, equality, justice, and topics in the ethics of education.

Has analytical philosophy of education survived? Does the movement any longer have any shared tenets? Or has analytical philosophy of education evolved into what Elliott (1986, p. 83) defined as the "older style" of philosophizing: "synthetic, comprehensive, directive, concerned with matters of the highest generality and the highest importance, encompassing both a metaphysical 'world-view' and a philosophy of life"?

We see two possibilities. (1) One might hold that analytical philosophy of education was always in fact practiced within the context of a tacit synthetic perspective of the older kind. Some have described this perspective as "rationalistic," as having inherited assumptions of the Enlightenment. On this view, analytical philosophy's encounters initially with phenomenology and existentialism and more recently with critical theory, feminism, and postmodernism have made its tacit commitments explicit. Philosophy of education has returned to the various "schools" prevalent prior to the analytic movement, with analytical philosophy staking out one perspective among others. Its promise to put an end to the schools has not been fulfilled. (2) A second and, we think, more plausible assessment emphasizes the methodological commitments of analytical philosophers. While many analytical philosophers of education may have shared a common perspective, these substantive commitments are not inherent in analytical practice. What is essential to analytical practice is clear, defensible arguments, rational modes of persuasion that are appropriate to the kind of conclusion to be established, and infusions of analytical resources from related domains of philosophy. Because the conclusions to be established in philosophy of education pertain largely to what is desirable and just in the realm of educational practice, analytical philosophers of education generally recognize (as Edel did) that significant results are impossible without both normative and factual premises. While they look to philosophy as a domain of disciplined inquiry into the credentials of normative premises, they also recognize, as practical ethicists do, that one can make little headway without getting the facts right, and that one must often look beyond philosophical research in order to get them right. Some critics do hold that even these minimal commitments are substantive, but it is that disagreement that makes analytical work distinctive in today's philosophical marketplace.

See also 13 FEMINISM; 16 THEORIES OF TEACHING AND LEARNING; 19 THE MEASUREMENT OF LEARNING; 20 KNOWLEDGE, truth and learning; 21 CULTIVATING REASON; 24 TEACHING SCIENCE; 25 TEACHING ELEMENTARY ARITHMETIC THROUGH APPLICATIONS; 26 AESTHETICS AND THE EDUCATIVE POWERS OF ART; 31 CHILDREN'S RIGHTS; 32 EDUCATION AND STANDARDS OF LIVING; 33 EDUCATIONAL EQUALITY AND JUSTICE; 36 THE ETHICS OF TEACHING; 41 ACADEMIC FREEDOM; 43 AFFIRMATIVE ACTION IN HIGHER EDUCATION; 44 THE PROFESSOR–STUDENT RELATIONSHIP AND THE REGULATION OF STUDENT LIFE

References

Archambault, R. D. (1972) Introduction. In R. D. Archambault (ed.), *Philosophical Analysis and Education*. New York: Humanities Press, pp. 1–13.

Austin, J. L. (1962) *Sense and Sensibilia*. Oxford: Oxford University Press.

Austin, J. L. (1970) *Philosophical Papers*, 2nd edn, ed. J. O. Urmson and G. J. Warnock. Oxford: Oxford University Press.

Ayer, A. J. (1948) *Language, Truth, and Logic*, 2nd edn. London: Gollancz.

Baier, K. (1958) *The Moral Point of View: A Rational Basis for Ethics*. Ithaca, NY: Cornell University Press.

Baier, K. (1973) Moral autonomy as an aim of moral education. In G. Langford and D. J. O'Connor (eds), New Essays in the Philosophy of Education. London: Routledge & Kegan Paul, pp. 96–114.

Baier, K. (1995) *The Rational and the Moral Order: The Social Roots of Reason and Morality*. Chicago: Open Court.

Baldwin, T. (1998) Analytical philosophy. In E. Craig (ed.), *Routledge Encyclopedia of Philosophy, volume 1*. London: Routledge, pp. 223–9.

Black, M. (1946) *Critical Thinking*. New York: Prentice Hall.

Callan, E. (1997) *Creating Citizens: Political Education and Liberal Democracy*. Oxford: Clarendon Press.

Curren, R. (2000) *Aristotle on the Necessity of Public Education*. Lanham, MD: Rowman & Littlefield.

Edel, A. (1956) What should be the aims and content of a philosophy of education? Reprinted in C. J. Lucas (ed.) (1969), *What Is Philosophy of Education?* London: Collier-Macmillan, pp. 140–7.

Edel, A. (1973) Analytic philosophy of education at the crossroads. Reprinted in P. H. Hirst and P. White (eds) (1998), *Philosophy of Education: Major Themes in the Analytic Tradition, volume 1*. New York: Routledge, pp. 39–60.

Elliot, R. K. (1986) Richard Peters: a philosopher in the older style. Reprinted in P. H. Hirst and P. White (eds) (1998), *Philosophy of Education: Major Themes in the Analytic Tradition, volume 1*. New York: Routledge, pp. 79–102.

Ennis, R. (1962) A concept of critical thinking. *Harvard Educational Review*, 32(1), 81–111.

Ennis, R. (1996) *Critical Thinking*. Upper Saddle River, NJ: Prentice Hall.

Evers, C. W. (1993) Analytic and post-analytic philosophy of education: methodological reflections. Reprinted in P. H. Hirst and P. White (eds) (1998), *Philosophy of Education: Major Themes in the Analytic Tradition, volume 1*. New York: Routledge, pp. 120–32.

Feigl, H. (1955) Aims of education for our age of science: Reflections of a logical empiricist. In N. Henry (ed.), *Modern Philosophies and Education: The Fifty-forth Yearbook of the National Society for the Study of Education*. Chicago: University of Chicago Press, pp. 304–41.

Feigl, H. and Sellars, W. (eds) (1949) *Readings in Philosophical Analysis*. New York: Appleton-Century-Crofts.

Frankena, W. (1965a) *Philosophy of Education*. New York: Macmillan.

Frankena, W. (1965b) *Three Historical Philosophies of Education*. Chicago: Scott, Foresman and Co.

Green, T. F. (1971) *The Activities of Teaching*. New York: McGraw-Hill.

Greene, M. (2000) The sixties: the calm against the storm, or, levels of concern. *Educational Theory*, 50(3), 307–20.

Hardie, C. D. (1942) *Truth and Fallacy in Educational Theory*. New York: Teachers College Bureau of Publications.

Heslep, R. A. (1996) Analytic philosophy. In J. J. Chambliss (ed.), *Philosophy of Education: An Encyclopedia*. New York: Garland, pp. 18–25.

Hirst, P. A. (1963) Philosophy and educational theory. Reprinted in C. J. Lucas (ed.) (1969), *What Is Philosophy of Education?* London: Collier-Macmillan, pp. 174–87.

Hirst, P. H. (1974a) Liberal education and the nature of knowledge. Reprinted in P. H. Hirst and P. White (eds) (1998), *Philosophy of Education: Major Themes in the Analytic Tradition, volume 1*. New York: Routledge, pp. 246–66.

Hirst, P. H. (1974b) *Knowledge and the Curriculum*. London: Routledge & Kegan Paul.

Hirst, P. H. (1983) *Educational Theory and Its Foundation Disciplines*. London: Routledge & Kegan Paul.

Hirst, P. H. (1986) Richard Peters's contribution to the philosophy of education. In D. Cooper (ed.), *Education, Values and Mind: Essays for R. S. Peters*. London: Routledge & Kegan Paul, pp. 8–40.

Hirst, P. H. and Peters, R. S. (1970) Education and philosophy. Reprinted in P. H. Hirst and P. White (eds) (1998), *Philosophy of Education: Major Themes in the Analytic Tradition, volume 1*. New York: Routledge, pp. 27–38.

Hirst, P. H. and Peters, R. S. (1971) *The Logic of Education*. London: Routledge & Kegan Paul.

Hirst, P. H. and White, P. (1998) The analytic tradition and philosophy of education: An historical perspective. In P. H. Hirst and P. White (eds), *Philosophy of Education: Major Themes in the Analytic Tradition, volume 1*. New York: Routledge, pp. 1–12.

Kaminsky, J. S. (1993) *A New History of Educational Philosophy*. London: Greenwood Press.

Levinson, M. (1999) *The Demands of Liberal Education*. Oxford: Oxford University Press.

Lucas, C. J. (1969) Introduction. In C. J. Lucas (ed.), *What Is Philosophy of Education?* London: Collier-Macmillan, pp. 1–16.

Martin, J. R. (1981) The ideal of the educated person. Reprinted in P. H. Hirst and P. White (eds) (1998), *Philosophy of Education: Major Themes in the Analytic Tradition, volume 1*. New York: Routledge, pp. 311–27.

Nagel, E. (1930) *On the Logic of Measurement*. Privately printed. (Cited in Smith, 1938.)

Neurath, M. (1951) Report on the last years of Isotype work. *Synthese*, 8, 22–7.

O'Connor, D. J. (1957) *An Introduction to the Philosophy of Education*. London: Routledge & Kegan Paul.

Passmore, J. (1980) *The Philosophy of Teaching*. London: Duckworth.

Peters, R. S. (1965) Education as initiation. In R. D. Archaumbault (ed.), *Philosophical Analysis and Education*. New York: The Humanities Press, pp. 87–111.

Peters, R. S. (1966) *Ethics and Education*. London: Allen & Unwin.

Peters, R. S. (1973) *Authority, Responsibility and Education*, 2nd edn. London: George Allen & Unwin.

Phillips, D. C. (2000) Interpreting the seventies, or, Rashomon meets educational theory. *Educational Theory*, 50(3), 321–38.

Philosophy of Education Society (1954) The distinctive nature of the discipline of the philosophy of education. Reprinted in C. J. Lucas (ed.) (1969), *What Is Philosophy of Education?* London: Collier-Macmillan, pp. 111–13.

Piaget, J. (1970) *Genetic Epistemology*. New York: W. W. Norton.

Pincoffs, E. (1986) *Quandries and Virtues*. Lawrence : Kansas University Press.

Rawls, J. (1971) *A Theory of Justice*. Cambridge, MA: Harvard University Press.

Rawls, J. (1993) *Political Liberalism*. New York: Columbia University Press.

Robinson, J. H. (1921) *The Mind in the Making*. New York: Columbia University Press.

Russell, B. (1903) *The Principles of Mathematics*. London: Cambridge University Press.

Russell, B. (1905) On denoting. *Mind*, 14, 479–93.

Russell, B. (1914) *Our Knowledge of the External World*. London: George Allen & Unwin.

Sayre-McCord, G. (1988) *Essays on Moral Realism*. Ithaca, NY: Cornell University Press.

Scheffler, I. (1954) Toward an analytic philosophy of education. Reprinted in H. W. Burns and C. J. Brauner (eds) (1962), *Philosophy of Education: Essays and Commentaries*. New York: The Ronald Press Company, pp. 333–40.

Searle, J. (1969) *Speech Acts*. Cambridge: Cambridge University Press.

Searle, J. (1995) *The Construction of Social Reality*. New York: Free Press.

Sellars, W. (1963) Empiricism and the philosophy of mind. In *Science, Perception and Reality*. London: Routledge & Kegan Paul, pp. 127–96.

Smith, B. O. (1938) *Logical Aspects of Educational Measurement*. New York: Columbia University Press.

Soltis, J. F. (1978) *An Introduction to the Analysis of Educational Concepts*, 2nd edn. Reading, MA: Addison-Wesley.

Soltis, J. (ed.) (1981) *Philosophy and Education: Eightieth Yearbook of the National Society for the Study of Education*. Chicago: National Society for the Study of Education.

Strike, K. (1989) *Liberal Justice and the Marxist Critique of Education*. London: Routledge.

Strike, K. (1994) On the construction of public speech: pluralism and public reason. *Educational Theory*, 44(1), 1–26.

Stroll, A. (2000) *Twentieth-century Analytic Philosophy*. New York: Columbia University Press.

von Glaserfeld, E. (1995) *Radical Constructivism: A Way of Knowing and Learning*. London: Falmer Press.

Wittgenstein, L. (1922) *Tractatus Logico-Philosophicus*. London: Routledge.

Wittgenstein, L. (1958) *Philosophical Investigations*, 3rd edn. New York: Macmillan.

Wittgenstein, L. (1969) *On Certainty*. New York: Harper & Row.

13

Feminism

Jane Roland Martin

The Missing Women

In the 1970s a body of literature known as "the new scholarship on women" began documenting the ways in which intellectual disciplines such as history and psychology, literature and the arts, sociology and biology were biased according to sex – or gender, as it would now be said. Then in the 1980s this writer published a series of papers on the status of women in the subject matter of the philosophy of education (Martin, 1981a, b, 1982; cf. Martin, 1985, 1994a; Greene, 1978; Morgan, 1979; Nicholson, 1980). These essays showed that although throughout history women had reared and taught their young and had themselves been educated, they were excluded from the standard texts and anthologies of the field both as the subjects and as the objects of educational thought.

A glance at the table of contents of the standard texts demonstrated that women's philosophical works on education had been overlooked. The one exception was Maria Montessori, whose theory was discussed at length by one historian of educational thought. In other texts she was not even mentioned. Nor were Catherine Macaulay, Mary Wollstonecraft, Catharine Beecher, Charlotte Perkins Gilman, or the many other female educational thinkers of history cited, let alone anthologized.

Some might wonder if the philosophizing of these women is sufficiently weighty to be enshrined in the historical record. It should not be supposed, however, that all the men whose educational thought was being preserved by the standard texts were of the stature of a Plato or Rousseau or that all the works represented in the anthologies were as important as the *Republic* and *Émile*. On the contrary, a reader of those surveys will find discussions of the views of some relatively unknown thinkers and some writings of questionable educational value.

The question remains of whether women were excluded from the texts and anthologies because they were women or because of their interest in the education of their own kind. In the early 1980s, a glance at the indexes of the standard texts in the field confirmed the exclusion of women as the objects as well as the subjects of educational thought. Rousseau's account in Book V of *Émile* of the education of Sophie, who represented Everygirl, was edited out of most texts and anthologies and so was Plato's account of the education of women in Book V of the *Republic*. Johann

Heinrich Pestalozzi's praise of Gertrude, a mother and teacher of her young in his pedagogical novel *Leonard and Gertrude*, was also missing, as was John Dewey's discussion of coeducation, among other things. Thus, women thinkers were in double jeopardy. They were penalized for their interest in the education of girls and women and also for being women.

It should not be imagined, however, that in the discipline of the philosophy of education women were excluded only from historical narratives. On the contrary, the very definitions of education and the educational realm implicitly assumed by the standard texts, and made explicit by contemporary analytic philosophers of education, excluded women.

Feminist political philosopher Lorenne Clark once wrote that, from the standpoint of political theory, women, children, and the family dwell in the "ontological basement" (Clark, 1976). This apolitical status was due not to historical accident or necessity, she said, but to arbitrary definition. The "reproductive processes" of society – processes in which Clark included creation and birth and the rearing of children to "more or less independence" – were by fiat excluded from the political domain, which was defined in relation to the public world of "productive processes."

The analogy between political theory and educational philosophy is striking. Despite the fact that society's reproductive processes, broadly understood, are largely devoted to childrearing and include the transmission of skills, beliefs, feelings, emotions, values, and even worldviews, they were not thought to belong to the educational realm. Thus education, like politics, was defined in relation to the public world of productive processes, a move that rendered the status of women and the family "a-educational" as well as apolitical.

Philosophical analyses made the boundaries of the educational realm explicit. For example, the British philosopher of education R. S. Peters, whose work exerted a tremendous influence on the field in the second half of the twentieth century, distinguished two concepts of education: one encompassing "any process of childrearing, bringing up, instructing, etc." and the other encompassing just those processes directed toward the development of an educated person (Peters, 1972). Only this latter, he said, has philosophical significance. This claim presumably rested on his contention that the second concept of education involves the *intentional* transmission of something worthwhile, an element of *voluntariness* on the part of the learner, and some *comprehension* by the learner both of what is being learned and of the standards the learner is expected to attain (Peters, 1967).

Since young children frequently fail to meet these conditions, from the standpoint of the paradigms of the then dominant analytic philosophy of education, Gertrude's educational activities and those of mothers of young children in general were irrelevant. From that standpoint, so too was Rousseau's account of the proper education of girls. At the center of Peters's philosophy of education stood a concept of an educated person as one who has been initiated into the disciplines of knowledge – or, to use his colleague Paul Hirst's phrase, the forms of understanding (Hirst, 1965). The things Rousseau would have Sophie learn – modesty, attentiveness, reserve, sewing, embroidery, lace making, keeping house, serving as hostess, bringing up children – were not in Peters's view a part of disciplines whose impersonal cognitive content and procedures are "enshrined in public traditions" (Peters, 1964, p. 35). Hence, they fell outside the curriculum of an educated person.

Just as the accepted philosophical analysis of the concept of education cast Gertrude's efforts at getting her children to learn outside the educational realm, the accepted analysis of the concept of teaching placed them beyond the pale. Israel Scheffler, arguably the most influential philosopher of education in the USA at the time, characterized teaching as "an initiation into open rational discussion" (Scheffler, 1975, p. 62). The learner's rationality must be acknowledged in two ways, he said. To be teaching one must expose one's reasons to the learner so that the learner can evaluate them. In addition, one's aim must be that the learner also have reasons, and attain a level of learning involving understanding (Scheffler, 1960).

Occupying a central position in philosophy of education, this "rationality theory" of teaching embodied a Socratic conception of both teaching and learning. The give and take of Socrates and his friends philosophizing in the marketplace, the Oxford tutor and his tutee, the graduate seminar: these were the intuitively clear cases of teaching and learning on which the analytic paradigm was based. Pestalozzi's Gertrude teaching her children a song to sing to their father when he returns home or the neighbors to count as they are spinning and sewing, Louisa May Alcott's Marmee helping her daughter Jo to curb her temper, George Eliot's Mrs Garth making little Lotty learn her place – the activities and processes of childrearing which have traditionally belonged to women as mothers were at best considered to be peripheral cases of teaching and learning and were more likely thought not to qualify under these headings at all.

A Case Study of Cultural Loss

Given the findings of gender bias in other disciplines of knowledge, the discoveries about the philosophy of education were not unexpected. That members of the profession were loath to search for the missing women and bring them and what were historically and culturally considered women's concerns into the field should not have occasioned surprise either.

In 1914 a disciple of John Dewey wrote, "It would not be fair to Madam Montessori to say that she herself draws all of these objectionable conclusions from her doctrine of education. She does not. She has not thought consecutively enough." He concluded, "they are ill advised who put Madam Montessori among the significant contributors to educational theory. Stimulating she is; a contributor to our theory, hardly if at all" (Kilpatrick, 1914, pp. 66, 67). In 1984 a student of Israel Scheffler wrote similarly of Montessori that, "According to standard criteria such as quality of argument, connection with a certain literature, etc., Montessori's works would not count as examples of philosophy of education" (Siegel, 1984, p. 50).

Claiming to agree with the feminist critique that the then dominant overarching ideal of education put women in a painful double-bind, this skeptic regarding the new scholarship on women insisted that a philosophical analysis could disregard with impunity society's "genderization" of individual traits and qualities (Siegel, 1984, pp. 39–41). Announcing that "any writing produced in a reformist spirit is no longer philosophy, it is advocacy," a kindred spirit went so far as to consign the present writer to the class of practitioners who "have yielded to the human temptation to be relevant for practice, and have thereby wandered some distance from the philosophical fold" (Phillips, 1983, p. 22).

Those who made such arguments were as reluctant to allow topics associated with women into their field as to welcome the women thinkers themselves. "Why should 'reproductive processes' and the experiences connected with them be regarded as a topic of concern for philosophy of education? Why is philosophy of education mistaken for ignoring such processes, when physics or psychology is not?" asked one (Siegel, 1984, pp. 42–3). Others damned the attempt to include traits culturally associated with women in the received ideal of an educated person by attaching to it the label "female essentialism" (Walker and O'Loughlin, 1984, p. 338).

Does it really matter that women were excluded from the educational realm? What difference does it make that any number of philosophers of education considered the exclusion to be justified?

The discovery that women and topics culturally associated with them were missing from the theories and analyses, texts and anthologies in the philosophy of education was tantamount to the finding that a huge portion of Western culture's wealth had been lost, stolen, or mislaid (Martin, 1996). To be sure, for any given portion of a culture's wealth there are apt to be many guardians. Thus, if the books, journals, national meetings, and curricula of the field of philosophy of education were not preserving and transmitting a given portion of the wealth, perhaps some other custodians were. In the case at hand, however, the probable candidates are feminist publications, meetings, curricula, and the like. But just as there has been a woman gap in the philosophy of education text – or , if you prefer, a gender gap – except for an important literature on feminist pedagogy there has been an education gap in the feminist text (Martin, 1998, 2000).

The gap in the feminist text confirms the hypothesis of cultural loss and also the conjecture that the loss matters. The great Western political and social philosophers had no doubts about the importance of education. Feminist philosophers of the past also understood the significance for their own projects of educational theory and philosophy. Today, however, books in the field pay little attention to the subject of education and rarely cite feminist philosophical research in the area. Widely circulated bibliographies of feminist philosophy and overviews of the field have tended, in turn, to make the whole area of feminist philosophical research about education invisible. Yet the political, the social, and the cultural are still inextricably tied to education. Just as it requires an understanding of politics, culture, and society to change education, an understanding of education is needed to transform politics, culture, and society.

As Plato needed a theory of education for the male and female rulers of the just state he put forward in the *Republic*, feminist philosophers need a well thought out theory of the education of the male and female citizens and family members of the societies they envision. Be it war or peace, the workplace or the academy, violence against women or the abuse of children, racism or homophobia, poverty or teenage pregnancy, science or technology: feminist philosophy and theory can profit from that portion of our culture's wealth associated with women and education.

For example, consider the oft-made claim that gender equality can only be achieved if women and men engage equally in parenting. A good way to dispatch the objection that many men do not possess the traits parenting requires is to educate boys and young men in the nurturing capacities and the three Cs of care, concern, and connection. But there is a problem with this strategy. One of the most important discoveries that followed upon women's entrance into the educational realm was that education today is a highly gendered system. Comprising the culture's dominant educational practices and ideology, it includes institutional forms and structures, accepted pedagogies, standard approaches to curriculum and organizations of subject matter, definitions of the function of school, conceptions of an educated person, and more. Quite simply, the envisioned instruction stands in tension with an "education-gender-system" (Martin, 2000) that takes for granted the old, outdated theory of two opposed societal spheres, and conceives of an educated person as someone who has learned to be a member of only one of them – the public world of work, politics, and the professions. It does so because of the stereotypically gendered rendering of those spheres. When nurturance and the three Cs are thought to belong to the world of the private home and education is considered preparation for life in a world that is thought to be home's polar opposite, it will seem counterproductive to educate anyone in these traits. Insofar as the qualities in question are viewed as "feminine," which they are, it will seem positively dysfunctional to instill them in boys and men.

Those who wish to rethink social and political structures must sooner or later reckon with the discoveries made by feminist philosophers of education, for without matching theories of education, their visions will be but idle dreams. In addition, the philosophy of education can benefit from that portion of the culture's educational wealth relating to women. One of the severest critics of the new feminist scholarship spoke truly when he said: "If Martin is right, the entire enterprise of philosophy of education is off track and stands in [need] of radical revision" (Siegel, 1984, p. 36). Indeed, when girls and women are included in educational thought as both subjects and objects, the field stands to be transformed.

Most obviously, when girls and women are omitted from the picture, questions "of value, virtue, veracity, and validity" (Scheffler, 1980) cannot be directed at policies concerning the education of one half the population. And since boys and girls, women and men live in the same world and to a large extent are educated together, policies concerning the education of boys and men will also be deprived of illumination.

For another example of the transformative potential of the study of the education of girls and women consider the standard interpretation of Rousseau's great educational treatise *Émile*. Based exclusively on Books I–IV of *Émile*, where the education of boys is discussed, this reading informs us that Rousseau envisioned an education that follows nature. Read Books I–IV of *Émile* in relation to Book V, where Rousseau outlines the education of the girl Sophie, however, and one can see how misleading are that philosopher's many references to nature. In fact, it then becomes apparent that the model of education he adopts for both Sophie and Émile is one of planned production, not natural growth. Rousseau is also represented as offering a model for the education of a self-sufficient, self-governing, autonomous man. Yet the program for Émile's education only makes sense in relation to the one he formulates for Sophie. Look at Sophie and Émile together and there can be no doubt that the man who Émile is destined to become is neither as self-sufficient nor as self-governing as assumed. On the contrary, he will be as dependent on the woman Sophie as she is on him. In other words, contrary to accepted opinion, Rousseau designed a two-track educational system for the production of an interdependent heterosexual couple.

Perhaps most important of all, women's entrance into the educational realm exposes the poverty of the now generally accepted policy that the ideal guiding the education of both sexes should be the one Rousseau posited for Émile. When women are missing from the annals of educational thought, it is all too easy to overlook the fact that Émile's education was fundamentally incomplete in that it was intended as preparation for citizenship in a democracy, and not for family living. In contrast, Sophie's education, also incomplete, was designed with this latter function in mind. Had our society chosen to follow Plato's recommendations in the *Republic* and abolish the institutions of private home, family, and childrearing, it might make no difference that an education in the societal tasks and duties, knowledge and skills, and ethics of care traditionally associated with women and the world of the private home has been allowed to drop out of the picture (see, however, Martin, 1985). But given our continued allegiance to these institutions and the fact that the values and virtues, traits and dispositions required for membership in them is not innate, the neglect is serious indeed. To say this is not to reinstate Rousseau's gendered division of education or to accept his stereotypically gendered conceptions of home and world. Rather, it is to emphasize the importance of educating both sexes for life at home and in the world in full recognition of the changes in our education-gender-system that this entails.

Cultural Wealth Regained

Twenty years after women were discovered missing from the philosophy of education, how much of the wealth in their keep has been recovered? (cf. Leach, 1991; Stone, 1994) What new wealth relating to women, if any, has been created?

Over the protests of the skeptics, a number of women thinkers have been brought into the philosophical region of the educational realm (e.g. Martin, 1985; Chambliss, 1996; Palmer, 2001a, 2001b; also Baseheart, 1989; Atherton, 1994; Levinson, 1997; Rogers, 1999; Slattery and Morris, 1999). Not all of them have written about the education of their own sex, but among those who have there is a wide range of opinion.

Echoing Mary Wollstonecraft's critique of Rousseau in *A Vindication of the Rights of Women*, some would extend to females the education reserved in their day for males. This group then divides into those who, like Wollstonecraft, advocate coeducation and those who believe that the two sexes should be given separate but identical educations. A second group rejects Rousseau's misogynous account of Sophie's character, and especially his claim that women lack reason, but agrees with him that a two-track gender-based educational system is best. Like him they maintain that women and men are destined to play different societal roles and that the two sexes therefore require different educations. The difference is that in their eyes both men's and women's roles involve the exercise of reason. Emphasizing the importance for both the individual and society of traits and dispositions that their culture considers feminine, yet another group takes the far more revolutionary step of introducing these into the education of both boys and girls. Few in this category seem to realize, however, that the proposal entails a dismantling of the culture's education-gender-system.

The last word on women's education has certainly not been said. Rather, the value of this new wealth lies in the fact that it opens up a fruitful area of research that has for too long been closed to philosophers of education and in so doing sheds light on contemporary policy. Moreover, this value was significantly increased with the publication in 1999 of *Women's Philosophies of Education*. Until that date, most of the women whose educational thought was being reclaimed were white and middle class. Connie Titone and Karen Maloney set out to remedy this situation by including in their edited volume chapters on the educational thought of a Puerto Rican teacher, feminist, and social reformer; a woman born into slavery who at the age of 67 obtained a PhD from the Sorbonne; a Pomo dreamer, healer, and basket weaver; and a contemporary African-American feminist scholar. The result was a welcome expansion of the historical and contemporary conversation about women's and also men's education.

Along with the women thinkers who have to date been admitted into the philosophy of education come new topics: the education of girls and women, of course; but also, for example, the social settlement as educational agent, municipal housekeeping as a vital societal role, the place of home and family in historical philosophies of education. New questions also emerge. For instance: Should childcare be left to specialists? Should school take on some of home's functions? Is mothering an educational activity? At the very least, work on these new issues also promises to invigorate the field.

For more than 2,000 years philosophical discussions of gender and education have swung back and forth between two extremes: the one put forward by Plato in the *Republic*, namely that sex or gender is a difference that makes no difference; and the polar opposite endorsed by Rousseau, among others, that sex or gender makes all the difference. The four authors of *The Gender Question in Educatiuon* (Diller et al., 1996) have created brand new wealth with a collection of essays that provides helpful ways in which to think and talk about this subject. Should public education be gender free? Can gender be abolished? Is an androgynous classroom a liberatory or tyrannical ideal? Is a rapprochement between educational criticism and nurturance possible? Whether the topic be sexism or sex education, women's physical education or the ethics of care, political correctness or the androgynous classroom, or for that matter gender theory itself, Ann Diller, Barbara Houston, Kathryn Pauly Morgan, and Maryann Ayim unfailingly challenge dichotomous thinking with gender-sensitive analyses. In the process they invite further research into education's aims, curricula, pedagogies, practices, and institutional structures.

Philosophy of Education: An Encyclopedia, edited by J. J. Chambliss, has been hailed as a survey of the field. Yet although this tome contains a number of entries on women thinkers and also on women-related topics, it has no entry on what represents one of the most important acts of recovery of cultural wealth to date, namely the ethic of care. In 1977 Carol Gilligan discerned this moral stance in the course of interviewing women (Gilligan, 1982). Following the lead of Milton Mayerhoff in *On Caring* (1971), Nel Noddings developed and elaborated it in *Caring: A Feminine Approach to Ethics and Moral Education* (1984). Philosophers of education have articulated, criticized, and applied this ethic in a wide range of contexts. Is caring inherently good? Is it a democratic virtue? How is it related to justice? Is it good to teach it? (e.g. Noddings, 1988, 1989, 1992; Houston, 1989, 1993; Thompson, 1990; Diller et al., 1996; Applebaum, 1997, 1999; Katz et al., 1999; Gregory, 2000; Slote, 2000; Thayer-Bacon, 2000; Klein, 2001).

The ethic of care is at least cited in the Chambliss encyclopedia's entry on ethics. In contrast, the entry on teaching eschews feminist work altogether. Nonetheless, in a series of papers Susan Laird has recovered the experiences of girls and women in order to deconstruct the standard analysis of teaching and begin the far more difficult process of reconceptualizing that concept (cf. Grumet, 1988). Thus, for example, she uses Ntozake Shange's novel about the education of an African American schoolgirl to question analyses of teaching that take as their paradigm case Socrates' encounter with the slave boy in the *Meno*, and that think "acontextually about 'the' teacher as a single ideal figure, or ahistorically about one 'clear-case' teaching event" (Laird, 1989, p. 43). She brings data from three reports on girls' schooling published by the American Association of Women to bear on her topic (Laird, 1995b). And she reconstructs and then draws on the educational thinking of Louisa May Alcott (Laird, 1991, 1995a).

Laird's ongoing research program on teaching (see also Laird, 1988, 1994) spills over into the general area of curriculum and so does Megan Boler's *Feeling Power: Emotions and Education* (1999), a book that explores emotions as a site of social control and political resistance (see also, for example, Garrison and Phelan, 1990; Martin, 1991, 1992a; Bogdan, 1992; Sichel, 1993; Diller et al., 1996). In addition, two books published in 1992 focus directly on the school curriculum. Rejecting the widespread assumption that school's job is to educate minds but not bodies, feelings, or emotions, they call for the transformation of the aims, the methods, and the content of schooling (Martin, 1992b; Noddings, 1992).

Making the Cultural Wealth Work

The signs are encouraging. Twenty years later, a goodly portion of the culture's philosophical wealth relating to women has been recovered and new wealth has been created. To date, however, no sea change has occurred in the philosophy of education.

A brief glance at the pages of the Chambliss encyclopedia reveals that feminist scholarship has yet to be integrated into the mainstream. Consider that the long entry on Plato's philosophy of education ignores the feminist literature on the subject, indeed does not even mention his philosophy of women's education. Consider that although the equally long entry on Rousseau includes a discussion of Sophie, its author does not acknowledge that Books I–IV of *Émile* need to be read differently when Book V is taken into account. Consider that the article on Pestalozzi makes but one reference to Gertrude, and it is misleading. Consider that the entry on moral development, devoted mainly to Lawrence Kohlberg's stage theory, makes no mention of Gilligan's finding that it was based solely on data about men or of her revolutionary research on the different moral voice she heard when interviewing women. Consider that the entry on existentialism is equally silent on Simone de Beauvoir's contributions to that movement and that the one on epistemology takes no notice whatsoever of feminist work on knowledge.

To be sure, not all the silences about women in the Chambliss volume are the authors' fault. In many cases, the relevant feminist work remains to be done. Aristotle, Hegel, Froebel, Comenius, Cicero, Erasmus, Marx, Dewey, Sartre, W. E. B. Du Bois: one big gap in the present philosophy of education text is the absence of feminist deconstructions of these men's educational thought (but see Laird, 1988, 1994; Leach, 1995; Henry, 1999). Just as the Titone and Maloney volume recovered writings by women who have been excluded from the field, one or more companion volumes could be devoted to feminist critiques of the educational philosophies of men who are included.

Another gap in the text is the failure to connect the new feminist scholarship in philosophy of education to the standard literature of the field. Some of this research cannot be connected for the simple reason that it is on topics such as identity, sexuality, and gender equity that were heretofore ignored (e.g. de Castell and Bryson, 1993; Levinson, 1998; Martinez Alemán, 1999; Mayo, 1999; Stone, 1999). But research on well established issues like teaching and education has paid scant attention to mainstream constructions. This "separatist" approach allows a scholar to concentrate on the development of her own perspective. The benefit would seem to be outweighed, however, by those accruing from an "integrationist" approach such as the one adopted by Barbara Thayer-Bacon in *Transforming Critical Thinking* (2000). Filling in the intellectual background against which she wanted her own analysis to be understood with chapters on the Greek heritage, pragmatism, and current critical thinking theories, Thayer-Bacon made it possible for readers to determine the extent to which her approach challenged old assumptions. Without such efforts to relate new scholarship on women to old scholarship without women the new work will likely be regarded as a simple "add on" lacking transformative power.

A third gap in the philosophy of education text is the failure to elaborate and build upon the new feminist work in the philosophy of education. In one of history's ironic twists, relatively few feminist philosophers of education have conducted the kind of research on women and girls that the feminist critique of the field made possible. The literature on the ethics of care is a happy exception to this rule. A glance at the proceedings of the Philosophy of Education Society and at recent issues of the society's journal, *Educational Theory*, suggests, however, that a good deal of feminist distancing from feminist scholarship has occurred.

One form the distancing takes is non-citation. Obvious opportunities for citation have rarely been taken. The impression one gets from publications in the field is that except when they are working on the ethics of care, few feminist philosophers of education consider their research to be part of a collective enterprise, let alone to have transformative potential. Yet how much more powerful research on a woman's educational philosophy becomes when it is situated within an ongoing research program in which others also participate! Standing alone it represents a "free-floating" item of scholarship that can all too easily be ignored. Connected through citation and commentary to like-minded research and framed as part of a serious, systematic effort, as, for example, the Titone and Maloney (1999) volume is (see also Laird, 1988, 1989; Chamberlain and Houston, 1999; Mayo, 1999), it is far more likely to be regarded as a factor to be reckoned with.

Another form of distancing has been to adopt a double standard. The new scholarship on women showed that "mainstream" scholars tended to judge works by women more harshly than those by men. In one more of history's ironies, in the 1980s and 1990s feminist scholars in philosophy, literature, and other academic disciplines were apt to look tolerantly on the gravest mistakes of a Foucault, a Derrida, a Lyotard, while denouncing works by women containing far less egregious errors. A glance at recent philosophy of education literature reveals a similar practice. One finds countless appeals on the part of feminists and countless others to the authority of an Aristotle, Dewey, Foucault, Gadamer, Habermas, Merleau-Ponty, Rawls – despite what these men have said or have not said about either women or gender. At the same time, no matter how relevant it may be, the educational thought of those women who have only recently been admitted into the subject matter of the field is misread and misrepresented (see, for example, Thompson, 1997, 1998; Gosseling, 2000), if not discounted or disregarded altogether. This is scarcely a recipe for the hoped for transformation.

Agenda for the Future

To turn one's back on feminist scholarship in the philosophy of education is not necessarily to turn one's back on the study of girls, women, and gender. A glance at the relevant literature suggests, however, that feminist scholars in the field have done both, however unintentionally. One finds few discussions of the education of girls and women and little interest in gender as a category of educational analysis. Indeed, although in 1984 Noddings explicitly labelled the ethic of care "feminine," even it has tended to become detached from girls, women, and gender. Many contributors to its elaboration have proceeded without reference to its gendered connections, and Noddings herself has written that the gender issue "does not always attend to matters that should be of central interest to educators" (Katz, et al., 1999, p.7).

That feminist scholars in the philosophy of education have pulled back from the study of topics that only recently found their way into the educational realm is another one of history's ironies. No doubt one reason for this retreat is that in the late 1980s feminist scholars across the disciplines began accusing one another of essentialism, ahistoricism, and false generalization. Following in their footsteps, some feminist philosophers of education have attached the essentialist label – or else hinted at its applicability – to feminist work on women or gender (e.g. Thompson, 1997; Leck, 1998). Their main objection has been that the concepts or categories of girls, women, and gender mask difference and diversity. As it happens, all concepts do this. Furthermore, non-essentialist definitions of girls, women, gender, and other relevant concepts can be and have been constructed (Martin, 1994b). Sadly, although the accusations of essentialism are not well founded, they have functioned as official seals of disapproval.

201

Some feminist theorists believe that in an ideal future the category of gender will be dispensable, whereas others do not. There is no need to settle the question here, however, for at present it is self-defeating to dispense with gender in the study of education. Gender may not be a relevant category of analysis in every matter of interest, but it surely is in many. The problem is that there is no way of knowing in advance where and when gender is a difference that makes a difference to the growth and development of the philosophy of education. Needless to say, a sensitivity to gender is necessary if the recovery of the lost cultural wealth relating to women is to proceed apace. But a gender-sensitive approach to educational research can also make visible aspects of the educational landscape that are not new but have long gone unseen (see, for example, Martin, 2000). Furthermore, an acknowledgement of the education-gender-system that underlies Western culture's educational theory and practice is required if policies regarding the education of girls and women – and also of boys and men – are to be enlightened.

In other words, it is too soon for philosophers of education to forsake the study of girls and women, too soon to stop using analytic tools such as the concepts of gender, reproduction, mothering, and gender-identity that have only been developed and refined in the past twenty years. Furthermore, there is no point in recovering lost cultural wealth relating to women or creating new such wealth if it is not preserved and transmitted to future generations as living legacy. Yet insofar as mainstream practices of non-citation, negative citation, and the double standard have been embraced by feminist philosophers of education, how possibly can this last be achieved? If they do not cite feminist work in the field, include it on their course syllabi, and anthologize it in their texts, who on earth will?

It is not necessary to agree with everything a feminist scholar has said to build on her work or at least take it as one's point of departure. Yet it can be helpful to think of feminist scholars as engaged in a collective enterprise, one that has a welcoming spirit even as it keeps a watchful eye on mainstream research. This vision is of people who hold up high standards for themselves and each other but do not demand perfection. It is of scholars from different backgrounds and with quite different kinds of training who are expert enough to see the mistaken assumptions and the gaps in other women's research, generous enough to give constructive criticism and to recognize the positive contributions contained in the work of others, and wise enough to know that their way of doing research is not the only right way.

See also 6 ENLIGHTENMENT LIBERALISM; 7 ROUSSEAU, DEWEY, AND DEMOCRACY; 12 THE ANALYTICAL MOVEMENT; 32 EDUCATION AND STANDARDS OF LIVING; 35 EDUCATION AND THE POLITICS OF IDENTITY; 37 INCLUSION AND JUSTICE IN SPECIAL EDUCATION

References

Applebaum, B. (1997) "But that is not what I mean": criticizing with care and respect. In F. Margonis (ed.), *Philosophy of Education 1996*. Urbana, IL: Philosophy of Education Society, pp. 77–85.

Applebaum, B. (1999) Is caring inherently good? In S. Tozer (ed.), *Philosophy of Education 1998*. Urbana, IL: Philosophy of Education Society, pp. 415–22.

Atherton, M. (ed.) (1994) *Women Philosophers of the Modern Period*. Indianapolis: Hackett.

Baseheart, M. C. (1989) Edith Stein's philosophy of woman and of women's education. *Hypatia* 4(1), 120–31.

Bogdan, D. (1992) *Re-educating the Imagination: Toward a Poetics, Politics, and Pedagogy of Literary Engagement*. Toronto: Irwin.

Boler, M. (1999) *Feeling Power*. New York: Routledge.

Chamberlain, E. and Houston, B. (1999) School sexual harassment policies: the need for both justice and care. In M. Katz, N. Noddings, and K. Strike (eds), *Justice and caring: the search for common ground in education*. New York: Teachers College Press, pp. 146–66.

Chambliss, J. J. (ed.) (1996) *Philosophy of Education: An Encyclopedia*. New York: Garland.

Clark, L. (1976) The rights of women: the theory and practice of the ideology of male supremacy. In W. R. Shea and J. King-Farlow (eds) *Contemporary Issues in Political Philosophy*. New York: Science History Publications, pp. 49–65.

de Castell, S. and Bryson, M. (1993) En/Gendering equity: emancipatory programs. in *Philosophy of Education 1992*. Champaign, IL: Philosophy of Education Society, pp. 357–71.

Diller, A., Houston, B., Morgan, K., and Ayim, M. (1996) *The Gender Question in Education: Philosophical Dialogues*. Boulder, CO: Westview Press.

Garrison, J. W. and Phelan, A. (1990) Toward a feminist poetic of critical thinking. In *Philosophy of education 1989*. Champaign, IL: Philosophy of Education Society, pp. 304–14.

Gilligan, C. (1982) *In a Different Voice*. Cambridge, MA: Harvard University Press.

Gosseling, C. (2000) Girls want to walk in the sun. In R. Curren (ed.), *Philosophy of Education 1999*. Urbana, IL: Philosophy of Educaton Society, pp. 165–75.

Greene, M. (1978) *Landscapes of Learning*. New York: Teachers College Press.

Gregory, M. (2000) Caring as a democratic virtue. In R. Curren (ed.), *Philosophy of education 1999*. Urbana, IL: Philosophy of Education Society, pp. 342–51.

Grumet, M. R. (1988) *Bitter Milk*. Amherst: University of Massachusetts Press.

Henry, R. (1999) W. E. B. DuBois and the question of black women intellectuals. In S. Tozer (ed.), *Philosophy of Education 1998*. Urbana, IL: Philosophy of Education Society, pp. 401–10.

Hirst, P. H. (1965) Liberal education and the nature of knowledge. In P. H. Hirst, *Knowledge and the Curriculum*. London: Routledge and Kegan Paul, chapter 3.

Houston, B. (1989) Prolegomena to future caring. In M. Brabeck (ed.), *Who Cares?* New York: Praeger, pp. 84–100.

Houston, B. (1993) Are children's rights wrong rights? In H. A. Alexander (ed.), *Philosophy of Education 1992*. Urbana, IL: Philosophy of Education Society, pp. 145–155.

Katz, M. S., Noddings, N. and Strike, K. A. (eds) (1999) *Justice and Caring*. New York: Teachers College Press.

Kilpatrick, W. H. (1914) *The Montessori System Examined*. Boston: Houghton Mifflin.

Klein, J. T. (2001) When is teaching caring good? In L. Stone (ed.), *Philosophy of Education 2000*. Urbana, IL: Philosophy of Education Society, pp. 335–42.

Laird, S. (1988) Reforming "woman's true profession": a case for "feminist pedagogy" in teacher education? *Harvard Educational Review*, 58(4), 449–63.

Laird, S. (1989) The concept of teaching; Betsey Brown vs. philosophy of education? In *Philosophy of Education 1988*. Champaign, IL: Philosophy of Education Society, pp. 32–45.

Laird, S. (1991) The ideal of the educated teacher – "reclaiming a conversation" with Louisa May Alcott. *Curriculum Inquiry*, 21(3), 271–98.

Laird, S. (1994) Rethinking "coeducation." *Studies in Philosophy and Education*, 13, 361–78.

Laird, S. (1995a) Curriculum and the maternal. *Journal for a Just and Caring Education*, 1(1), 45–75.

Laird, S. (1995b) Who cares about girls? rethinking the meaning of teaching. *Peabody Journal of Education: Teacher Effectiveness*, 70(2), 82–103.

Leach, M. S. (1991) Mothers of in(ter)vention: women's writing in philosophy of education. *Educational Theory*, 41(3), 287–300.

Leach, M. S. (1995) (Re)searching Dewey for feminist imaginaries. *Studies in Philosophy and Education*, 13(3/4), 291–306.

Leck, G. M. (1998) The gender question in education. In S. Laird (ed.), *Philosophy of Education 1997*. Urbana, IL: Philosophy of Education Society, pp. 461–3.

Levinson, N. (1997) Teaching in the midst of belatedness: the paradox of natality in Hannah Arendt's educational thought. *Educational Theory*, 47(4), 425–51.

Levinson, N. (1998) Unsettling identities: conceptualizing contingency. In S. Laird (ed.), *Philosophy of Education 1997*. Urbana, IL: Philosophy of Education Society, pp. 61–70.

Martin, J. R. (1981a) The ideal of the educated person. *Educational Theory*, 32, 97–109.

Martin, J. R. (1981b) Sophie and Emile: a case study of sex bias in the history of educational thought. *Harvard Educational Review*, 51, 357–72.

Martin, J. R. (1982) Excluding women from the educational realm. *Harvard Educational Review*, 52, 133–48.

Martin, J. R. (1985) *Reclaiming a Conversation*. New Haven, CT: Yale University Press.

Martin, J. R. (1991) What should science educators do about the gender bias in science? In M. R. Matthews (ed.), *History, Philosophy, and Science Teaching*. Toronto: OISE Press, pp. 151–67.

Martin, J. R. (1992a) Critical thinking for a humane world. In S. P. Norris (ed.), *The Generalizability of Critical Thinking*. New York: Teachers College Press, pp. 163–80.

Martin, J. R. (1992b) *The Schoolhome*. Cambridge, MA: Harvard University Press.

Martin, J. R. (1994a) *Changing the Educational Landscape*. New York: Routledge.

Martin, J. R. (1994b) Methodological essentialism, false difference, and other dangerous traps. *Signs*, 19(3), 630–57.

Martin, J. R. (1996) There's too much to teach: cultural wealth in an age of scarcity. *Educational Researcher*, 25, 4–10, 16.

Martin, J. R. (1998) Education. In A. Jaggar and I. Young (eds), *A Companion to Feminist Philosophy*. Malden, MA: Blackwell, pp. 133–48.

Martin, J. R. (2000) *Coming of Age in Academe*. New York: Routledge.

Martinez Alemán, A. M. (1999) *Qué Culpa Tengo Yo?* Performing identity and college teaching. *Educational Theory*, 49 (1), 37–51.

Mayeroff, M. (1971) *On Caring*. New York: Harper & Row.

Mayo, C. (1999) Gagged and bound: sex education, secondary virginity, and the Welfare Reform Act. In S. Tozer (ed.), *Philosophy of Education 1998*. Urbana, IL: Philosophy of Education Society, pp. 309–317.

Morgan, K. P. (1979) Amazons, spinsters, and women: a career of one's own. In G. D. Fenstermacher (ed.), *Philosophy of Education 1978*. Champaign, IL: Philosophy of Education Society, pp. 11–19.

Nicholson, L. (1980) Women and schooling. *Educational Theory*, 30(3), 225–34.

Noddings, N. (1984) *Caring*. Berkeley: University of California Press.

Noddings, N. (1988) An ethic of caring and its implications for instructional arrangements. *American Journal of Education*, 96(2), 215–30.

Noddings, N. (1989) *Women and Evil*. Berkeley: University of California Press.

Noddings, N. (1992) *The Challenge to Care in Schools*. New York: Teachers College Press.

Palmer, J. A. (ed.) (2001a) *Fifty Major Thinkers on Education*. London: Routledge.

Palmer, J. A. (ed.) (2001b) *Fifty Modern Thinkers on Education*. London: Routledge.

Peters, R. S. (1964) *Education as Initiation*. London: Evans Brothers.

Peters, R. S. (1967) *The Concept of Education*. London: Routledge and Kegan Paul.

Peters, R. S. (1972) Education and the educated man. In R. F. Dearden, P. H. Hirst, and R. S. Peters (eds), *A Critique of Current Educational Aims*. London: Routledge and Kegan Paul.

Phillips, D. C. (1983) Philosophy of education: in extremis? *Educational Studies*, 14, 1–30.

Rogers, D. G. (1999) Hegel, women, and Hegelian women on matters of public and private. *Studies in Philosophy and Education*, 18(4), 235–55.

Scheffler, I. (1960) *The Language of Education*. Springfield, IL: Thomas.

Scheffler, I. (1975) Concepts of education: reflections on the current scene. In I. Scheffler (ed.) *Reason and Teaching*. Indianapolis: Bobs-Merrill.

Scheffler, I. (1980) Philosophy of education: some recent contributions. *Harvard Educational Review*, 50, 402–6.

Sichel, B. (1993) Education and thought in Virginia Woolf's To the Lighthouse. In H. A. Alexander (ed.), *Philosophy of Education 1992*. Urbana, IL: Philosophy of Education Society, pp. 191–200.

Siegel, H. (1984) Genderized cognitive perspective and the redefinition of philosophy of education. In R. E. Roemer (ed.), *Philosophy of Education 1983*. Normal, IL: Philosophy of Education Society, pp. 35–51.

Slattery, P. and Morris, M. (1999) Simone Beauvoir's ethics and postmodern ambiguity: the assertion of freedom in the face of the Absurd. *Educational Theory*, 49(1), 21–36.

Slote, M. (2000) Caring versus the philosophers. In R. Curren (ed.) *Philosophy of Education 1999*. Urbana, IL: Philosophy of Education Society, pp. 25–35.

Stone, L. (ed.) (1994) *The Education Feminism Reader*. New York: Routledge.

Stone, L. (1999) Experience and performance: contrasting "identity" in feminist theorizings. *Studies in Philosophy and Education*, 18(5), 327–37.

Thayer-Bacon, B. (2000) *Transforming Critical Thinking*. New York: Teachers College Press.

Thompson, A. (1990) Friendship and moral character: feminist implications for moral education. *Philosophy of Education 1989*. Champaign, IL: Philosophy of Education Society, pp. 61–75.

Thompson, A. (1997) Surrogate family values: the refeminization of teaching. *Educational Theory*, 47(3), 315–39.

Thompson, A. (1998) Not the color purple: feminist lessons for educational caring. *Harvard Educational Review*, 68(4), 522–54.

Titone, C. and Maloney, K. E. (eds) (1999) *Women's Philosophies of Education*. Englewood Cliffs, NJ: Prentice Hall.

Walker, J. and O'Loughlin, M. A. (1984) The ideal of the educated woman: Jane Roland Martin on education and gender. *Educational Theory*, 34, 327–40.

14

Postmodernism

David E. Cooper

"The Postmodern Condition"

The expression "postmodern education" is ambiguous. On the one hand, it is a broadly sociological one referring to trends in education that have evolved in the so-called "postmodern condition" of contemporary culture. On the other hand, it refers to conceptions, attitudes, and proposals inspired by the alleged insights of philosophers who, with or without their blessing, are labelled "postmodernists." (A shortlist would include Jean-François Lyotard, Michel Foucault, Jacques Derrida, Jean Baudrillard, Peter Sloterdijk, and Richard Rorty.) These conceptions, attitudes, and proposals are urged at various levels: they may concern the organization and adminstration of education, teaching methods, the nature of particular disciplines, the general "tone" or "spirit" of education, and so on.

The focus of this chapter is upon postmodern education in the second of those senses, postmodernist educational thinking. Nevertheless, a few remarks on "the postmodern condition" and its educational dimensions are in order, not least because there are close connections between that condition and postmodernist thought. On the one hand, postmodernist educators regard their conceptions and proposals as peculiarly suited to societies experiencing that condition. One finds it urged, for example, that schools should emulate postmodernist trends in architecture through the encouragement of variety, hostility to central planning, and so on (Standish, 1995, p. 127). On the other hand, the postmodern condition is itself deemed to be the outcome, in part, of an atrophy – articulated and endorsed by postmodernist thinkers – of older philosophical convictions, such as confidence in universal moral norms.

Unfortunately, the expression "postmodern condition" is itself ambiguous. Lyotard, who popularized the expression, sometimes uses it in a historical sense, to refer to the "condition of knowledge in the most highly developed societies" that has become increasingly distinctive of "the state of our culture" since the nineteenth century. But he also uses "postmodern" to refer to an aspect of any age whatever that is self-consciously "modern" – its "suspicion of the past" and "flight...out of the metaphysical, religious and political certainties" of the preceding age. So understood, the postmodern, Lyotard remarks, is "undoubtedly part of the modern," and distinguished from other aspects by an attitude of "jubilation," as opposed to one of "regret" or nostalgia, regarding the demise of the old "certainties" (Lyotard, 1984, pp. 79ff).

In *The Postmodern Condition*, Lyotard's focus is primarily upon the postmodern in the first, historical sense – on "the state of our culture." Like many chroniclers of this condition, such as Fredric Jameson, Lyotard draws attention to such salient features of developed societies as consumerism, global capitalization, eclecticism, and an "anything goes" attitude in the arts and private life, a veneer of variety masking an underlying monotony, and the hegemony of a "performativity principle" that subjects activities to the "techno-scientific" criterion of "optimalization of the cost/benefit (input/output) ratio" (Lyotard, 1993, p. 25). As his subtitle, "A report on knowledge," indicates, Lyotard's emphasis, however, is upon the changes in ideologies and our "cognitive condition" that have helped to generate a culture with those features. Crudely put, the big change has been "the end of ideology," the atrophy of beliefs and ideals, of confidence in the powers of reason and moral reflection, that once provided people with purposes capable of constraining "consumer choice" and taste, and of furnishing criteria to override those of "fun" and "performance."

A diagnosis of our "cognitive condition" that complements Lyotard's is offered in Peter Sloterdijk's *The Critique of Cynical Reason*. The cynicism referred to in the title is "a central feature of the postmodern condition" and defined by Sloterdijk as "enlightened false consciousness" (Sloterdijk, 1987, pp. xi, 5). Enlightened, since it is that of people who have "seen through" the traditional justifications – religious, metaphysical, and so on – for values and beliefs, but false or inauthentic, since lip-service is still paid to these. The postmodern age of cynicism is, therefore, marked by "the passing of . . . hopes" that brings in its train a "listlessness of egoism" and "apathy" (ibid., p. 6). Recognizing that values have "short lives" and saying "No thanks!" to "new values," the cynical person is resigned to the pursuits of material well-being and fun, while displaying an ability to control "the symptoms of depression" that glimpses of the emptiness of life occasionally induce (ibid., pp. xxvii, 5–6).

Both Lyotard and Sloterdijk apply their diagnoses of the postmodern "cognitive condition" to the state of education. For the former, education has fallen increasingly under the domination of "techno-science" and the "rule" of "consensus." The "cognitive statements" and "commitments" to be encouraged by education are those deemed acceptable by criteria of pragmatic, technological value, or that are "testified" to by widespread consensus (Lyotard, 1984, pp. 76ff). For Sloterdijk, we are in effect witnessing "the end of the belief in education" considered as something to "improve" human beings. What does not visibly contribute to prospects in the job market induces "*a priori* stupefaction" among those at school (Sloterdijk, 1987, p. xxix).

As the tone of their remarks indicates, the attitude of Lyotard and Sloterdijk toward the postmodern condition is mixed. Like many other observers of that condition, they endorse the "suspicion" of, and "flight" from, traditional certainties. They are, however, sharply critical of the social, cultural, and educational tendencies that have accompanied this "flight." The contemporary response to "the end of ideology" has, taken at large, been a perverse one. The form of a more appropriate response, and its implications for education, is something we can identify only after examining the character of postmodernist philosophy.

Postmodernism

"Postmodernist philosophy" is not an entirely comfortable expression, since many writers to whose work it gets applied – Rorty and Derrida, for example – are fond of pronouncing obituaries on philosophy (see Cooper, 1998a). Provided, however, that "philosophy" is taken blandly, and not invested with a loaded sense – the search for *a priori* knowledge of reality, for example – there is no harm in speaking of postmodernist philosophizing. It should not be assumed, however, that the expression names a single set of doctrines agreed upon by those dubbed "postmodernists." There are significant differences among the thinkers I shortlisted at the beginning, and some familiar attempts to identify a common core to their views are unsuccessful.

On one popular characterization, postmodernist thought is virtually equated with *relativism*. When Rorty encourages us to use " 'true' to mean 'what you can defend against allcomers' " (Rorty, 1982, p. 308), or when Lyotard (1984, p. 52) urges us to understand knowledge as what is "accepted in the social circle of the 'knower's' interlocutors," that equation is understandable. The effect of such exhortations is indeed to render truth or knowledge relative to such factors as forensic skill or the company one keeps. Still, the equation is unhelpful. Relativism is best understood as a theory of truth or knowledge, to the effect that the truth of any belief, or its status as knowledge, is relative to certain contingent conditions. Now not all postmodernist thinkers subscribe to such a theory, and those rather casual remarks of Rorty and Lyotard should not be taken as endorsing it. (Their more considered view is that notions like truth and knowledge have proved "unhelpful" in appraisal of our beliefs.) Certainly there are forms of relativism, including ones that have enjoyed popularity in educational circles, uncongenial to postmodernist thinkers. Both "subjective" and "linguistic" relativism, which respectively relativize truth to individual subjects or selves and to languages, are rejected by those with a typically postmodernist hostility both to the notion of the subject and to the image of languages as fixed, more or less incommensurable sets of rules (see Blake et al., 1998, pp. 11–18). Merever, if one persists with the "relativist" label, the task still remains of identifying what is distinctive about the postmodernist brand of relativism, what considerations inspire relativistic remarks of the type cited, what views about truth and knowledge are reacted against, and so on. When that task is carried out, and those considerations and views are identified, whether to apply or withhold the label "relativist" is likely to seem a minor issue.

Another frequently quoted characterization of the postmodernist philosophical stance is Lyotard's, one which, moreover, essays an answer to the question of what that stance is a reaction against. He defines it as "incredulity toward metanarratives" – toward, that is, any "grand narrative, such as the dialectics of Spirit, the hermeneutics of meaning, the emancipation of the rational or working subject, or the creation of wealth," in terms of which, in modernity, each "science" has tried to "legitimate itself" (Lyotard, 1984, pp. xxii, xxiv). This characterization is at once too broad and too narrow. Too broad, since it fails to distinguish postmodernist attacks on "grand narratives" from those of philosophers no more congenial to postmodernists than are the champions of the discredited narratives. For example, the logical positivists gave short shrift to "the dialectics of Spirit" and related "narratives," but their equation of meaningful discourse with what is either empirically verifiable or true by definition is an explicit target of many postmodernist authors. Lyotard's definition is also too narrow, since it fails to include, as an object of postmodernist "incredulity," a position that is hardly a "grand narrative," but certainly is a target of postmodernist criticism. I refer to a "commonsense realism" – surely far more influential in the sciences than the "narratives" listed by Lyotard – according to which there is a way that the world objectively is, one that, with sufficient patience and intelligence, human beings may discover a great deal about. Rather few people, I suspect, have been wedded to the legitimating narratives mentioned by Lyotard: that hardly turns the rest of us, including commonsense realists, into postmodernists.

A clue to a better characterization of postmodernist philosophy is provided by the original employment of "postmodern" in the context of the arts. Here a striking theme was the hostility of postmodern artists to an alleged modernist concern for "depth." Postmodern works have a "contrived *depthlessness*," offer "no promise of a *deeper* intellectual experience," and are without any ambition to reveal "the true nature of a unified . . . *underlying* reality" (my italics; see Cooper, 1996, p. 466, for these and other quotes). Characteristic of such works, in architecture and painting, are pastiche and the importance attributed to façades or surfaces – the former without a concern for unity, the latter without one for structures underlying the immediately visible.

An analogous hostility toward "depth" is apparent in postmodernist philosophical writings. Here the target is no longer the pretensions of modern art to communicate something deep, but philosophical traditions that postulated something "below" or "behind" our linguistic and other practices by way of "grounding" these. "There is nothing deep down . . . except what we have put there" (Rorty, 1982, p. xlii), and "no deep significance that is not superficial" (Parker, 1997, p. 140). Such remarks prompt the accurate observation that "anti-" or "post-*foundationalism*," more than "relativism," captures the tenor of postmodernist philosophy (Blake et al., 1998, p. 18).

This hostility toward "depth" devolves into a number of antipathies. To begin with, there is the ubiquitous postmodernist antipathy to universalizing ambitions, in favour of "local" or "little" discourses, "narratives," and epistemic practices. What has been "wrong with philosophy, ever since Plato," is that "it has aimed at universal, ahistorical norms" (Rorty, 1987, p. 11). We should "respect," even celebrate, the existence of countless "*differends*" – differences or conflicts in judgment that cannot be settled, since there is no general "rule of judgment" available (Lyotard, 1988, p. xi). Beneath the surface differences that confront us, there is no reason to expect universal rules or structures capable of reducing them.

Second, there is antipathy to postulating anything "underlying" our discourses or "language games." Indeed, these are doubly "depthless." There is, for a start, no underlying logical structure, no "essence" of language, of which these discourses are manifestations, hence no common measure of their adequacy. It is therefore invidious to appraise a discourse – that of art, say – by criteria belonging to another, that of natural science, perhaps. Our discourses are "depthless" in the further sense that it is hopeless to seek foundations for them in the way the world objectively is. Language, wrote Wittgenstein – whose later writings are often appealed to by postmodernist thinkers – "is not based on grounds. It is not reasonable (or unreasonable). It is there – like our life" (Wittgenstein, 1969, s. 559). The point is not to deny that there is a world, but to reject the possibility of comparing language and world, given that any conception of the latter is inevitably shaped by our discourses. This, and not the mad claim that only language exists, is the point of Derrida's notorious remark that "there is nothing outside the text": we have, as he puts it, "access to ... 'real' existence only" through language (Derrida, 1976, p. 158).

A final antipathy devolved from a general hostility toward "depth" is toward the notion of a self or subject that underlies and unifies the motley of discourses and practices in which a man or woman engages during his or her life. The so-called self or subject is more a "function" of such discourses and practices than it is a unitary "agent and master" of them (Derrida, 1981, p. 28). Once again, as with a postmodernist building, "what you see is what you get" – the fragmented, diffuse human being, not a Cartesian self "below" or "behind" that diversity.

With these elements of a hostility to "depth" in place, and with some earlier points and some further strokes added, we might proceed to portray the "typical" postmodernist philosophical stance. This is not to be identified with that of any particular writer, and with certain features of the portrait, this or that writer would take issue. But it sketches, in characteristically postmodernist idiom, a position around which most postmodernist philosophical manifestos cluster. The "typical" postmodernist, then, subscribes to the following:

For millennia, but above all during the Enlightenment period, the project of western thought has been to establish through reason the fundamental universal and eternal truths that capture the objective nature of reality and the moral order. This "Enlightenment project" manifestly failed: no such set of truths were established. Through the writings of the great destroyers of the metaphysical tradition to which that project belonged, we now see that the project *had* to fail. It has been "exploded" by, *inter alia*, Nietzsche's (and later, Foucault's) "genealogical" exposures of the origins and conditions of beliefs and norms; Martin Heidegger's hermeneutic demonstration of the ineradicable role of "pre-judices" and "ground-plans" in our edifice of "knowledge"; and Derrida's deconstruction of a "logocentrism" that assumes our words and ideas mirror something "transcendentally signified" by them. When such destructive insights are assembled, it is evident that there is no Knowledge, only "knowledges," no Reason, only "reasons," and that these various knowledges and reasons are "constructed," not discovered. They are constructed in and through practices and discourses that bear the indelible mark of such "all-too-human" factors as the pursuit and exercize of power. Nor is there any prospect of people transcending such practices in order to obtain an objective grasp of truths and norms, for "the rational subject" of Enlightenment imagination is a myth. Human beings are themselves "inscribed" in the very discourses and practices they pretend to transcend.

Implicit recognition of the bankruptcy of the modernist Enlightenment project is characteristic of contemporary society, of our postmodern culture. Too often, unfortunately, this recognition assumes the form of nostalgia for lost certainties, apathy, or a "cynical" obsession with self-centered, pragmatic goals. Properly viewed, however, the destruction of tradition – what Nietzsche had in mind with his metaphor of "the death of God" – offers unprecedented opportunities for an emancipated form of human life. The recognition that no one discourse, like science, is more "grounded" than any other, and the appreciation of unresolvable *differends*, should induce a "celebration" of difference, playful thought, or healthy irony, and a new respect for "local," and long suppressed, views and voices.

Two things should be evident from this brief portrait of the "typical" postmodernist philosophical stance. First, the stance is one to invite criticism from many philosophers with more traditional allegiances. Second, it is one that looks to be replete with implications for educational thought and practice. I consider these two matters in reverse order.

Postmodernism and Education

Leaving aside for the moment those who find little or nothing to take seriously in the philosophical stance just sketched, writers on the significance of postmodernist philosophy for education have responded in four main ways. The most extreme response is indicated by Sloterdijk's reference to "the end of the belief in education" and by titles such as *The End of Education* (Giesecke, 1987). The point of the authors is not, presumably, that schools and universities will disappear. Instead they insist on two things. First, schooling in a postmodern era can no longer be "education" as traditionally conceived – induction into knowledge, for example – since the terms of that conception are now bankrupt. Second, it is not in schools and universities, which have become increasingly constrained by criteria of "performativity," but in "the university of life" that young people can best seek emancipation through "try[ing] out forms of living" and "oppose the cynicism of... official consciousness" (Sloterdijk, 1987, p. 120).

A second response by educationists who adopt the postmodernist stance is more optimistic, but scarcely less radical. In their view, it is both desirable and possible thoroughly to rethink and restructure education so that it fully reflects that stance. At the curricular level, subjects will be taught in a manner that reflects the "explosion" of erstwhile confidence in truth and objectivity. The teacher of history, for example, recognizing that "history is a constructed narrative" and that historical "truth isn't objectively there," will encourage pupils to "negotiate" historical "constructions" of their own. The mathematics teacher will stimulate a similarly "creative" and "constructive" attitude toward mathematical propositions, appreciating as he does that these can never furnish "an 'objective' representation of the world as it might 'exist' apart from us" (see Cooper, 1998b, pp. 39–40, for these quotes). At the organizational level, education will be decentralized, with schools regarding themselves as "communities" in which children, as much as parents and teachers, "create their own style, decide what... to learn... and what standards [they] will be judged by" (Parker, 1997, p. 159). Finally, the whole tenor or spirit of an education that fully reflects the postmodernist stance will be a radically new one. The venerable pedagogic ambition to initiate the young into generally accepted bodies of knowledge will, as Henry Giroux puts it, be "rejected as totalitarian and terroristic" (Giroux, 1988, p. 14). The whole ambience of the school will be one of "dissension" and "resistance" to received knowledge and norms. The radical character of these proposals may be gauged from one enthusiast's remark that we – and our children – should come to appreciate that Nazism is judged wrong only because "it offends *our* literary taste," not because "ethical reality itself is offended" (Parker, 1997, p. 154).

An obvious problem with this radical response is that, with all prospect of "discovering" scientific, moral, or other truth pre-empted, one wonders what the

211

purpose of frenetically constructing new narratives, negotiating different theories, engaging in unorthodox reasoning or maverick hypotheses, inventing "standards," and stoking up dissension is supposed to be. Is all of that just "play"? This is not a problem, its proponents allege, for a more moderate position that has been adopted in recent years. This is the position of several philosophers of education who, while sympathetic to some postmodernist insights, do not squarely adopt the postmodernist stance. Instead, they "want to advance ideas *after the style of* postmodernism" (Blake et al., 1998, p.186). These writers do not reject the possibility of objective agreement on truth, knowledge, and moral norms, but they share the postmodernist's hostility toward "depth" and rejection of "foundationalist" accounts of truth, etc. That hostility and rejection, they argue, is sufficient to impugn familiar and once received "legitimations" of the educational endeavour, in particular those offered by older champions of "liberal education." The aim of education cannot, to begin with, be initiation into "forms of knowledge," not at any rate if these are conceived of as bodies of beliefs "grounded" in an independent way the world is. Nor can the aim be the development of the rationally autonomous individual, able to stand back from and critically appraise all discourses and practices, for "the radical displacement of the centrality of the autonomous human subject" (Smeyers, 1995, p. 116) is a laudable achievement of postmodernist or poststructuralist thought. Moreover, while educational thought "after the style of postmodernism" need not countenance the radical proposals described in the previous paragraph, it will certainly include criticism of several current tendencies – the obsession with "performativity," for example, and the privileging of scientific knowledge as something allegedly free of all ideological and normative entanglements. Whether or not this relatively moderate position that, so to speak, cherry-picks certain elements from the postmodernist stance while discarding others is a stable one is a question I address at the end.

A final response by people more or less sympathetic to the postmodernist stance – one at an opposite extreme from the first – is that it should have few, if any, implications for educational practice. This response has taken two forms. The first of these is suggested by the distinction insisted upon by Rorty between the "private" and "public" realms (Rorty, 1989). Rorty's postmodern individuals are "ironists" who dispense with "foundationalist" aspirations and feel free, therefore, to create more or less unconstrained "redescriptions" of themselves and their world. However, they are also liberals and democrats who wish neither to be "cruel" to less sophisticated people by challenging their conceptions, nor to impugn bodies of understanding, notably the sciences and everyday morality, which, however "ungrounded," have contributed pretty well toward tolerance and material security in democratic societies. The postmodern individual, consequently, should restrict his or her "irony" to "private" life. At the "public" level, which includes the institutions of education, the ironist will endorse the practices and discourses that, by and large, serve our societies well.

According to a second and very different "conservative" response (Cooper, 1998b), the insights of postmodernist philosophy, where valid, are of a kind that, properly understood, "leave everything as it is." That phrase is Wittgenstein's and reflects a sense – shared by other "heroes" of postmodernist thought, such as Heidegger – that these insights into truth, objectivity, rationality, and so on in no way threaten those notions as ordinarily employed, but only certain mistaken accounts of them. The sensible response of the teacher to the news that mathematical systems, say, or historical narratives are inevitably shaped by contingent human practices and "fore-conceptions" is to carry on business as usual, for that is news about how such disciplines *must* be and so cannot have revisionary implications, *per se*, for their conduct and transmission. Again, that at some deep level no final distinction is to be made between fact and value, or between decision and logical compulsion, does not entail that such distinctions are dispensable at a less ultimate level. For example, there should, in the classroom, be no erasing of the distinction between the "creative" proposal of some hypothesis and the necessity of drawing a certain conclusion from certain premises. For the "conservative," the insights of postmodernism should be reflected where one might expect them to be – in the philosophy seminar, and neither in the maths, history, or science class, nor in the organizational aspects of the school.

Questioning Postmodernism

None of the above educational responses to the postmodernist philosophical stance will be of much interest to philosophers and educators who simply dismiss it. Critics of the "full-blown" postmodernist stance have tended to focus on three alleged deficiencies:

1   Its parody of "traditional" philosophy – one that lends it a spurious air of originality.
2   The weakness of many of its arguments, due in most cases to a failure to heed elementary distinctions.
3   Its self-stultifying character.

"Typical" postmodernists, we saw, regard themselves as "exploding" an "Enlightenment project" that, they claim, has given to modernity its distinctive stamp. In countless postmodernist writings, that project is described in terms of a faith in the power of reason to discover *a priori* the objective nature of a world and moral order as they are independent of human perspectives and interests. But this is a parody of Enlightenment thought. It is especially odd to find that project foisted, as it frequently is, on Immanuel Kant. The two central claims of his first *Critique*, after all, are that, despite "dogmatist" pretensions, reason is incapable of discovering *anything* about the world as it is "in itself," and that the world of which there can be any understanding is dependent upon the structures of our cognition and perception. More generally, the emphasis of Enlightenment thinkers was not upon the powers of unaided reason, but on the ability of empirical investigation, freed from various theological and metaphysical prejudices, to furnish understanding of the world and human nature. Moreover, as Jürgen Habermas (1987) has stressed, it was precisely during the Enlightenment period – in the writings of Kant, Fichte, and, above all, Hegel – that the question of how we should respond to the fact that we ourselves are responsible for our values, purposes, and nature first became salient: the very question, that is, which postmodernist writers give the impression of being the first to confront.

Twentieth-century "analytical" philosophy is often portrayed by postmodernists as continuing the Enlightenment project. But in the writings of, *inter alia*, Wilfred Sellars, Donald Davidson, and John McDowell, there is no less hostility than in the postmodernist camp toward the image of a given reality "out there" with which our conceptual and linguistic schemes might be compared. In moral philosophy, especially, the dominant analytical tendency has been a rejection of "moral realism," while in the philosophy of science, it is difficult to think of an English-language thinker of note who has not anticipated postmodernist attacks on the image of science as a value-free inquiry that establishes, with infallible certainty, the nature of reality as it presents itself to the unprejudiced mind (see Mackenzie, 1998).

That postmodernist writers are often guilty of historical parody, and that, as a result, the novelty of many of their claims is exaggerated, are not perhaps of great moment in themselves. They do, however, invite the suspicion that postmodernist proclamations against objectivity, truth, rationality, moral autonomy, and so on are themselves exaggerated responses to insights that are neither new nor, when properly grasped, apt to inspire such radical rhetoric. Suspicion, for some critics, turns into certainty when one examines the arguments deployed by postmodernists in support of those proclamations. These arguments, the critics allege, are feeble ones that reflect blindness to various, sometimes obvious, distinctions.

Consider, for example, the insistence that the world as described by the sciences is not an "objective," but a "constructed," one. Often the only reason given for this is the truism that scientific *theories* are human constructs. Obviously we should distinguish between X and a theory of X, and from the fact that the latter is constructed, it does not begin to follow that the former is. Or consider the claim that since all inquiry presupposes social practices and interests, we must abandon the pretension to provide a correct representation of an independent reality. This fails to distinguish the unobjectionable thought that representations are *causally* dependent on social factors from the contentious one that they are necessarily *infected* by them, that representations can never transcend the interests and perspectives that made them possible (see Siegel, 1995). Or consider, finally, the claim that once something is shown to be "invented" or "constructed," rather than "natural," then it no longer "constrains" us and we are free to "create" or "invent" something else in its place. One should not, however, confuse the natural with the fixed, or the "invented" with the optional. The structures of English syntax are, in a sense, "invented" by human beings, but no speaker can ignore them without paying the price of unintelligibility. Nor does one establish that certain moral rules are not binding merely by observing that, in a similar sense, they are of human "invention."

A final line of criticism is that the postmodernist stance is self-defeating. At its simplest, this criticism takes the form of identifying the paradox generated by denials of truth and rationality. How can such denials themselves be true or reasonable to endorse? And if they cannot be, they should be ignored. Radical postmodernists respond to this in one of two ways. They may take it on the chin, but add that charges of paradox belong to a "logocentric" tradition that should anyway be "deconstructed." In effect, they are happy to regard their own assertions and proposals as "moves" in a game that we are free to join in or stay away from. Alternatively, they may reject the suggestion that they are denying truth and rationality, insisting that it is only traditional conceptions of these that are being rubbished and that their own assertions can be true or rational in senses acceptable by postmodernist lights. They can, for example, accord with standards or rules that we have "created," or, like "Nazism is wrong," suit our present "literary taste." Neither response will impress critics. The first marks a blunt refusal of the constraints of intelligent, and intelligible, discourse. The second divests notions like standards and values of sense, for ones that we may create and undo at will, or according to taste, cannot play that role in the guidance of behavior and judgment that standards and values, to be such, must possess.

"The Last Word"

Many writers who, without adopting the full postmodernist stance, are nevertheless sympathetic to aspects of it, and seek to think about education "after the style" of postmodernism, accept much of the criticism just described. Perhaps postmodernists are guilty of historical parody, feeble arguments and failures to heed vital distinctions, and self-stultifying pronouncements. However, these sympathizers continue, such deficiencies can be repaired. A better historical story would show that postmodernist insights, while anticipated by many philosophers, are effective against received, popular images of, say, scientific enquiry that are still entrenched in education, and that they bring out implications to which earlier champions of anti-foundationalist, fallibilist conceptions of truth and objectivity have been blind. Better arguments than those often offered might, without ignoring crucial distinctions, succeed in securing the conclusions postmodernists draw – for example, the claim that no account of the world could transcend, and be "uninfected" by, "all-too-human" perspectives and interests. Better formulations of the postmodernist position might protect against charges of paradox or senselessness.

Some such attitude – that, in effect, of the "moderates" discussed in my section on postmodernism and education – should be taken seriously. But so should the question of whether such a "moderate" position is a stable one, whether there is a comfortable place to occupy between an "absolutist" or foundationalist conception of truth and value and a "whole hog" embrace of a "playful," anarchic or nihilistic attitude to our beliefs and commitments – an attitude congenial to those postmodernists who proclaim "the end of education."

Consider, in order to illustrate this question, one educational philosopher's defense of a "moderate" postmodernist endorsement of the democratic, "emancipatory values" long held dear in the tradition of liberal education. With all prospect of "*a priori* philosophical foundations" for such values now destroyed, they need not, however, be abandoned. Instead we can recognize that "what justifies our continuing allegiance to [these] values is their congruence with our present understanding of ourselves" (Carr, 1995, p. 81). The problem is whether this "congruence" can serve as *any* sort of justification. After all, a similar congruence with "our" present understanding, if "we" were Chinese or Iranians, would "justify" continuing allegiance to very different educational values indeed. (A point sometimes made is that the position of Rorty and other postmodernists – with their celebration of freedom and

215

creativity – sounds strikingly "Eurocentric" (Herwitz, 1998, p. 61).) If that is right, the attempt to justify certain educational practices or ideals – as distinct from a self-confessedly unwarranted "choice" of, or "taste" for, them – sounds bogus. Certainly it sounds like bootstrapping to "justify" democratic commitments by appealing to a self-understanding that has itself been shaped by those commitments.

The more general issue, put in Thomas Nagel's (1997) terms, is whether "the last word" in attempts to justify or give reasons can rest with anything other than truths and norms that obtain quite independently of "our" understanding and commitments. If "the last word" rests with convictions that we have simply decided to adopt, or that for purely contingent reasons we happen to find ourselves with, it is surely arguable that the whole enterprise of justification and reason-giving collapses. And if that argument is right, there is, perhaps, no firm ground to occupy between the poles of traditional philosophical realism and virulent, "whole hog" postmodernism.

See also 6 ENLIGHTENMENT LIBERALISM; 11 CRITICAL THEORY; 12 THE ANALYTICAL MOVEMENT; 15 THE NATURE AND PURPOSES OF EDUCATION; 20 KNOWLEDGE, TRUTH, AND LEARNING; 21 CULTIVATING REASON; 25 TEACHING ELEMENTARY ARITHMETIC THROUGH APPLICATIONS; 27 TEACHING LITERATURE

References

Blake, N., Smeyers, P., Smith, R., and Standish, P. (1998) *Thinking Again: Education after Postmodernism*. Westport, CT: Bergin & Garvey.

Carr, W. (1995) Education and democracy: confronting the postmodernist challenge. *Journal of the Philosophy of Education*, 29, 75–91.

Cooper, D. (1996) *World Philosophies: An Historical Introduction*. Oxford: Blackwell (rev edn 2002).

Cooper, D. (1998a) Postmodernism and "the end of philosophy." In J. Good and I. Velody (eds), *The Politics of Postmodernity*. Cambridge: Cambridge University Press, pp. 61–72.

Cooper, D. (1998b) Interpretation, construction and the "postmodern" ethos. In D. Carr (ed.), *Education, Knowledge and Truth: Beyond the Postmodern Impasse*. London: Routledge, pp. 37–50.

Derrida, J. (1976) *Of Grammatology*, trans. G. Spivak. Baltimore: Johns Hopkins University Press (originally published in 1967).

Derrida, J. (1981) *Positions*, trans. A. Bass. Chicago: University of Chicago Press (originally published in 1972).

Giesecke, H. (1987) *Das Ende der Erziehung: neue Chancen für Familie und Schule* [*The End of Education: New Opportunities for the Family and School*]. Stuttgart: Klett-Cotta.

Giroux, H. (1988) Postmodernism and the discourse of educational criticism. *Journal of Education*, 170, 5–30.

Habermas, J. (1987) *The Philosophical Discourse of Modernity*, trans. F. Lawrence. Cambridge: Polity Press (originally published in 1986).

Herwitz, D. (1998) Postmodernism: a historical and conceptual overview. In M. Kelly (ed.), *Encyclopedia of Aesthetics*, volume 4. Oxford: Oxford University Press, pp. 58–63.

Lyotard, J.-F. (1984) *The Postmodern Condition: A Report on Knowledge*, trans. G. Bennington and B. Massumi. Manchester: University of Manchester Press (originally published in 1979).

Lyotard, J.-F. (1988) *The Differend: Phrases in Dispute*, trans. G. van den Abbeele. Minneapolis: University of Minnesota Press.

Lyotard, J.-F. (1993) *Political Writings*, trans. B. Readings and K. Geiman. Minneapolis: University of Minnesota Press.

Mackenzie, J. (1998) Science education after postmodernism. In D. Carr (ed.), *Education, Knowledge and Truth: Beyond the Postmodern Impasse*. London: Routledge, pp. 53–67.

Nagel, T. (1997) *The Last Word*. Oxford: Oxford University Press.

Parker, S. (1997) *Reflective Teaching in the Postmodern World: A Manifesto for Education in Postmodernity*. Buckingham: Open University Press.

Rorty, R. (1982) *Consequences of pragmatism: Essays 1972–80*. Brighton: Harvester.

Rorty, R. (1987) Posties. *London Review of Books*, September 3, 11–12.

Rorty, R. (1989) *Contingency, Irony, and Solidarity*. Cambridge: Cambridge University Press.

Siegel, H. (1995) "Radical" pedagogy requires "conservative" epistemology. *Journal of the Philosophy of Education*, 29, 33–46.

Sloterdijk, P. (1987) *Critique of Cynical Reason*, trans. M. Eldred. Minneapolis: University of Minnesota Press (originally published in 1983).

Smeyers, P. (1995) Education and the educational project (1): the atmosphere of postmodernism. *Journal of the Philosophy of Education*, 29, 109–19.

Standish, P. (1995) Postmodernism and the education of the whole person. *Journal of the Philosophy of Education*, 29, 121–36.

Wittgenstein, L. (1969) *On Certainty*, trans. D. Paul and G. Anscombe. Oxford: Blackwell.

Further reading

Barnett, R. and Griffin, A. (eds) (1997) *The End of Knowledge in Higher Education*. London: Cassell.

Boghossian, P. (2001) What is social construction? *Times Literary Supplement*, February 23, 6–8.

Carr, D. (ed.) (1998) *Education, Knowledge and Truth: Beyond the Postmodern Impasse*. London: Routledge.

Cooper, D. (1983) *Authentivity and Learning: Nietzsche's Educational Philosophy*. London: Routledge & Kegan Paul.

Cooper, D. (2002) *Humanism, Humility and Mystery*. Oxford: Oxford University Press.

Harvey, D. (1989) *The Condition of Postmodernity: An Enquiry into the Origins of Cultural Change*. Oxford: Blackwell.

McDowell, J. (1996) *Mind and World*. Cambridge, MA: Harvard University Press.

Nagel, T. (1986) *The View from Nowhere*. Oxford: Oxford University Press.

Peters, M. (ed.) (1995) *Education and the Postmodern Condition*. New York: Bergin & Garvey.

Siegel, H. (1997) *Rationality Redeemed? Further Dialogues on an Educational Ideal*. New York: Routledge.

Usher, R. and Edwards, R. (1994) *Postmodernism and Education: Different Voices, Different Worlds*. London: Routledge.

Part II

TEACHING AND LEARNING

15

The Nature and Purposes of Education

Paul Standish

The Ends of Education

In Roger Marples's useful collection *The Aims of Education* (1999), a number of contributors sketch the different ways in which the question of aims has been addressed in educational theory. Kevin Harris's approach is indicative. Recognizing the salience of such questions in the study of education, he explains: "in the first lecture of every course I give, I stress that 'education' is a changing, contextual and often highly personalized, historically and politically constructed concept." To illustrate this Harris reads some dictionary definitions and gives examples of stated "aims of education," what R. S. Peters called, with some disparagement, "high level directives for education":

When students hear that D. H. Lawrence claimed that education should aim to "lead the individual nature in each man and woman to its true fullness," that for Rousseau the aim of education was "to come into accord with the teaching of nature," that R. M. Hutchins saw the aim of education as "cultivation of the intellect," that A. S. Neill believed the aim of education should be to "make people happier, more secure, less neurotic, less prejudiced," and that John Locke claimed "education must aim at virtue and teach man to deny his desires, inclinations and appetite, and follow as reason directs"; hopefully the penny has dropped. Just in case it hasn't I add in that while Pope Pius XI was declaring that the aim of education was to "cooperate with divine grace in forming the true and perfect Christian," Sergei Shapovalenko insisted that education should aim "to inculcate the materialist outlook and communist mentality." That usually does the trick. (Harris, 1999, p. 1)

The unease that Harris stimulates serves to reveal not only the contested nature of the concept of education but also the strange trajectory of the question of aims.

While Peters was skeptical about high level directives for education, a different criticism has emerged in the assumption that aims are in fact uncontroversial, even commonsensical. Thus, the European Union's White Paper *Teaching and Learning: Towards the Learning Society* confidently asserts that debates over the aims of education are now at an end (European Commission, 1996): the purpose of education is to serve the economy. Philosophers of education may be scandalized by this, though some, resigned in their frustration, will have come to savor the outrage: their worst fears are confirmed! Yet what seems crude philistinism on the part of the Commission may not be so remote from the assumptions of the public at large. We need, do we not, a healthy economy – the *sine qua non* of everything else? And one thing we are routinely told is that the way to secure this, now as never before, is through education. So of course the ends of education must now be self-evident.

Expanding state provision of education requires huge expenditure, and hence a certain degree of economic prosperity. That prosperity depends upon equipping learners with the skills the modern economy needs. Society at large has a right to expect some kind of return along these lines for the investment it makes. Society *qua* democracy seems to require universal access to education. But where provision at higher levels is extended, especially where opportunity is uneven, the case for an economic return is more pressing. Expansion along these lines in recent decades warrants, so the thinking goes, a concomitant adjustment in educational aims.

As Marples's book makes apparent, there have been countless attempts to define the aims of education. The present chapter does not attempt to enumerate these. The idea that this might be done – that there should be some kind of categorization of aims, perhaps the better to identify the ones that best suit our circumstances – seems to distort what is at issue here. For it gives the impression that aims are things that might be chosen and then attached to means adopted or developed in order to realize them. To many the good sense of such a procedure will seem as clear as the light of day. But what goes wrong here has to do with a failure to understand the extent to which aims are internally related to certain kinds of practice.

Michael Oakeshott's celebrated conception of education as a kind of conversation is apposite here (Oakeshott, 1989, p. 96). Oakeshott argues that it is a mistake to suppose that behaving purposefully and meaningfully in important aspects of life such as education depends upon determining a goal and then calculating how to act to realize that goal. Instead, it is the other way about: it involves knowing how to behave in a certain way and trying to behave in that way. To speak of the goal or aims of such an activity will then be a kind of shorthand expression of this knowledge and behavior. It will not be a program – or the basis of a program – of action. Educational institutions are not contrivances of some sort with a particular function, appropriately stipulated by a statement of intent. To see them in such terms is already to have thrown something valuable away. Oakeshott's understanding of aims cannot even come into the picture if aims are imagined to be enumerable in the way considered above. Such enumeration precludes certain possible ways of addressing the topic that are the concern of this chapter. The predominantly utilitarian climate in which educational practice is currently conceived makes the occlusion of views or approaches such as Oakeshott's all the more probable.

While there can be no tidy classification of aims, in what follows I draw upon two commonly made distinctions. The first concerns liberal and vocational education. The second is of a slightly different order in that it relates not to a conceptual distinction but to theoretical constructions: the relationship between liberal education and progressivism.

Before embarking on this, however, I want to say something about the trajectory of the question of the aims of education as this has developed in educational theory and practice. There is little doubt that the direct consideration of the question of aims, which was once a staple component of courses in philosophy of education, has been partly displaced. At an institutional level, philosophy of education appears less prominently in many teacher education programs. In terms of broader cultural change, there has been the development of the kind of technicism identified above that regards the questioning of aims as a somewhat self-indulgent armchair pursuit standing in the way of real progress. Is it still possible to find a language in which something like the aims of education can be addressed, or has the whole thing now been sewn up and sorted, so it is imagined? It is no surprise that, with notable exceptions such as Marples's book, there has been less academic writing directly about the question in recent years than was common twenty or thirty years ago. In the main this is to be regretted: its absence has made all the more commonplace the facile and seemingly unobjectionable technicist assumptions represented here.

Sometimes the question has been seen as the issue *par excellence* for philosophy of education. There is considerable merit to this view but also dangers of portentousness and pomposity. The preoccupation with aims may stand in the way of the more patient characterization of good educational practice that is of real benefit to practitioners. It tends to predicate the consideration of education on a teleological metaphysics, harboring a fallacy of essentialism. And it can deflect attention from the diversity of education, from the fact that it is not just one thing. When the assumed focus of much philosophy of education was on schooling, this was understandable, if regrettable; with the growing sense of urgency about education beyond school age, with the expansion of higher education, and the new hype for lifelong learning, inattention to this diversity is inexcusable. And this should carry with it a more prominent acknowledgment of the ways in which education takes place outside institutions and beyond formal attempts to educate. In sum, the implications are not that the question of aims should be avoided but that it should be broached with greater reservations and sensitivity to this diversity.

Liberal Education and Vocational Education

What we now think of as education is the result not of an initial unity that has diversified but of the confluence and overlapping of multiple practices. Much thought has been given to the cogency and legitimacy of the range of schools, colleges, and other institutions that is now common, and to the social and cultural effects that follow from this. Many discussions here turn on the distinction between vocational and liberal education. This, however, is less clear than it might seem.

The distinction all too quickly becomes tied to a dichotomy between the intrinsic and the extrinsic. The identification of the vocational with external ends has a superficial plausibility and in some activities seems entirely reasonable. Learning word-processing seems to have little point aside from its usefulness. If the example raises doubts, however, consider typing, the predecessor of word-processing, in which more than a generation of girls was trained. Perhaps some may gain satisfaction from such an activity, but it would be odd to find fulfillment in it regardless of its usefulness. In contrast, vocational studies such as medicine or engineering incorporate a potential for inquiry and understanding that have their own forms of satisfaction, their own never-ending possibilities of growth. Studies in medicine and biology overlap in such a way that students or researchers working in these respective disciplines may be engaged in the same activities. Hence, there is no reason to suppose that the ultimate usefulness of certain activities should make them any the less intrinsically rich. Moreover, the apparent uselessness of studies such as ancient Greek or Latin conceals the possibility that they may train the mind in ways useful in various fields of work.

In *The Wealth of Nations* Adam Smith presents a picture of society as an efficient system in which educational institutions play a crucial role, justified in terms of their utility. Smith recognizes that a division of labor is necessary for economic progress and the creation of a civilized society. Yet a consequence of this is that the minds of workers will be dulled by the repetitiveness and narrow range of their tasks, dulled in a way that does not occur in more primitive societies: this is a basis of moral and intellectual decay. So a civilized society is undermined by the very measures set up to bring it about. As a palliative to the alienated condition of the majority in such a society, however, Smith turns again to education, and now the training in geometry and mechanics thought a proper preparation for employment is supplemented by an introduction to "sublime" useless pursuits. Because of the way degeneration is, as it were, built into the system of utility, we have the paradox that the useful becomes useless for the society it was designed to create. Conversely, the pursuit of useless sublime knowledge becomes useful in ameliorating those worst effects of utility, and hence in sustaining the society. The opposition between usefulness and uselessness begins to fall apart (see Young, 1992, pp. 121–2).

The intrinsic/extrinsic dichotomy is then clearly less stable than has commonly been supposed. But the point here is more general and profound: the dichotomy may itself be tied in to a means–ends thinking that rules out in advance certain ways of thinking about education. What seems clear is that the relation of means to ends differs with different practices. Typing is a means to the production of printed letters, where alternative processes would serve equally well. Engineering is not dispensable in this way. The range of practices covered by this term is infinitely greater than is the case with typing, encompassing the design and mastery of machines, however they may develop. Human beings by their very nature live in a world increasingly shaped by design and manufacturing practice so that, while typing may be obsolescent, engineering itself cannot be. Engineering involves a mastery of technical means that incorporates some larger ethical sense of purposes and effects. Aspects of engineering may be pursued in educational institutions in far more limited, and indeed obsolescent, ways, but anyone who is trained merely in a specific technique without reference to these larger considerations is scarcely doing engineering at all, any more, that is, than is the typist.

With changing practice in vocational education these larger ethical considerations are coming to be recognized in curricula. Following a period in which the term "vocational" had an aura of robust, hard-headed practicality, and following recognition of the uselessness of much vocational training, there has been some rethinking of the field at large. But the tendency has been to incorporate ethical considerations in the manner of bolt-on components. Typically the ethical is understood first and foremost in terms of *issues*. Thus, courses in medical or business ethics have burgeoned. The isolation of the ethical in discrete components of courses may have the effect of reinforcing the belief that there is a brute objectivity, the real business of the vocational, to which these considerations are attached. What is less evident is attention to the ways in which some sense of the good must characterize such practices, must give them their very sense. Current discourse about vocational education is almost completely devoid of any richer sense of what a vocation might be. The loss of the sense of *calling* is not the replacement of idealism with down-to-earth practicality. That a vocation might give meaning to a person's life as a whole is understood in only the most limited degree.

Liberal Education and Progressivism

While the disjunction of liberal and vocational education is less clear than is commonly supposed, the connection between liberal education and progressivism needs to be called into question. The term "liberal education" is itself controversial, connoting origins in both the thought of Ancient Greece and the political liberalism of the modern world. The looseness of the term "liberal" means that "liberal education" is at its clearest when the phrase is used stipulatively.

A divergence persists between, roughly, American understandings of this phrase and those in other parts of the anglophone world. For while a congruence between liberal education and progressivism is often assumed in the former context, in the latter these are commonly understood to be opposed in important respects. Congruence is assumed especially where Dewey is the dominant figure. Opposition is apparent in such a context as the UK of the 1960s and 1970s, where the child-centered practices promoted by both educationalists and government reports (the Plowden Report and the Primary Memorandum in Scotland) were called into question by philosophers of education working in the analytical tradition. R. S. Peters, Paul Hirst, and Robert Dearden undertook to restate the claims of liberal education in the face of its erosion by progressive practices. Their targets included what they regarded as sentimentalization in progressivist conceptions of play, happiness, creativity, integration, and discovery learning. Peters famously expressed the view that child-centered education was too much concerned with the *manner* of education, insufficiently with the *matter* of education. With the attention on the learner, there was a tendency to lose sight of the nature and importance of traditions of inquiry, of the forms of knowledge that constitute the conversation of mankind. These thinkers developed a body of ideas at a crucial time of expansion for teacher education, attracting attention from around the world. Nor was this in any sense a peculiarly British project. In the United States, and at about the same time, Israel Scheffler developed an analytical approach to education to similar effect.

Liberal education and progressivism are united in their opposition to the instrumentalization of education, obviously sharing a commitment to freedom, to some kind of emancipation of the learner. It is perhaps in their understanding of what freedom consists in, however, that their difference can most clearly be seen. In progressivism the assumption tends to be that children's natural freedom needs to be cherished and allowed to develop in its own way, guided perhaps but not curtailed. In liberal education, freedom is a state to be worked toward, and this can be done only through an initiation into public forms of knowledge, a process through which mind is realized, no less, and human nature properly comes into its own. The influence of modern political liberalism on liberal education is reflected in its partial departure from its classical counterpart. Plato's concern, in respect of those most capable of education, is ultimately with a freedom from illusion, in the direction of attention toward the good – a theme running through the dialogues and given particularly vivid expression in the Myth of the Cave. There is no questioning the importance in modern liberal education of seeing things truly, but, to the extent that the ideal of rational autonomy is central to its concerns, the good life that is celebrated is understood in terms of agency. This contrasts with the receptivity in contemplation of the good that is Plato's concern, and it parts company in some degree with other aspects of this tradition of thought, including that of Oakeshott on whom these thinkers explicitly draw.

It is surely an understatement that neither liberal education nor progressivism is in the ascendancy at present. Reactionary tendencies have combined with frenetic "innovation" in service of the unpredictable demands of the economy and in the face of globalization. With the rise of notions of efficiency and effectiveness, with the importing of quality control from industrial practice, with the mantras of standards and excellence, there has been a stifling of serious debate about the nature and purposes of education. With the vacuum of values that these words conceal, a kind of nihilism is manifest (see Blake et al., 2000).

Information and Communications Technology

In 1979, in *The Postmodern Condition: A Report on Knowledge*, Jean-François Lyotard showed remarkable prescience of the threat to education that these changes constituted, aptly encompassing them in the term "performativity." A dimension of the pervasive managerialism that characterizes the contemporary world, performativity is heavily shaped by information and communications technology. The spreadsheets and databases that the computer so readily makes available facilitate accounting in new ways and on an unprecedented scale, profoundly influencing managerial practice and thinking. So too in curricula, the computer becomes something more than a technical aid to teaching and learning. More than an instrument, it is a site of the restructuring of these very processes.

The tendency in the philosophical literature has been to bemoan the effects of the computer in education: it reduces knowledge to information, and learning to skills of information access; it rewrites curricula as programmed learning, in consequence deskilling (if not dispensing with) the teacher; it weakens contact between teacher and learner, between fellow students; it distorts the very idea of education for teachers and learners alike. These are real dangers and, given the background managerialism, it is difficult to be optimistic that the tide of this change can be withstood.

Yet it would be wrong to deny the real benefit the Internet can bring. This is not just a matter of economies of scale and the extension of educational opportunities to people to whom they have previously been denied – including their extension in poorer parts of the world. It is also to be found in the new kinds of interaction, accessibility, and exploration that the technology makes possible. As a simple example, e-mail is a new form of communication, with limitations and possibilities different from, say, letter-writing or the telephone. Its practice is not predetermined but still to be developed, its potential in education still to be explored. So too, as searching of the web becomes more sophisticated, there may be rich, unprecedented possibilities of discovery, suggesting forms of enquiry at odds with the linear and closed structures of programmed learning. It is important to look imaginatively at such possibilities (see Blake and Standish, 2000). Increasing commercial involvement in education and the huge stakes that education represents for the information and communications technology industry make change unstoppable, with commercial interests best served where education is promoted along more or less programmed lines. It is imperative that other, richer possibilities of that technology are emphasized.

Programmed learning can be seen as the apotheosis of the principle that education requires the setting of clear objectives and the adoption of efficient means to their realization. It is education canned for convenience. Precisely against such assumptions Dewey argued that education must involve a "freeing activity." Aims imposed in advance in this way result in the intelligence of the learner being unfree, being confined to receiving aims laid down from above. The "dictation of authoritative supervisor, textbook on methods, prescribed course of study, etc." that Dewey feared can easily be intensified in certain modes of computer-assisted learning, however user-friendly these may appear. Under such circumstances the teacher is unable to "let his mind come to close quarters with the pupil's mind and the subject matter. This distrust of the teacher's experience is then reflected in lack of confidence in the responses of pupils" (Dewey, 1916, pp. 108–9).

The emphasis here is not just on the manner of education but on the teacher's coming to close quarters with the pupil's mind *through an authentic engagement with the subject matter*. Yet in progressivism's stress on freedom of activity this emphasis is not always apparent. Reduction in attention to content is likely to be amplified where a computer screen is the primary means of experience.

Ironically, for all that child-centeredness has been reviled by politicians as the root of the problems of society these past twenty years, there has been a resurgence of similar ideas in the contemporary rhetoric of student-centeredness in post-compulsory education. But here student-centeredness dovetails with the commodified, shopping-mall conception of education that is the managerialist and commercial dream. The duplicity of its vocabulary of choice, facilitation, ownership, and empowerment – muddling emancipation and consumerism – has lulled progressivist educators into cooperation, oblivious to the degenerate tendencies at work.

The unremitting teleological metaphysics that runs through these harmful practices, the miniature means-to-ends scenarios that they obsessively play out, are markedly at odds with the flow of activity, the constant renewal, that is Dewey's preoccupation. Teleological thinking becomes grotesque where it conceives of human beings and their politics as perfectible – in terms of ends that are in principle realizable. Sometimes, though in a manner far more benign, liberal education also becomes teleological, where, for example, it has been felt necessary to identify its end in terms of "the educated man." In what follows I want, with Dewey, to resist teleology but in a way that diverges from his pragmatism. It is in the contrast between teleological perfectibility and *perfectionism* that another way of thinking, of immense

227

potential for education, can be revealed. I explore this by way of the Emersonian moral perfectionism that has been developed by Stanley Cavell. Cavell traces a line of thought in Emerson that finds its way not only through American culture but, in one form or another, through Nietzsche and his legacy. This points to a reorientation of the very question of aims.

Perfectibility and Perfectionism

Cavell understands Emersonian perfectionism in terms of a loose set of features, all related to a kind of cultural conversion. The tone of moral urgency, elevated by the religious timbre of the prose, expresses the fact that morality is not a (limited) part of ourselves but more like something that runs through all we do. Perfectionism's most salient features are seen in a pattern whereby, through friendship and education,

each self is drawn on a journey of ascent . . . to a further state of that self, where . . . the higher is determined not by natural talent but by seeking to know what you are made of and cultivating the thing you are meant to do; it is a transformation of the self which finds expression in . . . the imagination of a transformation of society into . . . something like an aristocracy where . . . what is best for society is a model for and is modeled on what is best for the individual soul. (Cavell, 1990, p. 7)

Far from any crude individualism, this suggests aspiration toward our own best selves. What is aspired to is typically understood in terms of a new reality – the good city, the good society. It involves thinking how our world should be constituted, what words we can find for it, what practices should give it substance, what standards sustain it. Perfection's obsession with education, Cavell says, "expresses its focus on finding one's way rather than on getting oneself or another to take the way" (p. xxxii). Beyond the presumptions of freedom in progressivism and in resistance to the teleological and cerebral emphases in liberal education, it is necessary to ask what this finding of one's way might require.

Emersonian perfectionism requires a delicate adjustment between convention and individual: between an inevitable conformity – to the ways of being and vocabularies, the conventions that I must be initiated into in order to acquire a voice – and the voice that becomes my own. "What I require," Cavell writes,

is a convening of my culture's criteria, in order to confront them with my words and life as I pursue them; and at the same time to confront my words and life as I pursue them with the life my culture's words may imagine for me: to confront the culture with itself, along the lines in which it meets in me. (Cavell, 1979, p. 125)

It is not so much the *sovereignty* of rational autonomy that resides within the individual who has cast off the common motives of humanity: the suggestion is of something religious rather than regal, a light that illumines that person's character (Emerson, 1982, p. 194), and this light is derived from attunement to energies that, in their conduit through the self, are not diminished but amplified, intensified and given new radiance.

228

Any idea I have of myself as a whole is essentially only provisional: the soul is "an immensity not possessed and that cannot be possessed" (Emerson, 1982, p. 208). Imagining that I can construct myself incrementally, in a progressive acquisition of experience and skills, blinds me to this reality: "Our life is an apprenticeship to the truth that around every circle another can be drawn; that there is no end in nature, but every end is a beginning; that there is always another dawn risen on midnoon, and under every deep a lower deep opens" (Emerson, 1982, p. 225). Indeed, there is a kind of blasphemy in any attempt to approach such deeps directly. There is idolatry in the unswerving pursuit of fixed ends.

Living up to this recognition, which deprives me of an identity or attainment in which I might otherwise settle and hence saves me from complacency or hubris, is demanding in the extreme:

I have my own stern claims and perfect circle. It denies the name of duty to many offices that are called duties. But if I can discharge its debts it enables me to dispense with the popular code. If any one imagines that this law is lax, let him keep its commandment one day. (Emerson, 1982, p. 193)

Yet the popular code is not dispensable in any simple iconoclasm, still less in a kind of freedom *ab initio*. It is only on the strength of, and out of, initiation into the criteria that constitute the world in which I am brought up that I can rise to the demands of this sterner regime.

This aversion from conformity seeks also to uncover a possibility of what society might be. Democracy can only sustain its truth to itself by keeping alive the question of what democracy is, by way of its necessary voice within. It is aversion, not settlement (or "inclusion," one might say), that provides the possibility of movement toward a democracy that is always still to come.

A microcosm of this politics is seen in the individual's preparedness to be challenged by the other, by the friend or the challenging text. The friend does service by presenting back to me another, more exacting possibility of myself that otherwise only flickers in my vision. Emerson sees his own text as functioning as a friend does in setting up before us for our silent contemplation and response an *other* – a way of thinking in which we find our own thoughts, challenged. "My thought," writes Cavell,

is that a certain relation to words (as an allegory of my relation to life) is inseparable from a certain moral-like relation to thinking, and that the morality and the thinking that are insepar-able are of specific strains – the morality is neither teleological (basing itself on a conception of the good to be maximized in society) nor deontological (basing itself on an independent conception of the right), and that thinking is some as yet unknown distance from what we think of as reasoning. (Cavell, 1990, p. 46)

Unlike the (supposedly realizable) perfectibility envisaged in Leninism or National Socialism or Skinnerian behaviorism (contrast *Walden Two* with *Walden*), or the vapid satisfactions of the "end of history," Emersonian perfectionism involves the recogni-tion of our partial nature, our essential incompleteness, and this engenders at once a poignant sense of lack and an elevation by something ahead of us, beyond our grasp, something if not ineffable at least defiant of any tidy literal formulation. This – let it be emphasized – is an *essential* incompleteness, not an incompleteness to which we might add some missing component to make ourselves "complete." It suggests the messianism of a fulfillment that is always still-to-come. Utopian vision here functions as something non-real but visionary, and having such leverage on our real world as to enable the raising of standards in its pursuit, standards enabling us to live a life more fully realized.

This is a world apart from the free individual celebrated in political liberalism. It is not, of course, that rights and duties are of no account. It is that they are misunderstood if they are not seen in the light of the patterns of this conformity and aversion. We are founded in the ways that we find ourselves, in the culture with its givens, with the acknowledgment and observance that it requires of us. It is in relation to these given practices that we find our voice. In the culture we are schooled in we find the words that make possible our aversion from conformity, not least in the rich traditions of subjects of study. And this aversion, a kind of turning of the head (from our conformity, from the flickering images at the back of the Cave), is internally related to the possibility of our living better, of our orientation toward perfection. It is a moral imperative that comes from neither authority nor law but that speaks to our own best, attained yet unattained, selves. Finding our voice in this way is our most authentic engagement with the world.

The End of Schooling

That the friend or the challenging text is critical to this process raises new questions for educational practice increasingly shaped by information and communications technology, questions seldom understood by those at the forefront of its development. Conversely, that these relations are not necessarily obstructed by technology is not always recognized, especially by those most anxious to protect them. Understanding the importance of such relations and their congruence with certain possibilities of the technology should lay the way for imaginative developments in policy and practice.

Despite this note of optimism, however, the climate is bleak. Instrumental reason has emaciated the ethical language in which we consider our lives and education, distorting the public and private realms of our experience. Performativity constitutes the most grave threat. Although it is itself in part the outcome of new technology, although its agents see themselves as champions of that technology's hastening development, it also epitomizes the thinking that will most obstruct the technology's potential.

In the larger course of things, schools and colleges such as we know today are a relatively recent and local phenomenon, however much they may have become natural in the experience of recent generations. These institutions are now in the sway of a number of influences: the drive to adopt new technology more extensively; the global influence of commercial providers of information and communications technology and their interest in education as a growth market; the involvement of private companies in the running of schools and marketization of the post-compulsory sector; increasing indiscipline and disaffection within schools; the

230

constriction of the curriculum by multiculturalist and religious tensions; the growing practice of home-schooling; and governments eager to be seen to be doing something about education (and alert to potential economies of scale). It is now difficult to believe that in medieval Europe one in five people was employed by the Church. So too the demise of the institutions we now work in is difficult to entertain. But whatever their fate, outside the institution the issues addressed here must persist. Questions about the nature and purposes of education are ultimately questions about what it is to be, and about how we understand what it is to be, human.

See also 1 THE SOCRATIC MOVEMENT; 6 ENLIGHTENMENT LIBERALISM; 9 ROMANTICISM; 12 THE ANALYTIC MOVEMENT; 13 FEMINISM; 18 MOTIVATION AND CLASSROOM MANAGEMENT; 20 KNOWLEDGE, TRUTH, AND LEARNING; 21 CULTIVATING REASON; 22 MORAL EDUCATION; 28 THE AUTHORITY AND RESPONSIBILITY TO EDUCATE; 30 COMMON SCHOOLING AND EDUCATIONAL CHOICE; 32 EDUCATION AND STANDARDS OF LIVING; 39 ETHICS AND THE AIMS OF AMERICAN HIGHER EDUCATION; 40 UNIVERSITIES IN A FLUID AGE; 45 THE ROLE OF ETHICS IN PROFESSIONAL EDUCATION

References

Blake, N., Smeyers, P., Smith, R., and Standish, P. (2000) *Education in an Age of Nihilism*. London: Routledge/Falmer.

Blake, N. and Standish, P. (eds) (2000) *Enquiries at the Interface: Philosophical Problems of Online Education*. Oxford: Blackwell.

Cavell, S. (1979) *The Claim of Reason: Wittgenstein, Scepticism, Morality, and Tragedy*. New York and Oxford: Oxford University Press.

Cavell, S. (1990) *Conditions Handsome and Unhandsome: The Constitution of Emersonian Perfectionism*. Chicago: University of Chicago Press.

Dewey, J. (1916) *Democracy and Education*. New York: The Free Press.

Emerson, R. (1982) *Selected Essays*. New York and London: Penguin.

European Commission, Directorates General XXII and V (1996) *Teaching and Learning: Towards the Learning Society*, a White Paper on education and training. Luxembourg: Office for Official Publications of the European Communities.

Harris, K. (1999) Aims! Whose aims? In R. Marples (ed.), *The Aims of Education*. London and New York: Routledge, pp. 1–13.

Lyotard, J.-F. (1984) *The Postmodern Condition: A Report on Knowledge*, trans. G. Bennington and B. Massumi. Minneapolis: University of Minnesota Press.

Oakeshott, M. (1989) *The Voice of Liberal Learning: Michael Oakeshott on Education*, ed. T. Fuller. New Haven, CT: Yale University Press.

Young, R. (1992) The idea of a chrestomathic university. In R. Rand (ed.), *Logomachia: The Conflict of the Faculties*. Lincoln: University of Nebraska Press, pp. 97–126.

16

Theories of Teaching and Learning

D. C. Phillips

There is a close relationship between theories of teaching and theories of learning, although it is not a simple matter to give it adequate characterization. Many contemporary authorities see teaching (that is, good or effective teaching) as being parasitic upon some theory of learning. Bruce Joyce and his co-authors, in the most recent edition of a text widely used in teacher-training, *Models of Teaching*, write that "The models of teaching described in this book come from beliefs about the nature of human beings and how they learn" (Joyce et al., 2000, p. 29), and a National Research Council (NRC) report in the USA in 1999 explicitly sees "advances in research on human cognition, development, and learning" as ideally driving educational practice (NRC, 1999, p.2). However, it seems clear that this simple account will not quite suffice. Two complexities are mentioned here by way of introduction to the main discussion.

First, as William James so eloquently pointed out in 1899, "to know psychology" (of learning, for example) "is absolutely no guarantee that we shall be good teachers" (James, 1958, p. 24). As he said,

you make a great, a very great mistake, if you think that psychology, being the science of the mind's laws, is something from which you can deduce definite programmes and schemes and methods of instruction for immediate schoolroom use. Psychology is a science, and teaching is an art; and sciences never generate arts directly out of themselves. An intermediary inventive mind must make the application, by using its originality. (James, 1958, pp. 23–4)

In our contemporary world, echoes of James can be found in the work of philosophers of education such as Gary Fenstermacher and David Carr, who stress that practical reasoning – which cannot be reduced to following rules or applying theories – plays a central role in the thinking of effective teachers (Fenstermacher, 1986; Carr, 2000).

Another complexity arises from the fact that teaching very often takes place in institutions (schools, colleges, churches, families), and thus to some degree is shaped in its goals and methods by institutional demands. To the extent that these institutional demands are legitimate, they complicate and in some sense loosen the relationship between learning theory and good teaching.

These complications notwithstanding, the focus of this chapter is the teaching and learning of academic subjects, the relationship between teaching and such learning, and how views about the former have changed as understanding of the nature of the latter has progressed. It will be useful to open with a limited discussion of the influential views of Plato, John Locke, and Jean-Jacques Rousseau, before focusing on selected theories of learning and teaching that have attained prominence during the past century.

Classic Theories of Teaching and Learning

Plato and the Socratic method

Plato's dialogues offer several images of learning and teaching, most famously their various illustrations of Socratic questioning on the one hand, and of ascent to apprehension of transcendental objects of knowledge, the "Forms," on the other.

The *Apology* offers what was apparently Socrates' own understanding of the function of what we now call the *elenchus* or *elenctic* questioning, a method of instruction whose aim is to lead an interlocutor to see the inconsistencies or contradictions in his own beliefs. Socrates understood the purpose of this to be to purge the one questioned of false beliefs – above all, the mistaken belief that he already possessed knowledge or wisdom. Although several early dialogues illustrate the employment of the *elenchus* as a method of testing proposed definitions of various virtues, definitions which Socrates apparently regarded as the key to acquiring the moral knowledge he lacked, no adequate definitions are ever reached. It remains unclear how the *elenchus* could suffice in itself to distinguish truth from error, let alone yield knowledge. Plato displays its limitations in *Republic* I and abandons it thereafter (Reeve, 1988, chapter 1). (For discussions of teaching through Socratic questioning and dialogue see Scheffler, 1967; Lipman, 1988, 1991; Haroutunian-Gordon, 1991; Burbules, 1993; Reich, 1998.)

The *Meno*, with its much discussed questioning of the slave boy, shows Socratic method in a new light. In these pages (82a–86b), Plato depicts Socrates interrogating a boy untutored in mathematics about a form of the Pythagorean theorem, leading him to the correct conclusion through questions, while telling him nothing directly. This episode, prefaced by the announcement of a theory of learning as recollection of perceptions gathered in another life – a theory predicated on a belief in immortality and transmigration of the human soul – suggests the view that effective teaching acts as a stimulus to recollection or conscious recognition of what a learner already in some sense knows.

This model of teacherless learning (Woodruff, 1998) is evidently more Platonic than Socratic in its adoption of mathematics as a model of knowledge, and its optimism about the possibility of human beings acquiring knowledge. Socrates displayed no such optimism, and there is little reason to assume that he asserted his own ignorance merely as a pedagogical stance. By contrast, Plato develops in the *Republic* an account of the philosopher as one whose desire for wisdom, training in the abstract sciences, and sustained practice of dialectical inquiry may enable him or her to acquire knowledge – a knowledge of *reality*, as opposed to mere true beliefs about the world of *appearances*. He explicates this concept of learning through various analogies: the *line* (of ascent from opinion to knowledge; 509d–511e), the *sun* (an image of the "Form of the Good" as highest object of knowledge and "cause of all that is correct and beautiful in anything"; 517b, 507a–509c), and the *cave* (514a–519b). The point of Plato's famous allegory of the cave, in which prisoners in a cave can see only shadows of imitations of reality, is that education is not "putting knowledge into souls" (518b), but the craft of turning a person's desires away from bodily appetites and status-seeking toward the deeper pleasures of learning or contemplation (hence, an art of turning "the whole body" (518c) or "soul" (518d)). To teach, then, is not to transmit knowledge, but to lead students to search for it. Plato conceived of the culmination of that search, when successful, as "understanding," an intellectual perception or apprehension of the "Forms" or first principles of all knowledge.

Locke, associationism, and object lessons

John Locke, one of the great early figures in the school of British empiricism, also occupies an important place in the history of educational thought. In a variety of ways he influenced how learning and teaching were conceived by many educationists from the late eighteenth to the early twentieth centuries, and even beyond. The influential aspect of Locke's philosophy, so far as the theme of this chapter is concerned, is his line of argument that all "simple ideas" (the building blocks of "human understanding") originate in experience: either "external" experience that comes to a person via "sensation" through the sense organs, or "internal" experience obtained by "reflection"; the ideas of "yellowness," "hardness," "extension" come via the senses, while "pain" and "concentration" come from reflection. Simple ideas can be combined in various ways, or can be abstracted, to form "complex ideas," but an individual cannot invent or acquire simple ideas for which he or she has not had the requisite experience, nor any complex ideas of which those simple ideas are parts. Once the "understanding" is "furnished" with ideas, it can grasp relationships between various ideas or come to *know* things, through immediate apprehension of such relationships and through following out chains of reasoning (Locke, 1975, Book IV; 1996, pp. 169–81).

Locke's "sensationalism" helped to establish the educational principle that children need to have a solid background of experience upon which their formal education can draw; without experience, at best they will learn words but will not have mastery of the underlying concepts. Along these lines, educators in the late nineteenth century started to grapple with the following types of cases: children living in remote inland areas might learn the word "sea," but they are unlikely to acquire the concept of the sea as an entity if they have not experienced it; similarly, many city-dwelling children will have no real concept of the farm animals they have met only in picture books. In the last few decades of the twentieth century a similar realization underlay the development of the television series *Sesame Street*, which tries to give pre-school children a stock of ideas and experiences that can underwrite their learning when they enter the early elementary grades. (For further discussion of Locke's influence, see Cleverley and Phillips, 1986, chapter 2; Phillips and Soltis, 1998, pp. 13–19.)

Sometime in the late eighteenth century an educational practice emerged that was justified in Lockean terms; first espoused by the Swiss educational reformer Johann

Pestalozzi (1746–1827), so-called "object lessons" were a form of training of the senses that were widely used in the emerging elementary school systems throughout Europe and the United States. The idea was that, over time, the teacher would lead students through a graded series of lessons in which they carefully observed the qualities of objects presented to them. Many textbooks were published describing object lessons in detail, down to the precise series of questions the teacher should ask.

Object lessons bear a family resemblance to the sense training regimens adopted later in Montessori schools. Like her contemporaries Jean Piaget and John Dewey, Maria Montessori (1870–1952) objected to the passive, absorptive view of children that was implicit in the work of what she called "mechanistic psychologists" (presumably the associationists). She wrote that according to their theory of knowledge "the impressions which we receive from external objects knock upon and, as it were, force the gates of our senses." The child is treated as an "empty vase" waiting to be filled – apparently a reference to Locke's work which used the analogy of "furnishing" an empty cabinet (Montessori, 1972, p. 60). According to her own theory, the child is an active and insatiable reasoner; but she also stressed that young children pass through a sensitive period in which they assimilate images from the environment "in a truly prodigious fashion." Having, as she put it, a "more rational esteem" for the child's sensations than did other schemes of education, she was concerned that the child not be overwhelmed. Thus, she designed the strict regimen of sensory exercises that were used in her schools to allow the child to carefully discriminate between sensations, and to systematically order and "pigeonhole" them.

Rousseau and later "progressive educators"

Jean-Jacques Rousseau's book *Émile* (1762) stands as the foundation stone of the modern progressive education movement; it was a book that inspired many, and infuriated probably an equal number. Written to be read in conjunction with Rousseau's political treatise, *The Social Contract* (1762), it makes a graphic case for educational principles illustrated by incidents in the early life of the book's hero. Émile is a young boy whose family arranges for him to be educated on an estate in the country away from the harmful influence of contemporary civilization, which Rousseau decries in his opening sentence: "Everything is good as it leaves the hands of the Author of things; everything degenerates in the hands of man" (Rousseau, 1979, p. 37). Not surprisingly, then, the boy is given a "natural" education, one conducted in a "natural" (i.e. not urban) setting and intended to preserve his "natural" (i.e. innate or God given) goodness and freedom, and the book traces his progress from early childhood to manhood and marriage. Rousseau stresses that in all things Émile should be free from artificial restraint; he should be as free as nature intended him to be, and should only feel the "harsh yoke which nature imposes upon man, the heavy yoke of necessity," and should not suffer "the caprice of men" (p. 91).

Young Émile's education is in the hands of a tutor, and it does not take a perspicuous reader to notice how directive and manipulative the tutor is or how unnatural, in one sense, the whole set-up is. Rousseau envisions an education that is "according to nature" in the two senses noted above, but also in the sense that it follows the sequence and timing of Émile's "natural" or internally determined stages of intellectual and moral development: his progress from being moved by pleasure and pain and sharpening his senses, to grasping what is useful and reasoning instrumentally, to being moved by reason and discovering all that "natural reason" may reveal. This belief that the natural development of children occurs in stages was later adopted and developed by others, most famously by Rousseau's fellow Genevan Jean Piaget in the twentieth century, and suggests that for teaching to be effective it must match the material to be taught to the child's stage of development (see Phillips and Soltis, 1998, chapter 5).

Another sense in which Rousseau considers Émile's education "natural" is that he learns through discovery and the largely spontaneous exercise of his own faculties, motivated and moved along from one topic to another by his own curiosity. The tutor is to teach Émile nothing, but instead ask leading questions and contrive experiences which will increase the efficiency and frequency of the lessons Émile will draw from his experiences and the "natural" consequences of his actions. The consequences may be physical (if he breaks a window, he will not be protected from the cold), but also social. This is illustrated repeatedly, perhaps most importantly through a cleverly contrived lesson in the sanctity of property and its origins in labor, in which Émile both suffers the destruction of the beans he has cultivated and learns that he has inadvertently destroyed melons which had already been sown in the plot he has tried to make his own (pp. 98–9), and a lesson in magnetism and the perils of pride, in which his vanity leads (naturally) to public humiliation (pp. 172–5). Rousseau seems to conceive of these experiences as ones in which Émile acquires moral concepts and an intuitive grasp of moral laws, and they run parallel to Émile's discovery of the laws of nature. "Let him not learn science, but discover it. If ever you substitute in his mind authority for reason, he will no longer reason," we read in Book III (p. 168). Accordingly, Émile's tutor sets him a question, "I was thinking that yesterday evening the sun set here and that this morning it rose there. How is that possible?" and leaves him "to worry over it for a few days before he discovers it" (p. 169). Rousseau suggests that after some thought and observations Émile learns Ptolemaic astronomy for himself and, even more implausibly, that "Copernican astronomy will follow when he himself makes the observations which lead to it" (p. 486, n1). Other examples of envisioned discovery learning of scientific phenomena, laws, and explanatory models, are equally oblivious to the role in science of mathematics and exact observation, and trade on a spurious equation of scientific concepts and reasoning with concepts obtained directly from experience and "natural" reasoning.

There is an obvious link here to the "discovery learning" practiced by many of the so-called progressive educators of the twentieth century, which again hinged upon the negative idea that the teacher should not attempt to impose knowledge upon students but should arrange for them to inquire for themselves. This approach assumes that children *can* inquire meaningfully in a variety of subject domains; but for many educational theorists of the twentieth century – including Dewey and the constructivists – the issue of how much a teacher should actually *tell* her students remained a pressing one.

The progressives had much in common with Rousseau; perhaps most obviously in the case of A. S. Neill, headmaster of Britain's most famous "free school," Summerhill, which flourished during the last seven decades or so of the twentieth century. "My view is that the child is innately wise and realistic. If left to himself without adult suggestion of any kind, he will develop as far as he is capable of developing," wrote Neill (1960, p. 4). Borrowing liberally from Freud as well as Rousseau, Neill held that freedom is also therapeutic, and allows children to shed the inhibitions and life-hating attitudes that they acquire through bad parenting or from previous inadequate schooling. At Summerhill, attendance at classes was voluntary and the lessons seemed to be taught in a fairly traditional manner; Neill believed that when students decided that they wanted to learn, they would decide to come to classes and they would master the academic content easily, almost irrespective of how it was taught. Above all, like Rousseau, he trusted children and had faith that they were naturally good and self-regulating.

John Dewey's Theory of Learning and Teaching

There is little doubt that John Dewey was the most influential progressive educational theorist and philosopher of education in North America during the twentieth century. Dewey's conversion to pragmatism and away from Hegel dates to his reading of William James's landmark book *The Principles of Psychology* shortly after its publication in 1890, and it was from this source (and later shorter popularizations) that Dewey's theory of learning was largely acquired.

It is significant that the chapter of Dewey's small book *The School and Society* (1902) that discusses the "psychology of elementary education" bears remarkable similarity to passages in James's popular *Talks to Teachers on Psychology* (1899). James and Dewey both adopted an evolutionary approach to learning, in which the human capacity to think and to learn was seen as an adaptive feature that promoted survival by allowing actions to be guided by reason and experience. As James summarized it,

I shall ask you now ... to adopt with me, in this course of lectures, the biological conception, as thus expressed, and to lay your own emphasis on the fact that man, whatever else he may be, is primarily a practical being, whose mind is given him to aid in adapting him to this world's life. (James, 1958, p. 34)

From this biological perspective a learner should be active, both mentally and physically, and be engaged with material that is of direct (and preferably practical) relevance. In *Democracy and Education* (1916) Dewey wrote that

The effect [of evolutionary theory] upon the theory of knowing is to displace the notion that it is the activity of a mere onlooker or spectator of the world. ... For the doctrine of organic development means that the living creature is a part of the world, sharing its vicissitudes and fortunes. (Dewey, 1966, p. 337)

This led Dewey to be a particularly severe critic of what he called the "spectator theory of knowing," in which the learner was depicted as a passive receptacle or spectator. Indeed, he argued that all classic epistemologies were spectator theories: not only empiricist theories, but even Plato's, his conception of the intellectual

237

activity required to attain knowledge notwithstanding. All were guilty of believing that knowledge could be attained without acting in the world to affect the object that was to become known; as Dewey went to great lengths to explain in 1929 in his *The Quest for Certainty*, the spectator theorists as he understood them treated the object of knowledge as fixed and antecedent to inquiry (Dewey, 1988). He stressed that not only evolutionary biology, but also the development of the experimental method, had made the defects of the spectator theory apparent. (This crucial aspect of Dewey's work remains controversial; see Kulp, 1992.)

Dewey's pragmatic epistemology was, in his view, directly related to education, for he regarded philosophy as "the general theory of education" (Dewey, 1966, p. 328). It was on the basis of his biological, experimental approach to epistemology that he advocated the use of activity and discovery methods, and projects, in the classroom. Just how far Dewey regarded contemporary schooling as falling short of the ideal espoused by James and himself is revealed in this evocative passage:

Just as the biologist can take a bone or two and reconstruct the whole animal, so, if we put before the mind's eye the ordinary schoolroom, with its rows of ugly desks placed in geometrical order, crowded together so that there shall be as little moving room as possible . . . and add a table, some chairs, the bare walls, and possibly a few pictures, we can reconstruct the only educational activity that can possibly go on in such a place. It is all made "for listening." (Dewey, 1969, p. 31)

In sum, then, Dewey wanted students to be active inquirers, working on problems that were genuine problems for them (rather than being merely problems the teacher had imposed); and it is important to add that he also saw the classroom as a community.

There are points of close contact between Dewey's work, as just outlined, and two extremely influential models of teaching that emerged in the late twentieth century. The first of these needs a little by way of introduction. It would be a misapprehension to think that Dewey advocated allowing the students to do whatever they pleased (this, in his view, was one of the failings of the more radical progressive educators); schools had the responsibility of ensuring that students were acquainted with what he sometimes termed "the funded wisdom of the human race" – the wisdom that was embodied in the curriculum. But (like Émile's tutor) the teacher would not impose material on the students; instead, the teacher's role was that of a resource, a facilitator (or, in the con-temporary euphemism, an "instructional leader"). In *The Child and the Curriculum* he argued that the teacher needed to be a *psychologizer* of subject-matter, taking the material that was in the curriculum and ordering it (and arranging for the students' interaction with it) in such a way that it was appropriate to their current concerns and to their present developmental and psychological state (Dewey, 1969).

This aspect of Dewey's work served as inspiration to the contemporary educational theorist Lee Shulman, who was one of the strongest advocates in the USA in the late twentieth century for the professionalization of teaching. Shulman sees the teacher's role very much as Dewey saw it, and he revived interest in the field of "psychology of subject matter." Shulman suggested that, in order to be able to psychologize the subject matter or content of teaching, the teacher needs to have a different understanding of it than that which is possessed by scholars expert in the same material. Teachers need to have the material mentally ordered for pedagogical (rather than for "logical") purposes. They need to understand which topics are educationally central, in the sense that if a student does not grasp them, mislearning of the subject will occur. They need to be able to anticipate misconceptions that are likely to hamper student learning of the content. They need to know what topics students are likely to have problems grasping, and they need to have examples, analogies, and learning strategies available that are tailored for these difficult topics. Shulman called all this "pedagogical content knowledge" or "subject matter knowledge for teaching" (Shulman, 1986, 1987). Following Shulman's suggestions, researchers are now actively investigating the learning of school subjects, especially mathematics, science, history, and literature.

The second point of contact between Dewey and contemporary theories of teaching and learning lies in the fact that Dewey was a major contributor to the modern constructivist movement, in the sense that he stressed that when teachers attempt to transfer knowledge to their students this will be "cold storage knowledge" unless the students are active in using it in application "to their own purposes" (Dewey, 1966, p. 158). In short, for Dewey learning is an activity (physical as well as intellectual) engaged in by students, not an absorptive or even purely intellectual process.

In the years after Dewey's death the term "constructivist" came to have a variety of meanings and came to cover an extraordinary range of psychologists, philosophers, and educational theorists. As a consequence it is probably best to think of the word in terms of a set of Wittgensteinian "family resemblances" – various usages might have very little in common. It is worth departing from the historical sequence of the chapter at this point to discuss this movement in more detail.

Contemporary Constructivist Theories of Teaching and Learning

To bring some order to the vast spectrum of "constructivist" positions, it is useful to think in terms of several strands or themes. In the first place there are two quite different (but not completely discrete) foci of interest in contemporary constructivism: many constructivists have as their interest individual learners (such things as the psychological mechanisms that play a role in their learning, and to what degree social factors contribute); other constructivists focus upon the way in which the public bodies of knowledge (disciplines such as the sciences, mathematics, economics, history) are "socially constructed." This latter group played a prominent role in the so-called "science wars" of the 1990s, but will not concern us here. The former group (sometimes called the "individual or psychological constructivists"), with acknowledged influences reaching back into the past (to Vico, Kant, and Rousseau, for example, and also Plato and Locke), include in the twentieth century Jean Piaget, Lev Vygotsky, Maria Montessori, John Dewey, and Ernst von Glasersfeld (Phillips, 1995, 2000). These constructivists differ among themselves with respect to the mechanisms that they see at work in the learner. Piaget had a strong tendency to depict the young child as a solitary enquirer in which the biological processes of assimilation, accommodation, and equilibration were centrally important, and in his massive oeuvre he only devoted a little space to the discussion of social factors. Vygotsky, on the other hand, criticized this aspect of Piaget's work, and stressed the

239

role of parents, teachers, peers, and the cultural milieu – this position being nicely encapsulated in his concept of the "zone of proximal development," the "zone" in which children develop with the assistance of others, rather than by relying on their own independent efforts (Phillips and Soltis, 1998).

The second major focus of constructivism is arguably the central one, however, for it is this that many constructivists take as fundamental to their position: if one considers a continuum with respect to knowledge from "humans the creators" to "nature the instructor," constructivists deny that nature serves as an instructor or template that the knower merely "copies" or absorbs, and they hold that there is a sense in which knowledge is made, not discovered (Phillips, 1995, 2000). More generally, they deny that individual learners receive knowledge by instruction or transmission from "outside." It should be apparent – although it has not been apparent to many constructivists writing in the late twentieth century – that there is much need for philosophical refinement here, and it is far from clear which (if any) thinkers are actually ruled out by this element in constructivism. Locke's sensational-ism, for example, clearly seems anti-constructivist, but what happens in his theory after the simple ideas coming from experience have "furnished the understanding" is quite constructivist. Arguably there are both constructivist and anti-constructivist elements in Plato as well, and it is interesting to note that Ernst von Glasersfeld (1991, p. xiv) acknowledges Socrates as a forebear.

The third stream in modern constructivism is that the construction of knowledge is a process involving both physical *and* intellectual activity. Dewey, Piaget, Vygotsky, and von Glasersfeld, among others, are unanimous about this. Many of these theorists give a strong evolutionary justification for this view of learning, along the lines discussed above with respect to Dewey and James.

It is no surprise, then, that constructivist teaching has a strong Deweyan orienta-tion; the constructivist teacher encourages students to be active problem identifiers and solvers, and does not impose ready-made solutions on students but fosters discussion and inquiry. Consequently, constructivist teachers are concerned about how much they need to tell their students, particularly in science and math, where construction of all knowledge by inquiring students does not seem to be realistic. Many, following von Glasersfeld, believe that teachers cannot know how knowledge has actually been constructed by the students, as the minds of other individuals are unknowable (a solipsistic position von Glasersfeld evidently reached on the basis of his reading of the empiricist epistemologists; see Phillips, 2000, pp. 41–85, 161–92). But it is time to return to the mid-twentieth century.

The Contributions of Analytic Philosophy of Education

Analytic philosophy of education (sometimes known as APE) was heavily influenced by the so-called "ordinary language philosophy" practiced in the UK, North America, and Australasia around the middle decades of the twentieth century. The practition-ers of APE attempted to clarify the concepts that were central in educational discourse and central, also, to the theme of this chapter, often in the hope that this would eventually lead to advances in educational practice.

Although there was agreement with William James's point that the appropriate activities for a teacher were not fully determined by learning theory, there was some debate as to how tight the conceptual connection was between teaching and learning. Paul Hirst (along with Richard Peters and Israel Scheffler the leading proponent of APE) probably was speaking for the majority when he claimed that there was an extremely tight connection, for teaching always involves the intention that someone will learn (although it is not true that learning always involves teaching). He explicated the relationship as a triadic one:

A teaching activity is the activity of a person, A (the teacher), the intention of which is to bring about an activity (learning), by a person, B (the pupil), the intention of which is to achieve some end-state (e.g. knowing, appreciating) whose object is X (e.g. a belief, attitude, skill). (Hirst, 1974, p. 108)

This analysis entails an "intentionality criterion" for teaching, that a person engaged in the activity of teaching is *trying* to bring about learning. As the literature developed, controversies arose around other putative criteria, notably what came to be called the *criterion of reasonableness*, according to which the activity engaged in must be reasonably calculated to bring about the learning intended (Scheffler, 1960).

Hirst and others also stressed that teaching is a polymorphous activity: a large range of things can count as teaching activities, depending upon the context and on the specific nature of what is being learned. (Learning is also polymorphous, covering a large range of possibilities including facts, generalizations, intellectual skills, practical skills, and so forth.) Teaching, in short, could not be defined in decontextualized behavioral terms, a point of some significance for teacher evaluation (Scheffler, 1960; see also Hamlyn, 1978, chapter 10).

Another line of analysis on which a great deal of effort was expended was trying to clarify the "logical geography" of the family of related terms: "teaching," "instructing," "training," and "indoctrinating." The majority opinion was that, if the first and last of these are considered, there is a falling off in the centrality of appeal to reason. Perhaps this was most clearly expressed, in terms of teaching, by Israel Scheffler:

To teach ... is at some points at least to submit oneself to the understanding and independent judgment of the pupil, to his demand for reasons, to his sense of what constitutes an adequate explanation. To teach someone that such and such is the case is not merely to try to get him to believe it: deception, for example, is not a method or mode of teaching. Teaching involves further that, if we try to get the student to believe that such and such is the case, we try also to get him to believe it for reasons that, within the limits of his capacity to grasp, are *our* reasons. Teaching, in this way, requires us to reveal our reasons to the student and, by so doing, to submit them to his evaluation and criticism. (Scheffler, 1960, p. 57)

Contemporary Theories of Learning

In the past few decades there has been much fruitful empirical and theoretical work in the field of learning theory, work that – by and large – has been ignored by philosophers of education. There is a distressing tendency for members of the latter group to

241

write as if the dominant theory of learning is still the one developed by the classic behaviorists John B. Watson and, more notably, B. F. Skinner. Watson treated learning in terms of classic Pavlovian conditioning, and Skinner, more influenced by the work of E. L. Thorndike, approached learning in terms of operant conditioning. Both thought of learning in terms either of change of behavior or acquisition of new behavioral repertoires. Skinner was able to train rats and pigeons to do remarkable things (he even showed that the latter could steer a guided missile), and he also developed the so-called "teaching machine" (programmed learning) via which a student giving the correct response to a question was reinforced by immediately being informed that the answer was, indeed, correct. However, the work of Chomsky and the rise of modern cognitive psychology pushed Skinner's approach to the sidelines, and philosophers of education were extremely critical of his dismissal of "understanding" and his related refusal to consider learning as a rational activity of the kind so clearly described in the passage by Scheffler quoted above. (For further discussion, see Cleverley and Phillips, 1986, chapter 8; Phillips and Soltis, 1998, chapter 3.)

Three main lines of theory and research have tended to dominate in the last few decades of the twentieth century and the beginning of the twenty-first. One has been the work on cognitive development inspired initially by Piaget, to which Vygotsky's influence was added as his work became translated from its original Russian. The second has been the rapid rise of computer science and the interdisciplinary field of *cognitive science* it has inspired and facilitated. It has become natural to think of human cognition as analogous to automated information processing, indeed as different from such processing only in being executed by biological "wetware" as opposed to computing "hardware." Recent work in neuroscience and learning clearly has this as one of its sources. The third has been the field of cognitive anthropology, which has studied what Jean Lave (following Michael Cole and others) calls "outdoor psychology." She writes that "contemporary theorizing about social practice offers a means of exit from a theoretical perspective that depends upon a claustrophobic view of cognition from inside the laboratory and school" (Lave, 1988, p. 1). The work of Vygotsky has played a role in this approach as well, with his emphasis on socio-cultural factors.

A detailed cataloging of the achievements of recent work cannot be undertaken here; an excellent discussion of this territory produced by a National Research Council (NRC) committee in the USA is cited in the "Further reading" list below. It will have to suffice to say that much progress has been made – as Lee Shulman had hoped – on the learning of specific school subjects. There has also been headway: on transfer of learning, a topic of longstanding interest; on the design of learning environments, especially ones that effectively incorporate technology; on how motivation and learning interact; on the respects in which the learning processes of novices are similar to, and differ from, the learning processes of experts; and on how children gradually learn to monitor their own cognitive activities, including learning ("metacognition").

However, one interesting emerging line of work with special significance for reframing the role of the teacher is worth highlighting. Jean Lave and Etienne Wenger have focused on examples, gleaned from around the world, of how learning takes place in apprenticeships (for instance, becoming a tailor in Africa, becoming a midwife in the Yucatan). They studied how the student moves from being a legitimate but peripheral member of a community of practice to becoming a full participant (Lave and Wenger, 1991). This work has led to some experiments in the USA by Ann Brown and Joe Campione, and others, that have focused on recasting the school classroom as a "community of learners," with concomitant change in the role of the teacher along somewhat Deweyan lines (Brown and Campione, 1990). Closely related to this has been the work of the cognitive psychologist James Greeno and his co-workers, who have developed the theoretical position known as "situated cognition," which also portrays learning as being situated in social settings. According to this view, cognition, and thus learning, cannot be understood if regarded as situated solely in people's heads. This work quite closely follows the lead of John Dewey and his colleague George Herbert Mead, who regarded the psychological distinction of "inner and outer" – a distinction that goes back at least as far as the work of Descartes – as outmoded (see Greeno et al., 1996). The current scene with respect to theories of teaching and learning, then, is quite dynamic, and there is much grist here for the philosophy of education mill.

See also 1 THE SOCRATIC MOVEMENT; 4 THE EDUCATIONAL THOUGHT OF AUGUSTINE; 6 ENLIGHTENMENT LIBERALISM; 7 ROUSSEAU, DEWEY, AND DEMOCRACY; 12 THE ANALYTICAL MOVEMENT; 17 THE CAPACITY TO LEARN; 18 MOTIVATION AND CLASSROOM MANAGEMENT; 19 THE MEASUREMENT OF LEARNING; 20 KNOWLEDGE, TRUTH, AND LEARNING; 22 MORAL EDUCATION

References

Brown, A. and Campione, J. (1990) Communities of learning and thinking, or a context by any other name. In D. Kuhn (ed.), *Developmental Perspectives on Teaching and Learning Thinking Skills*. Contributions in Human Development, 21. Basel: Karger.

Burbules, N. (1993) *Dialogue in Teaching: Theory and Practice*. New York: Teachers College Press.

Carr, D. (2000) *Professionalism and Ethics in Teaching*. London: Routledge.

Cleverley, J. and Phillips, D. (1986) *Visions of Childhood: Influential Models from Locke to Spock*. New York: Teachers College Press.

Dewey, J. (1933) *How We Think*. Chicago: Henry Regnery.

Dewey, J. (1966) *Democracy and Education*. New York: Free Press (originally published in 1916).

Dewey, J. (1969) *The School and Society* and *The Child and the Curriculum*. Chicago: University of Chicago Press, Phoenix Books joint edition (originally published in 1902).

Dewey, J. (1988) *The Quest for Certainty*. Carbondale: Southern Illinois University Press (originally published in 1929).

Fenstermacher, G. (1986) Philosophy of research on teaching: three aspects. In M. Wittrock (ed.), *Handbook of Research on Teaching*, 3rd edn. New York: Macmillan, pp. 37–49.

Greeno, J., Collins, A., and Resnick, L. (1996) Cognition and learning. In D. Berliner and R. Calfee (eds), *Handbook of Educational Psychology*. New York: Macmillan, pp. 15–46.

Hamlyn, D. (1978) *Experience and the Growth of Understanding*. London: Routledge.

Hardie, C. (1962) *Truth and Fallacy in Educational Theory*. New York: Teachers College Press.

Haroutunian-Gordon, S. (1991) *Turning the Soul: Teaching through Conversation in the High School*. Chicago: University of Chicago Press.

Hirst, P. (1974) *Knowledge and the Curriculum*. London: Routledge.

James, W. (1958) *Talks to Teachers on Psychology; and to Students on Some of Life's Ideals*. New York: Norton (originally published in 1899).

Joyce, B., Weil, M., and Calhoun, E. (2000) *Models of Teaching*, 6th edn. Boston: Allyn and Bacon.

Kulp, C. (1992) *The End of Epistemology*. Westport, CT: Greenwood.

Lave, J. (1988) *Cognition in Practice*. Cambridge: Cambridge University Press.

Lave, J., and Wenger, E. (1991) *Situated Learning: Legitimate Peripheral Participation*. New York: Cambridge University Press.

Lipman, M. (1988) *Philosophy Goes to School*. Philadelphia: Temple University Press.

Lipman, M. (1991) *Thinking in Education*. New York: Cambridge University Press.

Locke, J. (1975) *An Essay Concerning Human Understanding*, ed. P. H. Nidditch. Oxford: Clarendon Press.

Locke, J. (1996) *Some Thoughts Concerning Education* and *Of the Conduct of the Understanding*, ed. R. Grant and N. Tarcov. Indianapolis: Hackett.

Montessori, M. (1972) *The Secret of Childhood*, trans. M. Costelloe. New York: Ballantine.

National Research Council (1999) *Improving Student Learning*. Washington, DC: National Academy Press.

Neill, A. (1960) *Summerhill: A Radical Approach to Child Rearing*. New York: Hart.

Phillips, D. (1995) The good, the bad, and the ugly: the many faces of constructivism. *Educational Researcher*, 24(7), 5–12.

Phillips, D. (ed.) (2000) Constructivsm in education: opinions and second opinions on controversial issues. In *99th Yearbook of the National Society for the Study of Education*. Chicago: University of Chicago Press.

Phillips, D. and Soltis, J. (1998) *Perspectives on Learning*, 3rd edn. New York: Teachers College Press.

Plato (1976) *Meno*, trans. G. M. A. Grube. Indianapolis: Hackett.

Plato (1992) *Republic*, trans. G. M. A. Grube and C. D. C. Reeve. Indianapolis: Hackett.

Reeve, C. D. C. (1988) *Philosopher-Kings: The Argument of Plato's Republic*. Princeton, NJ: Princeton University Press.

Reich, R. (1998) Confusion about the Socratic method: Socratic paradoxes and contemporary invocations of Socrates. In S. Tozer (ed.), *Philosophy of Education 1998*. Urbana, IL: Philosophy of Education Society, pp. 68–78.

Rousseau, J.-J. (1979) *Émile*, trans. A. Bloom. New York: Basic Books.

Rousseau, J.-J. (1987) *On the Social Contract*, trans. D. Cress. Indianapolis: Hackett.

Scheffler, I. (1960) *The Language of Education*. Springfield, IL: Thomas.

Scheffler, I. (1967) Philosophical models of teaching. In R. Peters (ed.), *The Concept of Education*. New York: Humanities Press, pp. 120–34.

Shulman, L. (1986) Paradigms and research programs in the study of teaching: a contemporary perspective. In M. Wittrock (ed.), *Handbook of Research on Teaching*. New York: Macmillan, pp. 3–36.

Shulman, L. (1987) Knowledge and teaching: foundations of the new reform. *Harvard Educational Review*, 57(1), 1–22.

von Glasersfeld, E. (1991) Introduction. In E. von Glasersfeld (ed.), *Radical Constructivism in Mathematics Education*. Dordrecht: Kluwer, pp. xiii–xx.

Woodruff, P. (1998) Socratic education. In A. Rorty (ed.), *Philosophers of Education: New Historical Perspectives*. London: Routledge, pp. 14–31.

Further reading

Green, M. (1986) Philosophy and teaching. In M. Wittrock (ed.), *Handbook of Research on Teaching*, 3rd edn. New York: Macmillan, pp. 479–501.

Green, T. (1971) *The Activities of Teaching*. New York: McGraw-Hill.

National Research Council, Committee on Developments in the Science of Learning (2000) *How People Learn: Brain, Mind, Experience, and School*, expanded edition. Washington, DC: National Academy Press.

17

The Capacity to Learn

Carol Wren and Thomas Wren

As every teacher knows, there are individual differences among students such that some students learn less, or learn more slowly, than others do regardless of their motivation, their teacher's pedagogical approach, features of the learning situation, and other extrinsic conditions. In short, few would deny that some children seem smarter than others, though there is no consensus about why this is so. Some educational psychologists have explained these differences in terms of the construct of "general intelligence," which quantifies the commonsense notion of intellectual capacity as well as the classical notion of a psychological faculty advanced by Aristotle, Thomas Aquinas, and British empiricists such as John Locke. More recently, social psychologists and philosophers such as Rom Harré and Paul Secord (1972) have revived the classical notion of "powers" to account for individual differences in the capacity to learn, and cognitive psychologists such as Howard Gardner (1983) and Robert Sternberg (1985) have introduced the notion of "multiple intelligences." These approaches, like faculty psychology, understand human cognition in general and learning capacity in particular in qualitative rather than quantitative terms, and attempt to go beyond sterile, purely behavioral descriptions in their efforts to represent in a systematic way the life of the mind. However, such approaches are not problem free, and have been accused of circularity, violating the principle of parsimony, and otherwise failing to give a productive account of what they attempt to describe.

In what follows we use the expression "the capacity to learn" as synonymous with "intelligence." However, the capacity to learn is problematic for at least three reasons. There is no consensus as to (1) what it means *to learn* something, (2) the extent to which the student comes to a learning situation with a determinate natural capacity, i.e. *intelligence*, and (3) how to account for *individual differences* in the capacity to learn.

To address these problems we begin with a short historical review of the concepts of learning and intelligence, and then move to the question of individual differences, which we believe are best understood in terms of the distinction between *cognitive abilities* and the learning outcomes usually called *knowledge* and *skills*. We then illustrate this distinction and show its utility for understanding individual differences by turning to five specific issues in educational theory: the *biological conditions* and *sociocultural conditions* for learning, *conative-affective factors*, *multiple intelligences*, and *learning disabilities*.

Learning

In ordinary parlance as well as in most philosophical traditions, learning consists in coming to know something. How one comes to know is a separate question, to which philosophy has provided quite different answers over the centuries. The earliest and most striking answer is Plato's doctrine of *mnemesis*, according to which learning is the recollection of things perceived in a previous existence. As he explains in the *Phaedo*, during this earlier existence the soul, unfettered by a physical body, had direct knowledge of the eternal "Forms." In the *Republic* he offers a related but distinct account of a philosopher coming to know these otherworldly objects through training in the abstract sciences and sustained dialectical inquiry. Later still, the Forms drop out of his account, and he conceives of knowledge as a product of analysis which locates a proposition or idea within a larger network of propositions or ideas, enabling the learner to provide an *account* of the object of knowledge. By contrast, Aristotle adopts a more commonsense and empirical view of learning and knowledge, which assigns a more significant role to perception and the role of *nous* or intellect in grasping the intelligible form or nature of things perceived.

Plato and Aristotle were also aware that propositional knowledge and knowledge of things and their natures through direct acquaintance are not the only outcomes of learning: many sorts of expertise and dispositional attributes are learned, including skills in the usual sense and virtues or "excellences," both intellectual and moral. Aristotle seems to have regarded these kinds of learning as arising in part from imitation, habituation, and practice, and in part from coaching, conversation, and (ideally) instruction in general principles or the sciences corresponding to the arts to be mastered.

The differences between Plato's and Aristotle's conceptions of learning foreshadow the opposition in modern philosophy between rationalists such as René Descartes and empiricists such as John Locke. Like Plato, Descartes and his rationalist successors Baruch Spinoza, Gottfried Leibniz, and (with important qualifications) Immanuel Kant subscribed to the view that our natural endowment includes certain ideas, or (in Kant's case) pre-established categories and conceptual relationships. These cognitive structures constitute rational thought by providing interpretive mechanisms that organize sensory data and regulate learning processes, including the acquisition of language itself. In contrast, empiricist philosophers such as Locke, Thomas Hobbes, David Hume, and J. S. Mill held that the mind is an empty slate and the only principle of organization for sensory data is that of simple association. Learning results from perceptual experience, not the imposition of intellectual templates. Concrete perceptions generate simple ideas that become more and more strongly associated with each other in the course of further experiences. The strength of the association among these ideas, as well as their complexity, is a function of the intensity of the original perceptual experiences as well as their frequency, duration, and similar factors. Like Aristotle, the empiricists also regarded general concepts as the product of abstraction from particular experiences from perceptual experience, though unlike Aristotle they did not posit a special intellectual faculty as the active source or agent cause of the abstractive process. Instead they expanded the concept of association to include what

247

they called "reflection," viz. the collection and comparison of several ideas in order to discern commonalities and make deductive and inductive inferences.

It was from the empiricist principle of association that behaviorist theories of learning evolved in the twentieth century. However, it is important to note that British empiricism came to American psychology by way of Germany. In the latter half of the nineteenth century Wilhelm Wundt, H. Ebbinghaus, and other German associationists used introspective methods to examine perceptual experiences from the inside, e.g. by asking their subjects, who were themselves trained observers, to report what they were seeing under different lighting conditions. When E. L. Thorndike used this German associationist psychology as the basis for his own "connectionism," he dropped its introspective methodology and thereby set the stage for John Watson and later behaviorists to declare internal states and processes off-limits for psychological investigation. At this point learning ceased to be a "coming to know" – since knowing is itself an internal state – and was redefined as a change in (purely external) behavior.

The emergence of cognitive psychology from rationalist philosophy has a similar history, at least as far as its geography is concerned. Early in the twentieth century German psychologists dissatisfied with Wundt's associationist suppositions developed the school known as Gestalt psychology, which influenced the American cognitive psychologists' reaction to behaviorism. About the time that behaviorism was becoming the dominant theory of learning in the United States, three German psychologists, Max Wertheimer, Kurt Koffka, and Wolfgang Köhler, were arguing that learning involved "emergent" properties that are not reducible to its elements. Like the early rationalist philosophers, these theorists argued that novel problems cannot be solved simply by applying existing knowledge or behavior patterns to new situations, nor can the way data are organized be explained entirely in terms of the data themselves. Instead, they argued, learning takes place thanks to the learner's understanding of the entire situation; it is not just the repetition of previously learned responses to specific stimuli provided in the situation. Innate tendencies to organize data in certain ways, such as in figure-ground configurations, were necessary conditions for learning to take place. The exact nature of these tendencies is still under discussion, but there is now little doubt among American psychologists and educational theorists that a strictly behavioristic account of learning is not sufficient to explain how people learn, especially when the learning in question involves higher order cognition. Cognitive accounts of learning are now thoroughly respectable and theories of learning now address the old questions of knowledge and skill acquisition that Plato and Aristotle once struggled with. Learning is still described as a change, but an internal change in the way knowledge is structured in the mind.

Following mid-century developments stimulated by theorists such as Noam Chomsky, Ulrich Neisser, and George Miller, and working within the increasingly powerful metaphor of the mind as a computer-like information processing system, cognitive psychologists now focus their attention on meaningful learning and acquisition of complex bodies of knowledge and skills rather than on simple acquisition of facts or routines. They have come to understand it as a constructive process in which the learner actively structures and restructures knowledge, organizing propositions into concepts and these in turn into schemata. This active construction of knowledge is mediated by a number of cognitive abilities (also called cognitive processes or cognitive functions). Though there is no consensus on the type or number of these constructs, most cognitive psychologists agree that learning is mediated by some lower-order abilities such as attention, perception, and memory, as well as various forms of encoding, and higher-order abilities such as analysis, evaluation, synthesis, and metacognition. In this view, learning depends on one's prior knowledge and skills as well as on one's present cognitive abilities. Learners determine what is learned as they perceive and construct mental representations of the new information, appreciate the contexts in which it is embedded, interpret it in terms of what is already known, integrate it into current knowledge schemata, and thereby restructure the schemata themselves. To be sure, this theory has its critics, who argue that a strictly cognitive view of learning is limited in important ways. In response, cognitive psychologists are currently expanding its scope by addressing social and cultural influences on learning as well as the role of conative factors such as affective states and learning styles. Others are addressing "authentic" learning in naturalistic settings and the domain-specific nature of some learning.

Intelligence

Until recently, most philosophers understood intelligence (from the Latin word *intellegere*, to understand) primarily if not exclusively in terms of its "intellectual" dimension, which involves perception of the way things are, abstract reasoning, propositional knowledge, logically coherent justification of beliefs, and so on. While they may have conceived of intelligence in this sense as a prerequisite for autonomous and prudent action, they did not conceive of action as essential to the exercise of intelligence, and they regarded intelligence as primarily theoretical and only secondarily practical. The beginnings of an alternative view are discernible in Jean-Jacques Rousseau's suggestion in his eighteenth-century classic *Émile* that human beings are curious or naturally inclined to engage in inquiry because it has survival value. However, it was not until the twentieth century in the work of John Dewey that philosophers began to understand intelligence itself prospectively, as an instrument for making things happen rather than simply grasping how they are. On Dewey's account, intelligence is inherently practical, and human beings would not be endowed with it if it were not.

Dewey's reversal of the priority of perceiving over doing and theory over practice is echoed in Gilbert Ryle's famous distinction in *The Concept of Mind* (1949) between knowing-how and knowing-that, by which he meant respectively the deliverances of practical intelligence and the propositional (theoretical) knowledge that he thought was derived from them. Over the next five decades philosophers debated this issue and added many qualifications to Ryle's claim, but it is now generally agreed that the old priority of theory over practice was too simplistic. Most would agree with Ledger Wood (1963, p. 147) that intelligence is "the capacity of the mind to meet effectively – through the employment of memory, imagination and conceptual thinking – the practical and theoretical problems with which it is confronted." However, to define it as a "capacity of the mind" begs the question as to whether intelligence is a unitary, cross-situational disposition. There are at least two alternatives here: intelligence may be a superordinate concept, a kind of conceptual resultant that is really nothing more than a shorthand way of designating the combined operations of attention, memory, and other cognitive abilities, or it may be a cognitive ability in its own right, perhaps so basic that it underlies all other cognitive abilities. Philosophers such as Ryle and, more recently, those interested in metatheoretical issues generated by cognitive science (e.g. Daniel Dennett and Jerry Fodor) continue to debate this question.

Similarly, among psychologists there is no consensus about whether intelligence is a unitary or multiple phenomenon. They have been trying for over a century to understand the underlying structure of what Harré and Secord have called natural powers, i.e. intelligence. Some psychologists have approached the topic indirectly, by administering a variety of tests or test items and then using statistical factor analysis to look for clusters of responses where performance scores are uniformly high or low, assuming as they do so that this uniform performance results from some underlying common factor. However, this line of research has yielded no clear factor or set of factors that constitute intelligence, at least in part because very different types of ability tests and different statistical procedures have been used. In any case, its reliance on statistical correlations reflects the underlying classical empiricist assumption of this approach, which as we saw above is that the general principle of mental functioning is association. This *psychometric approach* to intelligence is often considered atheoretical in that its primary focus is on measurement, not theory construction, though many psychometricians have also proposed theoretical accounts of the nature of intelligence. For example, in 1904, a year before the Binet–Simon test appeared, the English psychologist Charles Spearman published a paper that is still cited today, in which he argued that "general intelligence" (Binet's concept of "IQ" was still unpublished) has at its core a comprehensive and cross-situational intellectual ability that he called the "g factor." Spearman, who has been called the father of factor analysis, did not develop any assessment instruments of his own, but his statistical work continues to influence intelligence testing a century later. He thought of general intelligence as a biologically based trait, reflecting neural energy that enables the brain to operate effectively in roughly the same way that greater horsepower enables a car to operate more effectively. Later in the century P. E. Vernon argued for a variant of this idea, proposing a hierarchical theory that included not only a g factor, but also verbal and spatial/mathematical factors on a second level and several less important factors on a third level. R. B. Cattell proposed a developmental theory that culminates in two general factors, crystalized and fluid intelligence. However, some psychometricians have rejected the very idea of a general factor, arguing instead for one or another multiple-factor theory. For example, L. L. Thurstone identified seven "primary mental abilities," and J. P. Guilford developed a three-dimensional model with 150 factors.

Other psychologists take a more direct approach to the nature of intelligence, beginning at the level of theory and then conducting experiments – which study many sorts of behavior – designed to test their theories for accuracy, coherence, and comprehensiveness. This *cognitive approach* focuses on mental abilities rather than behaviors or performances, and rests on the rationalist assumption that intelligence operates with pre-established structures or ways of constructing knowledge. Contemporary cognitive theories of intelligence divide into two major groups: those inspired by Jean Piaget's cognitive-developmental theory and those which rest on the model of information-processing. Earlier in the twentieth century Piaget studied intelligence in terms of logical thought and argued that the major function of intelligence is to enable one to adapt to the environment through processes of assimilation and accommodation. He was particularly interested in the way in which the structures of logical thought appeared to develop as a series of increasingly comprehensive stages, each of which was a relatively stable and internally coherent holistic structure. More recently, neo-Piagetians have extended and modified his approach in order to answer criticisms of narrowness and inaccuracies, and in doing so have loosened the model of stage-sequential structures. In contrast, the information-processing approach considers processes rather than static stages and structures, and attempts to understand the underlying structure of intelligence in terms of universal cognitive abilities. Using the metaphor of the computer, these theorists try to understand what happens as information enters the mind, becomes integrated with what is already known, and is then used in specific intellectual responses. Several decades of work, dating back well before computers to Wundt's exploration of visual perception in 1873 and Ebbinghaus's study of memory and forgetting in 1913, have yielded abundant research on large pieces of the information-processing model, mainly concerning the lower-order abilities of attention, perception, and memory. More recent research has emphasized higher-order abilities such as reasoning, problem-solving, and metacognition. However, since much of this work has been very narrowly focused, singling out one or another specific aspect of cognitive functioning, only a few general theories of intelligence have emerged so far from this research. As we will see below, the two most prominent ones at this time are Sternberg's triarchic theory and Gardner's theory of multiple intelligence. Sternberg's theory is compatible with Gardner's but it emphasizes processes, whereas Gardner emphasizes domains of intelligence. Sternberg himself now believes that the processes described in his triarchic theory are embedded within each of Gardner's domains (Spear-Swerling and Sternberg, 1996). However, Sternberg's focus on processes lies more squarely within the mainstream of cognitive psychology.

As this brief review suggests, theories of intelligence have developed alongside theories and methods of assessment, and it is not always clear whether they are related or, if they are related, in just which direction the line of influence runs. On the one hand, most psychometricians cheerily accept E. G. Boring's wry comment that intelligence is what intelligence tests measure, though as noted above some have proposed theoretical accounts of intelligence that summarize their statistical findings. A few assessment instruments were developed based on these factor-analytic theoretical accounts, e.g. L. L. Thurstone's Test of Primary Mental Abilities (PMA) and more recently the second edition of the Woodcock–Johnson Psycho-educational Battery (WJ-R), which was revised in light of the theory of intelligence developed much earlier by R. B. Cattell and J. Horn. On the other hand, theory-oriented psychologists who set out to understand the nature of intelligence often find it difficult to operationalize their theories as assessment instruments, probably because of the complexity of the task, though Gardner rejects the very idea of a psychometric approach to measuring multiple intelligences. One may hope that future work in the area of intelligence testing will contribute to the understanding of intelligence and vice versa, but it would be a mistake to dismiss theories of intelligence simply because they are not easily operationalized. After all, as cognitive psychologists are quick to point out, high scores on intelligence tests are uncorrelated with many other sorts of achievement usually considered part of what it means to be intelligent, such as knowing how to deal with complex social situations or even knowing how to learn. Like the debate about learning, the debate about intelligence continues with little agreement about either its structure or its unitary/multiple nature.

Learning, Intelligence, and Individual Differences

In general, professional philosophers have shown little interest in the question of individual differences in intellectual abilities, perhaps because so many of them have been unduly influenced by the classical Aristotelian view that the basic principle of individuation is "material" – in this case sensory processes, which are considered extrinsic to the non-material intellect even though they supply its primitive data. To this historical explanation of the lack of interest philosophers have shown in individual differences one may add methodological and sociological explanations. For instance, the nature of philosophical inquiry emphasizes universal structures rather than particular cases. Fortunately, the picture is changing among contemporary philosophers, who have been influenced by developments in the cognitive sciences such as those we discuss below.

Among psychologists the picture has always been much different. Questions of individual difference have driven most of the empirical research on intelligence and intelligence testing. Early work on sensory processes – in England by Francis Galton, in Germany by Wundt, and in France by Hippolyte Taine – provided the background for the American psychologist James McKeen Cattell (not to be confused with R. B. Cattell, mentioned above) and the French psychologist Alfred Binet to develop their respective instruments for measuring intelligence. Cattell administered a preliminary battery of test items to 500 American college students who had already been ranked as bright or dull by their teachers, and then selected those items that best distinguished between the dull and bright students. Using a somewhat different methodology, Binet and his colleague Théodore Simon published in 1905 the first systematic intelligence test for large populations: like much of the subsequent work on intelligence it was designed to solve a practical problem, in this case identifying French schoolchildren who required special intervention. The Binet–Simon test, which introduced the idea of IQ as the quotient of Mental Age divided by Chronological Age, was revised several times over the following years, and was adapted to the American school scene by L. M. Terman in 1916 and 1937. Other tests were developed along the same lines, most notably the Wechsler Intelligence Scale for Children (WISC) in 1949. Within this approach, individual differences are conceived of quantitatively; that is, a gifted person simply has more of whatever it is that intelligence tests measure than a "retarded" person does.

While these and similar tests may measure the *magnitude* of individual differences in learning capacity (leaving aside the unresolved question of whether there is really such a thing as general intelligence, not to mention the many controversies surrounding its assessment), we believe it is at least as important if not more so for teachers in the twenty-first century to understand the *sources* of these individual differences. Since philosophy and psychology have not yet provided a comprehensive and generally accepted theory of either learning or intelligence and hence of the capacity to learn, it is all the more important that teachers understand the complex nature of individual differences in learning capacity, so that they can adjust instruction to meet the needs of all children.

To structure this discussion of individual differences we return to Harré and Secord's notion of natural powers in order to highlight their distinction between natural powers and acquired abilities – although we prefer a somewhat different nomenclature, in which the term *ability* is reserved for one's (natural) cognitive activities in contrast to the (acquired) *knowledge and skills* that are also called "learning outcomes." Using this distinction, it is possible at least in principle to construct an accurate and meaningful profile of a person's natural powers (i.e. cognitive abilities), which can then be compared to other persons' profiles. Ideally, such comparisons could pick out people whose cognitive abilities are uniformly low relative to those of others in the same age and social cohort, people whose abilities are uniformly high, and people whose ability levels are not uniform at all. Furthermore, in the ideal case, someone whose profile showed perfectly uniformly elevated cognitive abilities – acute attention, keen perception, strong memory, and so on – would show a correspondingly elevated profile of acquired knowledge and skills, including both academic skills such as reading and writing and non-academic skills such as social competence, being well organized, and so on. However, in real life uniform correlation of strong/weak cognitive abilities with strong/weak learning outcomes is rare. At one end of the spectrum, we find many highly intelligent people whose learned knowledge and skills are dramatically non-uniform, e.g. a brilliant physician with dreadful social skills. Similar non-correlations exist at the other end of the spectrum, e.g. a person of relatively low cognitive ability may (for reasons we take up below) be a surprisingly good reader.

Individual differences may be accounted for in a variety of ways that are not mutually exclusive. These might be grouped into five types of explanation concerning the gap between learning capacity and what is actually learned. These five accounts, each of which has its own vast literature, center on *biological* and *sociocultural* conditions for learning, *conative-affective* factors, *multiple intelligences*, and *learning disabilities*.

Biological Conditions

Biological sorts of explanation deal with physiological processes and structures relevant to learning. Most obviously, sensory impairments such as limited vision or hearing or other physical disabilities make learning difficult, especially in traditional classroom settings. Many sorts of neurological damage would fall into this general category, though it is often difficult to identify the extent and nature of the physical disability or to distinguish it from the environmental conditions that an unsympathetic society might create for persons with this or other manifestly physical disabilities (see Silvers et al., 1998). Other biological explanations, which are problematic for conceptual as well as medical or diagnostic reasons, focus on genetic endowment. Although it seems clear that what we have called natural cognitive abilities are biologically based, it does not follow that they correlate in any meaningful way with allegedly group-specific genetic structures, or that phenotypic differences in learning capacity correspond to genotypic categories. This point seems to have been lost in much of the discussion of whether IQ is inherited. For instance, many psychologists have resisted the arguments of Herrnstein and Murray's *The Bell Curve* (1994) because they regard as racist its conclusions that some racial groups have generally low IQ test scores. However, their counterarguments focus on the book's methodology, e.g. the authors' excessive reliance on a few dubious testing instruments, and never address the much more basic question of whether "race" is a meaningful category or valid scientific construct. As Lawrence Hirschfeld (1996, p. 31) has observed, in the flurry of criticism of Herrnstein and Murray's volume "virtually no psychologist has publicly suggested that their claims about a racialized or biologically cognitive underclass are implausible in the extreme."

Sociocultural Conditions

Even if one is raised by wolves, learning is socially situated. Discussions of learning environment can have many frameworks, ranging from the traditions of the learner's cultural or ethnic group to the interpersonal atmosphere of small institutions such as the family or school. Similarly, these discussions can have many centers of emphasis, including economic factors, class and gender issues, and so on. Cultural psychologists as well as multicultural educators have much to say on these matters, which we need not repeat here. However, in light of what is argued above about racially indexed IQ scores, it is worth noting that although the concept of race as a biological category was rejected long ago by geneticists (Lewontin, 1972, 1991), public discourse and professional educational practice routinely use racial and ethnic categories to discuss student populations, school policies, and classroom environments. For better or worse, this discourse creates a set of self-fulfilling predictions of group differences (as well as individual differences) in learning capacity and, perhaps more important to the classroom teacher, in *learning style*. For instance, Ramirez and Castañeda (1974) suggested that learning style is related to world view and that consequently certain learning styles tend to be prominent in certain cultures. Using the construct of "field sensitivity" found in the widely used Embedded Figures Test (EFT), they argued that Mexican-American schoolchildren tend to take a field-dependent or global approach to learning, in contrast to mainstream Anglo-Americans, who take a more inductive approach that begins with isolated facts and then puts them together to construct rules or conclusions. Subsequent studies, using this or related constructs such as global versus analytical thinking, have often focused on the learning styles of other non-mainstream groups such as African-American children, though other studies such as the *Learning Style Inventory* (LSI) have been more interested in individual differences than group differences (see Dunn and Dunn, 1993). Even so, differences in learning styles, be they group or individual differences, constitute an important part of the classroom environment. In a school whose learning culture is marked by sensitivity to these differences, one may expect greater across-the-board academic success than in less sensitive learning environments.

Conative-affective Factors

Until recently, research on learning has not dealt with individual differences in motivation and other non-cognitive aspects of intelligence, perhaps because these do not fit well into behavioral accounts of learning (black boxes have no emotions) or the computer model of information processing (computers have no emotions either: they just compute). However, studies on the relationship between motivation and learning began to appear in the early 1990s and seem to be filling the theoretical gap between these two research areas. For instance, Pintrich and De Groot (1990) have proposed three sorts of linkage: the learner's belief that he or she has the ability to accomplish a learning task, the reasons for engaging in the task, and the emotions produced in reaction to the task. This sort of research continues the earlier work on achievement motivation in the 1950s by David McClelland and others, by focusing on the motivations for specific tasks rather than general tendencies such as mastery striving or the need to feel competent. Similar studies on the relation between affect and learning show that cognitive processes such as attention and memory are profoundly influenced by affective states such as anxiety (Revelle, 1989). Affective factors also play a role in learning styles, though since affectivity is usually understood as a transitory affective state its influence on learning style is necessarily indirect. However, psychologists of learning often deliberately blur the venerable distinction between affect and conation in order to discuss cognitive dispositions such as focus and persistence, which are of clear relevance to learning capacity and learning styles. Especially relevant here is the heavily researched difference between two styles of processing information, often called impulsivity and reflectivity (the tendencies to prefer speed over accuracy or vice versa), and the statistical correlation between these two constructs and the IQ construct (Messer, 1976).

Multiple Intelligence

As noted above, the notion of "multiple intelligences" is not new. The currently prominent theories of Sternberg and Gardner echo earlier work on multiple-factor accounts of intelligence done by people like Thurstone and Guilford who rejected the notion of a unitary cross-situational intelligence or g factor without denying that when the multiple components operate well together they can give the appearance of a single intelligence. Gardner and Sternberg also dismiss traditional psychometric intelligence tests, claiming that they measure only small parts of what is postulated by their theories. In educational contexts, multiple intelligences theories are especially attractive because they provide explanations of the above-mentioned non-correlation between natural powers and acquired knowledge and skills, as when Gardner identifies the eight different domains in which a person can perform and within which his or her cognitive abilities operate in unique ways.

Sternberg's triarchic theory of intelligence describes the formal structure of intelligence rather than its range of contents or domains, and comprises three subtheories. The *contextual subtheory* involves the notion that different cultures value and identify different abilities and skills as intelligent behavior; thus intelligence is, in part, purposeful adaptation to the cultural environment. The *experiential subtheory* attempts to explain intelligence in terms of learning from experience, and discusses how the learner moves along a continuum between utterly novel situations and very familiar ones involving expertise and/or automization. The *componential subtheory* involves the mental abilities that underlie intelligent behavior and the way it develops within the context of a particular culture and across the experiential continuum just mentioned. Sternberg sorts these cognitive abilities under three triarchic categories: metacomponents (planning, monitoring, evaluation, etc.), performance components (attention, memory, encoding, logical reasoning, etc.), and knowledge-acquisition components necessary to learn how to solve problems and execute tasks (selective and strategic combining of old and new information, etc.). In the triarchic theory, individual differences are explained in terms of variations in the several components of intelligence. For instance, Sternberg views mental retardation as "due primarily to deficient functioning of metacomponents – the planning, monitoring, and evaluation processes of the human mind" (Spear-Swerling and Sternberg, 1996, p. 261). Giftedness, then, might be conceived of as generalized strength in these metacomponents. In the case of persons with more typical or "normal" abilities, strengths and weaknesses within and among these components are less extreme but account for individual differences in learning.

Gardner takes a somewhat different approach although it is compatible with Sternberg's process orientation. He originally identified seven "intelligences" or, more properly, domains of intelligence and has recently added an eighth: he calls them the linguistic, logical-mathematical, spatial, musical, bodily-kinesthetic, interpersonal, intrapersonal, and naturalistic intelligences. Each of these eight intelligences is relatively independent of the others and can operate effectively even if they do not. At the extremes, mental retardation can be conceptualized as generalized poor performance in all domains, while giftedness can be more variable. A person may be extremely gifted in a single domain while functioning adequately in all the others. Among people with more typical abilities, variations among these domains manifest themselves in facility with domain-specific symbol systems and in one's repertoire of acquired skills. In other words, even "normal" people have peaks and valleys and hence a wide range of learning capacities, all of which contribute to the wide variety of individual differences found in any classroom. For most if not all learners, there is always some non-correlation between their natural powers and the knowledge and skills they have acquired. One of the virtues of models of multiple intelligence is that they take this non-correlation as the natural situation within which learning takes place.

Learning Disabilities

Among the explanations for individual differences in learning capacity, one of the most important – and least well understood – is the concept of learning disabilities

(LD), whose theoretical research is located squarely within the framework of cognitive psychology. Its central idea is that some children – probably far fewer than those formally identified as learning disabled – have information-processing problems, i.e. serious weaknesses in those psychological processes that we referred to above as cognitive abilities. These processing difficulties show up in standard learning situations in fairly predictable ways. For example, problems with auditory short-term memory typically make it difficult to follow oral directions in class. Problems with visual motor perception or memory make learning cursive handwriting difficult. This is not to say that people with learning disabilities are unable to learn, but learning is more difficult for them, often requiring compensatory strategies.

From the outset LD researchers have looked "inward" for the source or sources of the learning difficulty. The development of the field has a chronology much like that of psychology's investigations into cognitive abilities: investigations into the sources of LD began with lower level perceptual and perceptual-motor processes (Orton, 1937; Kephart, 1960) and moved along through memory (Ross, 1977), language, and other symbolic functions (Kirk, 1968), to higher-order thinking, especially meta-cognition (Reid and Hresko, 1981). Dysfunctions in each of these areas were studied and subsequently proposed as explanations for seemingly anomalous learning difficulties. Unfortunately, theoretical work in the field could not provide schools with methods of identification that were at once adequate to the complex nature of learning disabilities and also simple or inexpensive enough for school systems to adopt. Even worse, it provided no systematic and proven methods of instruction for students with LD. Consequently, in the late decades of the twentieth century educators virtually abandoned the attempt to understand the phenomena of LD in terms of cognitive processes. The reasons for this abandonment were manifold. Some were patently political or economic, but other reasons had to do with the ways that professionals had proceeded in the early days of LD research. They tied cognitive processes to indeterminate neurological deficits, accepted naive arguments for a single cognitive disability as *the* source of all learning disabilities, and made simplistic assumptions about the relationship between specific learning outcomes and remedial instruction aimed at single cognitive abilities. In addition, researchers designed studies that had serious methodological problems, especially in subject selection. As a result, school personnel came to understand and identify children as learning disabled almost entirely in terms of the peripheral (and much more easily operationalized) notion of a discrepancy between actual and expected achievement – or sometimes even more simplistically on the basis of any sort of underachievement. As might be expected, children were identified as learning disabled in unprecedented numbers (some estimates ranged as high as 50 percent of all school children), a situation that continues to be aggravated in the United States by the fact that special education is now one of the few options available when children are failing in school, even though it is usually a very inappropriate one. The effect of this educational malpractice on LD theory has been heavy skepticism on the part of educational policy-makers as well as the general public concerning the utility if not the very intelligibility of the concept of a learning disability.

Despite heated public controversy and the bankruptcy of the concept as it has been used in most public school systems, the current outlook is not entirely bleak. Some theorists and researchers are returning to the key idea that learning disabilities are manifestations of processing disorders (Kavale and Forness, 2000). For example, within the past decade phonemic awareness, an aspect of auditory processing, has been shown to underlie many instances of reading problems. Our own view follows this approach. Instead of conceiving LD as a neurological deficit, and thus a condition which one either has or does not have, we believe LD are best understood within a framework like that of Sternberg's theory of triarchic intelligence. We think that each of the cognitive abilities described in Sternberg's componential subtheory can be located along a continuum ranging from substantial strength to substantial weakness or inadequacy, such that within the general population there is considerable normal variability as described above in the section on multiple intelligences. A learning disability, then, is a matter of degree. A serious inadequacy in one or more of what Sternberg calls metacomponents, performance components, or acquisition components of intelligence makes it difficult for a person to learn fairly specific knowledge and skills. Thus LD are characterized by significant variation not just among individuals but *within* an individual's cognitive abilities and acquired skills. For example, a student with a serious weakness in short-term memory may have difficulty remembering what the teacher just said, but may easily remember what he or she has read because written material can be reviewed and studied. Such deficiencies in cognitive components affect the learning disabled student's ability to move along the learning continuum from novice to expert (experiential subtheory), as well as to adapt to the sociocultural environment when the student's learning difficulty is in a highly valued area such as reading (contextual subtheory).

Implications for Teaching

By definition, successful teaching entails successful learning, but the converse does not hold. Learning can take place in the absence of, or even despite, any activity of the part of a teacher, and it can certainly take place in the absence of any *theory* held by learners or teachers concerning what it means to learn. We have already proposed that intelligence is basically the capacity to learn, and would now add that this capacity is the paradigm case of the cognitive disposition that Ryle called knowing-how. Teachers can enhance this capacity by helping their students to learn how to learn, which requires in turn that the teachers themselves learn, and continually relearn, how to teach. Part of what they must learn is how to suspend their theoretical commitments when the pedagogical situation requires that they mix and match different conceptions of learning. This may seem paradoxical, but it is really just common sense. As Robert Gagné showed more than 30 years ago, neither behaviorist nor cognitive theory completely explains how people learn. Some learning tasks – and some learning styles – are better matched with associative learning strategies, and others are better matched with the sort of holistic strategies and metacognitions that are associated with information processing models. Successful teaching, like successful learning, requires knowing which is which.

See also 16 THEORIES OF TEACHING AND LEARNING; 18 MOTIVATION AND CLASSROOM MANAGEMENT; 19 THE MEASUREMENT OF LEARNING; 37 INCLUSION AND JUSTICE IN SPECIAL EDUCATION

References

Dunn, R. and Dunn, K. (1993) *Teaching Secondary Students through Their Individual Learning Styles: Practical Approaches for Grades 7–12*. Boston: Allyn & Bacon.

Gardner, H. (1983) *Frames of Mind: The Theory of Multiple Intelligence*. New York: Basic Books.

Harré, R. and Secord, P. F. (1972) *The Explanation of Social Behavior*. Oxford: Blackwell.

Herrnstein, R. J. and Murray, C. (1994) *The Bell Curve: Intelligence and Class Structure in American Life*. New York: Free Press.

Hershfeld, L. (1996) *Race in the Making: Cognition, Culture, and the Child's Construction of Human Kinds*. Cambridge, MA: MIT Press.

Kavale, K. and Forness, S. (2000) What definitions of learning disability say and don't say: a critical analysis. *Journal of Learning Disabilities*, 33(3), 239–56.

Kephart, N. C. (1960) *The Slow Learner in the Classroom*. Columbus, OH: C. E. Merrill.

Kirk, S. A. (1968) *Illinois Test of Psycholinguistic Abilities*. Urbana: University of Illinois Press.

Lewontin, R. C. (1972) The apportionment of human diversity. *Evolutionary Biology*, 25, 276–80.

Lewontin, R. C. (1991) *Biology as Ideology: The Doctrine of DNA*. New York: Harper Perennial.

Messer, S. B. (1976) Reflection–impulsivity: a review. *Psychological Bulletin*, 83, 1026–52.

Orton, S. T. (1937) *Reading, Writing and Speech Problems in Children: A Presentation of Certain Types of Disorders in the Development of the Language Faculty*. New York: W. W. Norton.

Pintrich, P. R. and De Groot, E. V. (1990) Motivational and self-regulated learning components of classroom academic performance. *Journal of Educational Psychology*, 82(1), 33–40.

Ramirez, M. and Castañeda, A. (1974) *Cultural Democracy, Bicognitive Development, and Education*. New York: Academic Press.

Reid, D. K. and Hresko, W.P. (1981) *A Cognitive Approach to Learning Disabilities*. New York: McGraw-Hill.

Revelle, W. (1989) Personality, motivation, and cognitive performance. In R. Kanfer, P. L. Ackerman, and R. Cudeck (eds), *Abilities, Motivation, and Methodology*. Hillsdale, NJ: Erlbaum.

Ross, A. (1977) What have we learned from research: the unrealized potential. In *Learning Disability: The Unrealized Potential*. New York: McGraw-Hill.

Ryle, G. (1949) *The Concept of Mind*. London: Hutchinson & Co.

Silvers, A., Wasserman, D., and Mahowald, B. (1998) *Disability, Difference, Discrimination: Perspectives on Justice in Bioethics and Public Policy*. Lanham, MD: Rowman & Littlefield.

Spear-Swerling, L. and Sternberg, R. (1996) *Off Track: When Poor Readers Become "Learning Disabled."* Boulder, CO: Westview Press.

Sternberg, R. J. (1985) *Beyond IQ: A Triarchic Theory of Human Intelligence*. Cambridge: Cambridge University Press.

Wood, L. (1963) Intelligence. In D. Runes (ed.), *Dictionary of Philosophy*. New York: Philosophical Library.

18

Motivation and Classroom Management

Richard Ryan and Martin Lynch

Educational philosophies of motivation and classroom management have never been more polarized than they are today. With respect to learning, policy-makers advocate the use of rewards and sanctions, teacher-centered instruction, and "high stakes" evaluations to induce teacher "accountability" and raise student achievement. What is assumed is that students are motivated to pay attention and study by the social and economic value of a high school diploma and admission to college, and that the requirements for promotion and graduation can be manipulated to control what and how much students will study and learn. Opposing them are educators emphasizing student-centered instruction, personalized teaching, "constructivism," and "authentic" assessments. What is assumed by this group is that children are inherently motivated to learn and that the primary motivational task of educators is to rely on, nurture, and not extinguish that inherent motivation. Debates over student discipline and classroom management are similarly divided between advocates of more emphasis on discipline, "zero tolerance" of student infractions, and harsher penalties, and on the other side philosophers and psychologists who argue that a student's acceptance of norms and expectations begins in care, attachment, and an appreciation of the reasons that make those norms and expectations legitimate.

While many may think of these contrasting views of motivation and management as a modern issue, in fact they represent poles of a perennial argument. As John Dewey wrote:

The history of educational theory is marked by opposition between the idea that education is development from within and that it is formation from without; that it is based upon natural endowments [versus] that [it] is a process of overcoming natural inclination and substituting in its place habits acquired under external pressure. (Dewey, 1938, p. 1)

This argument runs so deep that it is reflected even in the etymology of the term "education." Amelie Rorty writes that our word "education" derives from both *e-ducare*, to bring out or draw forth, and from *e-ducere*, to lead out (Rorty, 1998). Whether learning most optimally proceeds from leading through external controls, or through drawing out inner initiative, is a debate that continues in today's psychological sciences (Ryan and Deci, 2000). Perhaps no theoretical issue is more relevant to actual teaching practices than this one, which concerns the core orientation of educational practice.

Autonomy versus Control

Clearly, students can be motivated by either internal or external forces. That is, learners can be "moved" by a variety of means, some of which foster initiative, engagement, and self-regulation, and some of which are experienced as alienating, and are dependent on the impetus and power of others. The issue of *autonomy* is particularly germane. Autonomy literally means "self-governing," and implies, therefore, regulation by the self. Its opposite, heteronomy, refers to regulation from outside the self, by alien or external forces. An understanding of the experience of autonomy versus heteronomy is therefore relevant to the understanding of what it means for educators to support learning from within or force it from without.

Alexander Pfander (1967), using phenomenological methods drawn from Brentano and Husserl, provided one of the earliest attempts to distinguish autonomous acts from other forms of striving or motivation. According to Pfander, self-determined or autonomous acts are those experienced "precisely not as an occurrence caused by a different agent but as an initial act of the ego-center itself" (p. 20). He argues that, although external pressures or influences may supply "grounds" for behaving, self-determination is nonetheless characterized by an *endorsement* of the behavior or the values it represents by the self or "ego-center."

Paul Ricoeur (1966) further examined this issue in *Freedom and Nature*. Like Pfander, Ricoeur argues that autonomy concerns acts that are fully endorsed by the self. Yet such acts need not imply an absence of external influences or even mandates to act in a particular way. One could be autonomous even under external pressure, provided one concurs with it. That is, one can consent to act in accord with an external force (such as a teacher's instruction) insofar as the circumstances also *engender in one* good reasons for acting (e.g. one understands the value of the activity). One does not necessarily lose autonomy when complying with that which, under other circumstances, one would voluntarily do. Thus autonomy applies not only to "independent" choices, but also to acts of consenting to actions that originate in external forces.

Autonomy pertains to all acts that are freely done or endorsed by the self. This of course applies to behaviors that are easily chosen (e.g. reading an interesting text for fun), as well as to more difficult choices (e.g. working on an arduous but valued task). In the latter case the self endorses the behavior because of its experienced value, and therefore it feels volitional.

Existential phenomenologists similarly distinguish *authentic* from *inauthentic* actions. The term authentic means literally "really proceeding from its reputed source or author" (cf. Wild, 1965). Authentic actions are thus those that one identifies as one's own, and for which one takes responsibility. A person's actions, even intentional ones, can be inauthentic insofar as they are experienced as not truly reflecting, or emanating from, the self. This is the use of the term in discussion of *authentic assessments*, in which evaluation proceeds from the self of the student.

261

These phenomenological approaches thus specify that for learners to be autonomous they must be willingly "behind" their actions. These characterizations also convey that autonomy is *not* defined by the absence of teachers' influences, but rather by one's subjective consent or assent to such influences. Autonomy is not equivalent to "independence" or complete self-direction.

In an analytical approach to autonomy, Gerald Dworkin (1988) arrives at similar conclusions. Dworkin argues that autonomy cannot simply mean behaving without constraint. Clearly one can assent to certain constraints, and in doing so still be autonomous. I may feel constrained, for example, in stopping for a traffic light. But, at the same time I may assent to the idea that traffic laws are useful in insuring my, and everyone else's, safety. I therefore may willingly consent to follow them, and in doing so have lost no autonomy. Indeed, I enact my autonomy with this higher-order, reflective commitment. Therefore, Dworkin argues that autonomy does not definitionally entail "being subject to no external influences." Instead, what is salient is whether the following of external inputs reflects mere obedience or coercion or reflects an acceptance of the direction or guidance that these inputs provide. Dworkin points out that there is no possible world that is free of external influences. Hence, it is in one's subjective assent to some influences and not others that autonomy becomes meaningful.

The Psychology of Autonomy

Given the definition of autonomous activity as volitional (i.e. done willingly) or assented to, rather than being forced or arbitrarily induced to act, the question practically is "when does such activity occur?" Psychological theories of motivation have addressed this question, theoretically and empirically (Deci and Ryan, 1985).

The most obvious instances of autonomy occur when actions are *intrinsically motivated*. Intrinsic motivation refers to doing an activity for its inherent interest or enjoyment. Reading an engaging book that is not assigned or playing a math "game" would be examples of such intrinsic motivation. Intrinsic motivation is common in learning activities in childhood. Children are curious to learn, and under appropriate conditions enjoy tackling challenges and acquiring skills. The literature in psychology, indeed, suggests that intrinsically motivated learning is perhaps the richest type of learning – characterized by persistence, integrative depth, and transfer. Remarkably, intrinsic motivation for learning *in school* wanes with age, mainly as a function of the presence of increasing controls, evaluations, and pressures that undermine the sense of fun and interest that learning can entail. However, intrinsically motivated learning occurs at all levels of education when education proceeds from students' interests.

Yet not every volitional action is intrinsically interesting. A second category of autonomous actions consists of those stemming from *internalized values*. Some activities that are instrumental and even arduous are done because the actor believes there is a good reason for doing them and personally grasps their importance. For example, if a student understands why learning a difficult skill will be useful later, more volition can result. Such learning occurs when teachers provide rationales and explanations for the relevance of lessons or behaviors. Research suggests that learning that proceeds from more internalized valuing is not only more autonomous, it is better maintained and transferred, and accompanied by more persistence, effort and interest (Ryan and LaGuardia, 1999).

The absence of autonomy has also been specified in motivational terms. People attribute an absence of autonomy to activities where the *perceived locus of causality* is clearly external. In schooling, this typically occurs when teachers use salient controls, either aversive or rewarding, to induce behavior. Students experience less autonomy in their behavior when teachers use gold stars, public grading, rewards, or aversive motivators such as humiliation or punishments. Indeed, two forms of motivation are characterized by an absence of autonomy. One is called *external regulation*, where the student behaves only "because of" salient reward or punishment contingencies (and fails to behave when they are absent). The second is *introjection*, when a student behaves not out of interest or value, but because of needs for approval or praise, or out of fear of suffering blows to self-esteem. In introjection learning is thus based not on volition, but on the perceived contingencies of self-regard. Both external regulation and introjection have been empirically shown to be associated with more superficial processing, less persistence, and less continuing interest in related activities (Ryan and Deci, 2000).

Questions Concerning Autonomy

Having defined autonomy and heteronomy, and specified, in brief, the forms of motivation characterizing them, we now turn to how these are related to philosophies of education, and their conceptions of motivation. We approach this historically, because, as Dewey observed, the debate concerning autonomy and control is perennial.

Views on autonomy and control in education are strongly connected with answers to some prior questions. If one assumes humans are naturally inclined to learn, allowing students to learn autonomously makes sense. However, if it is assumed that students are inherently unmotivated or disinclined, then control is more readily justified. If one believes that society depends on a specific body of knowledge or skills that must be disseminated, or character traits that must be inculcated, then using force to compel learning might be in order. However, if one assumes that useful knowledge takes many forms and is ever changing, then controlling what must be learned makes less sense. Similarly, if one's goal is not obedience but moral autonomy, one will be less concerned with control, though one may regard moral autonomy as the ultimate goal while holding that some degree of control must be exercised in preparing children for later autonomy. Philosophers' views of the matter have divided especially around the matter of what motives are spontaneously present in children and whether control is helpful or unhelpful in educating children for autonomy.

The Theory and Practice of Externally Controlled Learning

Sparta was almost alone in the Ancient Greek world in having a public system of education, and for this reason it was much admired by ancient moralists. Those

263

moralists included Plato (c.427–347 BCE) and Aristotle (384–322 BCE), who held that human happiness and freedom can and should be advanced through systematic control of what children are exposed to, the games they play, the stories and music they listen to, and the practices they engage in. Plato held that "it is better for everyone to be ruled by divine [i.e. unerring] reason, preferably within himself and his own, otherwise imposed from without" (*Republic*, IX 590d), and he described in both his *Republic* and *Laws* systems of public education designed to cultivate responsiveness to reason and a disposition to rely on reasoning in speech and action alike. His view was that rational and truthful persuasion should be relied upon as much as possible in dealing with others and governing a society, but that people are only *potentially* and not *naturally* disposed to listen to reason, and thus must first be *civilized* by training that is not optional. Education should be "a process of attraction" (*Laws*, II 659d), but it may have to be imposed using a measure of force. Accordingly, in Book VIII of the *Republic* he condemns the practice of engaging young people in philosophical discussion, and he rejects the Socratic vision of an open society in which primary moral education is handled privately and philosophers are free to encourage subsequent moral improvement through self-examination.

At the root of these views was a "developmental" view of human rationality, according to which it is not a foregone conclusion that people will *listen* to reasoning. Plato argued in the *Republic* that the human *psyche* encompasses three springs of action or kinds of desires: the desire for bodily pleasures, the desire for honor, status, and to prevail over others, and the desire to know or understand. There is a natural sequence of development in human motivation, and one can only progress through this sequence with the right education, training, and habituation. Most people, despite the best efforts of their parents, teachers, and communities, will never rise above the desire for bodily pleasures. They will never be motivated to seek understanding for the pleasure of understanding itself, and will never become fully rational or autonomous.

Early Christian views of education were Platonic in assuming that most people will not, on their own, come to the kind of knowledge that was necessary in order to be autonomous or truly self-governing. As outlined by Saint Augustine, it was incumbent upon the Church, as the guardian of the message of salvation, to provide the content of this message unerringly to its followers. For more than a millennium of Western history the little formal schooling that occurred was overseen by the Christian Church, and it relied on recitation, repetition, and drill. This relatively controlling style of education was also justified by a conception of human nature even more pessimistic than Plato's: human nature was viewed as "fallen" and depraved, being weakened by sin, both "original" (i.e. common to all humanity) and personal, and thus needed to be disciplined. This emphasis was only slightly tempered by thinkers such as Thomas Aquinas, who felt that providing students the tools of reason could also provide a scaffold to support faith. In fundamental respects, little changed in Christian education during the Reformation and into the nineteenth century, despite the spread of literacy promoted vigorously by Martin Luther. Indeed, Calvinists, whose view of human nature was perhaps even more pessimistic, were particularly prone to controlling approaches to schooling, which they felt all children should receive.

However, the nineteenth century brought important, new developments in the sphere of controlling approaches to education. Utilitarian philosophers formulated principles of motivation based upon hedonic principles and associationism: most notably, Jeremy Bentham (1748–1832) and James Mill (1773–1836) suggested systematic use of rewards and punishments to establish good learning habits. The English Parliament put this into practice, passing numerous laws intensifying examination structures to ensure literacy, including the Revised Code of Regulations (1862), which advocated a "payment by results" scheme that linked the funds awarded to schools to students' performance on the exams. While the Code promoted a wider national school system, it also prompted a rigid narrowing of curricula, and an escalation of teacher-centered, drill- and repetition-focused instruction. The ideas of "streaming" or segregation of students, evaluation by exams, and the resultant conservative methods instituted by the British system in the nineteenth century continued into the modern era.

In the twentieth century, after philosophy gave birth to psychology, advocates of controlling techniques became even more forthright in asserting theoretical rationales for externally controlled learning. Behaviorists, emerging from a blend of British associationism and naive positivism, insisted that learned behaviors were always a function of external controls, and that educators should utilize these external factors in regulating learning. Perhaps the most influential of behaviorist educators was Edward Thorndike, whose theory is labeled *connectionism*. Thorndike applied his famous "law of effect," which argues that if a behavior is followed by a satisfying consequence it is more likely to occur in the future under similar conditions. Conversely, if a behavior is followed by an unsatisfying consequence its probability of recurrence will wane. Another principle was that of "frequency": the more frequently an association is repeated, the more likely it is to recur in similar conditions. Together these "laws" of learning underwrote educational practices focused on the use of external reinforcements, coupled with practice, drill, and repetition. Although these techniques had characterized conservative education across history, connectionism gave them a specific theoretical rationale.

Thorndike's behaviorism was influential in education for decades, but eventually gave way to the "radical behaviorism" of B. F. Skinner, which similarly advocated the systematic application by teachers of consequences, principally rewards, to induce learning. Skinner also promoted the idea of "programmed learning," which viewed instruction as based not in relationships or interests, but in a well structured and systematic application of contingent reinforcements.

Today conservative educators continue to advocate the use of rewards to control learning, both at the classroom and school system levels. Behaviorists argue that teaching is most effective when based on control through reinforcements. At the systems level, Chester Finn has argued that "the problem is that academic success yields such few rewards – and indolence brings few penalties" (Finn, 1991, p.120). He and a broad array of conservative spokespersons from Admiral Rickover to William Bennett have cast the job of educators as that of disseminating essential knowledge, and motivating its assimilation through classroom discipline, backed by rewards and sanctions. This type of thinking has deeply influenced recent educational reforms in several nations focused on "high stakes" testing. In this view, instruction should be regulated by measurement, and the outcomes of measurement should be the basis of rewards and sanctions for both teachers and learners (Popham, 1983).

Conservative reforms set in motion teaching methods that focus on imposing learning on students rather than attempting to cultivate it from within. One primary result has been more and more testing, and, not surprisingly, less learning through activity, experience, and experimentation. Correspondingly, motivational techniques have become more controlling, because, as research suggests, when teachers are pressured to achieve specific outcomes they tend to pressure students through both reward and punishment strategies (Ryan and LaGuardia, 1999). Thomas Toch (1991, p. 240) thus argues that the new reforms have "made the joy of learning and rewards of teaching incomprehensible," a result that may, in itself, not concern those for whom accountability is the *sine qua non*.

The Theory and Practice of Autonomous Learning

The educational philosophies that have advocated autonomous or internally motivated learning have tended to regard children as inherently good and interested in learning, and have been receptive to rearranging the environment to suit the needs and interests of the child rather than forcing the child to adjust to the environment.

Although Aristotle's developmental and educational views resembled those of Plato in many respects, his conception of the human potential for rationality and autonomy played a foundational role in the thinking of later developmental theorists (Rychlak, 1977). Nevertheless, among ancients it is the Roman orator Quintilian (*c*.35–*c*.90), who is most noteworthy as an advocate of internally motivated learning. In his *Institutio oratoria* (*The Training of the Orator*), he recognized that learners of different ages have distinct needs and interests, and he held that curriculum and methods should be tailored accordingly. He also devised a more humane conception of motivation, de-emphasizing the use of corporal punishment common in the Roman ludi, and highlighting instead the importance of making learning interesting and attractive.

Two noteworthy figures of the Renaissance and Reformation were Vittorino da Feltre (1378–1446) and John Amos Comenius (1592–1670). Vittorino emphasized both developmental stages for learning and an appreciation of individual differences, holding that students should not be forced into rigidly predetermined studies, but encouraged to develop their current capacities and interests. He emphasized close teacher–student relationships and he himself often recreated and dined with his pupils. Moreover, he argued that interest was the optimal motivator of learning, and he de-emphasized methods employing punishment and control. However, the outstanding liberal educator of this time was Comenius. Anticipating the ideas of Rousseau, he believed in the unfolding Godly nature of the child, and the need to trust in the inherent processes of growth. Although Catholic, he did not adhere to the traditional Christian view of child depravity, and rejected teaching methods based on discipline and punishment. Instead he stressed the need to make learning attractive and intrinsically compelling, and advocated teacher attitudes of warmth and acceptance.

More philosophically prominent were the autonomy promoting views of René Descartes (1596–1650) and John Locke (1632–1704). Rejecting the artificial discipline of scholastic higher education, Descartes championed the free exercise of individual reason as not only the surest path to knowledge, but a natural, desirable, and *liberating* fulfillment of human nature. Although his conceptions of reason and knowledge owed much to those of Plato and Augustine, they were revolutionary in being completely egalitarian – an invitation, to all who dared, to think for themselves and direct their own inquiries and education for themselves. These Enlightenment themes were incorporated by Locke into a more systematic conception of liberal learning, noteworthy for its insistence that children should be given reasons appropriate to their age as soon as they can speak, and for counseling a gentle non-punitive approach. "None of the things they are to learn should ever be made a burden to them or imposed on them as a *task*," Locke insisted (Locke, 1996, p. 51).

Despite these precedents, Jean-Jacques Rousseau is frequently credited with formulating the liberal or *naturalistic* view of education in its classical form: that (1) human nature is not fundamentally lawless and depraved, but good, and will remain good unless it is corrupted by a corrupt society; (2) the child's natural curiosity and naturally maturing powers of observation and reason will enable him to acquire all the knowledge he will need without direct instruction by anyone. Rousseau's *Émile* (1911), which exerted a profound influence on subsequent educational thought and practice, develops these themes through an account of a child educated through natural means by a benevolent tutor who provides a structured, but never authoritarian, environment for growth.

One of the pre-eminent figures in the dissemination of naturalistic teaching methods was Swiss educator Johann Heinrich Pestalozzi (1746–1827), who held that education consists not in "imposing on the child fixed doctrines and alien concepts but in helping him to develop his own constructive powers" (Silber, 1973, p. 274). His educational methods, developed and displayed in several model schools, entailed above all an atmosphere of emotional security, based in a warm and caring relationship between teacher and child. Following Rousseau, Pestalozzi held that knowledge should be transmitted whenever possible through direct experience, discovery, and the natural growth of knowledge, and he disparaged the use of punishment and of creating fear of evaluation. In short, he was a strong advocate of a more nurturing and child-centered education.

Pestalozzian educational ideas were widely disseminated during the nineteenth century in Europe and the USA, and became a major influence on diverse theorists including Friedrich Froebel (1782–1852) in Germany and Maria Montessori (1870–1952) in Italy, both of whom regarded an educator as properly a facilitator of learning through spontaneous self-activity. Montessori's approach was innovative in its appreciation of developmental readiness, or "sensitive periods" in childhood, and attempted to provide resources timed to the budding capacities of children to afford maximal growth.

John Dewey represents, to many, the culmination of the liberal tradition, although in many ways he explicitly attempted to transcend the liberal/conservative debate. Although his own emphasis on development through interest, experience, and child-centered inquiry was robust, he was troubled by the conceptualization of learning as simply "natural," or as occurring without external inputs and structure. In *Experience and Education*, Dewey's struggle to resolve the question of methods is particularly apparent. There he resisted the idea that teachers should "stand out of the way," arguing that their role is to engage, guide, select materials, and provide challenges. Yet while acknowledging that teachers are authorities and societal agents, Dewey argued that they should use their authority in the interests of the learner and classroom group. He also sought a middle ground between an imposed curriculum and one deriving entirely from "the child's interests." As he argues in *Human Nature and Conduct*, the teacher is a conveyor of societal heritage, but if the latter is to be assimilated, it must be made relevant to the learner and grist for the kind of pragmatic problem-solving activities that represent the heart of Dewey's educational process.

Was Dewey successful in this synthesis? Clearly most readers have rightly appreciated the strong autonomy-supportive emphasis in Dewey's methods. He saw knowledge as achieved by learners who are actively grappling with interesting, personally relevant, and practical problems rather than being externally regulated to absorb predetermined materials. However, in seeking a middle ground between radical Rousseauian naturalism and the conservative focus on implanting "essential" knowledge, Dewey opened himself to the subsequent critiques of Paul Goodman, Ivan Illich and others on the left that his approach fell short of a liberating model for education, and the critiques of conservatives like E. D. Hirsch (1987) that his progressivism leads to a neglect of the basic knowledge every good citizen needs.

Among American teachers, a popular influence with Pestalozzian overtones has been the humanistic psychology of Carl Rogers. In his *Freedom to Learn* (1969) Rogers juxtaposed traditional (controlling) and student-centered approaches. He argued that significant learning is an expression of students' inherent tendencies toward "actualization," and that it happens best when they are treated with unconditional positive regard, provided with support for exploration and experiment, and allowed to evaluate their own work from an "internal locus." The optimal role for teachers is to act as facilitators, nurturing the actualization and growth of learners by providing inspiration and guidance, but not controls, he held.

Constructivism has more recently emerged as a paradigm for education that is hospitable to autonomy-support. Although constructivists may not endorse liberal philosophies *per se*, when it comes to classroom methods there is a convergence between constructivism and the liberal focus on student-centered methods, participatory process, and a resistance to predetermined, standardized knowledge. Constructivism not only rejects the conservative notion of there being a legitimate cultural literacy and justifiable control over the learner; it contrarily embraces multiple emergent formulations of ideas and productions and a need for a liberating nurturance of critical thought. Concretely this translates into interest in performance-based assessments such as portfolios of students' work, exercises in critical thinking, and open classroom exchange, rather than state-driven structured tests and preset content goals. Constructivist classroom contexts are characterized by caring and support for the learner's autonomy, rather than motivation by contingencies of reward.

In sum, the advocacy of autonomous learning is typically based on a naturalistic model: learning is growth, and growth depends upon an inner principle that mainly requires support and nutriments. The result is a focus on process, in which nurturance, mainly in the form of warm relationships and supports for initiative and interest, is the most common element. Critics of such approaches, however, cite the incompleteness of this metaphor of growth. Humans are not like acorns, they argue. Growth can occur in many directions – some constructive and beneficial and some not. Thus some educators have attempted to articulate conceptions of how supportive structure and guidance from teachers can complement intrinsic growth tendencies, without stifling the inner spirit that fuels learning and development.

As we have seen, the use of external controls to motivate students is often associated with a distrust of human nature that assumes students will not absorb, and teachers will not teach, what is essential unless strongly guided to do so through external controls. By contrast, the advocacy of autonomous learning depends on a view of humans as inherently desiring to know and disposed to assimilate ambient social values and knowledge, whenever they are properly cared for. In this view the controlling educator's attempt to control the learner spoils the very inherent tendencies upon which education optimally depends. Force, pressure and control stifle curiosity, breed rebellion and reactance, and undermine the processes that give rise to significant learning and care for community.

Classroom Management

This review of perspectives on motivation and teacher–student interaction yields important lessons for classroom management. Perhaps most salient is the idea that students can be motivated and socialized through external controls such as rewards and punishments, or through the provision of an atmosphere that nurtures basic psychological needs, including needs for relatedness and autonomy.

The impact of these differing approaches to classroom management has been directly examined in research stemming from Self-Determination Theory (SDT: Deci and Ryan, 1985; Ryan and Deci, 2000). The evidence suggests that teachers play the most influential role in creating a *classroom climate* that either facilitates or undermines autonomous forms of motivation, and improved self-regulation of behavior. Three aspects of teacher activity are viewed as particularly relevant. The first is that of *autonomy-support versus control*. Greater autonomy-support fosters students experiencing themselves as active initiators of learning, whereas greater control leads students to experience themselves as "pawns" or passive recipients. Autonomy-supportive teachers are those who embrace the students' perspectives, who make minimal use of salient rewards and punishments, and who attempt to foster motivation by means of enthusiasm and provision of material that is interesting or relevant from the student's viewpoint. The second aspect concerns *competence-supports*. Competence-supportive teachers attempt to provide optimally challenging lessons and tasks at which students can, with reasonable effort, typically succeed, and thereby experience efficacy. By contrast, some teachers focus on preordained or normatively determined levels of challenges, prescribed lesson plans, and competitive grading in which there are "winners" and "losers." Third, teachers differ on the dimension of *relatedness versus detachment* in their interactions with students. Providing warmth

269

and security leads students to want to assimilate and cooperate, whereas detachment and distance undermines this tendency, and thus leads to reliance on arbitrary motivators that tend to be based on authority and control. Research based on SDT (e.g. Ryan and LaGuardia, 1999; Ryan and Deci, 2000) has revealed considerable evidence that classroom climates that satisfy students' basic psychological needs in these ways foster greater intrinsic motivation, internalization of values for learning, and achievement. Conversely, classroom climates characterized by control, evaluations, or low relatedness and warmth result in less inner motivation and interest on the part of students.

This body of work further indicates that a teacher's philosophy of education and motivation readily results in a self-fulfilling prophecy. Teachers with controlling philosophies employ strategies of reward and punishment and in doing so "shape" students to be less active learners, to desire less rather than more challenge, and to find school more onerous and less engaging. Their students become control-dependent. Conversely, teachers whose view of education acknowledges the needs of students to experience relatedness and autonomy tend to be warmer and less controlling. In turn their students exhibit greater readiness to identify with the teacher's goals, and to internalize the value of learning, and accordingly they require fewer controlling interventions. Indeed, students whose teachers use nurturing, autonomy-supportive strategies have been shown to be more curious, interested, and challenge seeking in their approach to learning. In short, considerable evidence indicates that both controlling and autonomy-supportive approaches to learning and classroom management have validity, as each is self-confirming. Nonetheless, SDT suggests that because both the quality of experience and the depth of learning outcomes are more optimal in classrooms managed through nurturing versus controlling approaches, both practice and policy ought to be oriented toward the recognition and fulfillment of students' psychological needs.

A deeper question concerns the basis on which teachers and policy-makers adopt strategies of a controlling or nurturing sort. In part this relates, as we argued from the outset, to (a) one's view of human nature, and (b) the extent to which the goals of learning are predetermined or open. When one views humans as inherently active, curious, and ready to assimilate knowledge and social practices, then support for this positive nature makes sense. Along with this comes trust that the ultimate knowledge that is acquired will be significant and useful. However, if children are indeed indolent, depraved, resistant to reason, or unlikely to learn what they need to without external controls, as so many practitioners from Sparta to today's "high stakes" testing advocates have assumed, then it follows that educators need to strongly control and constrain them. Compelling arguments, in our view, support the more humane approach of autonomy-supportive classroom management styles for engendering quality learning and a more critically thinking, empowered citizenry.

See also 1 THE SOCRATIC TRADITION; 6 ENLIGHTENMENT LIBERALISM; 7 ROUSSEAU, DEWEY, AND DEMOCRACY; 8 KANT, HEGEL, AND THE RISE OF PEDAGOGICAL SCIENCE; 9 ROMANTICISM; 16 THEORIES OF TEACHING AND LEARNING; 17 THE CAPACITY TO LEARN; 19 THE MEASUREMENT OF LEARNING; 36 THE ETHICS OF TEACHING

References

Deci, E. L. and Ryan, R. M. (1985) *Intrinsic Motivation and Self-determination in Human Behavior*. New York: Plenum Press.

Dewey, J. (1938) *Experience and Education*. New York: Macmillan.

Dewey, J. (1922) *Human Nature and Conduct*. New York: Henry Holt.

Dworkin, G. (1988) *The Theory and Practice of Autonomy*. New York: Cambridge University Press.

Finn, C. E. J. (1991) *We Must Take Charge: Our Schools and Our Future*. New York: Free Press.

Hirsch, E. D. Jr (1987) *Cultural Literacy: What Every American Needs to Know*. Boston: Houghton Mifflin.

Locke, J. (1996) *Some Thoughts Concerning Education* and *Of the Conduct of the Understanding*. Indianapolis: Hackett Publishing.

Pfander, A. (1967) *Phenomenology of Willing and Motivation*, trans. H. Spiegelberg. Evanston, IL: Northwestern University Press (original work published 1908).

Plato (1975) *The Laws*, trans. T. Saunders. London: Penguin Books.

Plato (1992) *Plato's Republic*, trans. G. M. A. Grube and C. D. C. Reeve. Indianapolis: Hackett.

Popham, W. J. (1983) Measurement as an instructional catalyst. *New Directions for Testing and Measurement*, 17, 19–30.

Ricoeur, P. (1966) *Freedom and Nature: The Voluntary and the Involuntary*, trans. E. V. Kohak. Evanston, IL: Northwestern University Press.

Rogers, C. R. (1969) *Freedom to Learn*. Columbus, OH: Merrill.

Rorty, A. O. (ed.) (1998) *Philosophers on Education: New Historical Perspectives*. London: Routledge.

Rousseau, J. J. (1911) *Émile*, trans. B. Foxley. London: J. M. Dent & Sons (original work published 1762).

Ryan, R. M. and Deci, E. L. (2000) Intrinsic and extrinsic motivation: classic definitions and new directions. *Contemporary Educational Psychology*, 25, 54–67.

Ryan, R. M. and LaGuardia, J. G. (1999) Achievement motivation within a pressured society: intrinsic and extrinsic motivations to learn and the politics of school reform. In T. Urdan (ed.), *Advances in Motivation and Achievement, volume 11*. Greenwich, CT: JAI Press.

Rychlak, J. F. (1977) *The Psychology of Rigorous Humanism*. New York: Wiley.

Silber, K. (1973) *Pestalozzi: The Man and His Work*. New York: Schocken Books.

Toch, T. (1991) *In the Name of Excellence: The Struggle to Reform the Nation's Schools, Why It's Failing, and What Should Be Done*. New York: Oxford University Press.

Wild, J. (1965) Authentic existence: a new approach to "value theory." In J. M. Edie (ed.), *An Invitation to Phenomenology: Studies in the Philosophy of Experience*. Chicago: Quadrangle Books, pp. 59–78.

Further reading

Deci, E. L. and Ryan, R. M. (2000) The what and why of goal pursuits: human needs and the self-determination of behavior. *Psychological Inquiry*, 11, 227–68.

Ryan, R. M. and Stiller, J. (1991) The social contexts of internalization: parent and teacher influences on autonomy, motivation and learning. In P. R. Pintrich and M. L. Maehr (eds), *Advances in Motivation and Achievement: volume 7. Goals and Self-regulatory Processes*. Greenwich, CT: JAI Press, pp. 115–49.

Kellaghan, T. Madaus, G. F. and Raczek, A. (1996) *The Use of External Examinations to Improve Student Motivation*. Washington, DC: American Educational Research Association.

19

The Measurement of Learning

Andrew Davis

In the past few decades the use of written tests to measure learning has expanded on an unprecedented scale in parts of the developed world. At the same time, informal assessments together with practical and "authentic" approaches are also growing in importance. The link between assessment and teaching is increasingly explicit. There are strong pressures on teachers, schools, and other educational institutions to be accountable for the progress of their students.

This chapter begins by exploring two possible interpretations of accountability. It proceeds to investigate the problem of "teaching to the test" associated with making teachers accountable for student progress. The next topic it discusses is based on a classic question in assessment theory: can the measurement of learning be sufficiently reliable to hold education to account and yet at the same time possess any kind of validity worth having? Finally, some important questions about the fairness of assessment are examined.

Measuring Learning for Accountability Purposes

Assessment in the UK, the USA, and some other developed countries is said to be "high stakes." It is used to hold education to account, or in other words to hold teachers and schools responsible for student learning, or for their instructional decisions.

Accountability for pupil progress

To what extent can teachers be held *directly responsible* for pupil progress? Current assessment practices seem to assume a straightforward causal relationship between teaching and learning, but the actual relationship is more complicated and less certain. Many factors influence learning. It sometimes occurs without teaching, and more than one teacher influences the learning of any individual pupil. It is very difficult to determine the precise effect of a given teacher, or to know that pupils could have learned more from another teacher than their own. At best, teachers can use techniques that make it likely that their pupils come to know what they ought.

The responsibilities of teachers are also more complex than simply bringing it about that pupils come to know certain things. New knowledge must be connected to that which is already known, and this constrains the educational choices that can be appropriately made. More generally, pupils are persons capable of choice, emotion, and the exercise of reason, and must be treated accordingly. This implies that teachers should be answerable for the moral and educational appropriateness of their techniques, and so accountable to a wider set of professional requirements than standards of measurable pupil learning.

Furthermore, teachers are often attempting significant pupil developments that cannot be measured conventionally. Some aspects of the expressive arts and personal and social education fall into this category. Some forms of learning, including the mastery of abstract or theoretical concepts, develop over long periods and in the short term are not easily "measured."

All of this strongly suggests that accountability should not be restricted to standardized measures of pupil progress.

Accountability for learning outcomes increasingly emphasizes the "value added" to pupils' "progress." In the UK the progress of pupils in a particular school is compared to that of "similar" pupils elsewhere. The idea is that pupils start their schooling at very different points and with varying degrees of cultural and social capital (Bourdieu and Passeron, 1977). These factors should be discounted, or the relevant variables controlled for, so that the role of the school and teachers can be identified.

However, this whole procedure invites a number of challenges. No suggested criteria for "similarity" can be provided with a robust and conclusive defense. Socio-economic background is identified through proxies such as the proportion of students receiving free school meals, and even the postcodes of pupils' home addresses. While these moves seem sensible, it is surely impossible to establish that all the significant factors affecting achievement have been accounted for. The unpredictable "chemistry" of particular student groups may influence learning, as might subtle cultural influences that are not consistently linked to any particular socio-economic status.

There is a related special problem for whole-school accountability. If to obtain a fairer picture progression data are gathered over several years rather than with respect to just one pupil cohort, it becomes increasingly unclear what is to count as the "same school." Staff come and go, and change roles. Students also come and go, sometimes very rapidly.

When teachers and schools are held accountable for pupil progress as "measured" by tests, there is considerable pressure to discover how best to improve scores. The most effective means of so doing may not coincide with those needed even for the most instrumental of educational intentions. For "learning" in effect becomes redefined and identified with the performances accessible to examiners rather than the rich "connected" understanding essential for citizens using and applying their knowledge intelligently and flexibly in the diverse circumstances of "real life" and the workplace. "Teaching to the test" thereby offers pupils a distorted conception of learning (Davis, 1998).

If teachers seek to elicit those performances demanded by examinations regardless of the development of any kind of connected understanding that might ground

273

relevant pupil achievements, then according to a consistent theme of "effective teaching" research they should make this plain to their pupils at the beginning of their lessons. Teachers also ought to be honest with pupils about such objectives. They should not pretend to offer a diet of rich learning if they actually intend to sideline understanding, supporting instead the development of skills that will maximize examination performance. Such hypocrisy is wrong in itself. Moreover, it would be detected by many students and seems likely to undermine their commitment to learning.

Accountability for teaching approaches

Some years ago, Hugh Sockett (1980) advocated accountability for what he called "principles of procedure." On the face of it, this is fairer to teachers than holding them responsible for student progress. Teachers can choose how they will teach, whereas they cannot directly "decide" that their pupils will learn. They can only, in the last analysis, *try* to teach them. Moreover, inspectors can apparently observe whether teachers are adopting specified teaching approaches, whereas they often cannot "observe" that the pupils have achieved a given learning outcome.

However, one might define these teaching "approaches" and "'principles of procedure'" in different ways. For example, teachers might be required to use "interactive whole-class teaching" or, much more specifically, to seat pupils in a "horseshoe" configuration and present material using an overhead projector, an approach fashionable recently in the UK. So the possibilities range from the highly specific to much broader injunctions about teaching styles.

On the face of it, the justification for holding teachers to account in this way should appeal to empirical evidence about which approaches maximize pupil progress. The question of how such outcomes are "measured" thus reappears, as does the concern about whether the seemingly measurable in effect excludes other nonmeasurable yet significant educational achievements. Consider in addition the sheer difficulty of the research design required. Pupil performance in classrooms with specific organizations would have to be compared with "similar" pupils in classrooms without them. Both sets of classrooms would need to vary in many other ways so that the effect of the approach under investigation could be detected.

Moreover, only some teaching approaches in this category are readily identifiable. The horseshoe configuration is one that is. Others, such as interactive whole-class teaching, can appear in a great variety of guises. Teachers will make decisions minute by minute when interacting with a particular group, and no one lesson precisely resembles another even when the same material is being taught to the same age group. One teacher's decisions are likely to differ from another's even when handling similar content and similar groups, and of course the character of teaching groups varies enormously. "Interactive whole-class teaching" does not seem to be a sufficiently clear category for evidence favoring it to exist.

This is a very serious obstacle to the justification of a wider range of approaches for which teachers might be held to account, including styles of "effective questioning," letting pupils know at the start of lessons what they are about to learn, and other favorites from the effective teaching research stable. The problem of identifying the approach concerned could be avoided, in theory, by being entirely specific about what teachers are to do. For instance, they could be required to use certain forms of words expressed in a given tone. However, this rigid kind of accountability is not being promoted at present in the developed world.

If all these difficulties could be surmounted, we would be left with a paradoxical situation as regards accountability, namely that those holding the teachers responsible for the approaches in question ought themselves to be held to account for the relevant pupils' progress. Having taken it upon themselves to decide what is effective teaching, rather than leaving it to teachers' professional judgments, they would be "responsible" for whether children are learning, much more than the teachers themselves would be. To the extent that teachers are denied the opportunity to exercise professional judgment, they would be reduced to instruments in the hands of those who dictate the approaches they are expected to adopt.

Sockett's "principles of procedure" could be interpreted rather differently, however. They could, for example, specify the values appropriate to the relationship between teachers and pupils, such as mutual respect, proper exercise of authority, or respect for pupils' rights to privacy. A third interpretation of them might be to identify *processes* that ought to be salient within teacher–pupil interactions. Examples might include whether pupils are investigating, engaged in critical thinking, or making choices about the level and even the timing of their learning.

The Theory of Assessment

As indicated at the outset of this chapter, assessment is now seen as extending far beyond traditional written examinations. In "authentic" approaches candidates are asked to perform in "real world" contexts. Two key concepts linked to written tests are *reliability* and *validity*, but these are often now applied more widely to a range of assessment practices, including the appraisal of practical performances and of group presentations. In this section, some of the complexities in these ideas are examined, together with the philosophical questions they provoke.

Reliability is defined in a variety of ways, but is supposed to relate to consistency. We will consider three ways of interpreting it.

Reliability[1]: Would pupils perform at the same level if the test were administered more than once?

An understandable insistence on high levels of reliability in this sense might exclude significant achievement, since it lacked stability over time. Since teachers and others invariably assume that they can make predictions about the future behavior of students on the basis of assessment results, they may well feel that such exclusion is of no importance. They are only interested in abilities or knowledge that persist. This point is linked to the idea of construct validity, which we examine below.

Clearly, practical obstacles confront any attempts to measure reliability in this sense, for pupils might well remember earlier administrations of the test. A traditional approach here is to split the test into halves, with one half given on the first occasion

275

and the other on the second. Some assessment devices, such as the essay question, could not be dealt with in this way.

Another way around the problem is to allow that "administration of the same test" does not imply the setting of a test on more than one occasion with identical questions, but can involve "equivalent" questions. Judgments about "equivalence" can appear to be straightforward, simply involving inspection of possibilities by relevantly qualified professionals. However, we need to ask whether there are independent objective criteria of equivalence. It is well known that performance on apparently "similar" test items can vary considerably. Speculation about the causes of these differences centers on the precise detail of wording, format, and even the position of the item with reference to the rest of the test. With differential performances, some will conclude that the test items were not "really" similar even though they appeared to be. Conversely, it is sometimes claimed that apparently dissimilar test items are "really" similar since they elicit highly correlated performances. There are no obvious independent criteria to which we can appeal to settle this question.

Reliability[2]: Would students receive the same scores even if particular test responses were assessed by different graders?

Let us consider the philosophical questions provoked by the possibility that responses involve "practical performances" such as teaching a class, explaining an essay answer in an oral examination, presenting a research paper to a seminar group, or arguing a case in court. The interesting issues center on what precisely *counts as the performance*, or what features of the performance fall within the proper scope of judgment, and under what criteria of judgment. Differences in judgment may arise from a variety of sources, including differences of social class and culture, different assumptions about what constitutes a proper understanding of the subject being taught, different ideals of performance, and differences of taste. Any of these factors might lead to differing judgments about whether a teacher is conducting "effective questioning," for instance.

Reliability[3]: To what extent would a particular grader respond consistently to the same test response if required to do so more than once over a period of time?

In practice, if graders are dealing with very many test papers or essays, they may be quite unable to remember how they scored earlier answers. Indeed, it has been established that in such contexts scores are influenced by "sequence effects," or the order in which answers are graded. For example, the score of a good answer that follows a string of poor ones will tend to be inflated relative to what it would otherwise have been.

This brief treatment of reliability reveals that the notion of *consistency* in assessment embraces some importantly different ideas. When scrutinizing any form of assessment for its degree of reliability we need to be clear about which of these forms of consistency is relevant. We have seen no reason to believe that they will necessarily all be found together. Yet if the assessment concerned is a "high-stakes" one, then surely it should be strongly consistent in at least the three senses touched on here.

Validity

The degree of validity of an assessment is conventionally characterized as the extent to which it measures what it is intended to measure. Many validity "types" figure in the literature, but Samuel Messick (1989) highlighted three. "Content" validity appeals to experts to judge whether the test is "about" that which it purports to measure. The experts basically inspect the tests and make a judgment directly. "Criterion-related" validity is concerned with the correlations between the test concerned and *another* measure or "criterion." For instance, results from a test purporting to measure qualities required for a job might be checked against supervisors' ratings as a way of investigating its validity. "Construct" validity focuses directly on what the test is supposed to measure. Assessment is supposed to probe *something about the student* that explains the performance and is expected to persist and ground related future performances. It should detect some underlying trait, ability, knowledge, or competence that is reasonably stable over time. These are the "constructs." They cannot be observed directly, but are invoked to explain observable behavior.

Defenders of construct validity face some challenging philosophical questions. The first such question pertains to the basis on which diverse performances are assumed to manifest a singular enduring construct. A bewildering variety of constructs have been postulated, from the very general notion of intelligence to specific "skills" involved in reading or mathematics. The constructs are often described using language deriving from the characterizations of performances purportedly manifesting the said construct or underlying trait. For instance, Jane recharges her car battery, clears out the gutter so that rainwater stops pouring down near her front door, and completes a logic problem in her daughter's puzzle book. All these are classified as solving problems. The relevant "construct" is then said to be a "problem-solving ability." On what principled basis can one draw *these* and not other diverse performances together as manifestations of a singular underlying ability? Jane "solves a problem" today when she convinces her quarrelsome neighbors to speak to each other. Does this exhibit the *same* competence or ability that she allegedly demonstrated in the earlier examples, or must we hypothesize diverse problem-solving abilities, distinguishable by problem types, solution types, or something else?

In the absence of an adequate science of the mind, we simply do not know what any of the alleged constructs we are trying to measure amount to, and not knowing what they amount to we must remain in some doubt as to whether we have carved at the true joints of the mind as it were, and are not "measuring" a mere artifact of the choices made in constructing the exam. Our ability to name classes of complex social performances and to describe those performances as arising from enduring mental dispositions far outstrips our ability to say what those dispositions would amount to. From this perspective, the concept of test validity seems to thrust us right into the most difficult questions surrounding the ontology of the mind, cognitive science's limited progress toward computational models of cognition, the status of "folk psychology" *vis-à-vis* neuroscience, and the like. Perhaps, on the other hand, it is enough for the purposes of test validity that we carve not at the joints of the mind, but at the joints of the curriculum: if we know well enough what we are trying to teach and should expect students to learn, might we reasonably settle for establishing – what is

277

in any case hard enough to establish – that test performances are strongly predictive of the kinds of future performances that we care about? Predictive validity of this sort is all that the much-maligned US Educational Testing Service's (ETS's) SAT (formerly "Scholastic Aptitude Test," now "Scholastic Assessment Test") has ever claimed by way of validity. Whether such predictive validity is a satisfactory surrogate or substitute for construct validity in general, however, I will not presume to judge. Intuitively, we do use our evaluations of student performances to judge not only what they can *do*, but what they *understand*, and it is as true now as it was in Augustine's time that we can neither say what such understanding amounts to, nor directly cause it to occur (King, 1995, 1998).

Human performances occur in specific contexts, and further questions about construct validity arise from this, because the very idea of construct validity is that a test with such validity enables us to infer from a limited range of performances elicited within a specific context – namely, in the context of taking the exam – that the exam taker does or does not have knowledge or abilities that would be appropriately manifested in other quite different contexts. One line of argument holds that because "transfers" of learning are known to be limited, students should be allowed to demonstrate their learning in any of a number of ways, or contexts. Otherwise, they are penalized unfairly by the examiner's choice of format or performance context, and the exam may be said to lack construct validity in the sense that it is subject to an unacceptable risk of "false negatives." The essence of this line of argument is that: (1) learning is context-laden; (2) exams sometimes demand that students manifest their learning in ways they cannot, even though they have learned what is being tested; (3) what matters is that the essential learning has taken place; so (4) the fairness and validity of student evaluations would be enhanced by providing alternative means by which students could demonstrate their learning (see Wiggins, 1989). This argument impugns construct validity without impugning constructs.

Another line of argument from the context-ladenness of learning seeks to impugn construct validity precisely by impugning the constructs, not because we cannot identify any such constructs without an adequate science of the mind, but because one may doubt that abilities or knowledge as such can be properly distinguished from the grasp of the specific contexts in which they are acquired or learned. This argument arises from the consideration that demonstrations of learning always occur in some context, and in one way or another the inference to the presence of the construct, understood as having a kind of generality or applicability in various contexts, always involves a form of abstraction which sets aside the particularities of the context or the grasp of it that grounds the performance. This abstraction may be suspected of separating in description what is inseparable in fact.

We can distinguish two cases: examiners may be content with *any* demonstration of learning, or they may want to test for a more significant degree of understanding or skill in performing a task or solving a given kind of problem in a variety of contexts. In the former case, examiners infer a general though minimal ability from a performance which is generically described. For instance, an "ability to throw a ball" is inferred from any successful demonstration of throwing a ball that a person can offer, or "an understanding of subtraction" from any demonstration of ability to subtract. In the latter case, the skill would be the construct to be measured, but it would have to be observed across a variety of contexts of application, deployed with a grasp of the divergent features of those contexts. Here the reliance on understanding of the divergent contexts, and in some cases reliance on ancillary skills, may be very striking. The student who throws a ball may be called upon not just to throw any ball, but to throw a baseball within a batter's strike zone, *also* throw an American football to a receiver running a slant pattern, and throw a cross court bounce pass in close man-to-man coverage during a basketball game. Any one of these might be considered a demonstration of some skill in throwing a ball, and the combination of the three, each requiring very different movements, abilities, and ancillary understanding, would demonstrate a more advanced level of skill. Similarly, a good test of skill in subtraction might require applications of subtraction involving not only abstract numbers, but money in the context of shopping, measuring out lengths of rope, and coming up with an answer to "$2 - 7 = \ldots$" In either case, the abstraction involved in hypothesizing an ability or skill that is unitary and separable from all else that grounds the disparate performances is suspect.

A response to this might be to hold that there is some "core" grasp of subtraction, perhaps identifiable in principle as some kind of brain state, though we are unable to say at present what it amounts to. This "core" grasp of subtraction would need to be supplemented by a grasp of appropriate contexts for it to be applied in such contexts. Alternatively, one might doubt the existence of any such "context-free" knowledge of subtraction as an enduring and well defined trait of an individual. On this view, one might hold that all knowledge of subtraction is knowledge of how to do subtractions in specific contexts of application. One might hold that when "transfer" of learning to new contexts occurs it is rooted in training which provides learners with "paradigm" or model problem solutions and practice in subsuming new cases under those "paradigms" (Kuhn, 1977), but this does not amount to a context-neutral ability that can be properly abstracted from the various context-laden performances.

Combining reliability and validity

Empirical researchers point to the difficulty of combining reliability and validity when measuring learning. I have advanced a more general related argument (Davis, 1995, 1998) that applies to any attempts to describe achievement in standard language, whatever the evidence for such achievement might be. Examples of such standard languages include descriptions of "competences" in vocational courses, the National Curriculum of England and Wales and even some attempts to provide students with assessment criteria in higher education. The common language of criterion-referenced systems purports to be applicable to the achievement of any student, and claims to describe knowledge, understanding, and skills "objectively."

At this point it is easiest to take the argument further by means of an example. It is drawn from a version of the UK mathematics National Curriculum (Department for Education, 1995): "Pupils understand and use an appropriate non-calculator method for solving problems that involve multiplying and dividing any three-digit number by any two-digit number."

Despite its apparent precision this statement is open to interpretation. Teachers and others will construe it in a wide variety of ways according to their circumstances *unless they are constrained.* "Appropriate" might mean a method deemed to be sensible by the Qualifications and Curriculum Authority, the government agency that oversees the National Curriculum. Such an agency might well accept that the method might need to vary *according to the numbers in the calculation.* Thus 20×300 would be calculated in a different way from 38×966, which in turn would be calculated differently from 25×450. If "appropriateness" is not laid down by the "authority," matters might become even more complicated, since it could be judged at least in part with reference to a given pupil's knowledge, understanding, and skills. Thus a method appropriate for one pupil might be inappropriate for another. The term "problem" throws up a new set of issues, since the calculations could be presented in abstract numerical forms in a variety of formats, the most obvious of which would be either horizontal or vertical. However, it is not unreasonable to interpret "problem" as "realistic" or "practical" applications of multiplication. Only a moment's thought is necessary to appreciate that such challenges could come in an almost infinite variety of guises.

Can steps be taken to prevent the standard language characterizing performances from being open to a variety of interpretations? Offering linguistic alternatives is arguably doomed to failure, since these alternatives would have to be interpreted themselves. A regress threatens, because it seems in principle that continued attempts to supply interpretive guidance must themselves require interpretation. The design of assessment instruments has escaped this problem, as well as the time and expense involved in human scoring, by resorting to machine scorable examinations. This is accomplished by requiring students to choose one of several proposed answers to a question, the examiners having endeavored to ensure that *only* one of those answers is correct. Such tests are in practice overwhelmingly limited to probing factual recall and specific problem-solving skills, and it seems unlikely that they can be successfully adapted to adequately measure all the learning that matters to us. There are many kinds of performances that we prepare students for, which these tests can neither elicit nor observe, and they are insensitive to variations in the quality of thinking behind answers that are alike in being "correct" or "incorrect."

The dilemma that emerges, then, is that high reliability seems to require that scoring become mechanical, but restricting student responses to what is mechanically scorable seems to reduce validity by precluding the measurement of much that we should be concerned to measure. The claim that the reliability required for accurate accountability is incompatible with the validity essential to supporting meaningful learning is thus not surprisingly a familiar theme in the assessment literature. The TGAT Report in the United Kingdom (Department of Education and Science, 1988) famously tried to achieve what some regarded as squaring the circle in this respect, but work in the United States and Canada has begun to focus more on developing alternative forms of standardized assessment suitable to a "thinking" curriculum.

This work is proceeding along several paths. One approach is to more fully exploit the potential of machine scorable multiple choice tests by applying greater effort to designing prompts that demand more accomplished forms of thinking (Traub, 1993; Norris, 1995). Another approach, with several variants, is to use tests which allow students to construct their own responses, often in the form of essays, and develop methods for improving the consistency of the judgments made by human graders.

One approach, developed by ETS, involves the training and supervision of graders brought together at a scoring site (College Entrance Examination Board, 1993). Another widely used approach relies on sample answers representative of what is required to earn different scores. A third, used for several years now by the biology division of the California Assessment, has achieved slightly higher reliability than the 0.8 or 80 percent consistency claimed by ETS and considered sufficient by psychometricians. The approach used there is to ground both the development of essay prompts and the instructions provided to graders in an account of the forms of scientific thinking – explanatory, investigative, and confirmatory – that the essay questions are intended to measure. The prompts ask students to offer alternative possible explanations, critique experimental designs, suggest methods for investigating questions, and the like. The scoring instructions, mailed out with exam papers to teacher-graders across the state, explain how the prompts are intended to elicit broad forms of scientific thinking, and focus the attention of graders on the form and scientific plausibility of the answers, rather than discrete matters of factual correctness.

To the extent that training and supervision, model answers, and explanatory instructions only succeed in directing the attention of graders to superficial features of students' answers, or fail to yield consistency of judgment, they will fail. On the other hand, if they succeed in yielding the consistency and quality of judgment essential to adequate validity and reliability, it will be through building on a prior shared understanding of the content being tested and inducing a more specific understanding of the tests themselves. The educator of test graders can no more guarantee the timely occurrence of this understanding than the educator of test takers can guarantee that pupils will understand all that *they* will be tested on.

In their everyday dealings with pupils, teachers gather detailed, personalized, and context-sensitive information about pupil performance. They do so to enable them to support pupils in the development of understanding, particularly of concepts that take shape only gradually and uncertainly over longer periods of time. Characteristic examples include ideas about energy and force in science, place value in mathematics and the notion of a sentence in English. Although teachers' approaches to such information gathering may include the use of written tests of various kinds, they invariably employ a much wider range of interactions with their pupils. Would it be possible to gain equally accurate and comprehensive information about pupils' grasp of such complex and abstract ideas by using approaches with the level of reliability required for a "high stakes" accountability system?

The question is a philosophically interesting one. Is it simply a matter for empirical inquiry? Or is there, for instance, an incompatibility in principle between assessment for the kind of learning exemplified above, and assessment achieved with the degree of reliability appropriate for accountability? This remains a matter for debate, although I have argued elsewhere that there is a necessary incompatibility (Davis, 1998).

Assessment and Fairness

Notions of "bias" and "fairness" in tests are complex and raise a number of interesting value questions. They have not escaped the notice of empirical researchers (e.g. Gipps and Murphy, 1994), and are nicely illustrated in a paper on the assessment of physical education by Douane MacDonald and Ross Brooker (1997). The rhetoric of assessment is that students compete "on an equal footing," and without this presumption the consequences of the success and failure measured by the assessments we use would be understandably perceived as unjust. Assessment must be perceived as fair, to legitimize the reproduction or imposition of social and educational disparities.

Teachers in Macdonald and Brooker's study were concerned that students with certain characteristics would be advantaged in the assessment process. Examples of the features they had in mind were strength, size, and sex.

We would need to know the purpose of the assessment even to grasp the nature of these teachers' concerns, let alone to evaluate them. If the assessment process is designed to discover whether candidates can achieve given physical challenges objectively described, it would seem odd to *complain* that "stronger" candidates would do better. An analogous complaint in tests of cognitive achievement would be that candidates who could learn mathematics more easily (for whatever reason – we need not assume some dubious notion of fixed inherited ability such as the intelligence or IQ construct) would be unfairly advantaged in a mathematics test.

Returning to the physical education example, if the test determines access into teacher training courses for physical education specialists then complaints of unfairness have more weight. However, what is unfair here is the test's *use*, rather than its content. Arguably very high levels of physical prowess should not be deemed necessary for candidates aspiring to teach physical education to the whole range of pupil talent and motivation. On the other hand, the tests may be perfectly fair if intended to check on whether candidates can achieve specific athletic feats – for instance, if they are being selected to join some kind of sports academy promoting high levels of sporting and athletic achievement. The ultimate *value* of the promotion of such achievement might be contested but this has nothing to do with the fairness of the entry test.

In the United Kingdom the 2001 National Curriculum tests in English for eleven-year-olds have been said to be "unfair" in that they advantaged boys. The tests included very little in the way of story and narrative. Instead they incorporated "fact-filled non-fiction text in magazine format, chopped into bite-sized chunks" (*Times Educational Supplement*, May 25, 2001, p. 3). Critics assume that boys like this approach while girls prefer fiction, and that boys will score better in tests involving material they enjoy.

The notion of "fairness" here seems to be closely linked to validity. A test cannot be fair unless performance reflects *levels of relevant knowledge, understanding, and skills*. The majority of boys in our culture are socialized into certain literacy preferences and the test critics hold that these are contributing to superior performance when only the relevant knowledge, understanding, and skills ought to figure. Hence the accusation that the test is unfair. Moreover, insofar as the test fails to strike a balance between different types of writing and concentrates on non-fiction it is not a valid assessment of an appropriately broad aspect of literacy.

Can the criticism that a test is unfair because influenced by candidates' preferences be sustained? If the *preferences* of subgroups of candidates were held to damage the test's validity and fairness, draft tests would need to be scrutinized for *any* content that might impinge on preferences not shared by all candidates. Many tests could never aspire to validity in such circumstances. In practice, for a variety of political and social reasons test constructors will be expected to attend to the preferences of particular subgroups. If, for instance, the images and examples represented in test content affect the motivation and therefore the performance of groups with a given ethnic origin, then the test would fail to measure properly their relevant knowledge, understanding, and skills. It would to that extent lack validity and be deemed "unfair."

Ideas of meritocracy, equal opportunities and competing "on an equal footing" have been linked to other questions about fairness and bias. It has sometimes been assumed that if some groups perform worse than others on a particular test then it *must* be unfair because everyone begins on the same starting line. As Gipps and Murphy (1994) point out, this assumption may well be false, and attempts to secure equal outcomes across all groups would damage the test's validity. For example, boys as opposed to girls, or members of one social class or ethnic group rather than another, may differ in motivation and "cultural capital."

Conclusion

All attempts to measure learning are imperfect. The gravity of these imperfections depends on the purposes of the assessment. One of the key questions here is whether the advantages of high-stakes assessment outweigh the disadvantages. This chapter has rehearsed some of the arguments that must be considered to arrive at a measured answer. "Advantages" must in the end be interpreted in the light of a defensible set of aims for education. Each country also has its own special contextual features that should be taken into account. In my view, the current approaches to assessment in the UK and the USA are counterproductive even if education is seen as the servant of a competitive economy.

See also 4 THE EDUCATIONAL THOUGHT OF AUGUSTINE; 16 THEORIES OF TEACHING AND LEARNING; 17 THE CAPACITY TO LEARN; 18 MOTIVATION AND CLASSROOM MANAGEMENT

References

Bourdieu, P. and Passeron, J. (1977) *Reproduction.* London: Sage.

College Entrance Examination Board (1993) *1993 AP Biology: Free-response Scoring Guide and Sample Student Answers.* New York: The College Board and Educational Testing Service (ETS).

Davis, A. J. (1995) Criterion-referenced assessment and the development of knowledge and understanding. *Journal of Philosophy of Education,* 29, 3–23.

Davis, A. J. (1998) *The Limits of Educational Assessment.* Oxford: Blackwell.

Department for Education (1995) *Mathematics in the National Curriculum.* London: HMSO.

Department of Education and Science (1988) *National Curriculum Task Group on Assessment and Testing: A Report.* London: HMSO (known as the TGAT Report).

Gipps, C. and Murphy, P. (1994) *A Fair Test?* Buckingham: Open University Press.

King, P. (1995) *Augustine: Against the Academicians and the Teacher*. Indianapolis: Hackett.

King, P. (1998) Augustine on the impossibility of teaching. *Metaphilosophy*, 29, 179–95.

Kuhn, T. (1977) Second thoughts on paradigms. In *The Essential Tension*. Chicago: Chicago University Press, pp. 293–319.

Macdonald, D. and Brooker, R. (1999) Assessment issues in a performance-based subject: a case study of physical education. In P. Murphy (ed.), *Learners, Learning and Assessment*. London: Paul Chapman Publishing, pp. 171–90.

Messick, S. (1989) Meaning and values in test validation: the science and ethics of assessment. In R. McCormick and C. Paechter (eds), *Learning and Knowledge*. London: Paul Chapman Publishing, pp. 154–69.

Norris, S. (1995) Format effects on critical thinking test performance. *Alberta Journal of Educational Research*, 41, 378–406.

Qualifications and Curriculum Authority (1998) *English Tests Mark Schemes*. London: HMSO.

Sockett, H. (1980) Accountability: the contemporary issues. In H. Sockett (ed.), *Accountability in the English Educational System*. London: Hodder and Staughton, pp. 5–24.

Traub, R. (1993) On the equivalence of the traits assessed by multiple-choice and constructed-response tests. In R. Bennett and W. Ward (eds), *Construction versus Choice in Cognitive Measurement*. Hillsdale, NJ: Erlbaum, pp. 29–44.

Wiggins, G. (1989) A true test: toward more authentic and equitable assessment. *Phi Delta Kappan*, 71, 703–13.

Further reading

Greeno, J., Moore, J., and Smith, D. (1993) Transfer of situated learning. In D. Detterman and R. Sternberg (eds), *Transfer on Trial: Intelligence, Cognition and Instruction*. Norwood, NJ: Ablex Publishing Corporation, pp. 99–167.

Lave, J. and Wenger, E. (1991). *Situated Learning: Legitimate Peripheral Participation*. New York: Cambridge University Press.

Torrance, H. (1997) Assessment, accountability and standards. In A. H. Halsey, H. Lauder, P. Brown, and A. S. Wells (eds), *Education, Culture, Economy, Society*. Oxford: Oxford University Press, pp. 320–31.

20

Knowledge, Truth, and Learning

Jonathan E. Adler

Education, especially liberal education, aims at transmitting *knowledge* (Goldman, 1999, chapter 11). This traditional view holds that students should be taught subject-matter in a number of disciplines (e.g. literature, biology, history, mathematics), as well as the intellectual skills or abilities requisite for learning in those disciplines (e.g. reading, writing, arithmetical computation) (Hirst, 1973). In this chapter, I take up the traditional view and its closely related interpretation as the *aim of truth*, as a way to pursue the topic of knowledge and education. The *knowledge-aim* is a fundamental one. For this reason, as well as because it is an aim that *we share*, it is capable of justifying various basic educational practices.

Still, the knowledge-aim has been challenged, particularly by those who promote aims that are more formal, methodological, or process-oriented, or directed to ideals of character or citizenship. Arguing against a constricted, but popular, rendition of the knowledge-aim, William Kilpatrick declared that "Education must primarily seek character and behavior, all-round character of a kind to lead to proper behavior" (Kilpatrick, 1951, p. 226). Another form of challenge to the knowledge-aim arises from suspicions about the concepts of knowledge and truth. I will defend the knowledge-aim against these challenges, though it will necessarily be only a limited and schematic defense. Ultimately, even those who oppose the knowledge-aim must concede a great deal to it. Any general education that did not involve teaching students a variety of major disciplines would be a non-starter.

I will also show that the knowledge-aim has substantive educational applications. Although transmitting knowledge is not the only aim of education, it is surprisingly substantial in its ramifications. Because we can compare various educational practices to determine which ones better advance students' knowledge, the knowledge-aim offers educational guidance, justifies central educational practices, and exposes complexities in the educational policies it supports.

I begin with some background on the nature of truth and knowledge.

Epistemological Background

Doubts about the concept of truth cast doubt upon the truth-aim. If truth is *correspondence* with facts or states of affairs, to take the most well known explication, we can

285

easily make sense of teaching that, say, "DNA is a double-helix." But if truth or knowledge is to be the aim of education generally, it must apply to the arts and humanities as well as to the sciences (Rorty, 1998, chapter 3). It must apply to "Hamlet suffers an Oedipal complex," "Classical music is not appreciated by modern youth," and "Picasso is technically much more accomplished than Chagall" as well. But it is far less easy to understand any of these statements as corresponding to facts or states of affairs.

The conception of truth that builds confidence of application across subject-matters is the "deflationary" theory (Horwich, 1990). On a deflationary view of truth, there is no difference between asserting

(1)   "Snow is white" is true

and asserting

(2)   Snow is white.

On this theory, there is no more to understanding a statement's being true than to understanding that statement, and so no philosophical difficulty with the concept of truth that could be an obstacle to pursuing the truth-aim across diverse educational subject-matters.

Knowledge was traditionally analyzed as implying truth and as equivalent to *true justified belief*. (For an introduction to epistemology for educators, oriented toward the justified true belief analysis, see Scheffler, 1965). But the adequacy of this analysis was refuted by counterexamples due to Gettier (1970).

Here is a variant of a Gettier example. A student learns from her teacher that the music assembly is scheduled for next Thursday. The student concludes (believes) that there will be an assembly next Thursday, and she is justified in believing what the teacher said because sincere testimony is ordinarily an excellent reason to believe. Now imagine that the music assembly has been cancelled, unbeknownst to the student's teacher. Yet, the student's belief is actually correct because an earlier theater assembly has, in fact, been rescheduled for next Thursday. The student's justified belief is true, but that is only an *accident* from her point of view, and so she does not know. (Some claim that there are Gettier-type counterexamples that show that the traditional analysis also fails because it disregards a *social* aspect of knowledge. See, for example, Harman, 1973.)

Reliabilist analyses of knowledge handle this case as well as the original Gettier cases with the simple condition that, roughly, someone **S** knows that **p** just in case **S**'s believing that **p** is reliably connected to the fact that **p** (Goldman, 1986, chapters 3–5). The student's belief that there is an assembly next Thursday is not reliably connected to the fact that there is an assembly. (For a related type of analysis that is *subjunctive* or counterfactual, see Nozick, 1981, chapter 3.)

The lesson of the Gettier examples is that to know something, the basis upon which one believes must connect to what renders or establishes the belief as true. Truth is an *external* condition of knowledge. Whether it obtains depends upon conditions that the agent need not grasp.

Because it is an external condition for knowledge, truth has been of less educational interest than the justification condition, which is an *internal* one. The standard view is that a belief **p** is *justified* for an agent **A** just in case **A**'s epistemic reasons establish **p**'s truth. However, the Gettier examples undermine the conclusion that what is educationally, as well as epistemically, central is the justification condition. Indeed, if the Gettier problem can be solved by adding another necessary condition for knowledge, it will not be an internal condition. So, for example, one response is to add a *fourth condition* that rules out justification on the basis of a derivation from a false assumption. According to this fourth condition the student cannot know because his justified true belief *derives* from a justified belief that is false (that there is a music assembly next Thursday). But whether such a derivation exists will depend upon conditions that the agent need not comprehend.

It is knowledge's external property of being a *factive* that explains why it is a core or central concept. A factive is a complex statement that contains another statement in it, and implies the latter's truth. If "X knows that **p**" it follows that **p**. (By contrast, if "X believes that **p**" it does not follow that **p**.)

Now consider any number of propositional attitude statements, e.g.

Jones is angry that Mary ignored him.

"Angry" is a factive, as it follows that

Mary ignored him.

But this factiveness seems to rest on the telling implication that

Jones knows that Mary ignored him (Unger, 1975).

The result favors the view that we cannot just replace knowledge with some non-factive epistemic notion, like justification or warranted assertibility, without loss or alteration in the semantics of natural languages.

The view to which I adhere is that although there are internal and external facets to knowledge, the internal conditions must satisfy external demands. One's reasons must genuinely establish one's belief as true. Knowledge requires a process or method connecting the knower to the truth of, or indicators of the truth (or existence) of, the object of knowledge. The knower must have at least a minimal understanding or grasp of this connection which explains his attitude (belief, confidence) toward the object.

The vagueness of the phrase "object of knowledge" is intended to accommodate kinds of knowing other than knowing-that – knowledge of, knowing how, knowing why, knowing what. When a student acquires knowledge of the alphabet, he has reasons to believe that "ax" precedes "axle," and the reasons are facts that imply, given the nature of alphabetization, that "ax" does precede "axle." When someone has know-how on fixing a flat tire, he engages in controlled activities whose intended, and typically successful, result is that the flat tire is fixed.

All these kinds of knowing seem to require some knowledge-that, as do related notions. *Understanding* any subject-matter generally involves lots of knowledge-that.

You do not understand the New York City subway system unless you know that, for example, West 4th Street is a major stop. However, we can obviously have knowledge-that without understanding. You can know that $e = mc^2$ without understanding it. (On understanding's centrality in epistemology, see Elgin, 1996, and in education, see Gardner, 1991.)

Our truth-aim and the ethics of belief

Our truth-aim is the aim of having true *beliefs*. Knowledge that **p** (e.g. Bill is in Alaska), which implies the truth of the belief that **p**, is how we realize our truth-aim as believers. If you believe that Mary is in Alaska, your aim is to believe it only if it is true.

Because belief aims at truth (Williams, 1973), we cannot shape our beliefs according to our desires. Just as we are (conceptually) unable to willfully believe whatever we fancy, so too we cannot discard beliefs willfully. We cannot directly believe that, for example, the number of stars is even, so too we cannot just cease to believe that, for example, Lincoln was President.

Since belief aims at truth you cannot get anyone to believe (hence, *learn*) something directly by threat or offer: "Believe that the Civil War took place in 1786 or I'll shoot you"; "Cease to believe that I am a bad teacher and I'll be your buddy." We cannot obey either of these threats or offers directly because in each case the inducement to belief could not be a reason for it. At most, these inducements provide *non-epistemic* reasons to want to believe (to acquire the attitude of believing). But they are not *epistemic* reasons for the truth of the belief (the proposition believed). Since teaching aims at learning, and since these "*cannot*"s are manifest, no one can teach in these ways. You cannot intend what you recognize to be impossible.

These "cannot"s reflect the concept of belief. They lead us to *evidentialism* as the centrally contested answer to the central question of the *ethics of belief* ("what ought one to believe?") (Dearden, 1974; Adler, 2002). Traditionally, evidentialism holds:

Strength of belief ought to be apportioned to one's evidence.

However, evidentialism should be stated in the more general form:

Strength of belief ought to be apportioned to one's epistemic reasons.

For we have beliefs whose content is not empirical, e.g. torture is wrong; $2 + 6 = 8$. Since these also claim truth, they too must be backed by truth-relevant (i.e. epistemic) reasons. Evidence is only the most prominent epistemic reason.

Our truth-aim really is to aim at the *growth of significant truths* plus those truths requisite for comprehension of the significant ones. Consider that the largest collection of truths about the bricks on the school building – e.g. $brick_1$ has three chinks and it is located at position 451, $brick_2$ has seven chinks and it is located at position 464 – would not advance architectural understanding compared to a brief account of the design structure together with a survey of the building's composition.

We do not simply want more true beliefs regardless of our interests. Indeed, it often annoys us that we are compelled to acquire numerous trite beliefs which stick with us, e.g. that one commuter said to another that she has to catch the Flushing line. We want our beliefs to have systematic organization for easy access and storage and to make sense of phenomena and facts. The requisite structuring is how any decent teacher and curriculum tries to transmit knowledge of a subject.

However, the knowledge we seek educationally must meet loftier standards than what we seek individually. Individually we care that our beliefs respond to some interest of ours, however lowly, like gossip about our neighbor. But the educational aim is to select knowledge that is most valuable or fundamental. In an extended or indirect way, individuals still share this loftier aim, as discussion below indicates.

Growth of significant truths is an aim that is then both descriptive and normative. Descriptively, it accounts for a number of basic educational practices. We do teach students texts and discoveries across a number of disciplines, and we would regard an education that did not as impoverished. One that taught subjects indifferent to truth would be intolerable. Normatively, we regard these practices as worthy ideals. Liberal education attempts to teach the most worthy knowledge and texts, as well as to provide models of how to acquire knowledge and to nurture the intellectual virtues that promote that acquisition.

Belief, detachment, and epistemic "bad faith"

The knowledge-aim is the aim of *inquiry*. Broadly, inquiry is the systematic search through rational means for truths that resolve problems, perplexities, or puzzles, or fill gaps in our understanding. The methods of inquiry – from observation and experimentation to impartial evaluation and critical discussion – have commonsense roots, as methods of reason to which we are all committed.

Taking the viewpoint of inquiry as central, the truth or knowledge-aim has been disparaged because we have no access to truth over and above our reasons or evidence. Richard Rorty (1998, p. 19) writes:

Pragmatists think that if something makes no difference to practice, it should make no difference to philosophy. This conviction makes them suspicious of the distinction between justification and truth...assessment of truth and assessment of justification are, when the question is what I should believe now, the same activity.

But, on its own, truth has almost nothing to tell us:

the entire force of the cautionary use of "true" is to point out that justification is relative to an audience and that we can never exclude the possibility that a better audience might exist, or come to exist, to whom a belief that is justifiable to us would not be justifiable. (Ibid., p. 22)

The proposal to treat the successful end of inquiry as realized in "warranted assertibility" or "justification" rather than "truth" or "knowledge" – the *replacement* proposal – is already cast under suspicion by our earlier observation about the centrality of knowledge. Here we redouble that suspicion. When inquiry successfully concludes with the acceptance of a hypothesis as true, it issues in a *full* belief. When, instead, inquiry is aborted or fails to reach a successful terminus, we suspend judgment. We are consigned to only some degree of *partial* belief in the hypothesis. *Full belief* is ordinary, unqualified belief, and it is the truth of one's full belief that is what we aim at. Only full belief eventuates in a *transparent* attitude toward its content. We look through the belief to the world, but not to our attitude of believing it. However, when one holds a partial belief, one cannot look through one's attitude to the content as expressing a feature of the world, since one just does not (yet) take the world to be that way.

Since full belief claims truth, there is no reason for one's actual evidence to be retained. We find corroboration in the practice of *assertion*. Asserting is, roughly, the unqualified saying or uttering (or writing) of a declarative sentence. The parallel between assertion and belief is that the requirement of the speech-act of assertion is to state what is true, as it is the constitutive claim of belief that its content is true. To assert that "Joe is in Alaska" is to express the (full) belief that Joe is in Alaska. By contrast, the qualified assertion "I'm pretty sure that Joe is in Alaska" corresponds to a partial belief.

The assertion, not the speaker's reasons for believing it, is of focal interest. So, normally, from the hearer's point of view what matters is that the speaker has adequate reasons for what he asserts. The specifics of those reasons are not of focal interest (e.g. how the speaker knows that Joe is in Alaska). By contrast, since partial belief is an unsatisfactory state, seeking resolution as full belief (or disbelief), it cannot unburden itself of its evidential base. For the specific evidence one has will affect how one evaluates further evidence.

The replacement proposal implies that justification to some audience is the best we can do. The upholder of the knowledge-aim is then accused of entering the contradictory demand that we do better than our best. But the upholder should respond that the replacement view does not accord with our willingness to risk error, to go beyond our evidence, to claim truth or knowledge, as the elimination of the possibility of error.

The recommendation to set aside truth or knowledge is a recommendation for the evasion of commitment or (intellectual) responsibility – a kind of Sartrean epistemic "bad faith." For it is to withhold commitment to **p**'s being the case, so that one is not responsible should **p** turn out false, unless one has been negligent. When Rorty denies that truth is "something we might realize we had reached" he is not acknowledging that it is something that we *must* claim to have reached, if we take our reasons as genuinely adequate.

Certainty, assertion, and the alleged demandingness of knowledge

Knowledge as the *elimination of the possible ways* one can be mistaken (Lewis, 1996) has clear application to the natural and social sciences. We establish a hypothesis by systematically drawing out its vulnerable implications. The negation of each of these is a possibility that the hypothesis is mistaken. If by research and experimentation we show that each negation fails, we establish the hypothesis. But the conception readily applies to other inquiries. A student is revising her paper, and she generates several alternative ways of expressing a proposition. She then critically eliminates those alternatives (possibilities) which do not sound right or convey the wrong meaning.

In emphasizing the versatility of this understanding of knowledge, I am also hinting at my doubts about the complaint that knowledge is *too demanding* as a criterion either for ordinary knowing or for the cognitive achievement sought in education. If it is assumed that knowledge requires *certainty*, then it might seem to follow that knowledge is impossible, and skepticism is warranted. However, there is no good reason to hold that knowledge requires certainty. Certainty, as an attitude of the strongest assurance, is an associate of knowing, but not essential to it. As one eliminates more possibilities of error, one's confidence normally grows accordingly. Yet elimination of possibilities is at root an epistemic activity, not a psychological aid. The intellectually nervous or meek student can learn, just as the self-assured one, that $a^2 + b^2 = c^2$.

Yet how, more specifically, do we reconcile our fallibility with knowledge, as the elimination of possibilities of error, and inquiry as its main means? Eliminating possibilities of error does capture how inquiry proceeds and ends, as the opening paragraph of this section indicates. It seems to accord as well with our own judgment. If you ask Sally, "Where is Bill?" and she answers "Bill is in Alaska, though there is some possibility that he isn't," you would take her to be actually withdrawing to something like "Well, I'm pretty sure that Bill is in Alaska."

The form of reasoning just invoked is derived from *Moore's Paradox*. Moore's Paradox is that assertions of the following form are heard as contradictory, yet the assertions themselves are consistent:

p, but I do not believe that **p**.

For example,

It is raining, but I do not believe that it is raining.

A rough account of the contradiction is that since an assertion is proper only if the speaker holds the corresponding belief, the whole thought would be that I both believe that **p** and that I do not believe that **p**. But no such belief is possible, since its content is an overt contradiction. The Moore's Paradox test is a *first-person* test: one cannot think *of oneself* that one believes **p** and that one does not believe **p**. Using Moore's Paradox, we can defend further the ordinariness of knowledge.

The following seems to generate a Moore's Paradox:

John is in Detroit, but I do not know it.

By parity of reasoning, an assertion is proper only if the speaker has knowledge of what he asserts, and so we have the contradiction of affirming and denying knowledge of the same proposition (propositional content). Correspondingly, the standard form of challenge (or query) to a speaker's assertion that **p** (e.g. the cat is in the yard) is for the hearer to ask, "How do you know that **p**?"

We should mark this spot: assertion is an ordinary activity that we engage in regularly. Yet each of the numerous, everyday statements we sincerely and unself-consciously utter, we utter taking ourselves to know what we assert. Correspondingly, you as a hearer accept, without further proof or evidence, a speaker's assertion. For instance, you ask a stranger, "What time is it?" and the stranger replies "6:10." Normally, you readily accept (come to believe) that it is 6:10 because you take the stranger to know that it is 6:10.

Assertional exchanges are governed by a *default rule*: accept what a speaker asserts, unless you have special reason to object. Since the rule is a tacit one, not codified or explicitly taught, compliance with it appears to reflect our endorsement of it as conversationally necessary or rational. Harry asks a stranger, Sally:

H: How do I get to the Brooklyn Museum?
S :   Take the number 2 or 3 downtown to Eastern Parkway.

Sally implies that she knows that the right way to get to the Brooklyn Museum is to take the 2 or 3 subway to Eastern Parkway. Now consider the following retort by Harry

H: How do you know? [Are you sure?]

Meant as a challenge, the default rule implies that Harry's question requires backing (e.g. "I thought that the numbers 2 and 3 trains run express, but that the Eastern Parkway is a local stop"). Otherwise Sally can reject it. If Harry's challenge had to be accepted by Sally without backing, it would amount to imposing an unfeasible demand on speakers that they always retain the reasons that justify their assertions, and it would unnecessarily restrict the transfer or communication of knowledge. So, as a reflection of the default rule, H's question, as a challenge, would generally be considered rude:

S: If you didn't trust me, why did you bother to ask? [Why don't you take my word for it?]

Despite this, we also hear as a Moore's Paradox-like contradiction:

John is in Detroit, but it's possible that he isn't.

The speaker implies that he knows that John is in Detroit, and he cannot do so while acknowledging that it is possible that he is wrong. Having knowledge, then, may appear to be incompatible with there being any possibility of error. But how does one eliminate all possibilities of error? Notoriously, in inductive cases, we enter claims about the future based on past observations. Surely, as David Hume taught, even if the sun has risen every day, we cannot rationally exclude the possibility that tomorrow a cataclysmic event will stop the sun from rising. Again, how can we reconcile our fallibility with how easy it is to obtain knowledge? The ease of obtaining knowledge is a fact of life that theories of knowledge must do justice to, but so too is our fallibility.

First, it is important to recognize that knowledge is compatible with the *defeasibility* of a claim to knowledge. Externalists rightly insist that we must distinguish knowing from knowing that one knows. Similarly, we must distinguish the conditions for having knowledge or justification from our showing or knowing or justifying that those conditions are met. It is enough to know that Kate is in her office that the door is open and the person I see there looks exactly like Kate. Of course, if, unbeknownst to me, Kate has an identical twin, who could be in her office instead, then I fail to know. But it does not follow that I have to exclude Kate's having a twin, before I can know that she is in her office.

Second, we do not regard all logical or conceptual possibilities as real or serious ones. If I flip a coin, it is logically possible that it will land on its side. But we ignore this possibility as irrelevant, and claim that the coin *must* land either on its head or its tail. Similarly, it is an unproblematic commonplace that hypothesis-testing requires that we ignore many alternative hypotheses compatible with the same data.

Standards for what possibilities of error must be excluded for inquiry, justification, or knowledge are *context-sensitive* (Lewis, 1996). Return to our fragment of dialogue about the New York City subways above. Just as H could not simply challenge the assertion without reason, so too the following is unacceptable:

H: Isn't it possible that the conductor will have a heart attack, and so not stop at Eastern Parkway?

Now, another, and different kind of, challenge is the following:

H: Are you really sure? My elderly grandmother is waiting for me at the toll booth.

Where the health of the grandmother is presumed at stake, the challenge is appropriate, even though no specific possibility of error has been offered. Given the presumed vulnerability of H's grandmother, the standards for adequate reasons (for knowledge) rise, and so more evidence or grounds are necessary. Possibilities for error that are ignored originally are not ignored in the more demanding circumstance.

The context sensitivity of standards for knowledge chips away further and mightily at the charge that conditions of knowledge, particularly as the elimination of possibilities, are too demanding – so demanding that we should be tempted by skepticism. There are some further problems with the charge that I address at the end of this chapter.

Educational Applications

Given this epistemological background and orientation, let me try to show that the truth or knowledge-aim has substantive educational applications. Its major curricular implications mesh with those of the traditional liberal arts education, an education that takes the teaching and learning of knowledge in a range of disciplines as fundamental, as noted above. But the knowledge-aim is also central to intradiscipline choices. For an easy illustration: how can we justify the teaching in biology of evolution and not creationism except by invoking, as a premise, that we know evolution is basically correct and that creationism is not?

293

Justifying and motivating educational practices

In education, starting with the aim of truth has the great advantage of being an aim that is *ours* already. We aim at the truth of our beliefs, and we care intrinsically and extrinsically to reach that aim. Intrinsic concern is evidenced in curiosity, and extrinsic concern is related to our grasp of the utility of truth. Students should care about education because they care that their beliefs are true, and they seek to enlarge their set of true beliefs. The "should" here is that of their own commitments, and so it is a matter of consistency or the effectiveness with which they pursue their own aims, not the imposition of an outside standard. Students are committed to liberal education at least implicitly or by implication, however much they dissent from its specifics, because it is the only feasible means to satisfy their knowledge-aim. Hence, the requirement of a liberal education can be justified by open appeal to the reasonableness and critical judgment of students themselves.

Liberal education as realizing the knowledge-aim claims eventually to be *intrinsically* motivating. Intrinsic motivation for an activity is motivation that stems from the inherent rewards of pursuing the activity without outside inducement, whether through extrinsic rewards or threats (see Deci, 1975). Intrinsic motivation in the content of what is taught is at the heart of liberal education.

But it is an embarrassing romanticism to set a goal that education should be intrinsically motivating all the way through. Central to education and learning, within formal schooling, is regular testing and assessment. Yet, even if students do not want tests, as we may presume, they have *higher-order* wants which provide the opportunity to justify testing to them by appeal to their own wants. The (first-order) motivation is external: to pressure students to study and to give teachers a basis for assessment and grading. But since this external motivation is out in the open, testing is not manipulative (for further related analysis see Curren, 1995). Moreover, if testing is a necessary external motivator to realize the knowledge-aim, as we can safely assume, then we can expect it will foster pleasure in educational activities. Testing coerces students to study. But the result is an improvement in *competency*, and competency itself is a powerful motivator. Assuming some antecedent inclination toward an activity, we tend much more to pursue those activities in which we are skillful, since we find them easier to engage and more pleasurable.

Extending the internal justification: "why should I learn this stuff?"

Our knowledge or truth aim, we observed, is an aim for the growth or increase of knowledge or true beliefs. We care not just that our beliefs are true, but that we systematically expand and deepen our comprehension. In everyday life, the optimum way to accomplish this is to be fairly *profligate* about acquiring new beliefs, as contrasted to filtering or selectively accepting beliefs. You move around an environment, and you willy-nilly, rapidly acquire numerous beliefs: it's a rainy day, the newspaper was thrown under the car, etc. The profligacy is not *credulity* because by-and-large our belief-forming processes – perception, simple reasoning, memory, testimony – yield true beliefs (i.e. are *veridical*). Credulity, like hasty generalization, is a fault characterized by too readily acquiring beliefs where we know we should be hesitant.

Appeal to such profligacy affords us an answer to the student's pointed question, "Why should I learn this stuff?" even if we accept the presumption that our answer must rest on the extrinsic value of learning. The brief answer is that the profligacy creates the possibility of surprise and success in answering unanticipated questions. The first step to introducing a fuller version of this answer is to distinguish the question "Why should I care to be educated?" ("Why should I want to learn 'stuff' at all?") from the question "Why should I care to be educated in *this* way?" (where "this" picks out some determinate curriculum). The former, *indeterminate* form of the question is presupposed by the latter, *determinate* form of the question. This *indeterminate* form of the question is answered by the truth-aim: we can be very sure that some particular facts or subjects, among all that the student is taught, will be useful at some time, even if we regard each particular one as unlikely to be useful. We are constantly entering new informational or environmental settings. The great value of profligacy in learning is to provide us with a guide to acting and judging in situations that we do not anticipate. Traveling to a new town, working on a crossword puzzle, going to a dinner party, reading an op-ed piece call on us to act or to judge, and to do so we are likely to rely upon beliefs that we acquired without expectation of their usefulness on these occasions.

The unpredictability or limited predictability of one's future, dependent as it is on happenstance, also encompasses the limited predictability of one's future wants, ends, and objectives. Our knowledge-aim properly includes expanding our self-knowledge. Suppose that a student now sees no point in studying algebra, the civil war, the plant cycle, or Picasso's "Guernica," and that none of these has any bearing on the student's interests, as he currently conceives them. Nevertheless, there can still be a high probability that some one of these will awaken an interest in him that he does not now recognize, or would otherwise not exist, or will become relevant to his interests as those interests evolve with the changing circumstances of his life.

Knowledge, recognition, and understanding

With this answer to the "why should I learn this stuff?" question in hand, let us consider now what counts as learning. There are different ways of *possessing* knowledge, some more useful than others, and what we generally want is knowledge that is accessible and adequate to tasks that matter to us. Consider, first, that one can memorize all the conjugates for the French verb *être*, and then, for each addressee, know the proper form of *être* to use. But this knowledge-that, or propositional knowledge, is not sufficient for competence in using that verb in casual conversation, which may be one's goal. Consider also that a teacher can get students to achieve the legislated level of proficiency in a topic-module, yet find, when that learning is assessed through realistic exercises varied from the original teaching and tests, that the students' performance falls short of expectations.

The discrepancy is particularly perplexing when students overlook occasions that call upon their recent learning. Here's an example, originally offered for different purposes, which illustrates the problem: Consider the question, "What five-letter word contains the letters 'i', 's' 'l' in that order and not at endpoints?" Many will be

295

stumped. But none will be stumped by the same question with multiple choice answers, one of which is "aisle." The problem cannot be an informational one, since, by hypothesis, the student knows the relevant proposition – the student will assent to the query "Is 'aisle' a five-letter word?" Rather, the student does not *recognize* the answer's applicability to the case at hand. The student needs a cue to memory to access his knowledge, but the question as posed does not provide one.

The remedy cannot take the form of a further rule to apply this knowledge. Because, to recall an obstacle that Wittgenstein suggests, that rule itself would have to be recognized as applicable. So, if the same reasoning applies, a further rule would be required and so a regress is generated. The implication of this is that if we cannot always activate learning by rules, some learning must be activated *automatically* or *spontaneously*.

These considerations expose the error in criticism of teaching for skills, especially in programs to foster critical thinking, which can be expressed in slogans like "Evaluate arguments for their validity" or "Assess opinions impartially." The criticism is that these slogans are self-evident (McPeck, 1990; but see Scheffler, 1973; Siegel, 1988). However, even conceding that such directives are self-evident, it does not follow that students will have them available or be able to act on them at the appropriate time and in the appropriate way. Teaching and practice can render such directives *salient* and so available to students in ways they can act on, by yielding qualities of perception and judgment that bring the directives and related propositional knowledge into play at the right time and in the right way – not through applications of rules.

The root problem here pertains to the role of categorization in human cognition, and the fact that we must first *spontaneously perceive* or *understand* something as belonging in some category, or as subsumable under some rule or proposition, in order to bring our relevant knowledge to bear on it usefully. The problem applies to science as well as in everyday life, and makes for interesting comparison with Meno's *Paradox of Inquiry*: that one needn't search for what one knows, and can't search for – would not recognize the discovery of – what one doesn't know (Plato, 1981, 80e). Christopher Cherniak recounts the following example:

at least a decade before Fleming's discovery of penicillin, many microbiologists were aware that molds cause clear spots in bacteria cultures, and they knew that such a bare spot indicates no bacterial growth. Yet they did not consider the possibility that molds release an antibacterial agent. (Cherniak, 1986, p. 50)

The problem here is one of being able to see a phenomenon in the right way – to recognize it as the solution to a problem one would like to solve. Studies of reasoning in psychology show that recognition, even when one knows, may be blocked by everyday assumptions. Our intuitive picture of motion holds that if a solid object tied to a string is swung in a circle, and then released, the object will continue the circular path, though ever more loosely as its energy dissipates, until it drops. Despite how often we must have actually viewed this experiment or similar ones, our assumptions (beliefs) obscure from us their regular falsification – the solid object heads off on a tangent. The results hold for students who have done well in a course in elementary mechanics (see Gardner, 1991, chapters 8 and 9).

In sum, it is evident that if we share the truth-aim, we care to satisfy it at a level that is useful or serviceable. By reference to this need for learning to be serviceable in realistic and varied settings, I can now clarify the role assigned to the knowledge-aim. The key role so far is that of the justification of educational practices to students, given that the aim is theirs. But I assign it only a very weak, background role in students' actual learning, particularly in the early years. The most obvious reason is that students, unlike teachers and administrators, are not competent to wield the knowledge-aim as a basis for making curricular decisions. A further reason is that the student may realize his knowledge-aim better by his aiming – or more plausibly, his teacher's aiming – at a different, closely related, aim such as to gain *understanding*. The preceding comments suggest that there is a crucial distinction to be drawn between whether the teacher or text selects what is relevant to a topic, or whether the student must herself discern what is relevant from a mass of information. My claim is that the ability to discern relevance is itself part of the understanding that students must be taught and acquire in order to use effectively the knowledge they acquire, and cannot be taken for granted. As an illustration, consider learning about baseball for a new parent coach of a children's baseball team. The coach has to select the batting order in advance. The claim is that she will be well equipped to discern who should bat third by understanding the logic of the batting order. She has to determine from detailed descriptions of various players who should bat third. For each particular player, there will be a wealth of information, most of little relevance. But with understanding, the coach is equipped to zoom in on the pivotal qualifications. Previously, the coach could know that James is a power hitter without knowing that James is a candidate to bat third, even though being a power hitter is precisely the qualification for batting third. Given that she is in a context where information is not filtered to her for relevance, our new coach succeeds (acquires knowledge within the usual practical pressures) because she has an understanding of batting order. The understanding confers salience on the sought for properties.

Intellectual virtues, autonomy, and diversity

Adherence to the truth-aim implies that teachers, like students, are beholden to discoveries and learning that they *do not control*. What is discovered to be true constrains what is to be taught. By contrast, indoctrination, propaganda, preaching, and advertising are typically less constrained by truth – the content of the message is controlled by those who disseminate it to serve other aims than the growth of knowledge. If Kleenex does not work better than other tissues, the advertiser still wants us to believe it does.

Charles Sanders Peirce took the method of science to be advantageous over other methods for fixing beliefs because it is a method that scientists do not control: "To satisfy our doubts, therefore, it is necessary that a method should be found by which our beliefs may be determined by nothing human, but by some external permanency" (Peirce, 1957, p. 24). To accept the ideals of liberal education, and its goal of transmitting the knowledge and methods valued in the disciplines, is itself to impose an external permanency on one's study and teaching. We are bound to teach traditions, ideas, and texts, even if we do not presently judge them correct or best.

297

To respect liberal education is to allow its traditions to shape, in good part, one's educational judgments. As a consequence, intellectual humility and an appreciation of one's fallibility are constants of teaching for the truth-aim.

Peirce's conception of the method of science, particularly its *self-corrective* nature, points us toward the close relation between controls on one's judgments (beliefs) and the pursuit of the knowledge-aim. Teaching that impedes the development of critical thinking, humility, and honesty conflicts with the truth-aim because these are *intellectual* or *epistemic virtues* that encourage us to check on our beliefs. Good teaching would encourage the development of these virtues.

The intellectual virtues merit our attention here, and I will focus on *open-mindedness* because it nicely brings out the scope and complexities in taking the truth-aim seriously (on open-mindedness and education generally see Hare, 1979). Since we know that some of our beliefs will be mistaken and we care to know which, we need to be open-minded to be in a position to discover our errors. Open-mindedness is most familiarly exhibited in presenting one's view to others as a prompt to their critical response. Those others are, in Peirce's terms, one's "external permanency": the sources of critical controls on one's judgments that one does not determine. Our ceding of control to others, however, is usually problematically limited. The one who is opening his mind to others is usually the one who selects both what to be open-minded about and the weight to accord the critical judgment of others.

There is a puzzle here: if I believe something, why should I be open-minded about it? We generate something like a Moore's Paradox when we affirm

Racism is wrong, but I have an open mind on it.

The source of the heard contradiction seems to be the implication

Racism is wrong, but it's possible that it is not.

We have already argued that this assertion generates a Moore's Paradox. However, although one knows there is no real possibility of error, it is possible that one is mistaken that one knows. If a good bulk of the political morality we endorse is correct, as we properly take it to be, then racism is wrong. Nevertheless, our morality is defeasible. Perhaps, we are all suffering from some massive social delusion. But, of course, that possibility is a possibility of error in us, not in the belief that racism is wrong. Consequently, I can have reason to be open-minded about whether racism is wrong, even though I regard it as not possible that it is wrong.

In being open-minded about my belief that **p**, I need not consider **p** just from my own point of view as believing it. I can *detach* or *step back* from my own belief. From this perspective, I recognize that my arguments for **p** are defeasible, and, more pointedly, that my peers, similarly placed, have been mistaken. I can adopt a policy of open-mindedness toward this belief, while still lacking any ground to doubt it.

However, there is a complexity in teaching for open-mindedness that applies to "*virtue epistemology*" generally. Virtue epistemology is a recent theoretical development that models itself on Aristotelian "virtue ethics" (Zagzebski, 1996). The locus of moral evaluation in virtue ethics is the agent, not the act. We evaluate the agent's character as, for example, courageous or cowardly. Analogously, virtue epistemology takes the locus of epistemic evaluation to be the agent as, for example, open-minded or dogmatic, rather than the holding of specific beliefs.

A main presupposition of virtue epistemology is that an epistemic community is better (at furthering its own aim of truth) as more of its members are intellectually virtuous and lack the vices. But knowledge or truth is a goal independently specifiable from the virtues or vices. Could the goal of advancing knowledge be better achieved in social inquiries with a substantial, even if minority, mixture of epistemic virtues *and* vices?

Social inquiries work well only if there is a diversity of opinions or hypotheses. An implication of Mill's (1978) fallibilist defense of free speech is that diversity of ideas is necessary not only to increase the chances of finding the truth which may lurk among competitors. But, more pointedly, Mill argued that only by facing a wide range of competitors would the dominant view, even if correct, remain vital. The competition compels supporters of the correct view to meet criticisms posed by competitors, as well as to continue to argue their position so as to persuade the recalcitrant.

The conjecture is that an epistemic community works better if at least a few of its members are inclined to sometimes adhere to views *dogmatically*. We need (a few of) those who stick to their positions, despite being surrounded by reasonable dissenters.

The "need" is a persistent property of inquiry, not dependent on contingencies of particular ones (as it could be contingent that under certain circumstances a community is better off if some act on an ethical vice, e.g. lying to avoid a dire threat). We each have reasons of humility and respect for our epistemic community to accord a presumption of warrant to its consensus judgments. If there is no inherent opposing force to this deference, it is unlikely that divergent positions will be developed. The result will be homogenization of positions. Homogenization lessens competition, and it is competition that promotes criticism and the drive for producing original ideas, which is the healthy environment of fruitful inquiries. A dogmatism among some of us is a way to offset the homogenizing tendency of a well founded deference to dominant judgments. (Of course, the dogmatist must be a forceful opponent without being obstreperous, for otherwise he will just divert attention and energy.)

This line of argument applies to other epistemic virtues, and it is susceptible to testing. Imagine that teachers in the same grade divide up their classes into fairly large groups, and give them each projects of research, culminating in a group paper. Members of some groups all share a "mean" of carefulness and prudence. These students are all *reasonably careful*. They work hard and diligently on their projects, but they do not get hung up on getting every detail just right. Imagine that the other groups are composed mostly of members who are reasonably careful, but that some of their members do not share this virtue. These other groups have small minorities of students who regularly demand that research continue. They irritate their partners without thoroughly disgusting them. The dissension is not fanatical. Still another small minority of these groups deviate in the other extreme: they pretty regularly want to abort research, so that the project is quickly wrapped up.

Our mixed groups in regard to the virtues experience much less consensus and much more conflict than those groups homogeneously virtuous. To reach the conclusion sought our basic contrast would have to be developed on two fronts. First, psychologically, the tendency to "group-think" would be more severe for the homogeneous group. The vices in the mixed groups, though harmful, remain beneficial overall, in large part because only very few need suffer those vices. Second, epistemically, the inclination to accept the dominant judgment out of respect for one's community of inquiry would overwhelm reasons arrived at through the exercise of individual autonomy. The latter, plurality of reasons, arise naturally from the diversity of participants' experience, interests, and attitudes. The resistance that is then required to stave off homogenization would amount to a dogmatic adherence to one's minority position (e.g. to continuing some research project that others reasonably regard as exhausted). If these lines of argument can be made out, so that it is plausible that the heterogeneous groups are regularly more successful, especially in receiving better grades, than the homogeneously virtuous ones, then it is credible that the epistemic virtues work much better at fulfilling their truth-aim if they are not completely shared and only impurely promoted. The truth aim asks us to encourage inquirers to (sometimes) have or exhibit contrasting epistemic vices.

On Not Addressing Epistemological Controversies

Although I explored the knowledge-aim with an ax to grind, I have steadfastly avoided central epistemological issues, including ones that have enlivened recent philosophy of education. I want to explain the basis for this skewed presentation, and in particular, why I do not discuss "postmodernism." (For a "postmodern" critique of educational practices, see Blake et al., 1998.)

My primary excuse is limited space, and that some of these topics are addressed elsewhere in this volume. But also I am skeptical about the educational relevance of the major epistemological disputes. (For other doubts see Schrag, 1992.) These disputes are too abstract to have special relevance to educational practices. Even radical skeptics, like Hume, distinguish between the conclusions reached in their study (that, say, good inductive reasons are impossible) and what they believe and how they act practically, outside their study.

The main target of postmodernist criticism is *foundationalism*, understood as implying the certainty of various types of beliefs, e.g. sense-data, and that all other knowledge depends upon these. Above, we denied the significance that has been attributed to certainty, particularly by those who want to reject it. Something postmodernists have not noticed or acknowledged is that contemporary foundationalists claim that it is sufficient for their purpose that there is a ground level of beliefs that are either *self-supporting* or do not require support from further beliefs (it being enough that they arise from veridical experiences). This breed of foundationalism can accept both defeasibility and a lack of absolute certainty for basic beliefs.

So long as there are self-supporting basic beliefs, foundationalists have what they seek, namely a positive response to the *infinite regress problem*. The problem is that if a belief is to be justified, there must be some further (different) belief that justifies it; otherwise there is circularity. However, that further belief can only have justificatory force if it is itself justified. So, in order to be a justifier, a belief must be justified by another belief, which itself must be justified. But an infinite chain cannot provide a justification, since it can never be completed. Foundationalists conclude that to avoid skepticism there must be certain beliefs that are self-supporting. Postmodernists are unanimous in rejecting foundationalism, but how do they answer (or erase) problems like the regress?

Yet however foundationalism is expressed, it lacks educational relevance simply because there is no good reason to assume that, roughly, *the order of learning (teaching) is the order of knowledge.* Foundationalists can allow that learning should be sensitive to motivational and developmental issues, and should respect the autonomy of the disciplines for the foreseeable future. Moreover, even foundationalists who claim that the foundations of knowledge must be certain can allow for doubts about educational policies that we, nevertheless, must act upon, or about specific subject-matter knowledge-claims that there are reasons to doubt. As often occurs, we are just acting on a balance of reasons without knowledge. Cannot foundationalists take calculated educational risks, like everyone else?

In my presentation of foundationalism, I have construed it narrowly. Postmodernists, however, usually have a much broader target that they place under the label "foundationalism." They oppose the (alleged) Enlightenment conception of a "universal, *a priori* and absolutist conception of reason" and "a disembodied 'rational autonomous subject'," as well as its "distinction between the 'knowing subject' and an 'objective world' to be known" (from Carr, 1995, pp. 79–80; for critical discussion see Siegel, 1998). Even though I do not address this broader target, a number of concerns, already voiced, apply to it. First, numerous assumptions, some empirical, must be ascribed to this broadened foundationalist conception to yield educational implications. I am doubtful that the foundationalist is committed to these ascriptions. Second, to present these positions isolated from the perplexities that motivate their adoption (i.e. to strip them from their context) is to misrepresent them. Worse, it undeservedly relieves those who oppose these positions of the burden of explaining how they would answer these perplexities.

Postmodernist doubt is caught up in a dilemma: postmodern doubt is meant either to have thoroughgoing application or to be highly selective. In the former case, it is not credible; and in the latter case, it does not pose a bold challenge to modernism and its Enlightenment ideals of reason.

By "thoroughgoing" I mean that it applies to all, or just about all, knowledge claims or educational policies. In an article that skillfully and modestly defends a postmodernism for education that is a matter of *incredulity* (doubt, uncertainty), rather than a matter of specific doctrines, Nicholas Burbules writes

Error...is a dimension of *every* learning moment....Here difficulty, uncertainty, and error come to be seen from the postmodern view, not as flawed states to be overcome, but as ongoing conditions of the educational process itself – indeed, as educationally beneficial conditions, when they can serve as correctives to complacency or arrogant surety...

...a far-reaching postmodern doubt confronts the recognition that from the vantage point of some future realization, the successes celebrated today will come to be seen as tragic errors, or laughable ones, or as rueful blunders. (Burbules, 1996, p. 46)

These remarks are unqualified, so let us take them, initially, as meant to be thorough-going or having a comprehensive scope of application. On this interpretation, doubts are cast on the broad, unexceptionable, indeterminate view of education that I defended above via the knowledge-aim. The indeterminate view implies that we should teach in a number of major disciplines, but not, for instance, that every class will be X minutes long. We will teach to promote respect for intellectual authority and for the development of intellectual virtues, but it remains an open question whether we shall have sex education classes starting in grade 4. Here are some further, hardly contestable, practices of schools in liberal democracies, consonant with the know-ledge-aim, though not as close to it:

- There will be qualified teachers, who have completed a high level of education.
- Students will be assigned homework, and their progress will be assessed.
- Teachers have authority over the students, but are bound to teach in ways that avoid propaganda, coercion, or indoctrination.
- As students progress they move to higher grades (roughly corresponding to age) and the material that they will be expected to master becomes more sophisticated and complex.
- Schools should promote good ethical and intellectual values, particularly those related to democratic citizenship, yet minimize incursions on the privacy of students and the prerogative of their parents.
- The school curriculum is packed. Consequently, any proposal to incorporate a new topic into the curriculum, rather than to test it out, must be evaluated not simply for its inherent merits, but in contrast to topics that would be removed or cut down if the proposal is implemented.
- Among educational and pedagogical methods or programs that are acceptable, the "proof" of their value must ultimately be shown empirically, through re-search. Current research leaves a number of proposals open as serious candidates (e.g. tracking), and so choice between them now is uncertain.

These practices account for much of democratic schooling. There is little plausibility (or else, substance) in holding either that "difficulty, uncertainty, and error" apply to them or that in some near-by future we will declare these practices to be filled with, in another of Burbules's phrases, "tragic errors."

But if the modest postmodernist surrenders thoroughgoing application, so that his doubts are directed much more selectively to detailed and specific educational policies, e.g. extensive standardized testing, then the opposed danger surfaces: who dissents from the claim that these decisions are fraught with uncertainty? Similar consider-ations apply to the substance of what is taught: thoroughgoing skepticism, though perhaps irrefutable, has nothing to recommend it, while caution regarding propos-itions that we have specific reasons to doubt is uncontroversial.

I am not looking at the educational "glass" and saying that it is half-full, and attributing to postmodernists the claim that it is half-empty. Rather, I am claiming that the glass is at least four-fifths filled. This is not to say that we should not be anxious and concerned with the fifth that isn't filled. That's what all the debate, research, and excitement is rightly about. But, it is, first, to extend hope that a range of competing proposals to "fill" the remaining fifth stand a good chance of success insofar as they build upon the solid four-fifths. Second, it is to acknowledge that, with the exception of radical skepticism and nihilism, this limited scope for genuine doubt and intellectual anguish undermines neither any serious epistemological position nor, more assuredly, the knowledge-aim.

See also 1 THE SOCRATIC MOVEMENT; 6 ENLIGHTENMENT LIBERALISM; 12 THE ANALYTICAL MOVEMENT; 14 POSTMODERNISM; 16 THEORIES OF TEACHING AND LEARNING; 17 THE CAP-ACITY TO LEARN; 18 MOTIVATION AND CLASSROOM MANAGEMENT; 19 THE MEASUREMENT OF LEARNING; 21 CULTIVATING REASON; 24 TEACHING SCIENCE; 25 TEACHING ELEMENTARY ARITHMETIC THROUGH APPLICATIONS; 26 AESTHETICS AND THE EDUCATIVE POWERS OF ART; 40 UNIVERSITIES IN A FLUID AGE

References

Adler, J. (2002) *Belief's Own Ethics*. Cambridge, MA: The MIT Press.

Blake, N., Smeyers, P., Smith, R., and Standish, P. (1998) *Thinking Again*. London: Bergin and Garvey.

Burbles, N. (1996) Postmodern doubt and philosophy of education. In A. Neiman (ed.), *Philosophy of Education 1995*. Urbana, IL: Philosophy of Education Society, pp. 39–48.

Carr, W. (1995) Education and democracy: confronting the postmodern challenge. *Journal of Philosophy of Education*, 29, 75–91.

Cherniak, C. (1986) *Minimal Rationality*. Cambridge, MA: The MIT Press.

Curren, R. (1995) Coercion and the ethics of grading and testing. *Educational Theory*, 45, 425–41.

Dearden, R. F. (1974) Education and the ethics of belief. *British Journal of Educational Studies*, 22, 5–17.

Deci, E. L. (1975) *Intrinsic Motivation: Research and Theory*. New York: Plenum Press.

Elgin, C. Z. (1996) *Considered Judgment*. Princeton, NJ: Princeton University Press.

Gardner, H. (1991) *The Unschooled Mind*. New York: Basic Books.

Gettier, E. L. (1970) Is justified true belief knowledge? In M. D. Roth and L. Galis (eds), *Knowing*. New York: Random House, pp. 35–8.

Goldman, A. (1986) *Epistemology and Cognition*. Cambridge, MA: Harvard University Press.

Goldman, A. (1999) *Knowledge in a Social World*. Oxford: Oxford University Press.

Hare, W. (1979) *Open-mindedness and Education*. Montreal: McGill-Queen's University Press.

Harman, G. (1973) *Thought*. Princeton: Princeton University Press.

Hirst, P. H. (1973) Liberal education and the nature of knowledge. In R. S. Peters (ed.), *The Philosophy of Education*. Oxford: Oxford University Press, pp. 87–111.

Horwich, P. (1990) *Truth*. Oxford: Blackwell.

Kilpatrick, W. H. (1951) *Philosophy of Education*. New York: Macmillan.

Lewis, D. (1996) Elusive knowledge. *Australasian Journal of Philosophy*, 74, 549–67.

McPeck, J. (1990) *Teaching Critical Thinking*. London: Routledge.

Mill, J. S. (1978) *On Liberty*. Indianapolis: Hackett.

Nozick, R. (1981) *Philosophical Explanations*. Cambridge, MA: Harvard University Press.

Peirce, C. S. (1957) The fixation of belief. In V. Thomas (Ed) *Essays in the Philosophy of Science*. New York: Bobbs-Merrill, pp. 3–30.

Plato (1981) *Five Dialogues*, trans. G. M. A. Grube. Indianapolis: Hackett.

Rorty, R. (1998) *Truth and Progress*. Cambridge: Cambridge University Press.

Scheffler, I. (1965) *Conditions of Knowledge*. Glenview, IL: Scott, Foresman and Company.

Scheffler, I. (1973) *Reason and Teaching*. London: Routledge & Kegan Paul.

Schrag, F. (1992) Conceptions of knowledge. In P. W. Jackson (ed.), *Handbook of Research on Curriculum*. New York: Macmillan, pp. 268–301.

Siegel, H. (1988) *Educating Reason: Rationality, Critical Thinking, and Education*. London: Routledge.

Siegel, H. (1998) Knowledge, truth and education. In D. Carr (ed.), *Education, Knowledge and Truth: Beyond the Postmodern Impasse*. London: Routledge, pp. 19–36.

Unger, P. (1975) *Ignorance*. Oxford: Oxford University Press.

Williams, B. A. O. (1973) Deciding to believe. In *Problems of the Self*. Cambridge: Cambridge University Press, pp. 136–51.

Zagzebski, L. (1996) *Virtues of the Mind*. Cambridge: Cambridge University Press.

21

Cultivating Reason

Harvey Siegel

In the Western philosophical tradition, reason and rationality have long been regarded as important intellectual ideals. In the philosophy of education, their culti-vation has been similarly esteemed as a central educational aim or ideal. Historically, philosophers of education whose positions otherwise diverge dramatically have con-sistently articulated, endorsed, and defended educational visions to which the culti-vation of reason, or the fostering of rationality, has been central. Socrates is perhaps the clearest example of a philosopher who urged that education should encourage in all students and persons, to the greatest extent possible, the pursuit of the life of reason. Plato similarly venerated rationality, although he was a bit less sanguine concerning the degree to which the ideal could be successfully realized. Aristotle too championed rationality, both in theory and in practice, and uttered remarkably modern-sounding ideas concerning education's duty to develop the character traits we now associate with the rational person. The great philosophers of the Middle Ages, no less than those of Antiquity, similarly championed an education aimed at the fostering and development of rationality, believing it to be requisite for a full realiza-tion of Christian faith. Descartes, Locke, Hume, Kant, Mill, and other great figures of the Modern and Enlightenment periods also venerated rationality and praised it as an educational aim, the realization of which would enable humans to achieve their full potential as rational beings. More recently, Bertrand Russell extolled the virtues of an education in service of the cultivation of reason, and John Dewey developed a highly refined philosophy of education which placed rationality at its center. More recently still, R. S. Peters and his British associates endorsed a version of the ideal of the cultivation of reason, and placed reasons and rationality at the heart of their educa-tional philosophy. The pre-eminent contemporary philosopher of education, Israel Scheffler, has similarly urged that rationality, reasons, and reasoned criticism be made basic to educational endeavors. Although no doubt an oversimple historical generalization, it seems clear that the overwhelming majority of philosophers of education from Socrates to the present – despite sometimes dramatic differences in their overall views, and with various reservations and qualifications – have cham-pioned rationality and its cultivation as fundamental educational desiderata. No other proposed aim of education – knowledge, happiness, community, civic-mindedness, social solidarity, docility and obedience to authority, creativity, spiritual fulfillment, the fulfillment of potential, etc. – has enjoyed the virtually unanimous endorsement of historically important philosophers of education that reason and rationality have.

In contemporary discussions the cultivation of reason continues to be defended by many as an important educational aim or ideal. Unlike some historical predecessors, contemporary advocates of the ideal do not understand reason as a special psychological "faculty"; in defending rationality, they do not align themselves with the historical movement known as Continental Rationalism, according to which knowledge is based on the perception or intuition afforded by such a faculty. Rather, what is advocated is that education should have as a fundamental aim the fostering in students of: (1) the ability to reason well, i.e. to construct and evaluate the various reasons which have been or can be offered in support or criticism of candidate beliefs, judgments, and actions; and (2) the disposition or inclination to be guided by reasons so evaluated, i.e. actually to believe, judge, and act in accordance with the results of such reasoned evaluations. Students (and people generally) are rational, or reasonable, to the extent that they believe, judge, and act on the basis of (competently evaluated) reasons. Consequently, to regard the cultivation of reason as a fundamental educational aim or ideal is to hold that the fostering in students of the ability to reason well and the disposition to be guided by reasons is of central educational importance.

The two aspects of the ideal just mentioned deserve further comment. The first – the ability to reason well – presupposes an account of the constitution of good reasons upon which the ideal must inevitably rest. How do we determine that a proposed reason for some belief, judgment, or action is a good or forceful one (or not)? What are the guidelines, or principles, in accordance with which the goodness of candidate reasons are to be ascertained? What is the nature of such principles? How are they themselves justified? These questions are epistemological in nature; they call for a general account of the relationship between a putative reason and the belief, judgment, or action for which it is a reason. Such an epistemological account will have to grapple with deep questions concerning the nature of epistemic justification, the relationship between justification and truth (and so the nature of truth), the relativity (or absoluteness) of principles of reason evaluation, and so forth. In this sense, the educational ideals of reason and rationality depend, for their own justification, on an adequately articulated and defended underlying epistemology. (Some of these questions are addressed below; see also Siegel, 1988a, 1989b, 1997, 1998.)

The second aspect of the ideal mentioned above – the disposition or inclination actually to be guided by the results of the reasoned evaluation of reasons – has broader philosophical implications. Here the ideal recommends not simply the fostering of skills or abilities of reason assessment, but the fostering of a wide range of attitudes, habits of mind, and character traits thought to be characteristic of the rational or reasonable person (Siegel, 1988a; Scheffler, 1989). This extends the ideal beyond the bounds of the cognitive, for, so understood, the ideal is one of a certain sort of *person*. In advocating the fostering of particular dispositions, attitudes, and character traits, as well as particular skills and abilities, the proponent of this educational aim denies the legitimacy, or at least the educational relevance, of any sharp distinction between the cognitive and the affective, or the rational and the emotional. The ideal calls for the fostering of certain skills and abilities, *and* for the fostering of a certain sort of character. It is thus a general ideal of a certain sort of person whom it is

306

the task of education to help create. This aspect of the educational ideal of rationality aligns it with the complementary ideal of *autonomy*, since a rational person will also be an autonomous one, capable of judging for herself the justifiedness of candidate beliefs and the legitimacy of candidate values.

Critical Thinking

In the contemporary educational literature, these ideas are often discussed in terms of *critical thinking*. Advocates of efforts to foster critical thinking in schools sometimes conceive this aim narrowly, in terms of imparting skills which will enable students to function adequately in their jobs, and in so doing to be economically productive. More often, however, proponents of the educational aim of critical thinking have in mind the broader view of critical thinking as more or less equivalent to the ideal of rationality. In any case, it is only when understood in this broad way that this educational aim can be adequately analysed and defended (Bailin and Siegel, 2002; Siegel, 1988a, 1997). So understood, critical thinking is a sort of *good* thinking, so the notion of critical thinking is fundamentally a *normative* one. This distinguishes this understanding of critical thinking from those, common in psychology, which treat the notion as descriptive (Bailin et al., 1999).

To regard critical thinking as a fundamental educational aim is to hold that educational activities ought to be designed and conducted in such a way that the construction and evaluation of reasons (in accordance with relevant criteria) is paramount, throughout the curriculum. As Israel Scheffler puts the point:

Critical thought is of the first importance in the conception and organization of educational activities. (Scheffler, 1989, p. 1)

Rationality . . . is a matter of *reasons*, and to take it as a fundamental educational ideal is to make as pervasive as possible the free and critical quest for reasons, in all realms of study. (Ibid., p. 62, emphasis in original)

The fundamental trait to be encouraged is that of reasonableness. . . . In training our students to reason we train them to be critical. (Ibid., pp. 142–3)

To accord reasonableness central importance in education is to say not that other aims and ideals might not also be of serious importance, but that none outrank the primary obligation of educational efforts and institutions to foster critical thinking.

Why should the fostering of critical thinking be considered so important? There are at least four reasons. First, and most importantly, striving to foster critical thinking in students is essential to treating students with *respect as persons*. The moral requirement to treat students with respect as persons requires that we strive to enable them to think for themselves, competently and well, rather than to deny them the fundamental ability to determine for themselves, to the greatest extent possible, the contours of their own minds and lives. Acknowledging them as persons of equal moral worth requires that we treat students as independent centers of consciousness, with needs and interests not less important than our own, who are at least in principle capable of determining for themselves how best to live and who to be. As educators, treating them with respect involves striving to enable them to judge such matters for themselves. Doing so competently requires judging in accordance with criteria governing the quality of reasons. Consequently, treating students with respect requires fostering in them the abilities and dispositions of critical thinking.

A second reason for regarding critical thinking as a fundamental educational ideal involves education's generally recognized task of preparing students for adulthood. Such preparation cannot properly be conceived in terms of preparing students for preconceived roles; instead, it must be understood to involve student self-sufficiency and self-direction. In this the place of critical thinking is manifest. A third reason for regarding the fostering of critical thinking as a central aim of education is the role it plays in the rational traditions that have always been at the center of educational activities and efforts – mathematics, science, literature, art, history, etc. All these traditions incorporate and rely upon critical thinking; mastering or becoming initiated into the former both requires and is basic to the fostering and enhancement of the latter. A fourth reason involves the place of careful analysis, good thinking, and reasoned deliberation in democratic life. To the extent that we value democracy, we must be committed to the fostering of the abilities and dispositions of critical thinking, for democracy can flourish just to the extent that its citizenry is sufficiently critical (Siegel, 1988a).

These four reasons can and should be spelled out at greater length, but they are sufficiently powerful to justify regarding critical thinking as a fundamental educational ideal. Efforts to foster critical thinking aim at the promotion of independent thinking, personal autonomy, and reasoned judgment in thought and action. These particular aims are themselves in keeping with broader conceptions of knowledge, reasons and persons: for example, that all knowledge is fallible, that it is possible to objectively evaluate the goodness of reasons, and that personal autonomy is an important value (Bailin, 1998, p. 204).

These aims, and the broader conceptions in which they are grounded, are philosophically contentious; it is no surprise, then, that they – and the educational ideal of critical thinking itself – have been challenged. Several aspects of critical thinking are controversial. As already noted, while philosophers generally understand it normatively, psychologists and others often understand it descriptively. Philosophers debate its specifically epistemological dimensions, e.g. whether criteria of reason assessment should be understood as "absolute" or as relative to culture, context, or some other relativizing factor. Also contentious is the status of such criteria *as* epistemological, rather than political. A further, hotly debated controversy concerns the *generalizability* of critical thinking: are the skills and abilities of critical thinking generalizable in that they apply across a variety of disciplines, problems and contexts, or are they domain- or context-specific? Theorists also offer and debate the merits of conflicting accounts of key elements of critical thinking, e.g. concerning the nature of skills and dispositions. The place of subject-specific content knowledge in critical thinking is also controversial, as is the alleged distinction between critical and creative thinking. There is a large literature concerning all of this, which cannot be discussed here but is treated in Bailin and Siegel (2002).

Many approaches to teaching critical thinking have been developed. These too sometimes occasion controversy, consideration of which is not possible here. Worth mentioning in this context, though, is the *Philosophy for Children* program, pioneered by Matthew Lipman (1991). In this approach, classrooms become *communities of inquiry*, and students' critical thinking is developed through open discussion of fundamental philosophical issues (at age-appropriate levels of sophistication). In this and other programs, the close connections among critical thinking, rationality, and philosophy itself are made manifest.

Given the contentious nature of critical thinking, it is no surprise that the ideal of reason itself, and the desirability of its cultivation, also face important challenges. I turn to them next.

Critiques of Reason

Relativism and the philosophy of science: the case of Paul Feyerabend

Science is often conceived as the most impressive application and product of reason, and the apex of rational activity. It is perhaps surprising, then, that some of the most pressing and important critiques of reason emanate from its philosophy. The past several decades of work in the philosophy of science have produced a range of challenges to science's claims to be the embodiment of rationality and the archetypical model of rational inquiry. These challenges include the critique of textbook models of "the scientific method," and of related accounts of the rationality of science; problems concerning the "underdetermination of theory by data," the "theory-ladenness of perception," and the rationality of theory choice; and various defenses of epistemological relativism. The literature on these matters is vast; I cannot do even minimal justice to it here (see Siegel, 1985, 1987, 2002). Instead, I will address one of the most well known critics of reason, both in science and more generally: Paul Feyerabend.

Feyerabend's book is called, provocatively enough, *Farewell to Reason* (1987). In it he argues that objectivity, rationality and reason are false, destructive ideals which serve narrow and particular interests only, and which are valued by some traditions but by no means all (pp. 5ff); that 'Reason' is without content, and is politically and culturally destructive because of its discouragement of diversity and its indefensible advocacy of "a right way of living" (p. 11); that reasons have no objective force that is binding on all; and that rationality is just a "tribal creed" masquerading as a general ideal – "rationalists clamouring for objectivity and rationality are just trying to sell a tribal creed of their own" (p. 301). On Feyerabend's view, "It is time we bid it [i.e. Reason] farewell" (p. 17; see pp. 13, 319).

Is Feyerabend right that there are no such things as objective reasons; that rationality is but a "tribal creed"? These claims, though bold and in some ways intoxicatingly radical, are not well supported by Feyerabend's arguments. It is worthwhile to review those arguments in some detail, because doing so will reveal some general difficulties which plague any such attempt to criticize reason.

Consider Feyerabend's rejection of objective reasons:

I assert that there exist no "objective" reasons for preferring science and Western rationalism to other traditions. Indeed, it is difficult to imagine what such reasons might be. Are they reasons that would convince a person, or the members of a culture, no matter what their customs, their beliefs or their social situation? Then what we know about cultures shows us that there are no "objective" reasons in this sense. Are they reasons which convince a person who has been properly prepared? Then all cultures have "objective" reasons in their favour. Are they reasons referring to results whose importance can be seen at a glance? Then again all cultures have at least some "objective" reasons in their favour. Are they reasons which do not depend on "subjective" elements such as commitment or personal preference? Then "objective" reasons simply do not exist (the choice of objectivity as a measure is itself a personal and/or group choice – or else people simply accept it without much thought). (Feyerabend, 1987, p. 297)

Note, first, that this passage runs roughshod over the is/ought distinction – the distinction between what people *do* do and what they *ought* to do – in its suggestion that reasons which fail in fact to convince people therefore ought not to convince them. But there are many clear cases in which people ought to be convinced by reasons, even though they in fact are not. For example, I should have been convinced by prior experience that I should have begun work on this chapter earlier than I did if I wanted to meet the deadline, although, regrettably and irrationally, I was not so convinced. Second, and more significantly, it presupposes that choices and judgments are necessarily "subjective" or non-objective insofar as they are made by *subjects*, i.e. people with interests, attitudes, etc. Grant that choices and judgments are made by subjects and are in this sense "subjective." Does it follow that such judgments cannot be objective?

Obviously not. Consider a case. Alicia is a philosophy major about to graduate with her undergraduate degree. She has narrowed her options to the following: apply to graduate school in philosophy, apply to law school, or take a position in a local computer company. Does she have any objective reason to choose from among these options?

We can go two ways here. On the one hand, we can say that Alicia has perfectly objective reasons to (for example) apply to graduate school. Her intense love of the subject, the pleasure she takes in reading philosophy books and articles and in writing papers, her desire to be a publishing scholar and teacher of students like herself, her professors' encouragement and declarations of her likely success as a professional philosopher, and her dread of the prospect of a life in which she cannot spend time engaging in these activities, all provide objective reasons for her applying. Her assignment of utilities to the alternative outcomes – that is, her valuing of the life of the philosopher more highly than those of the lawyer and computer company employee – may be subjective, but once those subjective utilities are assigned, the calculation of expected utility, and the choice of the future course which maximizes it, is as objective as can be. In this case, if she chose not to apply to graduate school despite her own valuations, she would be choosing irrationally. Her choice would not reflect the objective reasons she has to apply.

On the other hand, we can say that Alicia has no objective reason to apply to graduate school in philosophy, to apply to law school, or to take the computer job. She has subjective reasons – her love of philosophy, her dread of law school and her worries about the glutted job market for lawyers, her mixed emotions about working with computers, etc. – and those are the only sort of reasons there are. If Alicia applies to graduate school, she acts on the basis of her reasons; if she applies to law school or takes the computer job, she likewise acts on that basis. All reasons are subjective, and all acts are subjectively reasonable.

This second response to Alicia's situation is Feyerabend's. But it is problematic. For according to it, no judgment, choice, or action, however local, is better than any of its alternatives. All reasons are "subjective" and as good, subjectively, as their contraries; no one can be judged to have chosen or acted unreasonably. This is quite implausible, since examples of unreasonable actions and choices are, alas, all too common. But it is the bind one gets in when one insists that all reasons, because they involve human choice and judgment, are subjective, and therefore that all judgments, actions, and choices are subjectively reasonable.

The issue is not whether "subjective elements" accompany or are part of all judgment and choice – Feyerabend may well be right about that. The issue is instead whether some considerations have force, and ought to move judgers/choosers/actors, even when those considerations are not recognized by them as having such force. Given Alicia's attitudes toward her alternatives, however "subjective" those attitudes might be, her decision whether to apply to graduate school or not is as "objective" as can be. If the case is as I have described it, she has strong, perfectly objective reasons to apply to graduate school, and equally objective reasons not to apply to law school or take the computer job. Of course the cases for each could be more equal in strength than I have presented them. That would make Alicia's choice more difficult, but not less objective.

In the end this dispute turns on what is meant by "objective." Feyerabend takes it to mean something like "lacking subjective elements"; and he argues that, so taken, no reasons are objective because reasons always function in ways which engage such subjectivity. But if "objective reason" is taken to refer instead to considerations which are relevant to, and ought to be taken into account and assigned due weight by, people making choices and judgments – and whose force ought to be recognized by those subjective choosers/judgers, even if they are not so recognized – then Feyerabend is mistaken in claiming that there are no objective reasons. Moreover, the defense, and so the consistency, of his position requires that there be reasons which are objective in just this sense. That is, his case that there are no objective reasons itself requires that there are such reasons – for if there are no such reasons supporting that case, we will have no objective reason to embrace his conclusion that there are none.

At bottom, Feyerabend has confused two quite different questions concerning the objectivity of reasons: whether they necessarily involve human subjectivity; and whether they might rightly be regarded as forceful, authoritative, and compelling even for those persons who are not convinced by them. The subjectivity issue is irrelevant to the objective forcefulness issue. Feyerabend has failed to provide any good reason to reject the claim that reasons can be objectively forceful. He has also failed to realize that his own positive view requires that some reasons have objective force. Thus his claim that there are no objective reasons fails.

Is rationality but a "tribal creed," whose dictates have no force on the members of other tribes? Here we can be brief. Feyerabend is perhaps right that rationality may be regarded as a tribal creed in the sense that only some people and cultures accept or respect it while others do not. But that some people fail to be moved by or respect rational considerations in no way entails, as we have seen, that they ought not to be so moved. Feyerabend has failed to secure his contention that rationality is *just* another ideology or tribal creed.

In the end, then, Feyerabend's relativistic critique of reason and its cultivation fails to upend that ideal (Siegel, 1989a). Other relativistic challenges face similar and additional difficulties (see Siegel, 1987, 2001, 2002).

Epistemic dependence

One prominent feature of education aimed at the cultivation of reason is its embrace of the value of personal autonomy, in its insistence that students should come to be able to determine for themselves the worthiness of candidate beliefs, judgments, values, and actions. Many philosophers have questioned the *individualism* inherent in such a view. Critiques of individualism are many and varied; most relevant here are those which challenge the idea that students – and believers generally – are rightly thought to be able to "drive their own epistemic engines" and determine by themselves, from among candidate beliefs, which are worthy of embrace. Such *epistemic individualism* is challenged by advocates of what has come to be called *social epistemology*: the systematic study of the ways in which knowledge is irredeemably social, because knowers are dependent on others for their knowledge. Because epistemic agents are *epistemically dependent* on others, epistemic individualism, it is argued, is a chimera.

Why think that we are epistemically dependent on others? The most important reason for thinking that we are so dependent is that most of our beliefs, including those that seem to qualify as knowledge, appear to depend upon the *testimony* of others, and require us to *trust* those others. It is clear enough that many of our beliefs *originate* in the testimony of others – the newspaper, the TV reporter, our parents, our teachers, etc. – and that these beliefs are overwhemingly *sustained* by that testimony as well. It appears that relatively few, if any, of our beliefs are free from such dependence. Many of us believe, for example, that the sun is 93 million miles from Earth (on average), but how many have carried out that measurement ourselves, or have any non-testimonial evidence for that belief? Similarly, many of us believe that the HIV virus causes AIDS, and that smoking tobacco increases one's risk of heart disease and stroke, but have no familiarity with the relevant scientific evidence for these claims. A final example is the common belief (among citizens of the United States at the time I write, at least) that a particular person, Osama bin Laden, bears significant responsibility for the destruction of the World Trade Center in New York. What is our justification for this belief? Most believers have no direct evidence for these (and most other) beliefs, but believe them on the basis of the testimony of others. Our thoroughgoing reliance on the testimony of others, and our need to trust that testimony, has suggested to some that we must give up any pretense to epistemic individualism and to individual responsibility for belief, and so must reject the idea that getting students to think for themselves is an important educational directive. As John Hardwig puts it, our systematic epistemic dependence on others forces the conclusion that "it is sometimes *irrational* to think for oneself – that *rationality* sometimes consists in deferring to epistemic authority and, consequently, in passively and uncritically accepting what we are given to believe" (Hardwig, 1985, p. 343, emphases in original).

It is controversial that we are as epistemically dependent on others as Hardwig and others claim (e.g. Coady, 1992; various authors collected in Schmitt, 1994). Jonathan Adler, for example, claims that we are not, since beliefs of ours which are generated by the testimony of others are typically justified by our evidence concerning testimony's general reliability, and are moreover typically sustained and justified by being confirmed for us in ways which do not depend upon the testimony of others. Adler argues, first, that we each have overwhelming evidence for the general reliability of testimony conceived as a social process, since from our earliest days we have been recipients of testimonial reports, the vast majority of which have turned out to be correct. Our own evidence for the general reliability of testimony thus offers us a significant measure of epistemic *independence*, even concerning beliefs we accept solely on the basis of testimony. In addition, Adler discusses a variety of ways in which beliefs that originate in testimony can be non-testimonially confirmed, and argues that this kind of account can be given for a large majority of beliefs. For example, many of us believe that smoking tobacco increases one's risk of heart disease and stroke. Typically, we will have formed the belief on the basis of the testimony of others – reading it in a book or the newspaper, learning it in school, hearing it from a relative or friend, etc. At the moment we acquire it, Adler argues, that belief is supported by our knowledge of the general reliability of such testimonial reports. However, it is typically subsequently confirmed for each of us routinely as we read both scientific and popular reports, speak with physicians, biologists, and others who do have direct familiarity with the details of research, hear pronouncements on the matter from government officials, talk to our doctors, etc. Because it is confirmed in this way, each of us has non-testimonial evidence which justifies our belief, despite the fact that we first acquired it through testimony. In light of both our justified belief in the general reliability of testimony, and the subsequent confirmation of specific beliefs which originate in testimony, Adler concludes that we are far less epistemically dependent than we might appear at first glance (Adler, 2002).

I find Adler's case against an overwhelming epistemic dependence compelling. But let us grant, for the sake of argument, that we are, as many authors claim, highly epistemically dependent upon others. What follows concerning the ideals of rationality and critical thinking? Does it follow from our alleged epistemic dependence that we should give up the commitment to epistemic individualism, and instead discourage students, and people generally, from thinking for themselves or exercising their reason?

It seems clear that this does not follow. For one thing, determining when we are in fact epistemically dependent and when not – when we should uncritically accept expert testimony and when we should endeavor to think for ourselves – itself requires critical thinking and the exercise of independent judgment. For another, we need to acknowledge a distinction between *rational* and *irrational* deference to the opinion of others, and to guard ourselves against the latter. Here too independent judgment and thinking for ourselves are necessary, and so the cultivation of reason is appropriate (Siegel, 1988b).

313

The issues here are more complex than this brief discussion suggests, but I hope I have said enough to indicate why the phenomenon of epistemic dependence does not compromise the educational aim of cultivating critical rationality (see Hardwig, 1985; Siegel, 1988b; Coady, 1992; Schmitt, 1994; Goldman, 1999; Adler, 2002).

Feminist and postmodernist critiques

Deep challenges to the ideal of reason have been articulated by feminist critics, who argue that, as standardly conceived, the ideal harbors deep masculinist biases; and by postmodernist critics, who argue that the ideal is prototypically modernist and retains all the flaws associated with modernism. Central to these criticisms is the claim that reason, at least under dominant-culture conceptions of it, favors the values and practices of dominant groups in society and devalues those of groups traditionally lacking in power. Here, as earlier, the range of relevant literature and argument is enormous. I consider here only two challenges: the feminist complaint that reason privileges the perspectives and interests of men, and is biased against the perspectives and interests of women; and the postmodernist complaint that reason constitutes an objectionable "totalizing metanarrative" that reflects and advances the interests of culturally dominant groups, and marginalizes and oppresses members of non-dominant groups. (For further discussion of these and other challenges, see Bailin, 1995; Siegel, 1997; Bailin and Siegel, 2002.)

Is reason problematically "male"? Is the advocacy of its cultivation similarly "masculinist-ly" biased? Feminist writers frequently answer in the affirmative. The central contention is clearly articulated by Louise M. Antony and Charlotte Witt:

Feminist challenges have, indeed, reached into the "'hard core' of abstract reasoning" itself, with charges that the most fundamental elements of the Western philosophical tradition – the ideals of reason and objectivity – are so deeply corrupted by patriarchy that they must be greatly transformed (if not utterly abandoned) by any philosopher committed to the development of conceptions of knowledge and reality adequate to the transformative goals of feminism. (Antony and Witt, 1993, p. xiii, quoting Harding and Hintikka, 1983, p. ix)

It is also challenged by Sally Haslanger: "a rational stance is itself a stance of oppression or domination, and accepted ideals of reason both reflect and reinforce power relations that advantage white privileged men" (Haslanger, 1993, p. 85). Catharine MacKinnon argues similarly that:

If feminism is a critique of the objective standpoint as male, then we also disavow standard scientific norms as the adequacy criteria for our theory, because the objective standpoint we criticize is the posture of science. In other words, our critique of the objective standpoint as male is a critique of science as a specifically male approach to knowledge. With it, we reject *male criteria* for verification. (MacKinnon, 1987, p. 54, emphasis added)

What follows from the rejection of "male criteria"? There seem to be only two possibilities: either that there are *no* criteria in terms of which theories can be evaluated, or that there are *different* criteria which should be appealed to in theory evaluation. The first of these is deeply problematic. If there are no criteria in terms of which we can legitimately evaluate theories, then the very possibility of evaluation is rejected. But this option is self-defeating: if evaluation in general is rejected, then we are unable to evaluate, or rationally prefer, the suggestions that male criteria should be rejected or that evaluation itself should likewise be rejected. But then we have no reason to accept these suggestions.

On the other hand, the rejection of "male" criteria of theory evaluation in favor of other, incompatible, "female" criteria must itself – if the preference for the latter is to be itself defensible and non-arbitrary – rely upon (meta-)criteria in accordance with which these two rival sets of criteria can themselves be fairly evaluated. Standards and criteria of rational evaluation are in this way *required* for the conducting of any sort of serious scholarly endeavor, including that of criticizing particular conceptions of reason as problematically "male." In short, one cannot coherently embrace this particular feminist critique of reason and at the same time reject reason or rational standards entirely.

Furthermore, MacKinnon's specific rejection of the standards of science, and so science itself, as male implies an abandonment of the benefits of science, including benefits that accrue to the oppressed themselves. Noretta Koertge has argued in this connection that "science – even white, upperclass, male-dominated science – is one of the most important allies of oppressed people" (Koertge, 1981, p. 354). Martha Nussbaum has argued similarly with respect to reason and objectivity that:

Convention and habit are women's enemies here, and reason their ally. Habit decrees that what seems strange is impossible and "unnatural"; reason looks head on at the strange, refusing to assume that the current status quo is either immutable or in any normative sense "natural." The appeal to reason and objectivity amounts to a request that the observer refuse to be intimidated by habit, and look for cogent arguments based on evidence that has been carefully sifted for bias. (Nussbaum, 1994, p. 59)

Of course, to say that standards are required for the rational defense of reason, or that rational standards are required for any sort of serious intellectual work whatever, is not to say that particular standards, or particular understandings of them, are themselves beyond critical challenge. On the contrary, one major sort of intellectual advance is precisely the sort which allows us to realize that our standards, or our interpretations of them, have in one way or another been defective and stand in need of criticism and improvement. Indeed, one of the main contributions of feminist scholarship has been precisely to establish that particular standards, or particular applications of them, have been problematically biased against women. But it cannot be wise, as Nussbaum (1994, pp. 60–1) points out, to reject a standard on grounds of its misuse. We can debate the merits of particular standards and criteria, and particular understandings, interpretations, and applications of them, of course. But we cannot reject the standards and criteria of reason altogether – not, at least, if we wish to uphold the virtues of feminism and the value of women's perspectives.

Postmodernist challenges to reason and its cultivation are varied but equally fundamental. According to at least one version of this challenge, the cultivation of reason depends on a "totalizing" or "universalizing" conception of reason which both illicitly presupposes the perspective of dominant groups and denies the particularity of those who are members of other groups, thereby marginalizing and oppressing them. Accordingly, "reason" must be seen not as a universal form or criterion of proper thought, but instead merely the form in use, and favored, by dominant groups, whose power is enhanced by imposing it upon dominated others. Reason, that is, is not any sort of ultimate authority or arbiter, but is rather simply one ideology among others, which must be recognized as a source of unjust power and privilege rather than a legitimate source of epistemic authority; its cultivation among marginalized others is a political act of cultural hegemony rather than an effort to liberate, empower, and enhance the rational autonomy of all students and persons.

This is clearly a very fundamental challenge. Like those already considered, however, it is not without difficulties, the most basic of which is that any such challenge to reason must, if it is to establish its case, itself be based on good reasons and provide good reasons for accepting its challenge as worthy. Consequently, the rejection of reason, to be epistemically forceful, must itself presuppose the legitimacy of reason (Siegel, 1997, chapters 9–12).

The reader who has followed the discussion to this point will have noticed a recurrent theme, to which I turn next.

The Fundamental Reply to All Critiques of Reason

All critiques of the ideal of reason, like those just considered, can and should be considered on their own merits. But it is of considerable comfort to friends of the ideal that there is available a general reply to all attempts to reject the ideal, one that appears to be effective against them all, and which is manifested in the discussions of each of the specific critiques considered above. This reply, if successful, establishes the impossibility of rationally rejecting reason – and so preserves the legitimacy of regarding its cultivation as an educational ideal. I conclude this discussion by rehearsing the reply and assessing its effectiveness.

Reason can be rejected in two ways. First, it can be rejected without thought or argument – indeed, it can be rejected without the question of whether it should be rejected ever being recognized or addressed. Alternatively, it can be rejected on the basis of some reasoned challenge to it (e.g. that it fosters patriarchy, aids and abets oppression, depends upon a problematic individualism, rests on an inadequate conception of objectivity, or whatever). In the former case, rejection doesn't threaten the legitimacy of the ideal, since no challenge is made. It is the latter, philosophical sort of rejection that genuinely challenges the ideal's cogency.

But if such a challenge is made, it is forceful, and successful, just to the extent that it is based upon good reasons for rejecting the ideal. The challenger is arguing, in effect, that there is good reason to reject the ideal of reason. Any such argument against reason, if successful, will itself be an instance of the successful application of reason. That is, the reasoned rejection of the ideal is itself an instance of being guided by it. In this sense, the ideal appears to be safe from successful challenge: any successful challenge will have to rely upon it; any challenge which does not cannot succeed. While challenges to the ideal might succeed in refining our understanding of it, none can succeed in overthrowing it. Thus the ideal cannot be successfully challenged.

Transcendental arguments like this one are notoriously controversial philosophically; I cannot provide a general defense of them here. But I should note that the argument does not prove too much. It does not suggest that other ideals are not important. Nor does it suggest that people cannot reject or live contrary to the ideal – though that they can (and do) does nothing to challenge its legitimacy, or the claim that they ought to be guided by it. The argument obviously will not persuade one who rejects reason independently of an argument against it. But such an "argument-less rejection" fails as a critique, since it offers no criticism of the ideal or argument in favor of its rejection.

The proponent of rationality and its cultivation must, to be consistent, regard challenges to it as centrally important, and must regard the obligation to take such challenges seriously as integral to rationality itself. Hence, deep criticisms of the ideal, and reasoned consideration of both its praiseworthy characteristics and its indefensible ones, are exactly what the ideal itself recommends. Whether the ideal survives extant criticisms will always be, in some sense, an open question; such criticisms may well succeed in altering our understanding or defense of it. Nevertheless, there is a limit beyond which any proposed criticism of rationality cannot go without undermining itself. Hence, the ideal of rationality (at least in some formulation of it) cannot be coherently rejected (Siegel, 1997, chapter 5, epilogue).

See also 1 THE SOCRATIC MOVEMENT; 6 ENLIGHTENMENT LIBERALISM; 8 KANT, HEGEL, AND THE RISE OF PEDAGOGICAL SCIENCE; 12 THE ANALYTICAL MOVEMENT; 13 FEMINISM; 14 POSTMODERNISM; 20 KNOWLEDGE, TRUTH, AND LEARNING; 24 TEACHING SCIENCE

References

Adler, J. (2002) *Belief's Own Ethics*. Cambridge, MA: MIT Press.

Antony, L. M. and Witt, C. (eds) (1993) *A Mind of One's Own: Feminist Essays on Reason and Objectivity*. Boulder, CO: Westview Press.

Bailin, S. (1995) Is critical thinking biased? clarifications and implications. *Educational Theory*, 45, 191–7.

Bailin, S. (1998) Education, knowledge and critical thinking. In D. Carr (ed.), *Education, Knowledge and Truth: Beyond the Postmodern Impasse*. London: Routledge, pp. 204–20.

Bailin, S., Case, R., Coombs, J. R., and Daniels, L. B. (1999) Conceptualizing critical thinking. *Journal of Curriculum Studies*, 31, 285–302.

Bailin, S. and Siegel, H. (2002) Critical thinking. In N. Blake, P. Smeyers, R. Smith, and P. Standish (eds), *The Blackwell Guide to the Philosophy of Education*. Oxford: Blackwell.

Coady, C. A. J. (1992) *Testimony: A Philosophical Study*. Oxford: Oxford University Press.

Feyerabend, P. (1987) *Farewell to Reason*. London: Verso.

Goldman, A. I. (1999) *Knowledge in a Social World*. Oxford: Oxford University Press.

Harding, S. and Hintikka, M. B. (eds) (1983) *Discovering Reality: Feminist Perspectives on Epistemology, Metaphysics, Methodology, and Philosophy of Science*. Dordrecht: D. Reidel.

Hardwig, J. (1985) Epistemic dependence. *Journal of Philosophy*, 82, 335–49.

Haslanger, S. (1993) On being objective and being objectified. In Antony and Witt (eds), *A Mind of One's Own: Feminist Essays on Reason and Objectivity*. Boulder, CO: Westview Press, pp. 85–125.

Koertge, N. (1981) Methodology, ideology and feminist critiques of science. In P. D. Asquith and R. N. Giere (eds), *PSA 1980: Proceedings of the 1980 Biennial Meeting of the Philosophy of Science Association, volume 2*. East Lansing, MI: Philosophy of Science Association, pp. 346–59.

Lipman, M. (1991) *Thinking in Education*. Cambridge: Cambridge University Press.

MacKinnon, C. (1987) *Feminism Unmodified: Discourses on Life and Law*. Cambridge, MA: Harvard University Press.

Nussbaum, M. (1994) Feminists and philosophy. *New York Review of Books*, 41(17), 59–63.

Scheffler, I. (1989) *Reason and Teaching*. Indianapolis: Hackett (first published 1973).

Schmitt, F. F. (ed.) (1994) *Socializing Epistemology: The Social Dimensions of Knowledge*. Lanham, MD: Rowman & Littlefield.

Siegel, H. (1985) What is the question concerning the rationality of science? *Philosophy of Science*, 52, 517–37.

Siegel, H. (1987) *Relativism Refuted: A Critique of Contemporary Epistemological Relativism*. Dordrecht: Kluwer.

Siegel, H. (1988a) *Educating Reason: Rationality, Critical Thinking, and Education*. London: Routledge.

Siegel, H. (1988b) Rationality and epistemic dependence. *Educational Philosophy and Theory*, 20, 1–6.

Siegel, H. (1989a) Farewell to Feyerabend. *Inquiry*, 32, 343–69.

Siegel, H. (1989b) Epistemology, critical thinking, and critical thinking pedagogy. *Argumentation*, 3, 127–40.

Siegel, H. (1997) *Rationality Redeemed? Further Dialogues on an Educational Ideal*. New York: Routledge.

Siegel, H. (1998) Knowledge, truth and education. In D. Carr (ed.), *Education, Knowledge and Truth: Beyond the Postmodern Impasse*. London: Routledge, pp. 19–36.

Siegel, H. (2001) Incommensurability, rationality, and relativism: in science, culture, and science education. In P. Hoyningen-Huene and H. Sankey (eds), *Incommensurability and Related Matters*. Dordrecht: Kluwer, pp. 207–24.

Siegel, H. (in press) Relativism. In I. Niiniluoto, M. Sintonen, and J. Wolenski (eds), *Handbook of Epistemology*. Dordrecht: Kluwer.

Further reading

Bailin, S. (1992a) Culture, democracy and the university. *Interchange*, 23, 63–9.

Burbules, N. C. (1991) The virtues of reasonableness. In M. Buchmann and R. E. Floden (eds), *Philosophy of Education 1991*. Normal, IL: Philosophy of Education Society, pp. 215–24.

Burbules, N. C. (1995) Reasonable doubt: toward a postmodern defense of reason as an educational aim. In W. Kohli (ed.), *Critical Conversations in Philosophy of Education*. New York: Routledge, pp. 82–102.

Ennis, R. H. (1998) Is critical thinking culturally biased? *Teaching Philosophy*, 21, 15–33.

Kohli, W. (1995) Educating for emancipatory rationality. In W. Kohli (ed.), *Critical Conversations in Philosophy of Education*. New York: Routledge, pp. 103–15.

Nussbaum, M. (1997) *Cultivating Humanity: A Classical Defense of Reform in Liberal Education*. Cambridge, MA: Harvard University Press.

Robertson, E. (1995) Reconceiving reason. In W. Kohli (ed.), *Critical Conversations in Philosophy of Education*. New York: Routledge, pp. 116–26.

Robertson, E. (2000) The value of reason: why not a sardine can opener? In R. Curren (ed.), *Philosophy of Education 1999*. Urbana, IL: Philosophy of Education Society, pp. 1–14.

Talaska, R. A. (ed.) (1992) *Critical Reasoning in Contemporary Culture*. Albany: State University of New York Press.

22

Moral Education

Graham Haydon

In discussing moral education within the context of philosophy of education there are several questions about how to delineate the field. First, moral education has been discussed by philosophers whose primary work has not been in philosophy of education as such; the present chapter, while making no attempt at comprehensive coverage, is about the philosophy of moral education, rather than what might be more narrowly construed as the discussion of moral education as a topic within philosophy of education.

Then, more substantially, there is a question of the relation between moral education and education in general. There are many possible positions between two extremes: that, on the one hand, moral education is a rather peripheral part of education in general; or, on the other, that all education is in a sense moral education.

The earliest written philosophy of moral education in the West, that of Plato, takes the latter position. Famously, if obscurely, for Plato in *The Republic* the form of the Good stands above all, and all education is aimed ultimately at the realization of the Good. Further, that holds true in two senses: that education culminates, for certain capable individuals, in understanding of the Good; and that education aims to make the Good real in the structure of human society. Even the many who will never themselves be able to understand the form of the Good will be taught (and as we might now say, socialized or trained rather than educated) to play their proper role within society and hence to play out an aspect of the Good in their way of living.

There is still room today for the position that all education is moral education in the sense of having an overriding moral end, and since there are various such ends (not to mention dispute over what kinds of ends might count as moral), there is more than one approach to educational thought that could be seen as a version of that position. There can, for instance, be religious versions, in which all education aims at the glorification and service of God, and secular democratic versions, in which all education aims at the realization of a democratic form of life. The common feature of such approaches lies in the fact that while they can include, within formal education, studies which have no obvious or direct moral import (such as the learning of mathematics), the reason for including such studies is ultimately the contribution these studies can make to the moral development either of individuals or of society.

320

While it is important to recognize that the connotations of "moral education" can in this way be extremely broad, it is clear that the present chapter cannot pursue the idea of all education being moral education – not only because space does not permit it, but also because it would overlap with so many other topics. The rest of this chapter, then, assumes, in accordance with the thinking that is dominant in the modern world in both practice and theory, that moral education is but one aspect of education.

Distinguishing Moral Education by Its Aims

The latter claim above can itself still be understood in at least two (not incompatible) ways: as a claim about the aims of education, or as a claim about content and processes. First, "moral education" may be understood as picking out some range within the totality of the aims of education; education may have many aims – developing the rationality of individuals, promoting a knowledge of certain subjects for its own sake, contributing to the economic flourishing of society, and so on – and among these moral education will itself be one aim (or one set of aims). Second, "moral education" may be understood as picking out some range of content or process within the totality of teaching and learning. Thus it might be said that certain subjects within a school curriculum are part of, or contribute to, moral education, but others not; or that certain activities within classrooms, or certain aspects of school organization, contribute to moral education while others do not.

Of these ways of identifying moral education as one aspect of education, the first – in terms of aims – seems to have logical priority, since it is hard to see how we could identify aspects of content or process as contributing to moral education, other than by seeing whether these aspects contribute toward the realization of certain aims which we have recognized as being those of moral education.

There is a possible counter to this, namely that moral education, or aspects of it, might be something that happens, rather than something consciously aimed at. It is certainly true that there are many factors in people's upbringing and wider experience that influence how people turn out (in ways that concern moral educators), and that many of these factors are not part of the conscious endeavors of educators. What is questionable is whether all such factors should be included under the heading of moral *education*. Here, moral education will not be taken to include factors of acculturation or socialization – such as the influence of mass media – which educators as such can have little direct influence over. For example, the commercial culture of a modern society may tend in various ways to make people think of themselves as consumers first and citizens second; and this is an outcome which might well be reckoned relevant to the aims of moral education. Here, moral education will not be taken to include the cultural influences themselves, but it may well include measures by which teachers consciously try to influence their students' response to such influences.

Thinking of moral education in terms of aims which teachers can consciously pursue also helps to distinguish moral *education* from moral *development*. The development of attitudes, patterns of behaviour, and espoused values is something that can

321

be studied empirically, and whether there is some universal pattern to such development – across genders and cultures, for instance – seems itself to be an empirical question. But while the empirical evidence may be relevant to educators in several ways, it does not dictate the aims of moral education. It does not have to be held, for instance, that moral education is basically – as Lawrence Kohlberg (1981) used to argue – a matter of taking people further and faster along a route which they would in any case have been following. Suppose it is found empirically that moral development tends to follow a different pattern in girls and in boys. Then various aims are still open to educators, including: reinforcing and extending the patterns of development in the two cases (thus possibly increasing the difference); endorsing just one of these patterns of development and trying to promote it in both girls and boys; trying to ensure that students of each gender understand the ways of thinking of the other; and so on.

How, then, can the aims of moral education be conceived? In popular thinking there are many views, but it may be that dominant among them are views which see the aims of moral education centrally in terms of promoting one kind or another of conformity: conformity to rules widely recognized within a society, or adherence to the norms of a tradition, or deference to authority. And behind such aims is often the idea that moral education is something that a society should engage in for the sake of the general social good – for its own protection, in effect. Philosophical writing has more often concentrated on the identification of certain capacities or qualities which are to be developed deliberately in individuals; but how these capacities or qualities are identified and characterized has varied, not only with wider conceptions of what it is to be educated, but perhaps more importantly with conceptions of the domain of the moral itself. The philosophical literature on moral education has often taken its cue from the concerns and approaches which are predominant at the time within moral philosophy, though it is doubtful whether this tendency (insofar as it is a following of academic fashion) has always been helpful in a field which seeks some influence on educational practice.

Rationalistic Accounts and Their Critics

Thus, it is broadly true that for much post-Enlightenment moral philosophy, the moral life was essentially a life of reason, at least in the sense that rational reflection was thought capable of establishing the credentials of some overarching moral principle (whether Kantian or utilitarian) and could go on (with or without the help of empirical evidence) to derive more specific conclusions about right and wrong action. Moral education, then, could be seen as part of the education of reason, which would lead to a person rationally holding certain principles and rationally deciding on the basis of these principles what to do in particular circumstances.

This approach readily cohered with a broader liberal emphasis on individual liberty, including freedom of thought. It enabled moral education to be seen as the deliberate development of rational moral autonomy; individual agents had to be able, when necessary, to do their own thinking and make up their own minds on moral issues. Not to be able to do this was tantamount to being indoctrinated, and indoctrination was above all to be avoided. But it could only be avoided through individuals being able to work out and endorse moral commitments for themselves, if necessary from first principles.

Such an approach made moral education fully compatible with other areas of education; not co-extensive with education in general, but a compartment of education, sharing the essentially cognitive aims of other compartments. The apogee of this approach was in the theory of liberal education propounded by the English philosopher of education Paul Hirst (1974) in the 1960s and 1970s. Liberal education was the development of the rational mind, which consisted in the development of understanding in each of seven or eight logically distinct forms of understanding, of which moral understanding was one.

On such an approach, then, moral education was not about the transmission of the values of society, still less about the molding of behavior – such activities would not have been considered educational at all – but about equipping people with the knowledge and understanding to enable them to think for themselves on moral matters just as they should be able to think for themselves on matters of history and mathematics.

Such views were never without their critics. In a practical vein, the emphasis on the cognitive reinforced an expectation among theorists that moral education in schools would proceed through instruction or discourse in the classroom, to the neglect of wider factors in the ethos and organization of schools which might seem to teachers to have obvious relevance. But behind such practical distortions there were philosophical deficiencies in the rationalistic approaches.

For one, such views assume, or at least reinforce, a narrow view of the scope of morality. Much as historical or mathematical thinking is something which most persons will engage in only on occasion, so moral thinking is something for specific occasions. Again, consistently with some strands of broader liberal thinking, what individuals do with their lives is a matter of their own choice and not a moral matter at all, provided they respect the rights of others and are equipped to handle moral dilemmas when they arise (which in a well ordered society might be rarely). On such a view, how one lives one's life is for the most part not directly a moral issue at all, and hence not within the scope of moral education.

Even where these rationalistic views should have been strongest, in their treatment of moral thinking about particular issues, they were still open to criticism. They often assumed, rather than argued, that the proper structure of moral thinking is the deductive move from general principles to their application to a particular instance. They largely neglected the possibility that seeing situations through the lens of general categories, intellectually grasped, might on the one hand presuppose, and on the other hand limit or distort, the perception of what is morally salient in particular circumstances.

More generally, such views, in concentrating on reasoned thinking, said little about the role of feeling. Something was surely missing from accounts on which the moral agent could be a perfect reasoner, making admirable assessments of interests or rights, but feeling nothing – or, if not nothing, then nothing in particular which was the business of moral education.

Part of what was missing was that in saying little about feeling such accounts also said little about motivation; and given that lack, they said little about how people would actually behave, though much about how they might think. That people would act in accordance with their own judgments – however rational and justifiable these might be – was either simply assumed, or thought not to be the concern of moral *education* as such.

In saying little about behavior, such approaches often seemed naive in at least two ways about the relationship between education and the context and expectations of the society in which the education took place. First, the expectations of society might be not so much that people emerging from schools should be persons who would think critically for themselves, but that, as mentioned above, they should conform to certain public norms. This did not necessarily mean that conformity was valued for its own sake; instead, conformity to publicly recognized principles or rules might be perceived as a necessary means to ensuring that people would conduct themselves in constructive or at least non-destructive ways. Though theorists had arguments against such points – cast in terms of the avoidance of indoctrination or the positive value of autonomous thinking – the philosophical discussion sometimes failed to engage seriously with popular concerns.

Second, the societies in which the education was going on were plural, multicultural ones. It was not that theorists did not recognize this. Indeed, rational moral autonomy could even be seen as an appropriate response to pluralism, for if there were so many competing values in society, then it might seem that the best aim was that individuals should make up their own minds. But this stance, in supposing that individuals could take a view "from nowhere" and still have some basis for making up their own minds, was naive about the sources of value in the individual.

Moreover, the very pluralism of society, the existence of competing and sometimes apparently incommensurable approaches on values, called into question whether there could be any one stance on values with better rational grounding than others.

A number of theoretical tendencies contributed to the making of these criticisms, and sometimes to attempts to remedy them. Thus the narrowness of certain rationalistic views of morality was a point made influentially by writers such as Bernard Williams (1985) and Charles Taylor (1989). The questioning of the possibility of showing *any* particular value stance to be rationally defensible owes a lot not only to specifically emotivist and subjectivist tendencies in metaethics, but also to a wider questioning of the role of ethical theory and of foundationalism generally. Not all of this broader climate within philosophy can be counted postmodern in any useful sense, and where professed postmodernists have contributed to thought about moral education it has often been the case that their constructive points are ones which would already be accepted by philosophers who, without counting themselves postmodernists, have seen the limitations of enlightenment aspirations.

Such philosophers, in looking at moral education, have been open to sources outside of moral philosophy narrowly construed, including empirical work on moral development. Particularly significant has been criticism within the moral development literature of Kohlberg's research. Two of the elements mentioned above – the emphasis on perception of and response to the particularities of a situation, and the role of feeling as interacting with cognition – have been especially pertinent within this criticism, and they have come together in the development by some writers, often but not necessarily distinctively feminist, of the idea of "an ethic of care" (Noddings, 1984). Here, what is seen as fundamental in the life of a moral agent is an attitude of care toward others, and most especially toward others with whom a person is involved in ongoing relationships.

Virtue Accounts and Their Limitations

But perhaps the strongest influence on the philosophy of moral education in the last two decades of the twentieth century was the rise of virtue ethics. This seemed to offer an answer to the criticisms made of rationalistic approaches. Virtues, whatever else may distinguish them, are complex dispositions of human beings which involve feeling and motivation as well as perception and reason. The virtue of benevolence, for instance, involves a sensitivity to the discomfort or flourishing of others – the benevolent person may notice in the particular circumstances the signs of distress, say, which the abstract moral reasoner misses; it involves the disposition to be pained at others' discomfort and pleased at their flourishing; and it involves the motivation to act in a way conducive to the well-being of others. So to see moral education as essentially involving the development of virtues is already to say something about the very aspects of moral response on which the rationalistic views were deficient.

If virtue ethics seems in this way to offer a rounded account of the aims of moral education, it needs to be supplemented by accounts of the processes by which virtues can develop, and of the role of teachers in promoting that development. Recent discussions by philosophers of the development of virtues have often drawn on Aristotle's account in the *Nicomachean Ethics*, and have perhaps sometimes put an unbalanced weight on his own stress on early habituation into right response and action. Following that line of thought, it can come to seem that the role of teachers in moral education will not be one of developing rational and principled thought at all. Their role will be simply to insist on certain ways of behaving, while trying themselves to be exemplars of the virtues; and since the same claims can be made for the role of parents and other adults in daily contact with the child, it can seem that teachers as such have no special contribution to make. But such a view not only ignores some of the opportunities for moral education which schooling makes available (on which more will be said below), it downplays too much the roles both of reasoning and of the public promulgation of rules and principles.

If it is right to look at virtues, this is not because one can thereby avoid saying anything about reason at all, but because looking at virtues can enable us to give a better and more comprehensive account of an ethical life in which rationality and other aspects are seen in balance. To imagine that a person, imbued with certain virtues, could go through life never having to think about what to do in some problematic situation would be to imagine a kind of life which probably no one in the modern world could lead. Equally, to imagine that the virtuous person can dispense with any regard for rules and principles would be to neglect the fact that the public acknowledgment of shared expectations on conduct can itself have valuable coordinating, predictive, and motivational functions.

The virtuous person will no more be a blind follower of rules than will the rationally autonomous person; but an adherence to broad principles of conduct (such as ideas of justice and of human rights), which do not attempt to prescribe the details of conduct in advance, can be part of the dispositions of the virtuous person as well as of the rationally autonomous. The picture of the virtuous person, however, attempts a fuller and more realistic understanding of how recognized principles can influence specific judgment. Principles will not be formulae brought in as premises for specific acts of deduction. Instead the principles will be present as part of the under-lying commitments of the agent, coloring her perception of the particularities of situations. Since the commitments and sensibilities of the virtuous person are part of an underlying disposition, they will be operative throughout her life, not only when there is an obvious need for a decision to be made.

In dealing with underlying dispositions, virtue ethics is not inherently confined to matters in which the interests of others are liable to be affected. There may be self-regarding as well as other-regarding virtues, or the same virtues may make a positive difference to the quality of life both of their possessor and of others with whom she has dealings. So a virtue approach to moral education questions the restriction of morality to other-regarding contexts. By the same token (and there is room for debate over the desirability of this), a virtue approach may lead to a blurring of boundaries between moral education and other aspects of education.

Once the inadequacy of a purely rationalistic approach is recognized, it would be difficult to deny that some form of virtues approach has more to offer. But it would be a mistake to suppose that thinking in terms of virtues resolves all the philosophical questions about moral education, let alone the practical issues about how to pursue moral education. Here are some of the issues outstanding.

First, the philosophical basis of virtue ethics is by no means definitively secured. As more philosophers have turned their attention to virtues, so differences of interpret-ation, justification, and even definition of virtues and of virtue ethics have emerged. Virtue ethics has been an ongoing research program, and one which is interacting with other established traditions within moral philosophy (one of the most interesting of these interactions being the increasing exploration by Kantian scholars of the interpretation and role of virtue within Kant's own ethics). So long as the philosoph-ical debate continues, it would be rash to suggest that no developments within moral philosophy could challenge the assumptions of work on moral education. Neverthe-less, virtue ethics appears to give a theoretical backing to the many and ongoing attempts in schools to develop approaches to moral education which build on the almost inevitable intuition of practical experience mentioned above, that the whole of the ethos and practices of a school, not just teaching as such, needs to be taken into account.

Second, and also bearing on how teachers should conceive the relationship be-tween their roles as moral educators and as academic instructors, there is a philo-sophical issue of the relationship between intellectual and moral aims. The rationalistic approaches, as we have seen, had an answer to this, but a deficient one. It is a merit of the virtues approach that in investigating this issue it can draw on discussion of the relationship between moral and intellectual virtues. A key Aristotel-ian insight here, and still one focus for philosophical discussion, is that a virtuous character cannot be fully developed without practical wisdom. One issue for philoso-phers of education is whether established areas of a school's academic curriculum can themselves have a role in developing practical wisdom. The ultimate goal here might be a unified account of educational aims in terms of the development of virtues, both intellectual and moral.

Third is the question whether virtue ethics provides a basis for moral education which can be acceptable within a plural and multicultural society. Discussion of this issue within philosophy of education overlaps with the continuing debate in political philosophy between a Rawlsian theory of justice for liberal-democratic and plural societies and its communitarian critics. Communitarians and some theorists of virtues have emphasized the rootedness of virtues in specific cultural traditions (MacIntyre, 1981). Where education itself is conducted within such traditions, this poses no problem of legitimation within the cultural groups which maintain those traditions. Christians running their own schools will be committed to the development of Christian virtues, socialists to the development of socialist virtues, and so on. But if we are looking for forms of moral education which can be shared in common across common schools in a plural society, there are problems. It may be possible to meet the qualms of liberal thinkers about the dangers of indoctrination, through a proper understanding of the role of reason and judgment within the virtues. But if it appears within a plural society that the virtues of any one tradition are being taken as a model for all, there will still be problems of legitimation across the society as a whole.

At this point there are several possible moves. One, within the ongoing research programme of virtue ethics, is to attempt to argue that there are indeed certain virtues which can be seen to be of universal value, desirable for human beings whatever their cultural circumstances. Another, which may be more likely to succeed in answering the actual legitimation challenge, is to argue that, whether or not there are universal virtues, there are virtues which are essential to life in a modern, plural, and demo-cratic society. This approach, adopted in some form by many contemporary theorists of liberalism, leads to an important overlap between moral education – insofar as it can be undertaken in common schools – and what may be variously called civic education or education for citizenship. Common schools may be expected to promote the virtues of citizenship, but if there are other virtues, rooted within specific trad-itions, it may be left to the communities embodying these traditions to cultivate these virtues in their own ways.

To this point, then, it may seem there is good reason for holding that the overall aim of moral education – if indeed there is to be one overall aim – is the development of virtues, even if the statement of such a broad aim inevitably leaves issues still to be settled. But this is not to say that there is any reason to be sanguine about the realization of such an aim. One practical difficulty is that theorists of virtues still have a wider public to convince. Even if it is true that virtue ethics gives the most rounded account of ethical life, the non-philosophers who fund and run schools may need to be persuaded of this fact. They may want certain rules to be taught, or certain patterns of behavior stamped in. Notions of character education, for instance, may have gained popularity recently in some parts of the world because they have become associated with the (socially conservative) inculcation of patterns of conduct rather than with any more comprehensive understanding of virtues.

As we have seen, talk of virtues may be favored philosophically over rationalistic approaches precisely because such talk captures the multidimensionality of ethical life better than any narrower approach. This very multidimensionality complicates the issue of how to go about the deliberate development of virtues. Even where the aim is the development of integrated character traits, one task that philosophical analysis can carry out is the conceptual breaking down of virtues into components, so that educators can consider how they might influence the development of particular components. (The results of such work might turn out to be not dissimilar to the analyses of "moral components" offered by the English philosopher John Wilson (e.g. Wilson, 1990), even though Wilson did not consider himself a virtue theorist.) Clearly, philosophy will not by itself issue in reliable practical guidelines for educators, but it has an essential contribution to make in conjunction with an increasing body of evidence available both from developmental psychology and from practical experience of what appears to work in schools.

There is also a variety of institutional and cultural constraints to be recognized. It is possible that the factors which account for one person developing certain virtues to a high degree and other persons showing little such development lie largely outside the reach of anything that formal education can do. It is even possible that the realization in individuals of the kind of unified structure of settled dispositions that Aristotle described in the *Nicomachean Ethics* is dependent on settled and culturally homogeneous social conditions which do not exist today. Even in present cultural conditions, if we could start afresh to design institutional structures conducive to the development of virtues, it might well be that we would not design schools as we know them.

Schools and Dialogue

Nevertheless, schools in modern plural societies do have features on which moral education can build. They bring together persons who for the most part would not otherwise meet, let alone interact in any ways other than the most casual or instrumental; and they rely for their educational activities very heavily on verbal communication, especially talk. Practical developments in schools which appear so far to be effective in moral education are often building on these two features of schools. For instance, Kohlberg's "just community" approach (Power et al., 1989) set up institutional arrangements (often within a larger school) by which a group of around a hundred students and teachers could take collective responsibility for matters of fairness and welfare within the group. The intention was that these persons would come to identify themselves as members of an explicitly recognized moral community, deciding on its norms, and willing to implement or accept sanctions when the norms were broken. The method was primarily democratic discussion, with a degree of formalization. Unlike Kohlberg's earlier reliance on responses to hypothetical dilemmas, this was discussion on which real consequences turned.

Many other practical approaches to moral education in schools have given an important role to discussion and dialogue. Indeed, it is arguable that one of the things which schools can do especially well as a contribution to moral education (better than other institutions including families and religious communities) is the promoting of disciplined, open-minded, and critical discussion, within a setting of ongoing interaction which makes the dialogue of more than academic interest. Here philosophy has a role not only in clarifying and justifying overall aims, but also in articulating ways in which the form and conduct of discussion can help to realize those aims. Indeed, doing philosophy with children can itself be a form of moral education (cf. Pritchard, 1996).

Reasons for advocating discussion as an aspect of moral education seem to fall into two main groups, but these are not incompatible with each other or with virtue approaches. First, discussion may be seen as potentially leading to a consensus by which norms or particular virtues can acquire a kind of authority. At one level, many practical approaches have started with an attempt within schools or wider communities (at local or in some countries at national level) to reach agreement on the values to be promoted. Politically, such agreement can provide legitimation for practical programs in schools, though philosophers may dispute whether consensus as such gives any other kind of authority to normative claims. Within a school, discussion among the students may lead (as in the "just community" model) to individuals acknowledging the authority over them of the norms which they have had a hand in formulating. Some philosophers would give a quasi-foundational role in moral justification to agreement arising out of dialogue, as in the communicative ethics of Habermas (1990), where norms can only be justified by surviving critical dialogical scrutiny.

The second kind of reason for advocating discussion and dialogue stresses understanding and associated dispositions. Through discussion, more than through direct instruction or unaided self-reflection, students may come to an appreciation of the role of moral norms, virtues, and commitments in their lives and the lives of others. Dialogue with others whose values are different, who use a different kind of language (say, religious rather than secular), or who put a different interpretation on the same virtues can lead in hermeneutical fashion to deeper understanding both of what is held in common and of why in certain ways people differ. At the same time it can promote the development of respect, willingness to listen, and tolerance.

Alongside their role in seeking to develop appropriate dispositions in individuals, schools have a role in preparing citizens to engage with the many public issues which have an inescapably moral dimension. Modern societies face issues of social justice, genetic engineering, human influence on the environment, and many others, on which it makes little sense to say that individuals should or can simply decide for themselves. We have already seen that within virtue theory there can be an overlap between moral and civic education, but it is not plausible to suppose that even if all citizens possessed any theorist's favoured civic virtues to the highest degree, the individual judgments of citizens on morally controversial issues would somehow coincide. Schools can give experience of the kind of dialogue on moral matters in which citizens have to engage, and can at the same time help to ensure that such dialogue is well informed.

The possibility of promoting dialogue across differences – both in structured classroom settings and in informal conversation – remains one of the strongest arguments for favoring common schools as a vehicle for moral education, rather than devolving responsibility for moral education solely to schools and other settings, including the family, which are culturally more homogeneous.

Conclusion

The philosophical consideration of moral education can be instructive in the more general consideration of the interface between the concerns of philosophers and of practicing educators. Philosophers often are not satisfied if they cannot produce a theory or at least some sort of systematic overview of an area. In recent decades, some of the moral philosophers who first wrote about virtues were offering a critique of the very idea that an ethical life could be captured in any sort of theory; but (not surprisingly, within the context of academic philosophy) virtue ethics came to be itself a theoretical approach competing with others. So it is tempting to think that what educators need from philosophers is the right ethical theory, which can then be applied to moral education.

This is unlikely to be fruitful in practice, however, not only because of the lack of consensus among philosophers, but also because of the multidimensional nature of moral education. Even the idea that the aim is to develop virtues needs, I have suggested, to be broken down into subordinate aims, and even then the whole field will not have been captured. There can be many aims for moral education. Some will complement each other or at least be mutually compatible. Others – such as conformity to publicly recognized norms of conduct, and individual autonomous judgment – will be in tension with each other, at least on first examination. Yet there may be good, if not conclusive, reasons for pursuing all of these aims. The contribution of philosophy here is likely to be not so much in building a unifying theory as in clarifying in a more piecemeal way the nature of these aims, showing how far they are mutually compatible when properly understood, and where they are not compatible, arguing for priorities among them.

See also 1 THE SOCRATIC MOVEMENT; 2 STOICISM; 3 THE JUDAIC TRADITION; 4 THE EDUCATIONAL THOUGHT OF AUGUSTINE; 6 ENLIGHTENMENT LIBERALISM; 7 ROUSSEAU, DEWEY, AND DEMOCRACY; 8 KANT, HEGEL, AND THE RISE OF PEDAGOGICAL SCIENCE; 9 ROMANTICISM; 15 THE NATURE AND PURPOSES OF EDUCATION; 23 RELIGIOUS EDUCATION; 26 AESTHETICS AND THE EDUCATIVE POWERS OF ART; 27 TEACHING LITERATURE; 28 THE AUTHORITY AND RESPONSIBILITY TO EDUCATE; 29 CHURCH, STATE, AND EDUCATION; 36 THE ETHICS OF TEACHING; 38 SEX EDUCATION; 39 ETHICS AND THE AIMS OF AMERICAN HIGHER EDUCATION; 45 THE ROLE OF ETHICS IN PROFESSIONAL EDUCATION

References

Habermas, J. (1990) *Moral Consciousness and Communicative Action*. Cambridge: Polity Press.

Hirst, P. (1974) *Knowledge and the Curriculum*. London: Routledge and Kegan Paul.

Kohlberg, L. (1981) *The Philosophy of Moral Development: Essays on Moral Development, volume 1*. San Francisco: Harper & Row.

MacIntyre, A. (1981) *After Virtue*. London: Duckworth.

Noddings, N. (1984) *Caring: A Feminine Approach to Ethics and Moral Education*. Berkeley: University of California Press.

Power, F. C., Higgins, A., and Kohlberg, L. (1989) *Lawrence Kohlberg's Approach to Moral Education*. New York: Columbia University Press.

Pritchard, M. (1996) *Reasonable Children*. Lawrence: Kansas University Press.

Taylor, C. (1989) *Sources of the Self*. Cambridge: Cambridge University Press.

Williams, B. (1985) *Ethics and the Limits of Philosophy*. London: Fontana.

Wilson, J. (1990) *A New Introduction to Moral Education*. London: Cassell.

Further reading

Carr, D. (1991) *Educating the Virtues: An Essay on the Philosophical Psychology of Moral Development and Education*. London: Routledge.

Carr, D. and Steutel, J. (eds) (1999) *Virtue Ethics and Moral Education*. London: Routledge.

Green, T. (1999) *Voices: The Educational Formation of Conscience*. Notre Dame, IN: University of Notre Dame Press.

Halstead, J. and McLaughlin, T. (eds) (1999) *Education in Morality*. London: Routledge.

Peters, R. (1981) *Moral Development and Moral Education*. London: Allen & Unwin.

Pincoffs, E. (1986) *Quandaries and Virtues*. Lawrence: Kansas University Press.

23

Religious Education

Gabriel Moran

Religious education is an area that has struggled throughout the past century to become an academic discipline or at least a topic worthy of academic discussion. The topic, of course, is not what has struggled; various groups at different times in several places have tried to establish a field of religious education. Given the inherent complexity of this task, the difficulties of development are perhaps not surprising. Some people, however, think that a field of religious education is an impossibility. The skeptics come from both sides: religious people who doubt the value of being linked to education, and educators who doubt that religion is compatible with education.

On the religious side, one can distinguish between those relatively few people who simply reject education and those people who believe that a religious life is irreducibly particular. That is, a Christian education or a Muslim education makes sense to this latter group, but a religious education would be a vapid generality. On the educational side, some people think that education and religion are contradictories, that education is the modern world's replacement of religion. Other people in education think that religion is a topic worthy of study but that the term "religious education" suggests involvement in the practice of a religion. They might acknowledge the academic legitimacy of "religious studies" in the university while opposing religious education in a high school.

These multiple objections to the existence of religious education cannot be answered here at the beginning. In the final section of this chapter I propose what might be an academically and religiously defensible concept of religious education. My starting premise is that as a practical matter, religion touches the lives of a majority of people in the United States and throughout the world. As a part of the philosophy of education, religion's relation to both philosophy and education has been and continues to be an important question. Education in the twentieth century did not succeed in replacing religion.

While it is possible to propose a logical and comprehensive meaning for "religious education," the idea will not succeed unless it emerges from the actual use of this expression by people who have some commitment to what they are doing under that rubric. Thus, much of this chapter is an attempt to gather up the shards that are entitled "religious education." While many of them may be lacking in logic, that is less important than the fact that a conversation has occurred or is taking place in which religious education is what people are looking for. It is crucial to follow the words and to ask in each setting how that meaning of "religious education" may fit into the overall puzzle. In this chapter I cannot survey all uses of "religious education" in the English-speaking world and the approximate translations of "religious education" in other languages. I concentrate on two main strands of the story, one in the United States and the other in England. After that I point out some further variations in other countries as well as the use in United Nations documents. Only then do I try to piece together the whole puzzle.

The United States

The adjective "religious" can be found as a modifier of "education" from the earliest period of the British colonies in North America. In the seventeenth century, Increase Mather wrote "that a Religious Education is a great mercy, yea, and to many of the Elect it is the great means of their Conversion." Mather's use reflects the meaning that "religion" had from the time of the Roman Empire until the end of the sixteenth century; that is, the practice of piety. "Christian religion" was not one of the set called religions but the practice of the Christian life. When Yale was established in 1701 it was based on the conviction that "the Liberal and Religious Education of Suitable youth is under the blessing of God, a chief and most probable expedient."

A new meaning of "religious education" began emerging in the second half of the nineteenth century. The Unitarian movement, conceiving itself to be the progressive transcending of denominational differences, began referring to religious education and has consistently done so ever since. The program of their national conference in 1872 is filled with papers discussing aspects of religious education. In the 1890s when William Rainey Harper at the University of Chicago looked for a way to describe a revolution in the church's approach to education, he adopted the term "religious education." The term suggested both academic and ecumenical possibilities. That is, "religious" could signify a diversity of religions and "education" could be a meeting place for church schooling and the new system of public schools.

The Religious Education Association was founded in 1903, an organization that at its origin represented the great hopes of the people who were responsible for the use of the term "religious education." What was announced at the beginning of the twentieth century was not a new organization but a new *movement* that would bring the forces of education and religion into a dynamic new relation. When four hundred religious, educational, political, and business leaders met to found the Religious Education Association, it seemed to the people in attendance that history was on their side. They listened to a keynote address by a young professor named John Dewey on the exciting possibilities of the new field of psychology (Schmidt, 1983). The aims of the movement were: cooperation among Catholic, Protestant and Jewish educators; a bridging of the gap between the state school and the religiously affiliated school; and the professionalizing of instructional efforts in church and synagogue.

When any group lays claim to a vision that will change the world, the background and assumptions of the founders inevitably exercise a greater constraint than they are aware of. Almost immediately, the movement of religious education found it

333

impossible to keep all the parties under one organizational umbrella. Among Jews, not surprisingly, all but the most liberal minded distrusted an organization that had Christian trappings and Christian leadership. A bigger blow, from the standpoint of numbers, was the unwillingness of the Roman Catholic church to participate. Just as important a drawback to a religious education movement was the absence of the conservative wing of United States Protestantism. The result was that "religious education" became a name for liberal Protestant education.

A parallel liberal movement to establish a religious education occurred in Germany early in the century. But a reaction, closely identified with Karl Barth, arose in Germany after the disillusion of the First World War. Although the influence of that Barthian reaction to liberal theology was delayed in the United States until the 1930s, the religious education movement by 1950 was widely perceived to be finished even though the Religious Education Association struggled on (Miller, 1950).

A new burst of life was given to the Religious Education Association in 1965. After a decade of coaxing by the Association's executive secretary, the Roman Catholic bishops endorsed Catholic participation in the group. The Second Vatican Council was about to conclude and the Catholic school system was at its most expansive. Although the religious education movement in the first half of the century was mostly Protestant, Catholics found it easy to work with the terms "religious," "religion," and "religious education." The term "religion" had passed from its ancient and medieval meaning of external piety to its modern meaning of an institutional system, and Catholics were comfortable in drawing upon its external and institutional connotations. The Catholic Church in the United States took over "religious education" with such enthusiasm that Catholics often sound as though they own the term. Thus, instead of religious education being a venture to which Catholics contribute, it is spoken of as one element within the Catholic Church's education.

Jews share with Catholics an appreciation of external rituals but the term "religion" is sometimes regarded by Jews as foreign. That is, the Jew's relation to Jewishness is said to be more intimate than "having a religion." Some Reform and Conservative Jews have been associated through the years with the Religious Education Association and are comfortable in referring to religious education when they converse with Christians. In Israel the "religious" is sharply opposed to the secular, so that religious education is a sign of orthodoxy; however, "religious education" can be found on the religious left as well as the right (Rosenak, 1987).

The missing piece in the picture of religious education in the United States is the place of religion in the state schools. In the 1960s, several decisions of the Supreme Court were intended to remove the vestiges of Protestant piety from the schools. At the same time, the Court tried to encourage a properly academic treatment of religion. Unfortunately, the Supreme Court had no language ready at hand to express this support. The Court employed a distinction that went back to the 1940s between "teaching religion" and "teaching about religion." This awkward language was immediately frozen into a complete separation, and the teaching of religion was henceforth assumed to be unacceptable in the state school (Piediscalzi, 1977).

A distinction between teaching something and teaching about something could be helpful in some educational discussions. In elementary school and early years of high school, students are not ready to study psychoanalysis or pre-Socratic philosophy;

likewise, they are not ready to study the discipline of religion. However, teachers might introduce elements of psychology, philosophy, or religion within material taught in elementary and secondary schools. One could thus distinguish between teaching about religion in a history or literature course and teaching religion in a religion course. Whether a seventh- or a twelfth-grade student is ready for a religion course is an educational issue worth exploring.

England

The term "religious education" probably migrated from the United States to England by way of missionary congresses (Priestley, 1991). The term was known but not frequently used in the 1930s. However, the Education Act of 1944 gave a legal meaning to the term, making religious education a requirement in every school of England and Wales. The religious education section was guided through the legislative process by Archbishop William Temple. "Religious education" was a term chosen for both its ecumenical and academic possibilities. One of the participants, Lord Fisher, wrote at the time: "Willie Temple and I were schoolmasters; that tells you all you need to know" (Niblett, 1964, p. 22).

There were two parts to the religious education provision in section 25 of the Education Act. The first provided that "The school day in every county school and in every voluntary school shall begin with collective worship on the part of the pupils in attendance at the school, arrangements made therefore shall provide for a single act of worship attended by all such pupils." The second provision was that "Religious instruction shall be given in every county school and in every voluntary school."

By the 1960s both provisions of the 1944 Act were facing a crisis. The assumption that the schoolchildren were Anglican or at least Christian began to unravel. The requirement of a common worship service faced increasing opposition; many educators had doubted from the beginning that the school is the proper place for worship (Hull, 1975). The other element, religious instruction, faced a different kind of crisis, one that could lead to a strengthening of the school's proper work. If the population of the school is nearly all Christians, religious instruction can slide into being instruction in Christian doctrine. If the classroom holds a mixture of Hindu, Christian, Muslim, and Buddhist students, then the teacher is unlikely to confuse the classroom with a factory for the production of good Christians.

There arose in the late 1960s two contrasting approaches to religious instruction. On one side there was attention to "world religions." John Hull at the University of Birmingham became the chief force for realizing this approach in the curriculum (Hull, 1984). The approach was commonly called objective or phenomenological. On the other side there was a search for a universal ground of religion that would allow ordinary experience and school subjects other than religion to be related to religious education. The student's experience was to be tapped for an "existential" encounter with the essence of religion.

Throughout the 1970s the phenomenological approach seemed to have the upper hand, at least among syllabus makers. One might wonder how many teachers were well prepared to render the fine points of difference between Hinduism and Sikhism. A document of the time describes religious education as a "procedurally neutral approach, wherein the teacher is ready to portray sympathetically and without bias any viewpoint which he may be required to teach." The hoped-for result from such teaching was "to create in boys and girls a more sensitive understanding of their own beliefs and the different beliefs by which others govern their lives" (School Council, 1971, pp. 38, 18).

By the beginning of the 1980s there was some qualifying of this objective approach. The other tradition, the existential or experiential, had not disappeared. It represented a valid concern that religion be intelligible, interesting, and relevant to the students' lives. The logic of religion may not be the same as the student's logic; someone has to mediate the understanding. The most prominent voice in this attempt to bring the competing traditions into conversation was Michael Grimmitt. His way of formulating the issue was to say that the student should learn about religion and learn from religion. In the former, the student evaluates "impersonally," asking about the meaning and inner logic of the religious system. In the latter, the student evaluates "personally," asking about the persuasiveness of that religion in his or her life. Grimmitt was acknowledging that on educational grounds a personal evaluation by the student is part of the study of religion (Grimmitt, 1987; Flood, 1999).

The Education Act of 1944 had said that religious education consists of worship and religious instruction. When the Act was being revised in 1988 what was discussed was worship and religious education. By then, "religious education" had collapsed into religious instruction but instead of being the name of the process or the name of the department, "religious education" came to be used for the curriculum subject. Religious education, especially when it is regularly referred to as RE, is not just encapsulated in the school but is narrowed down to one subject taught in the classroom.

"Religious education" used as the name of the object of teaching is a peculiar form of speech. The parallel in the United States is the practice of putting "education" after what many people doubt is a genuine academic subject. Thus, we have sex education, driver education, and drug education as things put into the school's curriculum. The word "education," instead of strengthening the topic, has the effect of casting doubt on its legitimate place in the school. A somewhat similar pattern can be seen in Australia, where a course is called "study of religion." Thus, the students don't study religion; they study the study of religion. These peculiar uses of language indicate an unwillingness to defend religion as something that can be taught in an academic setting.

A comparison between the United States and England brings out one fact clearly, that "religious education" can mean quite different things. In England, the most common meaning is the name of a curriculum subject in the state school. In the United States, "religious education," whatever its various meanings, never refers to a subject taught in state schools. For the development of religious education as an academic field, the English use of the term offers more to build upon. There is a corps of people who identify professionally with the teaching of religious education.

The clarity of the English usage has been at the expense of a narrow meaning for what people in England call "RE." United States usage offers a confusing but larger context for religious education: the school and not just the classroom subject; the work of religious bodies as well as academic instruction; the family as first teacher and continuing source of formation. An examination of religion and religions in the classroom should be part of a complete religious education, a fact that the United States must some day address. But the classroom of the state school should not be asked to carry the whole burden of a nation's religious education.

Variations: National and International

It seems unlikely that England and the United States will learn from each other's use of "religious education." Educators in each country have shown almost no interest in considering the religious education of the other. The countries that offer interesting case studies are ones that make use of literature from both the United States and England. For example, Canada is dominated by cultural influences from the United States; Canada has been a partner in the Religious Education Association from the beginning. However, the English meaning of religious education has had influence in several provinces, including Ontario, and especially in the "Protestant school system" of Quebec (Government of Quebec Education Ministry, 1984; Meyer, 1989). Other countries, such as Ireland, New Zealand and South Africa, show influence of religious education writing from both England and the United States. The case I will take for more extended comment is Australia.

Australia until the Second World War was populated mainly by descendants from Britain and Ireland. Since then there has been a diversifying of the culture. The United States has been a major contributor and there is a steady influx from the Asian nations to the north and from continental Europe. Australians are quick to say that, unlike the United States, Australia is a very secular country. The church has never played the role it has had in United States history. Nevertheless, in today's language Australia has a distinctive "spirituality." The people are related to the sea and the land, especially the desert, in a way that situates human life in relation to the marvelous diversity of species in Australia. The Aborigines, who have inhabited the land for tens of thousands of years, have emerged into a new relation with white Australia that gives a distinctive edge to Australian art, culture, and religion (Kelly, 1991).

As early as 1880 the Public Instruction Act in New South Wales proposed inclusion of "general religious teaching" (Clark, 1987, p. 151). Although the proposal was defeated by Catholic and Anglican opposition, it came back in a new form in 1964. The Department of Education approved "general religious and moral education." The churches were still critical of a general teaching of religion, but over the past thirty-five years there has continued to be interest in such courses in Victoria, New South Wales, and Queensland (Lovat, 2001). The language of religious education is widely used in these states; there is evident influence from Catholic educators who have studied in the United States. But unlike Catholics in the United States, who tend to restrict "religious education" to parish education, Australian Catholics use the term to refer to schools and curriculum. The integration of the Australian Catholic schools within the state system means that the British writing on religious education can be assimilated better than it can be in the United States.

South Australia, where Anglican and Roman Catholic influences were never as strong as in the eastern states, has been most open to the use of the British way of speaking of religious education and developing a curriculum subject (Crotty, 1986;

Clark, 1987, p. 84). In Western Australia, Brian Hill has sought the compatibility of the British approach to religious education and evangelical Christianity. In surveying other nations, Hill dismisses the United States as having practically nothing to say on religious education (Hill, 1999). The Australian Association of Religious Education has tended to assume a British meaning of "religious education," while the *Journal of Religious Education*, mostly under Catholic direction, has a broader usage for the term than curriculum in state schools. Australia may never be able to arrive at a well structured synthesis of religious education, but its distinctive environment, democratic tradition, geographical location, religious mixture, and educational commitment make it a place to watch for the future of religious education.

In looking for a meaning of "religious education" that would transcend the nation state, some attention should be given to the United Nations. Philosophers, educators, and other groups may have a tendency to dismiss UN documents as airy rhetoric. Nonetheless, the UN has had remarkable success in getting the world, including philosophers and ethicists, to pay attention to human rights. The world is still at the beginning of establishing enforceable policies on human rights but the progress in the past fifty years is impressive. The UN from its beginning has been aware that religion is unavoidably a part of the human rights story. Article 18 of the Universal Declaration of Human Rights includes the right to freedom of thought, conscience and religion. Freedom of religion includes the right to change one's religion or belief, as well as to "manifest" one's religion or belief. This last element has been a source of continuing struggles; one person's manifesting of religion (buildings, holy days, diet, clothing) can intrude on someone else's rights (Brownie, 1992; Evans, 1998).

This complicated story implies the need for a worldwide religious education that would include not only a study of academic concepts but a realistic give and take on religious practices. The UN has commissioned surveys of education, first in 1959 and most recently in 1998 (Lerner, 2000, pp. 11, 32). Not surprisingly, the surveys have shown education in religious matters to be undeveloped in most countries. States still tend to be insensitive to the rights of minorities who are subjected to instruction in the official or dominant religion of the state.

The UN actually uses the term "religious education" in several key documents, particularly the Covenant on Civil and Political Rights and the Covenant on Economic, Cultural and Social Rights, both adopted in 1966. These two documents assert that parents have a right to "the moral and religious education" of their children as they wish (Lerner, 2000, pp. 15, 20). I think it is encouraging that the UN puts forth moral and religious education as something to be understood and practiced universally. A surprising offshoot of this assertion of parental rights is a protest in several parts of the world against "anti-homophobic" courses in schools. These parents maintain that it is a violation of their right to control the religious education of their children. It is a fascinating development to have right-wing political groups appealing to UN documents to protect their rights.

The biggest drawback in the UN language is the assumption that moral and religious education is an affair of young children and their parents. The wishes of the parents should have primacy when the child is six years old. When the student is 19 years old – or 59 years old – the student's own wishes take centerstage, and the moral and religious dimensions of education may not fit together as they did when the person was six years old. As UN documents recount in painful detail, religious education is going to be needed not just to induct children into the religion of their parents but as a continuing process to cope with the world's political, cultural, and environmental problems.

Conclusion of a Beginning

Can any comprehensive and consistent pattern for religious education be drawn from this confusing array of meanings? Religious groups throughout the centuries have all trained their members in the practices of the group. A general name for these particular exercises could be "religious education." But every religious group today faces the challenge of a modern culture and the critical mindset of modern education. The critical study of religion could be called "religion education," similar to the way we speak of science education, art education, or mathematics education. A dichotomy could be imagined between the closed, "subjective" world of a religious group's discipline and the secular world's "objective" attempts to explain religion and religions.

In practice, however, there is tension and overlap rather than a total separation between these two forms of education. Most religious groups today make an attempt to come to terms with modern tools of education. The struggle around particular issues by particular religious groups can obscure the fact that the major religious traditions are not functioning in encapsulated, "subjective" worlds. Religious educators not only in the secular schools of England but in most religiously affiliated schools are exposing students to a diversity of beliefs and a search for intelligible answers. Anyone who assumes that only indoctrination happens in these classrooms is simply not acquainted with those schools, students, and teachers.

From the other direction, an educator need not be a member of a religious body to be able to teach religion. But neither should it be supposed that a schoolteacher's ability to be fair to evidence is hindered by being a practicing member of a religious body. Someone can teach political science even if he or she is a registered Democrat. Someone can teach ethics while being a firm adherent of utilitarianism. The tension may be greatest in religion but some experience of participation in religious activity should help a teacher in explaining religion. The teacher's relation both to the material and to the students is not captured by the word "objective." The teacher has to imagine what it is like to see the world as a Hindu or a Muslim or a Christian does.

I am suggesting that there is a healthy challenge that operates in both directions. While there are great risks for a religious group to open its intramural education to the tools of modern psychology, the critical study of history, archeology, and anthropology, a religious group today that tries to avoid modern education can survive only by turning increasingly inward. A Christian education or a Buddhist education cannot ultimately be successful in the twenty-first century without some interreligious conversation and a dialogue with secular culture.

The challenge to modern education is less obvious but just as real. When modern education is equated with rational explanation, much of what is valuable in human

339

life can be overlooked or explained away. The religious life of a people involves interiority, puzzling symbols and paradoxical uses of language. Anyone who tries to teach religion in a classroom has to pay great attention to the ambiguities of interpretation. A religion teacher needs a wide range of linguistic, historical, artistic, and philosophical skills. Understanding always involves comparison, so the phrase "comparative religion" is usually redundant.

The peculiar assumption in the literature of the United States, and echoed elsewhere, is that "teaching religion" is equivalent to indoctrination and proselytizing. This assumption raises questions not just about "religion" but about "teaching." If to teach religion means to tell people what to think, what does teaching history, literature, or ethics mean? An academic exploration of how to teach religion in private, religiously affiliated and state schools would be a worthwhile contribution to the classroom teaching of every subject.

For the individual, religious education is a process that begins at birth and continues throughout life. At a very early age, a child is immersed into a set of religious or quasi-religious practices. Parents or guardians have an ineluctably large part in how anyone takes up a stance toward a religious way of life. What goes on in school should not be a denial of the religion that students bring with them. But the classroom, from the first grade on, should be a place where every question is allowable and a student learns to think critically about all phases of life. There should be an increase of criticism as a student moves from primary to secondary to tertiary schools but nonetheless a continuity in the teaching of religion. If this school form of religious education is successful it should prepare students to take up an intelligent and freely chosen attitude to religious participation in adult life. From then into old age, a balance of activity and continued critical study should be available for every person.

See also 3 THE JUDAIC TRADITION; 4 THE EDUCATIONAL THOUGHT OF AUGUSTINE; 22 MORAL EDUCATION; 26 AESTHETICS AND THE EDUCATIVE POWERS OF ART; 29 CHURCH, STATE, AND EDUCATION; 38 SEX EDUCATION

References

Brownie, I. (ed.) (1992) *Basic Documents on Human Rights*. New York: Oxford University Press.

Clark, M. (1987) *A Short History of Australia*. New York: New American Library.

Crotty, R. (1986) Teaching religion in a secular school: the South Australian experience. *Religious Education*, 81, 310–21.

Evans, T. (1998) *Human Rights Fifty Years On*. New York: St Martin's Press.

Flood, G. (1999) *Beyond Phenomenology: Rethinking the Study of Religion*. New York: Cassell.

Government of Quebec Education Ministry (1984) *Protestant Moral and Religious Education*. Montreal: Government of Quebec Printing Office.

Grimmitt, M. (1987) *Religious Education and Human Development*. Great Wakering: McCrimmon.

Hill, B. (1999) Can religious education be theologically neutral? *Christian Education*, 42, 1–13.

Hull, J. (1975) *School Worship: An Obituary*. London: SCM Press.

Hull, J. (1984) *Studies in Religion and Education*. London: Falmer Press.

Kelly, T. (1991) *A New Imagining: Toward an Australian Spirituality*. Melbourne, Dove Publications.

Lerner, N. (2000) *Religion, Beliefs and International Human Rights*. New York: Orbis Books.

Lovat, T. (2001) The ideological challenge of the public syllabus in religious studies. In M. Ryan (ed.), *Echo and Silence: Contemporary Issues for Australian Religious Education*. Katoomba, NSW: Social Science Press, pp. 1–13.

Meyer, J. (1989) Shaking the foundations – religion and schooling in Ontario. *Religion and Public Education*, 63, 63–78.

Miller, R. C. (1950) *The Clue to Christian Education*. New York: Scribner's.

Niblett, R. (1964) The religious education clauses of the 1944 Act: aims, hopes and fulfillment. In A. G. Wedderspoon (ed.), *Religious Education 1944–84*. London: George Allen and Unwin.

Piediscalzi, N. (1977) *Teaching about Religion in Public Schools*. Niles: Argus.

Priestley, J. (1991) A new era – beginning from Jerusalem? Some reflections from 1928 on matters pertaining to 1988. *British Journal of Religious Education*, 13, 143–51.

Rosenak, M. (1987) *Commandment and Concern: Jewish Religious Education in Secular Society*. Philadelphia: Jewish Publication Society.

Schmidt, S. (1983) *A History of the Religious Education Association*. Birmingham: Religious Education Press.

School Council (1971) *Religious Education in Secondary Schools*. London: Evans Methuen.

Further reading

Coe, G. A. (1920) *A Social Theory of Religious Education*. New York: Scribner's.

Fowler, J. (1981) *Faith Development*. San Francisco: Harper and Row.

Groome, T. (1980) *Christian Religious Education*. San Francisco: Harper and Row.

Harris, M. (1987) *Teaching and the Religious Imagination*. San Francisco: Harper and Row.

Moran, G. (1989) *Religious Education as a Second Language*. Birmingham: Religious Education Press.

Rossiter, G. (1981) *The Practice of Religious Education in Government Schools*. Canberra: Curriculum Development Center.

Schreiner, P. (ed.) (2000) *Religious Education in Europe*. Munster: Comenius Institute.

Schweitzer, F. (1987) *Lebensgeschichte und Religion*. Munich: Kaiser.

24

Teaching Science

Michael R. Matthews

Science teaching occasions philosophical questions which thoughtful teachers and curriculum writers have long engaged. These questions encompass educational ones about the place of science in the curriculum, and how learning science contributes to ideals of an educated citizen and to the promotion of a modern and mature society. The questions also cover the subject matter of science itself. What is the nature of science? What is the status of its knowledge claims? Does it presuppose any particular world view? The first category of questions constitutes standard philosophy of education (PE); the second category constitutes philosophy of science (PS) or history and philosophy of science (HPS). PE questions in science education cannot be answered without answers to PS questions, as Israel Scheffler recognized thirty years ago when he wrote:

> I have outlined four main efforts through which philosophies-of might contribute to education: (1) the analytic description of forms of thought represented by teaching subjects; (2) the evaluation and criticism of such forms of thought; (3) the analysis of specific materials so as to systematize and exhibit them as exemplifications of forms of thought; and (4) the interpretation of particular exemplifications in terms accessible to the novice. (Scheffler, 1973, p. 40)

Just a sample of relevant PE and PS questions have included: what are the aims and purposes of science education? What should be the content and focus of science curricula? How do we balance the competing demands of professional training versus everyday scientific and technological competences versus understanding the past and present interactions of science with society, culture, religion, and world views? What is the structure of science as a discipline and what is the status of its knowledge claims? What are the ethical constraints on scientific research and what are the cognitive virtues or intellectual dispositions required for the conduct of science? What is the meaning of key scientific concepts such as theory, law, explanation, and cause?

This chapter surveys recent developments in the philosophy and practice of science education, documenting and illustrating the importance of PS and HPS for science education.

342

Contemporary Curriculum Reform

Fundamental debate about the aims and curriculum content of school science has been occasioned in recent years by a widely perceived science literacy crisis. Some curriculum developers and educators want to continue business as usual with discipline-based, professional-initiation curricula, in effect abandoning the 1970s goal of "science for all." Others want to substitute various vocational and applied science courses for the dominant professional curricula in schools. Others want to promote forms of Science-Technology-Society (STS) programs. Finally, some wish to resurrect aspects of the minority liberal education tradition in science teaching, a tradition that gives more recognition to the history and philosophy of science in science programs.

Commitment to aspects of this liberal educational tradition is manifest in numerous international reform reports and curricula (McComas and Olson, 1998). Among these are the American Association for the Advancement of Science in two of its influential reports, *Project 2061* (AAAS, 1989) and *The Liberal Art of Science* (AAAS, 1990); the USA National Science Education Standards developed by the National Research Council (NRC, 1996); the British National Curriculum Council (NCC, 1988, 1991); the Science Council of Canada (SCC, 1984); the Danish Science and Technology curriculum (Nielsen and Thomsen, 1990); and the Norwegian Core Curriculum (RMCER, 1994).

The American Association for the Advancement of Science (AAAS) in 1989 published *Project 2061: Science for All Americans* (AAAS, 1989), which was its blueprint for the long-term reform of science, mathematics, and social science education in the USA. This report bristles with philosopical claims and assumptions bearing on the work of science educators. For example, chapter 1 is on "the nature of science" and it includes discussions of objectivity, the mutability of science, the possible ways to demarcate science from pseudo-science, evidence and its relation to theory justification, scientific method, explanation and prediction, ethics, social policy, and the social organization of science. The report recommends that these themes be developed and discussed within the existing structure of science courses, without adding additional topics or substituting HPS content for science content, and that pupils completing school science be expected to know something of these themes.

The Norwegian National Curriculum says of science education that:

Teaching must also illuminate the ethical issues raised by science itself, and the moral judgements which are required when new knowledge engenders new choices. The human thinking that transcends the limits for what is possible, must be met with the humanistic tradition which sets the limits for what is possible. (RMCER, 1994, p. 15)

Clearly all these curricular exhortations depend on teachers having philosophical acumen and knowledge in order to understand, appraise, and enact them. This requires a mixture of philosophy of science (to understand the substantial claims), and of philosophy of education (to interpret and embrace the objectives of the curricula).

The Liberal Tradition

Proponents of this liberal tradition share, for the most part, the following commitments:

1 Truths about the natural world can be ascertained by the human mind.
2 Science provides our best understanding of the natural world.
3 Science endeavors to make truthful factual and theoretical claims about the world, not just useful or instrumental ones.
4 Science is rational in its methodology and processes, and scientific processes are the best available for ascertaining truths about the world.
5 Science is a cultural achievement of immense worth, and its factual claims cannot be countermanded by social or cultural authorities.
6 The scientific world view needs to inform our understanding of ourselves and our place in the world.
7 Science is crucial for solving countless personal and social ills.

There are of course legitimate issues about the interpretation of these seven claims – for instance, whether or not science lays claim just to factual truths or to theoretical ones as well – but their basic thrust is agreed to by adherents to the longstanding liberal tradition in science education. This liberal tradition in science education is an heir to more general Enlightenment movements of the seventeenth and eighteenth centuries (Shimony, 1997). To this extent the liberal tradition has seen school science education as having an important cultural role, impact, and responsibility. Science classes are not merely introducing students to truths about the world, but are also introducing them to a certain cultural tradition, the tradition of the Enlightenment. Perhaps the best known liberal programs are Harvard Project Physics (Rutherford et al., 1970; Holton, 1978), the Yellow Version of BSCS Biology (Schwab, 1963), and Conant's Harvard Case Studies in Experimental Science (Conant, 1957).

John Dewey expressed well this tradition's hope for science education when he said:

Our predilection for premature acceptance and assertion, our aversion to suspended judgment, are signs that we tend naturally to cut short the process of testing. We are satisified with superficial and immediate short-visioned applications.... Science represents the safeguard of the race against these natural propensities and the evils which flow from them.... It is artificial (an acquired art), not spontaneous; learned, not native. To this fact is due the unique, the invaluable place of science in education. (Dewey, 1916, p. 189)

In England, and contemporary with Dewey, Fredrick Westaway, a member of His Majesty's Inspectorate and an author of books on scientific method and on history of science, was also advocating the liberal view of science teaching, believing that such teaching contributed to individual rationality and, ultimately, to a more mature society. In his 1929 text, which was widely used in teacher education programs, he wrote that a successful science teacher is one who:

knows [his or her] own subject...is widely read in other branches of science...knows how to teach...is able to express [himself or herself] lucidly...is skilful in manipulation...is a logician . . . is something of a philosopher . . . is so far an historian that [he or she] can sit down with a crowd of [students] and talk to them about the personal equations, the lives, and the work of such geniuses as Galileo, Newton, Faraday and Darwin. More than all this, [he or she] is an enthusiast, full of faith in [his or her] own particular work. (Westaway, 1929, p. 3)

It is clear that, for Westaway, the philosophy of education that enables him to identify a "successful" science teacher leads straight into the history and philosophy of science.

In the USA, the National Science Foundation curricular reforms of the early 1960s brought back into science education some of Dewey's and Mach's concerns about the nature of science. (They notably left aside the earlier conviction that history of science bore upon our understanding of the nature of science.) Most of the NSF curricula stressed the importance of understanding the *structure of science*, which they regarded as synonomous with the nature of science. In this respect they again display the interweaving of PE and PS concerns. The famous Woods Hole conference of 1959, elaborated in Jerome Bruner's Conference Report, *The Process of Education*, maintained that:

the curriculum of a subject should be determined by the most fundamental understanding that can be achieved of the underlying principles that give structure to that subject. Teaching specific topics or skills without making clear their context in the broader fundamental structure of a field of knowledge is uneconomical in several deep senses. (Bruner, 1960, p. 31)

Joseph Schwab, the Chicago biologist, educational philosopher and driving force behind the Biological Science Curriculum Study, was one of the most eloquent and forceful advocates of the importance of teachers understanding the conceptual structure of science. In another influential essay, on inquiry learning and its connection to conceptual structure, he remarked that:

enquiry has its origin in a conceptual structure. . . . It is this conceptual structure through which we are able to formulate a telling question. It is through the telling question that we know what data to seek and what experiments to perform to get those data. Once the data are in hand, the same conceptual structure tells us how to interpret them, what to make of them by way of knowledge. Finally, the knowledge itself is formulated in terms provided by the same conception. (Schwab, 1964, p. 12)

A good example of a 1960s science educator who took such arguments seriously is James T. Robinson, who aptly observed that in the post-Sputnik era the infusion of reading materials and "packaged laboratory exercises" into classrooms in the USA had proceeded without a well grounded conception of how those readings and exercises would yield a better understanding of science (Robinson, 1965, 1968).

Some, if not all, of the tenets of the liberal tradition have been severely challenged by contemporary anti-scientific movements, by postmodernist writers, and by numerous sociologists of scientific knowledge. Science teachers and curriculum writers have a stake in the Science Wars. One prominent science educator, for instance, has claimed that recent HPS studies have established that science is: "mechanistic, materialist, reductionist, empirical, rational, decontextualized, mathematically

345

idealized, communal, ideological, masculine, elitist, competitive, exploitive, imper- sonal, and violent" (Aikenhead, 1997, p. 220). In other words, not such a nice thing, and something whose very teaching would need to be justified. Again the PE questions will depend upon answers to PS questions, in this case: how correct, if at all, are modern critics of science?

Not surprisingly, the Science Wars have been fought out within curriculum writing teams. This has been especially so in the United States, where even the National Science Education Standards are somewhat ambiguous about the claims of rational, realist liberalism versus those of relativist, instrumentalist postmodernism (Good and Shymansky, 2001).

HPS and Science Pedagogy

Twenty-five years ago Robert Ennis listed six questions that science teachers con- stantly encounter in their classrooms and staffrooms. What characterizes the scien- tific method? What constitutes critical thinking about empirical statements? What is the structure of scientific disciplines? What is a scientific explanation? What role do value judgments play in the work of scientists? What constitute good tests of scientific understanding? (Ennis, 1979). These questions are of perennial concern to science teachers, and clearly their answers depend upon views about the nature of science.

Philosophy is not far below the surface in any science classroom. At a most basic level any text or scientific discussion will contain terms such as "law," "theory," "model," "explanation," "cause," "truth," "knowledge," "hypothesis," "confirm- ation," "observation," "evidence," "idealization." Philosophy begins when students and teachers slow down the science lesson and ask what these terms mean and what the conditions are for their correct use. All of these concepts contribute to, and in part arise from, philosophical investigation of epistemological and metaphysical questions: questions about what things can be known and how we can know them, and about what things actually exist in the world and how they are related to one another.

Students and teachers can be encouraged to ask the philosopher's standard ques- tions about these concepts: "What do you mean by...?" and "How do you know...?" Such introductory philosophical analysis allows greater appreciation of the distinct empirical and conceptual issues involved when, for instance, Boyle's Law, Dalton's model, or Darwin's theory is discussed. This analysis is the beginning of students' understanding of the nature of science.

Attempts to introduce students to scientific methods through laboratory work and experimental inquiries have been a staple of science teaching, and provide a basis for further elementary philosophical reflection on the nature of science. The potential of such an approach is rarely fulfilled, however, in some instances because the labora- tory experiences students are offered rely crucially on mistaken conceptions of science. An example of this is the common assumption that students equipped with simple pendulums will be able to set those pendulums in motion and discover the laws of pendular motion by induction from what they observe. This is an assumption encouraged by textbook accounts of Galileo's discovery of the law of pendular isochrony (that the duration of passage through an arc is invariant, whatever the length of the arc, for a pendulum of a given length), which hold that he made the discovery during a church service by timing with his own pulse the arcs of a chandelier set in motion by the breeze. The message which often accompanies such accounts is that Galilean kinematics and the rise of modern science in general were made possible by nothing more complicated than a willingness to learn the ways of nature by *observing* them. Implicit in this are two faulty assumptions about the nature of science which have figured importantly in the theory and practice of school science: (1) that scientific thinking is *natural* and continuous with everyday thinking; (2) that science is straightforwardly empirical and inductive – that scientific concepts are straightforwardly obtainable through perceptual experience and scientific laws are inductively derived from observation. These are not inconsequential errors. Students have difficulty observing pendular isochrony, because *actual* pendulums are not isochronic – a point lodged in opposition to Galileo's idealized mathematical proof, his "world on paper," by many of the experimentalists of his day. The oft repeated account of Galileo's discovery of pendular isochrony in the church at Pisa is apocryphal, and the true story of pendular motion and its role in his invention of classical mechanics is far more interesting. It is a story deeply interwoven with not only the lingering influence and overthrow of Aristotelian empiricism, but also the history of timekeeping, navigation, and global exploration. An accurate sense of this history would not only spare students the frustration of attempting to repeat what never happened in the first place, but would enable teachers to lead students toward a much richer understanding of science as a human enterprise. (For details see Matthews, 1994, chapter 6, and especially 2000b.)

Contemporary Philosophical Concerns

In the past two decades the quantity, if not always the quality, of philosophical work in science education has been unprecedented. There have been at least four hundred papers published (Bell et al., 2001); one journal, *Science and Education*, is dedicated to the subject; a number of books and anthologies have been published (Duschl, 1990; Matthews, 1991, 1994, 2000a; Duschl and Hamiliton, 1992); and at least ten international academic conferences have been staged, each with substantial proceedings. In 1998 an *International Handbook of Science Education* (Fraser and Tobin, 1998) was published that included among its ten sections a section titled "History and Philosophy of Science." The titles of the eight essays in this HPS section are suggestive of the range of current philosophical concern: "The Nature of Science and Science Teaching," "Science and the Ideals of Liberal Education," "The History of Physics and European Physics Education," "History and Philosophy of Science in the Science Curriculum," "Conceptual Change in Science and in the Learning of Science," "Feminisms and Science Education," "Values in Science and in Science Education," "Preservice Teachers' Classroom Practice and Their Conceptions of the Nature of Science," and "Constructivism: Value Added."

Traditionally, as in the above liberal programmes and texts, it has been deliberations about curricular content that have moved science educators to engage with the historical and philosophical dimensions of science (HPS). These curricular

347

deliberations have embraced not only the subject-matter content of the curriculum, but also the all-important areas of scientific methodology, processes, and attitudes that the curriculum was supposed to cultivate. From the time of Dewey's seminal essay (Dewey, 1910), if not before, most advocates of science education believed that both scientific subject-matter knowledge and scientific method or ways of thinking should be cultivated in schools. And clearly the specification of these methodological, process, and attitudinal matters involves philosophical considerations.

These curriculum-driven concerns with HPS have continued. In the 1980s and 1990s knowledge of the nature of science was written into most countries' definitions of science literacy. It was no longer just an internal matter for students who were to pursue science studies, but became a hoped-for part of the education of all citizens, part of what was called "Science for All." In 1993 Yvonne Meichtry wrote: "The definitions of scientific literacy reported in the literature over the past three decades all emphasize the importance of an understanding of the nature of science" (Meichtry, 1993, p. 429).

But it is no longer just curricular matters that are driving philosophical investigations of the teaching of science. Questions about the nature of science have spread from their standard niche in curriculum theory to discussions about learning theory, conceptual change studies, teacher education, women and science, multicultural science education, environmental ethics, and constructivist theory. There is hardly an area of science education that is not touched by epistemological considerations such as: What is human knowledge? What is the difference between student belief and student knowledge? What is distinctive about scientific knowledge? Is there a scientific method? In what sense is science objective? How does science relate to mathematics and other areas of human knowledge? How do metaphysical commitments or world views affect the creation and learning of scientific knowledge? Is science value-free? Is there a feminine way of knowing? Do scientific theories make claims about the world or merely about experience?

The creation science debates and trials in the USA in large part hinged upon answers to the question: what is the nature of science? This was explicitly the case in the 1981 Little Rock trial over the constitutionality of Arkansas's Act 590 requiring equal time for the teaching of creation science and evolutionary science (see Ruse, 1988). These issues have been notoriously replayed in the more recent Kansas evolution debates.

Likewise, the widespread debates occurring at the present time over multicultural science also, in part, hinge upon answers to the question: what is the nature of science? That is, there is an epistemological question at issue in the debate. If one can establish that non-Western sciences or world views are indeed scientific, then their inclusion in the science curriculum is more easily justified.

That these epistemological debates concerning the nature of science are not educationally idle has been dramatically shown in decisions by a string of major cities in the USA to adopt the *Portland Baseline Essays* in their science programs (Martel, 1991). The science component of these essays lists a number of commitments that are flatly at odds with a Western-scientific view of the world (see Good and Demastes, 1995). But the claim is made that the Western view is just one of a number of equally valid scientific views, and this is thought to justify including in the curriculum the purportedly African science contained in the *Portland Baseline Essays*.

Constructivism and Philosophy

Perhaps overshadowing all of the foregoing claimants for philosophical attention in science education is constructivism. Constructivism is a major influence in contemporary science education: indeed, many would say it is *the* major influence. It is also a significant influence in mathematics, literary, artistic, social science, and religious education. Frequently, feminist and multiculturalist proposals in science education are put forward in a way that simply *assumes* constructivist pedagogical, epistemological, and ontological positions. For many, constructivism has become part of educational orthodoxy. And although constructivism began as a theory of learning to the effect that knowledge cannot be transmitted from teacher to learner but must be constructed anew by each learner, it has expanded its dominion, becoming a theory of teaching, a theory of education, a theory of educational administration, a theory of the origin of ideas, a theory of both personal knowledge and scientific knowledge, and even a metaphysical and ideological position. Constructivism has become education's version of a grand unified theory.

Many in the education community have not merely adopted constructivism in teaching method, or constructivism in learning theory, or constructivism in curriculum development, but they have also adopted constructivist epistemology, whereby truth is abandoned and knowledge claims are judged by their instrumental value, and a constructivist account of the nature of science, whereby consensus among scientists constitutes scientific knowledge. The spread of constructivist interest, or theorizing, is apparent in the remarks of one adherent who writes that "this approach [constructivism] holds promise for the pursuit of educational objectives other than those associated exclusively with cognitive development... the constructivist point of view makes it possible to develop a vision of the whole educational phenomena [*sic*] which is comprehensive and penetrating" (Pépin, 1998, p. 173). Another writes that "Constructivism is a postmodern theory of knowledge with the potential to transform educational theory" (Fleury, 1998, p. 156). It is thus not surprising that, "For several years now, across the country [USA], preservice and in-service teachers have been considering constructivism as a referent for their philosophies of education" (Bentley, 1998, p. 244). Constructivism is not just a theory about learning, teaching, and philosophy of education – significant though those subjects are. It is also put forward as a theory of science. As Bentley says, "Indeed as an epistemology, constructivism speaks to the nature of science" (Bentley, 1998, p. 243). If it does so speak, then it has a claim to our attention: few things are more important than understanding the nature of science.

Constructivist philosophy of education claims roots in philosophy of science. Joseph Novak, in the preface to his pioneering constructivist work, *A Theory of Education* (Novak, 1977, p. 5), writes that: "In philosophy, a consensus emerges that positivism is neither a valid nor a productive view of epistemology.... What is emerging is a *constructivist* view of epistemology, building on ideas of Kuhn, Toulmin and others." Most leading constructivists acknowledge Kuhn as the fount of their relativist epistemology and their constructivist view of science. Derek Hodson wrote: "It has been argued earlier that Kuhnian models of science and scientific practice have a direct equivalent in psychology in the constructivist theories of learning. There is, therefore, a strong case for constructing curriculum along Kuhnian lines" (Hodson, 1988, p. 32). And David Hawkins, in an article on the history of constructivism, wrote that Kuhn's *Structure* provided "'constructivist' justification" for "philosophies of relativism and subjectivism" (Hawkins, 1994, p. 10).

In 2000, Cathleen Loving and William Cobern conducted a citation analysis of two major science education journals for the thirteen-year period 1985–98 and, not surprisingly, found that there were numerous citations of Kuhn covering such Kuhnian themes as: paradigms (30 articles), conceptual change theory, constructivist epistemology, incommensurability, authenticity of textbooks, the social components of science, and the philosophical comparison of Kuhn and other methodologists of science (Loving and Cobern, 2000). Tellingly, they comment that in all of the Kuhnian-inspired corpus of science education articles there is not a single critical voice; the science education community has turned into an "admiration society for Thomas Kuhn" (Loving and Cobern, 2000, p.199).

The presumption that Kuhnian historicism is all the philosophy of science that the philosophy of science education needs is misguided, and there have been trenchant criticisms of constructivist epistemology in general, and of its Kuhnian roots in particular (Suchting, 1992; Matthews, 1994, chapter 7, 1998, 2000a; Phillips, 1995, 1997; Nola, 1997). What must be recognized, however, is that constructivism has propelled nature of science considerations onto centerstage in science education, and that the position is a further example of a philosophy of education being dependent upon, or at least interwoven with, a philosophy of science.

Conclusion

Science programs in any scheme of liberal education will include discussion of the nature of science – its history, methodology, philosophy, social and cultural impacts, and relation to other forms of knowledge. And all but the most impoverished technical programs will also include some aspects of the nature of science, its methodology, and the meaning of such central concepts as law, theory, model, confirmation, idealization, and so on. It is not surprising that a wide range of contemporary curricula are incorporating nature of science topics. But as Marx asked in the nineteenth century, who will educate the educators? Taking seriously the nature of science requires an alteration in the curriculum of most teacher education programmes, or else the provision of appropriate in-service courses. It remains to be seen how this can be done.

See also 6 ENLIGHTENMENT LIBERALISM; 16 THEORIES OF TEACHING AND LEARNING; 20 KNOWLEDGE, TRUTH, AND LEARNING; 21 CULTIVATING REASON; 25 TEACHING ELEMENTARY ARITHMETIC THROUGH APPLICATIONS; 42 THE ETHICS OF RESEARCH

References

Aikenhead, G. S. (1997) Towards a first nations cross-cultural science and technology curriculum. *Science Education*, 81(2), 217–38.

AAAS (1989) *Project 2061: Science for all Americans*. Washington, DC: American Association for the Advancement of Science.

AAAS (1990) *The Liberal Art of Science: Agenda for Action*. Washington, DC: American Association for the Advancement of Science.

Bell, R., Abd-el-Khalick, F., Lederman, N. G., McComas, W. F., and Matthews, M. R. (2001) The nature of science and science education: a bibliography. *Science and Education*, 10(1/2), 187–204.

Bentley, M. L. (1998) Constructivism as a referent for reforming science education. In M. Larochelle, N. Bednarz, and J. Garrison (eds), *Constructivism and Education*. New York: Cambridge University Press, pp. 233–49.

Bruner, J. S. (1960) *The Process of Education*. New York: Random House.

Conant, J. B. (ed.) (1957) *Harvard Case Histories in Experimental Science*, two volumes. Cambridge, MA: Harvard University Press (originally published 1948).

Dewey, J. (1910) Science as subject-matter and as method. *Science*, 31, 121–7. Reproduced in *Science and Education*, 1995, 4(4), 391–8.

Dewey, J. (1916) *Democracy and Education*. New York: Macmillan Company.

Duschl, R. A. (1985) Science education and philosophy of science: twenty-five years of mutually exclusive development. *School Science and Mathematics*, 87(7), 541–55.

Duschl, R. A. and Hamilton, R. J. (eds) (1992) *Philosophy of Science, Cognitive Psychology, and Educational Theory and Practice*. Albany: State University of New York Press.

Ennis, R. H. (1979) Research in philosophy of science bearing on science education. In P. D. Asquith and H. E. Kyburg (eds), *Current Research in Philosophy of Science*. East Lansing, MI: PSA, pp. 138–70.

Fleury, S. C. (1998) Social studies, trivial constructivism, and the politics of social knowledge. In M. Larochelle, N. Bednarz and J. Garrison (eds), *Constructivism and Education*. New York: Cambridge University Press, pp. 156–72.

Fraser, B. J. and Tobin, K. G. (eds) (1998) *International Handbook of Science Education*. Dordrecht: Kluwer Academic Publishers.

Good, R. G. and Demastes, S. (1995) The diminished role of nature in postmodern views of science and science education. In F. Finley et al. (eds), *Proceedings of the Third International History, Philosophy, and Science Teaching Conference*. Minneapolis: University of Minnesota Press, pp. 480–7.

Good, R. G. and Shymansky, J. (2001) Nature-of-science literacy in *Benchmarks* and *standards*: postmodern/relativist or modern/realist? *Science and Education*, 10(1/2), 173–85.

Hawkins, D. (1994) Constructivism: some history. In P. Fensham, R. Gunstone, and R. White (eds), *The Content of Science: A Constructivist Approach to Its Teaching and Learning*. London: Falmer Press, pp. 9–13.

Hodson, D. (1988) Toward a philosophically more valid science curriculum. *Science Education*, 72, 19–40.

Holton, G. (1978) On the educational philosophy of the project physics course. In *The Scientific Imagination: Case Studies*. Cambridge: Cambridge University Press, pp. 284–98.

Loving, C. C. and Cobern, W. A. (2000) Invoking Thomas Kuhn: what citation analysis reveals for science education. *Science and Education*, 9(1/2), 187–206.

McComas, W. F. and Olson, J. K. (1998) The nature of science in international science education standards documents. In W. F. McComas (ed.), *The Nature of Science in*

Science Education: Rationales and Strategies. Dordrecht: Kluwer Academic Publishers, pp. 41–52.

Martel, E. (1991) How valid are the Portland Baseline Essays? *Educational Leadership*, December/January, 20–3.

Matthews, M. R. (ed.) (1991) *History, Philosophy, and Science Teaching: Selected Readings*. New York: Teachers College Press.

Matthews, M. R. (1994) *Science Teaching: The Role of History and Philosophy of Science*. New York: Routledge.

Matthews, M. R. (ed.) (1998) *Constructivism and Science Education: A Philosophical Examination*. Dordrecht: Kluwer Academic Publishers.

Matthews, M. R. (2000a) Constructivism in science and mathematics education. In D. C. Phillips (ed.), *National Society for the Study of Education 99th Yearbook*. Chicago: National Society for the Study of Education, pp. 161–92.

Matthews, M. R. (2000b) *Time for Science Education: How Teaching the History and Philosophy of Pendulum Motion Can Contribute to Science Literacy*. New York: Kluwer Academic Publishers.

Meichtry, Y. J. (1993) The impact of science curricula on student views about the nature of science. *Journal of Research in Science Teaching*, 30(5), 429–44.

NCC (1988) *Science in the National Curriculum*. York: National Curriculum Council.

NCC (1991) *Science for Ages 5 to 16*. York: National Curriculum Council.

Nielsen, H. and Thomsen, P. (1990) History and philosophy of science in the Danish curriculum. *International Journal of Science Education*, 12(4), 308–16.

Nola, R. (1997) Constructivism in science and in science education: a philosophical critique. *Science and Education*, 6(1/2), 55–83.

Novak, J. D. (1977) *A Theory of Education*. Ithaca, NY: Cornell University Press.

National Research Council (1996) *National Science Education Standards*. Washington, DC: National Academy Press.

Pépin, Y. (1998) Practical knowledge and school knowledge: a constructivist representation of education. In M. Larochelle, N. Bednarz, and J. Garrison (eds), *Constructivism and Education*. New York: Cambridge University Press, pp. 173–92.

Phillips, D. C. (1995) The good, the bad and the ugly: the many faces of constructivism. *Educational Researcher*, 24(7), 5–12.

Phillips, D. C. (1997) Coming to terms with radical social constructivisms. *Science and Education*, 6(1/2), 85–104.

RMCER (1994) *Core Curriculum for Primary, Secondary, and Adult Education in Norway*. Oslo: Royal Ministry of Church, Education and Research.

Robinson, J. T. (1965) Science teaching and the nature of science. *Journal of Research in Science Teaching*, 3, 37–50.

Robinson, J. T. (1968) *The Nature of Science and Science Teaching*. Belmont, CA: Wadsworth.

Ruse, M. (ed.) (1988) *But Is It Science? The Philosophical Question in the Creation/Evolution Controversy*. Albany, NY: Prometheus Books.

Rutherford, F. J., Holton, G., and Watson, F. G. (eds) (1970) *The Project Physics Course: Text*. New York: Holt, Rinehart, & Winston.

SCC (1984) *Science for Every Student*. Report 36. Ottawa: Science Council of Canada.

Scheffler, I. (1973) Philosophy and the curriculum. In *Reason and Teaching*. London: Routledge, pp. 31–44.

Schwab, J. J. (1963) *Biology Teacher's Handbook*. New York: Wiley.

Schwab, J. J. (1964) Structure of the disciplines: meaning and significances. In G. W. Ford and L. Pugno (eds), *The Structure of Knowledge and the Curriculum*. Chicago: Rand McNally & Co.

Shimony, A. (1997) Some historical and philosophical reflections on science and enlighten-ment. In L. Darden (ed.), *Proceedings of the 1996 PSA Meeting*. East Lansing, MI: PSA, pp. 1–14.

Suchting, W. A. (1992) Constructivism deconstructed. *Science and Education*, 1(3), 223–54.

Westaway, F. W. (1929) *Science Teaching*. London: Blackie and Son.

25

Teaching Elementary Arithmetic through Applications

Mark Steiner

Philosophers since Plato (recall the slave boy in the *Meno*) have tried to draw insight into mathematics, the infinite, and philosophy in general from mathematics instruction – indeed, from the very fact that we can teach mathematics to children. As far as I know, the only major philosopher who actually engaged in mathematics instruction on the primary school level was Ludwig Wittgenstein, and the experience profoundly influenced his positions. For example, the *Philosophical Investigations* (Wittgenstein, 1968), Part I, is largely devoted to rules and rule following. (For an enlightening discussion see Kripke (1982). I maintain that this emphasis derives from his experience as a teacher, and hope to develop this theme elsewhere.)

It is only natural, then, that educators will attempt to do the converse: to gain insight into teaching mathematics from philosophy. Philosophers, certainly, have not been averse to advertising their own theories by drawing educational conclusions from them. For Plato, the road to mathematics instruction is to lift the soul from the muck of sensory experience; for John Stuart Mill, the trick is, on the contrary, to drag it back down from the heaven of Platonic Ideas to the firm ground of empirical reality. For René Descartes the role of the mathematics teacher is to inculcate "clear and distinct ideas." Bertrand Russell claims (at the conclusion of Russell, 1924) that before his own work in "showing" that arithmetic is nothing but formal logic, no one had really understood why $2 + 2 = 4$.

Where educators have taken philosophy seriously, the results have been mixed, or so it seems to this outsider. The "new math" in the United States, I believe, was an attempt to apply Russell's "logicist" program to education. Educators, however, did not seem to know that by the time they got around to doing this, the logicist idea had largely been repudiated by the philosophical community, because of the failure of Russell (and his collaborator Alfred North Whitehead) to make good on their promise to reduce arithmetic to a formal system that could plausibly be called "logic." In the case of what is called "social constructivism," often attributed to Wittgenstein, we also have the possibility that educators may be misreading the philosopher (as I argue below).

Even where the philosophy is true and understood properly (as I hope mine is in this chapter), caution must be exercised. Philosophy, I hold, is a discipline by itself; a search for truth. One cannot rule out the possibility that philosophical distinctions sometimes impede mathematical skill, just as unphilosophical conflations may well have greased the wheels of mathematical invention. Thus, the educator must read this chapter, on the distinction between mathematics and its applications, at his or her own risk.

Logical Applications

The power and importance of arithmetic, but also the difficulties that arise in teaching it, have a common source: the natural numbers can be viewed both as cardinals and as ordinals. This means, roughly, that we can determine the size of a set of objects by counting them (in any order): $1, 2, \ldots, n$ – and then n, the last number in the list, is the cardinality of the set. It also means that cardinal and ordinal arithmetic on the natural numbers are equivalent.

Consider, for example, the operations of addition and multiplication on the natural numbers. There are two equivalent and indispensable definitions for each of these operations on natural numbers (though the proof of the equivalence is not elementary). Each definition corresponds to an educational, as well as a mathematical, goal: one of them allows calculation; the other, application.

We can, first, define addition and multiplication by *recursion*, because we think of addition as repeating the successor operation, and of multiplication as repeating the addition operation. (Definitions by recursion are associated with the role of the natural numbers as ordinals, as Carl Posy pointed out to me.) We sum up these ideas in the recursion equations:

$$m + 0 = m \tag{1}$$

$$m + Sn = S(m + n) \tag{2}$$

$$m \times 0 = 0 \tag{3}$$

$$m \times Sn = m \times n + m \tag{4}$$

Strictly speaking, these are not definitions, because the signs $+$ and $\times$ appear on both sides of the equations (2) and (4), respectively, but each set of equations can be proved to characterize a unique function. Furthermore, these equations are in effect algorithms which allow the calculation of the value of the functions when the arguments are given in the form $SSSS \ldots S0$. (The arithmetic of infinite cardinals, on the other hand, lacks algorithms for calculation; as a result, set theorists cannot compute even the simplest results in cardinal arithmetic such as the value of 2 to the power $\aleph_0$.)

Where the arguments are given in the decimal notation, other algorithms are used, and these can be derived from the basic recursion equations as above, using standard mathematics (e.g. "Peano's" – really Dedekind's – postulates, which include mathematical induction). Standard mathematics also enables us to prove the basic laws of arithmetic, such as the commutativity of addition and multiplication and the distributive law. These standard laws of arithmetic are what is needed to validate the usual algorithms we use in decimal arithmetic – once we regard each decimal number as a polynomial in 10 (cf. Wu, 1999; compare Steiner, 1975, chapter 2). Unfortunately, the proof of these laws from the recursion equations (and mathematical induction) is far beyond the scope of grade school arithmetic. My experience in teaching formal arithmetic is that most college students (I won't say where) cannot discover unaided the proof of the commutativity of multiplication by induction, and many cannot reproduce it after they learn it (for details, see Mendelson, 1997).

Now, although the definitions by recursion provide algorithms for calculation, they do not by themselves account for the application of arithmetic: though $3 + 2$ is determined to be 5 ($SSSSS0$), and 4×3 to be 12, by the recursion equations, it is not yet clear why 3 apples and 2 apples make 5 apples, or why 4 children with exactly 3 candies each have exactly 12 candies. Thus, teaching algorithms alone is insufficient (though necessary).

Enter the second series of definitions. The natural numbers are identified as the cardinality of (finite) sets. Arithmetic is now understood as determination of the cardinality of some sets, given those of others. For example, if

$$\text{card } (X) = m,$$
$$\text{card } (Y) = n,$$
$$X \cap Y = \phi$$

then we *define* $m + n = \text{card}(X \cup Y)$.
We can also define

$$m \times n = \text{card } (X \times Y)$$
$$X \times Y = \{\langle x, y \rangle \mid x \in X, \; y \in Y\}$$

From this definition, unlike the recursive one, it is obvious that multiplication is commutative. Also, from the definition, we can prove, using elementary set theory, that if we have m disjoint sets each of cardinality n, the cardinality of the union of all the sets is that of $m \times n$, and this is therefore also the cardinality of the union of n disjoint sets of m elements each. This yields a more useful, though still set theoretical, definition of multiplication, one which befits the expression "m times n," meaning iterating the union of a set with n objects, m times.

To "apply" addition and multiplication, according to these definitions, is nothing but specifying the sets X and Y. Put another way, the logical operations of disjoint union and cross products of two sets are represented by addition and multiplication by a homomorphism: the sets are mapped to the cardinals; and disjoint union and cross products are mapped to addition and multiplication. Because the operations represented are logical operations, I call this an example of *logical application*.

Empirical Applications

There is another kind of application, in which the arithmetic operations represent empirical operations or relations; accordingly, we call these *empirical applications*. An example would be weighing. Define the "fusion" of two objects, A and B, A $\oplus$ B, as the "smallest" thing such that A and B are parts of it. More precisely, following David Lewis and others, A ⊕ B is that thing such that A and B are part of it, and such that no part of it is distinct from both A and B (Lewis, 1991, pp. 72–4). (Lewis's untimely death prevents me from expressing my deep gratitude personally.) If A and B are physical bodies (cf. definition below), we have a homomorphism: Weight(A ⊕ B) = Weight(A) + Weight(B). This is an empirical statement, which could turn out to be false (indeed, according to Einstein's theory of relativity it is in fact false, since the gravitational field is not quite linear).

Another example is tiling a rectangular floor, or areas. The number of equal square tiles we need along the base, times the number of tiles we need along the altitude, gives us the number of tiles we need to cover the rectangle.

When I say that tiling is an empirical application of multiplication I am adopting the modern point of view, which differs from Euclid's in two ways. First, for Euclid, multiplication is itself a geometrical operation, where lines are "multiplied" to get areas. It is true of course that these lines can have integral lengths, but even in those cases, what we are really multiplying are magnitudes, not natural numbers in the modern sense. As an example of the difference, note that magnitudes are not closed under multiplication. The second difference between Euclid's treatment and ours is that we today tend to regard Euclidean geometry as a physical hypothesis. That we can calculate in advance the number of tiles we need to cover a floor by multiplying presupposes that the floor is, or approximates, a Euclidean rectangle. Where the floor is non-Euclidean (i.e. some other surface), we will not be able to use simple multiplication.

The upshot of these two remarks is: once the natural numbers have been divested of their garb as magnitudes, i.e. once they are pure numbers, and once we realize that Euclidean geometry is a contingent (and probably only approximately true) description of the spatial world, we reach the conclusion that tiling is an *empirical application* of multiplication, where the operation is understood in the modern sense.

The concept of area applies even when the sides of a rectangle are incommensurable, as the Greeks found out to their dismay. The corresponding extension of multiplication to an operation on the "reals" was, it seems plausible, an abstraction of the concept of area to give it a quantitative description in all cases. We say that area is a *canonical empirical application* of *real* multiplication. Once multiplication becomes an operation on abstract objects ("real numbers"), it can be applied to magnitudes other than length and area; for example, to get the gravitational force between two mass points M and m, we multiply the two masses, and apply the gravitational constant, arriving at GMm, where all three numbers need not be rational. This is a simple example of a general point: beginning with an empirical phenomenon, we construct a mathematical theory which describes the phenomenon. Then, abstracting out the mathematical structure from this theory, we find new applications for the mathematics which may be quite remote from the original one. There is thus an important role for abstraction and the study of formalisms in mathematics education – this is the legacy of "structuralism" in the philosophy of mathematics, whatever we are to make of its more sweeping claims.

Nevertheless, the teaching of elementary arithmetic seems to rest on applications, not abstractions, and I now explore the ways and the extent to which different kinds of applications are used in mathematics instruction.

A useful distinction can be drawn between strong and weak uses of empirical applications in mathematics instruction. Strong uses of applications persuade the students that a mathematical proposition is true by way of an empirical application. Empirical facts thus become, as it were, evidence for the mathematics. Weak uses of applications use empirical applications to awaken mathematical intuition, to make mathematical propositions obvious or perspicuous to the student, but do not serve as the ground for believing the propositions.

The use of geometry in arithmetic gives some good examples of both strong and weak use of applications. Tiling, for example, could be used to teach, not only to apply, multiplication. Suppose we replace the tiles by dots, as is often done in teaching arithmetic, and we count the dots in a rectangular array by multiplying the number of dots in the base by the number in the altitude. We are still tacitly relying on the Euclidean nature of the plane; if space were severely warped, we could not arrange the dots in an array which is even close to the rectangular lattice. This is no longer, however, an *application* of multiplication to geometry. Geometry is here being used not to prove anything, or even to argue for anything, but simply to make the proof surveyable or perspicuous in the sense invoked by Wittgenstein in his *Remarks on the Foundations of Mathematics* (RFM) (Wittgenstein, 1978, Part III). Aside from lining up the dots in rows and columns, we could, as Wittgenstein suggests, improve further the surveyability of the proof by making loops around the rows or columns.

There are, however, things a teacher could do with dots which do count as true empirical applications of multiplication. For example, one could teach the commutativity of multiplication by drawing a rectangular lattice of dots, making the canonical connection between the number of dots and the area of the rectangle, and then pointing out that the area remains constant when the rectangle is rotated a quarter turn, permuting the base with the altitude.

This particular argument by rotation is, to be sure, not necessary (as Stanley Ocken pointed out to me). Without rotating the dots, we could still teach commutativity by putting loops around the rows, and then loops around the columns – so that we have a picture of, first, the union of m sets of n members each, and then the union of n sets of m members each.

Nevertheless, the argument using geometry has the great advantage that multiplication, an operation on two like entities (i.e. numbers), here represents the Greek operation of "multiplying" lines by lines; the area later being marked by dots. The diagram with "loops," by contrast, is a model of the concept of multiplication where "$m \times n$" means the cardinality of the disjoint union of m sets with n members each, so that, although multiplication is "extensionally" a commutative binary operation on the natural numbers, the "intensional" or "conceptual" *role* of the first operand is different from that of the second. (The discrepancy in the role of the operands is always present in recursive definitions; what is new here is a discrepancy in the set theoretical definition of the operations.)

It is becoming clear that the operation of multiplication is in some sense more set theoretical than that of addition. True, addition is set theoretical in that numbers are regarded as characteristics (cardinalities) of sets. Without this, as we have argued, addition could not be applied. Yet multiplication is set theoretical in a much deeper sense, which I must now describe (with thanks to Carl Posy for helping me clarify the issues).

A set S of physical objects is not a physical object. What is often mistaken for the set S, and what is a (perhaps scattered) physical object is the sum or "fusion" of the elements of S, which we have defined above. The mistake is understandable; the fusion of the elements of S bears an analogy to the set S, to the extent that we can think of the fusion as an empirical application of the set.

We think of the set S as a collection of physical objects, abstracted from details of order or place. (Of course there can be sets of non-physical objects, but they will not concern us.) The set S itself is not a physical object. Now, the fusion of these very objects *is* a physical object, but the part/whole relation plays, to some extent, the role of the membership relation in the set S. For example, we have the following principle, which Lewis (1991, p. 74) calls the *principle of unique composition*: it never happens that the same things have different fusions. For example, consider the fusion $A \oplus B$, of two blocks, A and B, where A is on top of B. Had B been on top of A, this would not have been a different fusion of A and B; rather, the fusion $A \oplus B$ would have been in a different position or configuration.

There are two main differences between the set S and the fusion of its members. One is that the members themselves have no members; they are not sets, but objects – but they do have parts. Hence the fusion $A \oplus B$ has many more than two parts (how many depends on what physical theory you believe), while the set $\{A, B\}$ has only two members. The other difference is that the set S is atemporal (according to most philosophers), while the fusion isn't; it can go out of existence if one of its parts does.

As for the first difference, often we think of certain of the parts of a fusion (scattered object) as units, indivisible in thought. (As Gottlöb Frege, 1980, points out, any object can serve as a unit.) Consider ordinary "bodies." I think (with thanks to Shmuel Weinberger for clarifications) that what most people would call a "body" or "physical object" is a solid mass which (a) can be approximated by a polyhedron of suitably large number of surfaces (call this a *smooth* solid mass); and (b) is not part of a larger smooth solid mass. The idea is that the fusion of two distinct bodies is not a body, and part of a body is not a body; just as the set of those bodies is not the body, and a part of the body is not an element of the set.

Of course, mathematicians have defined pathological spaces that are nowhere approximable by polyhedra. A famous example is the Mandelbrot set, which, though connected, has an "infinitely rough" border of "fractal dimension." Nevertheless, even a physicist like David Ruelle, who took part in the development of the theory of chaotic systems (for which fractal geometry is often necessary), admits that "It is, of course, an idealization to see our world as three-dimensional, and containing objects limited by surfaces... this particular idealization was encouraged by evolution and has been hard-wired into our brains" (Ruelle, 1991, p. 194fn). Ruelle goes on to argue that the concept of a body has survival value and contributed to the development of geometry. I would argue the same for arithmetic and set theory, for which the existence of fractal geometry is in any case not so relevant.

As for the atemporality of the set concept, we note that "bodies" typically have temporal stability; they remain in existence for lengths of time that are useful to human beings and other creatures, which certainly enhances the survival value of the concept of a body. Hence, we can say that, to a useful approximation, fusions of bodies are also atemporal.

We can thus speculate that the concept of a set is abstracted from that of a fusion; and that fusions are canonical applications of the set concept.

The application of set theory, and hence of arithmetic, to the empirical world, therefore, rests primarily on the relative stability of bodies. This ensures that the fusion F of n bodies will continue to *be* a fusion of n bodies, for a long enough time.

What is interesting about our application is that fusion can *also* be regarded as an application of disjoint set union, and thus ultimately of arithmetic addition. (Fusion, not "concatenation"; the latter is an abstract operation which forms the elements of a set into an ordered series.) This is obvious enough: set union is, intuitively, collecting the elements of two small sets to make a large one. Fusion mimics this "collection" by a "mereological" (i.e. empirical part/whole) relation. (Of course, historically this might get it backwards, if our view that set union is an abstraction from fusion is accepted.) This is the deeper reason why we can "add" candies to candies; we are doing nothing but fusing the elements of two sets of candies. The parts of the fusion which are whole candies are typically stable parts which remain candies. For this reason we can use addition to achieve an empirical conclusion: if we throw two candies into an empty hat and three more we will probably have five candies. All this says is that candies left alone usually don't disappear; the rest is given by the representation of fusion by set union. (For more on this see Steiner, 1998, chapter 2.)

Furthermore, the fusion relation, as a binary relation on scattered objects, is obviously commutative: it is obvious that the fusion of 2 with 3 objects is the same as the fusion of those 3 with 2.

Unfortunately for our students, there is no natural physical operation or relation that mimics the cross product, *except* for "constructing a rectangular area." (And, as we have seen, the mathematical operation that this represents is not the multiplication of numbers, but the multiplication of magnitudes, in the Greek, or pre-Cartesian style.) Rectangular arrays of dots are easy to *see as* the elements of m sets with n elements each, or the elements of n sets with m elements each. This does not, however, give any *empirical* operation that applies *multiplication*. Geometry is being used here, as I put it above, only "weakly."

This is what is meant, then, by saying that multiplication is more heavily involved with set theory than is addition: there is no canonical empirical relation which multiplication represents.

I conclude that there is a fundamental distinction between addition and multiplication: addition, though a theory of abstract "objects," may yet be considered an abstraction or idealization of empirical facts; multiplication cannot so be considered, for there are no empirical facts so to be abstracted; instead, multiplication is set theoretical from the beginning – if you will, mathematics applied to itself. In multiplication we deal not just with sets of material bodies, but with sets of such sets.

Another way of putting this is that addition (itself a mathematical operation) is the primary application of multiplication; whereas the canonical application of addition is an empirical operation, that of fusion. So the canonical *empirical* application of multiplication is, as it were, at two removes; the application of an application – the first being logical (repeated union of sets), the second, empirical (representing fusions by sets).

At the risk of repeating myself, I would sum up my view of the relationship between arithmetic operations and their applications as follows. We define the canonical empirical application of an arithmetic operation as the empirical operation or phenomenon the arithmetic operation was "abstracted" from. The canonical application of addition is fusion, where we "add" objects to objects. (A non-canonical application of addition is weighing.) Fusion is also the canonical empirical application of the concept of set itself. Multiplication, on the other hand, does not seem to have a canonical empirical application at all. Tiling is certainly an empirical application but does not strike me as canonical. On the other hand, the application of multiplication, where we calculate the total number of m disjoint sets each of cardinality n, may be canonical but it is not empirical. Furthermore, since in this application we reach sets of sets, the calculation in question is not even a straightforward empirical application of set theory either.

This explains why multiplication is harder to teach than addition: the most useful applications are not canonical empirical ones. As an example, the commutativity of multiplication can be taught only by awakening in the students the abstract concept of a set of sets.

Wittgenstein: A Social Constructivist?

Though Wittgenstein would have certainly balked at the Platonism of the above account of arithmetic, there is nevertheless something Wittgensteinian about it. My account shares with Wittgenstein's philosophy of mathematics the view that there is an "internal" (a Bradleyan phrase which Wittgenstein hijacked to mean stipulated) connection between mathematics and its canonical applications. (For the record, and with apologies to the uninitiated, I prefer interpreting the connection in terms of "rigid designation" in the sense of Kripke, 1980.) A connection like this makes it impossible to regard mathematics as a "social construction," whatever that may mean. The characterization of Wittgenstein as a "social constructivist" is an erroneous inference from his view that mathematical theorems are really rules imposed by society, to the invalid conclusion that society could have imposed other rules than the ones it did. All such rules, according to Wittgenstein, are "hardened regularities" (Wittgenstein, 1978, VI, 22). That is, we elevate empirical regularities of counting and measuring into norms for *correct* counting and *correct* measuring. This nevertheless means that mathematical rules are grounded in these regularities; where there are no regularities, there are no norms. For example, there is no "alternative" mathematics where $2 + 2 = 7$, because such a rule could not be grounded in facts. It might be thought that one could alter the meaning of "+" in such a way as to allow for "$2 + 2 = 7$," but Wittgenstein does not allow cavalier changes of meaning like this, because the practice underlying addition and the other arithmetic and logical operations meets objective human need.

It is a philosophical confusion, then, to regard Wittgenstein as the patron saint of social constructivism in mathematics, despite works like Bloor (1991) and Ernest (1998). However, it is also a philosophical confusion to regard mathematics, though grounded in empirical facts, as about those facts. Both on Wittgenstein's view and mine, mathematics as it is today is an abstraction from, and is therefore different from, its canonical empirical applications. Where my view perhaps differs from Wittgenstein's (apart from the Platonism of my own approach) is that I do not believe that mathematics remains eternally tied to its canonical, prehistorical, applications. As Eugene Wigner (1967) put it, the applicability of mathematics in natural science (i.e. to the world) is "unreasonable" in that once discovered, or abstracted if you prefer, mathematical ideas "pop up" again and again. The concept of addition appears in both classical and quantum physics as the "principle of superposition," in which the "sum" of two phenomena is again a phenomenon; or that phenomena can be analyzed in this way as a sum. In these applications, the notion of "sum" is abstracted further, till we get the concept of an "additive structure," i.e. we have a structure rather than a mere operation. This structure can be (and is) instantiated by phenomena very remote from the canonical applications from which we began.

We laud mathematics for its multifarious applications, and applications are the main motivation for teaching mathematics at every level of education. Even Plato, who despised the empirical world, felt constrained to point out that it was precisely the most abstract of sciences which turns out to be the most "practical" in the end. This essay has argued, however, that the applicability of mathematics is more than one thing: we have looked at logical applications and empirical applications, canonical and non-canonical.

And the "abstractness" of mathematics is also not one thing: for example, multiplication is abstract, in that it makes direct reference to "abstract objects," i.e. sets, and even sets of sets. Group theory is abstract in that, unlike arithmetic, it involves an uninterpreted set of postulates (i.e. any set equipped with any binary associative operation, relative to which every element is invertible and one of the elements plays the role of identity, is by definition a group), which defines an abstract structure. In other words, group theory is about nothing in particular.

The philosophy known as "structuralism" (see Worrall, 1989; Parsons, 1990; Resnik, 1997; Shapiro, 1997), to be sure, defines all mathematics as a collection of abstract structures. But this definition obscures the real differences between mathematics and its applications. Group theory, for example, is applied in a way in which multiplication is not.

Though the value of philosophical analysis (even good philosophy, to say nothing of bad philosophy) in mathematical education is debatable (see below), I humbly offer some educational conclusions from my own studies of mathematics and its application. Given the very different things we call the "application" of mathematics, and the very different meanings of the term "abstract" as applied to mathematics, pluralism in mathematics education seems in order. For example, one must obviously take into account the difference between what we call "applications" of mathematics in daily life and what we call "applications" of mathematics in science, if we are to do justice to the needs of society and the individual. What is less obvious is the variegated role of mathematics in science itself, and the different kinds of thing we call "application" in science.

Most lay people think of scientists as using mathematics to make complicated calculations that go far beyond addition and multiplication; but they are unaware of a crucial role that mathematics plays in scientific discovery. This role is to provide *analogies*, which then allow scientists to make educated guesses, which then can be checked by experiments. Take, for example, the phenomenon of electronic spin: it is known that the electron is a little magnet, as though it were a charged ball spinning on its "axis." Suppose we have an electron whose north pole is perpendicular to the floor; if we rotate the axis 180 degrees then, of course, the north and south pole change positions. If we rotate the axis 360 degrees, then the north and south pole revert back to their original positions, but something very subtle happens – the electron does not quite return to its original state, but rather its state is multiplied by -1.

In 1932, Heisenberg guessed that the relation of the proton and the neutron in the nucleus of an atom is, mathematically, the same as the two directions of the north and south pole of the electron. This is a purely abstract analogy, based only on the assumption of a common mathematical structure (i.e. based on group theory), not based on some physical or mechanical hypothesis. Obviously, nobody can turn a neutron into a proton by standing on his head. This correct guess, however, has physical consequences, yet no one has been able to explain why this analogy worked (cf. Steiner, 1998).

The surprising conclusion, then, is that even if we were to restrict mathematics education to future scientists, we would still have to approach the subject pluralistically. This is, after all, in keeping with the protean nature of mathematics itself. I believe that Wittgenstein was right when he said, "I should like to say: mathematics is a MOTLEY of techniques of proof. – And upon this is based its manifold applicability and its importance" (Wittgenstein, 1978, III, 46).

See also: 1 THE SOCRATIC TRADITION; 6 ENLIGHTENMENT LIBERALISM; 16 THEORIES OF TEACHING AND LEARNING; 24 TEACHING SCIENCE

References

Bloor, D. (1991) *Knowledge and Social Imagery*. Chicago: Chicago University Press.

Ernest, P. (1998) *Social Constructivism as a Philosophy of Mathematics*. Albany: State University of New York Press.

Frege, G. (1980) *The Foundations of Arithmetic: A Logico-mathematical Enquiry into the Concept of Number*, trans. J. L. Austin. Evanston, IL: Northwestern University Press.

Kripke, S. (1980) *Naming and Necessity*. Cambridge, MA: Harvard University Press.

Kripke, S. (1982) *Wittgenstein on Rules and Private Language*. Cambridge, MA: Harvard University Press.

Lewis, D. (1991) *Parts of Classes*. Oxford: Basil Blackwell.

Mendelson, E. (1997) *Introduction to Mathematical Logic*. London: Chapman & Hall.

Parsons, C. (1990) The structuralist view of mathematical objects. *Synthese*, 84, 303–46.

Resnik, M. (1997) *Mathematics as a Science of Patterns*. Oxford and New York: Oxford University Press.

Ruelle, D. (1991) *Chance and Chaos*. Princeton, NJ: Princeton University Press.

Russell, B. (1924) *Introduction to Mathematical Philosophy*. London: Allen & Unwin.

Shapiro, S. (1997) *Philosophy of Mathematics*. Oxford: Oxford University Press.

Steiner, M. (1975) *Mathematical Knowledge*. Ithaca, NY: Cornell University Press.

Steiner, M. (1998) *The Application of Mathematics as a Philosophical Problem*. Cambridge, MA: Harvard University Press.

Wigner, E. (1967) The unreasonable effectiveness of mathematics in the natural sciences. In *Symmetries and Reflections*. Bloomington: Indiana University Press, pp. 222–37.

Wittgenstein, L. (1968) *Philosophical Investigations*, trans. G. E. M. Anscombe. Oxford: Basil Blackwell.

Wittgenstein, L. (1978) *Remarks on the Foundations of Mathematics*, ed. G. H. Von Wright, R. Rhees, and G. E. M. Anscombe. Cambridge, MA: MIT Press.

Worrall, J. (1989) Structural realism: the best of both worlds? *Dialectica*, 43, 99–123.

Wu, H. (1999) Basic skills versus conceptual understanding: a bogus dichotomy in mathematics education. *American Educator*, Fall, 14–19, 50–2. Available at http://www.aft.org/publications/american_educator/fall99/wu

26

Aesthetics and the Educative Powers of Art

Noël Carroll

Throughout the ages and across cultures, the educative powers of art have been taken to be self-evident. In his *Ars Poetica*, Horace says the role of poetry is to "instruct and delight," where delight, I take it, is supposed to facilitate instruction. In his "Epistle to Augustus," Horace expands on this theme, writing: "The poet forms the young child's stammering mouth, and turns his ear at a timely hour from obscene discourse; next he also shapes his heart with friendly precepts, castigating harshness, resentment and wrath. He tells of deeds honorably done, instructs rising generations by the examples of famous men, and consoles the sick and helpless." Until the eighteenth century in the West, such thoughts were virtually commonplace and have even been referred to as the "Horatian platitude" (see "Horace" in Leitch, 2001, pp. 121–37).

Horace emphasizes the importance of poetry in particular and art in general ("*ut pictura poesis*") to educate the young. Art, in this regard, is an especially powerful means for transmitting the ethos of a people. Art is notably advantaged in this respect, because it standardly does not merely address cognition with abstract information, but also generally engages, by way of the sensuous, the feelings, including feelings of pleasure, the emotions, perceptions, memory, and imagination of its audience. Thus, the knowledge that art imparts, where it does so, is redundantly imprinted across several dimensions of the individual, thereby making it easier to access and to retrieve. Art, so to speak, can educate the whole person by involving many of our powers at once and in interrelated, mutually reinforcing ways. And this makes it a formidable instrument for the transmission of culture.

That art typically (not always, but typically) engenders feeling is one of its recurring features that can scarcely be disputed. But art does not simply promote feeling in a random or haphazard way. Most frequently it elicits the same or very similar feelings in disparate viewers, listeners, or readers (Dissanayake, 2000, chapter 2). When sitting in a concert hall, most feel pretty much the same thrill at Copland's *Fanfare for the Common Man*. When seeing or reading *Othello*, most recoil in the same or converging ways as Iago's machinations unfold.

Moreover, it is in its capacity to mobilize common feeling that art's potential as a transmitter of the shared ethos of a society primarily originates. For through song, dance, procession (including marches), dramatic enactment, decoration, festivals, architecture, sculpture, image, and word, art enlists a community of response, a communion of fellow feeling. Furthermore, this initial form of social cohesion can then serve as a platform for the development of richer bonds of attachment through the propagation of common values, ideals, doctrines, folklore, emotions, information, attitudes, knowledge, and so on. And since, as already noted, the sensuous mode of address in which art typically specializes activates multiple human powers – rather than just cognition, very narrowly construed – the imprint it leaves on its consumers is deeply embedded in their being.

Because of its interrelated capacities to promote fellow feeling, to induce social cohesion, and to transmit a common ethos in a profoundly sedimented way, art appears to be a universal or nearly universal phenomenon across human cultures. This should come as no surprise, since these factors provide evolutionary advantages to any human group. That is, the reason that art is so widespread is that, despite the obvious costs and sacrifices it incurs, it is adaptively beneficial. Art is useful or has utility or is instrumentally valuable, perhaps no more obviously than in its role as the educator of peoples – as the inculcator and transmitter of the ethos of a society. Moreover, art's role in this regard does not leave off with tutoring the young, but continues as we age, reinforcing, cultivating, and refining our understanding – cognitive, emotive, perceptual, and moral – of the human world we inhabit. Art, that is, affords a continuing process of enlightenment.

That art can perform this function – that art possesses such utility – is undoubtedly the reason that it has survived. Art emerges and develops coevally with ritual, both religious and civic. It is a means to commemorate historic events, to recall the founding of nations and their victories, to advance vivid exemplars of virtue and vice, to remind audiences of their values and responsibilities, to dispense advice, to sharpen perception, moral, psychological, and otherwise, to make sense of events and circumstances, and so much more. Societies gravitate naturally to artistic expressiveness because it is useful, and at the core of art's usefulness is its capacity to promote education in the ways of one's culture. Of all of the functions art discharges, at none is it more effective than in its transmission of the ethos of the pertinent lifeworlds. Indeed, art may excel most in this function, of all the functions within its reach, and, arguably, it also outstrips other sources of enlightenment, such as social science, in this regard.

A Catholic church, for example, is both a remembrance of the saint or the aspect of God for which it is named and an inspiration or call to emulation of its namesake (Visser, 2000, pp. 88–9). Its stained glass windows, altar pieces, stations of the cross, statues, frescoes, paintings, and decorated side chapels are virtually encyclopedias of Catholic culture, supplemented during services by word, prayer, narrative, song, and sermon, which function as redundant channels of information, predicated on prompting the faithful to recollect the exemplary moments, values, and doctrines of Christianity. The church as a whole is a teaching machine, skillfully orchestrated by the priest during rituals to rehearse the tenets of Christian culture, or working silently while the faithful sit in quiet meditation on the icons and scriptures that surround them. As Martin Heidegger suggests of the Greek temple, the Catholic church discloses an ethos to its audience (see "The Origin of the Work of Art," in Krell, 1977; also the excellent commentary by J. Young, 2001).

Of course, art traditionally serves not only religious education, but education more generally. Through art, political and social values are also taught, as well as norms of interpersonal relations, appropriate and inappropriate goals and emotions, folk psychology, custom, desirable and undesirable character traits, attitudes toward historical and contemporary events, manners and carriage, personal style, including even one's style of movement, and so on. That the arts could be so serviceable in all these arenas of education has made them virtually indispensable socially, not only for the prestige that possession of artworks might connote, but as a source, perhaps the most comprehensive and effective source, of enculturation.

Until the eighteenth century, in what we might call the premodern period, art's value, in this context, was thought to be functional. Art was a means to transmit culture and value. Art was esteemed not for its own sake, but because it was useful for promoting a society's ethos, primarily through processes that we may broadly call educational, albeit education frequently leavened with delight. That is, during the premodern period, the proposition that art had utility to both instruct and delight was an unobjectionable presumption. Indeed, such a "premodern" understanding is probably still shared by most ordinary consumers of art even today. However, something coalesced in the eighteenth century that sundered the untroubled relation between the utility of art, notably, for our purposes, in terms of education, on the one hand, and the value of art, at least as it was conceived by a vocal majority of experts, on the other hand.

What happened around the eighteenth century was the consolidation of the modern system of the arts and the emergence of modern aesthetics (see Shiner, 2001). Both these phenomena contrast with the "premodern" dispensation alluded to in the previous paragraph. Whereas the premodern view prizes art for its utility and functionality, especially in virtue of its powers of education and enculturation, the modern system of the arts distinguishes between the fine arts, on the one side, and the useful arts, on the other (on this distinction between premodern and modern views of art see Berger, 2000). If on the premodern conception of art, the values of art were heteronomous, the value of the fine arts, on the modern conception, was autonomous, presaging the notion of art for art's sake. On the latter view, art is its own locus of value, and should not be subservient to other sorts of value, such as educational value.

Hand in glove with the consolidation of the modern system of the arts was the emergence of modern aesthetics. "Aesthetics" itself was an eighteenth-century neologism, coined by Alexander Baumgarten. It came to be the label for a certain sort of experience, specifically the sort of experience one might undergo upon exposure to beautiful prospects in nature or in response to successful artworks. Indeed, artworks came to be regarded as objects expressly designed to promote aesthetic experiences, and, for that reason, particularly suited for eliciting them.

But what are aesthetic experiences? According to the ur-theory of modern aesthetics, they are experiences valued for their own sake, not valued for the ordinary, interested pleasures they afford nor their utility; neither the personal benefits (such as prestige) they bestow, nor the cognitive, moral, religious, political, social, scientific, or practical advantages they promise. Aesthetic experience was construed to be its own reward, not the handmaiden of other values, such as education. The contemplation of the artwork, especially in terms of formal properties like unity, promoted disinterested pleasure as it was called, or, even more ethereally, an experience valued for its own sake and nothing else.

The modern conception of aesthetic experience served the modern system of the fine arts well. For if one wanted to know how to identify an instance of fine art, the test was to ask whether the item in question was such that it was designed to promote aesthetic experience, an experience valued for its own sake, and not for anything else. This theory of art, which we might call the *aesthetic theory of art*, isolates the fine arts as distinct from all others, including all the useful arts, at a stroke. The fine arts, or what today some might simply call Art, are identified, by definition, by an experience that itself is distinguished from everything other than its own intrinsic value. Thus, the autonomy of art, so to speak, falls out automatically from the autonomy of aesthetic experience, which is art's identifying mark.

The aesthetic theory of art was, in one sense, a response to changing social circumstances. Whereas under the premodern dispensation, artists were craftspersons commissioned to make things that secured values that "were primarily not internal to the practice of art itself, but rather internal to other, nonartistic social activities of art consumers" – such as the display of political power, the communication of social mores, attitudes, and ideals, the inculcation of cultural ethos and identity, the building of moral communities and their reproduction through education – market conditions changed with the advent of the modern period (Berger, 2000, p. 5). The link between artists and patrons – whether individual patrons or larger social entities (like the church or the state) – loosened. Along with the precariousness of becoming a free-market agent, the artist was also liberated to pursue his own ends and values rather than those of his patrons. Artmaking, or at least some of it, came to be seen as an autonomous activity, rather than a heteronomous one (Berger, 2000, p. 5). And with that, a new understanding of art seemed to be called for.

At the same time that art appeared to sever its ties to social function, it also felt the pressure to defend its value on two fronts. Historically, insofar as art was often correlated with representation, it was thought to be in the same ballpark as science as a purveyor of knowledge. But with the rise of modern science, art hardly seemed a viable competitor in the knowledge game. Art would have to establish its credentials in some other way. And, in addition to staving off the encroachment on its authority by modern science, art also felt the threat of bourgeois philistinism, which, it was believed, tended to reduce all value to instrumental value.

The modern artworld responded to these challenges with the aesthetic theory of art. This theory denied that art's value resided in its contribution to knowledge or to any other form of instrumental value, and it ostensibly explained how art could be autonomously valuable, rather than heteronomously so. For according to the aesthetic theory of art, art was valuable for the kinds of contemplative experiences it was designed to promote – experiences that were themselves intrinsically valuable ones, irrespective of their consequences. This view of art, moreover, informed the evolution of artistic institutions from the nineteenth century through the twentieth.

Whereas traditionally artworks like frescoes and statues were situated in places where they had ritual, social, functional, and/or cultic significance, they began to be collected in museums and galleries, where they were isolated from external distractions and entanglements and were set forth free-standing for aesthetic contemplation. Exempt from social life and implication in ongoing affairs, artworks communed only with other artworks in the museum. Likewise, whereas prior to the modern period much music was married with song in religious rites, serious music mutated into absolute music to be sequestered in newly emerging concert halls, designed to focus contemplation on the musical fabric of the composition. (For a discussion of these institutional changes, see Shiner, 2001.) That is, the aesthetic theory of art began to shape the very institutional structures of reception in the modern period, at the same time that it converted successive generations of art theorists, including Gautier, Schopenhauer, Pater, Wilde, Bell, Fry, Stolnitz, Osborne, and Beardsley. Thus, a very powerful feedback loop evolved between the conditions of artistic reception and the articulation of aesthetic theory – a feedback loop that continues to exert its grip on the contemporary artworld.

For want of a better term, I will call this phenomenon "modern aesthetics." Modern aesthetics, as I have indicated, locates the value and identity of art, properly so-called, in the putative function of promoting experiences that are valuable for their own sake, and not for any utility, social or otherwise, that art may possess. This places art in an anomalous relation with education theoretically. For according to modern aesthetics, the educative potential of art is at best irrelevant to its nature, and, at worst, a perversion of the true aims of art. Whereas the premodern conception of art, to which I presume most people worldwide still adhere, takes the contribution of art to education, especially as a transmitter of ethos, to be self-evident, the most entrenched approaches of modern aesthetics regard this viewpoint as virtually a category mistake. There is more than a disconnect between common sense and theory here. There is an outright clash.

This clash, of course, might be dissolved easily, if the only reasons for the rise of modern aesthetics were the socio-historical ones sketched above. However, modern aesthetics also has some impressive arguments with which to defend its banishment of usefulness, especially educational usefulness, from the realm of art. Broadly speaking, these arguments can be called *aesthetic arguments* (arguments that purport to demonstrate that art, properly so-called, should have no traffic with education) and *epistemic arguments* (arguments that are designed to show that art cannot perform the function of education). In what follows, I will attempt to outline these arguments and then refute them. For in refuting them, we will not only establish that art has an important role in education, as the premodern viewpoint has it, but also we will be in a position to limn some of the precise ways in which art contributes to education.

Against the Educational Pretensions of Art: The Aesthetic and Epistemic Arguments

Though it appears obvious that art contributes to education, some of the most entrenched views of modern aesthetic theory deny that this is appropriate (the aesthetic arguments) or even possible (the epistemic arguments). Both sets of arguments are tied up with the project of attempting to characterize art as a unique realm of activity and value, distinct from other practices. As indicated above, this project

369

became especially pressing in the eighteenth century, when the system of the fine arts – the list of things we count as art (poetry, music, painting, etc.) – was established in its present form. This project mandated identifying a way in which to determine what sorts of things belonged on the list and which did not. Why was painting on the list, but not chemistry (despite the fact that in earlier times artists and chemists were in the same guild, since both ground pigment)? In short, what made art art? The answer was that it afforded a unique type of experience.

Something is art, on this view, because it is designed to facilitate aesthetic experience. This theory, the aesthetic theory of art, is a very elegant one. For not only does it enable its defender to define art, but by deploying aesthetic experience as a fulcrum, so to say, it also enables its proponent to answer in a highly systematic manner quite a lot of other questions we have about art. The notion of aesthetic experience not only enables one to say what works are art and what not, but additionally to isolate the reasons we have for saying an artwork is good or bad. A work is good to the extent that it promotes aesthetic experience and bad to the extent that it deters it. Thus, the aesthetic theory of art also putatively enables us to separate sound critical reasons from irrelevant ones. Sound criticism attends to those features of artworks that contribute to the promotion of aesthetic experience. Irrelevant criticism focuses on other issues, such as the utility of the work in the promotion of education.

How does the aesthetic theorist reach the conclusion that artworks are such as to be designed to promote aesthetic experience? Here is where the first aesthetic argument plays a role. We can call it the *common denominator argument*. It goes like this. Historically, artworks have had many different properties – displaying power, teaching catechism, brightening rooms, and so on. Whichever property or set of properties makes something art must be shared by every instance of the category. But not all artworks teach catechisms; indeed, many artworks teach nothing at all, such as many exercises in pure musical form and abstract pictorial design.

Similar tests can be run on other supposed candidates for the defining feature of art. Not all art, for example, affords pleasure, since some is designed to elicit horror. And so on. Ostensibly only one property is shared by everything we are prepared to call art – the power to engender contemplative experiences, valued for their own sake, of the design of the works in question.

That is, everything we call art has been made with a primary intention to command our attention to its mode of organization and presentation. This is the only constant that threads its way through everything we call art. It is the common denominator. Therefore, art is that which is created in order to absorb us in contemplation of a certain sort, namely in aesthetic experiences, which are their own reward. Or, more succinctly, the promotion of aesthetic experience is an essential condition for art status.

The conclusion of the common denominator argument, then, serves as a premise in a further argument, which we can call the *aesthetic argument* proper. If art *qua* art is essentially about the affordance of contemplative experiences of design, then considerations of other properties of the works in question, such as their political function or their educational messages, are not art-appropriate ones. The only appropriate response to an artwork *qua* art is the contemplation of its design. Other considerations are, at best, irrelevant, and, at worst, a distraction from the proper exercise of aesthetic attention. That is, we should appreciate the stained glass window for its pictorial unity and ignore its religious address. If we become too preoccupied with its message, we will leave off contemplating its formal organization.

Artists discharged many duties over history, including education. But putatively, when they were working as artists as such, they were fabricating designs that would engage contemplation. Their work as teachers was adventitious to their real work as artists, which was the promotion of aesthetic experiences. Likewise, when we, the audience, engage with their productions *qua* art, we should restrict our attention to their artistry, to the designs they created for our contemplative delectation. To do otherwise is artistically inappropriate, a perversion of the artistic contract that underwrites our relationship to the artwork *qua* art.

Moreover, the implications of the aesthetic argument proper for the educational pretensions of art are straightforward. Education is not an essential feature of art; facilitating aesthetic experience is. And aesthetic experience, unlike education, is not valuable for its utility. Therefore, whatever educational content an artwork may possess, it is at best irrelevant to artistic appreciation as such and, at worst, an impediment to it. Consequently, the best policy is to bracket educational considerations from our intercourse with artworks *qua* art. That is, education, even with artworks that once served that purpose, *should not* be our concern when we engage artworks properly.

The aesthetic argument proper maintains that in our commerce with artworks *qua* artworks, we should have no truck with their utilitarian values, such as their capacity to promote education. This argument at least concedes that artworks can promote education, however inadvisably. Nevertheless, the next set of arguments, the epistemic arguments, denies even this, contending instead that art is incapable of educating anyone.

There are at least three epistemic arguments against the pretensions of art to serve the purposes of education. The first is the *banality argument*. This argument begins with the observation that most of the knowledge that art critics allege artworks teach audiences is of a trivial or truistic sort – so well known that saying that artworks teach it to anyone is absurd. For example, in the 1960s critics frequently claimed that various modernist paintings taught spectators that pictures are really flat surfaces. But didn't ordinary audiences already know that? Furthermore, in order to interpret an otherwise obscure modernist painting as an affirmation of the conviction that all painting is flat, an exegete would already have to know that this is a theoretical commitment of modernist painting. So, in both the case of the ordinary viewer and the case of modernist exegete, the alleged knowledge that the painting has to offer is already known. And you can't learn what you already know. That much is built into the concept of education.

Likewise, the Christian already knows that Christ died for her sins; it is a commonplace of her faith. She doesn't learn it from the fresco. Indeed, in order to understand the fresco, she already probably needs to know this. Much art is like this in operating on the viewers' antecedent knowledge. Therefore, it makes scant sense to claim such art is educative.

The second epistemic argument against the educational pretensions of art is the *no-evidence argument*. Whereas the banality argument allows that an artwork may present some beliefs that it is designed to share with the audience, the no-evidence argument maintains that art cannot communicate knowledge, properly so-called. For knowledge involves warranted or justified belief, and, though artworks may present beliefs to audiences, the artworks in question typically do not propose evidence on their behalf. Let us suppose that one theme of *The Scarlet Letter* is that the repression of guilt is unhealthy. The novel does not support that conviction with any real evidence. At best, it offers one case study and a made-up one at that – indeed, one made up to carry that point, and, therefore, of somewhat dubious evidential value. To support an empirical generalization about guilt would require an altogether more substantial warrant of the sort that a psychological study, rather than a novel, would provide. Novels and similar fictional artworks are not the sorts of things suited to justify the various empirical generalizations that critics are always commending them for revealing.

So, despite all that critical cant, artworks are not genuinely educative, because that would require not only signaling a commitment to some or another general belief, say, about human nature, but also supplying the evidential warrant for that belief. Since art almost never does that, and, in the case of fiction, perhaps cannot do that, most artistic pretensions to education are empty. Whereas the banality argument challenges the educational claims of art on the grounds that what art supposedly teaches is already well known, the no-evidence argument questions art's license to teach by saying that what art offers its audience is not knowledge at all.

The third epistemic argument can be called the *no-argument argument*. It resembles the no-evidence argument inasmuch as it alleges that art has no knowledge at its disposal and, therefore, nothing to teach. But whereas the no-evidence argument contests art's claim to tutor us in empirical generalizations for which it provides no evidence, the no-argument argument maintains that art lacks the kinds of argumentation and analysis that are required to justify knowledge claims. *The Brothers Karamazov* is supposed to tutor us in the belief in God's existence. But where are, the skeptic asks, the argument and analysis to support that conviction? The novel may advance that belief, the skeptic contends, but it doesn't demonstrate it. It altogether lacks the apparatus of proof. So, like the no-evidence argument, the no-argument argument concludes that inasmuch as art fails to justify the beliefs it proposes, it falls short of knowledge, properly so-called, and insofar as it lacks knowledge, it has no claim to being educative.

Of course, these three epistemic arguments may not succeed in foreclosing every artistic claim to educate. Perhaps there are some examples of Conceptual or installation art, replete with lists of data, photographic documentation, and numbered proofs, which advance knowledge-claims unfamiliar to the general audience. However, with respect to most art, these three arguments at least initially appear to be onto something: namely, that most art cannot legitimately claim to be educative.

So, once again, we find ourselves in an anomalous position. Common sense indicates that education is a primary function of art. But probably the most entrenched convictions of modern aesthetics deny this. Something has to give.

Refuting the Aesthetic Arguments

According to the aesthetic argument proper, it is inappropriate to attend to artworks except as vehicles for securing aesthetic experiences. This conclusion is, in effect, supposedly the moral of the common-denominator argument. Allegedly the affordance of aesthetic experience is the only function that we can identify as common to all artworks; as such, it is the only standard of evaluation that can be brought to bear on artworks *qua* art. But even if this argument established that the intended promotion of aesthetic experience is common to artworks (something we shall dispute anon), this argument would not show that it is the only relevant response, and the only relevant standard of evaluation here.

At best, the common-denominator argument establishes a necessary condition for artistic evaluation. It ostensibly locates a generic source of value in every artwork. However, this does not preclude the possibility that certain kinds of artworks have additional, more specialized functions with related standards of evaluation. It is the generic function of knives to cut, but some knives are designed to cut steak, others to slice butter, and some to stab people. The fact that these knives share a generic function does not make it inapposite to evaluate these utensils differentially in terms of their more specialized functions.

Importing this analogy to the realm of art, we can argue that even if art has the alleged aesthetic function, some kinds of art – certain genres and modes – may have more specialized functions. Some art, for example, may be designed to promote education, and in such cases it cannot be inappropriate to respond to the artwork in the way in which it solicits attention.

If it is part of the specialized purpose of *Oedipus Rex* to show that it is impossible to call anyone happy until they are dead, then whether it enlightens us on this score is an appropriate consideration to contemplate when assessing the value of the play. The fact that this would not be an appropriate consideration to raise with respect to some string quartets is irrelevant. *Oedipus Rex*, given the kind of work it is, has educational ambitions and this warrants our responding to its teachings and evaluating them. The common-denominator argument does not close down this alternative.

Of course, it is also questionable whether the common-denominator argument has discovered a generic feature of or necessary condition for all art. Certain tribal artifacts, like shields, have a just claim to being artworks, given their representational and expressive properties and the evident skill it took to produce them. But they are designed to frighten off the enemy, not to invite him to contemplate their formal unity. Thus, not all artworks are designed with the intention to promote aesthetic experience. Some artworks are designed with the primary intention to secure practical ends, which may include not only intimidating invaders, but education as well.

Moreover, it is not clear that the aesthetic argument proper achieves its goal – to hive off artistic value from other sorts, like educational value. It aspires to this end by identifying art with the intended promotion of self-rewarding aesthetic experience. But if one identifies aesthetic experiences with those valued for their own sake, then, if you believe in intrinsic value, surely you must concede that learning that no one can be called happy until they are dead might be something that someone subjectively values for its own sake.

This shortcoming, needless to say, might be repaired by specifying the nature of aesthetic experience more precisely; by stipulating, for example, that aesthetic experiences involve the self-rewarding contemplation of the design of the artwork. This is called *formalism*. But formalism will not distinguish artworks from certain

373

mathematical proofs, where the mathematician in question attempts to develop a more elegant way of reaching a solution than is already known. In such a case, the aim is to promote our appreciation of the design of the argument. But a mathematical proof is not an artwork. That is, the formalist version of the aesthetic theory of art does not really isolate a sufficient condition for art status.

Nor, as we have seen, does it identify a necessary condition, even where the ruling notion of aesthetic experience is the contemplation of design. For the tribal shields alluded to above were not intended to elicit that sort of response. In short, the notion of aesthetic experience that the proponent of the aesthetic argument proper deploys is inadequate to define art *qua* art. Therefore, the argument cannot circumscribe the ambit of art-appropriate responses in the way it is intended to. Consequently, the argument does not successfully rule out that responding to the educational address of artwork may be an art-appropriate reaction to it.

At this point, the skeptic about the educational potential of art may change his tack. Instead of attempting to declare that interest in learning from art is inappropriate due to the essential nature of art, the skeptic may agree that art can be legitimately appreciated for its educational address, but then nevertheless go on to argue that it is still inadvisable to make and to appreciate art as a contribution to education, because this is not the very best thing art has to offer. Of all the functions art can discharge, the promotion of aesthetic experience is what it excels at. All other functions pale in comparison. Thus, to make the most out of art (the artist's imperative) and to get the most out of art (the audience's imperative), all we should expect from art is the promotion of aesthetic experience. Compared to art's capacity to afford aesthetic experience, what art has to contribute educationally is paltry.

This argument presupposes that promoting aesthetic experience is the function, of all art's functions, that art is best suited to implement. But why suppose this? In the opening passages of this chapter, reasons were produced to indicate that enculturating an ethos has at least as good a claim, if not the best claim, to being art's most efficacious service. Until that hypothesis is defeated, it is not obvious that the promotion of aesthetic experience should trump the promotion of education in our interactions with artworks. And, in any event, even if education were only a secondary benefit to be derived from art, that alone provides no reason for us to look this particular gift horse in the mouth. Moreover, in many cases where art affords both aesthetic satisfaction and educational value, the aesthetic dimension in the work may, in fact, operate ultimately to enhance instruction.

Lastly, the aesthetic approach to art contends that the cognitive and educational elements in artworks are always at best irrelevant to an appropriate response to art. This, however, cannot be correct, even where one is convinced that aesthetic experiences of the unity of the artwork are paramount. For often one can only discern the unity and design of the artwork when one comprehends its cognitive messages and educational purpose. One only grasps the form of *Oedipus Rex* – the principle of selection that led Sophocles to choose the incidents of the legend he did for inclusion in his drama – when one realizes that the point of the play is to teach that no one can be called happy until after death. Furthermore, reflection on that maxim, as guided by the play, is, in large measure, what invests it with its unifying aesthetic property of profundity, its pervasive *gravitas*.

Pace the aesthetic arguments rehearsed, there are not compelling reasons for us to ignore or disavow the educational dimension of art. Nevertheless, it will only be possible for us to learn from art if art has something to teach. Consequently, in order to be confident on this score, we must now confront the epistemic arguments against art's pretension to educate.

Refuting the Epistemic Arguments

A common presupposition of the skeptical epistemic arguments against art is that if art does educate, then it would have to do so in virtue of some worthwhile propositions that it conveys to its audiences (Reid, 1985). According to the banality argument, the propositions that art has to offer are not worthwhile, since they are of the nature of commonplaces – things people already know. According to the no-evidence argument and the no-argument argument, the pertinent propositions are not worthwhile, since they are unwarranted; they are not really knowledge at all. So art has nothing to teach – no educational role – because it has no propositions, notably no general propositions, of the relevant sort to dispense.

Inasmuch as these arguments depend upon the premise that if art is to educate, it must broker worthwhile propositional knowledge, they clearly exhibit a blindspot. Specifically: why suppose that the only form education takes is the communication of a certain sort of proposition? That is, the conception of education assumed by these arguments is too narrow. Perhaps the education that art has to impart is not a matter of communicating propositions, but of something else.

Above we stressed the relation of art to feelings, including the emotions. Even if art lacks the wherewithal to teach worthwhile propositional knowledge, it may possess the resources to educate the emotions. Emotions can be correct or incorrect. As Aristotle pointed out, correct emotions require the right feelings directed at the appropriate objects with a suitable level of intensity. The emotions, then, are educable, at least along these three dimensions.

Through art, one can learn that homeless people are appropriate objects of pity, that "tsking" in response to the Holocaust is incommensurate with its enormous depravity, and that *sang froid* is the wrong sensation to correlate with displays of wanton cruelty. (The role of art in educating the emotions is discussed at length in the exquisite article by Hepburn, 1998.)

Among other things, art may educate the emotions through representations that cultivate our abilities to recognize what our culture designates as the appropriate objects of the pertinent states, as well as the proper correlative inner feelings and corresponding levels of excitement that go with them. At the same time, artistic representations can also tutor us in what our culture counts as incorrect emotions. Moreover, art can educate us in the apposite kinds of behaviors, including expressive behaviors, that the emotion in question is supposed to elicit, and it can foster the kinds of desires that enable us to recognize and evaluate the appropriate objects of our emotions. In this way, art, at the very least, can attune us to our cultural world, by affording a certain *savoir faire* and emotive nuance in the ways of the heart.

375

Of course, what I have just said may suggest a way of rehabilitating the banality argument, as a complaint not about cliched propositions, but about cliched emotions. That is, art does not, it may be said, educate the emotions because it essentially trades on emotions already shared by the participants in a culture. But two things need saying here. First, art plays a major role in investing us with culturally converging emotional responses. If art is not our first instructor in matters of the heart, it nevertheless not only reinforces and strengthens the inclinations we may obtain elsewhere, but, importantly, it also substantially refines our emotive perceptiveness and powers of emotive management by elaborating what Ronald de Sousa calls "paradigm scenarios" (de Sousa, 1987, p. 182).

Art may not only encourage a common loathing of hypocrites like Tartuffe, but enable us to recognize the correctness of a similar kind of aversion, where we were previously oblivious, toward apparently disarming but equally vicious character types, like Skimpole in Dickens's *Bleak House*. Art, that is, may alert us to the appropriateness of a certain kind of wariness toward a species of charm, which wariness, although it builds on a fund of common feeling, need not be a "canned" emotional response, but an incremental expansion or sharpening of our powers of emotive discernment.

Second, art should not be construed as merely reinforcing emotions we already have. It may nurture new emotions by calling to our attention saliently features of situations heretofore unnoticed, as Kafka did for many in *The Trial* by highlighting the horrific, dehumanizing aspects of modern bureaucracy. That is, artistic representations may bring forth new feelings, as well as showing us that some feelings, previously beyond our ken, are possible ones, such as ambivalence toward beloved parental figures. John Cheever's short story "The Swimmer" not only enabled some to feel alienation where they were hitherto complacent, but, in doing so, apprized them of the existence of an emotion that was off their radar sceen, or perhaps only duly felt for being antecedently unarticulated. Thus, the rehabilitated banality argument does not stand; art need not simply recycle canned emotions. (For related discussion see Currie (1995, pp. 250–9) on art as a stimulus to simulated emotion, and J. O. Young (2001, especially chapter 2) on music and the emotions.)

By restricting the concept of education to the dissemination of a certain sort of proposition, the epistemic arguments overlook the possibility that art may educate abilities, such as our powers of emotional sensitivity. However, it is not only our emotional talents that art may nurture; it may also improve certain of our cognitive skills. With respect to morality, for example, we have been taught many maxims and concepts, such as concepts of virtue and vice, that are very abstract and often difficult to know how to apply to concrete situations. In some sense, we already know these maxims and concepts, but putting them to work is another matter. We may know that justice requires giving people their due, but what they are due in a certain context is often hard to determine. It cannot be done algorithmically on the basis of the maxim; it requires judgment.

Judgment, moreover, is a skill that art can augment. Narrative artworks, for instance, involve readers, viewers, and listeners in constant processes of moral judgment – constant assessments of which characters are virtuous and vicious and of whether what they are doing is good, bad, better, or worse. In this regard, art exercises and thereby accentuates our powers of judgment, our ability to apply abstract maxims and concepts to complex circumstances.

Even if we already know that people ought not be treated as means, we may not have a handle on how that applies to quotidian circumstances. A novel such as *Emma*, by enabling us to apprehend the wrongfulness of Emma's intrusiveness in Harriet's love affairs, gives us a complicated and vivid example of a violation of that maxim in a way that not only illuminates the moral status of Emma's behavior, but which can have transfer value in the judgments we make of comparable interpersonal relations in our own lives.

The novel, that is, induces us to reflect on important variables and interconnections that enable us to apply abstract maxims to concrete circumstances judiciously. Nor is this simply a matter of equipping the reader with a template to bring to real-life situations. For in guiding the reader in a process of shifting through the specifics of the case, the novelist exercises and refines the reader's general capacity for making the relevant kinds of judgment. By contemplating fictional situations, our powers of judgment are increased through practice, which, in turn, promises carry-over advantages in daily encounters. (For further discussion of the ways in which art contributes to the cultivation of moral judgment, see Carroll, 2001.)

Moreover, the kinds of capacities that art exercises are not simply those of moral judgment. We may know in an abstract way what a mid-life crisis is, but a fictional portrayal of one by an author like John Updike may help us to be able to recognize it when we see it. That is, art may give us a purchase on applying abstract psychological concepts and patterns as well as moral ones.

Surely training skills such as these should count as education. Since we are talking about skills rather than propositions, neither the no-evidence argument nor the no-argument argument has any leverage here. And though in one way we may already know the maxims and concepts that underwrite these skills, the banality argument is not pertinent, since what we are learning is not the maxims and concepts, but how to apply them. What we are acquiring is a certain finesse that we previously lacked. The epistemic arguments stipulate that the ambit of education is the communication of a certain *product*, worthwhile propositions. However, this ignores the educative contribution that the *process* of interacting with artworks may afford, such as the augmentation of our facility in rendering judgments.

According to the banality argument, the problem with art is that it recycles commonplaces or truisms. In many cases, this sounds correct, at least *prima facie*. But it overlooks the fact that quite frequently truisms, no matter how commonplace, are often forgotten, neglected, or even suppressed. Many middle-class Americans are well aware of the plight of illegal immigrant workers – aware that they are exploited and denied their rights. But it is easy to lose sight of these people's immiseration and our responsibilities to them. In this regard, a film like *Bread and Roses* may serve as a pertinent reminder. A viewer may already know about this kind of exploitation and, in addition, know that this should concern her. Yet the film serves as an occasion for her to remember what she knows and to think about what it implies about her position in our social system. Being jogged out of this kind of unmindfulness and being confronted with the relevance of what one already knows to one's own situation is hardly a trivial affair, as the banality argument suggests.

"Education" derives from the Latin *educere*, which means "to bring out" or "to draw forth." In this respect, education is often a process of drawing forth what is already known, even commonplace, but which has been forgotten or repressed. Art serves the purposes of education in this light, since it is often concerned with recollection – with recalling to mind often simple truths that, however obvious, lie latent in our consciousness.

This is not only the case with works of social protest like *Bread and Roses*. It is also the ambition of so many public monuments and religious icons whose function is to commemorate the historic events, convictions, and commitments of the relevant communities. The banality argument wrongly presumes that education is always a matter of acquiring a new piece of knowledge, thereby disregarding the possibility of one's being enlightened by being reminded of what one already knows and its relevance. Moreover, in cases where art educates by reminding audiences of what they already know, the no-evidence and no-argument argument are idle.

The no-evidence argument and the no-argument argument contend that art cannot educate, since art has no warranted beliefs, no knowledge, to transmit, because, on the one hand, it lacks supportive evidence for whatever general propositions it advances, and, on the other hand, it fails to confirm them with argumentation and analysis. This may be correct for much art, but not for all. For many works of art, especially narrative ones, resemble philosophical thought experiments, and, inasmuch as philosophical thought experiments can be educative, so can artworks that function comparably (Carroll, 2002). Philosophical thought experiments, which are generally fictional and narrative in nature, are not compromised by the no-evidence argument, since they present conceptual knowledge (*a priori* knowledge or the knowledge of how to apply concepts), not empirical knowledge. Nor do they fall foul of the no-argument argument, since philosophical thought experiments, examples, and counterexamples are themselves modes of argumentation that operate on our antecedent cognitive stock in ways that bring auditors maieutically to a certain conclusion by reflecting on what they already know in combination with the strategically designed particularities of the imagined case.

Moreover, the fact that such thought experiments depend on what the listener already knows does not open them to charges of banality, since they make what is already, in some sense, known explicit; they render our knowledge about how to apply concepts explicit – that is, they transform our know-how into statable propositions about the criteria and/or considerations relevant to the application of our concepts. Thus, insofar as some artworks – particularly fictional narratives – are analogous to philosophical thought experiments, examples, and counterexamples, they too can evade the banality argument, the no-evidence argument, and the no-argument argument.

The function of many philosophical thought experiments, is to present conceptual possibilities, in order to undermine universal claims that, upon reflection, we see are hardly exceptionless. If told that justice is a matter of helping one's friends, the philosophical skeptic imagines a case of friendship and loyalty between heartless murderers. That the case is made up is not a problem, since listeners can recognize it, by reflecting on their antecedent cognitive stock, as a possible one, and its possibility is enough to reject the ostensible definition of justice.

Likewise, artworks can function as counterexamples. Andy Warhol's *Brillo Box*, for instance, challenged the theory that art is always a direct function of something one can see, like significant form, since *Brillo Box* is indiscernible from non-art counterparts, such as ordinary Brillo boxes. *Brillo Box* does not require a supplemental argument, for it is the argument in the form of a counterexample that will bring the prepared spectator to the intended conclusion. Similarly, *in Hard Times*, Dickens imagined a fictional scenario that illustrated the limitations of a relentless positivist educational program, just as for generations modernist authors have intentionally subverted rosy beliefs in the utter rationality of human persons by parading before us a diverse array of plausibly drawn, psychologically creditable characters, driven by irrational forces.

The artwork as counterexample plays an important role in our culture. It is a means by which the general beliefs, theories, nostrums, and prevailing doctrines about morality, sexuality, justice, personhood, business, the good life, and so on can be interrogated. Often these generalizations are not of the order of thought-through philosophies, but more of the nature of presiding folk wisdom. Nevertheless, their less-than-rigorous credentials in no way undercut their influence in society. That artists imagine fictional counterexamples to resist them is one of art's more important functions in the dialogue of our culture. And like the philosopher, the artist may avail herself of the fictional narrative – the thought experiment – as her argumentative strategy.

Of course, philosophical thought experiments are not merely employed to refute universalizations. They may also be used to perform conceptual analyses. Kant imagines the case of two shopkeepers whose outward behavior in honestly making change is the same, although one does it because it is right and the other because he does not wish to get a bad reputation (since that would be bad for business). By depicting this polarized contrast, Kant encourages the reader to grasp the categorical distinction between a moral act and a prudent one – to excavate the criteria by which we apply the concepts of morality and prudence. In this case, the thought experiment initiates a grammatical investigation into the conditions that govern our use of the relevant concepts, which investigation the reader completes on his own, under the guidance of the examples. Here the examples themselves function as the argument in behalf of Kant's conclusions.

Artworks as thought experiments, deploying comparable contrastive structures, can also function in this way. The film *The Man Who Shot Liberty Valence*, among other things, invites viewers to contemplate what should count as genuine manliness by introducing us to three characters: Ransom Stoddard, Tom Doniphon, and Liberty Valence. As we unavoidably compare and contrast their motives and behaviors, the question of whom among them we would call the best man – the one who most approaches the ideal of manliness – comes to the fore. It is easy to remove Valence from the running, since he is little more than an incontinent savage, but why Doniphon has a better claim to the title than Stoddard is less obvious. And inasmuch as the film prompts us to ask ourselves why Doniphon is more admirable, it enables us to zero in on and articulate to ourselves the kinds of considerations that govern our attribution of the concept. In this, it teaches us something about our own conceptual schema.

As we have seen, the fact that artworks can function as thought experiments, examples, and counterexamples, of the sort found in philosophy, gives us a way in which to defeat the no-evidence argument and the no-argument argument on their own rather demanding terms. However, before leaving this topic, it is worthwhile to note that the terms of these arguments are themselves suspect. For both arguments presuppose that the authentic communication of knowledge, and, therefore, education, properly so called, requires that the propositional knowledge at issue be justified at the same time that it is being advanced. If it is an empirical claim, the relevant evidence must accompany it. If it is a non-empirical claim, like a moral claim, it must be freighted with the appropriate form of argument. Otherwise it is not a a genuine knowledge claim, and, if it is not that, then it has no educational value.

But this is too austere a conception of knowledge communication. We do not expect knowledge claims in the standard case to come with all the evidence and argument on their behalf, written, so to speak, "on their sleeves." Newspaper editorials, historical narratives, and even philosophical essays may leave out much of the documentation and argumentation that buttress their conclusions, relying instead on the reader to test them by bringing what she knows about the subject and about the world to the text.

For example, an article about the current state of the economy may issue a summary diagnosis without citing all the statistics that might be necessary to support its thesis. A biologist criticizing creationism may leave the arguments bolstering evolutionary theory off the page. It is supposed that the reader will fill in the necessary evidence and argumentation on her own. But what is important here is that we do *not* discount these as knowledge claims because they lack much of the relevant evidence and argumentation and because they assign to the reader the task of filling them in. Yet if this is true of ordinary, non-artistic knowledge communication, why should the requirements change when it comes to artworks?

Of course, once we realize that the skeptic has set the bar too high for what would count as knowledge communication and education with respect to art, it should be evident that art can afford the opportunity to secure not only conceptual knowledge, but knowledge of all sorts. Art can provide insight into psychology by showing us character types, like Emma Bovary and Raskolnikov, that exemplify certain syndromes. And artworks, such as *Bonfire of the Vanities*, can reflect upon and inform us of the state of various sectors of society. In these cases, the novels themselves do not supply us with the evidence and argument, but beckon us to use what we already know about the world and the mind to confirm the hypotheses they advance fictionally.

Nor need this invocation of "what we already know" force us back into the snares of the banality argument. For though we may have all the facts and evidence concerning a certain topic, we may fail to apprehend their import (Jobes, 1974). That is, the facts may be well known to us, but we may be blind to their significance, perhaps because they are so familiar to us and we have become so habituated to them that we have lost sight of their implications. Art, in this regard, can make us see things afresh; can enable us to notice things distinctly where previously we saw only a blur. By strategies such as amplification, simplification, idealization, juxtaposition, comparison, association, metaphor, contextualization, correlation, and so on, the artist can bring us to a new understanding of the facts already in our possession

(J. O. Young, 2001, pp. 80–8). We may have already been witnesses to many cases where rejection leads to rage, but Mary Shelley's *Frankenstein* may provide an occasion for us to grasp the pattern vividly at the same time we use the evidence we already have to confirm the plausibility of her hypothesis. To the degree that artworks induce us to re-explore and reconfigure what we already know, they are of exemplary educational value.

One way that artworks enable us to reconfigure our understanding is by organizing what may be familiar under a clarifying perspective that selectively emphasizes aspects of situations which might otherwise be lost in the fog of familiarity. In *Bleak House*, Dickens, for example, makes the soul-benumbing mechanism of the Court of Chancery stand out by articulating the perspective or point-of-view that underlines certain recurring aspects of the legal process, encouraging us to see it in a new and indignant light. And by giving us this perspective on the Court of Chancery, Dickens equips us with a framework for assessing other legal procedures. That is, artworks may provide us with ways of seeing and ways of approaching phenomena which, even if these ways of seeing are not themselves propositions, facilitate our discovery of propositions about our world under their guidance (for more on this theme see J. O. Young, 2001).

So far I have reviewed a number of ways in which the educative potential of art can be defended against the banality argument, the no-evidence argument, and the no-argument argument. I do not mean to suggest that these are the only ways, or that the considerations I have raised are always mutually exclusive. Nevertheless, the weight of my discussion should be sufficient to shift the burden of proof to the proponent of the epistemic arguments against art.

Insofar as those arguments depend upon reducing education to the communication of a certain sort of proposition, they forget that art can educate by enhancing our talents – our powers of emotive discernment and judgment. Art may not always provide new knowledge, but education is also served by recalling to mind forgotten, neglected, or repressed knowledge. And art may even sometimes be the occasion for obtaining new knowledge: sometimes new knowledge about the criteria that govern the application of our concepts and sometimes new knowledge about the world (where the artwork in questions leads us to notice afresh something about facts already at our disposal).

According to the leading epistemic arguments, the educative value of art is nil. However, though those arguments may pertain to some artworks, as we have seen, they scarcely apply across the board. Much art is educative, although often in diverse ways. Perhaps it is the fact that art is educative in so many different ways that obscures its educational value for many philosophers, since philosophers like to reduce phenomena to tidy, unified formulae. But neither art nor education is as simple as that.

Conclusion

We began this discussion by noting that with regard to the relation of art to education, there is a surprising, maybe even scandalous, disconnect between common sense and common practice, on the one hand, and modern aesthetic theory, on the other. For we typically presume that art possesses educational value and, for that reason, include it not only throughout the formal curriculuum, but also in our private projects of continuing self-education; nevertheless, some of the most entrenched prejudices of modern aesthetics maintain either that we should not look to art for education, or, even more ominously, that we cannot look to art for education. Thus, our practice appears wildly at odds with our theory.

Aesthetic reasons why we should not expect educational value from art have to do with the modern conviction that art is valuable because of the self-rewarding aesthetic experiences it affords, usually conceived of as a contemplative response to the design or form of an artwork, and not because of any utility the artwork might possess, such as the enhancement of education. Though we have stressed the theoretical threat this position poses for our practices, it also may have unfortunate consequences for educational policy. For it privileges one kind of response to art – the contemplation of form in isolation from other concerns – and this is apt to make an interest in art seem beside the point, or too specialized, or too rarefied for our students.

Luckily, however, as we have seen, these aesthetic reasons are not ultimately decisive. Though some art may be designed to afford self-rewarding aesthetic experience, not all art is for art's sake. Some art is expressly designed to foster such useful activities as inquiry, education, and learning, and there is no reason to suspect that these functions and the responses they elicit are any less art-appropriate ones than the contemplation of form.

Moreover, this result may even be important for educational policy. For it suggests that arts education is perhaps best pursued not by isolating art and its experience from everything else, but by integrating it with other cultural practices. In the past, art was folded into a wide variety of social functions, and it was probably more accessible, more intelligible, and more a part of people's lives for not being hived off in its own realm. This is a possibility that arts educators today should seriously reconsider, instead of emphasizing the arts as specialties in a way that accords with the admonitions of modern aesthetics.

The epistemic arguments we have rehearsed deny an educational role to the arts on the grounds that art has no knowledge to teach. But these arguments falter, because the concepts of knowledge, education, and knowledge communication that they presuppose are too restrictive and unrealistic. This, too, is a happy result, since art – insofar as it addresses so many aspects of the person (her senses, feelings, emotions, cognition, and imagination) at once – is one of the most effective devices in our possession for transmitting and embedding knowledge in its audiences. Indeed, with regard to certain forms of knowledge, such as knowledge of the heart and the ethos of a culture, art is probably our most serviceable mode of education. A play can often tell one much more about human motivation than a psychology textbook, because of the distinctive way it engages different aspects of our faculties simultaneously.

Modern aesthetics attempted to save art from the encroachment of other social initiatives, such as didacticism. The result was a commitment to art for art's sake, a viewpoint that lingers on, even where it is not voiced, in many of the presuppositions of modern aestheticians. One consequence of this is that art has become alienated, especially in our theoretical understanding of it, from the rest of society. Perhaps the

382

time has come now to save art from itself by recalling its connection to other cultural endeavors and functions, of which its role in education is among its most prominent.

See also 9 ROMANTICISM; 20 KNOWLEDGE, TRUTH, AND LEARNING; 22 MORAL EDUCATION; 23 RELIGIOUS EDUCATION; 27 TEACHING LITERATURE

References

Berger, K. (2000) *A Theory of Art*. New York: Oxford University Press.

Carroll, N. (2001) Art, narrative, and moral understanding. In *Beyond Aesthetics*. New York: Cambridge University Press, pp. 270–93.

Carroll, N. (2002) The wheel of virtue: art, literature, and moral knowledge. *Journal of Aesthetics and Art Criticism*, in the press.

Currie, G. (1995) The moral psychology of fiction. *Australasian Journal of Philosophy*, 73(2), 250–9.

de Sousa, R. (1987) *The Rationality of the Emotions*. Cambridge, MA: MIT Press.

Dissanayake, E. (2000) *Art and Intimacy: How the Arts Began*. Seattle: University of Washington Press.

Hepburn, R. W. (1998) The arts and the education of feeling and emotion. In P. Hirst and P. White (eds), *Philosophy of Education: Major Themes in the Analytic Tradition, volume 4*. London and New York: Routledge, pp. 171–85.

Jobes, J. (1974) A revelatory function of art. *British Journal of Aesthetics*, 14(2), 124–33.

Krell, D. F. (ed.) (1977) *Martin Heidegger: Basic Writings*. New York: Harper & Row.

Leitch, V. (2001) *The Norton Anthology of Theory and Criticism*. New York: W. W. Norton.

Reid, L. A. (1985) Art and knowledge. *British Journal of Aesthetics*, 25(2), 115–17.

Shiner, L. (2001) *The Invention of Art: A Cultural History*. Chicago: University of Chicago Press.

Visser, M. (2000) *The Geometry of Love: Space, Time, Mystery, and Meaning in an Ordinary Church*. New York: Farrar, Straus and Giroux.

Young, J. (2001) *Heidegger's Philosophy of Art*. Cambridge: Cambridge University Press.

Young, J. O. (2001) *Art and Knowledge*. London: Routledge.

27

Teaching Literature

Richard Smith

The teaching of literature, at whatever level of education, raises questions that are unmistakably philosophical. What is *truth* in literature? We often say approvingly of a novel, for instance, that it is "true to experience," yet the nature of this "truth" is unclear. If the novel reflects the "real world" this is likely to be in a more profound sense than that it echoes the banalities of daily existence, in which case some account of the novel's truthfulness needs to be given. Are our readings of literature inevitably personal, so that no kind of *objectivity* in the study or teaching of literature can be achieved? It might seem that such objectivity is supplied exclusively by the author's *intentions* in what she wrote, but the smallest reflection shows this cannot be so. The public meanings of words and conventions of syntax and expression often warrant people in finding meaning in our words that we did not consciously invest them with. How can we be *moved* by literature? It is clear that we are emotionally touched, shedding tears for Hecuba or for Anna Karenina, but these are fictitious characters, who never existed and so never suffered and do not need our sympathy or pity. What, in any case, do we mean by "literature"? What makes literature worthy of study in school? On what grounds if any is it possible to identify a canon of "great books" (the masterworks of Homer, Shakespeare, Dickens, Henry James et al.) that are so worthy of study that everyone with a claim to being "educated" must read them?

Over all these questions, however, there looms the larger question of the *value* of literature: why (or whether) we think it is worthwhile to help students of all ages to read and understand poetry, plays, novels, and other texts. This question would seem especially pressing in a world where the educational claims of such subjects as information technology, engineering, and mathematics are so much more easily made, and where English, as a school subject, has often been seen as a matter of "communication skills," of the "effective use of language," as if all writing were to be modeled on advertising or political propaganda. This is just one aspect of the widespread failure in the English-speaking countries in the past few decades to take seriously the question of what *education* is for. Debate on this subject has been stifled by the relentlessness with which governments have involved themselves in the details of the curriculum, shaping education primarily as an instrument of national economic competitiveness.

Our educational age can properly be called nihilistic in its lack of guiding values and visions of the educational enterprise. But the teaching of literature is in any case particularly difficult to justify. Trainee teachers, asked what is the point of teaching children to read stories, often reply brightly that reading is *fun*, or (in so many words) that it facilitates *escapism*. Leaving aside that *King Lear* is hardly fun (and neither are the darker myths and fairy stories), this leaves literature equivalent to, and replaceable by, a drug. If this is all that can be said in its defense it is hard to see why it should have a place in a required curriculum.

In what follows I offer a brief survey of some influential twentieth-century theories of the teaching of literature. Throughout, I foreground the question of just what good literature is for us, commenting on the complex issues of truth, objectivity, and representation only as space allows.

The Search for Objectivity

It is important to recall that at the beginning of the twentieth century English literature was a young discipline in academic terms. It was a recent arrival in the university, where it was treated as an upstart by comparison with such established subjects as classics and law. Fears were expressed that students of English would merely "chatter about books." It was natural therefore that English would seek to imitate the natural or "hard" sciences, which since the scientific revolutions of the seventeenth century had been the touchstone of intellectual respectability, with figures as different as David Hume and Adam Smith aspiring to be the Isaac Newton of their subjects. Accordingly, in the early part of the century we find two tendencies in literary criticism: an insistence on a species of realism, and an interest in what the new science of psychology could reveal about the reading of literature. These tendencies can both be found in the work of the critic I. A. Richards.

In *Practical Criticism* (first published in 1929) Richards analyzed the responses made by presumably sophisticated readers (they were Cambridge undergraduates) to what he called "protocols": short poems or extracts from poems, of varying degrees of literary merit. He showed convincingly that often these readers were responding not to the precise poem in front of them, but to an imagined or preferred version of the poem. Sometimes this is a matter of direct misreading. For example, D. H. Lawrence's poem "Piano" describes the narrator, as a child, sitting under the piano, while his mother plays, "in the boom of the tingling strings," an adjective which captures the powerful emotional affect of the scene. But for more than one reader these have become "tinkling strings": "to a great number of people a tinkling piano is execrating"; "we still have to satisfy ourselves that tinkling strings can boom" (Richards, 1973, pp. 105, 106). Other readers were distracted by what Richards called "mnemonic irrelevancies." Given a poem that describes the sun setting over the sea, for example, they recalled something similar from a recent holiday, again showing a lack of ability, or of willingness, to engage with the specific poem in front of them.

Two different but related lines of thought emerge from considerations such as these. One, the formalist way of thinking, emphasizes the separateness of literature and "life," and the need to bring an almost scientific detachment to the reading of literature. What matters in this view is the words of the text: there is nothing else that can be appealed to, whether personal experience or speculation about the

385

motivation of the characters of the play or novel; about how many children Lady Macbeth had, for example (see Knights, 1946). The other, more promising line of thought holds that much of the value of studying literature lies in its focus on the particular. The good reader is attentive to what is on the page: she reads in such a way as to resist the pull of fantasy or the self-indulgence of personal reminiscence. *Pride and Prejudice* is then not an opportunity to imagine what it would be like to go to bed with Mr Darcy, nor can a *literary* appreciation of the Lakes poets be spoiled by recollections of a miserable week spent by Ullswater. What then is it an opportunity for, and what does attentiveness earn the reader and teach the student? Richards, impressed by the science of psychology, regards the language of poetry as purely emotive, and thinks that the task of the reader is to recreate within himself the mental condition of the author. By recreating this mental condition the student will presumably acquire something of the author's (presumably valuable) sensibilities and perceptions.

Yet it is implausible to suggest that the language of poetry is merely emotive, as if words lose all their ordinary referential qualities when embedded in a poem, and there were no conventions of poetic expression that poets use to extend both the expressive and referential qualities of language. Similarly, one could argue, as philosophers following Ludwig Wittgenstein have, that is is not by approximating the author's state of mind that the reader succeeds. Hans-Georg Gadamer holds, for instance, that the "meaning of what is said is, when we understand it, quite independent of whether we can gain from the tradition a picture of the author" (Gadamer, 1985, p. 353). William Wimsatt and Monroe Beardsley insist, similarly, that the reader is not trying to reconstitute the meaning that was "in the writer's head" when he or she composed the poem, novel, or play (1946). In Wittgensteinian terms, the public meaning of language is a function of how words are used, not of the "private" or inaccessible contents of the speaker's or writer's mind.

Accordingly, there are those such as Wolfgang Iser who emphasize the way that text and reader together bring the work of literature "into existence." Literary works, Iser claims, contain blanks or gaps which the reader fills in the act of interpretation (Selden, 1988, p. 108). The reader's activity is by no means arbitrary, however, since the text has properties, both formal and semantic, that structure the reader's role. On this "reception aesthetics" readings are, as Catherine Belsey puts it, "neither given nor arbitrary" (Belsey, 1988, p. 36). There is an endless interplay, as the reader visits the text, producing readings that are themselves subject to further readings in turn, and no "closure," or point of authoritative termination.

Despite this open-ended quality of interpretation, however, there are arguably works that succeed in engaging the reader in valuable moral reflection.

Literature and Moral Education

This moral dimension of literature can be illustrated by drawing on the novelist Jane Austen. Her characters face the demand, among others, that they respond to each other honestly and accurately. The very titles of the novels point to this. In *Northanger Abbey*, for example, Catherine Morland must learn that the real world is not a gothic tale and General Tilney not a figure from one. In *Pride and Prejudice* Elizabeth Bennet must learn to make more measured judgments about situations and people (instead of yielding to the prejudice of the title), while Darcy must learn that accurate judgments are not enough: they must be made in a spirit of humility. And their challenge is also the reader's, who may take Mr Bennet as attractively droll and ironic in the opening pages of the novel but will find this judgment is too hasty. It becomes evident that Mr Bennet has to a great extent abdicated from his role of father for all of his daughters except his favorite, Elizabeth, with damaging consequences.

In an article of great interest, Duke Maskell (1999) shows how the characters' learning is also the reader's. The obnoxious Mr Collins writes to the Bennet family, indicating his intention of coming to stay with them for nearly two weeks. Their house is "entailed" to him; it will be his possession on the death of Mr Bennet. What do the various characters make of the letter? Mary comments on the prose style: the figures of speech are appropriate, if not particularly original. She is, we might say, a purely formalist literary critic. Jane thinks it is to Mr Collins's credit that he wants to make some atonement: she cannot penetrate beneath the surface meaning of the letter. The two youngest daughters, Catherine and Lydia, are interested only in flirting with the young officers in the neighborhood, and their interest in the letter extends no further than discovering that it promises no such opportunities. Only Elizabeth reads the letter with an intelligent scrutiny, detecting elements of humbug and hypocrisy, as well as evidence of Mr Collins's willingness to abuse the power he holds over them. "Can he be a sensible man, sir?" she asks her father, who responds that he has every hope of finding Mr Collins quite the opposite. Mr Bennet thus demonstrates his own inability to connect life and text: the letter is a further threat to the future security of his daughters, and even their neurotic and silly mother understands the need to find them suitable husbands as quickly as possible. Mr Bennet's only way of responding, however, is to retreat into irony just as throughout the novel he takes refuge in his study (the ambiguity of "study" should be noted).

To read literature in the way Maskell would have us do is to look for "truth to life" in it. F. R. Leavis, perhaps the most well known exponent of this approach, writes that the good novel is marked by "a vital capacity for experience, a kind of reverent openness before life, and a marked moral intensity" (Leavis, 1983, p. 18). Leavis's rejection of formalism extends to his famous denial that there are such things as purely literary values: "the judgements the literary critic is concerned with are judgements about life" (Leavis, 1972, p. 97). Bad works are shallow, sentimental; their characters are one-dimensional, perhaps as a consequence of the writer being in the grip of a *theory* (the characters of "existential" novels often seem thin for this reason). Good plays, novels, and poetry keep alive or make possible ways of thinking and feeling which are threatened by the debasement of language and the general philistinism of our time. Consider, for example, how the standard pop or rock lyric (which is of course to say there are exceptions to the standard) debases the complexities of human relationships, reducing them typically to the urgent desires and satisfactions of sex. Compare this to the subtle interplay between Wentworth and Anne in *Persuasion*. Here even the identities of the characters seem to merge and separate again, while the letters in which Wentworth confesses his love display a profound degree of attentiveness to his beloved, a kind of fitting of himself to her contours, a world away from the desire simply to take possession of another (see Blake et al., 1998, chapter 9). Thus Leavis's approach forms the basis for cultural criticism, and has been taken in this direction by writers such as Ian Robinson, Peter Abbs, and David Holbrook. They would have us scrutinize texts of all kinds (including advertising, politicians' speeches, and television programs) with the same care, and the same eye for what they hold in store for us, as Elizabeth Bennet scrutinizes Mr Collins's letter. Learning to do this is arguably a valuable preparation for thinking critically about one's society and its politics.

Art, then, extends and deepens our moral lives. Here there is perhaps an interesting answer to the question of how we can have feelings for and moral responses to characters of fiction. How can we blame Mrs Norris for her treatment of Fanny Price in *Mansfield Park* when Mrs Norris does not exist? Yet it seems quite inadequate to say that we "blame" her. Instead we find her domineering, callous, and hypocritical. We find Mary Crawford in the same novel brash, impulsive, utterly lacking in judgment (recall her remark, when someone alludes to the navy and its admirals during a dinner table discussion of careers, that she has seen her share of *rears* and *vices*). It would not do to say simply that we "disapprove" of her. Literature moves us away from "thin" moral ideas, such as those of praise or blame, to "thicker" moral notions (see Smith, 1992, p. 23). It teaches us to think in these richer and more particular ways, and so to see gradations and subtleties in the moral behavior and characters of those around us. We find similar arguments in the writings of Iris Murdoch, though the dominant influence on her is probably Simone Weil rather than F. R. Leavis. It is significant that Iris Murdoch was both a novelist and a philosopher. She warns us that we are too much inclined to "tame the world by generalising" (Murdoch, 1973, p. 82), preferring almost anything to "the horror of confronting a unique human history" (ibid., p. 15).

Content, Form, and Reference

Common to both the formalist approach and the Leavis line, which can be regarded as one of formalism's branches, is the insistence that in literature there is no way of separating form from content. *Hamlet* cannot be thought of as a way of expressing a truth that could be put in some other way. (This is what is wrong with student essayist claims of the form "What Shakespeare is trying to say here is..." The problem is not just that the student professes to express more satisfactorily what Shakespeare was stumbling towards in his amateurish manner.) Works of literature thus act, in the terms invoked in the previous paragraph, as very "thick" concepts indeed, and cannot be reduced to constitutive ideas of which they are the sum. When the modern Greek poet C. P. Cavafis writes the lines

> When you set out on your way to Ithaca,
> Pray that the journey be long

he alludes to the idea that Homer's *Odyssey* is emblematic of life's journey, the long and difficult passage to a kind of enlightenment and self-knowledge. But here you know little just by being told that "Homer's *Odyssey* is emblematic of life's journey."

To grasp this you must read the *Odyssey* itself. You must follow Odysseus through his trials and insights: that is the journey, and there is no substitute for it. Otherwise you would acquire knowledge only as some superficial proposition, and arguably it is precisely the move from knowledge in *that* form to knowledge as a deeper wisdom that the *Odyssey* enacts. Something similar is going on when we say "It's a *Catch-22* situation" or describe someone as "Prufrock to the letter." The allusion to Heller's novel or Eliot's poem conjures up a world that is expressed by the work of literature and not just described by it, as if it could have been described in some other way.

The inseparability of form and content can be illustrated by looking at cases in which the text seems to refer to specific events. It is tempting to think that we value the poetry of the Great War for its capacity to depict the suffering of the men in the trenches, the world of mud, gas attacks, and senseless slaughter, so that the poetry's meaning comes from the events it describes. It is instructive to take an example at random. In *Anthem for Doomed Youth* Wilfred Owen writes:

> What passing-bells for these who die as cattle?
> Only the monstrous anger of the guns.
> Only the stuttering rifles' rapid rattle
> Can patter out their hasty orisons.

The guns and rifles of the poem appear to refer to the guns and rifles of the soldiers of historical reality. The poem is "about" the horrors of that carnage, familiar from sepia photos and newsreel. We are encouraged to read the poem in this way – as a guide to *something else* – by editions that describe Owen's poems as "vivid studies in realism" (see, for example, Black, 1966, p. 36). But the reader who responds to the poem's flows of energy and cross-currents, its resonances and reverberations, notices many things which do not connect easily to Ypres or the Somme. The first eight lines are full of the imagery of sound (after the lines quoted above we have prayers, bells, voice of mourning, choirs, shrill, wailing, bugles), while the last six move to the imagery of visual perception, of colorless light (candles, eyes, shine, glimmers, pallor, dusk . . .). The reader of poetry, as opposed to someone knowledgable about the Great War, senses the balance, which is characteristic of the sonnet form. Attuned to this balance or contrast, we notice that the first eight lines give the sound of carnage in the language of the rites of the church: orisons, prayers, bells, choirs. All of these are horribly transformed, as in the line "The shrill, demented choirs of wailing shells." The last six lines begin with the question "What candles may be held to speed them all?" and appear to take us into the world of those who mourn for the dead soldiers. Yet here the language and imagery are in many places eerily evocative of the half-light of trench warfare, familiar to us from others of Owen's poems. The ambiguous lines

> Not in the hands of boys, but in their eyes
> Shall shine the holy glimmers of good-byes

confirm that the second part of the poem is not simply "about" the mourning in the homes the soldiers have left behind. Indeed, it is not clear that it would mean much less, carried back in time, to the reader of Browning or Keats who knew nothing of the First World War. That reader would know the sonnets of Shakespeare, for example, whose structure prepares us for "Anthem for Doomed Youth," and whose language and imagery Owen's poem often echoes. The poem is a making – the literal meaning of *poiesis* – and not simply a reflecting. It does not mirror the "real world," but brings something new into being. Roman Jacobson (quoted in Martin, 1975, p. 164) writes:

The function of poetry is to point out that the sign is not identical with the referent. Why do we need this reminder? . . . Because along with the awareness of the identity of the sign and the referent (A is A^1), we need the consciousness of the inadequacy of this identity (A is not A^1); this antinomy is essential, since without it the connection between the sign and the object becomes automatised and the perception of reality withers away.

But the perception of reality can be reinstated as more than that. The often-quoted example – of those who live by the sea growing so used to the sound of the waves that they cease to hear it – is misleading, for this mundane sense of reality is not what is in question. It is more the kind of hightened perception of reality that Eliot declared humankind cannot bear much of: the epiphany, the moment in intersection of the timeless moment with time.

The impossibility of separating content and form can be illustrated further from the poetry of Edward Lear:

> On the top of the Crumpetty Tree
> The Quangle Wangle sat,
> But his face you could not see,
> On account of his Beaver Hat.
> For his hat was a hundred and two feet wide,
> With ribbons and bibbons on every side
> And bells, and buttons, and loops, and lace,
> So that nobody ever could see the face
> Of the Quangle Wangle Quee.

That we call this "nonsense poetry" testifies to the difficulty we have in seeing that sense, or meaning, can come about in other ways than through "picturing" reality. The referential qualities of literature are thus complex. A poem or other composition is itself a creation. Many compositions – even those conventionally described as "nonsense" – though perhaps not all, also depict thought worlds, recognizable and coherent by degrees. Of these, some works populate their worlds with events and characters modeled – often complexly and multiply modeled – on actual people and events. Sometimes this is accomplished in ways that effectively explore aspects of "the human condition," without any obvious or intended reference to actual people or events. Sometimes it is done in ways that incorporate specific identifying references that give us reason to say the works are "about" a specific person or event. T. S. Eliot's "Mr Apollinax," for example, is almost indisputably a poem about Bertrand Russell. The important point, however, is that even in these cases, the aim and significance of the work lies not simply in being "about" the object of reference.

How We Are Moved by Literature

These considerations help us to understand how we can be moved by, as it is often put, the fate of Anna Karenina and other fictitious characters. It is necessary to examine an example in some detail. In the second book of Vergil's *Aeneid* the Trojan hero, Aeneas, is escaping the sack of Troy by the Greeks with his family when his wife, Creusa, becomes separated. He does not see her in the flesh again, but she appears to him in a vision, or as a ghost. She tells him that exile awaits him, and a new kingdom in the west, and a new queen there too. She herself cannot come with him, since "the great mother of the gods detains me / Here on these shores" (Robert Fitzgerald's 1984 translation), but at least she is spared the fate of so many of her compatriots, which is to be taken back to Greece as a slave. Her last words to Aeneas are "Farewell now; cherish still / Your son and mine."

If this is moving, what are we moved by? In Vergil's Latin her last words (line 789) are:

iamque vale et nati serva communis amorem.

Iamque vale translates as "and now, farewell." *Serva* is the imperative of the verb *servare*: Creusa is telling her husband to keep or preserve the love (*amorem*) of their common son, *nati communis*, the son that they share. Does this mean that Aeneas is to continue loving the bereaved child, or does it refer to the boy's love for his mother, so that she is asking Aeneas to make sure the boy never forgets her? *Nati amorem* is ambiguous, just as the English phrase "the love of a good woman" is ambiguous. As well as the boy's love for his mother it is also her love for her child. Furthermore, *nati serva communis amorem* can also mean "preserve *our* love," the love between Creusa and Aeneas, which *consists in* or is represented by the child who is the fruit and symbol of that love. Since this extraordinary line of poetry *can* mean all these things, it *must* mean all of them: all these meanings are there in the words. An adequate translation must be something like "Preserve our love in the form of the son whom it gave us." To be moved by the fate of Creusa (and of Aeneas, here, and of their son Ascanius) is to be moved by *these* words which express the fate of *these* people and their particular relationship, love, and desolation. It is precisely not to be moved by the general thought of death and bereavement (it is not even entirely clear that Creusa is dead: hence I wrote "vision or ghost" above), as if this were just another case of something that always excites our feelings. Even more than this, the good reader of the *Aeneid* knows that Aeneas will experience other partings and other sorrows in the remaining ten books, and that these produce the man who, in the last lines of the epic, behaves in the way he does to his enemy Turnus the Rutulian when he has him at his mercy. We would not be moved, as readers, by Creusa's words unless we had some general sense of what death, parting, and grief were, formed by our own experiences; what we are moved by *here*, however, is not something general. We are moved by *these words*, uttered in this context and no other, and not by "the fate of Creusa," as if that was something we could understand in some other way.

391

Destabilizing Meaning

Two tendencies in literary theory and critical practice flow from the ideas sketched in this chapter. The first is that the meaning of texts comes to seem unstable. If it is not guaranteed by authorial intention, dictionaries of contemporary usage, or any other means, just what does prevent a poem from meaning whatever a particular reader thinks it means? The second is that of the trio of author, text, and reader it is the reader that now moves to the center of interest. This is perhaps what we should expect in our democratic, consumer-oriented age. Where authority is routinely challenged it is natural to welcome the "death of the author" (in Roland Barthes's phrase) and to foreground the reader as one who actively participates in the play of possible readings set off by the text.

The resistance to "closure" referred to above means that, according to some, to be fully literate is to understand the open-ended nature of texts. It is to be alert to what Jacques Derrida calls their "desseminating" play: their constant repudiation of unity of meaning or privileged order of truth. He writes that "There are only, everywhere, differences and traces of differences" (Derrida, 1981, p. 26). Meaning is thus a function of the endless web of language itself, and, again, not of the relationship between language and anything else. Derrida regards attempts to secure stability of meaning with suspicion, seeing in them the operations of power attempting to secure its own base. They are thus fit objects for his deconstructive readings: readings which show how what the text represses or marginalizes returns to betray itself.

We do not have to be followers of Derrida to endorse such a view of literature: one that foregrounds attentiveness, engagement with text, skepticism toward received wisdom, and a tolerant yet still critical openness toward others' readings. It echoes many of the themes of literary criticism throughout the last one hundred years, as this chapter has attempted to show.

See also 5 HUMANISM; 9 ROMANTICISM; 10 HELLENISM, THE GYMNASIUM, AND ALTER-TUMSWISSENSCHAFT; 14 POSTMODERNISM; 22 MORAL EDUCATION; 26 AESTHETICS AND THE EDUCATIVE POWERS OF ART

References

Belsey, C. (1988) *Critical Practice*. London: Methuen.

Black, E. L. (1966) *Nine Modern Poets*. London: Macmillan.

Blake, N., Smith, R., and Standish, P. (1998) *The Universities We Need: Higher Education after Dearing*. London: Kogan Page.

Derrida, J. (1980) *Positions*. Chicago: University of Chicago Press.

Fitzgerald, R. (1984) *The Aeneid: Vergil*. London: Harvill Press.

Gadamer, H.-G. (1985) *Truth and Method*. London: Sheed & Ward.

Knights, L. C. (1946) *Explorations*. London: Chatto & Windus.

Leavis, F. R. (1972) *Nor Shall My Sword: Discourses on Pluralism, Compassion and Social Hope*. London: Chatto & Windus.

Leavis, F. R. (1983) *The Great Tradition: George Eliot, Henry James, Joseph Conrad*. Harmondsworth: Penguin.

Martin, G. D. (1975) *Language, Truth and Poetry*. Edinburgh: Edinburgh University Press.

Maskell, D. (1999) Education, education, education: or, what has Jane Austin to teach David Blunkett? *Journal of Philosophy of Education*, 33(2), 157–74.

Murdoch, I. (1973) *The Black Prince*. London: Chatto & Windus.

Richards, I. A. (1973) *Practical Criticism*. London: Routledge & Kegan Paul.

Selden, R. (1998) *A Reader's Guide to Contemporary Literary Theory*. Brighton: Harvester.

Smith, R. (1992) Thinking thickly. *Times Literary Supplement*, 4675.

Wimsatt, W. K. and Beardsley, M. (1946) The intentional fallacy. *Sawanee Review*, 54, 468–88.

Part III

THE POLITICS AND ETHICS
OF SCHOOLING

28

The Authority and Responsibility to Educate

Amy Gutmann

We are born weak, we need strength; helpless, we need aid; foolish, we need reason. All that we lack at birth, that we need when we come to man's estate, is the gift of education.

J.-J. Rousseau

So broadly understood as what we learn "from nature, from men, and from things," the gift of education may make us who we are, but is not ours to give (Rousseau, 1972, p. 6). Like Rousseau, we therefore direct our concern to that portion of education most amenable to our influence: the conscious efforts of men and women to inform the intellect and to shape the character of less educated people. We need to ask what the purposes of human education should be and where the authority to educate should lie.

We cannot determine the purposes of education by invoking an *a priori* theory of human nature. There are no doubt bounds of what is educationally possible at any given time, but these constraints leave societies a vast choice among competing educational purposes and authorities. Educational authorities may aim to *perfect* human nature by developing its potentialities, to *deflect* it into serving socially useful purposes, or to *defeat* it by repressing those inclinations that are socially destructive. We can choose among and give content to these aims only by developing a normative theory of what the educational purposes of a society should be.

We have inherited not one but several such normative theories. Three of the most distinct and distinguished of these theories can be drawn from interpretations of Plato, John Locke, and John Stuart Mill. In what follows I will not be concerned with the accuracy of these interpretations. My aim will be to use the theories of Plato, Locke and Mill, as they have been commonly understood, to illuminate the principles underlying three of the most common and compelling political understandings of education in our society. I call them (for reasons that will become apparent) theories of the *family state*, *state of families*, and *state of individuals*. Despite their differences, each treats questions of education (its purposes, distributions, and authorities) as part of a principled political theory. Building on the strengths and rejecting the weaknesses of each of these theories, I develop a theory of what I call *democratic education*, more fully supported in my book *Democratic Education*, that supports multiple educational authorities, who together are responsible for educating children to become free and equal persons (Gutmann, 1999). When parental, political, and professional authorities honor the principles of democratic education, which protect children against repression of ideas and discrimination on the basis of ascriptive characteristics (such as gender, race, religion, and ethnicity), they act responsibly in furthering the most justifiable aim of education in a democratic society: the education of free and equal persons.

The Family State

Can we speak meaningfully about a good education without knowing what a just society and a virtuous person are? Socrates poses this challenge to the Sophists in the *Protagoras*. Like most of Socrates' questions, it has remained unanswered after twenty-five centuries, but it is still worth re-asking.

In his critique of the Sophists and in the *Republic*, Plato suggests that we cannot speak about a good education without knowing what justice and virtue really are. Justice, Socrates suggests, is the concurrent realization of individual and social good. Since the good life for individuals entails contributing to the social good, there is no necessary conflict between what is good for us and what is good for our society – provided our society is just. The defining feature of the family state is therefore its claim to exclusive educational authority as a means of establishing a harmony – a constitutive relation – between individual and social good based on knowledge.

Citizens of a family state learn that they cannot realize their own good except by contributing to the social good, and they are also educated to desire only what is good for themselves and their society. Plato's most cogent defense of this ideal is that a peaceful and prosperous society will be impossible unless children learn to associate their own good with the social good. Unless the social good that they are taught is worthy of pursuit, they will grow to be unfulfilled and dissatisfied with the society that miseducated them. All states that fail to fulfill this responsibility over the education of children will therefore degenerate out of internal disharmony.

It is important to emphasize that Plato's family state provides no support for any educational authority that teaches children a way of life that cannot be rationally defended as morally superior to other ways of life. The state may not argue simply: "Because we wish to achieve social harmony, we shall indoctrinate all children to believe that our way of life is best." A reasonable response then would surely be: "But why should you have the authority to impose your way of thinking on the next generation. Why shouldn't I have the authority to impose my way?" And, of course, there will be many other people whose responses will be the same, but whose conceptions of the good life will be at odds with both my own and that of the state's educational authorities. On the Platonic argument, it is essential to the justice of the state's educational claims that its conception of the good life for every person be *the right one*. States that assume a parental role to educate according to false opinion are no better than Sophists who assume a professorial role to teach children virtue without knowing what virtue is. Indeed, sophistical states are worse than individual sophists because they can wield far more power.

The Platonic family state, however, has its own problems. A major one is the difficulty of someone or some group actually determining (in practice as well as in principle) the correct conception of the good for every person (Popper, 1971, pp. 18–34, 157–68). It is not that we know that a single conception of justice and the good *cannot in principle* be discovered. It is that we have no good reason to expect any political authority to be so wise in principle and impartial in practice.

Another, more telling criticism is one of principle: it proceeds by accepting the possibility that someone sufficiently wise and conscientious might discover the good. She would then try to convince the rest of us that she had discovered *the* good, not just another contestable theory of the good, and the good for us, not just the good appropriate to some other people. Were she to succeed in convincing us, there would be no need to rule over us. Were she to fail, she would need (as Plato recognized) to wipe the social slate clean by exiling "all those in the city who happen to be older than ten; and taking over their children, . . . rear them – far away from those dispositions they now have from their parents" (Plato, 1968, p. 220, 541a). That is not only an exorbitantly high price to pay for realizing a just society, it is a price that just authorities will be unwilling to pay. Socrates recoils from the idea on behalf of the philosopher king, suggesting that he would be unwilling to assume political power unless forced to do so. The people who are willing to exert such power are precisely those we ought to fear will wield it tyrannically and to bad ends (ibid., p. 274, 592a).

This objection to the family state is both practical and moral. A life that is good for a free person consists in part in a life that the person recognizes as good and therefore wants to live. Otherwise the life, however "objectively" good, will not be lived as such, and will be a misfortune for the person forced to live it. "That may be the best life to which someone – educated from birth in the proper manner – can aspire," I might admit, "but it's not the good life for me. And don't I have a claim to living a life that is good for me (provided I do not harm others by so doing)?" The objectively good life, defined as the life that is best for a person who is properly educated from birth, need not be the good life, or even the closest approximation of the good life, for people who are not so educated.

What about a state that insists on exclusive authority over children so they will not create the same problem for the next generation? The claim to *exclusive* authority over children is too great to entrust to a state, or to any authority (including parents, as we shall see when we consider the state of families). The freedom to raise children entails discretionary authority over the education of our children within the family, although that discretion is far from limitless and also must leave room for public education – for free and equal citizenship. Children are future citizens, but that does not make them mere creatures of the state.

As future citizens, children need to be educated to share authority over the collective decisions in their society. Placing exclusive educational authority in the hands of an unaccountable elite is an unpromising way of achieving free and equal citizenship. If citizens have a claim to free and equal citizenship, then part of that freedom will involve holding state educators accountable. The family state does not make room for such political accountability to the people who are governed. It rejects reciprocity, or mutual justification of mutually binding laws, which democracy defends.

The Platonic perspective refuses to recognize the force of the claims of reciprocity. Yet these claims constitute the most forceful challenge to anyone's exclusive authority over education. To be justified, the family state would need to recognize a realm of parental authority and it would also need to be democratically accountable. But then it would cease to be a family state.

The family state attempts to constrain our choices among ways of life and educational purposes in a way that is incompatible with the legitimate claims of parents and citizens. In its unsuccessful attempt to do so, it successfully presents the strongest case that educational knowledge should be translated into political power. But that case, as we have seen, is not strong enough to render illegitimate the claims of parents and citizens to share in educational authority.

The State of Families

States that aspire to the moral unity of families underestimate the strength and deny the legitimacy of any substantial parental authority over children. It is no coincidence that Plato's *Republic* required the wresting of children away from parents for the sake of educating them correctly. Radically opposed to the family state is the state of families, which places all educational authority ultimately in the hands of parents.

Theorists of the state of families offer two different justifications of parental educational authority, one based on consequences and the other based on rights. John Locke primarily maintained that parents are the best protectors of their children's future interests, while Thomas Aquinas claimed that parents have a natural right to educational authority. Some contemporary defenders of the state of families make both of these arguments, and they often add another weaker argument, based on the individual freedom of parents, without noting that individual freedom of choice ends where power over others begins. (For the first justification, see Friedman, 1962, pp. 85–107; Coons and Sugarman, 1978. For the second justification, see Schrag, 1971, p. 363.) Charles Fried argues that "the right to form one's child's values, one's child's life plan and the right to lavish *attention on* the child are extensions of the basic right not to be interfered with in doing these things for oneself" (Fried, 1978, p. 152). Fried bases parental rights over children on "the facts of reproduction" and the absence of a societal right to make choices for children.

Although the appeal of the state of families is apparent once we recognize the defects of a family state, *none* of these theoretical arguments justifies resting all educational authority ultimately in the hands of parents. It is one thing to recognize the right of parents to educate their children as members of a family, quite another to claim that this right of familial education extends to an exclusive and ultimate right of parents to insulate their children from exposure to ways of thinking and living that conflict with their own. The consequentialist argument is also weak: parents cannot simply be counted upon to equip their children with the education necessary to exercising freedom for themselves and becoming equal citizens of a democratic society. Some parents are unable (often through no fault of their own) and others are unwilling to accept such educational responsibility (see *Wisconsin* v. *Yoder*, 406 US 205, 1972). The widespread teaching of intolerance, which the state of families

400

would support as long as parents choose such teaching, would undermine the ability of a democracy to ensure all individuals the conditions of free and equal citizenship.

The strongest argument against the state of families is not that parents will teach intolerance – some will and others will not – but rather that neither parents nor states have a right to ultimate and exclusive authority over the education of children. Because the future freedom of children to live their own lives as they see fit is at stake – and implicit in the very claim that parents and other adults make to being treated as free and equal beings – the educational authority of parents has to be partial to be justified. Having already emphasized the danger of permitting a centralized state to monopolize education, it is now appropriate to recognize the danger of placing ultimate and exclusive authority in the hands of parents. (Locke himself, it should be noted, rejected the argument that children are the property of their parents.)

The same Lockean perspective that requires a state to grant adults a set of basic personal and political liberties also commits it to assuring children an education that makes those freedoms both possible and meaningful in the future. Dividing authority between parents and state is far less threatening to the future freedom of children than resting educational authority in parents or state alone. But a divided authority is not all that an education for freedom requires. It requires helping children to develop their faculties of reasoning and their capacities of discernment. Nevertheless, the aim of education that Locke recommends in his *Conduct of the Understanding*, moral freedom, is hard to reconcile with the means, namely exclusive parental authority, which Locke defends in the *Second Treatise*. Since schooling was overwhelmingly the province of the church in Locke's time, and Locke was an early defender of separation of church and state, it is not surprising that he looked to parents rather than the state to support schooling.

The fundamental oversight of the state of families is its assumption that the welfare of children will be safeguarded simply by securing the freedom of parents. Its fundamental insight is recognizing that parental freedom within the family can be consistent with the interests of children in becoming free and equal citizens of a democratic society, so long as the basic interests of children are safeguarded. What we have learned so far from the strengths and weaknesses of the family state and the state of families is that there is no simple way of resolving the tension between parental and political authority over the education of children, since both are necessary, yet neither is sufficient to secure the future of children as free and equal persons. The state may not grant parents absolute authority over their children's education in the name of individual freedom, nor may it claim exclusive educational authority in the name of communal solidarity. That there is no simple resolution to the tension between educational authorities should not deter us from searching for a better resolution than that offered by either the family state or the state of families.

The State of Individuals

John Stuart Mill argued that

It is in the case of children that misapplied notions of liberty are a real obstacle to the fulfillment by the State of its duties. One would almost think that a man's children were supposed to be

401

literally, and not metaphorically, a part of himself, so jealous is opinion of the smallest interference of law with his absolute and exclusive control over them. (Mill, 1977, p. 302)

Having exposed a central flaw in the state of families, Mill defended a more liberal conception of education. "All attempts by the State to bias the conclusions of its citizens on disputed subjects are evil," Mill argued, hence the government should "leave to parents to obtain the education where and how they pleased, and content itself with helping to pay the school fees of the poorer classes of children" and limiting the educational authority of parents through (among other things) a system of "public examinations, extending to all children and beginning at an early age." If a child fails the examination, Mill recommends that "the father, unless he has some sufficient ground of excuse, might be subjected to a moderate fine, to be worked out, if necessary, by his labor." To insure neutrality, the knowledge tested by the examinations should "be confined to facts and positive science exclusively" (Mill, 1977, pp. 302–3).

Some contemporary liberals extend the logic of Mill's argument to defend a state of individuals. They criticize all educational authorities that threaten to bias the choices of children toward some disputed or controversial ways of life and away from others. Their ideal educational authority is one that maximizes future choice without prejudicing children toward any controversial conception of the good life.

The state of individuals champions the dual goals of *opportunity* for choice and *neutrality* among disputed or controversial conceptions of the good life. A just educational authority must not bias children's choices among good lives, but it must provide every child with an opportunity to choose freely and rationally among the widest range of lives.

Neither parents nor states are likely to fulfill the ideal of neutrality. Parents are unlikely to resist passing some of their particular values and cultural prejudices on to their children. States are equally likely to subvert the neutrality principle: they will try to teach children to appreciate the particular values and cultural prejudices that hold their society together. Recognizing the power of these parental and political impulses, liberals dedicated to neutrality look for an educational authority more impartial than parents or public officials. They defend the authority of professional educators who are motivated by the interests of children in learning and unconstrained by parental or political authority.

Contemporary liberals often invoke the spirit of Kant or Mill to defend the ideal of neutrality, overlooking its moral limitations and the way both Kant and Mill diverged from defending neutrality in its pure principled form, which is unrealizable. In its pure principled form, neutrality is also undesirable. There is moral value in the desire of educators to cultivate basic virtues in children before they are capable of impartially considering all of the pros and cons of cultivating the basic virtues. By the time they learn to critically assess the virtues they have developed and the values to which they have been predisposed, the predispositions are already there. This does not mean that children who are taught certain virtuous habits (such as non-violence and honesty) before their critical capacities are fully developed are incapable of assessing those virtues. But it does mean that their education has not been neutral between virtues and vices. Nor should it be.

Nor can an education be culturally neutral, which is what the state of individuals in its pure principled form requires. When children learn to speak English rather than French, or Dutch rather than German, or when they are taught to be bilingual, they learn not by choice, but by cultural predisposition. And this cultural predisposition skews their future choices, even if it does not uniquely determine who they will be, or how they will decide to live their lives. Cultural predisposition of children through education (and socialization) can be justified by the need for cultural coherence, which is another name for a non-neutral education (Ackerman, 1980, p. 141).

What liberals rightly discern as a problem in using education to bias children toward some cultures and conceptions of the good life is not non-neutrality *per se* but the pretense on the part of those educators who claim, or teach as if they knew, that their culture is morally superior to others. Children are therefore biased into thinking, without actually subjecting their thinking to critical evaluation, that their language and culture are morally superior to all others. The antidote to this problem – and it is a problem that can accompany the necessarily selective nature of any education – is not to aspire to an impossible neutrality but rather to teach in a way that does not close children's minds to other cultures and ways of life. To teach open-mindedness, however, is not to teach in a morally neutral way. It is to teach an important democratic and liberal virtue. The virtue is democratically important because all democracies are culturally and morally pluralistic. The virtue is a virtue because it entails some moral commitments: the commitment to educate children in a way that encourages them to be open-minded at the same time as they are morally committed. Open-mindedness goes together with moral commitment once one recognizes that moral commitments can be subject to reasonable questioning, and through such questioning to affirmation (or rejection).

Liberals who say that freedom is the *correct* end of education cannot mean to defend a limitless freedom without moral limits. An education for equal freedom is not morally neutral. Freedom is a social good – indeed an individual right in a liberal democracy – when it is equal freedom of all individuals as free and equal persons. Equal freedom is also an individual good, but one whose limits are set by our social being and context. My freedom must be compatible with your equal freedom, and vice versa. My child's education for freedom must be compatible with your child's education for freedom, and vice versa. It follows that the state of individuals can only realize its defensible aim of educating for freedom if it recognizes the social context and constraints of educating for freedom. Among those constraints are the need to provide some kind of cultural coherence in education and the need to educate children to equal freedom, not the kind of freedom for some that effectively subordinates others.

The strength of the state of individuals is the high value it places on educating children so that they can live a free life and the life of a free people. The weakness of the state of individuals is its benign neglect of the fact that educating children for individual freedom entails also educating them in a social context that is conducive to such freedom. That context must also provide for political freedoms: the equal freedom of individuals to choose not only a good life for themselves but also to collectively decide as political equals on the shape of their society, which includes its culture. Cultures change partly as a consequence of political choices, such as what language and history curricula to teach children in schools.

403

An educated, self-reflective people must have both personal and political liberties. Political liberties distinguish democratic societies from undemocratic ones. Citizens of a democratic society are free only if the democracy also secures their personal liberties along with their political ones. Many personal freedoms, such as free speech, are also political freedoms. Taking individual freedom in all its dimensions seriously therefore means taking democracy seriously. And taking democracy seriously means taking democratic education seriously. We therefore need to move beyond the state of individuals to a democratic state of education that is committed to supporting a plurality of conceptions of the good life and a corresponding plurality of educational authorities. Without this, tyranny is more likely than not to prevail in education as in politics.

Democratic Education

The ideal of democratic education is what I call *conscious social reproduction.* "Conscious" means that education aims to cultivate the capacity in all children to reasonably reflect on their own lives and the society and world within which they live. "Social" means that such a capacity aims not only for personal but also for political freedom, since choices at the social level profoundly affect choices at the individual level. Without political freedom, individuals are not fully free. Reproduction does not mean replication, but is the aim of education to empower individuals to make choices within the contexts in which they find themselves. We cannot choose our personal or political lives *de novo.* Our choices are contextual, and therefore conscious social reproduction recognizes the need to empower individuals to think contextually about how they want to re-produce their society, rather than merely mindlessly replicate it.

Conscious social reproduction, like any educational ideal, is not self-evidently correct or uncontroversial. It is a morally defensible ideal because it leaves maximum room for citizens both to live their own lives as they see fit and to shape their society together as free and equal persons. A society committed to conscious social reproduction has a moral response to those adults who object to a way of education on grounds that it conflicts with their moral values. "The virtues of freedom, honesty, non-violence, critical thinking, and so on that democratic education teaches," educational authorities can reply in the first instance, "are necessary to give children the chance to live a free life as both individuals and citizens. The kind of character you are asking us to cultivate would deprive children of that chance, the very chance that justifies your own claim to living a good life and sharing as equals in educational authority."

Democratic education accepts the partial insight of the family state: education must have a social component and authorities that are not only parental. Democratic education accepts the partial insight of the state of families: parents must also share educational authority. The life of a free person includes the choice of being a parent, and being a parent entails having some educational authority over one's children. Parental authority must not be considered exclusive and ultimate authority, which would deprive children of the education they need in preparation for the freedom to live their own lives as adults as they see fit, and also deprive a democracy of the ability to educate children in preparation for exercising the political freedoms of free and equal citizens. Democratic education accepts two important partial insights of the state of individuals. One is that living the life of a free person is a basic aim of education. Another is that professional educators need to be well equipped and motivated to teach the deliberative skills that are essential to living such a life.

Why is democratic education committed to teaching skills for choosing among good lives rather than the single best way of life for each person? It would be an illegitimate pretension to educational authority on anyone's part to deprive any child of the capacities necessary for choice among good lives. Even if I know that my way of life is best, this does not entail a right to impose my way of life on anyone else, even on my own child, at the cost of depriving her of the ability to choose a good life for herself. Second, the same skills that are necessary to choosing among good lives are also necessary for the political freedom to share as free and equal citizens in a representative democracy. It would also be an illegitimate pretension on educators' part to think that they know precisely what political decisions citizens should make, and make those decisions for them, rather than educate them to be capable of holding their representatives accountable for political decisions, according to their own best lights.

Educating children to live the lives of free and equal persons, which includes being free and equal citizens, does not entail an education that itself values only freedom. Educational authorities must teach children those virtues that are conditions of the lives of free people, which include tolerance, justice, and reciprocity, without which democratic societies, and therefore freedom, cannot flourish. Teaching these virtues also entails educating children to develop their capacities to assess these virtues, and therefore to accept, reject, or revise their understanding of them through the use of their reason.

Cultivating moral character is therefore part of a democratic education. Who, it might be challenged, should decide what kind of character to cultivate? We have examined and rejected three philosophically forceful answers to this question. Theorists of the family state rest educational authority exclusively in the hands of a centralized state in an attempt to wed knowledge of the good life with political power. Theorists of the state of families place educational authority exclusively in the hands of parents, on the assumption that they have a natural right to such authority or that they alone are the educational authorities who can safeguard the welfare of their children. Theorists of the state of individuals refuse to rest educational authority in any hands without the assurance that the choices of children will not be prejudiced in favor of some ways of life and against others – an assurance that no educator can provide.

None of these conceptions of educational authority provides an adequate foundation for educating children to become free and equal persons and citizens. Yet each contains a partial truth. States, parents, and professional educators all have important roles to play in educating free and equal persons. A democratic state of education recognizes that educational authority must be shared among parents, citizens, and professional educators, even though such sharing does not guarantee that power will be wedded to knowledge, that parents can successfully pass their prejudices on to their children, or that education will be neutral among competing conceptions of the good life.

405

If a democratic education does not guarantee virtue based on knowledge, or the autonomy of families, or neutrality among ways of life, what is the value of its premise of shared educational authority? The broad distribution of educational authority among citizens, parents, and professional educators supports the core aim of democratic education: educating free and equal persons who are capable of engaging in conscious social reproduction. Unlike a family state, a democratic state recognizes the value of parental education in perpetuating particular conceptions of the good life, consistent with the future freedom of children to choose their own way of life for themselves and to share as free and equal citizens in the political life of their society. Unlike a state of families, a democratic state recognizes the value of professional authority in enabling children to appreciate and to evaluate ways of life other than those favored by their families. Unlike a state of individuals, a democratic state recognizes the value of political education in acculturating children in ways that are consistent with living the life of free persons and sharing the rights and responsibilities of democratic citizenship.

Democratic education is committed to the sharing of educational authority so as to provide all children with an education adequate to their becoming free and equal persons and citizens. They should be educated in a way that they can choose (or not) to participate as equals in democratic politics, choose among good lives (which include raising children, if they so choose), and join (or not) the many associations that partly shape the identities of free people.

Democratic education also acknowledges two reasons for permitting communities to use education to predispose children toward some ways of life and away from others. One reason is grounded on the value of moral freedom. All societies of self-reflective beings must admit the moral value of enabling their members to discern the difference between good and bad ways of life. Children do not learn to discern this difference on the basis of an education that strives for neutrality among ways of life. Children are not taught that bigotry is bad, for example, by offering it as one among many competing conceptions of the good life, and then subjecting it to criticism on grounds that bigots do not admit that other people's conceptions of the good are "equally" good. Children first become the kind of people who are repelled by bigotry, and then they feel the force of the reasons for their repulsion. Reasons to reject bigotry are quite impotent in the absence of such sensibilities: they offer no compelling argument to people who feel no need to treat other people as equals and are willing to live with the consequences of their disrespect of others. To cultivate in children the character that feels the force of reason is a justifiable aim of education.

Education for free choice cannot be the only justifiable aim of education in a democratic society, since part of free political choice is the freedom to pass on particular, non-neutral cultural understandings to children through education. Consistent with our being educated as free persons, we are also educated as people with particular cultural identities, which we have the capacity to affirm, revise, and reject. To focus exclusively on the value of freedom, or even on the value of moral freedom, neglects the value that people may legitimately place on educating children as members of families, communities, and the world today. Education is not timeless, and its time-bound quality orients us toward the world in ways that we value.

Children can be educated as free people who are also predisposed to particular ways of life, but those predispositions should not be taught (or held) as unquestionable prejudices. When children are taught particular languages, they should not be taught that those languages, or the cultures attached to them, are superior. Identifying strongly with language and culture should not be confused with moral superiority. To avoid teaching culture as prejudice, a democratic state should teach children in ways that help them develop their capacity to understand and to evaluate competing conceptions of the good life and the good society. A commitment to developing the capacity for critical deliberation among good lives and societies requires principled limits on all educational authorities, parents, public officials, and professionals.

One principled limit on all educational authorities is *non-repression* of reason. The principle of non-repression prevents the state, and any group within it, from using education to restrict the development of children's capacity for reasoning. Non-repression is completely compatible with also using education to cultivate those character traits that serve as foundations for developing the capacity for reasoning. Cultivation of a democratic character develops rather than represses the use of reason to assess the character traits that are cultivated.

Teaching the skills of reasoned deliberation remains the educational aim most distinctively critical to a democratic society of free and equal citizens. Although non-repression constitutes a constraint on educational authority, it is best conceived as a self-constraint in defense of democratic citizenship. The principle of non-repression derives from the primary value of democratic education, to educate individuals as free and equal persons who are able to hold their representatives accountable. Democratic education is not based on the view that individuals must participate in politics. This would choose a conception of the good life for people. Rather, it is based on the view that they must be educated as children to be capable of choosing a good life for themselves and sharing as free and equal citizens in democratic politics. Free and equal citizens participate in politics as they so choose (to participate) and are chosen (as representatives) by their fellow citizens. To repress the capacity for reasoned deliberation in children is to prevent them from having the opportunity to be free and equal citizens. Because *conscious* social reproduction is the ideal of democratic education, democratic educators constrain themselves from using education to stifle reasoned deliberation of competing conceptions of the good life and the good society.

A second principled limit on legitimate democratic authority, which also follows from the ideal of education for free and equal citizenship, is *non-discrimination*. For democratic education to support conscious *social* reproduction, rather than elite reproduction, all educable children must be adequately educated. Non-discrimination extends the logic of non-repression, since states and families can be selectively repressive by excluding entire groups of children from schooling or by denying them an education conducive to deliberation. Historically, repression in education has commonly taken the more passive form of discrimination in schooling against ethnic and racial minorities, girls, physically disabled, and other socially disfavored groups of children. The effect of discrimination is often to repress, at least temporarily, the ability of members of these groups to share as free and equal citizens in enjoying the social goods that democracy has to offer other more advantaged citizens. Non-discrimination can thus be viewed as the distributional complement to non-repression.

In its most general application to education, non-discrimination prevents the state, and all groups within it, from denying anyone an educational good on grounds irrelevant to the justifiable social purpose of that good. Applied to all aspects of education that are necessary to prepare children for future free and equal citizenship, non-discrimination entails non-exclusion. No educable children may be excluded from an education adequate to develop their capacities for free and equal citizenship.

Non-repression and non-discrimination are principled constraints on parental, popular, and professional sovereignty over education. Why consider such constraints democratic? Democracy is a moral and political ideal, and as such democracy cannot mean merely majority (or plurality) rule. Democracy entails the idea that mutually binding laws and policies should be mutually justified to free and equal persons. Free and equal personhood is therefore basic to democracy, as is the idea of sharing as equals in holding accountable those who make laws and policies in one's name. Free and equal persons must therefore be able to deliberate about their collective lives in order to hold their representatives accountable. The same skills of reasoned deliberation also enable individuals to choose among good lives for themselves, if they so choose. There is no force to be applied here; individuals are free not to participate in politics and not to deliberate about their own lives. But this freedom as adults makes it all the more important that children are educated to have the choice. Educational authorities cannot be allowed to make the choice for them, blocking their choice for the future and violating their democratic birthright.

The principles of non-repression and non-discrimination support deliberative freedom at both the personal and political levels. All citizens should be educated so as to have a chance to choose a good life for themselves and to share in self-consciously shaping the structure of their society. Democratic education leaves open a vast array of lives that may be chosen, but it is not therefore neutral among conceptions of the good life. No conception of education can be. A defense of democratic education does not depend on a claim to neutrality. It depends on the ideal of educating all children to be capable of free and equal personhood and citizenship.

Like the family state, a democratic state of education tries to teach virtues that can be reasonably affirmed, but it does not claim absolute educational authority. One democratic virtue is open-mindedness, and the corresponding capacity to question what one has been taught. Virtues that embrace open-mindedness might best be called *democratic* virtues. To educate all children to be able to reflect reasonably on their society supports their free and equal citizenship and its constitutive role in conscious social reproduction.

Like the state of families, a democratic state upholds a degree of parental authority over education, resisting the view that children are creatures of the state, but also resisting the view that children are the creatures of their parents (which was long taken to mean their fathers, despite the fact that mothers did most of the child-rearing). In recognizing that children should be treated not merely as creatures of a family state or a family, democratic education educates children as future free and equal persons. In this way, democratic education accepts the insight of the state of individuals, that no group can claim to assimilate the identity of children to its own, whether that group be public, parental, or professional.

Like the state of individuals, a democratic state defends a degree of professional authority over education, not on grounds of their neutrality or their exclusive or ultimate authority over children, but rather to the extent that professional educators can help teach children the skills and virtues necessary for free and equal personhood and citizenship. Democratic education therefore is committed to a combination of public, parental, and professional authority, as needed, to educate children as future persons and citizens.

Conclusion: Civic Minimalism and Multiculturalism

Two issues in democratic education have gained prominence in the past decade. The first is whether civic education that is publicly mandated must be minimal so that parental choice is maximal. The second concerns the way in which publicly subsidized schools should respond to the increasingly multicultural character of societies.

How extensive are the civic purposes of schooling? A view called "civic minimalism" defends teaching the minimal requirements that are necessary to permit a democracy to function, but requiring no more. For a democracy to require more than the civic minimum, on this view, constitutes an illegitimate exercise of political authority on the part of citizens over parents. A common corollary of civic minimalism is a voucher system, by which parents have the authority to decide how public monies are spent for their own children in schooling. Civic minimalism weds the "state of families" to a minimal defense of civic education.

By minimizing the civic component of schooling, civic minimalists suggest they can avoid the problem of achieving consensus about civic education. Civic minimalism seeks not to contribute to democratic deliberation but rather to offer an alternative to it. Even if democratic majorities support educational standards that are more than minimal, civic minimalists oppose their authority to implement those standards even in publicly supported schools. Civic minimalists would need to turn to judges to overrule state legislatures, school districts, and boards of education that impose higher standards than their minimalist conception.

Paradoxically, civic minimalists must still rely on democratic justifications: any legitimate law or constitutional amendment that defined and enforced the civic minimum would require democratic support. This creates a serious problem for civic minimalists, since there are so many competing conceptions of the civic minimum, some defending no more than literacy and numeracy, others teaching civic virtues such as toleration, racial and gender non-discrimination, and mutual respect. Who has the legitimate authority to impose a contestable conception of a civic minimum as a ceiling as well as a floor on democratic authority in the face of democratic disagreement?

For civic minimalism to work, its advocates would need to defend a specific, substantive conception of the civic minimum, and convince enough other people of its unique correctness that no other set of public requirements on schools would be justifiable. The problem is that all such substantive conceptions are subject to the same sort of reasonable disagreement that minimalists claim is grounds for rejecting democratic education in favor of civic minimalism. Because many people reasonably reject civic minimalism, its self-defense as a means of avoiding democratic disagreement is self-defeating.

The increasing multiculturalism of modern societies raises another important set of questions for democratic education. In the United States, students were once taught histories that systematically excluded the voices of minority groups, and were commonly expected, regardless of their religion, to participate in Protestant prayers and Christian hymns. I mention these practices here, rather than more positive ones, to illustrate two troubling features of a public schooling that does not appropriately recognize multiculturalism. The history books illustrate the first feature: disrespect of experiences of groups that have suffered discrimination. The second feature is reflected in the practices that pressure students to conform to Protestant religious practices: intolerance of dissenting beliefs and practices.

These two features of public schooling are indefensible from any moral and political perspective that would treat individuals as civic equals. They are impermissible in light of the principles of non-repression and non-discrimination. Public institutions should manifest and cultivate mutual respect among individuals as free and equal citizens. This aim is basic to every democratic ideal that defends free and equal citizenship. A democratic education that is consistent with these conceptions calls for two different responses to multiculturalism, responses that are united by a single principled aim of treating individuals as civic equals, free to live their own lives as they see fit – as long as they do not harm others – and empowered to share as equals in the collective decisions of their society.

The first response, in reaction to exclusions of the experiences of entire groups from the curriculum, is to publicly recognize the experiences of oppressed groups, rather than neglecting or denigrating those experiences and thereby exalting those of more dominant groups. The second response is similarly inspired by a commitment to mutual respect among citizens. This response is agreeing to disagree about beliefs and practices, such as sexual orientation, that are a matter of basic liberty. This is the response of toleration. Toleration substitutes for imposing any single substantive system of beliefs and practices on all students, regardless of their religious or other spiritual convictions. Multicultural democracies cannot afford to take for granted either of these two responses, for they are not the inevitable product of a democratic process. Instead, democratic education should work actively to support respect for individuals and their equal rights as citizens, rather than support the survival rights of traditional cultures or defend the dictates of any single authority – whether it be the state, parents, or professionals – simply because they posses decision-making authority (for a defense of survival rights of cultures, see Taylor, 1994).

See also 1 THE SOCRATIC TRADITION; 6 ENLIGHTENMENT LIBERALISM; 7 ROUSSEAU, DEWEY, AND DEMOCRACY; 29 CHURCH, STATE, AND EDUCATION; 30 COMMON SCHOOLING AND EDUCATIONAL CHOICE; 31 CHILDREN'S RIGHTS; 33 EDUCATIONAL EQUALITY AND JUSTICE

References

Ackerman, B. (1980) *Social Justice in the Liberal State*. New Haven, CT: Yale University Press.

Coons, J. E. and Sugarman, S. (1978) *Education by Choice: The Case for Family Control*. Berkeley: University of California Press.

Fried, C. (1978) *Right and Wrong*. Cambridge, MA: Harvard University Press.

Friedman, M. (1962) *Capitalism and Freedom*. Chicago: University of Chicago Press.

Gutmann, A. (1999) *Democratic Education*. Princeton, NJ: Princeton University Press.

Mill, J. S. (1977) *On Liberty*. In *The Collected Works of John Stuart Mill, volume 18*, ed. J. M. Robinson. Toronto: University of Toronto Press, pp. 213–310.

Murphy, W. F. (1980) An ordering of constitutional values. *Southern California Law Review*, 53(2), 703–60.

Plato (1968) *The Republic*, trans. A. Bloom. New York: Basic Books.

Popper, K. (1971) *The Open Society and Its Enemies, volume 1*. Princeton, NJ: Princeton University Press.

Rousseau, J. J. (1972) Émile, or On education, trans. B. Foxley. New York: Everyman (original work published 1762).

Schrag, F. (1971) The right to educate. *School Review*, 79(3), 359–78.

Taylor, C. (1994) The politics of recognition. In A. Gutmann (ed.), *Multiculturalism: Examining the Politics of Recognition*. Princeton: Princeton University Press, pp. 25–74.

29

Church, State, and Education

William Galston

The variety of political regimes and of religions makes it impossible to speak of "the" relation among church, state and education. To move toward greater definition, let us begin by considering three ideal-typical structures.

In a *theocratic* regime, the dominant religion will largely define the purposes and authority of state institutions, and state power will shape the content of education toward the ends of that religion. History offers many examples of this theocratic structure, an extreme form of which we encounter in contemporary Afghanistan.

As religions differ, so do theocracies. Traditional Judaism and Islam express faith through bodies of law that minutely regulate individual conduct, as contrasted with the Christian focus on doctrinal belief and theology. Within Christianity, differences between the hierarchical centralization of the Catholic Church and the more decentralized, congregational form of mainstream Protestantism have shaped the regimes these faiths have dominated. Contemporary Iran illustrates a tension characteristic of every revealed religion today, between literalist-fundamentalist tendencies and forces seeking a rapprochement with modernity to the extent that fidelity to essential religious concepts and categories will permit.

In a second ideal type, the *civic republic*, the state may invent, or select, a "civil" religion that serves public ends, and it will certainly try to restrict the activities of other religions to the extent that they undermine the power and purposes of the state. Accordingly, the civic republic may establish a monopoly system of public education. Short of that, it will do what it can to circumscribe the content of religiously based education and to squelch religious teachings contrary to the tenets of civil authority. The long struggle between the Catholic Church and a succession of post-Revolutionary French republics exemplifies these processes.

Liberal-constitutional democracy (hereafter LCD) presents a third ideal-type. In LCDs, many different religions are allowed to operate more or less freely, state power and purposes enjoy substantial autonomy from any particular religion, and public and non-public (including religious) systems of education coexist. Also characteristic of LCDs is a substantial though contested sphere of parental authority to make educational choices for one's own children. By contrast, civic republics from Sparta to the French Revolution have asserted near-plenipotentiary claims over children, denying the moral force of the intimate bonds between parents and children and working to minimize the political impact of those bonds. While theocracies may choose to allow parents of non-established religions to educate their children in the tenets of their faith, these regimes typically prevent the parents who adhere to the state religion from educating their children in any ways other than those the theocratic authorities may require.

One might infer that specifying a regime type eliminates the apparent indeterminacy of the church/state/education relation. To the extent that the choice of regime has normative consequences, one might conclude that this normativity extends to the appropriate division of educational authority among religion, state institutions, and families. So if we believe (as many theorists have claimed) that LCD is the best form of government under modern circumstances, then the educational arrangements characteristic of LCDs would enjoy a normatively preferred status as well. But this move turns out to be too quick. When we move from the general formal features of LCDs to actual LCD regimes, significant differences emerge among those regimes, making it difficult to identify empirically typical patterns, let alone normatively preferable educational practices.

The comparative research of Charles Glenn and others has revealed the extent of these differences. Some LCDs have established churches, while others do not. Some have a handful of dominant faiths and denominations, while others display much more dispersed patterns of religious affiliation. Most LCDs have national educational curricula and standards of educational achievement, with local educational authorities that implement rather than create educational policy. By contrast, the United States has a system of geographical differential and dispersed power over educational matters. (What national authority over education there is in the United States typically comes in the form of regulations imposed as conditions for the receipt of federal funds, which amount to less than 10 percent of total spending for elementary and secondary education.) In most LCDs, public funds are used to finance private (including religious) schools, often on equal terms with public schools. Here again the United States stands out; the US Constitution and the constitutions of most of the fifty states erect substantial barriers to the use of public funds for private (especially religious) schools (Glenn, 2000, 2001).

This diversity of educational structures reflects deep differences of national culture, history, and politics, as well as divergent weightings among various dimensions of fundamental values. Even if political philosophy can resolve age-old controversies among regime types in favor of LCD, educational philosophy may not be competent to go much farther in specifying normatively preferred educational structures.

To probe these limits, the following remarks consider both philosophical and legal sources, and move back and forth between claims applicable to all LCDs and claims applicable to the specific case of the United States. While decisions of the US Supreme Court necessarily draw on the specific provisions and traditions of the US Constitution, these decisions often make claims which, if correct, have general implications for educational practices across LCDs.

As we consider the tangled relations of religion, state and education in LCDs, two facts become clear. First, decisions about education inevitably spark tensions between public institutions and parents over the control of children. To understand these tensions, we must try to assess the competing claims of state and parental authority in this sphere. Second, we cannot clarify the claims of religion in the educational

413

arena without examining the appropriate role of religious discourse in the public dialogue of LCDs.

The thesis that I develop is roughly this: in establishing the aims of, and control over, education, three sets of interests must somehow be coordinated. First, the conditions for the normal development of children must be secured, their ability to become contributing members of the economy and society must be fostered, and the growth over time in their capacity for sound independent judgment must be recognized. Second, the liberal democratic state must act, not only to safeguard the developmental interests of children, but also to promote the effective functioning of its basic institutions. Third, the special relationship between parents and children must be reflected in the allocation of educational authority, and so must what I shall call the "expressive interest" of parents in raising their children in a manner consistent with their understanding of what gives meaning and value to life.

While each of these interests must find appropriate expression in practical decisions, there is no guarantee that they will fit together into a harmonious whole. Pressed to the hilt, any one of them will entail costs to the others that may well be judged excessive. Hence, sound education policy cannot be exclusively state-centered, parent-centered, or child-centered, and none of these interests can be given absolute priority, or function as trumps, in discussions of educational policy.

Education in the United States: Historical and Constitutional Developments

John Stuart Mill regarded the right of the state to compel parents to educate their children as "almost a self-evident axiom." Yet writing in 1859, he observed that in practice, few of his fellow citizens were willing to affirm its force. While most acknowledged the moral duty of parents to educate their children, they denied that the state had the right to enforce it (Mill, 1956, p. 128). Much the same situation prevailed on the other side of the Atlantic. Despite the spread of the "common school" ideal in the early decades of the nineteenth century, as late as the eve of the Civil War only two states (Massachusetts and New York) had enacted compulsory education statutes (Butts and Cremin, 1953, p. 415). Many citizens who conceded that this policy would promote the general welfare nonetheless denied that the state could properly, and constitutionally, go down this road.

Within decades, matters had changed radically. By 1900, thirty-two states had passed compulsory attendance laws. By 1918, such laws were universal throughout the United States. Despite its readiness to strike down a wide range of social legislation as infringements of individual liberty, not even the Lochner-era Supreme Court was willing to raise constitutional questions about the power of the states to enforce such laws.

It is instructive to review the kinds of arguments in favor of public education that gained currency in the century between the onset of the common school debate and the establishment of universal compulsory education. The first may be called "limited perfectionism": a certain measure of education was necessary for normal intellectual and moral development and for full participation in cultural and associational life.

414

The second revolved around basic social obligations: education enabled individuals to maintain their economic independence and to discharge their duties to family members. Third, education was thought to promote a range of public goods: economic growth, appropriate civic beliefs and virtues, national unity and "Americanization," and a strong national defense. The increased credibility of these claims arose from some key developments; in particular, the industrialization of the economy, the diversification of the population through immigration, and the emergence of the United States in world affairs.

Early in the twentieth century, the US Supreme Court acted to ratify, but also to limit, the evolving power of government in educational affairs. Three decisions handed down in the 1920s helped to define the constitutional context within which education policy has operated ever since.

Reflecting in part the nativist passions stirred by the First World War, the state of Nebraska passed a law forbidding instruction in any modern language other than English. Under this statute, a Nebraska trial court convicted a teacher in a Lutheran parochial school for teaching a Bible class in German. In *Meyer* v. *Nebraska* (262 US 390), decided in 1923, the Supreme Court struck down this law as a violation of the Fourteenth Amendment's liberty guarantee.

Writing for seven members of the Court, Justice McReynolds noted that "it is the natural duty of the parent to give his children education suitable to their station in life; and nearly all the States, including Nebraska, enforce this obligation by compulsory laws" (p. 400). This kind of legislation is not in itself constitutionally dubious: "The power of the State to compel attendance at some school and to make reasonable regulations for all schools . . . is not questioned" (p. 402). The question is whether the prohibition of all instruction in modern languages other than English meets this test. Justice McReynolds argued that it did not:

That the State may do much, go very far, indeed, in order to improve the quality of its citizens, physically, mentally and morally, is clear; but the individual has certain fundamental rights which must be respected. A desirable end cannot be promoted by prohibited means. (p. 401)

Nebraska's action represented such prohibited means, because it violated both Meyer's right to teach German and the right of parents to engage him to instruct their children in that language:

The desire of the legislature to foster a homogeneous people with American ideals prepared readily to understand current discussions of civic matters is easy to appreciate. But the means adopted, we think, exceed the limitations upon the power of the State. (p. 402)

In a remarkable if controversial passage, Justice McReynolds expanded the discussion beyond even constitutional bounds. He identified the underlying theory of the Nebraska law with the practices of Sparta and the pedagogical principles of Plato's *Republic*. But "their ideas touching the relation between individual and State were wholly different from those upon which our institutions rest" and could not be implemented "without doing violence to both letter and spirit of the Constitution" (pp. 401–2). Our constitutional conception of liberty guarantees parents a wide though not unlimited sphere of discretion to educate their children as they see fit.

415

The Supreme Court handed down a second key ruling just two years later. The background can be summarized briefly. Through a ballot initiative, the people of Oregon adopted a law requiring parents and legal guardians to send all children between the ages of eight and sixteen to public schools. In practice, this amounted to outlawing most if not all non-public schools. The Society of Sisters, an Oregon corporation that maintained a system of Catholic schools, sued, claiming that the law was inconsistent with the Fourteenth Amendment. In *Pierce* v. *Society of Sisters* (268 US 510), decided in 1925, the Court emphatically agreed. Justice McReynolds, this time writing for a unanimous court, declared:

we think it entirely plain that the Act... unreasonably interferes with the liberty of parents and guardians to direct the upbringing and education of children under their control.... The fundamental theory of liberty upon which all governments in this Union repose excludes any general power of the State to standardize its children by forcing them to accept instruction from public teachers only. The child is not the mere creature of the State; those who nurture him and direct his destiny have the right, coupled with the high duty, to recognize and prepare him for additional obligations. (pp. 534–5)

This is not to say that the state is devoid of authority over private education. As the *Pierce* court observed,

No question is raised concerning the power of the State reasonably to regulate all schools, to inspect, supervise and examine them, their teachers and pupils; to require that all children of proper age attend some school, that teachers shall be of good moral character and patriotic disposition, that certain studies plainly essential to good citizenship must be taught, and that nothing be taught which is manifestly inimical to the public welfare. (p. 534)

But how far may such regulation go? What does it mean to regulate "reasonably" rather than unreasonably? In this context consider the third of our cases, *Farrington* v. *Tokushige* (273 US 284), decided in 1927. Faced with a proliferation of schools teaching the Japanese language to students of Japanese ancestry, the Territory of Hawaii enacted a law strictly regulating all foreign language schools. Among its other provisions, the law imposed a per capita tax on these schools and gave the territorial government the right to determine hours, course of study, entrance requirements, textbook, and teacher qualification.

The Court found that this law and the administrative measures adopted pursuant to it "go far beyond mere regulation of privately supported schools.... They give affirmative direction concerning the intimate and essential details of such schools." Enforcement of the act, the Court concluded, would destroy most of the regulated schools and would deprive parents of a fair opportunity to obtain instruction, not obviously harmful, that they desire for their children. "The Japanese parent has the right to direct the education of his own child without unreasonable restrictions," but the law in question represents "a deliberate plan to bring foreign language schools under a strict governmental control for which the record discloses no adequate reason" (p. 298). Because the law is inconsistent with the liberty guarantees of the Fifth Amendment, it cannot stand. The Fifth Amendment rather than the Fourteenth applies because Hawaii was at that time a territory rather than a state, and the Fourteenth Amendment constrains only state governments (p. 299).

Taken together, these decisions establish three propositions. First, in the US Constitution's version of liberal democracy, there is in principle a division of authority between parents and the state. Government has the right to require parents to educate their children and to specify some basic features of that education, wherever it may be conducted. Parents, however, have a wide and protected range of choices as to how to discharge that duty to educate. Second, the state may not deploy its regulatory power to deny in practice what it grants in principle. In particular, government may not require non-public educational institutions to conform themselves to public schools as a condition of their continued existence. And third, there are some things the government may not rightly do, even in the name of forming good citizens. The appeal to the requisites of civic education is powerful, but not always dispositive when opposed by claims based on parental authority or individual liberty.

From History to Theory

As we have seen, John Stuart Mill regards it as virtually self-evident that the state "should require and compel the education, up to a certain standard, of every human being who is born its citizen" (Mill, 1956, p. 128). In his account, the state's authority derives from parental responsibility. The bare fact of causing the existence of another human being brings into play more responsibilities than does virtually any other human act. In particular, "it is one of the most sacred duties of the parents (or, as law and usage now stand, the father), after summoning a human being into the world, to give to that being an education fitting him to perform his part well in life toward others and toward himself." The failure to do so is a "moral crime, both against the unfortunate offspring and against society; and . . . if the parent does not fulfill this obligation, the State ought to see it fulfilled" (ibid.).

Mill assumes that this educational duty flows directly from the fact of biological generation, coupled with broad features of the individual and social good. Parents do not have the right to neglect the education of their children in ways that impose avoidable burdens on their fellow citizens; for example, by raising children unable to contribute to the economy or unwilling to obey the law. Nor do they have the right to deprive their children of what Mill assumes to be the profound and pervasive benefits of education: the development of human faculties is at the core of what he terms the "permanent interests of man as a progressive being" (ibid., p. 14). Mill accepts a version of the thesis I earlier termed "limited perfectionism"; the necessity of education reflects not only the contextually specific requisites of advanced economies, but also non-contextual features of the human condition. The state has a legitimate interest in enforcing parental responsibility, both to enhance social utility and to create human beings in the "maturity of their faculties" who are "capable of being improved by free and equal discussion" (ibid., pp. 13–14). Mill suggests that this parental responsibility is material as well as moral: parents must finance their children's education to the extent they can. His insistence on individual responsibility is striking: the "moral crime" lies not only in willfully depriving a child of education

417

but also in bringing a child into the world without a "fair prospect" of being able to afford a basic education. (He even endorses the legitimacy of European laws forbidding couples to marry unless they have the means to support a family (ibid., p.132).) But he also stresses the element of social responsibility: when the state makes education compulsory, it must provide sliding-scale subsidies for lower-income families and pay outright for the education of children whose parents cannot afford to contribute anything. So all members of the society must do their part to sustain a system of compulsory education that benefits society as a whole.

Mill distinguishes between state-enforced compulsory education and direct state provision of education. He opposes all policies that lead to state dominance over or monopoly of education. Diversity of character and opinion is the key to both individual flourishing and social progress. But a state-dominated system of education is a "mere contrivance for molding people to be exactly like one another" that "establishes a despotism over the mind." A state system of education "should only exist, if it exist at all, as one among many competing experiments, carried on for the purpose of example and stimulus to keep the others up to a certain standard of excellence" (ibid., p.129).

This is not to say that the state has no interest in defining a basic common education or no legitimate power to enforce it. A wide range of parental choice makes sense only in the context of publicly defined educational standards that can serve as regular and reliable benchmarks of educational attainment. Mill proposes a universal system of public examinations, beginning with basic literacy at an early age and widening out annually to ensure the acquisition and retention of core general knowledge. He is confident that these examinations can be structured to prevent the state from exercising an improper, homogenizing control over the formation of opinion through a strict focus on "positive science." To the extent that examinations on disputed topics such as religion and politics are administered, for example, they should be confined to facts about the views of specific authors or denominations and the stated grounds of those views (ibid., pp.130–1).

This defense of educational diversity and choice has much to commend it. Assuming, as Mill does, the diversity of human types, it is hard to see how any monopolistic system of education could accommodate them all equally well. The existence of a range of educational choices offers the possibility of a better fit between institutional settings and individual needs.

While children can be consulted, moreover, they cannot make these educational choices for themselves, especially in the early years. Either parents will make these choices, or the state will make them for them. While parents may often fail to choose wisely, there are reasons to believe that the state typically will do even worse. On average, parents understand their children's individual traits better than public authorities do, their concern for their children's well-being is deeper, and they are not subject to the homogenizing imperatives of even the best bureaucracies in the modern state. In practice, the legal system must create a presumption in one direction or the other, and the case for a presumption in favor of parents is strong.

This presumption in favor of parents is rebuttable, however. While the range of parental discretion is wide, the state properly enforces numerous limits on parental authority, and may act to prevent what amounts to educational abuse and neglect, through measures such as compulsory education statutes and basic standards of education attainment. It may not, however, define a child's best interests so expansively and in such detail that the enforcement of those interests would in practice eviscerate the power of parents to make decisions concerning their children's education (see Strike, 1982, pp. 157–61).

Eamonn Callan offers a useful example. Suppose that the parents of a musically talented child can afford either to buy a piano or to take her on an expensive holiday. Judged from the standpoint of the developmental best interests of the child, the right choice is reasonably clear. Yet we would not elect to grant a state the authority to compel parents to buy the piano instead of going to Disneyland. There must, it appears, be a protected zone of parental discretion, even when the judgments parents make look mistaken to outsiders (Callan, 1997, pp. 146–7).

Why should such a zone exist? One standard liberal answer is fear of the overweening state: even if the judgment of bureaucratic experts were systematically superior to that of parents, a government with the power to make us buy the piano is unlikely to leave any of our liberties intact. A fuller answer would appeal to the expressive interests of parents in raising children in a manner consistent with their own understanding, and it is to this theme that I now turn.

Expressive Liberty and Parental Interests

By "expressive liberty" I mean the absence of constraints imposed by some individuals or groups on others that make it impossible or significantly more difficult for the affected individuals or groups to live their lives in ways that express their deepest beliefs about what gives meaning and value to life. An example of such constraints is the Inquisition, which forced Iberian Jews either to endure persecution or to renounce their religious practices.

Expressive liberty offers us the opportunity to enjoy a fit between our inner and outer lives, our convictions and our deeds. Not all sets of practices will themselves rest on, or reflect a preference for, liberty as ordinarily understood. For example, being Jewish is not always (indeed, is not usually) understood as a matter of choice. But once that fact is established through birth and circumstance, it becomes a matter of great importance for Jews to live in a society that permits them to live in accordance with an identity that is given rather than chosen and that is structured by obligations whose binding power does not depend on individual acceptance. For Jews, and for many others as well, the ability to revise one's conception of the good is hardly a good thing. In short, because not all sets of beliefs and practices value (let alone give pride of place to) liberty, expressive liberty protects the ability of individuals and groups to live in ways that others would regard as unfree.

Expressive liberty is an important good, rightly infringed only to protect other important goods, because it is a precondition for leading a complete and satisfying life. The reason is straightforward: part of what it means to have deep beliefs about how one should live is the desire to live in accordance with them. Only in rare cases (perhaps certain kinds of Stoicism) do constraints imposed by other individuals and by social structures have negligible effects on the ability of believers to live in accordance

419

with their convictions. Most of us experience impediments to acting on our deepest beliefs as sources of deprivation and unhappiness, resentment and anger. The absence of expressive liberty is a misfortune that few would willingly endure.

Expressive liberty is possible only within societies whose members do not needlessly impede one another's opportunity to live their lives as they see fit. To be meaningful, the ethic of liberty requires a politics and sociology of liberty. Suitable institutional arrangements can help police a zone of mutual abstention, but these institutions must be bolstered by the pervasive belief among citizens that it is wrong to deprive others of expressive liberty. Citizens must internalize norms of self-restraint in the face of practices that reflect understandings of the good life that they reject. Fostering this self-restraint, this principled refusal to use individual or collective coercion to deprive others of expressive liberty, is a legitimate object of liberal civic action.

What I want to argue is that the ability of parents to raise their children in a manner consistent with their deepest commitments is an essential element of expressive liberty. As Eamonn Callan rightly suggests, parenting is typically undertaken as one of the central meaning-giving tasks of our lives. We cannot detach our aspirations for our children from our understanding of what is good and virtuous (Callan, 1997, p. 144). As Stephen Gilles insists, loving and nurturing a child cannot in practice be divorced from shaping that child's values in a way that draws upon "the comprehensive understanding that gives our values whatever coherence and grounding they may possess" (Gilles, 1996, pp. 960–7). Moreover, we hope for relations of intimacy with our children, as they develop and when they are grown, and estrangement is the enemy of intimacy. It is understandable for parents to fear that their children may become embroiled in ways of life they regard as alien and distasteful and, within limits, act to reduce the risk that this fear will be realized. Callan links these parental expressive interests with core liberal freedoms:

The rights to freedom of conscience and association are widely accepted as among the necessary requirements of any recognizably liberal regime. But the freedom to rear our children according to the dictates of conscience is for most of us as important as any other expression of conscience, and the freedom to organize and sustain the life of the family in keeping with our own values is as significant as our liberty to associate outside the family for any purpose whatever. (Callan, 1997, p. 143)

Conversely, one of the most disturbing features of illiberal regimes is the wedge their governments typically seek to drive between parents and children, and the effort they make to replace a multiplicity of family traditions with a unitary, state-administered culture.

The appropriate parental role is structured in part by the vulnerability, dependency, and developmental needs of children. The model of fiduciary responsibility developed by Locke and endorsed by contemporary thinkers such as Richard Arneson and Ian Shapiro well captures this dimension of the parent–child relationship (Arneson and Shapiro, 1996). But the expressive interests of parents are not reducible to their fiduciary duty to promote their children's interests. A better model is more nearly reciprocal: parents and children serve, and are served by, one another in complex ways. To quote Callan once more:

if a moral theory interprets the child's role so as to make individual children no more than instruments of their parents' good it would be open to damning moral objections. But parallel objections must be decisive against any theory that interprets the parent's role in ways that make individual parents no more than instruments of their children's good. We should want a conception of parents' rights in education that will not license the oppression of children. But we should also want a conception that will do justice to the hopes that parents have and the sacrifices they make in rearing their children. (Callan, 1997, p. 145)

As parent, I am more than the child's caretaker or teacher, and I am not simply a representative of the state delegated to prepare the child for citizenship. The hopes and sacrifices to which Callan refers reflect the intimate particularity of the parent–child bond, the fact that the child is in part (though only in part) an extension of ourselves.

Like any other value, the expressive interests of parents can be pushed too far. To begin with, as children develop, their own expressive interests must be given increased weight. Consider the well known case of *Wisconsin* v. *Yoder* (406 US 205, 1972). This case presented a clash between a Wisconsin state law, which required school attendance until age sixteen, and three Old Order Amish parents, who claimed that mandating their children's school attendance after age fourteen would undermine their community-based religious practices. While the Supreme Court decided in favor of the parents, a number of justices declared that the adolescent children had liberty claims independent of their parents'. If the children had expressed the desire to continue their schooling, these justices would have voted to uphold the state's enforcement of its attendance laws against the wishes of the parents. At a minimum, the children's freestanding religious claims imply enforceable rights of exit from the boundaries of community defined by their parents. I would add that the exit-rights must be more than formal. Communities cannot rightly act in ways that disempower individuals – intellectually, emotionally, or practically – from living successfully outside their bounds.

But should the expressed views of the children be taken as dispositive? Arneson and Shapiro say not: even if the children acquiesce, the parents may still be in violation of their fiduciary responsibility. A parent, they insist,

cannot pretend to speak for the child while really regarding the child as an empty vessel for the parent's own religious convictions. As a fiduciary, the parent is bound to preserve the child's own future religious freedom. (Arneson and Shapiro, 1996, p. 154)

Even if we accept this premise (and it may be questioned from several perspectives), it is by no means clear what practical conclusions we are compelled to draw from it. Does respect for a child's religious freedom mean that the parent is required to treat all comprehensive views (of what is good and right) equally, taking the child on a tour of different faiths and secular philosophical outlooks and then saying in effect, you choose? Few parents, whatever their outlook, would accept this proposition; even fewer would endorse its enforcement by the state; and I do not see considerations weighty enough to warrant such a sharp break with established practices. At the very least, parents are entitled to introduce their children to what they regard as vital sources of meaning and value, and to hope that their children will come to share this orientation. One might also argue that instructing children within a particular

421

tradition, far from undermining intellectual or religious freedom, may in fact promote it. Knowing what it means to live within a coherent framework of value and belief may well contribute to an informed adult choice between one's tradition of origin and those encountered later in life.

Now consider a thought-experiment at the other extreme. Suppose a group raises its children with the result that as adults none ever questions or rejects the group's basic orientation. To achieve this result, the group seals itself off from the outside world and structures its internal education so that children are not even aware of alternatives to the group's way of life. In effect, the group has become a kind of mental and moral prison. Because diversity and disagreement typically arise even in circumstances of considerable repression, their absence in this case is a sign of extreme suppression of individuality that warrants external scrutiny and perhaps intervention. Parents abuse their expressive liberty if they turn their children into automatons, in part because in so doing they deprive their children of the opportunity to exercise their own expressive liberty.

In this respect, I agree with Eamonn Callan's argument that servility is a vice and that parental actions fostering servility in children amount to illegitimate despotism. As a parent, I cannot rightly mold my child's character in a way that effectively pre-empts "serious thought at any future date about the alternatives to my judgment." Every child has a prospective interest in personal sovereignty (Callan's term) or expressive liberty (my term) that parents cannot rightly undermine (Callan, 1997, pp. 152–4).

There are, however, formative forces other than parental despotism that also foster servility. Children immersed in a culture defined by advertising, entertainment media, and peer pressure are often dominated by influences that they neither understand nor resist. In the face of such challenges, to have any realistic possibility of exerting countervailing formative power, parents may be compelled to take a strong counter-cultural stance that involves a substantial measure of family or communal separation from external influences. Parental actions that may be judged despotic in some circumstances may well be necessary, or at least justified, in others.

While these arguments clarify some moral intuitions, they also suggest that practical issues of educational authority cannot be resolved on the plane of moral abstractions. The acceptability of parental decisions must be evaluated within the full context of influences shaping children's awareness of alternatives and ability to weight them. And it is not enough to judge the intention of parents' educational decisions; we must also look at their concrete results.

These considerations highlight some relevant empirical dimensions of the *Yoder* controversy. The Amish community is not a prison. Young adults must explicitly choose to become full members. Substantial numbers decide not to join when they reach adulthood, and others leave later. While there are transitional difficulties for some, there is no evidence that many former members find themselves unable to cope with the demands of a modern economy and society.

This is hardly surprising. In a contemporary liberal-democratic society, it is impossible for small groups to seal themselves off from ways of life very different from their own. Even a coherent separationist community such as the Amish can serve at most as a counterweight to the dominant culture. It cannot prevent children from learning about alternatives, and while it can offer young adults various incentives to stay, it cannot prevent them from leaving.

Even if *Yoder* does not violate the present or potential expressive liberty of Amish young people, it may be argued that the decision gives inadequate weight to the state's interest in fostering good citizens. According to this line of argument, good citizens participate actively in public affairs, using developed powers of critical reason to deliberate on and decide among competing policies and representatives. But Amish education discourages both active participation and critical reasoning and thus fails to meet legitimate basic state requirements.

There are three sorts of reply to this line of argument. First, as we have seen, the proposition that *x* is instrumental to (or even necessary for) the creation of good citizens does not, as a matter of constitutional law or liberal democratic theory, warrant the conclusion that *x* is right or legitimate, given the other interests or goods at stake. Second, even if we accept the premise that critical reasoning is a *sine qua non* of liberal-democratic citizenship, the Amish have arguably demonstrated their capacity for critical reasoning in ways that it is publicly reasonable to expect (Keim, 1975). As I argue below in discussing deliberation, faith, and public reason, critical thinking *within* a tradition is what can be reasonably expected. Finally, the active deliberative/participatory virtues are not the only virtues of citizenship we should care about. Law-abidingness, personal and family responsibility, and tolerance of social diversity are also important for the successful functioning of contemporary liberal democracies (Galston, 1991, chapter 10). In these respects, among others, the Amish score high. They may not be the best of citizens, but may we not say that they are good enough?

Parental Authority, Expressive Liberty, and Public Education

Today, after decades of handwringing about the quality of public education, roughly 90 percent of all school-age children still attend public schools. There is no compelling reason to believe that the role I have carved out for expressive liberty and the role of parents, if taken as the basis for actual policy, would significantly erode the dominant position the public schools now enjoy. Nor does my thesis undermine the legitimate role of the state in requiring all parents to educate their children and in establishing basic standards for all educational institutions. Rather, my account merely makes explicit the moral and theoretical underpinnings of the longstanding US constitutional commitment to the principle that parents may choose among a range of options – public and private, secular and religious, heterogeneous and homogeneous – for discharging their obligation to educate their children.

Nonetheless, my stance does reflect an underlying understanding that some may find objectionable. I believe that in a society characterized by a deep diversity of moral and religious views, and accordingly by diverse family and communal ways of life, both social peace and normative legitimacy require that to the maximum extent consistent with the maintenance of civic unity and stability, all permissible ways of life be able to find expression in the key choices families and communities must make. Among these choices, the venue and conduct of education ranks high. I would argue

423

that genuine civic unity rests on unforced consent. States that permit their citizens to live in ways expressive of their values are likely to enjoy widespread support, even gratitude. By contrast, state coercion is likely to produce dissent, resistance, and withdrawal.

Granted, sometimes the state has no choice. If families, schools, or local communities are acting in ways that violate the basic rights of citizens, then the state must step in. And if the result is resistance, even "massive resistance" in the face of compulsory school desegregation, that is the price that must be paid for defending the rightful claims of all citizens. My point is rather that the state must be parsimonious in defining the realm in which uniformity must be secured through coercion. An educational program based on an expansive and contestable definition of good citizenship or civic unity will not ordinarily justify the forcible suppression of expressive liberty.

Indeed, there are limits on the polity's ability to enforce even core public commitments on subcommunities when these principles clash with religious convictions or "expressive" freedom of association (see, for example, *Roberts* v. *US Jaycees*, 468 US, 1984, pp. 622–3). Consider, for instance, that while many regret the exclusion of women from the Catholic priesthood and from the rabbinate of Orthodox Judaism, most would agree that anti-discrimination laws that are morally weighty and otherwise binding should not be invoked to end these practices. What blocks the extension of these laws is our belief that religious associations (and perhaps others as well) enjoy considerable authority within their own sphere to determine their own affairs and in so doing to express their understanding of spiritual matters.

Consider next Bob Jones University, whose students were prohibited on religious grounds from engaging in interracial dating. In this and other cases of conflict between First Amendment-protected associations and compelling state interests such as ending racial segregation, the flat prohibition of conduct judged obnoxious by public principles seems hard to square with the minimum requirements of Free Exercise. In such cases, the removal of all forms of otherwise applicable public encouragement and favor, rather than an outright ban, may well be the most appropriate course. As the Supreme Court declared in its decision denying Bob Jones's request for reinstatement of its federal tax exemption, "the Government has a fundamental, overriding interest in eradicating racial discrimination [that] substantially outweighs whatever burden denial of tax benefits places on petitioners' exercise of their religious beliefs" (*Bob Jones University* v. *United States*, 461 US 574, 1983, p. 604).

The case of *Ohio Civil Rights Commission* v. *Dayton Christian Schools, Inc.* (477 US 619, 1986) provides another example in which expressive freedom of association must be respected even when competing weighty interests are at stake. A private fundamentalist school decided not to renew the contract of a pregnant married teacher because of its religiously based belief that mothers with young children should not work outside their homes. After receiving a complaint from the teacher, the Civil Rights Commission investigated, found probable cause to conclude that the school had discriminated against an employee on the basis of religion, and proposed a consent order including full reinstatement with back pay. As Frederick Mark Gedicks observes, this case involves a clash between a general public norm (non-discrimination) and the constitutive beliefs of a civil association. The teacher unquestionably experienced serious injury through loss of employment. On the other hand, forcing the school to rehire her would clearly impair the ability of the religious community of which it formed a key part to exercise its distinctive religious views; not just to profess them, but also to express them in its practices. The imposition of state-endorsed beliefs on that community would be inconsistent with protecting the core functions of diverse civil associations. In this case and others like it, a liberal politics guided by moral pluralism and the mitigation of state power would give priority to the claims of civil associations (Gedicks, 1989, pp. 101–3).

Current federal legislation and constitutional doctrine reflect this priority to a considerable degree. Thus, although Title VII of the Civil Rights Act prohibits employment discrimination on the basis of religion, section 702 of the statute exempts religious organizations. In the case of *Corporation of the Presiding Bishop* v. *Amos* (483 US 327), decided in 1987, the Supreme Court not only upheld this accommodation in principle but also extended its reach to a wide range of secular activities conducted under the aegis of religious organizations.

This does not mean that all religiously motivated practices are deserving of accommodation. Some clearly are not. No civil association can be permitted to engage in human sacrifice: there can be no free exercise for Aztecs. Nor can a civil association endanger the basic interests of children by withholding medical treatment in life-threatening situations. But there is a basic distinction between the minimal conditions for human well-being, which the state must defend, and diverse conceptions of flourishing above that baseline, which the state must accommodate to the maximum extent possible. There is room for reasonable disagreement as to where that line should be drawn. But an account of liberalism built on expressive liberty and on moral and political pluralism should make us very cautious about expanding the scope of state power in ways that mandate uniformity.

Deliberation, Faith, and Public Reason in Liberal-constitutional Democracy

Let me now turn to one of the most discussed recent examples of the tension between the expressive and civic dimensions of liberal democracy, the controversy between Christian fundamentalist parents and the public schools that erupted in Hawkins County, Tennessee, a decade ago. The parents charged that textbooks selected by the school board conveyed teachings at odds with the faith they sought to transmit to their children. They therefore requested that their children be allowed to use alternative textbooks and (if necessary) study the contested subjects outside the regular classroom. After early efforts by individual school administrators to accommodate the parents' request collapsed, a legal process ensued that culminated in a pro-school board decision by the US Sixth Circuit Court of Appeals.

The most systematic philosophical analysis of this controversy is offered by Amy Gutmann and Dennis Thompson in the course of their path-breaking account of deliberative democracy. Gutmann and Thompson contend that fidelity to democratic deliberation as they define it entails the rejection of the fundamentalists' attempts to have their children shielded from reading materials they found offensive to their faith.

The question I want to raise is whether their conception of democratic deliberation proves in the end to be compatible with an understanding of liberal constitutional democracy that gives due weight to expressive liberty and moral and political pluralism. I conclude that it is not and offer in its place a more capacious account of liberal democratic public argument.

The linchpin of Gutmann and Thompson's account of deliberation is the idea of reciprocity. Building on the work of John Rawls and Thomas Scanlon, they say that the

> foundation of reciprocity is the capacity to seek fair terms of social cooperation for their own sake.... From a deliberative perspective, a citizen offers reasons that can be accepted by others who are similarly motivated to find reasons that can be accepted by others.... [Thus,] a deliberative perspective does not address people who reject the aim of finding fair terms for social cooperation; it cannot reach those who refuse to press their public claims in terms accessible to their fellow citizens. (Gutmann and Thompson, 1996, pp. 52–5, 55)

This understanding of reciprocity raises some deep questions (for example, about the nature of moral motivation), but I shall not pursue them here. Instead, staying within the bounds of Gutmann and Thompson's account, I want to offer three caveats. First, the phrase "social cooperation" tends to suggest a common course of action that all citizens (must) pursue. But there are other equally legitimate forms of cooperation, including agreements to disagree, to go our various ways without hindrance or cavil, to "live and let live."

In addition, there are different kinds of "public claims." Individuals may argue that the political community as a whole ought to pursue a particular course of action. This is, I think, the core case that Gutmann and Thompson have in mind. But individuals may also argue that the question at hand should not be treated as a public matter in the first place; or that even if it is a legitimate public matter, some individuals and groups may (or must) be exempted from the constraints of otherwise general decisions. Some public claims are "offensive" ("You (all) should do what I say"), while others are "defensive" ("I need not do what you say, even if you speak in the voice of the entire political community"). The kinds of reasons offered in support of defensive claims may rightly differ from those for offensive claims.

Finally, the requirement that the terms of public argument should be "accessible" to one's fellow citizens turns out to be highly restrictive: "any claim fails to respect reciprocity if it imposes a requirement on other citizens to adopt one's sectarian way of life as a condition of gaining access to the moral understanding that is essential to judging the validity of one's moral claims" (Gutmann and Thompson, 1996, p. 57). Over the past two decades, a substantial debate has developed over the nature of what Rawls calls "public reason." It may well make sense to urge all citizens to do their best to translate their commitments into terms that can be understood by citizens who do not share them. But the norm of reciprocity should not be interpreted to screen out the kinds of core beliefs that give meaning and purpose to many lives. This caveat is especially important in the United States, where levels of religious belief and observance are far higher than in any other industrialized democracy. It is difficult to imagine that any liberal democracy can sustain conscientious support if it tells

426

millions of its citizens that they cannot rightly say what they believe as part of democratic public dialogue.

I want to suggest that an inclusive understanding of public reason is especially appropriate in the context of what I have called defensive public claims. It is one thing to contend that the United States should be a "Christian nation" and should restore official Christian prayer to public schools. That was the situation that existed in the grade schools of my youth, when I (though Jewish) was compelled to recite the Lord's Prayer. I do not see how such a regime could possibly be defended through legitimate public reasons. It is quite a different thing to seek, on conscientious grounds, defensive exemption from general public policies that may be legitimate and acceptable to a majority of citizens. Suppose a fundamentalist parent said to a secular philosopher:

Because of the content of your deepest beliefs, you happen not to experience a conflict between those beliefs and the content of the public school curriculum. But if *you* believed what *I* believe, you would experience that conflict, and you would seek for your child what I am seeking for mine. Moreover, the accommodation I seek is one that I would readily grant, were our positions reversed. I am not asking you to enter into the perspective of my particular religious beliefs. But I am asking you to enlarge your sympathies by imagining what it would be like to be in my shoes.

This fundamentalist is offering as a public reason not the specific *content* of religious belief, but the *fact* of that belief and the resulting clash with secular public policies. The secular interlocutor is being asked to imaginatively experience that clash as part of a process that could create a wider shared understanding, even if the particulars of faith are not easily communicable. I do not see why such a request is outside the legitimate bounds of public reason, especially for Gutmann, who praises the cultivation of the imagination as an important (and politically relevant) goal of education (see Gutmann, 1995, p. 572).

Gutmann and Thompson insist that "There is a public interest in educating good citizens, and no citizen can fairly claim that what constitutes good citizenship is whatever happens to conform to his or her particular religion" (Gutmann and Thompson, 1996, p. 67). This proposition is true as far as it goes. But as applied to the clash between the fundamentalist parents and the public schools, it raises three issues that are specific instances of the broad questions with which I opened this chapter.

The first is empirical. Is it the case that the accommodation sought by the fundamentalist parents would significantly impair the development of democratic citizens? The Hawkins County School Board never offered evidence on this point, and it is hard to see how they could have done so. Besides, the fundamentalist parents are constitutionally permitted to withdraw their children from the public schools and send them instead to Christian academies. It is hard to believe that the consequences of such a choice for democratic citizenship are more favorable than a policy of accommodation within the public schools would have been.

The second issue raised by Gutmann and Thompson's assertion is conceptual. How is the good citizenship whose development we seek through education to be defined? The answer is contested, and in any event it is likely to be complex. As I have already suggested, the capacity for deliberation is surely one element, but there are others, including law-abidingness and the willingness to do one's share (through taxes, jury

427

duty, military service, etc.) to sustain a system of social cooperation. In comparing the civic consequences of different educational strategies, one must examine all relevant dimensions, not just one.

The final issue cuts even deeper. Suppose it is the case that a particular public policy is conducive to the cultivation of democratic citizenship. Does it follow that this policy is always right or permissible? For liberalism as I understand it, the answer is no, not always. Expressive liberty and political pluralism serve to limit the state's power to mold individuals into citizens. That is what it means to affirm a sphere of parental power not subject to state control. And as we saw, that is the clear meaning of *Meyer* and *Pierce*. There is, as Gutmann and Thompson rightly insist, an important public interest in educating good citizens. But there are other morally significant interests with which the formation of citizens sometimes comes into conflict, and to which the claims of citizenship must sometimes give way.

Conclusion: Education as and for Tolerance

I believe that a genuinely liberal society will organize itself around the principle of maximum feasible accommodation of diverse ways of life, limited only by the minimum requirements of civic unity. This principle expresses (and requires) the practice of *tolerance*: the conscientious reluctance to act in ways that impede others from living in accordance with their various conceptions of what gives life meaning and worth. Tolerance is the virtue sustaining the social practices and political institutions that make expressive liberty possible. Gutmann and Thompson criticize this way of thinking on the grounds that it

would not go far enough for the purposes of deliberative democracy. It provides no positive basis on which citizens can expect to resolve their moral disagreements in the future. Citizens go their separate ways, keeping their moral reasons to themselves, avoiding moral engagement. This may sometimes keep the peace....But *mere toleration* also locks into place the moral divisions in society and makes collective moral progress far more difficult. (Gutmann and Thompson, 1996, p. 62, emphasis added)

In my view, Gutmann and Thompson are far too optimistic about the actual possibilities of resolving moral disagreements, and much too grudging about the practical worth of toleration. In most times and places, the avoidance of repression and bloody conflict is in itself a morally significant achievement, all the more so if it is based on internalized norms of restraint rather than a *modus vivendi* reflecting a balance of power. The agreement to disagree is a way of dealing with moral disagreement that is not necessarily inferior to agreement on the substance of the issue. In the real world, there is nothing "mere" about toleration. As Michael Walzer says,

Toleration itself is often underestimated, as if it is the least we can do for our fellows, the most minimal of their entitlements. In fact,...[e]ven the most grudging forms and precarious arrangements [of toleration] are very good things, sufficiently rare in human history that they require not only practical but also theoretical appreciation. (Walzer, 1997, p. xi)

428

I do not deny that "collective moral progress" is possible. But it is much rarer than one would like and (if history is any guide) at least as likely to be achieved through the exercise of political power, or military force, or slow unplanned processes of social abrasion and influence, as through democratic deliberation. Liberals have never scorned (indeed, they have rightly prized) principles of social organization that "lock into place" *religious* divisions in society. A society that makes room for a wide though not unlimited range of cultural and moral disagreements is no less an achievement.

See also 6 ENLIGHTENMENT LIBERALISM; 23 RELIGIOUS EDUCATION; 28 THE AUTHORITY AND RESPONSIBILITY TO EDUCATE; 30 COMMON SCHOOLING AND EDUCATIONAL CHOICE; 31 CHILDREN'S RIGHTS

References

Arneson, R. and Shapiro, I. (1996) Democratic autonomy and religious freedom: a critique of *Wisconsin v. Yoder*. In I. Shapiro (ed.), *Democracy's Place*. Ithaca, NY: Cornell University Press, chapter 6.

Butts, R. F. and Cremin, L. A. (1953) *A History of Education in American Culture*. New York: Holt, Rinehart, and Winston.

Callan, E. (1997) *Creating Citizens: Political Education and Liberal Democracy*. Oxford: Clarendon.

Galston, W. A. (1991) *Liberal Purposes: Goods, Virtues and Diversity in the Liberal State*. New York: Cambridge University Press.

Gedicks, F. M. (1989) Toward a constitutional jurisprudence of religious group rights. *Wisconsin Law Review*, 99, 101–3.

Gilles, S. G. (1996) On educating children: a parentalist manifesto. *University of Chicago Law Review*, 63, 960–7.

Glenn, C. L. (2000) *The Ambigious Embrace: Government and Faith-based Schools and Social Agencies*. Princeton, NJ: Princeton University Press.

Glenn, C. L. (2001) Religion and education: American exceptionalism? In D. Ravitch and J. P. Viteritti (eds), *Making Good Citizens: Education and Civil Society*. New Haven, CT: Yale University Press.

Gutmann, A. (1995) Civic education and social diversity. *Ethics*, 105, 557–79.

Gutmann, A. and Thompson, D. (1996). *Democracy and Disagreement*. Cambridge, MA: Harvard University Press.

Keim, A. N. (ed.) (1975) *Compulsory Education and the Amish: The Right not to Be Modern*. Boston: Beacon Press.

Mill, J. S. (1956) *On Liberty*, ed. C. V. Shields. Indianapolis: Bobbs-Merrill.

Strike, K. (1982) *Liberty and Learning*. New York: St Martin's Press.

Walzer, M. (1997) *On Toleration*. New Haven, CT: Yale University Press.

30

Common Schooling and Educational Choice

Rob Reich

The common school ideal is the source of one of the oldest educational debates in liberal democratic societies. The movement in favor of educational choice is the source of one of the most recent. Each has been the cause of major and enduring controversy, not only within philosophical thought but also within the political and social arena. This chapter investigates the relationship between common schooling and educational choice. Are these ideals in tension, because educational choice undermines visions of common schooling? If so, which should prevail and on what grounds? Can, or should, proponents of the common school embrace school choice?

At first glance, it would appear that the question is easily resolved by answering a single empirical question: Does educational choice lead to the creation and perpetuation of separate schools? If so, then choice conflicts with common schooling. If not, then choice and common schooling can coexist. But this is far too simplistic, for the specification of the common school ideal and the architecture of school choice are complex, and their relationship is quite complicated.

They are *complex* because it is not immediately clear what either common schooling or educational choice entails. Does common schooling demand only that publicly funded schools be open and available to all, or does it require a particular ethos for every school? Likewise, does educational choice refer to the availability of separate schools for different groups in society, or does it mean something like a charter school movement or voucher program? Their relationship is *complicated* because how we view the relationship and assess the weight of each aspiration depends on something external to each. In particular, it depends on the normative significance we attach to the fact of pluralism, by which I mean the existence of religious and ethical diversity in a society. Whether or not we see common schooling and educational choice as in fundamental tension, merely compatible, or mutually reinforcing turns on how we interpret the normative implications of pluralism. Showing that this is so, and demonstrating that there is no necessary conflict between aspirations to common schooling and educational choice when we understand pluralism in a certain way is the main aim of this chapter.

The chapter proceeds in four sections. First, I explain why we need to understand something about pluralism in order to understand common schooling and school choice. In the second and third sections, I explore the normative significance of

430

pluralism for common schooling and educational choice, respectively. In the fourth section, I show how the two can be reconciled, given a certain understanding of what pluralism demands.

I begin, however, with a cautionary note. Little about the justice of either common schooling or educational choice can be settled decisively at the level of philosophical theory or principle. This is so for two reasons. First, the practice of schooling rests inevitably within particular social settings and historical traditions where the institutional structure of schooling reflects the community of which it is a part. Authority over education in the United States, for instance, is far more localized than in most other countries. Second, philosophy does not furnish a complete educational blueprint for all educational practice. At best, philosophy can provide a theoretical framework that shapes the making of policy and the particulars of practice. For these reasons, my goal here is not to spell out what happens when we combine common schooling with educational choice but instead to map out the key philosophical considerations involved in determining whether the ideals are reconcilable, and to provide an argument to show how they are.

The Fact of Pluralism

Pluralism is a sociological fact in liberal societies. The natural outcome of the use of human reason within free political and social institutions is a multiplicity of values and ways of life. People will be divided by their adherence to a diversity of religious and ethical doctrines that differ in their understanding of what constitutes a good life. As a result, liberal societies house citizenries divided by religious and philosophical traditions which are sometimes in conflict or even incompatible. It is the distinguishing feature of liberal societies that they attempt to secure the legitimacy and stability of political institutions amidst such pluralism. Indeed, many interpret the rise of liberalism as a response to pluralism, specifically religious diversity.

How, then, is the fact of pluralism related to common schooling and educational choice? Quite simply, both represent attempts to cope with the political complications that arise in a pluralistic society. Let's start with common schooling. The movement to create common schools arose in the mid-nineteenth century in the United States as an effort to instill in diverse citizens a set of common values and allegiances in order to forge an *unum* from the *pluribus*. Common schools would be the vehicle in which children of all groups would be educated for democratic citizenship, in which the social cement of national identity would be laid. At times, as I describe below, the movement to create common schooling was unjustly oppressive of diversity because its leaders understood citizenship and nationalism in narrowly ethnic terms. But history also provides examples of common school defenders with views of citizenship and nationalism that are civic rather than ethnic. Consider, for instance, John Dewey's aspiration for the American common school: "The intermingling in the school of youth of different races, differing religions, and unlike customs creates for all a new and broader environment.... The assimilative force of the American public school is eloquent testimony to the efficacy of the common and balanced appeal" (Dewey, 1916, pp. 21–2). The fact of pluralism, in short, makes the common school necessary, in that the schoolhouse is perhaps the best vehicle available to the state to unite a diverse citizenry under common ideals and to help to forge a common national identity.

If the ideal of common schooling represents an effort to respond to and shape the diversity that attends a pluralist society, the movement for educational choice must be equally understood as a response to pluralism. But rather than an effort to *shape* diversity, school choice represents the appropriate *accommodation* to such diversity. If the liberal state must refrain from compelling uniform convergence on a single set of values or one way of life, it ought to respect diverse approaches to raising children rooted in particular ways of life. Educational choice is thought to be warranted because the fact of pluralism requires that parents and communities be permitted to create schools that accord with their own values and ends. Forcing all students to attend common schools not only fails to respect the choices of parents who wish for particularistic school environments, it also runs the risk of sowing the seeds of discord in the populace. Consider, for example, the view offered by US Supreme Court Justice Robert Jackson: "Probably no deeper division of our people could proceed from any provocation than from finding it necessary to choose what doctrine and whose program public educational officials shall compel youth to unite in embracing" (*West Virginia Board of Education* v. *Barnette*, 319 US 624, 1943, at 641). School choice, in short, is an effort in keeping with liberal principles that seeks to accommodate parents and groups with diverse convictions.

On this view, there seems to be an ineradicable tension between common schooling and educational choice. Efforts to inculcate common values in common schools run headlong into efforts to respect and accommodate the diverse convictions of citizens. But must it be so? In the next sections, I examine the normative significance of the fact of pluralism for common schooling and educational choice as a prelude to showing how they can be reconciled.

Common Schools and the Normative Significance of Pluralism

Historically, the movement to establish common schooling was driven by the task of creating citizens. Early proponents of common schooling hoped through schooling to produce a unified citizenry capable of democratic self-governance. Advocates such as Thomas Jefferson, for instance, thought common schools were a prerequisite for safeguarding individual and collective liberties. "It is an axiom in my mind," Jefferson wrote to George Washington in 1786, "that our liberty can never be safe but in the hands of the people themselves, and that too of the people with a certain degree of instruction. This it is the business of the state to effect, and on a general plan" (quoted in Conant, 1962, p. 98). Later proponents such as Horace Mann thought common schools were necessary not only for the general diffusion of knowledge but for the transmission of common virtues among an increasingly diverse populace. Schools would serve to educate children from all religious and class backgrounds, including the many newcomers to American soil, and to inculcate in them civic virtues and allegiances. The common school crusaders of the mid-nineteenth century were heavily motivated by a religious ethic, however, and they understood civic virtue to be infused with Protestant Christianity. This orientation was naturally felt to be oppressive by the increasing number of Catholics in the United States, and led to monumental struggles which culminated in the creation of a separate Catholic school system (Ravitch, 1974; Tyack and Hansot, 1982). Charles Glenn (1988) has shown that the common school movements in France and the Netherlands were similarly oppressive. As common schooling became established as a necessary vehicle for creating intelligent and loyal citizens from a diverse populace, then, it was an ideal that intertwined civic virtue with religious and ethnic allegiances.

This is the historical record. It is worth recounting because it registers the intellectual roots connecting the common school ideal with citizenship and the actual institutional practices that tended to impose a dominant cultural matrix on religious and ethnic minorities. I turn now to contemporary philosophers, who do not advocate, of course, that common schooling be cast in narrowly religious or ethnic terms. Yet debates among liberal theorists reveal how common schooling is still understood as a response to pluralism. Consider two approaches that interpret the normative significance of pluralism in different ways, each flawed.

Take first John Rawls's defense of political liberalism, in which the aim of the state is to secure political agreement about fundamental principles of justice while remaining neutral to the reasonable but sometimes clashing and incompatible worldviews professed and lived by citizens. Here the existence of pluralism constrains what the liberal state can do in order to establish social unity; it may not seek to unite people under any one religious, philosophical, or moral doctrine. Therefore, according to Rawls, "Society's concern with [children's] education lies in their role as future citizens..." (Rawls, 1993,p. 200), not in shaping their private identities, values, or allegiances. For Rawls, this implies that schools are common insofar as they all attempt to foster in children the political virtues of democratic citizenship. But they should not go beyond this. Common schools must instill a common political morality but leave private belief alone. In this vision of liberal society, because the state cannot endorse any particular comprehensive religious or moral doctrine, schools are authorized to cultivate a wide set of political virtues but must forbear from shaping the non-public identities of children and refrain from imposing any view of the good life on them.

But this sharp demarcation between shaping public identities and leaving private identities alone is both impossible and undesirable. It is impossible because education can never be morally neutral to private life, for decisions about even such mundane matters as coeducation or the identification of a language of instruction and school holidays transmit the importance of certain pervasive values (e.g. the equality of the sexes, the religious traditions worthy of public recognition). Moreover, the inculcation of political virtues such as political autonomy and reasonableness cannot be accomplished without making it possible for these to be activated in a child's private life; teaching only political virtues in common schools cannot avoid spillover effects (Gutmann, 1995; Callan, 1997; Macedo, 2000; Reich, 2002). These virtues require associated skills and habits such as rational reflection and evaluation, open-minded toleration of competing viewpoints, and a willingness to engage in collective deliberation, which possess alone and more strongly in combination a transformative potential, even likelihood, for the various private affiliations and allegiances of

433

individuals. Because pluralism must be shaped in light of important civic purposes such as the achievement of justice and the development of public reason in order to ensure the endurance of equality and freedom that make respect for diversity possible, it follows that the liberal state should not seek to be neutral in aim or outcome. Hence, the liberal state cannot and should not leave private belief untouched to the extent that Rawls suggests.

Another prominent strand of liberal theory takes the protection of diversity as the primary aim of the liberal state. William Galston, for instance, defends the "Diversity State," which "afford[s] maximum feasible space for the enactment of individual and group differences, constrained only by the requirements of liberal social unity" (Galston, 1995,p. 524). For those to whom diversity is of paramount importance, the fact of pluralism becomes the central point of departure for the liberal state, and these requirements of social unity are comparatively minor and unburdensome. On many such views, social unity can be achieved when public institutions convey the importance of law-abidingness and tolerance. Thus, Galston accepts the importance of a common civic education, but its aim is only to foster "social rationality," or the ability to participate in the main social and economic institutions of society. The promotion of autonomy or political virtues such as reasonableness are seen unduly to constrain diversity because they valorize choice-making, critical thinking, and secular rationality. So long as children learn to tolerate their diverse fellow citizens and learn social but not secular rationality, schools have no warrant to teach children anything that threatens to interfere with or undermine diversity. In this vision of liberal society, common schooling is necessary but its program of civic education is purposefully thin in order to allow maximum space for the flourishing of diversity.

But a vision of liberal society and common schooling put at the service of deep diversity fails for two reasons. First, when maximum feasible accommodation of diversity is the goal, the content of common civic education must be reduced to the lowest common denominator of what citizens can agree upon. This strategy may seem attractive inasmuch as it eliminates anything considered controversial, but as Eamonn Callan argues, it effectively undercuts any argument for common schooling at all (Callan, 1997, pp. 170ff). If the content of common schooling is little more than tolerance and law-abidingness, few if any citizens will be motivated to send children to such schools because they will fail to teach anything even remotely approaching their most valued convictions. Boring, anodyne educational environments are hardly inspiring or attractive places for any parent. Second, it fails because a threadbare conception of common civic education neglects the independent interests of children in developing into autonomous persons. The arguments in favor of autonomy are varied (see Callan, 1997; Levinson, 1999; Brighouse, 2000; Reich, 2002), but the essential point is that children have an interest in developing into autonomous persons first because the exercise of autonomy is necessary in the political domain in order to establish legitimate and free consent to principles of justice, and second because the achievement of autonomy makes it possible for a child to exit a way of life and thereby precludes the inculcation of ethical servility to one's parents or ethnocultural group.

Political liberals, such as Rawls, interpret the normative significance of pluralism as necessitating a kind of liberal neutrality which restricts the pursuit of common educational goals to the political domain. Liberals who identify the protection of diversity as the primary purpose of the state, such as Galston, assign greater weight to the normative significance of pluralism; they abjure the cultivation of political autonomy, secular reason, and related political virtues in schools. Each view insists upon an important role for a common education, but the breadth of this education is circumscribed by the respective importance attached to diversity. Each view is also, I have argued, mistaken: the first because political liberalism bleeds inevitably into the realm of the private and must engage anyway in a transformative educational project supportive of liberal democratic citizenship; the second because maximal space for diversity means an insipid educational environment that will attract no one and because the protection of diversity should not take precedence over the interests of children in their prospective autonomy.

How, then, should we interpret the normative significance of pluralism for the common school ideal? First, theorists must acknowledge that invocations of common schooling will have to contend with the past use of common schools to subjugate and coercively assimilate minority populations. The frequent result of such uses was not only social discord but, ironically, the stimulation of a separate system of schooling, as with the Catholic school system in the United States. Common schooling must be sufficiently responsive to the scope of diversity that it does not impose upon children a sectarian or ethnic conception of education. The task of the common school is not to overcome pluralism, but to shape it in light of public purposes.

Second, our consideration of both political liberals and promoters of diversity with respect to their common school ideals helps to illuminate an absolutely fundamental aspect of the common school. Within a liberal pluralist society, the common school ideal is distinctive not for its structural features but for its substantive educational ethos and aspirations. By this I mean that common schools are not necessarily schools whose funding is exclusively public or whose admission criteria are open to all. They are schools which might be privately funded or might welcome only some particular students but which pursue a conception of common education without regard to students' or their parents' ways of life. That a privately funded school might be considered common can be seen in the example of the contemporary state of Catholic schools in the United States. Many urban Catholic schools not only appear to achieve considerable success in civic outcomes but also admit students without considering their religious background (Bryk et al., 1993). Conversely, many publicly funded schools can hardly be said to deliver anything associated with the common school ideal. Consider the educational system in Israel, in which at least four separate systems of schooling are publicly supported, included the schools of the Ultra-Orthodox Jews, which are as good an instance of separate schooling as one is likely to find. That a school which limited admission to particular students might be considered common can be seen in the various and legitimate attempts to carve out forms of restrictive schools designed only for some students. Some schools pursue common educational goals but restrict entry in order to overcome certain forms of disadvantage. Consider, for instance, schools for disabled or ill children where teachers have special training and resources, or all-girl academies whose rationale is to promote science and math achievement more effectively. Arguments might be made to show that disabled children and girls are better off when schooled with all

435

other students. But the point is that common schooling is consistent with separating students, so long as the separation is done for reasons that accord with liberal justice.

What is fundamental to the common school ideal, then, is not its structure but its substance. A common school is marked by an educational environment that is open to ethical and cultural diversity and by a commitment to common educational goals. These common educational goals are twofold. First, schools are responsible for a civic education that teaches children what they need to know in order to be free and equal citizens in a pluralist liberal society. It is not my purpose here to settle what the scope and depth of civic education shall be; this is a matter of great controversy. My point is only to insist, as Terry McLaughlin has put it, that "The common school has an obligation to 'transmit' the basis or non-negotiable norms which constitute the framework of a liberal democratic society" (McLaughlin, 1995,p. 247), however one understands these norms. Second, schools owe to children as a matter of justice an autonomy-promoting education. Independent of a state's interest in civic education, children have an interest in becoming autonomous persons. As I argue in the final section, common schools that expose children to and engage children with cultural and ethical diversity are important in cultivating autonomy.

Educational Choice and the Normative Significance of Pluralism

The fact of pluralism provides both the inspiration for and limits to common schooling. The need for a unifying civic education must be carefully balanced against an unjust oppression of the diverse convictions of citizens. To understand the normative significance of pluralism for educational choice, consider once again two different views, each flawed.

One school of thought holds parental choice of schools to be inimical to the development of citizenship and the interest of children in autonomy. Bruce Ackerman, for instance, rejects vouchers out of hand because "most parents will refuse to spend 'their' vouchers on anything but 'education' that strives to reinforce whatever values they have...imposed on their children during infancy," and that vouchers would legitimate "a series of petty tyrannies in which like-minded parents club together to force-feed their children without restraint" (Ackerman, 1985,p. 160). Meira Levinson's argument about the demands of liberal education are similar, concluding that schools must be "detached" from parental and local control, and that all forms of religious schools in the United States and Britain should be closed because they are organized around divisive conceptions of the good (Levinson, 1999, pp. 144, 158). She also says that state regulation should be used to make private schools indistinguishable from public schools. Levinson endorses limited educational choice (among schools of different sizes and varying pedagogical approaches), but since schools cannot embody a particularistic ethos, it is choice that has virtually nothing to do with responding to the fact of pluralism. For Ackerman and Levinson, the deference to be accorded to the diverse convictions of parents concerning the best education for their children is small indeed.

But this is a cramped view of educational choice, for it is both unfairly dismissive and unduly suspicious of parents' interests in the education of their children. On the one hand, it fails to register the legitimate interests that parents have in the education of their children. Surely parents have some claim to influence the educational environment of their children, to be involved with their schooling, and to expect that schools will provide reinforcement for at least some portion of the child's home environment. It cannot be the function of schooling to oppose parental convictions at every turn; such an experience will only produce wanton moral confusion and rootlessness in children. On the other hand, the Ackerman and Levinson view assumes that given the opportunity all or most parents will seek to shield their children from anything except their own moral or religious universe. To be sure, some parents will do so, but how many is an empirical question and the existence of some should not rule out the possibility that others may choose schools on the basis of values fully consonant with liberal democratic citizenship. (Indeed, school choice experiments in the United States indicate that most parents seek an education for their children that will offer a stronger chance for academic achievement.) Regardless of the empirical matter, however, the point is that the existence of state interests in common schooling provides no reason to ignore parental preferences. Authority over schooling is properly shared between parents and the state (Gutmann, 1987), and that shared authority is not inconsistent with an educational choice plan responsive to parental preferences.

For a polar opposite view, take the position of legal scholar Michael McConnell. McConnell is an ardent proponent of school choice or, as he calls it, educational disestablishment. His argument rests on the claim that educational choice is required in order to maintain a free and liberal society in the face of wide cultural and religious diversity. He fears what John Stuart Mill worried about with respect to state-provided and regulated schooling: the imposition of a standardized uniformity on children that runs counter to liberal values supportive of diversity. Moreover, citing the battles between Catholics and the Protestantism of the American common school founders and contemporary strife between devout religious believers who see in public schools nothing but rampant secular humanism, McConnell says that common schooling sows the seeds of social unrest. Thus McConnell believes that a liberal pluralist society should organize education along pluralist lines, permitting parents to choose from a marketplace of educational options, including state, private, religious schools, and home schooling. For McConnell the deference to be paid to the diverse convictions of parents is vast, constrained only by "basic requirements of educational quality, and perhaps of minimal civic responsibility" (McConnell, 2001, p. 88).

However, rather than asserting that parents possess natural or legal rights of some sort to direct the upbringing of their children in accordance with their own understanding of the good, he thinks that citizenship and democratic values are not only consistent with but are best served by educational choice. In an interesting twist on the usual line of argument, not only pluralism requires educational choice, but so too does the transmission of democratic citizenship. If this is true, McConnell's argument would undercut one significant foundation of the common school ideal.

In developing this argument, McConnell makes three important claims. First, he endorses a minimalist set of political virtues that citizens need in a liberal democratic society: literacy and numeracy, a rudimentary understanding of history, and a tolerant live-and-let-live attitude. Second, he says that democratic citizenship requires a moral

437

and spiritual underpinning, a coherent rather than disjointed worldview. And third, he appeals to empirical research indicating that public schools are flooded by a moral tidal wave of consumerism and materialism and that non-public schools foster comparatively higher rates of civic participation, voting, and community service.

Even assuming these were true, however, the common school ideal with its attendant conception of common education would retain some force insofar as McConnell's argument does not address the child's independent interest in an autonomy-promoting education. Were educational choice to result in *autonomy-undermining* school environments, we would still have to weigh this result against the civic benefits of choice. But leaving this aside, McConnell's argument for educational disestablishment as conducive to civic virtue has its own internal problems. For starters, it makes of democratic citizenship a thin gruel consisting of little more than some basic academic outcomes and a healthy tolerance for the beliefs and values of others. This is not the place to offer a defense of a more robust conception of citizenship, but few theorists understand citizenship as capped by the lowly hillock of tolerance; most defend at least a sense of fairness and civility. What is more, McConnell strangely enlists Rawls's conception of overlapping consensus on his behalf, claiming that since political arrangements are to be endorsed for a variety of reasons from the range of citizens' diverse doctrines, educational choice will help to foster the comprehensive moral and religious worldviews of citizens undergirding the overlapping consensus. But McConnell neglects to mention that an overlapping consensus can form only through the use of so-called public reason, which requires citizens to abstract from their particularistic views and come to understand, sympathetically listen to, and learn to respond to – not merely tolerate – the diverse views of other citizens. Public reason demands far more than tolerance; it demands a settled disposition to treat fellow citizens fairly and with civility, and it demands, as John Tomasi has argued, a potentially taxing psychological reintegrative project to show how public reason can be supported by one's non-public affiliations and values (Tomasi, 2001). Rawls's overlapping consensus does not support, but undermines, educational choice of the sort promoted by McConnell.

More importantly, the consequences of educational disestablishment *do* threaten in some cases to compromise a child's interest in an autonomy-promoting education. McConnell prefers morally coherent school communities to public schools, because he thinks a deep grounding in particularistic views sets the foundation for democratic citizenship. But some parents and religious groups, such as the Amish, do not value autonomy, because they think its exercise may lead their children away from their religious or ethical beliefs and communities. If permitted to select schools for their children that mirror and reinforce their own beliefs in every way, some parents will not provide an education for autonomy. Deference to parental choice in education must end when parents wish to thwart the development of autonomy in their children that enables them to exercise the basic freedom of living a life other than that into which they were born.

Once again, we see how visions of educational choice are powered by a normative understanding of pluralism. The weight assigned to the authority of parents to choose an educational environment in keeping with their convictions depends on how one interprets what must follow from the fact of pluralism. The Ackerman and

Levinson view offers too little accommodation to parents and educational choice, McConnell's too much. Pluralism should not be discounted or exalted. Put differently, the fact of pluralism should neither wholly trump, nor wholly be trumped by, efforts to secure the basis of social unity and foster citizenship and autonomy. The function of schools is not to subdue or tame an unwelcome diversity of ways of life nor to be the institutional fertilizer that permits a thousand blossoms to bloom and sustains their reproduction over time. In some sense, they must do a little of each: schools must be common insofar as they secure unity, foster citizenship, and cultivate autonomy, which will inevitably cut against some ways of life and thereby narrow the range of pluralism that would exist if educational choice was a supreme value; and schools must be somewhat responsive to parental interests in education, which opens up space for some kinds of educational choice that would not exist if common schooling were a supreme value. With a proper understanding of pluralism – seeing it as one among several important values in a liberal state – we can honor both the common school ideal and calls for educational choice. The final section shows how.

Reconciling Common Schooling with Educational Choice

The fact of pluralism is, as Rawls says, not an unfortunate condition but a natural outcome of the exercise of freedom in a liberal state (Rawls, 1993, p. 37). But fostering pluralism is not the purpose of the liberal state, as if the only function of public institutions were to permit diversity to thrive, and the mark of a better or healthier liberal state were its ability to promote greater pluralism. Liberal states are committed in the first instance to ethical individualism, by which I mean that the fundamental unit of analysis is the individual and not the group or the state. Liberals view the freedom and equality of individuals as the highest political values, and the success of political arrangements is to be judged not on the basis of how they sustain or allow pluralism to thrive but on how they promote individual freedom and equality. Of course, the best understanding of freedom and equality can be contested, but the basic point is clear: individuals have equal entitlements to define for themselves what goods and ends are most worthy, according to their own lights and independent judgment, and to possess equal civic standing. Seen in this light, pluralism is the consequence of the liberal state's concern to protect individual freedom and equality, for individuals will make different choices about how to lead their lives, choices which are worthy of the state's and citizens' respect.

Given this understanding of pluralism, how should we understand common schooling and educational choice? As I suggested earlier, the fact of pluralism is a source of both personal and social meaning and enrichment but also sets up a foundational problem: what will provide the basis of the social unity of a diverse, free and equal citizenry, with shared commitments to justice, without unjustly oppressing the reasonable ways of life led by these diverse citizens? As I have argued, common schooling can be seen as an attempt to forge unity, while educational choice can be seen as an accommodation to diversity. But this is not an either-or proposition. Common schooling can coexist with educational choice, doing justice in the process to individual freedom and equality and to pluralism.

439

In the previous section I concluded that the liberal democratic state has an interest in common schools that are marked by an openness to ethical and religious diversity and a conception of common education consisting of developing citizenship and fostering autonomy. Let us consider what kind of educational choice is consistent with this understanding of common schooling.

First, following Callan and McLaughlin, we should distinguish between common schooling and common education (McLaughlin, 1995; Callan, 1997). Common schools are schools that are open to all and that as a result may attract a mixed student body. But what matters about the common school ideal is not, in the first instance, that a school accepts all comers and is diverse in population. What matters is the institutional ethos and common educational goals that are part of the common school ideal. The function of common schooling must be to promote common educational aspirations, and if they fail in this task they are not independently worthy of liberal approbation. To suppose that they are is to suppose, in Callan's apt analogy, "that hospitals are good or bad in a way that is independent of their effects on the health of patients" (Callan, 1997, p. 166).

So if an institutional ethos that is open to pluralism and a conception of common education consisting in fostering citizenship and cultivating autonomy are what matter about the common school ideal, then there exists wide room for parental discretion in choosing among schools which are distinguished in a variety of ways but that all embody this educational vision. At least in principle, public, private, religious, and even home schools can be successful in achieving the right ethos and common educational vision. Whether or not they do so in practice is an empirical question, and it is the proper task of the liberal state to set regulations on all forms of schooling such that the common educational goals are met.

Here, then, we see how common schooling and educational choice can be reconciled. Educational choice in a variety of contemporary forms – private and religious schools, charter schools, vouchers – are all potentially consistent with the demands of common education. As I noted at the outset, it is impossible to determine from the level of theory a specific institutional blueprint for the provision of schooling. What this analysis suggests is that so long as schools embody an ethos that does not shut out diversity and that develops citizenship and autonomy, parents should be free to choose among schools on the basis of how they want their children to be educated. This would include a great diversity of schools: public, private, religious, and home schools. To be sure, it rules out some undiscriminating forms of choice, such as McConnell's proposal, whose view of democratic citizenship is threadbare and ignores the child's interest in autonomy. And it rules out schools which would refuse to expose children to and engage them with value diversity. Democratic citizenship and autonomy can be fostered only when children become aware of the existence of other ways of life, and, moreover, when they engage intellectually with such value diversity. The liberal state should be wary of parents whose choices are made solely on the basis of shielding them from any and all competing views. To allow this would indeed establish a kind of parental despotism over children. As the liberal state seeks to protect the freedom and equality of all citizens, including children, it must make it possible for children to make decisions about the kind of lives they wish to lead. This does not imply the ridiculous claim that children deserve to be able to lead any life possible, or that the state should seek intentionally to increase the chance that children will be skeptical of their parents' deepest convictions. It simply means that children deserve the basic freedom to lead lives other than those into which they are born, or to contest and revise the values of their parents or cultural communities.

On some views, the achievement of these common educational goals might require side-by-side learning of diverse students. Randall Curren, for example, finds in an understanding of Aristotelian civic friendship that students must learn to exercise certain virtues in the practice of relating to diverse others (Curren, 2000). Similarly, Eamonn Callan believes that the exercise of the political virtue of reasonableness and the exercise of public reason can only be learned in deliberative settings in which students of diverse backgrounds encounter and engage each other (Callan, 1997). I believe there is a strong case to be made here, and that a diverse student body is an undeniable asset to both the democratic citizenship and autonomy-promoting goals of common education. Thus, to the extent that educational choice makes it likelier that schools will be divided along religious and moral lines, the prospects of realizing the common school ideal look dimmer. But again, the implication is not to forbid choice but to construct a framework for educational choice that does not lead to a system of schools marked by external pluralism and internal homogeneity.

Supporters of some form of educational choice include among them some of the strongest defenders of a common educational vision (McLaughlin, 1995; Callan, 1997; Macedo, 2000). Each is deeply concerned with the common school ideal yet sees room for educational choice that is controlled or constrained by the public purposes of education. One approach is to see separate education – schools which are not open to religious or ethical diversity and do not foster citizenship or autonomy – as permissible during the early ages when children depend most on their parents and need most a coherent moral universe to establish an initial identity. Another approach sees the common school ideal as the very rationale for endorsing choice. Richard Kahlenberg's proposal to create a choice system of schools integrated by socio-economic lines, for example, assumes that such schools will not only produce better academic outcomes but also result in a broader racial and ethnic diversity than currently exists in most American public schools (Kahlenberg, 2001). A great many institutional arrangements for pursuing common education and accommodating educational choice will be permissible, and liberal accounts should leave the resolution of these arrangements to democratic politics.

See also 28 THE AUTHORITY AND RESPONSIBILITY TO EDUCATE; 29 CHURCH, STATE, AND EDUCATION; 31 CHILDREN'S RIGHTS; 34 MULTICULTURAL EDUCATION; 35 EDUCATION AND THE POLITICS OF IDENTITY

References

Ackerman, B. (1980) *Social Justice in the Liberal State*. New Haven, CT: Yale University Press.
Brighouse, H. (2000) *Social Justice and School Choice*. Oxford: Oxford University Press.
Bryk, T., Lee, V., and Holland, P. (1993) *Catholic Schools and the Common Good*. Cambridge, MA: Harvard University Press.

Callan, E. (1997) *Creating Citizens: Political Education and Liberal Democracy*. Oxford: Clarendon Press.

Conant, J. B. (ed.) (1962) *Thomas Jefferson and the Development of American Public Education*. Berkeley: University of California Press.

Curren, R. (2000) *Aristotle on the Necessity of Public Education*. Lanham, MD: Rowman & Littlefield.

Dewey, J. (1916) *Democracy and Education*. New York: Free Press.

Galston, W. (1995) Two concepts of liberalism. *Ethics*, 105(3), 516–34.

Glenn, C. (1988) *The Myth of the Common School*. Amherst, MA: University of Massachusetts Press.

Gutmann, A. (1987) *Democratic Education*. Princeton, NJ: Princeton University Press.

Gutmann, A. (1995) Civic education and social diversity. *Ethics*, 105(3), 557–79.

Gutmann, A. (2000) What does school choice mean? *Dissent*, Summer, 19–24.

Kahlenberg, R. (2001) *All Together Now: Creating Middle-class Schools through Public School Choice*. Washington, DC: Brookings Institution Press.

Levinson, M. (1999) *The Demands of Liberal Education*. Oxford: Oxford University Press.

McConnell, M. (2001) Education disestablishment: why democratic values are ill-served by democratic control of schooling. In S. Macedo and Y. Tamir (eds), *NOMOS XLIII: Moral and Political Education*. New York: New York University Press, pp. 88–146.

Macedo, S. (2000) *Diversity and Distrust: Civic Education in a Multicultural Democracy*. Cambridge, MA: Harvard University Press.

McLaughlin, T. (1992) The ethics of separate schools. In M. Leicester and M. Taylor (eds), *Ethics, Ethnicity and Education*. London: Kogan Page, pp. 114–36.

McLaughlin, T. (1995) Liberalism, education, and the common school. *Journal of Philosophy of Education*, 29(2), 239–55.

Ravitch, D. (1974) *The Great School Wars: New York City, 1805–1973*. New York: Basic Books.

Rawls, J. (1993) *Political Liberalism*. New York: Columbia University Press.

Reich, R. (2002) *Bridging Liberalism and Multiculturalism in American Education*. Chicago: University of Chicago Press.

Salomone, R. (2000) *Visions of Schooling: Conscience, Community, and Common Education*. New Haven, CT: Yale University Press.

Tomasi, J. (2001) *Liberalism beyond Justice: Citizens, Society, and the Boundaries of Political Theory*. Princeton, NJ: Princeton University Press.

Tyack, D. and Hansot, E. (1982) *Managers of Virtue: Public School Leadership in America*. New York: Basic Books.

31

Children's Rights

James G. Dwyer

The purpose of this chapter is not to determine whether children are morally entitled to an education of a particular type or content, but to address the broader question of who has moral rights of any sort in connection with children's education, and to identify some of the formal characteristics of children's educational rights. My approach to determining who has moral rights in connection with children's education is in part deconstructive; I critique prevailing views holding that parents or the state possess rights concerning children's education. It is also constructive; I show that a proper understanding of the nature and purpose of rights supports attribution of educational rights to children, including both basic rights and equality rights.

Basic Principles Concerning Rights

I begin with a particular conception of what rights are and what they do. I draw this conception from the history of political and legal theory, and from widely shared moral precepts in our society. Under this conception, rights are claims that impose on others duties of forbearance or assistance, and that override interests and preferences that do not command the protection of rights. Rights carry the moral connotation of entitlement and deservingness; to state that one has a moral right is to make a strong statement about what others owe one as a matter of justice. Because of these characteristics of rights, they are properly ascribed only to protect certain interests. Interests that warrant the protection of rights are defined by their importance and their kind.

First, only interests of great importance command the protection of moral rights. The importance of the interest is determined not by the subjective value an individual places on it, but by reference to objective criteria that select for goods of the greatest intrinsic and instrumental value. Joel Feinberg distinguishes "welfare interests" from "ulterior interests" (Feinberg, 1984, p. 37). Welfare interests are those aspects of well-being, such as food and education, that one must have in order to carry on in life, that are preconditions for pursuing any higher aims. In Feinberg's terms, they are "the basic requisites of a man's well-being," "generalized means to a great variety of possible goals and whose joint realization, in the absence of very special circumstances, is necessary for the achievement of more ultimate aims." From an objective perspective, these are the most important interests a person has, even if most people take them for granted most of the time. And because of their great importance to an individual's well-being, they "cry out for protection, for without their fulfillment, a person is lost."

Ulterior interests, in contrast, are satisfactions of the higher, individualized aims people form for their lives. Though these aims have great subjective importance for those who hold them, frustration of them does not undermine a person's well-being in the same way or to the same extent as does harm to welfare interests, and frustration of one aim might be compensated for by fulfillment of another. They therefore do not warrant the protection of rights. Feinberg gives as examples of ulterior interests "such aims as producing good novels or works of art, solving a crucial scientific problem, achieving high political office, successfully raising a family, achieving leisure for handicraft or sport, building a dream house, advancing a social cause, ameliorating human suffering, achieving spiritual grace."

Second, some kinds of interests are ruled out as bases for rights. For example, although law and public morality support attribution of rights to ownership of property, they rule out attribution of rights to ownership of persons, even though ownership of a person could be of much greater subjective value and material benefit to a right holder than ownership of any thing. An interest whose satisfaction entails disrespecting the personhood of another cannot give rise to a moral right.

These two limitations on rights – the importance of interests and the kind of interests – generate a general principle that is reflected in all areas of law other than child rearing. That principle is that no individual is morally entitled to control the life of another human being. This principle rests on the empirical assumption that an interest in controlling the life of any other person – however strongly one might wish to do so – is objectively not an aspect of basic welfare, and on the moral premise that deeming one person the object of another's rights fails to accord that person the respect he or she is owed as a person. The principle also rests on a conceptual distinction between a right to self-determination and a right to "other-determination," the former being of fundamental importance and the latter not, the former resting on a sound moral premise of self-ownership and the latter finding no support in general moral principles. Finally, this conceptual distinction presupposes a moral and practical difference between having a right to something – that is, a moral entitlement – and simply being privileged to have or do something. We can recognize that sometimes practical circumstances require that one person direct the life of another person – specifically, when the latter is not sufficiently competent to direct his or her own life – while at the same time denying that having the power to do so is ever a matter of right: that is, is something the power-holder is himself or herself entitled to as a matter of justice.

Importantly, our legal system applies this principle to the lives of incompetent adults. Even though those persons must have others exercise control over their lives to some degree, such control is not bestowed or exercised as a matter of the guardian's right. Instead, the state confers on caretakers and surrogate decision-makers a legal privilege to exercise certain powers, subject to regulation and revocation by the state as the welfare of the incompetent adult requires. Guardians for incompetent adults occupy a fiduciary, rather than possessory, role; they are agents rather than owners.

444

They have legitimate power insofar as they act to effectuate the rights of the incompetent adult, and are subject to legal override and removal if they act contrary to the interests – as defined by the state – of the incompetent person. Thus, habilitation decisions on behalf of mentally disabled adults must conduce to the welfare of the incompetent adult. And if there is disagreement between interested parties – for example, a state agency and a ward's parents – courts or administrative agencies resolve that disagreement on the basis of what they find to be best for the ward, and attribute no rights to either the state agency or the parents in the matter.

Against Parents' Rights

Parents' child-rearing rights are of two kinds. Rights to recognition as a parent and to custody of a child are associational rights. They are analogous to rights to enter into other sorts of relationships, such as a marriage. These associational rights of parents are not at issue here. Rights to make decisions concerning specific aspects of a child's life, such as the child's education, are control rights or powers. These are distinct from custodial rights, and denying to parents the power to make certain decisions regarding a child's education does not affect their custodial, associational rights: that is, their right to have a relationship with, live with, and interact with their child.

The general principles relating to control rights identified above *prima facie* rule out parental control rights, while allowing for parents to exercise some authority over their children's lives as a matter of legal privilege and in a fiduciary capacity. Thus, the parental child-rearing rights the United States Supreme Court has fashioned from the First and Fourteenth Amendments to the Constitution (neither of which mentions parents or children) are presumptively morally (and on some views of constitutional interpretation, legally) illegitimate. In the controlling cases, the Court determined that parents have a legal right that trumps state education laws in some instances. The Court has not squarely held that parents have a constitutional right to make educational decisions contrary to their children's interests, because in each case it decided the Court found that the state had not shown its laws necessary to protect children's welfare. Nevertheless, the Court's reasoning in these cases allows for such a result, because the Court did not rest its decisions on the (false) assumption that parents must have rights (rather than simply fiduciary authority) in order to protect the interests of children, but attributed child-rearing rights to parents principally on the basis of parents' own interests. The Court has never addressed the apparent inconsistency between attributing other-determining rights in the parent–child context and refusing to do so in every other context, including contexts involving incompetent adults.

Putting aside what the Supreme Court has done, several moral arguments might appear to support attribution of parental control rights. These arguments can usefully be categorized on the basis of whose interests they champion – children's interests, parents' interests, or societal interests. First, many would argue that parents should have rights concerning their children's education because parents know their children best and are more committed to their children's welfare than anyone else. The alternative of a state right to standardize children for its own purposes is

445

unacceptable in a liberal society that respects the separateness of persons and places moral value on the welfare of the individual. This argument has the virtue of making children – the persons whose lives are directly at stake – the center of moral attention. Nevertheless, it is flawed.

The factual premises underlying this argument are themselves subject to dispute: for example, on the grounds that many parents are not very committed to their children's welfare and that education, like medicine, is a specialized field about which most parents know very little. But even if the factual premises were unassailable, they would not support the conclusion that parents must have rights to control children's education. They would support assignment of some decision-making authority to parents, but only if and to the extent that this is best for children, and as a matter of the children's right, not the parents' right. It is simply nonsensical to attribute rights to one person – that is, to say that moral duties are owed to that person – in order to protect the welfare of another person. If the moral foundation for attributing some rights is the welfare of children, then the rights should be attributed to the children themselves – rights to have decisions about their lives made in a particular way by particular people on the basis of particular standards.

Moreover, in the context of religious objections to state-imposed rules for public or private schools, where parental rights are most hotly contested, the issue is really not who is in the best position to know what is best for a child, but whose values will control. When parents object for religious reasons to some aspect of public school curriculum, such as a course in critical thinking, or to imposition of a particular regulation on private schools, such as one prohibiting sexist teaching and treatment of students, the contest is not between competing positions on empirical facts. It is between competing ideologies. As such, it is senseless in this context to speak of who knows the child best and cares most about the child. Knowledge of a particular child's characteristics is irrelevant to the question of whether her school should teach her that females have moral worth and social importance equal to that of males and can rightfully pursue all the same careers that males pursue. The answer to such a question turns on whose values will govern the child's schooling – the state's values or the parents' values. And what many people fail to realize is that it is the state that must answer that question, because it is the state that ultimately must determine who will possess legal power over the lives of non-autonomous persons and what the scope and standards for exercise of that power will be. And in making that determination, the state must rely on its own perceptions – from its necessarily secular perspective – of what interests are at stake and which are the most important.

Thus, anyone who accepts that children have the most important interests at stake in connection with their own education, and who believes that education law and policy ought to be driven by the interests of children, must recognize that at this second-order level, in deciding whose values will control a child's upbringing when a conflict arises – parents' religious values or the liberal state's secular values – the state must act on the basis of its own perception of what is, in general, best for children. If the state concludes that it is generally best, in terms of children's temporal well-being, that parents' religious values control their schooling, then it should establish legal rules that give effect to parental religious objections. If, on the other hand, the state concludes that it is generally best for children, in terms of their temporal well-being, that this one aspect of their lives be controlled by liberal secular values, then it should establish legal rules that do not give effect to parental religious objections. In either case, though, the legal rule would be predicated on rights of children, rather than on rights of parents or the state.

A second category of arguments for parental rights rests on interests of parents themselves. Many contend that parents have fundamental interests at stake in connection with their children's upbringing, and that those interests deserve the protection of child-rearing rights. Parents therefore *are* a proper locus of moral entitlement, they argue. The rest of society owes duties *to them* as parents, wholly apart from any duties owed their children. Here the empirical premise is clearly flawed. Parental interests in how their children's lives go are simply not fundamental. They do not constitute a component of basic welfare, satisfaction of which is a prerequisite to pursuing higher aims in life. Instead, they are related to one of the higher aims that many – but not all – adults choose to pursue. They are in the same category as interests in having a particular job (which one might be unable to secure) or in marrying a particular person (who might refuse the proposal) – interests that might be of tremendous subjective importance to a person but are not, from an objective point of view, fundamental in the true sense, such that they warrant the protection of a right. Non-fulfillment of such an interest does not undermine one's capacity for self-determination and pursuit of other ulterior aims.

This is even clearer when it is recognized that formal education is just one facet of a child's life, occupying less than 20 percent of a child's awake hours from birth to adulthood, and that denying parents a right to decide how their child will be educated does not amount to denying them the opportunity to be parents and to teach their children their beliefs. To say that parents have fundamental interests at stake in matters of state regulation of children's schooling is to say that parents have a fundamental interest in having exclusive dominion over their children's minds, and that assertion is utterly implausible as an empirical matter. This conclusion that the parental interest is not fundamental is borne out by the quite common practice in divorce law of completely denying one of a child's parents any authority whatsoever to make decisions concerning the child's education. Significantly, it is not regarded as a tragedy or a grave injustice that a non-custodial parent has no say at all in his child's education, where a court deems that to be in the child's best interests, and non-custodial parents carry on with their lives and maintain rewarding relationships with their children despite denial of that power.

In addition, no matter how important parents' interests in how their children's lives go are, for the state to attribute to them control rights in order to further those interests entails treating children instrumentally, as means to the furtherance of other persons' aims. With respect to any adults, whether competent or not, we regard it as morally inappropriate for the state to treat them instrumentally in this fashion. Thus, the law treats the interests of an incompetent adult's guardian as entirely irrelevant to decisions about the incompetent adult's living situation, training, and medical care. Absent a compelling argument for treating children anomalously in this respect, we should not do so. Children are persons, and the state should not treat them as instruments for furtherance of other persons' aims in life any more so than it should treat any adults in that fashion.

Finally, some defend parental control rights on the grounds that such rights are necessary to promote certain diffuse societal interests, such as interests in pluralism and in avoiding state tyranny. Entitling parents to depart from prevailing norms is said to promote diversity of beliefs and ways of life. Such diversity is valuable because it facilitates societal progress, expands the opportunities available to individuals to adopt beliefs and ways of life most conducive to their happiness, and simply makes for a richer, more stimulating and aesthetically pleasing cultural environment (at least for people who value diversity).

One problem with this line of reasoning is that the premise that parental power over children's education is necessary to preserve and promote diversity is false. On a liberal understanding of children's welfare, a state aiming to provide children the best education would provide an autonomy-facilitating education, one that fosters abilities to question received views – including those espoused by current government officials – and to develop one's own views about the world and matters of value (Levinson, 1999; Brighouse, 2000). Such an education would thus tend to produce greater diversity in our society. Parental rights are often asserted as an objection to that type of education, and in that respect actually tend to diminish diversity and to inhibit the progress said to come from the freedom to engage in experiments in living. A diversity of illiberal, authoritarian communities is not the sort of diversity a liberal state values. While a liberal state might properly leave adults free to form illiberal cultural communities for themselves, its interest in pluralism does not support a decision affirmatively to assist such communities in perpetuating themselves, by bestowing on their adult members plenary power over their children's lives, including the power to stifle children's freedom of thought.

Moreover, if and to the extent that the state itself acts illiberally, and itself denies children an education that facilitates their freedom of belief, expression, and self-determination, children's rights – asserted by themselves or by their parents – can serve as an appropriate and sufficient basis for moral condemnation and legal injunction. It is not necessary as a practical matter to attribute rights to parents in order to guard against ideological tyranny by the state. And to say that parents do not possess moral rights to control their education is not to say that they should have no voice in the formation of education policy. To the contrary, it is best for children in general that the process of formulating education policies be open to the public and that all concerned citizens be able to participate in public deliberations about children's welfare.

An additional problem with the argument based on societal interests is that it presupposes the appropriateness of sacrificing children's welfare for the sake of diffuse societal interests. The very point of attributing rights to parents on this basis is that there is a conflict between parents' ideological preferences and what the liberal state deems best for children, and it is supposed that deferring to parents will enable dissident, illiberal subcultures to survive. Those who make this argument never defend the implicit assumption that furthering a societal interest in pluralism by this means is of greater moral importance than protecting the educational interests of children. As an empirical matter, it seems clear that children's interests are weightier than any contrary societal interest at stake. A child's interest in receiving an autonomy-facilitating education is profound, while the interest of any person *qua* citizen in living in a society that contains pockets of illiberal resistance to prevailing norms is insignificant, at least in connection with any single instance of parent–state conflict, if not entirely illusory. Thus, this argument would have to rest on a moral premise that the collectivity is to be favored over the individual regardless of what a balancing of interests would dictate. That is a decidedly illiberal premise, entailing an instrumental view of persons whose basic welfare is at issue, and one to which few if any people would be willing to adhere consistently.

Against State or Citizen Rights

In recent decades, political theorists writing about children's education have been preoccupied with the notion of civic education, which is typically taken to mean the kind of education necessary to prepare succeeding generations to support the basic institutions of liberal democratic society. Some "liberal statists" speak of the state having a right to inculcate particular values in children in order to produce the correct sort of citizens. Others speak of current adult citizens having a right to participate in the process of "social reproduction," a right effectuated by having education policies determined by democratic decision-making, in order to ensure that their conceptions of the good persist in succeeding generations and that they have an opportunity to effectuate their preferences for how their society develops in the future (Gutmann, 1999). Some do not speak of rights, but simply of state or citizen interests, or of prerequisites for the stability of liberal political institutions, and implicitly treat these interests or needs as of greater importance than any other considerations.

The principal counterpoise to political theorists' emphasis on civic education or "democratic education" has been the sort of arguments rehearsed above for parental rights based on parental or societal interests. But there is a much stronger, child-centered objection that has been overlooked. Most apparent is the problem that liberal statist arguments treat children instrumentally; children's education is approached not as a service to the children, whose fundamental developmental interests are at stake, but as a means for furthering interests of society as a whole or of current adult citizens who want to share power over children's lives. As such, it fails to accord children the respect they are owed as persons. Were liberal statists to speak of habilitation decisions for incompetent adults in the same way – that is, with priority, if not exclusive attention, given to general societal interests or to the desires of competent adult citizens to share in power over incompetent adults' lives – they would be roundly condemned for treating the incompetent adults instrumentally, for failing to recognize that the personhood of those adults requires that their own fundamental interests be the primary consideration in decisions about basic aspects of their lives.

Of course, to the extent that liberal statists aim to serve interests shared by all members of society, they aim to serve some interests of today's children, because children are members of our society. A child born today will benefit over the course of her life from decisions today that bolster the foundational institutions of our liberal democracy. However, liberal statists do not even consider whether the diffuse societal interests they champion are consistent with other of children's interests, and if not whether children's other interests trump the particular societal interests at issue or whether some alternative means might be available for furthering those interests. For example, many believe toleration for illiberal ways of life conduces to the stability of liberal democratic society, and suppose that such toleration should include substantial deference to parental desires regarding their children's education, even to the extent of sacrificing to a significant degree what, from a liberal perspective, is best for the children. Some liberal statists would concede to parents the power to place their children in schools that engage in such illiberal practices as explicit teaching of sexist views and training of girls for lives of subordination to men.

Conflict between perceived state interests and children's interests is not inherent in the liberal statist approach. Some iterations of the liberal statist position on education could be entirely consistent with children's developmental needs. But nothing in the liberal statist position guarantees this or even makes it more likely than not. Proponents of civic or democratic education have yet to address adequately this potential for conflict between their positions and the interests and rights of children, or the fact that their approach treats children's lives in a purely instrumental fashion.

Formal Characteristics of Children's Rights

According children the respect they are owed as persons entails giving proper weight to the interests they have at stake in connection with their education. From an objective standpoint, their educational interests are clearly fundamental, and the most important among all the interests potentially affected by education policy. Schooling is about shaping minds, fostering skills, providing socializing activities, and otherwise preparing young people for adult life. The minds that are being shaped belong to the children, not to any adults. The skills reside in them and largely determine their life prospects, not those of current adults. They are the ones being socialized and they are the ones who will live the adult lives for which schooling is preparation. Ordinarily when we debate policies concerning the fundamental welfare of some group of individuals, those individuals – *their* rights, *their* interests, *their* claim to justice – are the focus of moral inquiry. And so it should be with children's education.

One would be hard-pressed to find any theorist who denies that children possess a moral right to an education of some sort. Disagreement arises principally as to the specific formal and substantive features of children's educational rights. Are children entitled to the best education feasible, or simply to a minimally adequate education, or to something in between? What is the content of a good education? Against whom do children's rights operate or, in other words, who owes duties to children to ensure that they receive an education of the sort to which they are entitled – the federal government, state governments, local communities, or only parents? And are children's rights only entitlements to what others think is best for them, so that paternalistic imposition of a curriculum is appropriate, or do children have choice-based rights, such that teachers owe children a duty to secure their assent to particular lessons before administering them? I will not attempt to answer these questions or even to rehearse the many arguments advanced by others, but instead offer just a few observations relevant to these questions.

First, it is generally assumed that any educational rights children have must, as a conceptual matter, be positive rights, rather than negative rights – that is, they are rights to assistance rather than forbearance on the part of others. This assumption colors much of the discussion among both philosophers and legal scholars as to the content of children's educational rights, in particular because many resist the notion that the state owes positive duties to any persons, rather than just duties of non-interference. A strong version of that position would hold that only private parties – specifically, parents – owe any duties to children relating to education. In the legal world, this distinction between positive and negative rights has figured most prominently in United States Supreme Court decisions addressing claims for a federal constitutional right to an education. The Court has largely rejected such claims, in large part because it views the Constitution as an embodiment of negative rights only. On the other hand, most state constitutions in the USA, the national constitutions of many other countries, and several international conventions and declarations contain an explicit affirmation of children's positive right to an education, suggesting that the libertarian view that the state bears only duties of non-interference is not the prevailing view in American society or in other societies.

In any event, the distinction between positive and negative rights is unclear at best, and in some contexts entirely illusory. One could argue, for example, that today's children have a *prima facie* negative right against the state ever imposing legal restrictions on their behavior, a right that is extinguished only insofar as the state ensures them an education adequate to prepare them for responsible self-governance. In the context of disputes between parents and the state over regulation of children's education, it is generally assumed that parents asserting a constitutional right to non-interference with their choices are asserting negative rights, while any claims on behalf of the children to enjoy the benefits of state-imposed standards are presumed to be claims of positive rights. But in fact what parents are demanding is that the state bestow on them a great benefit – namely, plenary legal power over their children's lives. Parents are not demanding that the state dissociate itself entirely from their children's lives, since that would leave them with no legal power at all, but that the state favor them in making the decision – which the state must make – as to who will possess authority over children's education. The parents' claim is therefore very much a positive right claim, a claim for state assistance in advancing their aims. And the claim on behalf of the children whose parents object to state requirements for education can be viewed as a negative right claim; it is a claim against interference with their statutory right to an education that satisfies state standards. The children's claim is essentially that the state – in the form of school officials or a court or a legislative body – must not act to exclude them from benefits they would otherwise receive, simply because their parents do not wish them to have the benefit. It is as much a negative rights claim as is the claim of a property owner against a change in zoning laws that diminishes the value of his or her property.

In addition, children possess equality rights, as a moral and constitutional matter, that significantly constrain state action relating to their education. Regardless of what basic rights children have in connection with their education – that is, what rights

451

they possess because of their developmental needs, children have rights arising from the state's obligation to act impartially and to treat equally persons who are similarly situated. This right is embodied in the Equal Protection Clause of the Fourteenth Amendment to the federal Constitution, and in similar provisions in every state's constitution. This right requires that if the state chooses to bestow particular educational benefits on children generally – for example, by enacting compulsory schooling laws and by providing schooling itself (i.e. public schools), even if it is not morally obligated to provide such benefits to anyone, the state must provide that benefit equally to all children, absent circumstances that make the benefit of no value to some children. Analogously, if the state chooses to provide the benefit of police protection, it must provide it equally to all citizens; it may not create a police force and then limit its operation to protecting only people who are white or male, for example.

Children's equality rights have numerous implications for their education. Because all states in the USA do confer on children the benefit of a statutory and, in many states, constitutional right to an education, they may not exclude any children from this benefit absent a showing that the children would not benefit from receiving an education. There might be circumstances in which this is the case for some children, but such circumstances would not arise simply from a parental objection on ideological grounds. The Supreme Court's decision in *Wisconsin* v. *Yoder*, which held, in effect, that the state may not guarantee to children of Amish parents the same education it guarantees for other children, thus violated the Equal Protection Clause and the equality rights of children whose parents are Amish. The Court ought to repudiate the *Yoder* decision on that basis.

The same is true when one looks beyond merely receiving some education to receiving an education of a particular quality or content. If the state determines that children's developmental interests require that they receive an education of a particular sort – for example, one that promotes critical thinking, trains children in the investigative methodologies of many disciplines, instills the knowledge they would need to pursue a higher education in the best universities, and teaches gender equality – and the state acts on this determination by fashioning regulations requiring schools to provide such an education, it bears a moral responsibility to ensure that *all* children receive such an education. To exclude any children from that benefit on the grounds that their parents object to it, or have chosen to place their child in a private school, is to violate the equality rights of those children. The children themselves have not, presumably, chosen to forgo that benefit, and the state cannot justifiably withdraw it from them because of other persons' preferences. Analogously, the state could not justifiably deny police protection to African-Americans on the grounds that some other persons do not want them to have that protection. The state would bear the burden of demonstrating that any children excluded from the protection of state-imposed standards for education would not benefit from that protection, or that providing that protection to them would inevitably entail countervailing costs to them that outweigh the benefits, because of the children's circumstances. Absent such a showing, the state would be precluded from exempting any children from aspects of the public school curriculum that further the objectives identified above, and would be required to extend all its academic standards to all private schools.

Finally, children's equality rights also have implications for state funding of education, which is a very large benefit that the state provides to children. When the state spends large sums of money to operate public schools, or where it funds public schools and some private schools (e.g. only non-sectarian schools, as with voucher programs in Vermont and Maine), it has a *prima facie* obligation to fund the education of all children. In other words, every child has a presumptive, equality-based right to a fair (as determined by need) share of state spending on education. This means that children in private schools, including religious schools, have a *prima facie* right to state-provided educational vouchers. With adults, we say that there is no equality-based entitlement to funding of private analogues to public services – for example, museums – because everyone is treated equally by the service being made available to all, and any who freely choose to forgo the state-provided service justifiably bear the consequences of doing so. This understanding of moral responsibility defeats equality-based claims for school vouchers on behalf of parents. But the same cannot be said of children in private schools, who generally do not themselves choose to forgo the state-provided service of public schooling. They should not be made to suffer, by losing out on the important state benefit of funding for education, as the result of other persons' choices, not even the choices of their parents.

This implication of children's equality rights leads to the startling conclusion that children in religious and other private schools are presumptively entitled, as a matter of moral equality rights and constitutional equal protection rights, to state-provided school vouchers. And were it the case that the state regulated private schools sufficiently to ensure that they all strive to provide a good secular education – that is, the kind of education the liberal state determines to be good for children, that right would be controlling. The problem today in the USA is that the state ignores its responsibility to children in private schools to extend to them the benefit of academic standards and rules for treatment of students. Private schools are virtually unregulated with respect to curricular matters and conduct toward students. Beyond requiring that private schools profess to teach certain subjects, states do nothing to ensure that private schools are academically sound. And beyond general criminal prohibitions against serious physical violence, states do nothing to ensure that private schools treat students with respect. As long as this remains the case, children's equality-based rights to state funding of private schooling cannot be effectuated. The state has no reason to believe that in funding any particular private school it will be benefiting the children in it. In fact, in funding some schools, the state would be harming the children in it, because the state would be supporting illiberal schooling practices – for example, stifling of critical and independent thought and teaching of sexist and racist views. Giving effect to the rights of children in private schools would require a major transformation of that sector of the US educational system.

Finally, a distinction can be made between children's welfare rights and their liberty rights or rights of self-determination. It is plausible to regard the value and moral force of rights of self-determination as varying with the capacity of their possessor to make competent decisions, because to the extent that one lacks this capacity one's freedom to make decisions for oneself will not enable one to effectively promote one's interests. Regard for well-being and respect for claims of self-determination converge by-and-large in the case of adults, and this convergence warrants a strong principle of respect for individual liberty rights. But what weight should be given to the claims of children to make decisions, such as educational decisions, on their own behalf? Children have been traditionally regarded as lacking the maturity of judgment necessary to be able to make decisions that will adequately protect their interests, including their developmental interests. Because proper attention to these developmental interests is vital to a child's *future* capacity for effective self-determination, it has been common to regard the promotion of these developmental interests as displaying a kind of prospective or forward-looking respect for the child's interest in self-determination or autonomy.

Against this traditional view, child liberationists have argued that children are rational enough to decide well for themselves, and that they should thus be morally entitled to the same rights of self-determination as adults. On this basis others have derived various conclusions regarding the moral impermissibility of imposing various aspects of schooling on children without their consent. This is not the place to review the evidence which has been brought to bear against this view of children's decisional competence (see Purdy, 1992). I will simply make two points. The first is that a proper respect for children does require that, to the extent education is imposed upon them involuntarily in public or private schools, that education should be one that enhances their autonomy on the whole in the long run (Pritchard, 1996; Brighouse, 2000). Given children's limited maturity of judgment and foresight, their present interest in making choices for themselves cannot be given the weight properly accorded their well-being and the development of their future capacities for competent self-determination. The second point relates specifically to contexts where parents who wish their children to have an authoritarian, illiberal upbringing object to liberal state requirements for education. The point is simply that, as an empirical matter, children of such parents tend to be delayed in their development of the capacity for free and fully informed, independent decisions about their lives. Thus, when children voice agreement with parental objections to liberal educational requirements, their choices are more likely to be heteronomous than autonomous, and heteronomous choices generally command lesser respect than autonomous ones. On the other hand, a child's disagreement with a parent's illiberal objections – for example, if a child says she *wants* to study evolution and other mainstream views in the sciences – might signal an independence that makes all of the child's views worthy of greater respect than if she appeared simply to be obeying parental commands to express a certain position.

Conclusion

While educational theorists and curriculum developers generally focus their attention on what kind of schooling is best for children in today's world, political and legal theorists in recent decades have been largely preoccupied with ideological battles between the state and parents or cultural communities and have given much greater attention and weight to parents' rights, group rights, states' rights, and adult citizens' rights than they have to children's developmental interests and rights. That needs to change. An impartial weighting of the interests at stake in connection with children's education, and full recognition of children's personhood and all that that entails, make clear that political and legal theorists ought to give priority of place to children's welfare and rights in their thinking about parent–state conflicts over children's education and about other political and legal issues relating to children's education. They should not speak to the interests or rights, if any, of other persons in any child-rearing context until they have determined whether children have any rights in the matter and, if so, what those rights require. And when a conflict arises between children's interests and interests of other persons, they should objectively and explicitly evaluate whose interests are weightier, giving children's interests their full due.

See also 28 THE AUTHORITY AND RESPONSIBILITY TO EDUCATE; 29 CHURCH, STATE, AND EDUCATION; 30 COMMON SCHOOLING AND EDUCATIONAL CHOICE; 33 EDUCATIONAL EQUALITY AND JUSTICE; 36 THE ETHICS OF TEACHING; 37 INCLUSION AND JUSTICE IN SPECIAL EDUCATION

References

Brighouse, H. (2000) *School Choice and Social Justice*. New York: Oxford University Press.

Feinberg, J. (1984) *The Moral Limits of the Criminal Law. Volume 1: Harm to Others*. New York: Oxford University Press.

Gutmann, A. (1999) *Democratic Education*, rev. edn. Princeton, NJ: Princeton University Press.

Levinson, M. (1999) *The Demands of Liberal Education*. New York: Oxford University Press.

Pritchard, M. S. (1996) *Reasonable Children: Moral Education and Moral Learning*. Lawrence: University of Kansas Press.

Purdy, L. (1992) *In Their Best Interests? The Case against Equal Rights for Children*. Ithaca, NY: Cornell University Press.

Further reading

Dwyer, J. G. (1998) *Religious Schools v. Children's Rights*. Ithaca, NY: Cornell University Press.

Dwyer, J. G. (2002) *Vouchers within Reason*. Ithaca, NY: Cornell University Press.

32

Education and Standards of Living

Christian Barry

Disagreements about educational policies, practices, funding, and assessment are sometimes purely empirical, with advocates of opposing positions differing only on the best means to achieve their shared aims. But the intensity of these debates is often due to deeper disagreements about the role that educational opportunity and achievement play in determining the quality of people's lives and the justice of social institutions. One such disagreement is foundational, concerning whether educational opportunities and achievements are important only as a *means* to other valuable things such as happiness or income and wealth, or whether they are themselves important *constitutive* elements of living standards. Other disagreements concern the relative importance of different kinds of educational opportunities and achievements. These are philosophical issues, but the ways we resolve them have practical consequences. Different understandings of the role of education in determining living standards may lead social scientists to concentrate on different facts when they attempt to measure the impacts of institutions and policies. Different emphases in research may affect claims not only about the living standards of individuals, groups, and countries, but also about inequalities in living standards *between* them and about trends in overall living standards over time. And different claims about overall trends in living standards and their distributional aspects will often lead to very different ethical evaluations of policies and institutions and sharp disagreements about how they should be reformed.

The intent of this chapter is to clarify the nature of some of these disagreements about the value of education by surveying the discussions of the "standard of living" that have figured prominently in the social sciences and the recent literature on social justice. Discussion of the standard of living provides a useful entry point, since this concept is generally intended to play a role both in discussions of *theories* of justice and in *practical* assessments of actually existing social arrangements. That is, the concept of the standard of living is often understood as an element in a theory of justice and a measurement tool for policy-makers. Given this dual role in social thinking, the evaluation of conceptions of the standard of living requires attention both to disputes among political philosophers concerning social justice and to questions about the potential use of such conceptions in practical assessment.

This chapter begins by exploring the concept of the standard of living and the nature and importance of disagreements about its interpretation, then goes on to

456

investigate four leading conceptions of the standard of living and the role that education plays in them. It reaches three main conclusions. First, education plays an essential constitutive role in any plausible conception of the standard of living. Indeed, even some widely held *implausible* views (such as those based on utility or income) that attribute only instrumental value to education seem, when combined with available empirical evidence, to indicate the need to stress education as a means to improve living standards. Second, the role of education in more plausible conceptions of living standards is complex and far-reaching. Illiteracy and other deprivations related to lack of basic education are significant obstacles to essentials of good living, such as participation in economic activities, political life, and decision-making within the family. Third, the plausibility of any particular conception of the standard of living (and the role that education is given within it) may depend on the practical or theoretical purposes for which it is intended.

The Concept of the Standard of Living

People often disagree about which of two persons, two groups, or two countries enjoys a higher standard of living. These disputes are often not straightforwardly empirical – two parties who disagree may be aware of all the same "facts" yet still disagree in their judgments, because they have different conceptions of the standard of living. Like other evaluative concepts such as "justice," "fairness," and "impartiality," the concept of the standard of living has no clearly definable and specific use that can be set up as "standard" or "correct." There are deep disagreements about how this concept should be more fully understood because it is inextricably linked to our general beliefs about how states of affairs should be judged and how societies should be arranged.

Consider, for instance, two persons X and Y. Suppose that X has a higher income than Y but that Y is literate while X is not. Which of the two has a higher living standard? If our answers to this question differ, it is because we evaluate the relative significance of literacy and income in determining persons' living standards differently. Income-based views, for example, would judge X to have the higher standard of living, while views that give significant weight to education might not. Still other views, such as utilitarianism, may hold that information about income and literacy *per se* is, strictly speaking, irrelevant, because the only thing that ultimately matters is how pleasant one's life is or the extent to which one's desires are satisfied.

These issues become even more complex when our interest is in comparing the overall living standards in different countries or groups. Consider, for instance, two countries A and B. Suppose that A has a higher per capita income than B and also produces more PhDs and Nobel laureates per capita, but that B secures universal primary education and has lower rates of functional illiteracy. It is easy to see how we might disagree about which of these countries has a higher overall standard of living. This disagreement might be linked to different views about:

- the relative importance of educational achievements and other goods in evaluating the standard of living;

457

- the relative importance of different kinds of educational achievements or opportunities for determining the standard of living of an individual;
- the way that individual educational achievements and other goods should be aggregated into overall measures of the standard of living of a country.

Adjudicating between different conceptions of the standard of living cannot, then, be delinked from broader questions of ethics and social justice. But it nevertheless is possible to specify the *concept* of the standard of living in terms of the rather abstract "common" content shared by more specific conceptions of it. For the purposes of this chapter I understand the concept of the standard of living as follows:

The standard of living denotes the aspect or aspects of persons' well-being that are of ethical importance for assessing either states of affairs or the justice of social arrangements.

Specifying the concept of the standard of living in this way indicates the common purposes of competing *conceptions* of the standard of living, while leaving open questions about both their content (the space that they specify) and purpose (the role that they are intended to serve in social evaluation). The standard of living identifies what Sen has called the "evaluative space" of an ethical theory (Sen, 1987, p. 4, 1991, p. 4, 1993, pp. 7–8). Specifying this space entails "a class of 'informational constraints' in the form of ruling out directly evaluative use of various types of information, to wit, those that do not belong to the evaluative space" (Sen, 1993, p. 32).

The Diverse Purposes of the Concept of the Standard of Living

A *conception* of the standard of living specifies the information about persons that is relevant for ethically evaluative judgments. *Substantive* disagreements about the informational bases are disagreements about the kinds of information that are relevant to these different kinds of judgments and about how this information should be interpreted to provide overall assessments of the standard of living for persons and groups. But in defending a conception of the standard of living it is also essential to determine what *purpose* we intend it to serve in the public political culture of a society. A conception of the standard of living can be used alternatively as:

- A part of a criterion of *goodness*, to be used in the ethical evaluation of states of affairs and distributions.
- A part of a theory of *justice*: a set of criteria to be used in the ethical evaluation of social rules and institutions.
- A part of a *public criterion* of justice, suitable for use by citizens in evaluating shared institutions.

The distinction between these purposes is not always taken to be very significant. Some consequentialist ethical theories, such as utilitarianism, regard the justice of social institutions, legislation, and other social rules to consist simply in their tendency to promote the overall goodness of states of the world. But a suitable conception of the standard of living for the purpose of constructing a theory of justice may not work well as a *public* criterion for the public assessment of institutions or as a mandate for political leaders. Such conceptions of the standard of living may be too complex for ordinary citizens to understand, too complex to serve as instruments for assessing how public institutions and policies are affecting living standards, and too broad to be useful as criteria to which politicians may be held accountable (Rawls, 1982, 1993; Pogge, 1989, pp. 110–13; Seabright, 2001). Many utilitarian thinkers have also stressed the need to separate ultimate from "use" or "public" criteria for moral assessment, fearing that widespread *acceptance* of the utility principle may undermine the *aims* of the principle. (On these distinctions see Hare, 1981; Parfit, 1983; Pogge, 1990.) Rawls, as we shall see, specifies the standard of living in terms of social primary goods (including basic liberties, opportunities, income and wealth, and the social bases of self-respect), intending this standard as a public criterion for evaluating social institutions, while denying its adequacy for providing a measure of the overall quality of life. Showing that social primary goods are inadequate as an overall measure of wellbeing does not then constitute a refutation of Rawls's position.

The importance of publicly verifiable criteria for the assessment of policies has been stressed in many recent debates on education. We may wish to preserve simplicity in our public criteria for assessing educational policies (perhaps through repeatable testing), while acknowledging that these criteria ignore ethically important aspects of education that might be captured by more complex criteria. One should note, though, that there might also be virtue in complexity, even in a public criterion. As Sen has pointed out repeatedly, the conflict between relevance and simplicity of use should not always be resolved in favor of simplicity and it is often better to be vaguely right than precisely wrong in our evaluations. Setting overly specific targets can not only miss much of what we want to capture, but also produce distorted estimations of achievement through pressure to show "results." These pressures and the distortions that they engender have often been particularly intense with respect to education (see, for example, Gardner, 2000; Lemann, 2000). In addition, a criterion of educational adequacy that is limited to improving test scores is likely to impoverish public discussion of the value of education by ignoring such factors as the encouragement of tolerance, community spirit, critical thinking, creative self-expression and open-mindedness.

The analytical importance of these distinctions between the potential purposes of a conception of the standard of living can be accepted without judging in advance their ethical or practical importance. Grasping these distinctions can also be helpful for diagnosing the nature of disagreements about the standard of living, which have often reflected differences of purpose as well as substance. It may be that no single conception of the standard of living will be adequate for all three of these purposes.

The Importance of Disagreement about the Standard of Living

Social scientists generally try to choose focal variables for their statistical studies that capture something of evaluative importance: they try to count what "counts." Different conceptions of the standard of living and the "evaluative spaces" they define will, then, often lead social scientists to concentrate on different things when trying to measure the impacts of institutions and policies. Indeed, social indicators, whether in the form of individual statistical indicators or composite indices, are usually chosen in order to serve the need for a concise overview of ethically relevant social trends. These assessments can have a significant influence on public perception about the adequacy of policies and institutional arrangements. A great deal of economic theory focuses on the development of per capita income levels over time, at least in part because per capita income levels are taken to be either *constitutive of* or at least good *proxies for* living standards. Philosophical criticism of the role that per capita income has played in evaluation of living standards and the desire to operationalize new conceptions of the standard of living have led to the construction of a plethora of new measures. Many of these measures have been offered as rough proxies of much richer conceptions of the standard of living. The concept of "human development," for instance, was developed through the work of Mabhub ul-Haq, based on the "capabilities" approach to the standard of living developed by Amartya Sen. This approach, which is discussed in more detail below, identifies living standards with enlarging people's choices and achievements (ul-Haq, 1995). This conception led to the development of the United Nations Development Program's "Human Development Index" (HDI) (UNDP, 2000, p. 157). Calculated annually for approximately 170 countries, currently ranked from Norway at the top to Sierra Leone at the bottom, the HDI combines four simple statistical indicators – life expectancy at birth, the adult literacy rate, school enrollment rates, and the average annual income per person – to create a composite index that gives a basic measure of the standard of living in a country on a scale of zero to one. Integrating concerns with health and education into this measure results in country rankings that are significantly different from rankings according to per capita income. And focusing on a broader range of social indicators has produced some surprising results. It seems more possible than was originally thought to achieve high rates of literacy, high life expectancy, and good nutrition without higher income levels. Costa Rica, Sri Lanka, and the Indian State of Kerala are the most often cited examples (Dreze and Sen, 1990). When countries are ranked from first to last, the difference between HDI rank and per capita income rank is often significant. In 1999, for example, South Africa was ranked 45th in per capita income but only 94 according to the HDI, while Sweden ranked only 17th according to per capita income but 4th according to the HDI. Recognizing differences of this kind, some development economists have investigated the commonalities between countries that consistently rank higher on the HDI and other social indicators than in terms of per capita income (see, for example, Jolly and Mehrotra, 1998).

Though, for reasons of simplicity and political impact, the HDI emphasizes adult literacy rate and school enrolment rates, Human Development Reports have repeatedly stressed the importance of other educational indicators in developing a fuller picture of overall living standards. These include the required level of teacher training, the percentage of government expenditure allocated to education and expenditure per pupil, and the cost of education for families. Attention to this broad range of social indicators reflects a pluralistic understanding of the concept of the standard of living with a strong emphasis on the role of education. It also expresses a pluralistic understanding of education itself – that simple indicators such as literacy do not fully capture the value of education. (For more on the HDI and its critics see Desai, 1991; Dasgupta and Weale, 1992; Raworth and Stewart, 2000; Sen, 2000.)

It is also important to emphasize the more general (and often indirect) role of conceptions of the standard of living in shaping the research priorities of social scientists. How the standard of living is conceived may help to provide a framework for inquiry even when there are significant practical constraints on its use. Even when data limitations appear to render their complete representation impossible in principle (as some have claimed for any approach that relies on the idea of counterfactual choice), conceptions of living standards can seek to accommodate and minimize these gaps. Adopting simple but implausible conceptions of living standards such as per capita income may, on the other hand, enable detailed precision in measurement only at the price of omitting other ethically relevant information and causing distortions in assessments of social arrangements.

Broadening the factual concentration of the social sciences often has other effects on public political culture. Impoverished conceptions of the standard of living and the factual concentration they encourage can lead to a more general blindness in social thinking. A long running dispute among economists has focused on the reality of the so-called Kuznets curve, which suggested that rising inequality was strongly correlated with economic growth at early stages of economic development (Kuznets, 1955; Chenery and Syrquin, 1975). Public discourse has seized upon this finding with some avidity, often making it the basis of unwarranted generalizations. Many interpret studies of this kind as demonstrating the general impossibility of promoting equality *and* growth or efficiency in any area, including health care and access to educational opportunities (Okun, 1975). Though some recent studies seem to have discredited the postulated "curve," it is perhaps more important to note how little relevance such a finding has to promoting equality in living standards more broadly conceived. By leading us to focus on more integrated sets of information, richer conceptions of the standard of living have often undermined received wisdom. The idea that there is a necessary and very significant tension between aggregative and distributive concerns seems to be a case in point (Sen, 1992, pp. 32–7). Indeed, in the areas of health and education there is considerable evidence that addressing distributive inequity is an important *means* to promoting aggregative goals (for discussion see Birdsall, 2001; Sen, 2001).

An understanding of the concept of the standard of living is also important for the interpretation of many other concepts of social evaluation, such as "poverty" and "deprivation." Judgments about whether people are poor or deprived or suffer from social exclusion rely on an informational base that specifies the objects that they lack, are deprived of, or are excluded from. A reorientation of factual concentration in the study of living standards, then, is also likely to engender additional changes in how these other concepts are understood and empirically investigated. The adoption of "human development" as an interpretation of the standard of living has, for instance, led the United Nations Development Program to devise other correlate concepts and measures in these areas. "Human poverty" is thus distinguished from "income poverty" and the Human Poverty Index (HPI) measures poverty in a way that incorporates concern with educational achievement. This more complex concept of poverty tends to encourage social scientists to study the effects of educational reform in different ways, focusing on the direct effects of such reforms, such as functional literacy rates, instead of their impact on incomes or asset holdings (Anand and Sen, 1997; UNDP, 1997; Sen, 1999).

How living standards are conceived can also be of great practical importance in guiding our judgments about whose needs and which needs should be given priority in the allocation of scarce resources. If educational achievement is taken to be an important element in the standard of living, then concern with improving the living conditions of less advantaged persons and groups might tend to focus more on securing their educational opportunities than attempting to increase household income. Substantial variation in the *kinds* of educational achievement and opportunity that are given weight in a conception of the standard of living can also give rise to practical conflicts about resource allocation. Two views of the standard of living that emphasize, respectively, achievement in higher education and achievement in primary education can lead to quite different assessments of regimes of public expenditure on education. Problems of this kind are often of particular importance in developing countries that are simultaneously trying to establish universally accessible primary and secondary education as well as to compete in sectors that require significant technical training, such as software development.

The Role of Education in the Standard of Living

The content of any particular conception of the standard of living can be understood, then, by how it answers three interconnected questions:

1 *What information is relevant to the evaluation of living standards?* What, according to the theory, are the objects of value, its "currency"? Are living standards fixed by happiness, educational achievement, income and wealth, some combination of these things, or something else?

2 *What is the relative importance of different kinds of information in determining an individual's overall living standard?* How are the objects of value within the theory – such as educational achievement, health status, income, enjoyment of basic liberties, or other information – to be weighted relative to each other? Does the conception adopt a strict intrapersonal aggregation function that fixes the exchange rates between these currencies (value objects) or does it leave these questions open, allowing for the possibility that a plurality of aggregation functions may play a role in determining living standards, the choice of which might be determined by the political process, or depend on the discretion of public officials on a case-by-case basis?

3 *How, if at all, is information about the standard of living of individuals combined to give aggregate measures of the standard of living within a group or a country?* Does the conception use familiar aggregation functions such as the arithmetic or geometric mean or sum-ranking? Does it use some indicator of inequality to determine the overall standard of living? Or does it either refrain from giving determinate answers of this kind or leave a robust role to the political process in deciding them?

Answers to these questions will determine whether and how education is taken to contribute to living standards. Question (1) is the most foundational of these three questions, and it is on this question that this chapter has primarily been focused. Four main answers to question 1 have been offered in the literature on the standard of living: income or commodity possessions, utility, Rawls's account of social primary goods, and Sen's account of capabilities. The roles of education in these four approaches are quite different.

Two prevalent conceptions of the standard of living focus on *single* types of variables: income or commodity possessions and utility.

- *Income or commodity possessions.* According to this view, a person's standard of living is determined by his or her income and or commodity possessions. This understanding of the standard of living has dominated much of the literature in the social sciences. Some economists adopt this conception explicitly, using the terms "living standards" and "per capita income" more or less interchangeably, and basing broad claims on trends in living standards on per capita income trends. The research priorities of economists also suggest that this view is often implicitly adopted. A great deal of economic theory focuses on the development of per capita income levels over time, at least in part because per capita income levels are taken to be either *constitutive of* or at least good *proxies for* living standards. And per capita income has been the predominant measure of living standards for some time (Maniw et al., 1992; Hobijn and Franses, 1999).

- *Utility.* Utilitarianism claims that the moral quality of states of affairs, human lives, and social institutions is reducible to a single value, utility. Utility, understood as, alternatively, preference satisfaction or pleasure, is the object of value that determines the worth of all human pursuits and activities.

Neither of these conceptions allows educational opportunity or achievement any *direct* role in evaluations of living standards. Utilitarian theorists, for instance, take utility (understood either as pleasure or as satisfaction of preferences) as *the* relevant information for assessing people's living standards. According to these views, information about non-utility features of persons, such as whether they are literate, well nourished, and free from sexual discrimination, are irrelevant for evaluation. Income-based conceptions of living standards are similar to utilitarian views in that they focus only on one variable, income, and hold that education is but one of many potential causal contributors to higher living standards. It should be noted, however, that even income-based views appear to justify significant emphasis on education for promoting living standards. A strong positive effect of educational investment on economic growth is now widely acknowledged. Better-educated workers earn higher incomes and education raises the output of farmers (Psacharapoulus, 1985). And income-based considerations would also appear to motivate increasing concern with gender equity in education. Educated women have fewer and healthier children, and the mortality of infants and children under five years old decline as the number of years that a mother has been in school increase (Birdsall, 1993; Shultz, 1993). All of these factors have been shown to have a significant long-term effect on economic growth and per capita income. Recent studies have also shown that inequality in education

463

appears to have a strong *negative* effect on growth, suggesting that even a rather simpleminded focus on per capita income would justify efforts to promote a more equal distribution of educational opportunities (Birdsall and Londoño, 1997).

Both of these monistic views of living standards have been under severe attack, and not without reason. Utilitarianism has been rejected as an overall ethical theory for many different reasons. But one criticism is particularly damaging for utility as an interpretation of the standard of living. Utilities, whether understood as satisfied preferences or pleasurable mental states, are fungible and often are adapted to people's circumstances. People are often conditioned by their circumstances to be satisfied with less than most would think necessary for a minimally decent life. Martha Nussbaum has recently noted how, in one desert area in India, women had no feelings of anger or protest about their own severe malnourishment, lack of basic education, or the lack of clean water supply. The utilitarian standard would, as she puts it, give "sanctity" to one's "quiet acceptance of deprivation" (Nussbaum, 2000, p. 139; see also Sen, 1987, pp. 8ff). Similar claims have also been made in the context of developed countries, where many citizens have come to accept large and increasing inequalities and deprivations as "fair" (Hochschild, 1981; Newman, 1988). This suggests that a utilitarian standard would be sharply at odds with many of our commonsense judgments about how well people's lives are going and the extent to which social arrangements are securing them what they are entitled to.

Income-based views appear to be inadequate in a different way. They seem to provide too thin a basis for judging personal advantage. Persons can have relatively high income but lack opportunities, suffer from various forms of social exclusion and suffer from severe health problems due to pollution, contaminated water supplies, and other socially caused environmental problems. Overemphasis on income as a public criterion of the standard of living has also distorted evaluations of policies and institutional arrangements, since countries such as Sri Lanka, Costa Rica, and Zimbabwe have managed to create a wealth of opportunities for their people without significant increases in income (see UNDP, 1996; Jolly and Mehrotra, 1998).

Recently, Amartya Sen and John Rawls have advanced two more plausible conceptions of the standard of living. Each differs from the two views discussed above by claiming that a *plurality* of non-utility and non-commodity features, including educational opportunities, achievements, and a broad range of freedoms, are relevant to assessments of living standards. Despite a common commitment to pluralistic assessments of living standards, these views differ in important ways. They differ theoretically, by specifying different objects of value in their accounts of living standards. And they may also differ practically due to differences in those aspects of educational achievement and opportunity that they deem to be important and in the weight they assign these factors in assessing the living standards of individuals, groups or countries.

Social Primary Goods

The social primary goods approach, developed by John Rawls, proposes to measure the standard of living for the purposes of a public criterion of justice only. Social primary goods are conceived as a complex bundle of resources available to persons.

Rawls describes them as "things which it is supposed every rational man wants whatever else he wants" (Rawls, 1971, p. 62). And the list of the types of these resources that this bundle includes suggests that referring to them as "goods" is somewhat misleading; they are not commodities or goods in any straightforward sense. Rawls distinguishes five types of social primary goods: (1) basic enumerated liberties, such as freedom of thought and liberty of conscience, freedom of association, and the freedom defined by the liberty and integrity of the person, as well as by the rule of law, and finally the political liberties; (2) freedom of movement and choice of occupation against a background of diverse opportunities; (3) powers and prerogatives of offices and positions of responsibility, particularly those in the main political and economic institutions; (4) income and wealth; and (5) the social bases of self-respect.

Different goods are governed by different principles. Type 1 goods are governed by the principle that each person has an equal right to a fully adequate scheme of equal basic rights and liberties, which scheme is compatible with a similar scheme for all. Type 2 goods are governed by the *opportunity principle*, which states that social and economic inequalities must be attached to offices and positions open to all under conditions of fair equality of opportunity. Goods of types 3, 4, and 5 are governed by the *difference principle*, which states that social and economic inequalities must be to the greatest benefit of the least advantaged members of society (Rawls 1999, p. 392). Rawls assigns lexical priority to goods of type 1 over all other goods, as well as lexical priority of goods of type 2 over the remaining goods. Given Rawls's weighting scheme, "all citizens in a well-ordered society have the same equal basic liberties and enjoy fair equality of opportunity. The only permissible difference among citizens is their share of the primary goods in [3], [4] and [5]" (Rawls, 1982, p. 162). The standard of living of a person is, for Rawls, a function of his or her possession of this complex bundle of social primary goods weighted according to Rawls's priority rules. Rawls thus addresses our question 2 above in a clear form. Since one principle does not come into play until those previous to it are either fully satisfied or do not apply, this ordering serves to indicate both when injustices are present in a social system and which injustice is most urgent (Rawls, 1971, p. 43; Pogge, 1989).

Education plays a direct and complex role in determining living standards within Rawls's theory. Minimally adequate educational achievement is constitutive of the highest priority social goods, since enjoyment of the basic liberties depends upon persons being sufficiently educated to understand and participate in their society's political, legal, and associational life (Rawls, 1971, p. 107). But Rawls also grants educational opportunity an important role in his conception by requiring (through his opportunity principle) that persons similarly endowed and motivated enjoy equal chances of education and culture (Rawls, 1971, p. 275, 2001, p. 43).

Rawls appears to claim that his opportunity principle requires rough statistical equality in educational achievement among similarly endowed and motivated persons regardless of socioeconomic class (Rawls, 1971, p. 73, 2001, p. 43). Educational opportunities, then, can improve the standard of living of persons who may not take advantage of them due to lack of either effort or ability. To understand the educational component of the living standard of a particular person, it is not sufficient to focus on her achievement, nor on any other individual information about her.

465

Instead, it is essential to investigate patterns of achievement within various social groups within her society.

By incorporating education in principles that are lexically prior to his difference principle, Rawls also appears to hold fairly strong views about the urgency of addressing injustices related to educational deprivation. Because lack of educational achievement may render many members of society unable to effectively participate in labor markets, the political process, and the legal system, Rawls's basic liberties principle would seem to entail that bringing citizens up to a certain threshold of educational achievement is of the utmost urgency. His view also suggests that we may be required to begin reform of social institutions by focusing on enlarging the educational opportunities of younger persons in disadvantaged social groups – since deprivation of such opportunities would appear to be a higher-order injustice than lack of income and wealth.

The Capabilities Approach

Sen has argued that the appropriate specification of the standard of living is not in terms of either utilities (subjective goods) or resources (income, wealth, or rights). Instead, he claims, we should assess social arrangements in terms of their effects on what he calls "*capabilities*." To have a capability is to be capable of achieving a range of what he refers to as "functionings." Functionings refer to things that a person manages to do or be in leading a life (Sen, 1992, pp. 39–41, 1993, p. 31). The capability set of a person is the set of functionings that she can choose or achieve. A person's standard of living consists in her overall ability to achieve states and activities that she has reason to value. Though they are often interrelated, capabilities vary significantly – from basic capabilities such as the abilities to meet nutritional requirements and to avoid preventable morbidity or premature mortality, to more complex freedoms such as enabling opportunities secured through education and the ability to participate in political and associational life. A person's standard of living is diminished if he comes to lack these capabilities, whether or not his preferences can adapt to accept these deprivations.

Sen's approach to specifying the standard of living is significantly less determinate than Rawls's. First, he has resisted prescribing *a list* of *functionings* that should be taken into account in all social assessment. (For a contrasting application of the capabilities approach, see Nussbaum, 2000, pp. 74–80.) Second, Sen has refrained from assigning relative *weights* to different objects of value. Indeed, he has stressed that, in many practical contexts, the question of weighting may not even be necessary in order to have a working index of the standard of living. In addition, he has insisted that questions concerning the precise identification and weighting of value objects should be partly left open for different communities to decide. "Individuals may differ a good deal from each other in the weights they attach to these different functionings – valuable though they may all be – and the assessment of individual and social advantages must be alive to these variations," he writes (Sen 1987, pp. 31ff). How much the capabilities approach and Rawls's resource approach ("resourcism") differ will depend in large part on how capabilities and their weights are specified. If the relevant capabilities are understood as "capabilities to have access to resources," then the approaches will differ in presentation but not content. Sen's criticisms of Rawls suggest that the former understands capabilities (in at least some contexts) as capabilities to *function* or *achieve*. And he charges resourcist theories, and societies governed by resourcist conceptions of justice, with systematically overlooking the fact that some people, due to differential natural endowments and special needs, will require more resources than others to achieve the same levels of functioning.

Like Rawls, Sen asserts an important and complex role for education in determining living standards. There are, for instance, many different ways in which school education may promote a young woman's living standards. Literacy may enhance her decisional power within the family, more generally affect her social standing and economic position and contribute to her capacity to participate in political decision making – all of which are valuable capabilities (Sen, 1999, p. 193–9). Sen often notes the multifaceted way that illiteracy engenders unfreedom: by depriving her of understanding of the outside world and the power to articulate ideas, and through creating barriers to participation in various forms of associational life.

Conceiving and Applying the Standard of Living

The approaches to the standard of living (and the role of education within it) developed by Rawls and Sen have much to recommend them. (For further discussion of the comparative merits of these approaches, see Sen, 1993; Cohen, 1993; Pogge, 1999; Nussbaum, 2000.) The major difference between them lies in how they incorporate concern with special needs due to differential natural endowments. Sen (and others who adopt the capabilities approach) affirm that social institutions, in order to be just, must bring people with different natural endowments up to the same level of capability to function. Rawls denies this. A society governed by a resourcist conception of justice can (and should) compensate for special educational needs due to poverty in order to ensure fair equality of opportunity (Rawls 1971, pp. 73, 301). It can also compensate in other ways as well: to ensure the fair value of the political liberties, for instance, or to ensure fair equality of educational access (Rawls, 1971, pp. 81, 226). But it denies that special needs due to natural inequalities should be compensated or corrected for. If, due to congenital differences alone, x and y convert the same educational resources into significantly different levels of educational achievements, this does not, for Rawls, indicate an *injustice* in the educational system, much as this may be an unfortunate *state of affairs*. By contrast, the capabilities approach suggests resources should be shifted to the congenitally disadvantaged in order to bring them up to some level of educational achievement. The choice between these theories does, then, make a difference to hard choices over the allocation of resources. How significantly they differ will depend on how the capabilities approach understands the education-related functionings that all congenitally disadvantaged persons must be enabled to achieve.

It is interesting to note that, despite their differences, these approaches share features that both contribute to their plausibility as criteria to be used in the ethical evaluation of social rules and institutions and make them rather difficult to use in

467

many practical contexts. Each view is enhanced by its recognition of the complex role of educational achievement and opportunity in promoting living standards, especially their importance for enabling the exercise of many other kinds of freedom. Both recognize the importance of freedom to living well. Yet it is precisely the focus on freedom that makes these views difficult to operationalize in practical contexts. Rawls's emphasis on opportunities imposes significant informational demands, particularly on our ability to measure social mobility (see Roemer, 1996; Birdsall and Graham, 1999; Bowles et al., 1999). How, according to Rawls's view, can we really determine whether life prospects in all sectors of society for those similarly endowed and motivated are equal? And how, indeed, can we determine whether motivation and endowment are not themselves shaped by one's position in a social order? (For discussion see Sennett and Cobb, 1972; Roemer, 1996; Bowles et al., 1999.) Can we really measure the extent to which "chances to acquire cultural knowledge and skills" depend upon one's class position (Rawls 1971, p. 73)? Even if we could confront these problems, is it really plausible that our measures of living standards should assign so much weight to deprivations due to social factors, and so little weight to those caused by natural handicaps? (For further discussion see Pogge, 1989, pp. 160–81.)

Measuring a person's capability requires information not only about the actual achievement, but also about unchosen alternatives that were available to the agent. How reliable are such hypotheticals and how is the information relevant to our claims about them to be ascertained? How are we to evaluate the standard of living of persons who have through their own choices (such as having children or enrolling in doctoral programs) significantly limited future options? (For discussion see Kanbur, 1987; Saith, 2001.) Statistical findings about groups also pose significant challenges to the applicability of the capabilities approach. In India the dropout rate of primary school children for the poorest households is about four times that of the richest ones (World Bank, 2001). And some researchers have argued that in the United States young people from poorer backgrounds tend not to take advantage of many educational opportunities that are formally open to them and where resources are available to them for enrollment. Many argue that the choices of poorer Indian families and poorer American students are constrained by their communities, which either provide no models for them or limit information about the potential benefits of education. Whether and how the capabilities approach embraces and can formalize these constraints on choice will significantly affect its practical assessment of existing institutions (for discussion see Roemer, 1996).

Because of the multiple roles it plays in social assessment, it is likely that there will remain a tension between the plausibility and practicality of different understandings of the concept of the standard of living. And because education is perhaps the most open-ended social good, attempts to characterize its value and capture it in practical assessment will remain an enduring and exciting challenge.

See also 15 THE NATURE AND PURPOSES OF EDUCATION; 33 EDUCATIONAL EQUALITY AND JUSTICE; 39 ETHICS AND THE AIMS OF AMERICAN HIGHER EDUCATION; 43 AFFIRMATIVE ACTION IN HIGHER EDUCATION

References

Anand, S. and Sen, A. K. (1997) Concepts of human development and poverty: a multidimensional perspective. In *Human Development Papers 1997*. New York: UNDP.

Birdsall, N. (1993) Social development in economic development. *World Bank WPS/123*. Washington, DC: World Bank.

Birdsall, N. (2001) Why inequality matters. *Ethics and International Affairs*, 15(2), 3–28.

Birdsall, N. and Graham, C. (1999) *New Markets, New Ideas: Economic and Social Mobility in a Changing World*. Washington, DC: The Brookings Institution and Carnegie Endowment for International Peace.

Birdsall, N. and Londoño, J. (1997) Assets inequality matters: an assessment of the World Bank's approach to poverty reduction. *Applied Economics in Action Papers and Proceedings*, May, 32–7.

Bowles, S., Gintis, H. et al. (eds) (1999) *Recasting Egalitarianism: New Rules for Markets, Communities and States*. London: Verso.

Chenery, H. and Syrquin, M. (1975) *Patterns of Development, 1950–1970*. New York: Oxford University Press.

Cohen, G. A. (1993) Equality of what? On welfare, goods, and capabilities. In M. Nussbaum and A. Sen (eds), *The Quality of Life*. Cambridge: Cambridge University Press, pp. 9–30.

Dasgupta, P. and Weale, M. (1992) On measuring the quality of life. *World Development*, 20(1), 119–31.

Desai, M. (1991) Human development: concepts and measurement. *European Economic Review*, 35, 350–7.

Dreze, J. and Sen, A. K. (1990) *Hunger and Public Action*. Oxford: Oxford University Press.

Gardner, H. (2000) *The Disciplined Mind: Beyond Facts and Standardized Tests, the K-12 Education that Every Child Deserves*. New York: Penguin Putnam.

Hare, R. (1981) *Moral Thinking: Its Levels and Point*. Oxford: Oxford University Press

Hobijn, B and Hans Franses, P. (1999) Convergence of living standards: an international analysis. *Econometric Institute Report 9534*, New York.

Hochschild, J. (1981) *What's Fair? American Beliefs about Distributive Justice*. Cambridge, MA: Harvard University Press

Jolly, R. and Mehrotra, S. (eds) (1998) *Development with a Human Face*. Oxford: Oxford University Press.

Kanbur, R. (1987) The Standard of Living: uncertainty, inequality and opportunity. In G. Hawthorn (ed.), *The Standard of Living*. Cambridge: Cambridge University Press, pp. 59–70.

Kuznets, S. (1955) Economic growth and income inequality. *American Economic Review*, 45(1), 1–28.

Lemann, N. (2000) *The Big Test: The Secret History of the American Meritocracy*. New York: Ferrar, Straus & Giroux.

Mankiw, G., Romer, D., and Weil, D. (1992) A contribution to the empirics of economic growth. *Quarterly Journal of Economics*, 107, 407–37.

Newman, K. S. (1988) *Falling from Grace: The Experience of Downward Mobility in America*. New York: Free Press.

Nussbaum, M. (2000) *Women and Human Development*. New York: Oxford University Press.

Okun, A. M. (1975) *Equality and Efficiency: The Big Tradeoff*. Washington, DC: The Brookings Institution.

Parfit, D. (1983) *Reasons and Persons*. Oxford: Oxford University Press.

Pogge, T. W. (1989) *Realizing Rawls*. Ithaca, NY: Cornell University Press.

Pogge, T. W. (1990) The effects of prevalent moral conceptions. *Social Research*, 57(3), 649–63.

Pogge, T. W. (1999) Human flourishing and universal justice. *Social Philosophy and Policy*, 16(1), 333–61.

Psacharapopoulus, G. (1985) Returns to education: a further international update and implications. *Journal of Human Resources*, 20(4), 583–604.

Rawls, J. (1971) *A Theory of Justice*. Cambridge, MA: Harvard University Press.

Rawls, J. (1982) Social unity and primary goods. In A. Sen and B. Williams (eds), *Utilitarianism and Beyond*. Cambridge: Cambridge University Press, pp. 159–86.

Rawls, J. (1993) *Political Liberalism*. New York: Columbia University Press

Rawls, J. (1999) Justice as fairness: political bot metaphysical. In S. Freeman (ed.), *John Rawls Collected Papers*. Cambridge, MA: Harvard University Press, pp. 388–414.

Rawls, J. (2001) *Justice as Fairness: A Briefer Restatement*. Cambridge, MA: Harvard University Press.

Raworth, K. and Stewart, D. (2000) Review of academic critiques of the HDI. Mimeographed, Human Development Report Office, New York.

Roemer, J. (1996) *Theories of Distributive Justice*. Cambridge, MA: Harvard University Press.

Roemer, J. (1998) *Equality of Opportunity*. Cambridge, MA: Harvard University Press.

Saith, R. (2001) Capabilities: the concept and its operationalisation. *QEH Working Paper QEHWPS66*. Oxford: Queen Elizabeth House.

Seabright, P. (2001) The road upward. *New York Review of Books*, March 29 (available at www.nybooks.com/articles/article-preview?article.id=14128).

Sen, A. K. (1982) *Choice, Welfare and Measurement*. Cambridge, MA: Harvard University Press.

Sen, A. K. (1987) The standard of living. In G. Hawthorn (ed.), *The Standard of Living*. Cambridge: Cambridge University Press, pp. 1–39.

Sen, A. K. (1991) The nature of inequality. In K. Arrow (ed.), *Issues in Contemporary Economics: volume 1, Markets and Welfare*. New York: New York University Press, pp. 3–21.

Sen, A. K. (1992) *Inequality Reexamined*. New York: Russell Sage, Harvard University Press.

Sen, A. K. (1993) Capability and well-being. In M. Nussbaum and A. Sen (eds), *The Quality of Life*. Cambridge: Cambridge University Press, pp. 30–54.

Sen, A. K. (1999) *Development as Freedom*. New York: Knopf.

Sen, A. K. (2000) A decade of human development. *Journal of Human Development*, 1(1), 17–23.

Sen, A. K. (2001) Foreword. In N. Daniels, B. Kennedy and I. Kawachi (eds), *Is Inequality Bad for Our Health?* Boston: Beacon Press.

Sennett, R. and Cobb, J. (1972) *The Hidden Injuries of Class*. New York: W. W. Norton.

Shultz, T. P. (1993) Economics of women's education. In J. K. Conway and S. C. Bourke (eds), *Politics of Women's Education*. Ann Arbor: University of Michigan Press, pp. 237–44.

ul-Haq, M. (1995) *Reflections on Human Development*. Oxford: Oxford University Press.

UNDP (1996) *Human Development and Economic Growth*. Oxford: Oxford University Press.

UNDP (1997) *Human Development Report 1997: Human Development to Eradicate Poverty*. Oxford: Oxford University Press.

UNDP (2000) *Human Development Report 2000: Human Rights and Human Development*. London: Oxford University Press.

UNDP (2001) *Human Development Report 2001: Making New Technologies Work for Human Development*. Oxford: Oxford University Press.

World Bank (1999) World Bank support for education in India. Available at http://wbln1018.worldbank.org

33

Educational Equality and Justice

Harry Brighouse

In common parlance and public policy educational equality is usually discussed as a relationship between predefined groups. We assess whether men and women are educationally equal by looking at the relative resource inputs devoted to, or educational outcomes achieved by, boys and girls. Similarly with equality between racial groups, or ethnic groups, or social classes. But if there is a reason to care about inequalities between these groups it is because they represent inequalities between the individuals who compose the groups. Educational equality, insofar as it is a forceful principle of justice, concerns the position of every individual relative to every other individual.

From the perspective of public policy it makes sense to be concerned with inequalities between groups because group membership often correlates with disadvantage in the real world, so that addressing these group-based inequalities turns out to be an efficient method for tackling inequalities between individuals. So, for example, in the United States, race is a major factor in the production of inequality: African-Americans overall have fewer educational resources devoted to their education (even to their public schooling) than do white Americans overall, and display considerably lower levels of educational achievement. Because of what we know about the role of race in our history and our present, inequalities between racial groups give us reason to suspect injustices between individuals.

This chapter is about educational equality, as a relationship between individuals, and its connection to justice. Justice is, as John Rawls puts it, the primary virtue of social institutions. Because people's life prospects are profoundly affected by the character of the institutions in which they are raised and in which they interact, and because these institutions govern the distribution of the benefits and burdens of social interactions, it is urgent to ensure that the institutions are governed fairly: that is, in accordance with the correct principles of justice.

Education, in its broadest sense, mediates between the overall social order and our individual prospects. How well I will do, even what sort of person I will become, in a given social order, will be significantly shaped by the kind of education I receive. That education will, in its turn, be profoundly affected by the character of the social order. If the government imposes compulsory schooling and taxes the citizenry to pay for it, many people will face different prospects than if it didn't. If it uses schooling to indoctrinate children in a favoured religious view, they will face different prospects,

471

and live different lives, than if it uses schooling to promote personal autonomy, or to promote an ethic of hedonistic enjoyment. So the issues of how to distribute education and what kind of education to distribute are pressing to the theorist of justice. I shall pursue the issue of what kind of education to distribute for most of this chapter, and concentrate on the distributive rule.

Why does justice suggest a principle of educational *equality*, rather than one of educational adequacy, say, or the distribution of education according to the willingness of parents to pay for it? I present an argument for a principle of educational equality, but for the moment it helps to note that education is a key mechanism for distributing opportunities for goods. If equality of opportunity is a central principle of justice, as it is on many theories, then there are likely to be reasons to seek an equal distribution of education, whatever that means.

Educational equality is not the *only* principle of justice regarding education, and acknowledging this helps to answer some otherwise apparently compelling objections, as I show below. But before looking at its relationship to other principles of justice, we should look at its content and the reasons for accepting it.

There is a great deal of public complaint about educational inequality, but much less clarity about what is meant by it. One confusion has already been mentioned: that between groups and individuals. Another concerns whether inequality is constituted by inequality of input or inequality of outcome. In the UK there is an annual debate lamenting the inequality of outcome between boys and girls at age 16 and 18: girls do slightly better overall than boys do in exams at these ages. Yet there is considerable evidence that, at least in terms of attention, boys get more resources than girls do in the process of schooling. The solution to the inequality of outcome problem is usually posed in terms of even greater compensatory inequality of input. But which inequality should we be concerned with? Outcomes or inputs?

More straightforwardly concerned with input is the charge frequently levelled at the US education system that, because of the system of local funding, the government spends vastly more on the education of children in wealthy communities than it does on children in poor communities. But, of course, these inequalities of input can be expected to have consequences for the outcomes, and a further charge is that test scores (outcomes) are unequal between blacks and whites (this very roughly correlates with an inequality of input, because black Americans disproportionately live in poor communities).

There is a third kind of complaint, though, which is usually posed in terms of equity, or inclusion, which concerns children with special educational needs. In most developed countries more money is spent, on average, on children with special needs than on children without them. Those who complain that children with special educational needs are underresourced are complaining neither abut unequal input (because the inputs are already unequally distributed in favor of the children with special needs, and the demand is that they receive even more) nor about unequal outputs, since the plaintiffs do not imagine that any amount of resource reallocation would lead to equal achievements between children with (some) special needs and children without them. Nor do they demand the disabling of the children without special needs that would be required to achieve equality of outcome. The complaint instead is that some level of resource allocation higher than that described, but not as high as would be needed to ensure equal achievement, is essential for the children to be educated equally.

A principle of educational equality need not be constrained by the judgments implied in the above complaints. But they help us to see what the problem is that a theory of educational equality has to address: it has to give an account of why inputs or outputs (whichever it is) are the proper measure of inequality, and give guidance as to the distribution of resources between less and more able children, and between socially advantaged and socially disadvantaged children.

I need to flag two complexities before presenting the argument for educational equality. The first concerns the distinction between education and formal schooling. This is an artificial distinction from the moral point of view. Much education goes on in the home and in other contexts outside the school, and how much and what goes on where depends on the institutional arrangements. If all children spent their entire childhood in school, twenty-four hours a day, then all education would go on in school, and none in the home. The principle of educational equality concerns education, not schooling *per se*. However, the distinction plays an important role in thinking about how to implement the principle, as I show below.

The second complexity concerns the kinds of opportunities education provides. For the purposes of justice there are two importantly different kinds of opportunity. First, education provides access to the world of work, and to the skills required to acquire income and wealth in a competitive economy. But it also provides access to less tangible rewards: the rich enjoyments of reading novels, cooking dishes, playing musical instruments, playing sports, and the like, which are valuable independently of their contribution to our access to income and wealth. I shall call the former the *instrumental* benefits and the latter the *intrinsic* benefits. This distinction is somewhat artificial: some valuable benefits of education fall into both categories, such as improving our ability to make good judgements. But the distinction is essential to seeing what is really at stake in debates about the distribution of education. What I shall call the basic case for educational equality is grounded in concern with the instrumental benefits. But, as we shall see, that case dissolves under conditions in which income and wealth are distributed equally. But still, there may be a case for an egalitarian distribution of education with respect to the intrinsic benefits, which is explored below.

The case for educational equality can be stated simply in what I shall call the *Basic Argument* (this is developed, and much improved, from Brighouse, 2000):

1 Where social institutions license unequal rewards it is a *prima facie* requirement for their fairness that the competition for them is to ensure that the individuals who benefit from the rewards deserve to in some sense.
2 Inequalities of outcome are deserved only to the extent that educational inequalities are not due to (i) family background circumstances or (ii) families' choices.

Conclusion. Educational inequalities due to (i) family background circumstances or (ii) families' choices are *prima facie* unacceptable.

Is there any reason to accept both premises of this argument? Premiss 1 seems unobjectionable: it is part of the idea of fairness that people in some sense deserve their situation. The premiss does, however, depend on the idea that social institutions are constructs of human agency: institutions such as markets, for example, are not unalterable parts of the social order of things, but social constructs which we are able consciously to reform through public policy.

Premiss 2 can be defended by appeal to what I shall call the *Desert Argument*:

(a) Unequal rewards are only deserved to the extent that the candidates can reasonably be held responsible for their level of success in the competition for them.

(b) To the extent that unequal inputs into a child's education are affected by (i) family economic background circumstances or (ii) his or her family's choices, labor market outcomes cannot reasonably be considered his or her responsibility.

Therefore 2.

I take premiss (a) to be relatively uncontroversial. There may be other reasons for thinking that people should get rewards that they don't deserve, and the more weight we give to those reasons the more acceptable we shall find educational inequalities to be. But it is part of the idea of desert that people deserve what they are responsible for and not what they are not responsible for. But premiss (b) needs more support, in the form of the *Responsibility Argument*:

(x) When someone's level of success in the labor market is due to some extent to (i) his or her family background economic circumstances or (ii) his or her family's choices, it is unreasonable to hold the competitor responsible for that level of success to that extent.

(y) Education significantly affects labor market outcomes – i.e. the level of success in competition for higher levels of income – and the quality of educational inputs affects the quality of educational outputs.

Therefore b.

Premiss x seems reasonable. None of us is responsible for having been born to the parents we have, or ending up in the adoptive family we ended up in. If the piece of fortune leads to benefits in the labor market, it is unreasonable to hold us responsible for having gained those benefits. This is not to say that we are not responsible for any of our success in the labor market. On most accounts, the extent to which we exert effort in pursuit of some goal is something for which we can be held responsible, and even accounts which deny that will usually accept that it is right to hold children somewhat accountable for the extent to which they exert effort, because in doing so we are shaping the extent to which they will exert effort. But the extent to which they can be held responsible cannot be isolated from the extent to which they cannot: we have no way of measuring exertion of effort independently of achievement. So if, as desert seems to require, reward should be calibrated to features for which the individual can be held responsible, in practice labor markets will only be fair if the competitors within them have received an equal education.

474

Premiss y, I take it, is a true empirical generalization. But it is worth noting that its truth is contingent on the economy being structured in a particular way. One can imagine an economy in which incomes are relatively flat, and in which, therefore, educational prospects would have little bearing on the pecuniary rewards individuals faced (though the non-pecuniary rewards would, presumably, remain unequal and be affected by education). It is widely assumed that there are powerful reasons for wanting labor market rewards to be unequal: reasons to do with the need to provide incentives for self-interested agents to be productive, and for signalling socially valuable work even to altruistic agents. I make no comment on these reasons, and assume the fact of inequality. Given that fact, it is true that education affects labor market outcomes, at least in capitalist economies.

The Basic Argument, and its supporting arguments, focus entirely on the instrumental benefits of education. But the case would dissolve if the ultimate goods for which education is instrumental were distributed equally. In that case, since income and wealth would be equally distributed, it would make no difference if educational resources were distributed in accordance with, say, the ability of parents to choose schooling well. It couldn't reasonably be said that those who were better educated did not deserve their success in material terms relative to those who were ill-educated.

Now, even egalitarian theories of justice do not usually call for an equal distribution of income and wealth. John Rawls's does not, and nor does Ronald Dworkin's. Dworkin's theory of equality of resources, in fact, requires that income and wealth be unequally distributed to reflect the choices individuals have made against a background of equal opportunity. So on his view, the case for educational equality I have described goes through (Rawls, 1971; Dworkin, 2000).

But imagining the dissolution of the argument forces us to focus more sharply on the so-called "intrinsic goods" of education and on what the rule should be governing their distribution. Suppose the instrumental benefits are not at issue. Still, surely, there would be a case that it would be unjust for the intrinsic benefits to be distributed wildly unequally? Perhaps. But the intrinsic benefits have a different internal structure from the instrumental benefits. To see this, think about the way in which education is a *positional good*, relative to the instrumental benefits it brings. It is true that if no one were educated, everyone would be worse off than if some were educated and others not. But, given that most people are somewhat educated, above some threshold of education the instrumental benefits go primarily to the person receiving it who is then in a better position to compete for income in the labor market. Suppose Julian and Sandy are equally talented and inclined to exert effort, but Julian is twice as well educated as Sandy. When they compete for a single job, Julian will have the same advantage over Sandy regardless of whether Sandy has been educated sparsely or generously. What matters (for getting the job) is that he has been educated better than Sandy, not how well he has been educated.

The intrinsic benefits display a much less noticeably positional character. My ability to enjoy playing soccer depends on there being a range of other people who can play roughly as well as I do, and is even enhanced by there being many around who are better than me but still willing to play against me. Enjoyment of literature and art is enhanced by the presence of many others who are educated in the relevant traditions, and depends on there being some who excel at the execution of, and others who excel at critical reflection on, the arts. Happiness is a non-competitive good. In fact, it is in most reasonably healthy circumstances a positive-sum good: the happier other people are, the easier it is for me to be happy. Our capacity for making and enjoying friendships or intimate lasting relationships depends in an even more obvious way on the similar capacities in others. This is reflected in the sense of parents that in raising a happy, well adjusted child they are not only benefiting *their* child, but are providing a public good. Because such goods are not competitive in the same way as the instrumental benefits of education, it is harder to make a case for the education that produces them being equally distributed.

Certainly for most children, though, any enjoyment of the intrinsic benefits of education depends on having *some* education. One must learn to read to enjoy literature; understanding and enjoyment of music require induction into certain traditions and practices; most sports employ skills which have to be taught, and all follow rules that have to be learned. There are, apparently a handful of mathematical savants, but for most of us the rewards of understanding, let alone deriving, a complex proof are hard won under the guidance of a teacher. A system which educates some, but not others, for the intrinsic benefits shuts some children out from their enjoyment. And education is a scarce resource. Even much of the informal education that goes on in the family demands the time and attention of adults that could be productively used in other ways, and this is certainly not sufficient to provide the level of intrinsic benefit that it is reasonable to expect in a modern wealthy society. So despite the non-positionality of the goods produced, there is an issue of justice attached to their distribution.

For this reason, there may be a *prima facie* case for the intrinsic benefits to be distributed without regard to parental wealth. The wealth of Julian's parents has no bearing on whether Julian's access to the intrinsic benefits of education will contribute to the access of others to those benefits. Of course, in the circumstances I am considering this is not an issue, since I have assumed away inequalities of income and wealth. But I have done so to help make vivid the proper considerations concerning education that yields these benefits, and the distributive rule will have some weight even when there is inequality of income and wealth, so that the rule concerning the instrumental benefits is operative. Consideration of the structure of the intrinsic benefits supports a rule that the unequal distribution of the education yielding them is justified in terms of the tendency of that distribution to promote the widest possible access to those benefits. This, interestingly, may support the policy that those with aptitude for some particular pursuits be given more attention and education regarding them, as long as there are mechanisms in place that make it reasonable to expect that this will enhance the enjoyment of those with less aptitude.

In practice, assuming there are inequalities of income and wealth, it is very hard to disentangle the kind of education needed to produce the instrumental benefits from that needed to produce the intrinsic benefits of education. One cannot teach a child to read only in order to read great literature – the same skills enable her to read a job application and a trade union manual. So policy-makers and practitioners are normally unlikely to be troubled by the potential conflicts between the two principles. But there will sometimes be conflicts, and when there are we need to know which principle should take priority. Here, I have only flagged the issue and the different kinds of consideration at stake.

Two difficulties with the conclusion of the argument for educational equality remain. The first is that it only has *prima facie* force. That is, weighty moral considerations prior to that of educational equality might, in principle, block educational equality. I address this difficulty below when discussing the objections to educational equality. The second is that it seems that a parallel argument could be made for the conclusion that educational prospects should be insensitive to the level of talent of the child, because the level of talent a child possesses is not something she can reasonably be held responsible for, any more than she can be held responsible for the wealth level or choice-making abilities of her parents. This presents profound difficulties for any conception of educational equality, because it is plain that there are, or could be, children with disabilities such that although their disabilities cannot be completely rectified, enormous resources could be devoted to their education before it is saturated: that is, before there is no further educational benefit to extra resources. This raises the possibility of a *bottomless pit problem* for egalitarians analogous to that posed in medical ethics: the possibility that in attempting to do the most we can for the least advantaged, we are forced to devote all our resources to them and none to those who are more advantaged.

Take the second difficulty first. I should start by admitting that what I have to say is tentative and unsatisfactory. Even these tentative comments require a brief detour into the debate among contemporary egalitarians about the moral significance of different inequalities.

Egalitarians typically distinguish three sources of inequality:

- *Individual agency.* Julian and Sandy have the same holdings. Julian risks (and loses) half of his in a lottery with a 1:4 chance of quadrupling his stake. Sandy now has double the holding because he did not enter the lottery.
- *Social agency.* Julian has double the holdings of Sandy, because, although they are equally talented and hard working, they live in a society that prevents people of Sandy's type (for example, known homosexuals, women, blacks) from entering the most highly rewarded labor markets.
- *Brute luck.* Julian is born disabled, Sandy is not; Julian's house is struck by lightning, Sandy's is not; (more controversially) Julian is untalented, but Sandy is talented.

In practice, it is difficult to distinguish these three sources, for three reasons: it is hard to disentangle choice and luck; the effects of brute luck can be affected by both individual and social agency (for example, through the existence of insurance markets and the purchase of insurance); it is hard to say whether society is responsible for a condition which has its source "in nature" but which society has the means to compensate for and chooses not to. But these difficulties aside, there are broadly two camps of egalitarians.

Luck egalitarians claim that any inequalities in people's conditions (well-being resources) must have their sources only in matters over which those people had autonomous choices available to them. The idea is that it is only these inequalities for

477

which we can reasonably be held responsible, and that people should get, roughly, what they deserve (what they can be held responsible for). So brute luck and social agency are treated exactly the same way. Luck egalitarians differ as to what counts as a person's "condition," and also as to what inequalities count as having their sources in personal responsibility, and so disagree among themselves about what should be the metric of equality. But for our purposes this debate among luck egalitarians is secondary (for examples of luck egalitarians see Arneson, 1989; Cohen, 1989; Dworkin, 2000).

Respect egalitarians focus, instead, on inequalities that have their sources in social agency. So rather than looking at what the individual is responsible for, they look at what society is responsible for, and try to correct for that (only for that, or that more urgently). The idea is that there is something specially demeaning about suffering from other people's choices, which is not present when one simply sufferers reverses of fortune. However, because what matters to respect egalitarians is that all individuals have the resources needed to respect themselves and be respected by others, they seek to compensate for misfortune of whatever source to the degree that is required for effective functioning in society (for examples of respect egalitarians see Fleurbaey, 1995; Anderson, 1999; possibly Rawls, 1971).

Respect egalitarians, then, unlike luck egalitarians, do not regard those inequalities that have their sources in brute bad luck as having the same urgency from the moral point of view as those arising from social agency. However, they recognize, as I hinted above, that some brute luck inequalities have a social dimension because society is capable of doing something to correct or compensate for them. Another difference, though, is that while luck egalitarians allow for radical inequalities of condition as long as they are the result of agents' choices against a background of equal opportunity, respect egalitarians reject inequalities when those disadvantaged fall below the level that is needed for them to function as self-respecting citizens in a democratic society.

With this brief summary of the debate in hand, it can be seen fairly easily that luck egalitarians have no ready answer to the bottomless pit problem. They are committed in principle to devoting resources to such children until those children are saturated with resources, before beginning to devote resources to other children. Respect egalitarians have a more straightforward response, but there are difficulties even with this.

Amy Gutmann presents an influential proposal through which she attempts to evade the bottomless pit problem. The following intuitions must be respected by any account of educational equality: it must focus on outcomes, since children cannot ultimately be held responsible for their degree of uptake of educational opportunities; it must demand that more resources be accorded to the disabled than to the ordinarily abled, and it must have something plausible to say about the bottomless pit problem. Gutmann (1987) proposes an interpretation of equal educational opportunity which meets all three of these criteria – she calls it the *democratic threshold principle*. Under the democratic threshold principle,

inequalities in the distribution of educational goods can be justified if, but only if, they do not deprive any child of the ability to participate effectively in the democratic process (which determines, among other things, the priority of education relative to other social goods). (Gutmann, 1987, p. 136)

478

Since the standard proposes a threshold, it is immune to the worst bottomless pit problems. Inequalities of educational achievement above the threshold are entirely acceptable, as long as every child reaches the threshold. Those inequalities might reflect differences of ability (or even, though I think Gutmann would reject this for other reasons, differences in parental wealth), and so as long as more than enough resources are devoted to education to ensure that all reach the threshold, there is no bottomless pit.

Assume for the sake of argument that Gutmann's threshold of "effective" democratic participation is well defined. A lesser bottomless pit problem re-emerges since there may be children who can be brought up to the threshold, but only with the devotion of extensive resources which might be thought to be better spent on others or even on enhancing other more intuitively central aspects of their own welfare. Furthermore, as Randall Curren points out, Gutmann's standard does not identify a fixed baseline: it may be that as the best educated individuals get more education, the least well educated need to get more in order to be able to participate effectively (Curren, 2000). This threatens to generate a further bottomless pit problem.

No satisfactory solution, then, seems to have been found to the bottomless pit problem. This may be because insufficient attention has been devoted to it, especially by luck egalitarians. One move is available to the luck egalitarian which diverts attention away from equality of opportunity, and toward the well-being of the least advantaged. Luck egalitarians commonly say that inequalities are permissible when they are arranged to the advantage of the least advantaged. This provides a possible solution to the bottomless pit problem, although it does so at the cost of eviscerating educational equality. It is plausible to suppose that devoting in principle limitless resources to educating persons with very severe cognitive disabilities could have the result of seriously draining the resources available for both educational and other opportunities. If this were not the case, then the bottomless pit problems would be nothing to worry about. But if it *is* the case, then presumably this redounds to the disbenefit of the least advantaged, which is likely to include the severely cognitively disabled. The luck egalitarian could say that our concern with the advantage of the least advantaged supports not saturating them with educational resources, but ensuring that educational resources are distributed to the overall benefit of the least advantaged – which may involve devoting far more educational resources to the more talented who can stimulate productivity and technical innovation to the overall benefit of the least advantaged.

Objections

I want to look now at a series of objections to the principle of educational equality.

Educational excellence

The first objection is that equality competes with educational excellence, and that where there are trade-offs excellence should be preferred. Proponents of the excellence objection are often not clear what, exactly, constitutes excellence, either individually or within a system (Cooper, 1980; Wilson, 1991). Rather than address the former

479

question, I ask the reader to use whatever they take to be the right standards of excellence. It may be high achievement in a wide range of academic subjects, high achievement in only those subjects that are truly important (mathematics, the arts, poetry, physics, whatever you prefer), the achievement of a range of desirable character traits, or any other standard. The first question to ask is, "What constitutes *systematic* achievement of excellence?" In order to address this question consider the following, highly stylized, table of scenarios, in which individual students' final "achievement" scores represent whatever you think it is important for people to achieve, and in which systems one, two and three are, by hypothesis, the only feasible systems.

	System one	System two	System three	Full Potential
Tony	165	135	90	175
Sid	70	110	90	115
Hattie	90	118	90	120
Total	325	363	270	

Most proponents of the excellence objection would favor system one over the others. But I shall argue here that *that* preference depends on a specific interpretation of educational excellence, which in most circumstances cannot plausibly be assigned so much importance that it would override egalitarian considerations.

Here are three possible interpretations of systematic achievement of excellence:

(i)   The system promotes the highest possible achievement overall.
(ii) The system promotes, as far and as widely as possible, individuals' achievement of their full potential (i.e. it minimizes the gap between potential and achievement for the person for whom the gap is greatest).
(iii) The system promotes the highest possible individual levels of achievement.

On none of these versions of the objection could system three, which has the most equal achievement, be chosen. But if (i) is the correct reading of the excellence objection, the objection prefers (in this scenario) system two to system one. Similarly, if (ii) were the correct reading, system two would be preferred. In system two Tony is 40 away from his full potential, rather than only 10 away in system one, but in system one Sid is 45 away and Hattie 30 away, while in system two they are only 5 and 2 away, respectively. So the largest individual gap is smallest in system two.

What are the reasons for believing (i)? High overall achievement matters because it is likely to have economic benefits, and because it realizes many of the intrinsic goods of education – self-fulfillment, personal enjoyment, public cultural benefits. These both matter a good deal: but they do not matter independently of distributive concerns. Reasons for caring about them are equally reasons for caring that they should be distributed fairly: and fairness is captured by the arguments I have already given.

By contrast, interpreting systematic excellence as minimizing the maximum gap between achievement and potential (ii) has considerable plausibility with respect to the intrinsic benefits of education, though not the instrumental benefits (as I explain below). So if all that were at stake were the intrinsic benefits, (ii) might be the right interpretation.

480

On (iii) system one is, of course, the preferred choice. But why prioritize the highest possible individual levels of achievement, at the expense both of overall achievement and of the ability of individuals to achieve their full potentials?

I can imagine three different reasons. The first is that the most able individuals deserve to have their talents fully developed. This is implausible, because no one is responsible for having their talents and so no one can reasonably be said to deserve anything on the basis of having them. But it is worth noting that someone who seriously advances this objection should be wary of rejecting the practices recommended by the principle of educational equality, given how limited is our ability to identify the highly talented, especially when they come from disadvantaged social backgrounds. Desert claims have great force, and if the highly talented deserve to have their talents developed it is very important that an education system be set up to ensure that no one falls through the cracks. This version of the excellence objection counts very strongly, for example, against the UK practice of allowing wealthy parents to lavish educational resources on their, often not highly talented, children; and against the US policy of high funding for schools in wealthy communities and low funding for schools in disadvantaged communities.

A second reason might be that it is supremely important that human excellences be realized at the highest possible level. Why think this? One reason might be that it is good that these excellences be realized even if no one other than those who realize them benefited from them. This view might appeal to the notion of goods which do not depend for their value on being observed by agents. However plausible this is as a view, it does not justify the state acting to produce such goods. The state has an obligation to guarantee goods for its citizens, and when the production of some free-floating good has opportunity costs for the production of goods for citizens, that decides against state involvement in its production. The purpose of an education system is not to produce excellence for its own sake, but to produce it for the sake of those who can achieve and benefit from it.

A different reason for placing high priority on realizing human excellences at the highest possible level is that human beings, for many generations, can sometimes benefit from these realizations. The achievements of Shakespeare, Mozart, and Einstein have benefited many millions of people, and will benefit billions more as time passes. These benefits are hard to quantify, and cannot be distributed by institutional guarantees such as the tax-benefit system. But they are no less real for that. This consideration might merit some weight. But in the light of the case for educational equality more needs to be said about how much weight to accord it: at best it supports a case for tempering, rather than undermining, educational equality. And, again, proponents of this reason should be wary of rejecting the practices recommended by educational equality: many of those who have realized the excellences in the arts and the sciences were not identified by their educators as highly talented, and would not have benefited from a systematic redistribution of educational resources to those predicted to achieve greatness.

A final, and related, reason, which I shall call the redistributive argument, for believing (iii) invokes the move I posited for the luck egalitarian at the end of the previous section. This is that the greater achievement of Tony can have greater economic benefits for society (in egalitarian terms – the least advantaged in society),

481

so that everyone will be better off if Tony is allowed to achieve at the highest possible level. The truth of this would be consistent with what we know.

But it is also consistent with what we know that the redistributive argument for believing (iii) is false. Whether it is or not is an empirical conjecture. If the redistributive argument were true, and there were clear mechanisms (for example, a highly progressive tax/benefit system) by which the least advantaged would benefit economically from Tony's higher achievement than by the higher overall achievement yielded by system two, that would indeed be a consideration in favor of (iii) and system one. But in practice we would want to see the empirical and strategic case for this made out very convincingly.

Assume that the reasons for preferring system one are not sufficient. System two still seems intuitively preferable to system three. But whether or not this is true depends on the extent to which the instrumental rather than the intrinsic benefits are being produced. Unequal distribution of the intrinsic benefits along the lines of system two does indeed benefit everyone. But if *only* the instrumental benefits were involved, the apparent benefits to Hattie and Sid of the inequality are illusory; because the education is bringing no intrinsic benefit, and is beneficial only for access to income and wealth, its unequal distribution only has the effect of diminishing their opportunities for income and wealth. Of course, in the real world the instrumental and intrinsic benefits cannot be pulled apart, so both sets of consideration apply. But insofar as the instrumental benefits are at issue, the standard redistributive case for inequality has no weight.

State incompetence

A second objection asserts that support for educational equality depends on a misplaced faith in the capacity of states to achieve effective redistribution of resources and opportunities. This objection has been developed against most of the redistributive activities of the state by so-called new right thinkers influenced by the intellectual power of the public choice economic analysis of politics. The public choice movement tends to see politics as an opportunity for rent-seeking activity, and criticizes states that engage in redistributive activities for inefficiency and distorting market processes. James Tooley presses this objection especially powerfully:

> We've noted empirical evidence from around the world which shows rampant inequity in public funding of education. But perhaps . . . with "the right sort" of government intervention it would all be different or . . . in any case, markets in education would be much worse. The problem here is that there is a huge literature which points to the problem of "middle class appropriation of welfare," which suggests that, if education is provided on a universal level, the middle classes will inevitably benefit more than the disadvantaged. (Tooley, 2000, p. 79)

Tooley also points to the evident failure of some states to provide effective and efficient public education universally. His own preferred case is India, where the rise of a market in very low-cost private schools is a response to the spectacular failure of public education, but there are many other examples from developing countries such as South Africa, Brazil, Peru, or Romania (Tooley, 1999).

The first thing to say in response to this objection is that, unlike the excellence objection, it is not an objection to the principle of educational opportunity at all, but an objection to the assumption that much can be done to honor it. The argument for educational equality could be entirely robust, yet it could be the case that not much, or perhaps even nothing, can be done to implement the ideal. So the objection is somewhat orthogonal to our concern here.

But something more can be said. It is absolutely clear that the South African state, for example, knowingly endangers the health, and even lives, of girls it forces to attend school, knowing the extremely high risks of rape they face, and the high incidence of HIV in the school population (Unterhalter, 2001). Educational inequality is not the worst evil involved here, but it is one that can be *somewhat* addressed: for example, by providing better security in schools, or by establishing single-sex schools. Maybe, even, by privatizing schools. The point of the principle of educational equality is that it guides states to do whatever they can to promote educational equality.

A second comment, though, is that the public choice critique of public provision of welfare goods, while it has some power, is highly limited in its applicability. First, because states vary enormously in how egalitarian their policies are in effect, and they vary partly by competence, partly by intent. Compare Sweden and Germany with the USA: the former countries have both achieved greater equality of condition than the USA, and have done so without apparent loss of productivity (Goodin et al., 1999). But the US government has not attempted to achieve equality of condition or anything like it: it has deliberately fostered inegalitarian outcomes, which it (apparently wrongly) sees as the precondition of healthy economic growth. UK governments throughout the post-war period till 1979 did try to foster greater economic equality, and did so less successfully than did the Swedish governments in the same periods. But crucial to Swedish success in achieving equality (and probably to its success in avoiding deleterious effects on economic growth) was that governments largely eschewed means-tested benefits with their concomitant disincentives for individuals to be economically prudent. The second reason why the public choice complaint about "middle-class appropriation of welfare benefits" has limited applicability as an argument against the possibility of achieving greater equality is that there are issues of what counts as the baseline against which "appropriation" is measured. Many systems of welfare provision reliably make middle-class people better off than they would be under equality, but nevertheless achieve greater equality than there would be in the absence of the provision. I think that in advanced industrial economies state funding of education has this effect, but that is not the point here. The point, again, is that whatever action or inaction best promotes educational equality consistently with other more fundamental values should be adopted.

The family and its value

Perhaps the most common objection to educational equality, and equality of opportunity in general, is that its achievement is incompatible with the integrity of the family (Fishkin, 1982). This objection takes several forms. Some argue that parents have a right to spend their money on their children in ways incompatible with achieving educational equality (Fried, 1978); others that they have a right to pursue activities with their children that will have the effect of making them unequally well educated (Lomasky, 1987); still others that attempts to implement educational equality will undermine the incentive of parents to provide benefits for their children, to the detriment of the quality of the parent–child relationship (Tooley, 2000).

A couple of important comments by John Rawls, not about educational equality, but about the principle of fair equality of opportunity, lend credence to these objections:

> the principle of fair opportunity can only be imperfectly carried out, at least as long as the institution of the family exists. The extent to which natural capacities develop and reach fruition is affected by all sorts of social conditions and class attitudes. Even the willingness to make an effort, to try, and so to be deserving in the ordinary sense is itself dependent on happy family and social circumstances. (Rawls, 1971, p. 74)

He goes on to say, much later in the text, "Is the family to be abolished then? Taken by itself, and given a certain primacy, the idea of equal opportunity inclines in this direction" (ibid., p. 511).

Again, the first response to this objection is that, in whatever form it takes, it does not imply rejection of the principle of educational equality. At most it shows that there are two principles: that of the integrity of the family, and that of educational equality, and, with a plausibility that depends on the strength of the argument for the integrity of the family, asserts priority for that principle. If the integrity of the family has complete priority, then this shows that efforts toward educational equality are permissible only insofar as they do not violate (or, to put it more strongly, jeopardize the security of) the integrity of the family. Some indirect measures to promote educational equality seem intuitively unproblematic: for example, egalitarian redistribution of income and wealth, or requiring a minimal level of compulsory schooling for all children. In fact, in most advanced industrial countries, mandatory attendance at school from the ages of five to sixteen, with the option of a state-funded place free at the point of delivery, is virtually uncontroversial, and few of those who argue against these measures do so on the grounds of the integrity of the family.

However, a theory of justice will have to say something about the place of educational equality in justice: it is not enough to say it is a valid principle that sometimes conflicts with other principles, and give no guidance on how to manage the conflict. There are two matters at issue in the conflict between the integrity of the family and educational equality. The first concerns priority: what sort of priority, if any, should the integrity of the family have? But the other concerns the content of the principle of the integrity of the family, because this will have profound implications for the content of conflicts between the principles. It is quite possible for the integrity of the family to have lexical priority – such that whenever there is conflict educational equality must give way – but for it nevertheless to be the case that there is great scope to promote educational equality because the integrity of the family is a relatively undemanding principle.

Space does not allow for a full discussion of these issues here. There is, I believe, a strong case for the priority of the integrity of the family, which provides a range of goods to both parents and children that are fundamental to human flourishing and not available through any other institution. But the content of the ideal of the integrity of the family, while it does imply that many behaviors and activities that we know will transmit advantage unequally may not be discouraged or prohibited, allows for a great deal to be done to promote educational equality. So, for example, mandatory government funded schooling, high taxes on elitist private schooling, additional funding of schools attended by low-income children, and government-subsidized health and dental care for children all seem to be entirely consistent with maintaining the integrity of the family on the best available understanding of the content of that principle. My point here is not to prove this (which would take a great deal of argument concerning the normative content of the integrity of the family and empirical analysis of the putative conflicts between the principles), but by asserting it to illustrate the right way to think about the conflict.

But I shall finish by highlighting the most striking way of resolving educational equality and the integrity of the family in practice, because it tells us something about the relationship between equality of outcome, equality of opportunity, and the family. From what we know about the effects of inequality on the educational (and hence lifetime expected income) prospects of children, it is hard to imagine what mechanisms could achieve educational equality against the background of substantial inequalities of household income and wealth. Measures designed substantially to reduce inequalities of income and wealth do nothing to undermine the integrity of the family: wealthy parents have less money to spend on their children, but they have no less of themselves to share with their children. In fact, since poverty is a major factor in disrupting the smooth operation of the family, reducing inequalities should benefit the institution.

See also 28 THE AUTHORITY AND RESPONSIBILITY TO EDUCATE; 31 CHILDREN'S RIGHTS; 32 EDUCATION AND STANDARDS OF LIVING; 34 MULTICULTURAL EDUCATION; 35 EDUCATION AND THE POLITICS OF IDENTITY; 43 AFFIRMATIVE ACTION IN HIGHER EDUCATION

References

Anderson, E. (1999) What is the point of equality? *Ethics*, 109, 287–337.

Arneson, R. (1989) Equality and equal opportunity for welfare. *Philosophical Studies*, 56, 77–93.

Brighouse, H. (2000) *School Choice and Social Justice*. Oxford: Oxford University Press.

Cohen G. A. (1989) The currency of egalitarian justice. *Ethics*, 99, 906–44.

Cooper, D. E. (1980) *Illusions of Equality*. London: Routledge & Kegan Paul.

Curren, R. (2000) *Aristotle on the Necessity of Public Education*. Lanham, MD: Rowman and Littlefield.

Dworkin, R. (2000) *Sovereign Virtue*. Cambridge, MA: Harvard University Press.

Fishkin, J. (1982) *Justice, Equal Opportunity and the Family*. New Haven, CT: Yale University Press.

Fleurbaey, M. (1995) Equal opportunity or equal social outcome? *Economics and Philosophy*, 11, 25–55.

Fried, C. (1978) *Right and Wrong*. Cambridge, MA Harvard University Press.

Goodin, R. E., Headey, B., Muffels, R. and Dirven, H.-J. (1999) *The Real Worlds of Welfare Capitalism*. Cambridge and New York: Cambridge University Press.

Gutmann, A. (1987) *Democratic Education*. Princeton, NJ: Princeton University Press.

Lomasky, L. (1987) *Persons, Rights, and the Moral Community*. Oxford: Oxford University Press.

Tooley, J. (1999) *The Global Education Industry*. London: Institute for Economic Affairs.

Tooley, J. (2000) *Reclaiming Education*. London: Cassell.

Rawls, J. (1971) *A Theory of Justice*. Cambridge, MA: Harvard University Press.

Unterhalter, E. (2001) The capabilities approach and gendered education: an examination of South African complexities. Paper delivered at the conference "Justice and Poverty: Examining Sen's Capabilities Approach," St Edmunds College, Cambridge.

Wilson, J. (1991) Does equality (of opportunity) make sense in education? *Journal of Philosophy of Education*, 25, 27–31.

Further reading

Barry, B. (1988) Equal opportunity and moral arbitrariness. In N. Bowie (ed.), *Equal Opportunity*. Boulder, CO: Westview Press, pp. 23–44.

Barry, B. (2001) *Culture and Equality*. Cambridge: Polity Press.

Brighouse, H. (2001) *Egalitarian Liberalism and Justice in Education*. London: Institute of Education.

Hollis, M. (1982) Education as a positional good. *Journal of Philosophy of Education*, 16, 235–44.

Jencks, C. (1988) Whom must we treat equally for educational opportunity to be equal? *Ethics*, 98, 518–33.

Marshall, G., Swift, A., and Roberts, S. (1997) *Against the Odds? Social Class and Social Justice in Industrial Societies*. Oxford: Oxford University Press.

Roemer, J. (1998) *Equality of Opportunity*. Cambridge, MA: Harvard University Press.

34

Multicultural Education

Robert K. Fullinwider

The doctrinal stream making up the multicultural education movement in the USA represents the confluence of three tributaries. The first emerged as a by-product of the racial integration schools underwent in the 1960s and 1970s. Relative to their white classmates, black students performed poorly. Many social scientists adopted a "cultural deprivation" theory to account for the academic weakness of black students, pointing to the "disadvantaged" and "underprivileged" circumstances of the households in which they were raised. Government initiatives such as Head Start were designed to compensate for initial cognitive shortcomings in children raised in lower-class, i.e. "deprived," settings.

Against this standard approach to black underachievement, a counter-literature emerged, generated mostly by African-American scholars and educators who saw in talk of disadvantage and deprivation a not-so-subtle depreciation of black children and their families. This counter-literature adopted the slogan "difference, not deficit," insisting that the problem of black underachievement lay with the schools, not the children. Schools were unprepared to teach children who brought *different* norms, customs, and behavior to the classroom. Teachers and administrators were projecting their own failings onto minority children by labeling them as "deficient" and in need of remediation. Instead of "tracking" these pupils into classes for slow learners, educators needed to learn how to teach them effectively. Every child could learn. It was the educator's job to make sure every one did (see Gollnick and Chinn, 1986, p. 28; Bennett, 1990, p. 203; Sleeter, 1992, pp. 57–9; Banks, 1994, pp. 48ff; Nieto, 2000, pp. 231–5).

During these same decades, a second tributary sprang from the "new ethnicity" movement, which saw ethnic groups across the land assert a renewed pride in their distinctive customs, traditions, and languages, a renewed pride given official imprimatur (and federal funds) by the Ethnic Heritages Studies Act of 1972. The "new ethnics" challenged what appeared to be an oppressive social norm, namely that they shed their differences to become homogenized Americans. "Cultural pluralism" was the watchword of this movement, "assimilation" the foe.

A third tributary added force to the developing stream. In many parts of the country, the academic underachievement associated with ethnic and racial differences had a linguistic as well as a class component. Children – largely Hispanic – came to school speaking a language other than English. Pushed by advocacy groups, bilingualism emerged as the platform for propelling non-English speaking children to academic success.

The broad social terrain in post-1950s America was favorable to the flow of these tributaries into one large stream, as different "liberation" movements – forming around the categories of race, gender, youth, and sexual orientation – challenged various forms of authority and weakened the legitimacy of authoritative institutions. The multicultural education movement picked up definition and momentum in the 1970s and in the 1980s became institutionalized in the course work of teachers' colleges and the curriculum frameworks of state education departments (Gollnick, 1992, p. 247). The state of Maryland is an exemplar. Its current state-wide regulations require all school districts to carry out multicultural reforms in "curriculum, instruction, and staff development." These reforms must have as one of their goals student "understanding and appreciation for cultural groups in the United States." This goal is to be furthered by "correcting ... omissions and misrepresentations" in the curriculum of "African Americans, Asian Americans, Latinos, Native Americans, women, and individuals with disabilities"; by teaching the "history of cultural groups and their contributions" to community, nation, and world; by examining historical events and conflicts "from diverse perspectives"; by focusing on the "[p]olitical, social, and economic conditions which cultural groups have experienced and continue to experience"; and by taking up "issues of racism, sexism, bias, and prejudice."

A second goal of the reforms is "the valuing of cultural groups" by students and staff. Students should, through their school experience, come to value three things – their own heritage, "the uniqueness of cultures" other than their own, and the "richness of cultural diversity and commonality" generally. They should learn to respect "diverse cultural groups throughout the world," become sensitive to "individual differences within various cultural groups," and eschew "stereotypes related to race, ethnicity, region, religion, gender, socioeconomic status, age, and individuals with disabilities" (Maryland Code, 13A.04.05.04). Within these disparate aims and means one finds the main themes prominent in most multicultural literature:

- the celebration of diversity (appreciating and valuing cultural differences);
- the contributions of different groups (all cultural groups have contributed to contemporary society and made noteworthy achievements in the past);
- the importance of seeing events and conflicts from multiple perspectives;
- the importance of structuring classroom instruction around explicit discussion of how individuals are shaped by culture and around group experiences of discrimination and oppression.

Narrowing the Scope

The early formulators of multicultural orthodoxy were situated in colleges of education and education associations and drew much of their inspiration from the civil rights struggles and the new ethnicity movement. Indeed, at first, the shape of multicultural education was as inclusive as the idea of cultural pluralism itself. In the 1979 collection *No One Model American*, intended to give flesh to the official statement on multicultural education adopted by the American Association of

Colleges of Teacher Education in 1972, essays about African-Americans, Hispanics, and women nestled cozily next to ones about Appalachian folk, evangelists, Jews and Irish, Chinese and Gypsies (Lopez and Vogel, 1979). However, multicultural education soon took a form more narrowly bounded. In 1976, the National Council for the Social Studies – the leading American professional organization for social studies teachers – published its "Guidelines on Multiethnic Education," one of whose principal authors was James Banks, a writer whose influence on the development of multicultural education has been enormous. Banks tried to nip in the bud the newly emerging *multicultural* education movement, insisting that

The [NCSS] Guidelines should focus on *ethnic* pluralism and not on *cultural* pluralism. Cultural pluralism suggests a type of education which deals with the cultural contributions of all groups within society. Consequently, that concept is too broad and inclusive to set forth effectively the boundaries of an area encompassing both the contributions of ethnic groups and the problems resulting from ethnic discrimination in American society. (NCSS, 1976, p. 6)

For it was this last – the focus on ethnic discrimination, and more particularly on racial discrimination – that Banks wanted at the center of any new educational movement. A year later, giving up hope of stopping the new movement in its tracks, Banks sought to co-opt it for his original vision. "Anthropologically," he noted, "multicultural education suggests a type of education which is . . . concerned with all cultural groups in a society." However, such education sweeps too broadly, Banks warned. A properly tempered multicultural education "would focus on groups which experience discrimination in American society." It would dwell on concepts of discrimination, prejudice, and alienation and aim to reform "the total educational environment" so that schooling "would promote respect" for these victim-groups (Banks, 1977, p. 3).

As the Maryland regulations give evidence, Banks's gambit succeeded. The Maryland conception of multicultural education seeks to "correct" curriculum with respect to "African Americans, Asian Americans, Latinos, Native Americans, women, and individuals with disabilities," not Jews, Irish, mountain folk, and religious evangelicals. What holds the Maryland list together is not an idea of culture but a putative common history of past and/or present exclusion from, or marginalization within, major cultural, economic, and political institutions. A similar list adorns all standard multicultural education texts and the formal guidelines promulgated by private and public associations (see Bennett, 1990, p. 13; New York Report, 1991, p. 7). The conceptual center of gravity of orthodox multicultural education is "discrimination": its experience by certain groups; the conditions that caused it, and cause it still, to operate; and the compensatory strategies needed to combat it and its legacies (Bennett, 1990, p. 17; Davidman and Davidman, 1997, pp. 8, 53; Nieto, 2000, p. 4).

Culture

In one sense, then, the "culture" in multicultural education was not a concept well suited to the movement's objectives. In the UK, writers operating under conditions similar to those that spawned multicultural education in the US – that is, the growth of new populations of school children, largely of Caribbean or Pakistani background, who were underperforming in school – early on drew a distinction between multicultural and antiracist education (Sarup, 1986; Lynch, 1987; Klein, 1993). Education specifically targeted at reducing racial prejudice in the school, or at promoting antiracism more generally, had about it a transparent directness, undiluted by vague ideas of cultural diversity.

In another way, however, "culture" has served multicultural education well by encouraging easy equivocations that make its basic tenets seem deliverances of common sense. "Celebrate cultural diversity," "respect those who are culturally different," "learn to be bi-cultural" – these and similar injunctions require very little labor to buttress them, given the effortlessness by which one can move from an evaluatively neutral to an evaluatively honorific use of "culture." Every multicultural text begins by offering a descriptive, normatively empty definition of culture and then moves straightaway to presumed normative implications. Thus, culture is said to be "a way of perceiving, believing, and acting" (Gollnick and Chinn, 1986, p. 5) or "a system of shared knowledge that shapes human perception and generates social behavior" (Bennett, 1990, p. 47). These descriptions, which apply equally to Mafia "families," Mexican-American households, dangerous militias of xenophobic fanatics, and productive waves of earnest immigrants, offer no logical basis for the credal centerpiece of multicultural education, namely "acceptance and appreciation of cultural diversity" (Bennett, 1990, p. 30).

The credal conclusion is a non-sequitur, but useful. It plays upon an honorific sense of "culture" – a sense derived from using the term to refer to a people's "high culture" or its "civilization" – so that by describing a thought or action as "cultural," one dignifies it. As a consequence of such descriptions, the license of white teachers and administrators to criticize and penalize the behavior, attitudes, and performance of minority students gets estopped (rhetorically, at least). Such children don't fail by some reasonable, objective standard, they simply exhibit culturally distinctive learning styles. They don't lack discipline and self-control, they just have different ways of behaving (Bennett, 1990, p. 69; Ladson-Billings, 1992, p. 113). Refusing to accept and appreciate such difference marks one as an ethnocentric teacher, or worse. Such are the implications packed into the honorific use of "culture."

The conflation of the two uses of "culture" arises in part from collapsing together two further matters, respect for a person and respect for the person's culture. Multiculturalists are inclined to equate the two: "love me, love my culture." Consequently, their child-centered inclinations ("view what the child brings from home as a strength, not a weakness") push multicultural educators toward the insistence that all "cultures" must be respected and valued (Campbell et al., 2000, p. 39).

The failure of multiculturalists to keep in view the distinction between "high culture" and home culture leads to further difficulties beyond the general conflation just noted. James Banks, for example, has been insistent that multicultural pedagogy should focus on the "ideas and interpretations" of a culture rather than its "tangible" elements – dress, food, games, tools, and the like (Banks, 1992, p. 7, 1994, p. 39). When teachers concentrate on such shallow classroom activities as celebrating different national holidays, sampling food from different ethnic groups, and playing games from all parts of the world, they trivialize the idea of culture.

However, emphasizing the "non-trivial" – the deeper values and ideas animating different customs and ways of life – may take the multicultural classroom in unexpected directions. For example, if one wants to understand the family values of students whose parents were raised in Mexico, El Salvador, or Puerto Rico, one needs to know something about Roman Catholicism. This means setting forth on inquiries that can lead back to Plato and Aristotle, and to the Stoics, Epicureans, and Skeptics, whose moral and metaphysical views provided the framework – along with Scripture – in which theological views were forged in the early Christian Church. Quite obviously, a K-12 curriculum will not set students to reading Plato, Aristotle, Augustine, and Aquinas, but the general point remains: putting an emphasis on the ideational dimension of culture, *where culture is taken in the sense of "high culture,"* pushes curriculum toward the classical and modern roots of the different strands of our civilization – whether those strands derive from Iberia, the British Isles, Gaul, the Middle East, or Mediterranean Africa. Further, it highlights an important ambiguity in speaking of the "culture a student brings from home." Do we mean the elaborated and canonical versions of the Hispanic student's "home culture," say, or the particular, quite possibly corrupted and vulgarized, version actually possessed by the student and his family? If part of multicultural education involves helping students appreciate their *own* "cultures," what does this imply?

Learning Styles

Closely connected to the idea of "cultural difference" and the repudiation of the "deficit" model is the idea of "learning styles." The problem minority students face in schools reduces to a matter of cultural imperialism: schools are arranged, and classrooms conducted, in ways congruent with the cognitive styles of European Americans, styles at odds with those of the "people of color" among the student body. For example, "African American students," it is said, "tend to prefer oral communication and kinesthetic activities for taking in new information...[while] Native-Americans tend to have excellent visual skills" (Sleeter and Grant, 1994, p. 54). Yet the typical classroom "emphasizes verbal learning and written demonstrations of achievement," the style European-Americans favor (Gay, 1992, p. 179). In a successful multicultural classroom, the teacher will use many instructional styles, not favoring the dominant style over others.

Are there "culturally distinct" learning styles? Some multiculturalists explicitly warn educators away from this path. The research is too flimsy, they say (Ladsen-Billings, 1992, p. 108; Irvine and York, 1995, p. 485); the idea is too easily misused (Gordon, 1992, pp. 21–2; Nieto, 2000, p. 143); and talk of distinct learning styles can actually "hinder rather than facilitate communication" (Ford, 1999, p. 8).

Even so, the notion is widely embraced in the multicultural education literature. Most typically, it comes wrapped in the nomenclature of "field-dependent" versus "field-independent" styles of learning. Initially, these two concepts had to do with certain perceptual skills exhibited by children. Some, asked to pick out a specific geometrical shape from a more complex background pattern, were more easily able to do so than others. The successful children were termed "field-independent." The surrounding pattern didn't hinder their picking out the embedded shape. By contrast, for "field-dependent" viewers, the shape became lost in the pattern (Bennett, 1990, pp. 142–3). Soon enough, however, education theorists unmoored these notions from the narrowly perceptual context in which they arose, and began to attribute a range of personal attitudes, preferences, and capabilities to an underlying tendency to be field-independent or field-sensitive. As in astrological tables, whole clusters of capabilities and characteristics form under one's "sign." If you are a "field-independent learner," you are a self-motivated and independent student good at abstract thought and analysis of wholes into their parts; but you are also individualistic and insensitive to the emotions of others, possessing poorly developed social skills. By contrast, if you are a "field-dependent learner," you are responsive to social reinforcement and well attuned to the social environment, possessing highly developed social skills; but you are liable to take information as it comes pre-packaged and to be weak at analyzing it into its constituent parts (Bennett, 1990, p. 144).

It was inevitable that this promiscuous employment of field-dependence/independence would hook up with the growing idea that different ethnic groups had different ethno-cultural traits, and by the 1970s the deed was done (Bennett, 1990, pp. 144–7). Not surprisingly, African-American and Mexican-American students turned out to be field-dependent, white Anglo students field-independent (Ramírez and Castañeda, 1974, pp. 64–5). These divisions are, of course, related to putative deeper cultural cleavages. For example, one multiculturalist provides this instructive list of cultural attributes: African cultures tend toward spiritualism, harmony with nature, expressive movement, organic metaphors, interconnectedness, emotion, event-orientation, expressive individualism, talk-based communication, and an appreciation of uniqueness; while European cultures tend toward materialism, mastery over nature, impulse control, mechanistic metaphors, separateness, reason, clock-orientation, possessive individualism, print-based communication, and a preference for uniformity (Sleeter, 1992, p. 220). Another multiculturalist offers a similar account of African-American "cultural style." While African-Americans "respond to things in terms of the whole picture," Euro-Americans are preoccupied with parts and divisibility (indeed, they can't even learn to dance well since they insist on counting time with the music instead of letting themselves move spontaneously). Moreover, African-Americans "tend to prefer inferential reasoning to deductive or inductive reasoning." They "approximate space, numbers and time rather than stick to accuracy." They "prefer to focus on people . . . rather than things" (a preference illustrated by the tendency of African-Americans to work in the helping professions). They have a keen "sense of justice" and "lean toward altruism." They "prefer novelty, freedom, and personal distinctiveness." Finally, they are not "word" dependent, tending "to be very proficient in nonverbal communication" (Bennett, 1990, pp. 158–9).

Confronting Racism

The leading multiculturalists agree that racism (along with other "isms") must be confronted and discussed in the classroom (recall the Maryland regulations; see also Davidman and Davidman, 1997, p. 60). Indeed, insists one writer, "Antiracism

... [and] antidiscrimination in general, is at the very core of a multicultural perspective." And "To be antiracist ... means making antiracism and antidiscrimination explicit parts of the curriculum and teaching young people skills in confronting racism" (Nieto, 2000, pp. 305, 307). Two other multiculturalists maintain that the "entire school experience should be reoriented to address ... issues. .. [of] social inequality based on race, social class, disability, and gender" (Grant and Sleeter, 1989, p. 212). These admonitions stand in accord with the 1991 "Curriculum Guidelines for Multicultural Education" promulgated by the National Council for the Social Studies (and authored by James Banks), which declared that educators "have a professional responsibility to help students learn the basic facts and generalizations about the nature of race and ethnicity in the United States" (NCSS, 1992, p. 283).

But what are those basic facts and generalizations? It isn't as though they are straightforward and uncontentious. And how will their presentation in the classroom yield positive educational benefits?

James Banks thinks it vital that students "view American ... experience from the perspectives of different racial, ethnic, cultural, and gender groups" (Banks, 1994, p. 15). Now, letting different perspectives be voiced and discussed in the classroom, without forcing discussion to a definitive closure, avoids the problem of deciding whose version of the "basic facts and generalizations" about race and ethnicity gets the stamp of approval. Providing ample room in discussions and textbooks for "multiple perspectives" to be heard is a pedagogy endorsed even by those who count themselves as opponents of multiculturalism (Schlesinger, 1992, p. 15). The resulting educative experience might be positive: although students may disagree profoundly on the meaning of discrimination and its extent, causes, effects, and remedies, airing these disagreements could result in heightened awareness by all students of different ways of seeing society, and of the complexity of discrimination both as an idea and as a social fact. But it could also produce the opposite result, with students angrily withdrawing into their inital points of view, confirmed in their suspicion that their opponents are ill-informed and badly motivated.

Indeed, multiculturalists note that teachers are very reluctant to bring issues of racism and sexism into their classrooms for fear the issues are "too dangerous" to deal with fruitfully, and may divide the classroom into victims and victimizers. Indeed, by some accounts multicultural literacy *means* that one group in the classroom (white teachers and students) must work through a process others don't – acknowledging their status as "victimizers" and passing through the consequent emotional stages. White students must recognize their "personal participation in an unjust system" and confess their "white privilege" (Sleeter, 1992, p. 40; Howard, 1996, p. 229; Campbell et al., 2000, p. 66). For two influential multiculturalists, Carl Grant and Christine Sleeter, white students must take a back seat as multiculturalist teachers build coalitions inside and outside the classroom "among various oppressed groups" (Sleeter, 1991, p. 12; Sleeter and Grant, 1994, pp. 229–30). White students may support such "coalitions" as allies as long as they are willing to "take direction" from the "oppressed groups" and contribute their opinions "only when ... [they are] asked for" (Sleeter, 1991, p. 19).

James Banks evinces a "faith" that a course of instruction prompting white students to recognize "their own participation in a system of institutionalized racism"

493

will lead them to respect "marginalized ethnic groups." But unlike other multiculturalists, he also concedes that educators "have little evidence" to support the assumptions upon which this faith rests (Banks, 1988, pp. 189, 185).

The NCSS Guidelines authored by Banks gesture toward an approach which need not lead to students dividing themselves into "victimizers" and "victimized." "Both racism and sexism must be seriously examined in any sound multicultural curriculum," the Guidelines announce, but these topics need not be treated in a way that forecloses differences of opinion.

In a sound multicultural curriculum, emphasis should be neither on the ways in which the United States has "fulfilled its noble ideals" nor on the "sins committed by the Anglo-Americans" (or any other group of Americans). Rather, students should be encouraged to examine the democratic values that emerged in the United States, why they emerged, how they were defined in various periods, and to whom they referred in various eras. Students should also examine the extent to which these values have or have not been fulfilled, and the continuing conflict between values such as freedom and equality. (NCSS, 1992, pp. 275, 282)

Indeed, for all their emphasis on the importance of – and the importance of study about – ethnic and racial identification, the Guidelines also adopt as a sub-theme an important counterweight: while multicultural education should enable students to understand and appreciate their own ethnic identities, it should also enable them to *break free* from these identities, should they so choose (NCSS, 1992, p. 278). Taken at face value, this sub-theme pictures multicultural education fundamentally as an education in freedom (see Gollnick and Chin, 1986, p. 90; Banks, 1994, p. 1). Multicultural education provides students the intellectual tools to rethink or revise their identitites. It supports them in constructing their own individuality.

Multiculturalists also seem on firmer ground in recommending cooperative learning as a device for stimulating respect across races. In cooperative learning, a team of students works on a common project in which the contribution of each is integral to the outcome. When the team is racially mixed, it affords opportunities for mutual respect and cross-racial solidarity (see Schofield, 1995; Slavin, 1995).

Philosophical and Conceptual Issues

Philosophically, the main body of work undergirding the multicultural education movement in the United States has relied almost entirely on some of the trappings and language of critical theory and, more recently, postmodernism.

For example, Carl Grant and Judyth Sachs write that "postmodern theory can contribute" to multicultural education by supplying an "oppositional language" of "discourse" and "power" to show students "how discourses emerge to suit the interests of particular groups and deny other groups." Discourses "become the sites for struggle between dominant and subordinate groups." There is no "neutrality" in this struggle, "merely perspectives." Yet Grant and Sachs, while dabbling in this fashionably radical language, have no sense of its potentially corrosive sweep and retain their faith in quite old-fashioned goals framed in quite old-fashioned terms.

494

They want multicultural education to promote "equity and social justice," ideas they are not prepared to see dismissed as *mere* perspectives, *mere* effects of power, or *mere* interests of particular groups (Grant and Sachs, 1995, pp. 89, 94, 95, 97, 96, 101).

Likewise, James Banks argues for the thesis that "knowledge is constructed" and a matter of "positionality"; that is to say, a matter of one's social or ethnic "location" (Banks, 1995, p. 12, 1996, p. 6). Different locations produce different knowledge, even different reality (Ovando and Gourd, 1996, p. 298). This might seem on its face a radical challenge to our ordinary understanding of knowledge, but it isn't. The lesson conveyed in this language is a commonplace one about the formation of *beliefs* (Banks, 1996, p. 5). People acquire new beliefs based on what they already believe (Ovando and Gourd, 1996, p. 298). If their experiences and perspectives are limited, if their prior beliefs are not well founded, and if they are disinclined to be self-reflective, their new beliefs can be distorted by bias, unexamined interests, and incomplete information (Banks, 1994, p. 65). There are well known correctives to these pitfalls: if people make articulate the unexamined assumptions behind their views, if they consider interpretations from other people's perspectives, and if they broaden their information base, their beliefs are more likely to be true, accurate, and objective – more likely to *approximate what is actually the case* (Banks, 1996, p. 8). These goals to which Banks is explicitly committed – truth, accuracy, objectivity, actuality – are not the bread-and-butter of contemporary postmodernism. Thus, the mainline multicultural literature, though it appropriates some of the language of postmodernism, remains wedded to orthodox concepts of value (human dignity, respect for others) and truth (completeness, accuracy, objectivity).

This literature also frequently allies itself with a central tenet of critical theory. "Critical multiculturalists" focus on "culture" in a sense not rehearsed above, a sense having to do with the fine-grained disciplinary web of daily practices. These multiculturalists seek to uncover "how human relations are shaped in the workplace, the schools, and everyday life" by common routines of action, deference, and thought. They undertake this project for a reason.

Critical theorists want to promote an individual's consciousness of himself or herself as a social being. An individual who has gained such a consciousness understands how and why his or her political opinions, socio-economic class, role, religious beliefs, and racial self-image are shaped by dominant perspectives. (Kincheloe and Steinberg, 1997, p. 23)

When students understand the causes of their beliefs, and whose interests they serve, this is supposed to be liberating. How so? Because students are expected to make this inference: "seeing now that my beliefs were caused by and serve someone else's interest, I am free to abandon them for others."

However, like the inferences multiculturalists typically derive from normatively empty definitions of "culture," this one too is a non-sequitur. Suppose it is in the interest of the dominant class to get me to believe I live in a classless society (so I will not see myself as lower class and resist dominant arrangements) and to believe that 9:00 a.m. comes after 8:00 a.m. (so I will show up on time at my low-paid, dead-end job from which the dominant class reaps its profits). What follows? If the first belief is false, its falsity lies not in its causes; and regardless of its causes, the second belief is true and I am not free to abandon it at will. Whether there are sound *reasons* for accepting a proposition as *true* or rejecting it as *false* are matters independent of causes and interests. *Indeed, the illumination that comes from the causal stories about power and interests presupposes that I have already rejected the truth of a proposition: what I want to know is why I (or others) came to hold such a false belief.*

An unrelenting curriculum of "critical" stories about power and domination may provide a student with a platform for effectively acting on certain beliefs, but it provides her with no platform for assessing the soundness or accuracy of beliefs in the first place, a platform that education ought to provide. The deep infatuation of multicultural education with "critical theory" leaves out a vital dimension of education, a dimension which could be more productively developed were the literature of multicultural education more conversant with the recent traditions of political theory and philosophical reflection. This would include, most obviously, work on justice, multicultural citizenship, and civic education by John Rawls, Isaiah Berlin, Charles Taylor, Will Kymlicka, Amy Gutmann, Iris Marion Young, Nancy Fraser, William Galston, Stephen Macedo, Jeff Spinner-Halev, Eamonn Callan, Jeremy Waldron, Kenneth Strike, and others.

Recourse to this large and growing body of philosophical work would also enable multiculturalism to offer more sophisticated accounts of culture, race, and critical citizenship. For example, it might abandon the equation "respect me, respect my culture" if it had at hand an analysis of recognition and respect like that offered by Larry Blum, in which "recognizing" a group need not involve making evaluative judgments about its "culture" (Blum, 1998, p. 56). It might offer a more nuanced picture of the intellectual virtues that make up a generous and open mind and that underwrite effective democratic deliberation if it engaged the ideas in Gutmann and Thompson's *Democracy and Disagreement* (Gutmann and Thompson, 1996). It might enrich its theorizing about movements for social justice, and how they look through the prism of critical theory and postmodernism, by following the lead of Nancy Fraser's (1989) *Unruly Practices*. It might present more subtle treatments of race and racism were it to take notice of Anthony Appiah's (1992) *In My Father's House*, and of multicultural citizenship and education were it to consult Will Kymlicka's (1995) *Multicultural Citizenship* or Stephen Macedo's (2000) *Diversity and Distrust: Civic Education in a Multicultural Democracy*. (The literature in England has been less parochial, where the political theorist Bikhu Parekh (1986) has been a contributor for many years.)

Kymlicka, for instance, argued in *Liberalism, Community, and Culture* (1989) that people have a right to what he called a secure (if evolving) cultural structure, which he believed essential to self-respect and worthwhile choice. In response to the objection that this view protected too many unattractive cultures, he later in *Multicultural Citizenship* restricted this argument to what he called "societal cultures," or national minorities, having social, political, and economic structures, geographical concentration, and often distinct languages. Iris Marion Young developed an alternative view in *Justice and the Politics of Difference* (1990), according to which group rights must be understood through the concept of oppression. She holds that oppressed groups should be accorded a variety of rights, including special consideration in educational settings, but has been criticized for underplaying the importance of the common good and having too expansive a view of oppression. Two other important lines of argument have been developed by Joseph Carens (2000), who warns against general theories of cultural rights in favor of a more particularistic approach to group rights, and Jeff Spinner-Halev (2000), who argues that most theories of multicultural-ism ignore the interests of religious people, and endorse excessive interference in their exercise of religion, including in educational matters.

The failure of multicultural educators to make contact with other intellectual traditions is not limited to philosophy, however. It is acutely reflected in their treatment of "discrimination," where this pivotal concept – picking out both the content and context of multicultural education – is treated without any attention to salient legal developments.

A central target of multicultural educators is "institutional discrimination" (or "institutional racism"). Institutions exclude people not only through the deliberate and hostile designs of institutional actors but primarily through the "normal oper-ations" of the institutions themselves (Nieto, 2000, p. 37). The regular routines and practices of businesses, factories, schools, cultural organizations, and governments reproduce racial inequalities (Bennett, 1990, p. 45).

Any useful understanding of class, gender, and race in the United States or any other country needs some idea of "institutional discrimination." Thinking of discrim-ination or racism *merely* as an upshot of malicious intent by individuals is too limiting. However, looking at discrimination or racism *merely* as the institutional reproduction of inequality is similarly unsatisfactory. Such a conception provides no basis for drawing important distinctions.

To see why, contrast the undifferentiated idea of "institutional discrimination" at work in the multicultural literature with the standard employed in the law. Since 1971 the Supreme Court has construed the broad antidiscrimination mandates of the Civil Rights Act of 1964 to prohibit any institutional practice that adversely affects racial minorities *without a compelling reason*.

This last clause is crucial. Because of their generally lesser initial starting points in society, blacks will be adversely affected by almost any broad rule or requirement. For example, if school boards require that bus drivers not have drunk-driving convictions, this requirement will disqualify more blacks than whites. If states make teachers pass a competency exam, disproportionately more black teachers than whites will fail. If banks give better mortgage rates to home-buyers who make large down-payments, relatively fewer blacks than whites will get the better rates. May school boards, states, and banks adopt such policies?

The legal standard to apply to these cases is clear, although its application is often contentious. Generalized across all institutions and sectors, the legal standard says that those exclusionary practices count as discrimination *which it is reasonable for society to require institutions to eliminate*. Thus, the statutory standard involves an inherently judgmental component. Informed people of goodwill can disagree about which institutional practices society should discountenance and at what acceptable cost. Nevertheless, the standard supplies a basis for making moral and legal distinc-tions: those practices that *unnecessarily* burden minorities cannot pass legal muster; those practices that *unnecessarily* burden people who have already been disadvan-taged by past oppression morally cannot stand.

497

By contrast, the idea of "institutional discrimination" used in the multicultural literature blurs over the difference between practices necessary to vital institutional objectives and those not, making *any* practice producing adverse racial impact count as discrimination. Such a construal of "discrimination," far from advancing racial justice, robs the term of its critical force altogether. If everything is discrimination, then people simply will stop counting all discrimination as unacceptable.

The multicultural education literature's strength has been its unremitting commitment to closing the achievement gap and fostering respect across ethnic, racial, and "cultural" boundaries. Its weaknesses derive from its intellectual insularity and limited conceptual tools.

See also 11 CRITICAL THEORY; 14 POSTMODERNISM; 29 CHURCH, STATE, AND EDUCATION; 30 COMMON SCHOOLING AND EDUCATIONAL CHOICE; 33 EDUCATIONAL EQUALITY AND JUSTICE; 35 EDUCATION AND THE POLITICS OF IDENTITY; 43 AFFIRMATIVE ACTION IN HIGHER EDUCATION

References

Appiah, K. A. (1992) *In My Father's House: Africa in the Philosophy of Culture*. New York: Oxford University Press.

Banks, J. A. (1977) The implications of multicultural education for teacher education. In F. H. Klassen and D. Gollnick (eds), *Pluralism and the American Teacher: Issues and Cases Studies*. Washington, DC: American Association of Colleges of Teacher Education, pp. 1–30.

Banks, J. A. (1988) *Multiethnic Education: Theory and Practice*, 2nd edn. Boston: Allyn & Bacon.

Banks, J. A. (1992) Multicultural education: characteristics and goals. In J. A. Banks and C. A. M. Banks (eds), *Multicultural Education: Issues and Perspectives*. Boston: Allyn & Bacon, pp. 2–26.

Banks, J. A. (1994) *An Introduction to Multicultural Education*. Boston: Allyn & Bacon.

Banks, J. A. (1995) Multicultural education: historical development, dimensions, and practice. In J. A. Banks (ed.), *Handbook of Research on Multicultural Education*. New York: Macmillan, pp. 3–24.

Banks, J. A. (1996) The canon debate, knowledge construction, and multicultural education. In J. A. Banks (ed.), *Multicultural Education, Transformative Knowledge, and Action*. New York: Teachers College Press, pp. 3–29.

Bennett, C. I. (1990) *Comprehensive Multicultural Education: Theory and Practice*, 2nd edn. Boston: Allyn & Bacon.

Blum, L. (1998) Recognition, value, and equality: a critique of Charles Taylor's and Nancy Fraser's accounts of multiculturalism. *Constellations*, 5, 51–67.

Bull, B. L. et al. (1992) *The Ethics of Multicultural and Bilingual Education*. New York: Teachers Colllege Press.

Campbell, D. E. et al. (2000) *Choosing Democracy: A Practical Guide to Multicultural Education*, 2nd edn. Columbus, OH: Merrill.

Carens, J. (2000) *Culture, Community and Citizenship*. Oxford: Oxford University Press.

Davidman, L. and Davidman, P. T. (1997) *Teaching with a Multicultural Perspective: A Practical Guide*, 2nd edn. New York: Longman.

Ford, T. (1999) *Becoming Multicultural: Personal and Social Construction through Critical Teaching*. New York: Falmer Press.

Fraser, N. (1989) *Unruly Practices: Power, Discourse and Gender in Contemporary Social Theory*. Minneapolis: University of Minnesota Press.

Gay, G. (1992) Ethnic minorities and educational equality. In J. A. Banks and C. A. M. Banks (eds), *Multicultural Education: Issues and Perspectives*. Boston: Allyn & Bacon, pp. 167–88.

Gollnick, D. M. (1992) Multicultural education: politics and practices in teacher education. In C. A. Grant (ed.), *Research and Multicultural Education: From the Margins to the Mainstream*. Washington, DC: Falmer Press, pp. 218–39.

Gollnick, D. and Chinn, P. (1986) *Multicultural Education in a Pluralistic Society*. 2nd edn. Columbus, OH: Merrill.

Gordon, B. (1992) The marginalized discourse of minority intellectual thought in traditional writings on teaching. In C. Grant (ed.), *Research and Multicultural Education: From the Margins to the Mainstream*. Washington, DC: Falmer Press, pp. 19–31.

Grant, C. A., and Sleeter, C. E. (1989) *Turning on Learning: Five Approaches for Multicultural Teaching Plans for Race, Class, Gender, and Disability*. Columbus, OH: Merrill.

Grant, C. A. and Sachs, J. M. (1995) Multicultural education and postmodernism: movement toward a dialogue. In B. Kanpol and P. McClaren (eds), *Critical Multiculturalism: Uncommon Voices in an Uncommon Struggle*. Westport, CT: Bergin & Garvey, pp. 89–124.

Gutmann, A. and Thompson, D. (1996) *Democracy and Disagreement*. Cambridge, MA: Harvard University Press.

Howard, G. (1996) Whites in multicultural education: rethinking our role. In J. A. Banks (ed.), *Multicultural Education, Transformative Knowledge, and Action*. New York: Teachers College Press, pp. 323–34.

Irvine, J. J. and York, D. E. (1995) Learning styles and culturally diverse students: a literature review. In J. A. Banks (ed.), *Handbook of Research on Multicultural Education*. New York: Macmillan, pp. 484–97.

Kinchloe, J. and Steinberg, S. R. (1997) *Changing Multiculturalism*. Buckingham: Open University Press.

Klein, G. (1993) *Education toward Race Equality*. London: Cassell.

Kymlicka, W. (1989) *Liberalism, Community, and Culture*. Oxford: Oxford University Press.

Kymlicka, W. (1995) *Multicultural Citizenship*. Oxford: Oxford University Press.

Ladsen-Billings, G. (1992) Culturally relevant teaching: the key to making multicultural education work. In C. Grant (ed.) *Research and Multicultural Education: From the Margins to the Mainstream*. Washington, DC: Falmer Press, pp. 106–21.

Lopez, T. R. Jr and Vogel, A. W. (eds) (1979) *No One Model American*. Toledo, OH: College of Education, University of Toledo.

Lynch, J. (1987) *Prejudice Reduction in the Schools*. London: Cassell.

Macedo, S. (2000) *Diversity and Distrust: Civic Education in a Multicultural Democracy*. Cambridge, MA: Harvard University Press.

National Council for the Social Studies (1976) Curriculum guidelines for multiethnic education. *Social Education*, 40, supplement 1–48.

National Council for the Social Studies (1992) Curriculum guidelines for multicultural education. *Social Education*, 55, 274–94.

New York Report (1991) *One Nation, Many Peoples: A Declaration of Cultural Interdependence*. Report of the New York State Social Studies Review and Development Committee. Albany, NY: State Department of Education.

Nieto, S. (2000) *Affirming Diversity: The Sociopolitical Context of Multicultural Education*, 3rd edn. New York: Longman.

Ovando, C. J. and Gourd, K. (1996) Knowledge construction, language maintenance, revitalization, and empowerment. In J. A. Banks (ed.), *Multicultural Education, Transformative Knowledge, and Action*. New York: Teachers College Press, pp. 297–322.

Parekh, B. (1986) The concept of multicultural education. In S. Modgil et al. (eds), *Multicultural Education: The Interminable Debate*. London: Falmer Press, pp. 19–31.

Ramírez, M. and Castañeda, A. (1974) *Cultural Democracy, Bicognitive Development, and Education*. New York: Academic Press.

Sarup, M. (1986) *The Politics of Multiracial Education*. London: Routledge & Kegan Paul.

Schlesinger, A. M. Jr (1992) *The Disuniting of America: Reflections on a Multicultural Society*. New York: W. W. Norton.

Schofield, J. W. (1995) Improving intergroup relations among students. In J. A. Banks (ed.), *Handbook of Research on Multicultural Education*. New York: Macmillan, pp. 635–46.

Slavin, R. (1995) Cooperative learning and intergroup relations. In J. A. Banks (ed.), *Handbook of Research on Multicultural Education*. New York: Macmillan, pp. 628–34.

Sleeter, C. E. (1991) Introduction: multicultural education and empowerment. In C. E. Sleeter (ed.), *Empowerment through Multicultural Education*. Albany, NY: State University Press of New York, pp. 1–23.

Sleeter, C. E. (1992) *Keepers of the American Dream: A Study of Staff Development and Multicultural Education*. Washington, DC: Falmer Press.

Sleeter, C. E. (1995) An analysis of the critiques of multicultural education. In J. A. Banks (ed.), *Handbook of Research on Multicultural Education*. New York: Macmillan, pp. 81–94.

Sleeter, C. I. and Grant, C. A. (1994) *Making Choices for Multicultural Education: Five Approaches to Race, Class, and Gender*. New York: Merrill.

Spinner-Halev, J. (2000) *Surviving Diversity: Religion and Democratic Citizenship*. Baltimore: Johns Hopkins University Press.

Young, I. M. (1990) *Justice and the Politics of Difference*. Princeton, NJ: Princeton University Press.

35

Education and the Politics of Identity

Yael Tamir

Education and Politics

Political philosophy and the philosophy of education were born together in Plato's *Republic*, and their fates have remained entwined. Plato held in that formative work that the inculcation of civic virtue is essential to a just and harmonious political order, and the ensuing tradition has largely accepted this idea, especially with respect to democracies. No democratic republic can survive without active, responsible, informed citizens, and citizens of this kind must be trained to fulfill their role. Without a certain degree of literacy, basic knowledge of the structure and workings of political institutions, and information regarding the beliefs and policies of different candidates and parties, individuals are unable to make informed decisions, the kind of decisions democratic citizens must learn to make. For democracies, then, education is a major social and political tool.

The kinds of knowledge and skills required for responsible political participation are not the only ones that education systems transmit, however. It is impossible to teach democratic skills in the abstract. Such civic and political skills are necessarily taught in a certain language, grounded in a particular culture and a particular historical narrative that produce heroes to venerate, festivities to celebrate, days of national mourning as well as national feats.

This cultural bias of the curriculum raised no difficulties in the age of the nation state. National education was meant to place one national culture over and above all others. Its declared purpose was to enhance the transformation of a population into a nation by promoting the homogenization of language and culture, spreading the official historical narrative and fostering a common national vision.

More recently, however, the empowerment of national minorities, together with intense waves of immigration, has changed the nature of most states, eroding homogeneity and allowing cultural, lingual, and national differences to surface. An educational system constructed to fit this new political reality faces the most difficult educational task ever faced. It must respect diversity, allowing a plurality of cultures and languages to flourish, while teaching civic virtue and fostering social responsibility and political unity.

The Politics of Identity

The fact that personal identity is formed by membership in cultural, linguistic, and national communities was well known in the age of the nation state and was the main motive for nation building through the suppression of diversity. The politics of identity assumes this is true as well, yet endorses radically different policies. It seeks to secure an opportunity for all national, cultural, and linguistic communities to be present in the public and political spheres, and sees cultural suppression and identity misrecognition as harms ranked alongside inequality, exploitation, and injustice (Taylor, 1994, p. 64).

The politics of identity thus forces a reconstruction of the public and the political spheres and a redefinition of the role and scope of education. The changes it requires pertain to educational institutions ranging from "university humanities departments, where demands are made to alter, enlarge, or scrap the canon," to "secondary schools where an attempt is made to develop a curriculum which meets the needs of students coming from very different backgrounds" (Taylor, 1994, p. 65).

In fact, the politics of identity calls for nothing less than an educational revolution that touches upon each and every sphere of education. It obliges educational systems to rewrite their curricula, retrain teachers, rethink the degree of autonomy granted to parents in defining their children's education, and reconsider claims for educational segregation.

Rewriting the Curricula

The curricula taught in schools are one the most important sources of social legitimacy. They define the nature of social authority, constitute the relevant spheres of knowledge, and determine social and political norms, the cultural heritage(s), historical narrative(s), as well as the language(s) spoken in the public sphere.

From its moment of birth and until the emergence of the politics of identity, the primary purpose and effect of state-governed education was to erase differences and produce social and cultural homogeneity. Nationalists saw cultural and linguistic homogeneity as a means for nation building, while democrats endorsed it as a means of promoting democratic equality and popular political participation. These goals are different, but the consequences of pursuing them were surprisingly similar: schooling served to unify and harmonize public life, and it did so in a way that was invariably homogenizing.

The politics of identity challenges the homogenizing purposes and consequences of state-governed education, and demands the introduction of curricula that are culturally and linguistically diverse. It demands multicultural curricula that leave room for conflicting national narratives, place local and communal knowledge on a par with the national one, and encourage reflective cultural dialogue. Such curricula empower minority groups and undermine the power and authority of the ruling nation. The politics of identity thus seeks to change the distribution of social power, legitimizing the presence of a plurality of identities in the public sphere. It sees school reforms in general and the rewriting of the curricula in particular as tools of such reform.

The presence of a culture or language in the classroom indicates that the community whose culture or language is present is seen as worthy of respect, as a source of moral and social knowledge all children can share and benefit from. The absence of a culture or its presentation in a biased and unflattering manner has severe consequences. It engenders among members of that cultural community low self-esteem and a sense of inferiority and worthlessness. Moreover, it challenges traditional patterns of authority, as it fosters, among children, disrespect toward their parents and their community, who seem to have nothing worthwhile to teach or transmit either to their own children and members or to the society at large.

The purpose of multicultural education is not only to enhance the self-esteem of members of minority groups, or allow communities to learn about each other, but also to allow minority communities to protect their ongoing existence as distinct communities. Language, because it is one of the main defining features of most minority cultures, is often seen as one of the most important conditions necessary for cultural survival. The ability to use a language and teach it reinforces family ties, allows the child to identify with the community, and opens up cultural opportunities. A report of the *Minority Rights Group International*, reviewing the case of the Bengali minority in Britain, indicates that Bengali girls who had the opportunity to study Bengali in school were eager to learn the language. It's my first language, says one of them, "English is my second language, so I should know my first language more than my second language" (Minority Rights Group International, 1994, p. 23).

Yet how many languages should a child learn? What should be the curricula for children of mixed cultural – linguistic origins? What kind of language skills should children have in both the minority and the majority language? Is bilingualism (or trilingualism) an intellectual asset or a burden? The answers to these questions are yet to be determined.

There are many degrees of cultural knowledge, from superficial knowledge acquired by incidental encounters with a culture – watching a movie, spending a summer vacation, or reading a novel – to profound cultural competence and understanding which comes from a long, deep cultural experience. It is unclear how much cultural knowledge is necessary in order to use a culture as a moral or social framework of frame of reference, or as a reflective tool on one's own culture. Consequently, the task of designing a multicultural curriculum that is neither simplistic nor disrespectful of the richness of culture is a daunting task. When does diversity turn into no more than a symbolic gesture and when is it offering a real cultural experience? What are the limits of diversity within one classroom? How many cultures can be experienced meaningfully by a student or by one group of students? Is there a threshold number that determines the size of a community deserving representation in the curriculum? These questions will lie at the heart of educational research and controversy in years to come.

Retraining Teachers

Multicultural education places special demands on teachers, and thus on the training and retraining of teachers. The aim of multicultural education is twofold: to initiate children into their own communal heritage and to acquaint them with the history, culture, and language of other cultures. In so doing, multicultural education is meant to develop in children not only identification with their community of origin, but also an appreciation for the diversity of mankind. In order to accomplish this twofold aim teachers must first widen their own cultural – linguistic horizons, free themselves from prejudices and misconceptions and become the guardian of cultural pluralism, toleration, and respect.

The politics of identity places the teacher in a delicate position. In the age of the nation state the teacher was the bearer of the collective national message, and her authority derived from that message and the significance assigned to it by all social institutions. Now, like all other citizens, the teacher is identified as a member of a particular group that has a particular culture and values. For members of all other communities the teacher is no longer the embodiment of the state or the nation but simply "the other." Her authority over those who do not belong to her community is therefore severely curtailed. Moreover, when teaching minority culture(s) the teacher is likely to be culturally illiterate. Her knowledge is, at best, a second-hand one, inferior to that of some of her students, and this disparity may further erode her authority. The result of these changes is a restructuring of the power relationship between teacher, students, and parents.

In a multicultural school system teachers are likely to play an educational role that raises suspicion among members of minority and majority cultures alike. The former are likely to feel that their culture is not given enough attention and is superficially taught by unqualified teachers. The latter are likely to resent the "invasion" of the classroom by other cultures, suggesting too much time is dedicated to these cultures and traditions. Both groups are likely to rest their dissatisfaction on the shoulders of teachers. The teacher is thus transformed from the representative of social and political consensus to "the usual social suspect."

The teacher's unfamiliarity with the cultures of some of her students could inspire cultural misunderstanding, frustration, and finally alienation, which may lead children from minority cultures to drop out of school. For example, in some cultures it is a sign of honesty to look into the teacher's eyes, but in others it is a sign of disrespect to do so. Immigrant children from Ethiopia are educated at home to glance to the side or to the floor while talking to an adult. This is a sign of respect, an acknowledgment of the social hierarchy. In the Israeli classroom Ethiopian immigrants find, to their surprise, that their polite behavior is interpreted as avoidance, dishonesty, or inattentiveness. The response of the educational environment to a behavior guided by an unknown culture intensifies the child's feeling of "otherness" and yields dire educational consequences. Such cultural pressures *can* be eased, however, and one way to do so is through the employment of "cultural mediators" who facilitate the mutual adjustment of members of different cultures to a mixed environment.

The Minority Rights Group International concludes its report on respecting the rights and status of minorities in educational settings by making the following recommendations:

1   Teachers need to be trained to be aware of their own cultural biases and seek to modify them.

2   Teacher training should include learning about the cultures of their students and their experiences as members of minority groups.

3   Teachers should promote a climate of acceptance, mutual respect, and collaboration in the classroom, thus facilitating the expression of ideas, feelings, and different cultural values and experiences.

4   Minority views should be given the same critical hearing as majority views, and teaching should avoid stereotypical labeling of the attributes and competence of different minority groups (Minority Rights Group International, 1994, p. 33).

The politics of identity thus assigns teachers the almost impossible task of turning the necessity of pluralism into a virtue.

Rethinking Parental Choices and Demands for Segregation

In the early stages of the struggle for equal rights and integration members of minority cultures tended to reject any deviation from universalistic arguments, fearing that any such deviation would legitimize discrimination. Yet they discovered that being granted a set of formal, individual civic rights is insufficient to ensure their persistence as a separate cultural group. They had to decide which was the lesser of two evils: retaining their particular identity at the risk of remaining estranged and marginalized, or integrating at the price of cultural self-effacement.

Haunted by the shadows of "separate but equal" policies originally meant to preserve segregation and social inequality in education, members of cultural minorities were at first reluctant to demand special schools or classes aimed at fostering their own traditions, languages, and history. Demanding such measures would imply not only an acknowledgment, but also an acceptance, of their minority status, it was argued. It was only when it became clear that strict adherence to the principles of equal treatment in common schools tends to perpetuate assimilation that minority groups started raising demands in the name of equality for cultural diversity and special accommodations to preserve diversity. Such accommodations may involve opening up the general curriculum, or offering special language classes, Sunday schools, separate classes, or even separate educational systems.

One purpose of such demands is to initiate children into their own culture and language, as well as to introduce the general population to minority cultures. For some minority groups, achieving these aims is not enough; they wish to reform the educational system in ways that will allow them to "protect" their children from the temptation of assimilation or from what they consider morally or religiously corrupting influences. Members of such communities: find education that encourages reflection on values and comparison of cultures threatening; object to science classes on the ground that they teach a human history different than their own; find literature classes biased against their values; protest that history lessons exclude or distort their history; resent health and sex education as being too permissive; forbid the participation of girls in mixed classes; and prefer children to wear their traditional clothing rather than school uniforms.

505

Such communities demand certain freedoms to exclude children from parts of the curriculum or to introduce some changes in the national school system in order to allow the participation of their children in the national system without renouncing their traditions. Other communities make separatist claims meant to isolate children from the general school system. The two kinds of demands are distinct and at odds with each other.

The moral and political logic motivating the politics of identity suggests that demands for cultural variance with the common school system should be endorsed even at the cost of some inconvenience and compromise on the part of the larger community. Take, for example, the debate concerning the right of immigrant Algerian girls living in France to wear a *hidjab* (a head cover) in schools and universities. According to the French civic tradition educational institutions are public institutions and as such they must be culturally and religiously neutral. Before entering such institutions individuals should shed all distinguishing features, be they a *hidjab*, a skullcap, a turban, or any other traditional wear. These garments could, of course, be worn in the private sphere but not in the public one.

Hence the French education minister, François Bayrou, asked secondary school principals to ban "ostentatious signs" of religion, a code phrase for head scarves. The French, says a government official, want Muslims to behave like them. "If Muslims want to impose their costumes, wear veils, that generates a backlash. Muslims born in France who don't want to become French are fanatics or invaders." Our only ambition, replies Abdallah Ben Mansour, president of the Union of Islamic Organizations in France, "is to become at the same time good Muslims and good French citizens. But as long as people wage campaigns on the peril of Islam, as long as we let fear and frustrations accumulate, we will encounter all forms of radicalization" (Tamir, 1995, p. 9). The politics of identity sides with the immigrant parents demanding that the public sphere should be changed in order to allow members of minority groups to find their place within it.

Yet what about parents who, in the name of the preservation of a particular identity, wish to exclude their children from the general school system? The answer calls for a delicate balance between two kinds of considerations. The first weighs the rights of parents to retain their identity against the rights of children to become free agents able to make decisions that will shape their lives. The second weighs the interest of the community in retaining its particular identity against the interest of the state in fostering among its future citizens democratic knowledge, civic virtues and social responsibility.

The Limits of Diversity

Multicultural education inspired by the politics of identity is meant to "initiate the child not merely into the cultural capital of his own community but of the entire man kind in so far as it is possible and thus to humanize rather than merely socialize him" (Parekh, 1986, p. 19). Education must therefore be a three-layered system: the first layer includes general civic, democratic, humanistic education; the second particularistic communal education; the third a shared cross-cultural education.

506

This threefold structure is assumed to meet the cultural needs of members of minority communities, while preserving a somewhat fragile but nevertheless stable political union based on equal participation in a shared political culture.

Yet there are ample cases in which a community demands, in the name of respect and recognition of its own special identity, the right to isolate children from the larger society. An education isolating children from the larger society and forcing them to remain within their community of origin restricts their freedom and ability to determine for themselves their own cultural, communal preferences. If the child's interest in freedom is the overriding moral consideration, then most calls for segregation ought to be rejected. As members of such cultures insist on "bringing up their children in their own ways," Joseph Raz (1988, pp. 423–4) writes, they are, "in the eyes of liberals, like myself, harming them." According to an autonomy-based liberalism liberals have a right, or maybe even a duty, to promote the assimilation of illiberal cultures. Raz thus suggests that liberals are justified in taking actions to assimilate illiberal minority cultures, including the closing down of separate schools, even at the cost of allowing a culture to become diluted or die.

The endorsement of policies aiming to liberalize traditional authoritarian cultures leaves room for only "thin multiculturalism" (see Tamir, 1995), the kind of multiculturalism that offers respect and recognition only to those national and cultural communities that share a basic set of liberal democratic principles. There is, however, a second kind of multiculturalism, "thick multiculturalism," which raises far more difficult dilemmas, as it involves liberal egalitarian cultures as well as illiberal authoritarian ones. Can members of a thick multicultural society agree on the way future citizens should be educated? Probably not, as even the most modest forms of democratic education and multicultural experiences are rejected by most traditional authoritarian cultures.

Michael Walzer argues that democratic education demands that all children be taught the history, the philosophy, and the political practice of democracy. This demand is not as minimal as it might seem. Democracy, especially liberal democracy, "has a substantive character; it isn't a neutral procedure but a way of life" (Walzer, 1995, p. 183). Democratic education thus invokes resentment among those who adhere to traditional authoritarian values, and is seen as a program for either cultural subordination or cultural reform. Such resentment renders social agreement on matters of education impossible. Democratic education must then be forcibly imposed on members of traditional groups.

The politics of identity and its educational implications force liberal theory to admit its own limitations: it can foster a wide range of cultural and linguistic diversity but a rather limited normative diversity. Liberals may attempt to present multicultural education as embodying concessions to the demands and needs of members of traditional minorities, yet these concessions are motivated by liberal values that contradict the closed, authoritarian conception of the good life endorsed by the relevant minority cultures. Demanding that members of such groups open up their educational systems, respecting other ways of life, is demanding that they compromise their most basic beliefs and loosen up the communal authority they wish to preserve.

The politics of identity opens up the political and educational spheres in order to make room for members of minority groups. In so doing it changes the nature of these spheres and lessens the costs of preserving particular identities. For members of some national, cultural minorities – those who endorse a set of liberal democratic values – such policies will allow equal participation in public life. For members of other minorities – those who subscribe to closed, authoritarian beliefs – the politics of identity may appear to be no more than another form of a liberal attempt to socialize them into the ruling liberal-democratic culture. In a way such claims are justified ones: the politics of identity starts from a liberal premise, namely protecting members of minority cultures from external oppression and pressures of involuntary assimilation; it cannot, and should not, turn into a tool of internal oppression and pressures for involuntary segregation. A political theory that starts with individual rights and freedoms must not lose sight of what it is meant to protect, or else it will undermine its own justification.

See also 29 CHURCH, STATE, AND EDUCATION; 30 COMMON SCHOOLING AND EDUCATIONAL CHOICE; 34 MULTICULTURAL EDUCATION; 36 THE ETHICS OF TEACHING

References

Minority Rights Group International (1994) *Education Rights and Minorities*. London: MRG.

Parekh, B. (1986) The concept of multi-cultural education. In S. Modgil, G. K. Verna, K. Mallick, and C. Modgil (eds), *Multicultural Education: The Interminable Debate*. London: The Falmer Press.

Raz, J. (1988) *The Morality of Authority*. Oxford: Oxford University Press.

Tamir, Y. (1995) Two concepts of multiculturalism. In Y. Tamir (ed.), *Democratic Education in a Multicultural State*. Oxford: Blackwell, pp. 3–14.

Taylor, C. (1994) The politics of recognition. In A. Gutmann (ed.), *Multiculturalism: Examining the Politics of Recognition*. Princeton, NJ: Princeton University Press, pp. 25–73.

Walzer, M. (1995) Education, democratic citizenship and multiculturalism. In Y. Tamir (ed.), *Democratic Education in a Multicultural State*. Oxford: Blackwell, pp. 23–32.

36

The Ethics of Teaching

Kenneth A. Strike

The ethics of teaching is a disorderly topic. Since most ethical problems and issues can become classroom issues, the ethics of teaching could concern almost any ethical matter. Moreover, there are various sources of conceptions that might inform the ethics of teaching. These include the law, the constitutional principles of liberal democratic societies, an ethic of care, or various postmodern and critical theories. Yet there are ethical conceptions internal to the teaching profession, which would presumably define the core of the ethics of teaching. More specifically, there are (at least) three general norms that are internal to the practice of teaching and central to our topic. These are: (1) teachers must teach their subjects with integrity; (2) teachers must be exemplars of what I shall call the civic ethic and run their classrooms congruently with democratic principles; and (3) teachers must create a climate that promotes growth. These ideas provide a core of coherence for an otherwise messy domain.

Orientation

I maintain a file of articles about teaching and ethics that appear in the *Washington Post*. Consider a sample of issues. There is a rise of incidents of teachers cheating so as to enable their students to do well on standardized tests (Mathews and Argetsinger, 2000). A group of teachers was charged with hitting students (Blum, 2000). Teachers delivered a group of students to jail officials for a strip search in a "Scared Straight" program (Lengel, 2001). A teacher provided students with alcohol (Blum and Lengel, 2001). Schools ignored harassment of gay students (Bowman, 2001). A teacher was accused of purchasing child pornography and possession of drugs (Snyder, 2001). If one's view of the salient issues of teacher ethics were to be taken from the newspapers, drug use, sexual peccadilloes, cheating, abuse, and violence would be the order of the day. All of these are matters of ethics; when teachers engage in such conduct they are issues of teacher ethics.

If one were to construct a "person on the street" image of the concerns that should drive a discussion of the ethics of education based on such accounts, it might consist of the following kinds of questions:

- How can schools be made safe and secure?
- How can we make sure that children are not subject to abuse?
- How can discipline be made fair and effective?
- How can we have schools that are drug- and alcohol-free?
- How can we have teachers who will not steal from their schools or cheat on behalf of their students, who will perform their duties conscientiously, and who will be more concerned for their students than for their own advantage or advancement?

This issue list might be expanded by looking at a range of policy controversies concerning curriculum, religion, or the distribution of resources. What shall we teach about gays? Who can pray in schools when? Should we prefer high-need or high-ability students in allocating resources? Should schools take corporate advertising?

Such issues do not usually flow from any conception of the nature of good teaching or good education. Most of the crimes and misdemeanors enumerated above can occur outside of schools and independently of whether the perpetrators are teachers or the victims are students. Similarly, the curricular and policy issues tend not to be educational issues *per se*, but are broad social issues that have application to schools as well as other social sites.

Compare this to the idea that teachers should not indoctrinate their students or that teachers have a duty of fidelity to the subject matter they teach. These notions seem more internal to the activity of teaching. They tend to presuppose conceptions of the ends of a good education.

Care needs to be taken about what is meant. Consider grading. Teachers should grade fairly. Grading practices must respect norms of due process and must not be biased. Grading practices should also be educative. Teachers should provide useful feedback. Students should learn something from their tests and essays.

Suppose we say that the claim that grading should be educative is an ideal that is internal to the ethics of teaching, but that due process is not. When we grade we need to be fair because we are distributing a commodity that can be exchanged for other social goods such as additional education, jobs, and income. Grading has much to do with distributive justice, thus much to do with just educating, but little to do with good educating. If so, it does not follow that respecting norms of fairness in grading is unimportant, for grading must be done fairly. Yet it is not altogether clear that fairness in grading is external to justifiable conceptions of good teaching and good education. Suppose we view fair grading practices not only as being fair to students, but also as teaching students to be fair. To say this is to make modeling norms of justice internal to a conception of good teaching.

The philosophical literature on the ethics of teaching provides another entree into what the topic might be supposed to be about. One of the first books on the topic in the post-Second World War era was R. S. Peters's (1966) *Ethics and Education*. In this book Peters deals with such topics as the nature of worthwhile activities, the justification of educational authority and punishment, and freedom, democracy, and equality. The book is also distinguished by the development of a distinct form of ethical argument that Peters calls a transcendental argument. Let us ask, says Peters, what we must presuppose if we are seriously to engage in addressing the question

510

"Why do this rather than that?" Even to ask the question is to take on commitments to such notions as the importance of reason giving.

Peters's book has two noteworthy features. First, the discussion is rooted in metatheoretical claims. Peters begins with a general view of the nature of ethical argument and ethical justification. Second, Peters's book articulates a general philosophy of education. Peters's book is no mere attempt to lay down guidelines for ethical practice that might be subscribed to by practitioners of diverse persuasions about the larger purposes of education. It is intended to answer some of the deeper questions about the nature of a good education and indeed a good life. It might be described as *deeply rooted*, as distinguished from John Rawls's (1993) notion that a theory of justice should be *philosophically shallow* so it can be held by those who believe diverse comprehensive doctrines.

A conception of the ethics of teaching suitable for the public schools of liberal democracies needs to respect two forms of pluralism. It needs to recognize a pluralism of comprehensive doctrines, religions, and cultures, but it also needs to respect a diversity of values (see Gray, 2000). We should avoid the tendency in some of the literature on ethics that grows out of Lawrence Kohlberg's (1981) work on moral development and his feminist critics (see Gilligan, 1982; Noddings, 1984) to reduce ethics to justice or to caring or to some synthesis of these, just as we should avoid the assumption that all values come in discrete and integrated cultural or religious packets. There is a range of ethical conceptions that can inform teaching. There is kindness and decency and integrity and excellence and mercy, as well as justice and caring. There is a voice of craft as well as a voice of justice or of caring (Green, 1999). The diversity of moral conceptions cannot be reduced to some overarching moral theory. Attempts to do so constrain and distort our intellectual resources (see Strike, 1999).

These two kinds of pluralism suggest an approach to the ethics of teaching that seeks to avoid overly theorizing the discussion of particular ethical problems and believes that comprehensive moral doctrines and ethical theories have limited utility in the project. We need instead, so far as we are able, to appeal to a range of moral concepts and principles that are broadly understood and widely accepted and to attempt to resolve issues with minimal invoking of abstract philosophical theories. We may look to more deeply rooted conceptions for insight and wisdom or in desperation, but we should carefully avoid grounding a professional ethic in any one of them.

The work of Strike et al. (1988) and Strike and Jonas Soltis (1998) suggests a different approach. These books contain chapters on such topics as equal opportunities, punishment, educational authority, and intellectual liberty as they apply in educational contexts. They have four characteristics. First, they begin with an ethical code. The *Ethics of Teaching* begins with the *Code of Ethics of the National Education Association*. Since the *Ethics of School Administration* is modeled on the *Ethics of Teaching*, this is implicitly true of it as well. Second, these works do not flow from a deeply rooted philosophy of education. They aim to explicate a range of ethical conceptions that regulate the conduct of educators in the practice of their craft that are, arguably, capable of being ascribed to by practitioners of diverse philosophical positions. Typically, the focus is on ethical concepts that might be viewed as part of the political norms of liberal democracies. Third, while the conceptions they characterize are those that define the rights and role of citizens, they are not developed from

511

a stance that emphasizes the production of good citizens. Finally, theoretical concerns tend to occur in these works in a way that is interpretive and, in retrospect, largely unnecessary to the book. Strike and Soltis employ the distinction between consequentialist and non-consequentialist ethical theories to discuss how ethical conceptions such as due process and intellectual liberty are interpreted and how they may be applied to cases in different ways.

One concern with this approach is that the conceptions developed, while they do regulate the behavior of teachers in classrooms, are presented as external conceptions. Often the concepts discussed are those that regulate the interactions between governments and citizens in liberal democratic societies. While they apply to public school teachers, they are not inherently about the ethics of teaching any more than they are about the ethics of policing.

Amy Gutmann (1987) develops an approach to the ethics of education (and implicitly to the ethics of teaching) that falls between these two approaches. It is rooted in the question "What must education be like if it is to produce citizens for a democratic society?" Gutmann's starting point is Aristotle's insight that education must produce people whose character is suitable to the constitution of their society. Hence Gutmann begins with a defense of her view of democracy. Her work makes the question of legitimate authority central not only to the justification of educational authority, but also to the larger questions of the philosophy of education. While I have not asserted any precise measure that might be used to determine how deeply rooted or philosophically shallow an approach to the ethics of teaching might be, Gutmann's strategy recognizes both the fact and the legitimacy of what Rawls calls durable pluralism and seeks to balance the authority of the state, the family, and the individual. While at the end of the day one might wonder whether Gutmann has made democracy itself into a way of life, there is no attempt to root the ethics of teaching in some particular vision of a good life. Once the imperative of creating democratic character is satisfied, other goals can be chosen democratically for reasons that seem good to those who do the choosing.

Assigning schools the primary function of producing good citizens for liberal democratic societies has the consequence of making those moral conceptions that characterize liberal democratic societies internal to notions of good teaching and good education. Teachers need to regulate their conduct according to these principles not only because they are dealing with citizens, but also because they are creating citizens.

This discussion suggests that a core conception of the ethics of teaching should have these two characteristics: First, it should emphasize those ethical concepts that are internal to good teaching and good education. Second, it needs to find a path between a conception of the ethics of teaching that has no view of good teaching and good educating and one that has a conception that is philosophically deeply rooted.

Teacher Ethics and the Law

The education codes of many US states require for licensure that teachers be persons of good character. Most states also permit teachers to be dismissed for unethical conduct. What counts as good character is a contentious matter. Indeed, the law rarely discusses good character. Instead it emphasizes conduct bad enough to warrant dismissal or withdraw of licensure.

The kinds of misconduct dealt with by the law are usually acts that are unethical in any context (for discussion see Fischer et al., 1999). Teachers, like others, are expected not to steal, kill, commit assault, abuse children, or engage in sexual harassment. While the definition of immoral conduct in the law has not become coextensive with violations of criminal law, it seems headed in that direction. The law largely provides legal force to the "person in the street" view.

In years past, teachers have been sanctioned for a range of conduct that violates local community norms, but is often not illegal. Examples are homosexuality, sexual promiscuity, or drinking. In assessing whether teachers can be sanctioned for immoral conduct that falls short of violations of the criminal law, courts have often insisted that actionable conduct be job related. This expectation can be viewed as an attempt to find grounds for judging immoral conduct that are rooted in obligations that reasonable people will understand themselves to have taken on in virtue of having agreed to accept a position as a teacher. The formulation suggests that teachers are entitled to a private life that should be beyond the power of a public employer to regulate.

The protection afforded to teachers extends to rights that have constitutional standing under the US Constitution, such as the right to free speech or association. Teachers cannot be required to abandon their constitutional rights as a condition of employment.

Consider three issues. First, do we expect teachers to be good ethical role models? Answering affirmatively to this question threatens to make all conduct that might be judged immoral into job-related conduct. Answering negatively suggests that teachers can be held accountable only for the competence with which they teach their subjects and for not engaging in immoral behavior toward their employers or their students, but cannot be held accountable for being a bad example, no matter how egregious their out of school behavior.

A second issue concerns the exercise of such rights as free speech. Should teachers have the right to publicly criticize their employers? Should teachers have a broad right to teach what and how they wish? The US Supreme Court (*Pickering* v. *Board of Education*, 391 US 563, 1968) has held that public criticism of schools by teachers plays a useful role in deliberations about educational policy and hence should be afforded Constitutional protection. However, courts have tended to claim that the right of teachers to exercise their right of free speech in classrooms is constrained by the democratic authority. Free speech may entitle teachers to the occasional expression of a political view or unpopular opinion (*Tinker* v. *Des Moines Independent School District*, 393 US 503, 1969), but does not provide teachers a license to substitute their judgment for that of the school board or state legislature with respect to what may be taught or how.

A third issue concerns the extent to which teachers may promote what might be called "cosmopolitan" values when these conflict with the values of a local community. To what extent should teachers be Socratic gadflies questioning local customs and beliefs? Must teachers respect the values of the community that pays their

513

salaries? May they actively challenge them? Often teachers who are charged with exposing their students to immoral or offensive ideas view themselves as broadening the education of their students.

The lack of a clear conception of the nature of good teaching and the nature of a good education make it difficult to apply the law in these kinds of cases. The idea that teachers are role models tends to undermine the notion that teachers can only be sanctioned when immoral conduct is job related. If teachers must be good examples potentially all immoral conduct may be job related. This difficulty might be mitigated were we able to show that some kinds of conduct are internal to a conception of good teaching and others not. Similarly, apart from some conception of good teaching it is difficult to know how to strike a balance between the right of teachers to teach and the authority of administrators and school boards to decide what will be taught and how. How do we distinguish between opening students' minds and undermining local values? How do we decide when discussing a controversial idea is good education or insubordination?

The NEA Code of Ethics

The most prominent code of ethics for teachers is the National Education Association's (2001) *Code of Ethics for the Education Profession*. The "Preamble" to this code begins

The educator, believing in the worth and dignity of each human being, recognizes the supreme importance of the pursuit of truth, devotion to excellence, and the nurture of democratic principles. Essential to these goals is the protection of the freedom to learn and to teach and the guarantee of equal educational opportunity for all. (Strike and Soltis, 1998, p. ix)

The NEA Code has two sections with eight provisions in each. The first section, entitled "Commitment to the Student," promotes the freedom to learn, requires equal opportunity, protects students against disparagement, and protects students' privacy. The freedom to learn provisions prohibit teachers from *preventing* student inquiry, *denying* students access to diverse points of view, and *distorting* subject matter. There is no provision mentioning the freedom to teach.

The NEA Code's specific provisions do not assert *affirmative* duties for teachers to *create* an inquiry-oriented environment or to *pursue* educational objectives that might be associated with the pursuit of truth, excellence, or democratic principles. Implicitly, the Code's stance seems to be that students, as bearers of rights, may not be interfered with in the exercise of these rights; however, no affirmative duty is assigned to the teacher to promote an inquiry-oriented classroom. Similarly, the NEA Code interprets the requirement of equal opportunity narrowly. Provision number six essentially prohibits teachers from denying participation or benefits to students or from granting advantages to them on the basis of a list of "irrelevant" characteristics, such as race or creed. Hence, it prohibits overt discrimination. But it does not require teachers to establish a climate of tolerance and mutual regard or to create a democratic and multicultural community. It is also silent on how educational resources are to be allocated in relationship to need and ability.

The "Preamble," in contrast to the specific provisions, provides educational grounds for a more positive role for teachers. Respect for the dignity and worth of students may require that they be provided with an education that develops their autonomy. The dignity of students is not respected if they are left subservient to parochial values unreflectively held. Also, a conception of educational excellence that did not involve developing rational and critical capacities would be an impoverished one. Finally, the idea of equal opportunity, understood in an adequately expansive way, leads to the need for an educational environment that emphasizes openness to diverse ideas, the development of critical capacities, and equal participation in goal formation. An education that provides unimpeded access to a curriculum that reflects the culture of a dominant group falls short of the ideal of genuine equal opportunity.

The second section of the NEA Code begins with the comment that

the educator shall exert every effort to raise professional standards, to promote a climate that encourages the exercise of professional judgment, to achieve conditions which attract persons worthy of the trust to careers in education and to assist in preventing the practice of the profession by unqualified persons. (Strike and Soltis, 1998, p. x)

Among its specific provisions are prohibitions against misrepresenting one's own qualifications or those of others, prohibitions against assisting unqualified persons in entering the profession or assisting non-educators in the unauthorized practice of teaching, and prohibitions against defamation of colleagues.

Here too, the NEA Code's specific provisions fall short of what might be expected given the language with which the provisions are introduced. While the ideals expressed in the introduction of the second section of the code might lead one to expect specific provisions requiring conscientious professional development, the maintaining of qualifications, or the creation of collegial learning environments, no such ideas are found in the code's specific provisions. Indeed, these provisions lack any clear suggestion that teachers have a responsibility to pursue excellence in their craft and are largely oriented to gatekeeping.

The NEA Code, whatever the shortcomings and omissions of its provisions, provides a view of the ethics of teaching that is rooted in a conception of the activities intrinsic to teaching and to the basic aims of education. It is a view that, on a charitable reading, sees teachers as promoters of inquiry and excellence and as creators of citizens. Despite its lapse into occupational protectionism, it sees teachers as professionals who have a duty to maintain excellence in their craft. As we shall see, these ideals of professionalism, excellence, inquiry, and citizenship can be expanded upon, and can become the basis of a conception of the ethics of teaching that satisfies the criteria described in the previous sections.

Teaching with Integrity

Consider two ways that one might understand what it meant for teaching to be a profession. One view, I will call it the technocratic view, claims that teachers possess two basic forms of knowledge. One is knowledge of the subjects they are to teach. The

515

second is knowledge of various skills and strategies for imparting subject matter to students. These skills and strategies are certified through empirical research and are often thought to be rooted in an understanding of the psychology of learning. Knowledge of the aims of education, however, is not viewed as a part of the professional knowledge of teachers. This conclusion may have at least two sources. The first is the latent positivism that still pervades much of the social sciences. Facts can be known through empirical inquiry. Values are matters of personal preference. The second is a belief that the goals of education should be chosen either by individuals or, when they must be collectively pursued, democratically. If so, then the claim that teachers have some special and privileged knowledge about the aims of education can be viewed as both illiberal and undemocratic (see Strike, 1993). This conception of a profession of teaching tends toward a "person in the street" or an externalist view of the ethics of teaching because it has no resources for developing a conception rooted in norms that are internal to the activities of teaching and the aims that are central to education. Teaching is a technical, not a moral, activity.

A technocratic conception of a profession of teaching sets standards for what counts as a profession that teaching is unlikely to be able to meet. The subjects that teachers teach are often associated with professions. Chemistry and mathematics are professions. Teachers of chemistry and mathematics, however, do not claim to be professional chemists and mathematicians. They claim to be professional teachers. However, the claim that there is a technical knowledge base that underlies the practice of teaching is a doubtful one (see Strike, 1990). Consider a thought experiment. Suppose we were faced with the necessity of complex surgery, and we were given a choice of having this surgery performed by a mediocre graduate of an undistinguished modern medical school or by one of the greats of ancient medicine, Hippocrates or Galen perhaps, employing the techniques available to their age. Most of us would choose the mediocre graduate of the undistinguished medical school, recognizing that the intervening growth of medical knowledge makes the recent medical school graduate a better risk. Is there any knowledge about teaching that would similarly cause us to choose a mediocre graduate of an undistinguished teachers' college over one of the great teachers of history, Socrates or Jesus, perhaps? That there is such a body of technical knowledge about teaching that would lead us to prefer the recent graduate to Socrates or Jesus seems improbable.

More importantly, were we to be asked to make such a choice, we would make it on the basis of such things as the conception of worthwhile knowledge and the conception of human flourishing held by these different teachers. Socrates and Jesus taught in very different ways. Jesus' sermon on the mount is not a Socratic dialogue. The differences in their approach to teaching are not technical. They reflect the differences between an inquirer and a prophet, between one who uses reason to discover truth and expose error and one who claims to speak with the authority of God. Imagine the absurdity of running an experiment to see which method was most effective!

This illustration suggests the difficulty with supposing that the techniques of teaching could be merely technical matters. What counts as good teaching is, at least in part, determined by norms that are epistemological and ethical. We cannot know what counts as teaching well if we do not know what knowledge is like, how it is attained, and what its worth is. We need a vision resembling what Lee Shulman

516

(1986) calls "pedagogical content knowledge," but which includes not only a grasp of the substantive concepts and epistemology of knowledge, but also a grasp of its norms and worth (see Sockett, 1993; Carr, 2000).

Consider another thought experiment. Imagine that the board of education of the Bourgeois Independent School District decided that the sole purpose of education was to create effective employees for the national economy. It thus sent a directive to its teachers requiring them to revise their lesson plans and syllabi on this assumption and to provide a justification for the results to the board. Mr Adante was a high school English teacher. He proceeded to redesign his unit on poetry on the assumption that the main purpose of the study of poetry was preparation for positions writing greeting cards. He then proceeded to analyze what kinds of poems made for successful cards. He discovered that successful greeting cards had simple brief poems of limited vocabulary. They always rhymed. Moreover, they tended to be highly sentimental. They rarely involved a complex human emotion. Sometimes they aimed at crude humor. Mr Adante thus revised his poetry syllabus to include lessons with titles such as "Creating the simple rhyme," "Leaving space for the picture," "Don't confuse them with complexity," "Tear-jerkers made easy," and "Tasteless limericks for every occasion." His reading assignments were from top selling cards.

Mr Adante's treatment of poetry fails to teach it with integrity. It misrepresents poetry's aims and purposes. Moreover, Mr Adante fails to have the character required to teach poetry adequately. Good teaching requires that the teacher be an exemplar of the characteristics and commitments of a poet. It may not require that one be a good poet, but it does require that one care about, understand, and exhibit those things that people who love poetry find of value in it.

The coherence of these claims requires a certain view of academic subjects. It requires us to believe that they are not mere collections of truths, theories, and techniques. Science, art, literature, music, and history have aims that are internal to them and are essential to their character. Moreover, they demand certain excellences of their practitioners. A teacher of poetry who does not see in poetry what poets see and who does not exemplify the excellences of the poet or the poetry lover is like the clergyperson who can preach a good sermon, but does not care about piety or strive for righteousness. To teach subjects in such ways that deny their aims and fail to exemplify their excellences is to distort and misrepresent them. To faithfully represent one's subject matter is to teach with integrity.

The subjects taught in schools are what Alisdair MacIntyre (1981) calls practices. MacIntyre characterizes a practice as

any coherent and complex form of socially established cooperative human activity through which goods internal to that form of activity are realized in the course of trying to achieve those standards of excellence which are appropriate to, and partially definitive of, that form of activity, with the result that human powers to achieve excellence, and human conceptions of the ends and goods involved, are systematically extended. (MacIntyre, 1981, p. 175)

Examples of practices include: complex games and sports (e.g. chess and football); academic disciplines (e.g. mathematics or biology); the arts (e.g. musical performance, dancing, and painting); and many occupations (e.g. farming or engineering).

517

To see an activity as a practice is to say about it at least that: (1) there are goods internal to it that form part of its nature and are not merely preferences about it; (2) these goods are realized by mastering or following certain rules and standards of excellence; (3) and mastering a practice alters one's outlook, develops one's tastes, forms one's moral commitments, and shapes one's character.

Consider physics. The goods internal to the practice of physics include a certain way of understanding the world, but also the satisfaction that results from such understanding and the effect on the character of becoming the kind of person who is able to seek truth in this way and who deeply cares about doing so. Some goods that may result from physics – position, income, or prestige – can be acquired in other ways. But one can only understand the behavior of quarks or the evolution of galaxies through physics. To become a physicist is, in addition to mastering its concepts, techniques, and forms of inference, to become the kind of person who cares about quarks and galaxies. Mastery of a practice shapes character and taste and makes one a member of a community that holds to certain ideals. To become a physicist is to become a person of a certain sort.

Given this, what is wrong with teaching poetry as though it aimed at employment writing greeting cards? What is wrong is that to do so is to ignore the goods that are internal to the practice of poetry, to fail to submit to the standards that define poetic excellence, and to fail to shape character in the process of the pursuit of poetic understanding and accomplishment. Poetry aims at such things as beauty in the language, the unique perspective, the illumination of the human condition, and the display of subtlety in wit. To fail to aim at these things is not only to miss the potential that poetry has to enrich human experience, it is to misrepresent what poetry is and to fail to be an exemplar of poetry's excellences.

Part of the ethics of teaching is to faithfully represent one's subject and to exemplify its excellences, but teachers must also help their students to learn how to assess practices and discover a mix of practices and excellences that fit a reasonable conception of a good life. The goods internal to practices are not always suitable for everyone, every occasion, or every society. The selection and balancing of such goods is essential not only to a mature understanding of the practices themselves, but to a life well lived. In order to faithfully represent their subjects, therefore, teachers must help students to acquire the tools of appraisal essential to placing those subjects, and the practices and excellences associated with them, within a wider understanding of what it might mean to live a good life. Beyond this, the faithful representation of subjects and exemplification of their excellences places on teachers a professional responsibility to maintain and increase their depth of mastery of their subjects. Mastery withers without exercise, and the virtues of inquiry would scarcely be exemplified by a teacher who did not display continued curiosity and learning.

The claim that teachers must teach with integrity reaffirms the claim that the specific prescriptions in the NEA Code are too narrow. Teachers have the affirmative duty to display their subjects as practices and to exemplify the excellences intrinsic to those practices. This means that teachers must do more than avoid interference with students' right to inquire. It means that they must seek to transform their classrooms into communities where the excellences involved in practices are actively pursued. This will mean among other things that students are taught how to inquire. It means that part of the craft of being a teacher is to exemplify the virtues one's academic craft requires.

Teachers need some protection of their freedom to teach in this way. They may need more protection than what is often provided by the law. If teachers have a duty to teach with integrity, it follows that they require a right to do so. Attempts to mandate equal time for scientific creationism provide a useful illustration. Courts have rejected such attempts because they violate the Establishment clause of the First Amendment of the US Constitution (*Edwards* v. *Aguilard*, 482 US 587, 1987). However, insisting that teachers present evidence for both evolution and scientific creationism while maintaining a stance of neutrality between them also requires teachers to misrepresent biology and undermines their ability to teach with integrity. If teachers are entitled to the autonomy provided to other professions, the requirement to be permitted to teach with integrity is the principal justification. Such claims must be justified by appealing to the character of the subjects taught as practices and to the need to represent them faithfully.

Citizenship, Civic Norms, and Moral Education

The "Preamble" to the NEA Code asserts the importance of democratic principles for educators. In this section, I explore how we should understand the role of such principles in formulating a view of the ethics of teaching.

I want to begin by expanding the notion of democratic principles to a broader (if vaguer) notion that I shall call "civic principles." I will understand civic principles to include three kinds of (overlapping) moral notions. First, there are those principles that have constitutional status in liberal democratic societies. Such principles need not be explicitly recognized in a document called a constitution. Principles have constitutional status in liberal democratic societies insofar as they are central to the conception of such a society. Such principles include freedom of religion, speech, and assembly, respect for the rule of law, the equal protection of the law (including equal opportunity), a right to privacy, a right to democratically made decisions, and a right to fair procedures and just punishment. Second are moral conceptions that are a normal part of the criminal law. These include prohibitions against violence and dishonesty. Normally, as a matter of morality, we expect people to hold to a higher standard in these areas than the law requires. Lying is often immoral even when it is not illegal. Third, there are what might be thought of as consensual norms of civility and decency. Responsibility, trustworthiness, kindness, and politeness are examples. These are the lubricants of social interaction.

Such conceptions have a public character in that they enable people of different cultures and convictions to cooperate. Moreover, few religions, cultures, and worldviews find them problematic. They are not likely to be matters of contention when we consider questions of diversity and pluralism. The NEA Code contains examples of each. Teachers are expected to avoid discrimination, conflicts of interest, and the exposure of students to embarrassment or disparagement.

An ethic consists in more than a set of principles. It consists in those understandings, virtues, and moral sentiments that enable people to understand, competently

519

apply, and act on reasonable principles. We might think of civic principles along with such understandings and virtues as a civic ethic.

The role of these civic principles in the ethics of teaching can be conceptualized in three distinguishable ways. I shall call these the regulatory view, the civic education view, and the educational enabling view. I do not view these as inconsistent. However, as we move from the regulative to the enabling view the requirements become both more expansive and more internal to the role of teacher.

The regulatory interpretation of the civic ethic concerns teacher ethics because it is regulatory of the moral relations between citizens generally or between the state and its citizens. Teachers should not discriminate against or humiliate their students because generally people or citizens should not humiliate or discriminate against one another. People ought not to discriminate in their private dealings with others because it is wrong. Teachers should not discriminate against their students because, when they act on behalf of government, it is illegal as well.

Teachers may reasonably be thought to have a duty to teach the civic ethic to their students. If we claim this, the consequence is that the civic ethic becomes part of the curriculum and, thus, internal to the conception of the role of teacher. If teachers have such a responsibility, it becomes crucial to have a sharper view of the content of the civic ethic as well as a view of how it is to be taught.

Consider a view about the latter. I will call it the *congruence argument* (for discussion see Rosenblum, 1989; Strike, 1998). The congruence argument holds that to teach the civic ethic teachers must exemplify the civic ethic in their character and practice, and the organization of the classroom and how its affairs are conducted must be congruent with the principles of the civic ethic. The assumptions of the congruence argument are that the civic ethic is taught by modeling and practice more than by precept.

Such a view requires teachers to be exemplars of civic virtue in the conduct of their teaching. To say this is to say in a different way that teachers should be role models, and this way of saying they should be role models has the advantage of being rooted in the constitution of liberal democratic societies, in societies' legal conceptions, and in a consensual and relatively non-controversial ethic. It is possible to explain why being an exemplar of the civic ethic is job related and to do so in a way that does not permit the scope of role modelling to expand in a way that erodes teachers' rights to a private life.

Several comments on the connection between the idea that teachers are responsible to teach the civic ethic and that they are responsible to teach their subject matters with integrity are called for. First, both perspectives on the role of teacher provide reasons why teachers should be concerned to create classrooms in which ideas are freely explored and debated. Free inquiry is both an epistemological and a democratic necessity.

Second, teaching with integrity, as I have developed the idea, involves engaging students in the mastery of practices and all that that involves. It includes exploration of the goods internal to these practices, mastery of the standards that regulate competent performance, and the assessment of the worth of different practices. It is an education of this sort that liberates the intellect from parochialism and prejudice. Hence there are reasons to suppose that the goal of teaching with integrity and the goal of creating citizens are mutually supporting.

520

The juxtaposition of these two ideals suggests that the notion that classrooms must be congruent with the mores of liberal democracies needs to be accommodated to the notion that mastery of a practice requires submission to its standards of judgment and excellence. Such standards are rightly viewed as provisional. Indeed, they are regularly matters of dispute among competent practitioners. Nevertheless, they have authority over the education of novices. The exercise of this authority is vested in masters of the practice and is warranted by expertise, not democracy. Truth is not democratic. Constructing the educative classroom requires striking a sensitive balance between the rule of reason and the sovereignty of the people.

There is a third view of the role of moral conceptions in education that I have called the enabling view. One provision of the NEA Code says that educators "Shall not intentionally expose the student to embarrassment or disparagement" (Strike and Soltis, 1998, p. ix). One reason why embarrassment and disparagement are objectionable is simply that they are painful. Causing gratuitous pain is an evil. There are, however, educational reasons. If children are to grow and to learn, they require an environment in which they are emotionally safe, have the security needed to explore and take risks, and are valued, cared for, and even loved.

This is a claim that I am not able to develop here. I would not, however, have it thought unimportant. The claim might seem to expand the aims of education well beyond what has been suggested thus far. The promotion of growth seems a wide view of education and suggests a broader picture of the role of teacher and, hence, the ethics of teaching, than either the mastery of practices or the creation of citizens suggests. I am reluctant to support such an expansion. Public schools and public school teachers cannot be held responsible for every form of growth and human development. To say merely that teachers are responsible for an environment that produces growth could be construed to include responsibility for goals as diverse as religious and spiritual development, moral development of a kind that is well beyond the civic ethic, and mental health. To say this expands the tasks of schools and teachers in such a way that they cease to have any core functions. Such an expansion also takes schools and teachers into areas that, in liberal democratic societies, are better thought of as the educational functions of family, church, and community.

Such an expansion might have as a corollary the expansion of the ethics of teaching in a way that has the potential to undermine any distinction between the teacher's public role and the teacher's private life. If we say that teachers are to be role models and that this includes a responsibility to exemplify whatever principles and virtues people might wish children to acquire, the requirement becomes indeterminate and potentially all-consuming. Carr (2000) suggests that in the modern world we should view teaching as a profession rather than as a vocation (a calling) that dominates the whole of life. Permitting the ethics of teaching to be dominated by an unspecified notion of promoting growth moves it in the direction of a vocation.

The solution to this dilemma is to confine the notion of establishing a growth-promoting environment to the core functions of schooling in liberal democratic societies. This chapter suggests that there are two such core functions. The first is to teach the public ethic. The second is to help students develop an educational project that includes the selection and mastery of a set of practices that can sustain a life that is experienced as worth living. A teacher's obligation to create an environment that promotes growth can be understood as the obligation to create a climate that sustains the pursuit of these two core functions of schools.

Conclusion

I have argued above that the ethics of teaching has several core ideas that are internal to the conception of good teaching. These are: (1) teachers must teach their subjects with integrity; (2) teachers must be exemplars of what I shall call the civic ethic and create classrooms that are run congruently with liberal democratic principles; and (3) teachers must create a climate that promotes growth. If it has a core it also has a periphery – what I have called the "person in the street" view. The core should generally be central in the preparation of teachers, but there is an important caveat. The distinction between what belongs to the core and what does not is not coextensive with the distinction between what is important and what is not.

The discussion has also asserted or implied several criteria that should be kept in mind in justifying a conception of the ethic of teaching. I want to note and discuss two of these.

First, I took note of the difficulty that the law had in applying the notion that teachers could be sanctioned for immoral conduct only if that conduct was job related. This became particularly difficult when teachers were expected to be role models of good conduct. Apart from a clear conception of the moral content of teaching, such an expectation tends to eliminate any boundaries on what teachers can be held accountable for.

The view that teaching is a moral profession and that its core norms flow from the obligation to teach with integrity, to create citizens, and to promote growth suggests that teachers are expected to be role models, but constrains the scope of what they are expected to model. It suggests that teachers are expected to be exemplars of the excellences and virtues associated with their subjects and that they should act according to the requirements of the civic ethic. These are demanding standards and their boundaries are not sharp, but they fall short of making demands on the whole of life.

Second, I argued that a conception of the ethics of teaching should avoid, as far as possible, a philosophically deep justification that appealed to a comprehensive moral theory or a specific view of moral reasoning. Does my core succeed in being philosophically shallow? Here is an argument suggesting that it does.

The first part of the argument concerns the emphasis on the civic ethic. The civic ethic is a *civic* ethic because its concepts and virtues have some kind of public standing. The civic ethic involves the kinds of concepts and virtues that enable the diverse members of a pluralistic society to cooperate together. Moreover, the civic ethic tends not to be rooted in some particular religious or ethical tradition. Its norms can be widely shared.

The emphasis on the mastery of practices might be thought to involve a particular conception of a good life. And in one sense it does. However, this conception has the virtue of being substantive without being specific. It is substantive in that it assumes that the mastery of complex and sophisticated practices enhances the richness of experience and the capacity to appreciate and enjoy life. Not only that, but the mastery of practices creates in us virtues and capacities that make us, on reflection, the kinds of persons we would wish to be. This view is, however, unspecified in that it does not claim that any particular set of practices is essential to a good life, that any specific set of goods must be realized, or that any specific set of virtues and excellences is to be acquired. Moreover, while I have claimed that practices can be appraised, they may be appraised from the perspective of diverse traditions.

Finally, to suggest that human flourishing is enhanced through the mastery of practices is not the equivalent of claiming the superiority of the life of the mind. Farming and football are practices. Thus a substantive, but unspecified, view of the good can be cashed out in a variety of different ways and is likely to be supportable by most religious and cultural traditions. A substantive, but unspecified, conception of the good is the kind of conception that can sustain a worthy educational system in a pluralistic liberal democracy.

I doubt that this conception would meet the exacting standards for neutrality among reasonable conceptions of the good required by Rawlsian liberalism. But I doubt that any good education could met those standards, and I worry that the attempt to meet such standards is one of the things that pushes schooling toward a highly instrumental conception dominated by economic concerns. Nevertheless, an education that is dominated by a thick, unspecified conception of the good provides for the kind of openness, tolerance, and diversity that is consistent with good and ethical teaching.

See also 18 MOTIVATION AND CLASSROOM MANAGEMENT; 22 MORAL EDUCATION; 28 THE AUTHORITY AND RESPONSIBILITY TO EDUCATE; 29 CHURCH, STATE, AND EDUCATION; 31 CHILDREN'S RIGHTS; 34 MULTICULTURAL EDUCATION; 35 EDUCATION AND THE POLITICS OF IDENTITY; 37 INCLUSION AND JUSTICE IN SPECIAL EDUCATION; 38 SEX EDUCATION; 44 THE PROFESSOR–STUDENT RELATIONSHIP AND THE REGULATION OF STUDENT LIFE

References

Blum, J. (2000) DC teachers accused of hitting students. *Washington Post*, A01.

Blum, J. and Lengel, A. (2001) D.C. student drank with her teacher, officials say. *Washington Post*, B01.

Carr, D. (2000) *Professionalism and Ethics in Teaching*. London: Routledge.

Fischer, L., Schimmel, D., and Kelly, C. (1999) *Teachers and the Law*. New York: Longman.

Gilligan, C. (1982) *In a Different Voice*. Cambridge, MA: Harvard University Press.

Gray, J. (2000) *Two Faces of Liberalism*. New York: The New Press.

Green, T. (1999) *Voices: The Educational Formation of Conscience*. South Bend, IN: University of Notre Dame Press.

Gutmann, A. (1987) *Democratic Education*. Princeton, NJ: Princeton University Press.

Kohlberg, L. (1981) *The Philosophy of Moral Development*. New York: Harper and Row.

Lengel, A. (2001) Student searches at jail stir anger. *Washington Post*, B07.

MacIntyre, A. (1981) *After Virtue*. Notre Dame, IN: University of Notre Dame Press.

Mathews, J. and Argetsinger, A. (2000) Cheating on rise along with testing. *Washington Post*, A01.

National Education Association (2001) *Code of Ethics of the Education Profession.* http://www.nea.org/aboutnea/code.html

Noddings, N. (1984) *Caring: A Feminine Approach to Ethics and Moral Education.* Berkeley: University of California Press.

Peters, R. (1966) *Ethics and Education.* Atlanta: Scott, Foresman and Company.

Rawls, J. (1993) *Political Liberalism.* New York: Columbia University Press.

Rosenblum, N. (1989) *Liberalism and the Moral Life.* Cambridge, MA: Harvard University Press.

Shulman, L. (1986) Those who understand: knowledge growth in teaching. *Educational Researcher,* 15(2), 4–14.

Snyder, D. (2001) Frederick teacher freed in porn case. *Washington Post,* B5.

Sockett, H. (1993) *The Moral Base for Teacher Professionalism.* New York: Teachers College Press.

Strike, K. A. (1990) Is teaching a profession: how would we know? *Journal of Personnel Evaluation in Education,* 4, 91–117.

Strike, K. A. (1993) Professionalism, democracy, and discursive communities: normative reflections on restructuring. *American Educational Research Journal,* 30(2), 255–75.

Strike, K. A. (1998) Freedom of conscience and illiberal socialization: the congruence argument. *Journal of Philosophy of Education,* 32(3), 345–60.

Strike, K. A. (1999) Justice, caring, and universality: in defense of moral pluralism. In M. Katz, N. Noddings, and K. Strike (eds), *Justice and Caring: The Search for Common Ground in Education.* New York: Teachers College Press, pp. 21–36.

Strike, K. A., Haller, E. J., and Soltis, J. (1988) *The Ethics of School Administration.* New York: Teachers College Press.

Strike, K. A. and Soltis, J. F. (1998) *The Ethics of Teaching,* 3rd edn. New York: Teachers College Press.

37

Inclusion and Justice in Special Education

Robert F. Ladenson

The Case of Beth B

Beth B is a child with Rett syndrome, a form of autistic disorder involving multiple severe disabilities in the areas of cognition, communication, and motor functioning. Beth's parents, her private therapists, and the staff of professional educators who work with her at school estimate her motor abilities lie within the range of five to seven months. As for Beth's cognitive and communicational abilities, she expresses interest in people, especially in their faces. She smiles and laughs, responds positively to music, and has definite likes and dislikes concerning food, which she expresses through eye gaze, bodily movements, and facial expressions. This is because Beth cannot speak, but instead communicates primarily through her eye gaze. For this reason, educational efforts to help her develop her communicational and cognitive abilities rely to a large extent upon computer-based assistive technology equipment which presents her with arrays of pictures on an adapted keyboard, among which she may focus her eye gaze to make a choice.

Several years ago Beth's parents strongly urged that Beth be placed in a regular education kindergarten classroom, with a one-on-one aide, adaptive physical education, and the related service of speech and language therapy. Their school district agreed, and Beth's regular education classroom placement continued through second grade. At the end of second grade, however, the school district indicated that, in the opinion of its professional educators who worked with Beth, her needs would be served better through placement in a special education classroom with a small number of other students, all having severe cognitive disabilities. Beth's parents strongly disagreed and requested a hearing on the matter, to which they were entitled under federal and state laws regarding special education. After a lengthy hearing, over many days, that included testimony from numerous individuals, including Beth's parents, teachers, and private therapists, as well as expert witnesses called by each side, the hearing officer issued an opinion upholding the position of the school district. Beth's parents appealed. Recently the hearing officer's decision was upheld in federal court.

I was the hearing officer in the Beth B case. As noted above, the case called for evaluation of extensive testimony and evidence. The legal issues presented by the case were far from easy to resolve. I am sure that, more than anyone else in the world, I do not want to readjudicate the Beth B case in an academic, rather than a legal, forum. In this chapter, however, I want to examine certain key aspects of the case, not from a legal standpoint, but instead from an ethical one. Through such an examination, I hope, we might begin to achieve a clearer and deeper sense of what justice means relative to a major issue in special education – inclusion in regular education classrooms of children with severe cognitive disabilities. Although I discuss questions related to the idea of justice in this chapter, rather than the disputed legal issues that figured in the Beth B case, I begin by summarizing some fundamental aspects of American special education law that define the context in which these questions arise.

The Individuals with Disabilities Education Act (IDEA)

In 1975 the US Congress enacted the *Individuals with Disabilities Education Act* (IDEA). Under the IDEA States receive financial support for special education programs on the condition that they make available to every student with special educational needs a "free appropriate public education," provided "to the maximum extent appropriate" in the "least restrictive environment" (1412(a)(1)(c)). The IDEA delineates extensive procedures that states accepting funds under the Act must assure are followed by school districts. In this regard, school districts must initiate "child find" efforts to identify every student among those they serve who may have special educational needs. Having identified such students, school districts must then decide in each case whether to conduct a full evaluation to determine a student's eligibility for services. In the case of the students who are evaluated and found eligible, school districts must provide individualized educational plans (IEPs), developed through conference meetings of teachers and school staff who will implement the student's program. Under the IDEA a student's parents must be invited to participate in the IEP conference meeting.

The IDEA also provides for a range of parents' rights with regard to the evaluation and IEP conference processes. The most important of these is that states accepting IDEA funds must set up a system that enables parents who dissent from the IEP conference recommendations to challenge those recommendations at a hearing (referred to in the IDEA as a "due process hearing") before an impartial hearing officer. The IDEA gives parents, and school districts as well, a right of appeal to federal or state court from a hearing officer's decisions.

The most critical issues with regard to interpreting the IDEA concern the following two questions. First, what does the word "appropriate" mean in the context of a special needs student's right to a "free appropriate public education"? Second, how should one understand the IDEA's requirement that children with special needs be educated "to the maximum extent appropriate" in the "least restrictive environment"? The first of these questions was clearly and directly addressed by the United States Supreme Court in the case of *Board of Education of the Hendrik Hudson School District* v. *Rowley* (458 US 176, 1982). The Supreme Court set out in this case a two-part test for whether a school district has provided a free appropriate public education for a special needs student. The first part of the test concerns whether a school district has complied with the procedural requirements of the IDEA. The second part involves the question of whether the student's program "provides personalized instruction with sufficient supportive services to permit the child to benefit educationally from that instruction" (p. 203). In an often quoted statement that summarizes this two-part test, the Court said in *Rowley*:

A court's inquiry in suits brought under the . . . [IDEA] is two fold. First, has the State complied with the procedures set forth in the Act? And second, is the individualized educational program developed through the Act's procedures reasonably calculated to enable the child to receive educational benefit? If these requirements are met, the State has complied with the obligations imposed by Congress and the Congress and courts can require no more. (pp. 206–7)

With regard to the question of what the phrase "educational benefit" means in the preceding statement, the Court said:

By passing the [IDEA], Congress sought primarily to make public education available to handicapped children. But in seeking to provide access to public education, Congress did not impose any greater substantive standard than would be necessary to make such access meaningful. Indeed, Congress expressly recognized that in many instances the process of providing special education and related services is not guaranteed to produce any particular outcome. Thus the intent of the [IDEA] was more to open the door of public education to handicapped children on appropriate terms than to guarantee any level of education once inside. (p. 192)

The Court considered, but expressly rejected, a more stringent view of a school district's legal obligation, under which an "appropriate" free public education would mean an education making it possible for a student with an educational disability to achieve the level of progress she could attain but for her disability (pp. 198–200). Rejecting this more stringent standard, it held that a school district need only provide an education from which the student derives "some benefit" that is "meaningful" to the extent of "[opening] the door of public education to handicapped children"(p.192).

As for the second of the preceding questions, concerning what the phrase "least restrictive environment" means, the IDEA expressly requires that "special classes, separate schooling, or other removal from the regular education environment occur only when the nature or severity of the disability of a child is such that education in a regular classroom with the use of supplementary aids and services cannot be achieved satisfactorily" (1412(a)(5)). A crucial question remains, however, of the proper legal standards to employ for resolving disagreements that may arise about whether education of a child with disabilities "cannot be achieved satisfactorily" in the regular education environment.

Although several circuits of the US Court of Appeals have addressed this question, the US Supreme Court has not done so. In cases presenting the issue of regular education classroom inclusion of a child with severe cognitive disabilities, however, the above question tends to merge with that of how to interpret the IDEA's guarantee of an "appropriate education" in the circumstances of the case. This is because parents in such a case argue invariably that, given the particular educational needs of their child, only full regular classroom inclusion will meet the standard of an appropriate education set out in *Rowley* by the US Supreme Court. The school district in such a case invariably argues a polar opposite position, with the result that conflicting evidence and testimony about what is educationally appropriate always looms large.

Justice and Community

As noted above, school districts in states that accept IDEA funding are required to provide a free appropriate public education for every child eligible to receive special education services. The consensus of judicial opinion holds, what seems evident to me given the IDEA's essential purpose, that school districts may not consider the issue of expense in deciding upon the *educationally* appropriate placement for a child. The judicial consensus, however, also holds that, in the case of a choice between several placements, each of which is educationally appropriate in legal terms – i.e. which meet the standard set by the US Supreme Court in *Rowley* – a school district may consider their respective costs as a legitimate factor of decision.

Questions of distributive justice thus can, and do, enter into educational placement decisions for children with severe cognitive disabilities. So long as the program options considered for a student are all "reasonably calculated" to provide educational benefit, then questions may arise concerning the allocation of resources to the student's program, in relation to other areas of expenditure in the school district's budget. It seems to me, nonetheless, that in some important disputes between parents and school districts over these matters, issues of distributive justice are interrelated, in ways that can be difficult to disentangle, with questions about how to interpret, from a moral standpoint, the idea of an educational community. The nature of such entanglement is brought out, I believe, by a closer look at some of the sources of contention in the Beth B. matter.

Beth's parents found much to criticize about the school district's inclusionary efforts on behalf of Beth. They contended that the manifold problems (from their perspective) in this regard stemmed largely from the school district's refusal to work with them in ways they considered meaningful, as well as to work cooperatively with diverse educational specialists whom Beth's parents had retained privately. These specialists, in the opinion of Beth's parents, could have provided valuable advice and information to the school district on a wide array of matters important to developing a successful inclusionary placement for Beth in a regular education classroom.

The school district, in turn, recounted at the due process hearing the extensive efforts that, in its opinion, it had undertaken to develop and implement a successful regular education classroom inclusionary program for Beth. Both administrators and teachers testified to, what they considered, frequent interactions with Beth's parents concerning diverse aspects of her program. The teachers and other school district staff members who worked with Beth testified in great depth concerning the specific reasons they believed that Beth had not benefited educationally despite these efforts, and why, in their judgment, she would benefit from placement in a special education classroom, with opportunities for partial mainstreaming.

Parents who are motivated to pursue such disagreements with their local school districts to the point of a due process hearing often believe that anything other than full inclusion amounts to exclusion of their children, and themselves, from membership in the educational communities centered in their schools. Consistent with this outlook, they believe also that membership in an educational community is not just a matter of the child's physical presence in a home school regular education classroom.

Instead, they say, it also requires that the community members – that is, the students, teachers, administrators, and other school staff – undergo a change of spirit. They believe that these diverse groups must come to view the child with severe cognitive disabilities as integral to the community – that is to say, following John Dewey's (1954) definition of a community, in the moral sense – as someone whose good both enhances and is enhanced by the good of the other community members.

The parents' opinion is, thus, that an appropriate educational program for a child with severe cognitive disabilities usually requires a radical change of spirit on the part of other members of the educational community. Such a change, they believe, must begin with teachers, administrators, and other school district staff members. In contrast, however, the school district, in the above kinds of controversies, contests vigorously the reasonableness of the parents' perspective that anything other than full regular educational classroom inclusion of a child with severe cognitive disabilities amounts to the exclusion of the child, and her family, from the educational community. To the contrary, in light of its educational efforts on behalf of the child, the school district regards itself as having treated the child, and her family, as full-fledged community members. From the school district's standpoint, the question of whether a child with severe cognitive disabilities should be placed in a regular education classroom presents educational issues, not issues concerning whether a child has, or has not, been denied educational community membership status.

Questions about what it means for a classroom, school, or school district to be an educational community, and about the place of children with severe cognitive disabilities within such a community, thus loom large in controversies presenting the kinds of issues that figured in the Beth B. matter. It seems to me as well, for reasons I try to develop in the next two sections of this chapter, that from a moral standpoint the idea of an educational community admits of at least two interpretations. The first interpretation, which I term the "ethics of inclusionary care," tends to support the position of parents who favor full regular classroom inclusion of a child with severe cognitive disabilities. In contrast, the second interpretation, which I call the "morality of equal educational concern," tends to support the school district's position.

The Ethics of Inclusionary Care

The outlook I have termed the ethics of inclusionary care involves a commingling of ideas drawn from educational theory and moral philosophy. I should acknowledge at the outset that, to my knowledge, it does not correspond exactly to the expressed positions of supporters of regular classroom inclusion of children with severe cognitive disabilities. Nor can I say, based upon my experience as a special education hearing officer, that this outlook often hovers implicitly in the background of arguments presented on behalf of parents by their attorneys in cases posing issues similar to those in the Beth B. matter. Nonetheless, it represents my best effort to articulate a morally (as distinct from legally) coherent position incorporating important elements of the moral viewpoint commonly held by supporters of regular classroom inclusion of children with severe cognitive disabilities.

The ethics of inclusionary care approaches the subject of special education programs for children with severe cognitive disabilities from the standpoint of a wider ethical outlook often referred to as the ethics of care, which has been articulated in diverse ways by many contemporary philosophers and educational theorists (see Gilligan, 1982; Noddings, 1984; Ruddick, 1989; Held, 1993). Proponents of the ethics of care tend to emphasize important and pervasive elements of a typical human life, such as the following. Under normal conditions, a human life proceeds through stages, from infancy to old age, characterized by varying degrees, and kinds, of dependence and independence. Furthermore, at any give time any human being may suffer tragic, catastrophic events or conditions that result in sudden and/or irreversible losses of independence in crucial areas of life. The ethics of care keeps these facts in the foreground, thereby accommodating one's sense that the moral concerns of most human beings revolve, to a large extent, around relationships in which care is given and received – care such as that bestowed in raising children, providing needed assistance to severely disabled relatives and friends, and caring for elderly parents. Much of the philosophical writing that explores various aspects of the ethics of care attempts to analyze how the notion of care compares and contrasts with other important moral concepts, especially justice, responsibility, and obligation (see Held, 1995).

The notion of *inclusionary* care relates the preceding points to the topic of special education programs for children with severe cognitive disabilities in the following ways. According to this notion, a strong presumption, from the standpoints of both morality and educational methodology, favors placement of children with severe cognitive disabilities in environments that provide opportunities for meaningful inclusion in the educational community centered on a particular classroom, school, or school district. It follows that children with severe cognitive disabilities belong in regular education classrooms, and may be justly removed from them only when clear and convincing evidence makes it apparent that they cannot learn at all in regular education classrooms, but, instead, require more restrictive placements to derive educational benefit. The ethics of inclusionary care thus calls for developing ways to implement the IEP goals and objectives of a child with severe cognitive disabilities in the context of the diverse classroom activities, both academic and non-academic, of the regular education students. Otherwise, although physically present in a regular education classroom, the disabled child will not receive the educational benefits of social development, cognitive stimulation, and reinforcement to expend communicative effort that come from membership in an educational community with non-disabled students (see Stainback and Stainback, 1992).

Numerous manuals, books, articles, and in-service workshops are available that provide suggested teaching approaches and materials to assist educators in their efforts to implement regular education classroom inclusion of children with severe cognitive disabilities (see, for example, Mastropieri and Scruggs, 2000; Sands et al., 2000; Stokes and Hornby, 2000). Under the IDEA, however, such efforts cannot be generic, but, instead, must address the individual needs of particular students. Accordingly, the ethics of inclusionary care calls for deep commitment on the part of teaching staff and school administrators to adapt the above kinds of resources to meet the specific educational needs of individual children.

One may refer to this deep commitment as the *spirit* of inclusionary care. In the opinion of those who advocate the ethics of inclusionary care, educational initiatives undertaken in this spirit would benefit students with severe cognitive disabilities and their non-disabled classmates alike. Indeed, they maintain that with intelligence, creativity, teamwork, and perseverance in almost every case inclusionary approaches can be developed that do not interfere with, but, to the contrary, enhance the education of non-disabled students (see Gartner and Lipsky, 2000; Giangreco et al., 2000; Thousand and Villa, 2000). While recognizing that in some cases problems for non-disabled students may arise from specific details of a full regular education inclusionary program, the advocates contend that educators should always proceed upon the premise that children with severe cognitive disabilities belong in the regular education classroom, and that such problems can be resolved to the satisfaction of everyone concerned if approached with the spirit of inclusionary care.

Many among the supporters of regular education classroom inclusion for children with severe cognitive disabilities would concur, I believe, that educational measures reflecting the spirit of inclusionary care can make apparent to non-disabled students a valid and important outlook that, unfortunately, often gets ignored. Such measures can teach, by example rather than exhortation, that children with severe cognitive disabilities ought to be considered integral members of the educational community centered on a classroom, school, or school district. More broadly, the advocates would say, these kinds of measures can impart through direct personal, face-to-face, contact between non-disabled students and their severely disabled peers a deep understanding, in terms of character formation, as well as intellectual awareness, of the following morally essential point. Despite their immense importance as human values, independence and productive ability are not the sole elements in a fully flourishing human life. Such a life can take place only within a caring community that values the flourishing of all, without qualifications based upon whether an individual can "live on his own." Adverting to a key idea of Plato's, those who support the ethics of inclusionary care would thus say that when a non-disabled student comes to understand, and to internalize, the above outlook, he benefits in the critical respect of becoming a morally better person.

Attitudes toward children with severe cognitive disabilities have undergone a major transformation since the early 1970s, when one could have described the prevailing outlook, with only a few exceptions, as "full exclusion," rather than even partial, let alone full, inclusion. This transformation is reflected poignantly in the following passage from an essay by philosopher Eva Feder Kittay, whose daughter, Sesha, now past thirty, has severe cognitive disabilities. In this passage Kittay describes how she reacted in 1970 when her mother, upon first becoming fully aware of the severity of Sesha's disabilities, insisted that Kittay place Sesha in an institution.

Of all the traumatic encounters in that first year and a half of Sesha's life, none, perhaps not even the realization that Sesha was retarded, was as painful as these words from the woman that I loved most in my life. The woman who had taught me what it was to be a mother, to love a child, to anticipate the joys of nursing, of holding, and caring for another, of sacrificing for a child. . . . In time, my mother allowed herself to love Sesha with the fullness of a grandmother's love. And in time I forgave my mother and came to appreciate how her intense, if misdirected, love for me fueled her stubborn insistence that we "put Sesha away." (Kittay, 1999, pp. 152–3)

531

The deep emotion, and firm moral convictions, underlying Eva Feder Kittay's choice in 1970 not to "put Sesha away" incipiently reflected the major transform-ation of social attitudes that has taken place during the past thirty years toward children with severe cognitive disabilities. In the *Republic* Plato appears to have considered killing such children as consistent with, if not required by, his understand-ing of the conception of justice as social harmony (460c). By 1970 society in the United States had come to acknowledge that, as with all other children, those with severe cognitive disabilities at least ought not to be killed. The prevailing view at that time, however, reflected in the widespread institutional practice of "warehousing," barely, if at all, went beyond such an acknowledgment.

The Individuals with Disabilities Education Act, passed in 1975, however, has shaped the provision of special education services in the United States in ways that give far reaching effect to the idea that society has significant responsibilities in connection with educating all children, including those with severely limited poten-tial for independent and productive lives. The ethics of inclusionary care seems to its supporters to follow naturally and inevitably, in terms of both moral sentiment and moral logic, from the major transformation of attitudes toward children with severe cognitive disabilities that has taken place over the past thirty years.

The Morality of Equal Educational Concern

The preceding section sets out, in summarized form, the reasons why supporters of the ethics of inclusionary care think it should guide decisions about the education of children with severe cognitive disabilities. Many would disagree, however, looking upon the ethics of inclusionary care not as the sole morally required outlook, but instead as one of several perspectives allowed by morality. Furthermore, I think that a large number of the individuals who hold this view would include among these morally allowed perspectives an outlook I term the morality of equal educational concern.

This outlook relates K-12 education to a broader ethical viewpoint with the following three ideas at its core: (1) there are universal human rights; (2) such rights apply equally to every human being; (3) the most important responsibility of a government is to uphold the human rights of each individual subject to its authority.

The morality of equal educational concern applies the above moral viewpoint to the circumstances of K-12 children in general, and to children with severe cognitive disabilities in particular, by proceeding from the premise of a universal human right to an education. Those who support the morality of equal educational concern might say in this regard that the idea of such a universal human right has philosophical grounding in diverse considerations related to personal development, growth, fulfill-ment, and fostering of essential capacities needed for democratic citizenship. Support-ers of the morality of equal educational concern would advert to a vast body of classical and contemporary philosophical works (see, for example, Dewey, 1916; Aristotle, 1953; Rawls, 1971; Gewirth, 1978, 1982; Mill, 1978; Kant, 1981; Dwor-kin, 1986, 2000; Gutmann, 1986; Aquinas, 2000).

The powerful strain of philosophical thought underlying the idea of a universal human right to an education reflects a comparably strong consensus of moral judgment throughout the world, expressed, for example, in Article 26 of the *United Nations Declaration of Human Rights*. Article 26 states:

Everyone has the right to an education. Education shall be free, at least in the elementary and fundamental stages....Education shall be directed to the full development of the human personality and the strengthening of respect for human rights and fundamental freedoms.

Widespread (although not unanimous) agreement thus exists, in terms of both philosophical reflection and moral judgment, upon the status of education as a universal human right. Nonetheless, it is immensely difficult to arrive at a consensus interpretation of this right, applicable to substantive issues of educational resource allocation in connection with non-disabled K-12 children. Difficulties become even greater upon widening one's focus to consider the allocation of educational resources to children with severe cognitive disabilities.

It seems to me, nonetheless, that the morality of equal educational concern can be interpreted as applying in a reasonably clear way to the circumstances of public school teachers and administrators addressing the educational needs of children with severe cognitive disabilities. First, as noted above, an educator whose outlook corresponds to the morality of equal educational concern would proceed from the premise that, despite its substantive complexities and difficulties, the idea of a right to an education applies to every child. This means, I believe, that such an educator would consider the sole morally and intellectually defensible minimal qualification for membership in the group of right holders who possess this right to be the capacity to benefit from educational services, including those services especially relevant to children with severe cognitive disabilities.

Second, an attitude of equal educational concern toward children with severe cognitive disabilities would involve careful adherence to rules and regulations of federal and state law intended to provide educational benefit for such children. Third, it would require an informed understanding of the historical background behind these laws and regulations; that is to say, of the widely prevalent absence of educational concern for children with severe cognitive disabilities that the IDEA aimed to rectify. Such an informed understanding is essential, in my opinion, so that teachers and school administrators keep in mind, even when they have to meet the law's requirements under tight fiscal and temporal constraints, the reasons why children with severe cognitive disabilities need not only special services, but also special legal protections. Fourth, and finally, an attitude of equal educational concern would involve complete open-mindedness about educational approaches that might benefit a child with severe cognitive disabilities, and unfailing readiness to work with the child's parents to develop and implement a successful educational placement.

An educator imbued with the attitude of equal educational concern would always be prepared to consider seriously supporting full regular education classroom inclusion as a placement for a student with severe cognitive disabilities. However, she also would have an open mind toward supporting other educational placement options. In this regard, one must keep in mind that from the standpoint of the morality of equal educational concern the issue would never reduce to a simple choice between full inclusion and full exclusion. Given the evident educational value of meaningful interaction with non-disabled peers – in terms of socialization, cognitive stimulation, and a severely disabled child's motivation to communicate – any placement considered would have to provide significant opportunities in this regard. Such opportunities could include, for example, mainstreaming for lunch, physical education, and other strategically selected classes, as well as regular interaction with non-disabled students through a voluntary "peer buddies" or student helper program. The goal, from the standpoint of the morality of equal educational concern, would be to arrive at a just *balance* between concern for the educational needs of disabled and non-disabled students. One might point out, in this connection, the significant danger that schools may disregard, or marginalize, the needs of disabled students. According to the morality of equal educational concern, however, the appropriate means for society to address this danger is through adoption of social policies and institutional practices, such as those delineated in the IDEA, and through fostering among educators the dispositions, noted above, that comprise the attitude of equal educational concern.

From the perspective of the ethics of inclusionary care, American society must put in place transformative measures which will help it become a genuinely caring community, in order to approach more closely a harmonious balance between the perspective of parents concerned about the well-being of their own children with special needs and the perspective of those answerable for the well-being of every member of an educational community. Full regular classroom inclusion of children with severe cognitive disabilities is critical, from this point of view, as a means of expanding the scope of non-disabled students' personal sense of communal affiliation with individuals in extreme and perpetual conditions of dependency. In contrast, supporters of the morality of equal educational concern might consider the notion of a community whose members share a strong personal sense of communal affiliation with severely disabled individuals as a moving and powerful ideal, yet not as morally fundamental from the standpoint of justice.

In this regard, the morality of equal educational concern draws heavily upon another moral conception, which Ronald Dworkin (1986, pp. 211–15) terms "community of principle." Under this conception, the shared attitude at the core of the *morally* significant idea of community, relevant to contemporary American society, consists of commitment to principles of equality governing the entitlements of individuals as holders of important rights. These include the fundamental rights guaranteed by the United States Constitution, but others as well, among which is the right to an education specified in Article 26 of the United Nations Declaration of Human Rights.

In a community of principle, justice as harmony, relative to the education of children with severe cognitive disabilities, may not be expressed directly in a strong personal sense of communal affiliation with such children, shared by all, or most, of the non-disabled members of the community. It would express itself, however, in broad support for social policies intended to reflect the principle of equal educational concern, applied specifically to children with disabilities. Such support, however, also would recognize the extent to which this principle is subject to differing interpretations. Accordingly, the members of a community of principle would also support the institutional practices set up to resolve and settle disagreements in this regard, and they would exemplify a readiness to listen to, and consider with an open mind, interpretations different from their own.

534

Constitutional Democratic Proceduralism

My accounts of the ethics of inclusionary care and the morality of equal educational concern have attempted to explain how the combination of moral perspective and outlook on educational theory comprising each view leads to significantly different, although not diametrically opposed, approaches to regular education classroom inclusion of children with severe cognitive disabilities. In this regard, as noted above, advocates of the morality of equal educational concern might view the ethics of inclusionary care as an inspiring ideal, but not as a morally required outlook from the standpoint of justice. Alternatively, supporters of the ethics of inclusionary care might look upon the morality of equal educational concern as not essentially immoral, but instead a kind of moral minimalism, nowhere near sufficient to understand the moral dimensions of an educational community, especially with regard to the inclusion of children with severe cognitive disabilities.

I have sought in the preceding discussion to convey, at least partially, both the moral force and the intellectual depth of both the ethics of inclusionary care and the morality of equal educational concern. In this regard, given the detail and sophistication with which both viewpoints can be articulated, each of them provides its proponents extensive conceptual resources for criticizing, and for responding to criticism, from the other viewpoint. It seems to me that academic debate and discussion in this regard has the potential to continue for a long time. The problem of developing a (morally) just conception of the place of children with severe cognitive disabilities within an educational community, however, is not just a matter for controversy among academics. It arises most importantly with respect to concrete issues concerning educational placements of actual students. How then should one approach the problem, given that the two ways of thinking about it that seem most morally and intellectually credible differ in significant respects?

The analysis and discussion developed in this chapter indicate, I think, that the problem at issue equates in large part with the following question. By what means can our society establish a framework of rules and procedures to facilitate arriving, in particular cases, at reasonable approximations to a just balance of the following four considerations?

1　Educational programs for children with severe cognitive disabilities should provide significant opportunities for them to interact with non-disabled students in order to promote their socialization, cognitive stimulation, and motivation to communicate.
2　Such programs should address the individual educational needs of severely disabled children, which requires, in turn, that teachers and school administrators foster informative and productive communication with the students' parents.
3　Inclusionary educational programs for children with severe cognitive disabilities must not unjustly limit provision of educational services for non-disabled students.
4　The meaning of justice in connection with 3 above relates to diverse interpretations of the idea of a classroom, a school, or a school district as an educational community, about which there is significant moral disagreement.

Development of a suitable framework of rules and procedures for balancing these considerations presents immense challenges. It requires that parties with significantly differing moral perspectives, on a matter of great importance to them, participate in a process calling for extensive debate and discussion, toward the end of discovering areas of convergence in their (highly divergent) perspectives, which could provide the basis for a working framework. Furthermore, given the importance of the matters at stake to the participants in the debate and discussion, as well as the extent of divergence in their moral perspectives, no framework arrived at could ever come close to satisfying everyone. For this reason, one needs to understand the processes through which harmony is sought among parties with deeply divergent perspectives as operating necessarily over the long run, and tending, at any given time, to achieve only partial success. Thus, one must also understand the parties to proceed upon the premise that even if the processes of debate and discussion of the terms of a framework result in a statutory enactment, any proposal considered and rejected, no matter how much at odds with the one ultimately enacted, may always be brought up again at a later time for reconsideration.

For a society to develop rules and procedures reasonably addressed to the task of arriving at a morally just balance among the aforementioned factors, its governmental practices thus must include two elements that are not easy to combine. The society must be able both to make and to implement decisions on various controversial matters. At the same time, however, it must not only allow, but also positively promote, debate and discussion on such matters, even in cases where the society has arrived at closure on them for the purposes of collective action, through legislative enactment. That is to say, the processes of debate and discussion must be ongoing (literally) and always regarded by those participating in them as capable of generating meaningful results.

It seems to me that, far more than in any other kind of government, constitutional democracy combines the above-described two elements. A constitutional democratic government, like any other, has its procedures of decision-making, and it requires strong deference to their outcomes on the part of everyone subject to the government's authority (see Soper, 1989). At the same time, however, a constitutional democracy contains elements which allow and encourage, to a much greater extent than in the case of any other kind of government, the processes of ongoing and meaningful discussion needed to harmonize the perspective of parents concerned about their own children with special needs and the perspective of those answerable for the well-being of every member of an educational community.

The essential elements in this regard concern three synergistically related areas: (a) practices involving exercises of communicational rights, such as freedom of speech, press, and assembly, which make possible debate and discussion whereby individuals and groups may express their viewpoints in regard to the necessity, desirability, or appropriateness of contemplated legislative enactments; (b) procedures of democratic decision-making, through which a constitutional democratic government can demonstrate meaningful responsiveness to the activities of the individuals and groups exercising their communicational rights; (c) judicial practices and procedures that make possible the challenging of interpretations adopted by government officials of enacted rules and regulations in specific cases, and which, in virtue of the principle of *stare decisis*, provide for debate and discussion to take place even *after* the enactment of a law, with tangible effects upon how the law will be applied in the future (see Ladenson and Malin, 1998).

I do not mean to portray constitutional democratic government as an absolute prerequisite for developing a framework of rules and procedures to determine educational programs for children with severe cognitive disabilities. Frameworks for this purpose could be devised under other governmental systems, which might even have certain important advantages, such as clarity, consistency, and efficiency of administration, over the kind of framework likely to emerge under constitutional democracy (e.g. the IDEA). It seems impossible to me, however, that such frameworks could address satisfactorily the problem of *justice* with regard to regular education classroom inclusion of children with severe cognitive disabilities, as I have posed it.

The problem in this connection relates to harmonizing significantly divergent interpretations of the idea of an educational community, and of the place within such a community of children with severe cognitive disabilities. For Plato, such harmonizing would require that someone invested with authority to govern transcend the realm of mere opinion and gain the knowledge which can ground a correct understanding of what makes a classroom, school, or school district an educational community in the sense, articulated by John Dewey, of an association in which the good of any student enhances and is enhanced by the good of all the others. Another viewpoint (maybe postmodernism in some of its forms) would reject the idea of knowledge in the realms of morality and educational theory as in the worst cases pure myth, embodied within an ideology propagated by the powerful in society to maintain their dominant position.

A third outlook – the one I hold – says that unless we assume the reality of knowledge, in connection with morality and educational theory, the entire enterprise of K-12 education lacks a coherent point. What exactly it means to speak of knowledge in these areas, however, is very hard to explain (at least I can't). Nonetheless, some points in this regard seem clear to me. Knowledge about morality and educational theory, whatever it may be (and I consider it to be something; that is, I believe it exists), is immensely difficult to obtain. For this reason, at any given time, understandings of what it means for a classroom, school, or school district to constitute an educational community can only be partial and highly subject to change. One has to assume, however, that in the long run, with great effort, and despite – or more accurately, in virtue of – countless disputes, such understanding tends to advance both morally and intellectually. In this regard, for the reasons developed above, the institutions and practices of constitutional democracy, whatever their shortcomings, seem indispensable to me.

Conclusion

I expressed a hope at the beginning of this chapter that the discussion to follow might contribute to a "clearer and deeper sense of what justice means relative to a major issue in special education – inclusion in regular education classrooms of children with severe cognitive disabilities." As the chapter now concludes, it is apparent that I have not attempted to advance a specific recommendation about the meaning of justice in this context. Given the complexity and depth of the issue, however, such a recommendation would have been a bold or, more accurately, a wrongheaded objective on my part. If this chapter has helped to clarify and deepen our understanding of what justice means in this context, it has done so in a more modest way, through developing the following point.

Regular education classroom inclusion of a child with severe cognitive disabilities can raise difficult problems regarding allocation of the classroom teacher's time between the needs of the disabled student and those of her non-disabled classmates. Such problems raise issues of distributive justice of a kind that are deeply interconnected with questions about what it means for a classroom, school, or school district to constitute an educational community, from a moral standpoint. The resolution of these issues is complicated by the fact that there is no universal and objective combination of regular education academic objectives, teaching methods, and learning environment that can serve as a standard for assessing the effects upon non-disabled students of including a child with severe cognitive disabilities in a regular education classroom. Schools can make a wide array of choices concerning the educational programs for non-disabled students, influenced by many different factors. As I have stressed throughout this chapter, one such factor, of special importance in my opinion, is an understanding of what it means for a classroom, school, or school district to be an educational community. The questions of justice at issue here thus call for interpretation of the idea of an educational community.

In this chapter I have described two such interpretations, which I term respectively the ethics of inclusionary care and the morality of equal educational concern. I have attempted to characterize each conception in a way that brings out its moral force and intellectual depth. My discussion, however, does not proceed to the point of considering the question whether one, or the other, or a particular synthesis of these conceptions most closely approximates justice relative to the inclusion of children with severe cognitive disabilities in regular education classrooms. This is not because of reluctance to reveal my opinion on this matter. In that regard, to borrow a frequently used phrase in due process hearings, I will affirm "for the record" the following attitude, on my part, which I think is already apparent. I feel strongly pulled, albeit in differing directions, by both the ethics of inclusionary care and the morality of equal educational concern, but do not, at this time, have a clear idea of how to reconcile them. Be that as it may, I believe also that from the perspective of society, in contrast to that of any given individual, the reconciliation of these viewpoints, to the extent possible, must come through the processes of discussion, debate, legislative decision-making, and judicial adjudication distinctive of constitutional democratic government.

See also 13 FEMINISM; 17 THE CAPACITY TO LEARN; 28 THE AUTHORITY AND RESPONSIBILITY TO EDUCATE; 31 CHILDREN'S RIGHTS; 33 EDUCATIONAL EQUALITY AND JUSTICE; 36 THE ETHICS OF TEACHING

References

Aquinas, St T. (2000) *Treatise on Law* (*Summa theologia*, Questions 90–108), ed. R. J. Regan. Indianapolis: Hackett.

Aristotle (1953) *Nicomachean Ethics*, ed. J. A. K. Thompson. Baltimore: Penguin.

Dewey, J. (1916) *Democracy and Education*. New York: Macmillan.

Dewey, J. (1954) *The Public and Its Problems*. Chicago: The Swallow Press.

Dworkin, R. (1986) *Law's Empire*. Cambridge, MA: Harvard University Press.

Dworkin, R. (2000) *Sovereign Virtue*. Cambridge, MA: Harvard University Press.

Gartner, A. and Lipsky, D. K. (2000) Inclusion and school restructuring: a new synergy. In R. A. Villa and J. S. Thousand (eds), *Restructuring for Caring and Effective Education*. Baltimore: Paul H. Brookes, pp. 38–55.

Gewirth, A. (1978) *Reason and Morality*. Chicago: University of Chicago Press.

Gewirth, A. (1982) *Human Rights*. Chicago: University of Chicago Press.

Giangreco, M. F., Cloninger, C. J., Dennis, R. E., and Edelman, S. W. (2000) Problem solving to facilitate inclusive education. In R. A. Villa and J. S. Thousand (eds), *Restructuring for Caring and Effective Education*. Baltimore: Paul H. Brookes, pp. 293–327.

Gilligan, C. (1982) *In a Different Voice*. Cambridge, MA: Harvard University Press.

Gutmann, A. (1986) *Democratic Education*. Princeton, NJ: Princeton University Press.

Held, V. (1993) *Feminist Morality: Transforming Culture, Society, and Politics*. Chicago: University of Chicago Press.

Held V. (ed.) (1995) *Justice and Care*. Boulder, CO: Westview Press.

Kant, I. (1981) *Grounding for the Metaphysics of Morals*, trans. J. W. Ellington. Indianapolis: Hackett.

Kittay, E. F. (1999) *Love's Labor*. New York: Routledge.

Ladenson, R. F. and Malin, M. H. (1998) On the scope of legitimate authority. *Journal of Social Philosophy*, 29, 59–73.

Mastropieri, M. A. and Scruggs, T. (2000) *The Inclusive Classroom: Strategies for Effective Inclusion*. Upper Saddle, NJ: Prentice Hall.

Mill, J. S. (1978) *On Liberty*, ed. E. Rapaport. Indianapolis: Hackett.

Noddings, N. (1984) *Caring: A Feminine Approach to Ethics and Moral Education*. Berkeley: University of California Press.

Plato (1992) *Republic*, trans. G. M. A. Grube. Indianapolis: Hackett.

Rawls, J. (1971) *A Theory of Justice*. Cambridge, MA: Harvard University Press.

Ruddick, S. (1989) *Maternal Thinking*. New York: Beacon Press.

Sands, D. J., Kozleski, B., and French, N. K. (2000) *Inclusive Education for the Twenty-first Century*. Belmont, CA: Wadsworth.

Soper, P. (1989) Legal theory and the claims of authority. *Philosophy and Public Affairs*, 18, 209–37.

Stainback, W. and Stainback S. (1992) Schools as inclusive communities. In W. Stainback and S. Stainback (eds), *Controversial Issues in Special Education: Divergent Perspectives*. Needham Heights, MA: Allyn and Bacon.

Stokes, R. and Hornby, G. (2000) *Meeting Special Needs in Mainstream Schools: A Practical Guide for Teachers*. London: David Fulton Publishers.

Thousand, J. S. and Villa, R. A. (2000) Collaborative teaching: a powerful tool in school restructuring. In J. S. Thousand and R. A. Villa (eds), *Restructuring for Caring and Effective Education*. Baltimore: Paul H. Brookes.

38

Sex Education

David Archard

Children and young persons ought at some stage and in some measure to know about sex. Everyone can perhaps accept that much as true. However, what will be disputed are the answers to the following questions. How much should they know? When should they know it? What exactly should they be taught? Who should teach them? Sex education is disputatious because sex itself has a great significance in our lives yet we disagree profoundly about the values that should inform our sexual conduct. We can recognize that we ought to teach sex while being deeply divided on the best way in which we should do so.

Should sex be taught in school? There are a number of reasons for thinking that it should. First, evidence suggests that parents support the teaching of sex education within school. Even though they may express concerns about the manner in which it is taught and may reserve the right to impart their own sexual values to their children, they tend generally to believe that, in the first instance at least, sex education should be a part of the curriculum. The following qualification needs to be made. Children themselves may want to be able to talk with their parents about sex, and any irremediable conflict between what children learn at school and what they learn at home is undesirable. It is in consequence important that any sex education should allow for the possibility of a partnership between the school and parents. Second, we should teach sex in schools because the default position is unacceptable. In the absence of any sex education within the school children will still learn about sex from a variety of other sources – their peers, their family, the media (television, film, newspapers, and magazines) and the Internet. These sources cannot be guaranteed to provide children with accurate or helpful information about sex. Third, the state can claim a legitimate interest in ensuring that its future citizens learn about sex in the right way. This is explained further below. Fourth, when sex education forms a part of the curriculum it can in principle be taught with an assured degree of consistency, accuracy, integrity, and pedagogical skill. This is not certain if sex is taught outside the school.

Why should we sexually educate the young? A sex education serves directly those who are taught but it may also promote certain social desiderata. To see this consider first what a sex education is. It teaches about sex but may comprise any of the following elements: the imparting of information – that is, facts about sexual orientation, health, reproduction, and forms of sexual activity – the transmission of relevant skills, the consideration of salient values and attitudes, and the development of individual character strengths, such as self-esteem and self-confidence in one's relations with others. Those who receive a sex education may benefit from acquiring the information they need to make their own choices and to avoid harms that would otherwise befall them. They may benefit from acquiring the confidence to express themselves sexually in ways that are true to their own natures. They may benefit from being able to enjoy themselves sexually and thus lead fuller, more contented lives. They may benefit from learning the values in conformity with which any properly regulated sexual activity should be conducted.

Society gains in the following way. There are costs to the individual – but also to the society to which they belong – which are attributable to poor and uninformed sexual choices. Let us call these the public health costs. Most notable are the costs of unwanted pregnancies and those of the contraction of sexually transmittable diseases. Early unwanted pregnancies have further costs. The children of teenage mothers are more likely to suffer ill health and the mothers themselves are more likely to remain unsupported and to endure a lower standard of living. If a sex education of the right kind reduces the incidence of these public health costs, then the state has a legitimate interest in ensuring that all receive the right kind of sex education.

However, no degree of agreement on the need for some form of sex education amounts to – nor can it deliver – agreement on what form that education should take. This is for the simple reason that we are divided profoundly in our sexual morality. The most salient dividing line is between those who subscribe to a "traditional" view of sex and those who favor a "liberal" view. This should not simply be taken as equivalent to a "religious" versus a "secular" outlook, although there is evident overlap. The defenders of a traditional view may appeal to reasons that are independent of religious doctrine, and religious believers may espouse liberal views of sex. Moreover, the two sides of the divide do not exhaustively capture the possible moral understandings of sex. Nevertheless, the divide provides a convenient means of orienting oneself and others with respect to sexual morality.

On the traditional view the sole permitted, and morally esteemed, form of sexual activity is heterosexual coitus between a married couple. On the liberal view whatever is freely and knowingly consented to by competent adults and does not harm third parties is morally permissible. Masturbation, consensual adult homosexuality, and extramarital sex of any kind are prohibited on the traditional view but permitted on the liberal view. Some parents will subscribe to the traditional view, others to the liberal view. However, it will matter greatly to both sets of parents what view of sexual morality their children acquire. This is not for the simple and obvious reason that any parent wants her child to have just those values that she happens to think true and warranted. It is because in the case of sex these are values by which a person lives a central part of her life. A child who leads her sexual life by values her parents think mistaken leads a life her parents are apt to regard as blighted and unworthy.

The division between traditional and liberal views on sexual morality is likely to be a broader one inasmuch as the two sides will also hold opposed views on matters distinct from but closely related to questions of sexual conduct strictly construed.

541

Such matters include gender roles and identities, the centrality of the family as an institution, the nature of childhood, and the appropriateness of state regulation of "private" behavior. Acknowledging this fact shows the real difficulty of securing acceptance of a general program of sex education. It also exposes the more general implications this division of moral views may have for the rest of the curriculum, especially that part of it which may teach civic values.

Why should the state in its provision of a public education that includes teaching about sex acknowledge the parent's wishes that her child be taught her sexual morality, whether this is traditional or liberal? Parents might claim that they have a right to have their children educated in just those values they themselves hold. This claim, of course, has implications beyond sex education. It is unpersuasive to the extent that, first, it is acknowledged that the state already concedes to parents the right to bring up their children as they choose, subject to basic constraints, and, second, that the state itself has legitimate ends which can only be served by the teaching of an agreed curriculum.

Independently of claims about parental rights the liberal state is enjoined to be neutral, in the sense of not presuming the superiority of any particular moral viewpoint, in its enactment of law and policies. We belong to morally plural societies whose members espouse different and frequently incompatible values. A government that favors one set of values over others does not treat its citizens as equals. Consequently, any sex education program informed by a set of moral views about sex that the child's parents cannot endorse violates the liberal principle of neutrality. More generally, such a program may be said to show a lack of respect for the individual or for the group or community to which the individual belongs. It does so to the extent that it repudiates or discounts or undermines those values which the individual and the community hold dear.

Arguably it is consistent with the principle of neutrality, and that of equal respect, if the government is able to give as its justification for the offending sex education program not that its underpinning morality is true but that the program serves certain social ends all can agree are advantageous. Imagine then that everyone concurs that public health costs should be reduced. Imagine further that a "liberal" sex education program – one which provides young people with the maximum amount of information about possible forms of sexual activity and which emphasizes the centrality of informed choice to a good and healthy sex life – reduces these public health costs. In such circumstances the parent subscribing to a "traditional" sexual morality is provided with a reason for having her child undergo a liberal sex education that does not show disrespect for her own moral views and which she can herself acknowledge.

The success of this strategy for gaining general approval for a sex education program in the face of disagreement about sexual morality depends, however, on it being demonstrable that the *prima facie* contestable program does indeed serve agreed ends. This may be unlikely. Traditionalists will most probably argue that a sex education program informed by traditional sexual values will just as effectively, or indeed more effectively, reduce the public health costs of unwanted pregnancies and transmitted sexual diseases. After all, it will be said, a traditional sexual morality celebrates the virtues of sexual abstinence before marriage. What better guarantee of not getting pregnant or of not contracting a sexually transmissible disease can there be than simply not having sex before it is proper to do so? Defenders of a "just say no" message, for instance, can claim that teaching young persons to say "no" to sex is all that is needed by way of a socially effective sex education program.

There is another way in which it might be thought that those with divergent sexual moralities could nevertheless agree on a sex education program with a substantive moral content. This is by means of what might be termed a "bootstrapping" strategy. Such a strategy works by asking individuals to consider the implications of the basic democratic values they all endorse as citizens. The principal values in question are those of equality and individual liberty. It might then be argued – and herein consists the "bootstrapping" – that what it should mean for citizens to be equal is that *inter alia* their sexual lifestyles are equally respected. What it means to grant a citizen liberty is among other things to protect her sexual choices, whatever they might be, so long as the choices of others are equally protected. It would then follow from the initial concession of basic and agreed democratic values that homosexuals, for instance, have as much right to make *their* sexual choices as heterosexuals have to make theirs. A sex education program should acknowledge as much.

However, traditionalists will resist such a bootstrapping strategy. They will argue that a principle of equal political liberties is perfectly consistent with public recognition of some sexual choices as immoral. The homosexual, for instance, is not discriminated against as a citizen if his homosexual activity is morally condemned, so long as he can vote and run for office, and receives the equal protection of the law. A sex education program teaching that homosexuality is morally reprehensible does not, in itself, violate the principle of political equality which assures the homosexual the same civic status as the heterosexual.

There is, then, on the face of it an intractable problem. All are agreed that there should be a sex education program. Sex should be taught in school. Yet there is widespread and ineliminable disagreement about what the content of that education should be, a disagreement which directly mirrors a substantive moral dispute about sex itself. Appeal to agreed social ends, served by a sex education program, or to basic democratic values, will not solve the problem. What then is to be done? There are three broad possibilities.

The first is that the content of any sex education program should be exclusively factual, restricted to the bare biological facts and stripped of any contestable moral claims. Children should merely be taught what sex and its reproductive function is. Such a compromise is unacceptable to all parties, however. In the first place an entirely factual description provides, for both the traditionalist and the liberal, a wholly inadequate characterization of sex. For the traditionalist, heterosexual married sex is, beyond the biological facts, an expression of marital love and a means to reproduction. For the liberal, consensual sex is, beyond the bare facts, a mode of self-expression, a valued form of pleasure, and the realization of a freely made choice.

At a minimum both the liberal and the traditionalist can agree that a proper understanding of sex sees it as necessarily set within a broader context – of relationships, commitments, and values. Consequently, neither the liberal nor the traditionalist will view an education in just the facts of sex as being in any way sufficient to

543

guide a young person in her life. Both believe that a young person must be in a position not just to know what sex is, but to understand and appreciate the significance of each and every possible sexual act.

Second, it will be a matter of moral dispute between the traditionalist and the liberal as to what facts the young person should be apprised of. For the traditionalist will believe that there are some things that simply should not be told, and that there are other things that should not be told without comment. The traditionalist will not want her children to learn about every possible form of sexual activity, and will also believe that some forms of sex are so evidently depraved that children must be made aware of their wrongfulness. As the traditionalist sees it the mere listing of forms of sex, and their exhaustive factual description, implies that all forms of sex are, in some sense, morally equivalent. To offer everything without moral comment is to suggest that none is better or worse than any other is. This is something that the traditionalist fundamentally disputes.

The second possible way in which a sex education program might secure general support against a background of moral disagreement about sex is by teaching only what can be agreed are basic moral values or by teaching about only those forms of sexual activity which everyone can agree are permissible. This option too is unacceptable. In the first place the range of sexual activities which all can agree are licit is small indeed. Moreover, the liberal will be unhappy with the exclusion of those forms of sexual activity which she believes are perfectly appropriate yet are stigmatized by being put beyond the educational pale. If heterosexuality is taught as acceptable, homosexuality in not being taught is by inference represented as unacceptable. This portrayal of homosexuality is something the liberal fundamentally disputes.

With regard to the possibility of teaching only basic moral values the problem is that even where such values can be agreed upon their application is the subject of controversy. One cannot teach, for instance, "respect for persons" without specifying what merits respect. The traditionalist and the liberal deeply disagree as to whether someone who engages in homosexual sexual activity should be respected for what she does. Again, one cannot simply teach "responsible sexual behavior" without broaching the question of what counts as "responsible." This is, of course, a matter of serious disagreement.

The third possible manner in which moral disagreement about sex might be negotiated within a single-sex education program is by providing children with factual information about sex but supplementing this with a clarification of the various possible ways in which the different forms of sex are viewed. This is a concession to the fact of moral pluralism. It teaches children that not only are there different forms of sexual activity but there are also different moral views in respect of this varied activity. Such an education might thus consist of a neutral description of a sexual practice conjoined with a review of the different moral judgments concerning the practice in question.

Even this concession to moral pluralism will not satisfy everyone. For a traditionalist, for instance, it may not be enough to tell her children that some believe homosexuality is an immoral perversion. What is needed, she thinks, is that her children are taught that it *is* an immoral perversion. Moreover, the traditionalist will object to the idea that her child should learn about some forms of sexual activity even if it is accompanied by information about the strong disapproval some feel for such activities. Her child, she will insist, just should not and need not know about such activities. Moreover, both the liberal and the traditionalist can agree that a refusal to valorize any form of sex or sexual relationship amounts to a representation of all of them as in some sense morally equivalent. Such a representation is unsatisfactory to both the liberal and the traditionalist.

Sex education remains a battleground on which different approaches to sexual morality are contested. None of the suggested solutions to the problem will be satisfactory to all parties. There are also further issues that need to be addressed. The first is the proper mode of teaching about sex. An orthodox pedagogical style whereby information is straightforwardly imparted seems inappropriate in this context. After all, sex is not simply a matter of acquiring a store of knowledge or a cognitive capacity. Sex is something we do and something we engage in with other people. Thus a sex education must teach young persons so that they are able confidently and comfortably to act in the world on their own understanding of what matters to them. Interactive and participatory methods seem in consequence best suited to sex education.

A further issue is how one might practically accommodate the wishes of parents and communities about what their children are taught. Such wishes are likely, in the case of sex education, to be especially strongly felt. Moreover, as emphasized above, it is important to preserve the possibility of a partnership between parents and schools. One can envisage here a variety of appropriate practices. Parents may be properly consulted about the sex education program a school is using – the materials employed, the pedagogic mode, its role within the curriculum as a whole – and given an opportunity to propose changes or even to veto what is found utterly unacceptable. Where it is a question of religious views, especially if it is the religion of a well defined community, then it may be proper and helpful to allow a religious representative to make the children fully aware of that religion's views on sex. All of these practical concessions to the sensitivities of particular parental viewpoints may nevertheless be within the constraints of an insistence upon a basic, common curriculum, including sex education, that must be taught in *all* schools.

A further issue concerns the appropriateness of any sex education program for the age of those who are taught. Here the liberal and traditionalist may be divided further. For the traditionalist is likely to think that teaching children about sex too soon is not just pedagogically mistaken but corrupting of their childhood. The claim of corruption should be understood as in fact comprising three distinct claims. The first claim involves the view that learning about a subject serves to erode the capacity to make correct or sensible moral judgments in its domain. Learning about sex too early makes children incapable of subsequently exercising proper sexual judgment. The second claim of corruption involves the view that teaching children about some activity is tantamount to encouraging those taught to engage in that activity, or at least it conduces those taught about the activity to engage in it. A sex education leads children to be prematurely or promiscuously sexually active. The third claim of corruption involves the view that childhood is a time of innocence. To teach children about sex too early is to deprive children of their innocence, and thus their childhood, prematurely.

DAVID ARCHARD

These corruption claims are important and exercise considerable influence in the debate about sex education. A full and balanced evaluation of these claims would need to take account of both empirical and moral considerations. Thus, for example, comparative studies might reveal whether children are more or less likely to engage in sexual activity when they receive a sex education at a certain age. One would also need to consider to what extent any such sexual activity has certain outcomes, such as unwanted pregnancies or the contraction of sexually transmitted diseases. An evaluation of the corruption claims must address the understanding of childhood presupposed. For instance, what is characterized by some as a joyful innocence others may pejoratively view as a state of ignorance which only serves to sustain dependence and vulnerability. Finally, it needs to be determined whether sex is so essentially different from other subjects that may be taught. Is it, for instance, only the teaching of sex that disposes those taught to judge thoughtlessly and behave promiscuously? Or is this also true of other subjects? And if it is only true of sex why might this be so?

The final issues concern the context within which any sex education program is taught. There is a broad and a narrow social context. The broad social context is the way in which within a culture – the media especially – sex and sexuality are represented. We in the West now live within a highly sexualized culture in which representations of sex figure large. An important message conveyed by this culture is that sex is an important, indeed central, part of our lives and our identities. Such a "sexualization" of our culture may be regrettable but it is probably not reversable. Any desire to return to a more innocent, modest, decorous, and less explicit time should be tempered by the knowledge that such innocence was associated with sexual prejudice, repression, exclusion, and injustice. Nevertheless, if we do now seemingly talk about little else but sex we ought to be aware that a sex education program cannot ignore this context. Nor, importantly, can it go against the grain of our sexualized culture. This means that we cannot hope by education alone to put what some view as the genie back in the bottle. It also means that we should beware of giving mixed and confusing messages to children, telling them one thing at school and quite another in our magazines, films, advertisements, and television programs.

The narrow social context for any sex education program is the provision of ancillary facilities, such as family planning clinics, counselling services, help centers, and so on. It is, for instance, counterproductive to teach children about safe sexual practices if they cannot gain access to further extracurricular advice and material relating to contraception. The provision of such facilities is not, strictly speaking, an educational matter, but no sensible and practicable sex educational policy can be devised without an eye to this particular social context.

The issues considered above show how complex are the implications for sex education of the basic divisions in respect of sexual morality. These divisions are unlikely to disappear and any sex education program must negotiate rather than ignore them. The background fact of moral pluralism is not unique to sex education. But perhaps sex education does display this fact in a particularly dramatic fashion.

See also 13 FEMINISM; 22 MORAL EDUCATION; 28 THE AUTHORITY AND RESPONSIBILITY TO EDUCATE; 36 THE ETHICS OF TEACHING

Further reading

Philosophical analyses of sex can be found in:

Archard, D. (1998) *Sexual Consent*. Boulder, CO: Westview Press.
Belliotti, R. (1993) *Good Sex: Perspectives on Sexual Ethics*. Lawrence: University Press of Kansas.
Primoratz, I. (1999) *Ethics and Sex*. London: Routledge.
Soble, A. (ed.) (1980) *Philosophy of Sex: Contemporary Readings*. Totowa, NJ: Rowman and Littlefield.

Philosophical discussions of sex education can be found in:

Archard, D. (1998) How should we teach sex? *Journal of Philosophy of Education*, 32(3), 437–49.
Archard, D. (2000) *Sex Education*, Impact No. 7. London: Philosophy of Education Society of Great Britain.
Reiss, M. (guest ed.) (1997) Moral values and sex education. *Journal of Moral Education*, 26(3), special issue.
Reiss, M. and Mabud, S. A. (eds) (1998) *Sex Education and Religion*. Cambridge: The Islamic Academy.
van Wyk, R. N. (1993) Sex education, the family, the state, and political theory. In D. T. Meyers, K. Kipnis, and C. F. Murphy Jr (eds), *Kindred Matters: Rethinking the Philosophy of the Family*. Ithaca, NY: Cornell University Press, pp. 194–208.
White, P. (1991) Parents' rights, homosexuality, and education. *British Journal of Educational Studies*, 39(4), 398–408.

Part IV

HIGHER EDUCATION

39

Ethics and the Aims of American Higher Education

Minda Rae Amiran

College admissions brochures are eloquent testimony to the endurance of Plato's educational ideals. In his dialogues and through the figure of Socrates himself, Plato shows education molding citizens of the polity, leading students to pursue truth and justice, the Idea of the Good, preparing them for an examined life. In that educational world, the teacher-philosopher turns his students toward the light to see for themselves, pushes them to discover what they already know, and goads them to question received ideas. There is no campus and no administration: just somewhere with Socrates and one or more of his young men. Of course, Plato saw Socrates' students as future leaders, the guardians and the supreme rulers of the *polis*, a select few: in our time we see a need for a much larger educated public. So, in our homespun way, we transmute Socrates and the well born Glaucon in Piraeus into a respected teacher "at one end of a log" and an ordinary student at the other, but we keep Socrates' goals. Thus admissions brochures talk about faculty availability and concern for individual students, and speak of their students' developing "critical thinking" and a desire for life-long learning. There is usually something on providing a "rounded" education, usually something on preparing future leaders and citizens of a democracy in a changing world. The accompanying pictures show a teacher at the blackboard with a small group of students standing by, a teacher bending over a student at her microscope, maybe even a small class meeting outdoors. Vocational schools and certificate programs in community colleges or on the web may not present themselves in this manner, but it seems safe to say that most two-and four-year colleges and universities do. Moreover, research on teaching suggests that most faculty believe in the Socratic aims. (In what follows, I use the terms "institutions of higher education," "academy," "university," "college," and sometimes "school," interchangeably, from concern for the reader's ear. My discussion does not apply to narrowly vocational institutions such as secretarial schools, nor to programs that offer certificates in fields such as computer languages, small engine repair, or culinary arts. Nor, alas, to for-profit school.)

The academy, then, as it most often presents itself, aims to foster free and open inquiry guided by Socrates' values, or the values of free speech and action enshrined in the American Constitution, or broadly religious values of responsibility for ethical choices. It would thus act as an ethical agent for its students, helping them examine themselves and their place in the world, helping them develop their powers of reasoning and acting through intellectual discipline and self-government, getting them to question their society and its values independently – or even "subversively." On this view, undergraduates are future informed and active citizens of our democracy and graduate students are, additionally, future contributors to the fund of human knowledge, agents, it may be, of social improvement as physicians, teachers, city planners, judges, field biologists, psychologists. For faculty, the academy would also be an ethical agent, protecting a space for free inquiry, free research, in a self-governing, cooperative community of scholar-teachers. Through the actions and scholarship of its alumni and through the fruits of its faculty research and thought, the academy would thus also enlighten, shape, help transform the culture at large. Or so we say, and often profoundly believe, and so act.

However, it is not news that this view of the university's role is threatened today by the academy's economic problems – in fact, by its political–economic position in our late-capitalist global-economic society. This society, though its leaders are themselves college graduates, tends to see the nation's institutions of higher education as servants of the economy, as, for example, in *A Nation at Risk* (1983), a report by the US National Commission on Excellence in Education that accuses American colleges of producing inadequate employees. (College are factories with student products.) And this is not all: the academy is also under attack for inefficiency and lack of faculty productivity in numbers of students taught. (An unprofitable factory.) The colleges themselves have long operated like businesses, competing quite consciously for economic means, as Sheila Slaughter and Larry L. Leslie so thoroughly document in *Academic Capitalism* (1997). In our global marketplace, under conditions of sharply decreased public funding for higher education, colleges aim to retain or increase their viability by competing for money, students, and professorial "stars." The students bring the college their tuition payments or proportional (if reduced) public funding; the star professors attract more students, especially graduate students who pay more tuition or teach undergraduates for a pittance. Faculty stars also win more research or project grants from public or private sources, competing against peers at other universities. Colleges mount intensive efforts to lobby legislatures for funds, often competing with other colleges in their state. They engage sizeable officefuls of "development" personnel, where "development" means getting money from alumni, businesses, or foundations. In this connection, and with legislatures as well, colleges often compete with other cultural institutions – theaters, museums, libraries, orchestras, research hospitals. They also compete with businesses that train their employees through extensive classes at work or on the web. For the college as economic agent, undergraduates are future employees and graduate students cheap labor and future experts, and within the academy the community of scholars becomes a small jungle of programs, departments, schools, and institutes competing with one another for students and for funds from college administrators, outside grantors, and business partners.

It is usual to argue that we cannot close our eyes to reality, that to serve the Socratic ideals, to function as an ethical force in society, the university must maintain itself by canny behavior in the marketplace. Indeed, it is hard to fault an institution for seeking the funds it needs to survive. However, as I hope to show, in day-to-day campus decisions, decisions involving ethical, political, and social values, one rarely can serve both masters equally, the academic and the economic, much less make the market serve Socrates. And these everyday decisions, ordinary though they may be, are far from trivial. They involve the very questions philosophers have been asking about education throughout the centuries. In her essay "The Ruling History of Education" (1998, pp. 1–2), Amelie Oksenberg Rorty names these perennials: "What are the proper aims of education? ... Who should bear the primary responsibility for formulating educational policy? ... Who should be educated? ... What interests should guide the choice of a curriculum? ... How should the intellectual, spiritual, civic and moral, artistic, physical and technical dimensions of education be related to one another?" It may seem that these questions are quite distant from some of the smaller issues claiming attention in our time – accusations of "grade inflation" in higher education, for instance. Yet a moment's thought will show that almost every issue leads directly to the choice between Plato and Darwin. Thus while grade inflation has been blamed on our cultural coddling of layabout student narcissists, the argument from culture misses an important point. If a large number of students fail, the funding that depends on enrollment falls and colleges have to spend more of their decreased funds on recruitment. When students must maintain a C average for financial aid, "C" becomes the lowest passing mark, and teachers who give even "too many" C-minuses may be warned. So grades may rise ("inflation" is a telling term) in no necessary relation to the student's development or the professed aims of education. One for Darwin.

Of course, for a Marxist, the academy has always been an economic actor with intellectual illusions. In a capitalist economy, it is the servant of capitalist power and not its questioner, producing concepts to justify existing social relations. This is true even when the academy is not engaged in entrepreneurial behavior, even when it follows its Platonic ideals. A place that encourages free inquiry serves as a useful vent or distraction for the capitalist system, with the added benefit that it sometimes produces marketable goods. So capitalists support their alma maters or any handy college. If capitalism had not inherited the university it would have had to invent it. This view, most recently evident in certain attacks on academic postmodernism, is not the premise of this chapter. If it were true, there would be only an illusion of choice, an illusion of ethical issues. Daily experience in the academy shows otherwise, that decisions do change a state of affairs: they can be made this way or that, they lead to different outcomes for real people, including the Marxist social critics themselves, and make palpable differences in national as well as campus life. If this were not so (*pace* ontological issues), it would be pointless to discuss ethical problems in higher education.

What, then, are some of the problems that arise in the tension between the economic and ethical functions or aims of higher education? I begin with students, with Rorty's perennial "who should be educated?" Our professed national answer today is that any American high school graduate who so wishes should have access to higher education, and this answer is backed by government grants and loans for tuition and by support for open-admission community colleges. The principle draws upon the egalitarian values to which Americans at least pay lip service, but there are many problems with putting it into practice. One of these problems is the allocation of

553

students to colleges. Generally speaking, more selective colleges take the most promising students further in developing their abilities and acquiring knowledge than open admissions colleges would, for the selective colleges are better provided with means for learning. Now, these more selective colleges, whether public or private, actually compete with one another for better prepared students, and put resources into scholarships to attract them. And while some of these (even middle-class) students need the money to attend, others do not. Having "merit-based" scholarships sounds like an egalitarian idea, but in practice it most often favors the well-to-do. Partly, this is a result of the correlation in our society between superior attainments and socio-economic status. But colleges worsen the inequity by using the very money that might give promising working-class students a better education to attract bright wealthy students instead, students who would get that education anyway.

The desire for better students is justifiable. Research has shown that students learn a great deal from one another. There is a legitimate claim that one way to provide a fine education is to bring good student minds together, though, sadly, at present this translates into gathering students of higher socio-economic status (Gamson, 1993). Certainly teachers can go father and come closer to realizing their aims for education when such students are plentiful in their classes. So merit scholarships do promote the Platonic ideal, if one ignores the problem of justice. On the other hand, colleges whose entering students have high SAT scores – scores that correlate well with being white and affluent, though not very well with success in college – have "bragging rights" that attract more and better prepared students. Affluent students have affluent parents who contribute to the college, and they tend to become affluent alumni. Moreover, such students are more likely to stay in college and graduate in four or five years, and "retention" and graduation rates count among the measures that qualify state colleges for competitive funding awards. One might argue, then, that merit scholarships benefit everyone: the students get a better education, the faculty are better satisfied, and the college increases its resources – Plato and Darwin dancing together. Except that the valedictorian of an impovershed rural or a chaotic inner-city school may have lost her chance for a liberating education that espouses Socratic ideals, and all because of intercollege competition, the decisions of "enrollment managers." Possibly worse yet, in the competition for well-to-do students, some colleges have chosen to supplement merit scholarships with luxurious residence halls, riding stables, and other country-club attractions, using funds that might otherwise have gone to need-based scholarships or served other educational ends. College attendance rates of high school graduates are 32 percent lower for the least wealthy 25 percent of students (Lauter, 1995, p. 80). Even if my valedictorian attends a community college, as many low-income students do, it may greatly limit her choices, and she may have no access to Internet courses, or be unable to learn in that solitary mode.

A second set of ethical problems arises in connection with faculty recruitment and rewards: what qualities distinguish a professor who furthers the aims of higher education? On the Socratic model, this person should first be a teacher who inspires students to learn and think for themselves, and then a scholar who eagerly pursues knowledge, enriching his teaching and perhaps also making discoveries that benefit the society at large. Since educational research has shown that learning proceeds best in small classes, a college should aim to minimize its student/faculty ratio, hiring as many well qualified teachers as its means allow. Anyone familiar with recruitment and tenure procedures at any kind of college knows how far this picture is from reality. Often it is not the candidate's ability to open minds that counts in decisions on promotion, tenure, and merit awards, but her ability to open corporate or foundation purses, or failing that, at least her ability to publish papers that carry the college's name abroad. In decisions on hiring, any college that can afford it is likely to enter the race for academic stars, who command large salaries and often expensive equipment, and then to assign the star almost no teaching duties, so that he can devote his time to "high-profile" research, often commercial, "strategic," or "targeted" for corporate sponsors.

But I am oversimplifying: it is not easy to disentangle Socratic and economic aims here. A famous scholar may attract better graduate students and better junior faculty, even if he teaches very little, so both graduate students and undergraduates may benefit. Moreover, the grant-getter's department may be able to acquire valuable new equipment and support more graduate students as a result of his grants. Also, grant-getting much-published faculty may be ardent teachers as well. On the other hand, hiring two good faculty instead of the one famous scholar may result in smaller classes and better learning, and surveys have shown that most faculty are happiest teaching. Experience suggests that many very good teachers in certain fields publish little, though they read immensely. And most scholars prefer basic, curiosity-driven research (Slaughter and Leslie, 1997, p. 235), which is often less fundable and takes years to bring to publication. The Socratic aims of the college – but not its economic well-being – are less fulfilled when it denies such teacher/scholars tenure. One would think undergraduates would leave universities where they sit in huge classes and are graded by overworked teaching assistants, and of course some do, but if the school is prestigious enough through its stars and graduates, the value of its degree in the labor market keeps students there: no loss of tuition reduces its income from applied research, industrial partnerships, grant-getting, and the other enterprises Slaughter and Leslie describe.

Syracuse University has recently struggled with these issues in notable ways. Faced with falling enrollments and reduced revenues, in 1989 its faculty and administrators looked at the tension between its commitments to research and to students, and decided to become a "student-centered research university" (Wright, 2001, p. 39). Faculty not happy with this decision retired or left, tenure criteria were altered, resources were directed in accordance with the redefined aim, and the college won the prestigious Hesburgh Award for its balance between teaching and research. Enrollment and retention increased (and admissions became more selective) and revenues recovered. But in 2001 the new vice-chancellor and provost called for a change of direction again, noting that externally sponsored research had not increased over the past ten years, and calling for more "productivity" while pledging to maintain the campus concern for students. It is hard to serve both aims at once.

This problem of conflicting aims affects two groups of people in worrying ways: when economic aims lead, part-time temporary faculty ("adjuncts") are denied the rightful fruits of their labor and graduate students are both overworked and acculturated to an economic idea of their aims. A campus totally devoted to learning might well still hire adjuncts for specialized subjects like harp or international shipping law, and would pay the musician or lawyer well. But most colleges today hire adjuncts in subjects like freshman writing and mathematics, formerly taught by regular faculty. Paying small stipends by the course, with no benefits, they can cut faculty positions or hold them steady while "serving" more students. The adjuncts, often PhD graduates, and at present more than a third of all faculty, must forgo their own studies and teach five or six courses a semester to survive (often commuting between colleges) because the regular faculty positions for which they qualify have been eliminated. The plight of these wage-slaves, mostly in the humanities, is well known (Kean, 1994); many of them finally leave the profession, but there is always a new supply. Yet graduate programs continue to persuade their students toward the life of a publishing star, urging them not to apply for jobs that require more than two courses a semester. So the academy "produces" faculty that will perpetuate its economic strategies. Meanwhile, of course, it pays its graduate students relatively little for the number of undergraduates it asks them to teach and fights their efforts to unionize. It also continues, by and large, to maintain the size of its graduate programs, at least through the master's level, because it needs large numbers of teaching assistants to substitute for higher-paid faculty. Although the initial impetus for employing more adjuncts and maintaining the size of graduate programs was rising costs and declining public support for higher education, somewhat better times have not resulted in more regular faculty posts, as funds released from salaries are used for other ends. The educational, ethical decisions here have economic constraints, but they are also made with some degree of freedom, as Syracuse shows.

The tension between Socratic and economic aims of the academy has been evident also in a third set of issues, answers to the perennial question: "what interests should guide the choice of a curriculum?" Plato has Socrates argue for mathematics, music, astronomy, selective studies in literature, and, above all, philosophy as essential to the education of wise, civic-minded leaders. These same liberal arts and sciences, with due additions, were long the cornerstone of American higher education, though the land-grant colleges were created to offer programs in agriculture and engineering as well. The liberal arts tradition is still maintained at certain private highly selective four-year colleges. However, despite some evidence to the contrary, in general, economic considerations seem to have led universities to "starve" many of their liberal arts programs in favor of those that easily attract outside funding or those that attract students with the promise of immediate, well defined jobs. To some extent, the academy has been helpless here: the enormous cost of advanced laboratory equipment and the higher salaries available in the marketplace to scientists, computer scientists, and people with advanced degrees in engineering, accounting, and finance have meant that academic programs in these fields demand proportionally more of a college's finite resources, leaving less for programs in the humanities and social sciences. While some advanced institutes support themselves with grants most of the time, ordinary undergraduate programs in expensive fields are far from doing so. Of course, a college could decide not to offer business, accounting, and other professional programs that are relatively new to higher education, but most could scarcely afford the consequent loss of students, who have been led to view college as preparation for specific jobs. In fact, many colleges have been so eager to attract more students that they have offered undergraduate professional programs in fields such as social work and law, where jobs require graduate degrees, even though the graduate schools prefer their students to have majored in one of the liberal arts. Moreover, programs in certain liberal arts subjects, such as art, music, and theater, have become so professionalized that students in these fields barely meet the special reduced general education requirements that apply to them. The same is true for students in many undergraduate programs in education, engineering, certain specialities in the sciences, and allied medical professions. Thus the humanities and social sciences and any conceivable vision of an integrated world of knowledge are further starved.

Here the competition among internal units on campus becomes fierce. Without student "traffic," departments will not be allowed to replace faculty, much less expand, and in fields where outside funding for programs is scant, departments depend almost entirely on internal funds, though these often follow students at a lower rate in their fields. There is a great temptation to offer "gut" courses or meritricious topics that, it is hoped, will fill large lecture halls at minimal department expense, and to place these courses in the general education program, where they will get the most "play." Moreover, departments are under pressure to accept transfer credits from "feeder" two-year schools in lieu of general education courses, even when the courses scarcely qualify for the name ("Personal Finances" and the like). If the transferring students' credits are not accepted, the students may go elsewhere, and in many colleges, undergraduate transfer students constitute at least 40 percent of the graduating class. So liberal education is diluted from within.

Competition for students and for permission to fill faculty vacancies greatly increased pressure on junior faculty to publish and win grants, lest they be refused tenure, their places be reallocated, and programs be cut – all these have disastrous results for the campus community of scholars. People have no time or mind to meet people in other departments collegially, no time to serve in faculty governance, no time to consider general education or the curricular mix of the campus at large, little time to counsel students or mentor their organizations. Administrators have stepped into the breach: their ranks have increased nationwide in great disproportion to increases in students and faculty. While state and agency requirements for reporting and assessment ("accountability") have demanded some of this increase, much of it is related to "management" of curriculum, enrollment, faculty, "student affairs," and "development." And, of course, a larger administration means a smaller proportion of the college's budget can go to learning or be available to support newly marginalized liberal arts. The increasingly business-like approach of administrators, moreover, alienates faculty into further withdrawal. The answer to the question of what interests should guide a curriculum have been complex and varied, but decisions have tended to be market-driven, to the detriment of the liberal arts and a learning community among scholars. Tellingly, an earnest defender of higher education rests his case on market factors alone: "higher education is an investment in economic development – an investment which promotes better jobs and living standards for all" (Benjamin, 1995, p. 71).

This discussion has been proceeding as if all institutions of higher education were of one kind, with vocational exceptions. But higher education is sharply segmented, not so much into private and publicly funded schools as into the Carnegie classifications: roughly, research universities, doctoral-granting universities, comprehensive colleges, four-year liberal arts colleges, and two-year community colleges. The difference between research and doctoral universities is a difference in number of PhDs awarded each year and, until very recently, in federal research dollars per faculty member. Comprehensive colleges offer the master's degree in various fields and have many professional programs, typically in education and business. Although what has been said so far applies in varying degrees to all, the rivalry among them is a source of further ethical dilemmas.

In theory, each kind of institution is guided by a somewhat different set of educational aims: research and scholarship weigh heavily in the first two, undergraduate student education in the last three. However, in practice the five categories form a hierarchy in prestige, as research trumps teaching, and each of the lower three tries, in its own way, to resemble the "top." Thus, though community college faculty usually teach five courses a semester, on the ground that they are not required to be scholars, and though few of them hold doctoral degrees, because the colleges shun PhD salaries, still, publications and grants, limited though they be, "count" when administrators want to replace faculty with adjuncts, especially as the community colleges compete more fiercely with nearby comprehensive colleges for students. The teaching colleges, for their part, compete for students and faculty with the universities, and to rise in attractive prestige, try to be more like them. Faculty in these colleges regularly teach six to eight courses a year, usually without graduate student help, yet they are increasingly being required to publish and win grants nearly as much as their university peers, despite the disparity in laboratory and library facilities, let alone time. Class sizes also approach the university model, except in the richest schools, to the detriment of most teaching goals. And like universities, and for the same reasons, even public comprehensive colleges now offer merit scholarships. Why the comprehensive college aim of teaching undergraduates (usually less affluent), by faculty who keep abreast of their fields even when they publish less, should be less prestigious and hence less well funded than the aims of research universities is hard to understand on ethical grounds alone.

An interesting example of the ways issues of prestige and curriculum interact comes from the Phi Beta Kappa Society. Membership in this most prestigious of honor societies is awarded to outstanding students in liberal arts curricula, and the society actively promotes the liberal arts and sciences. But since the criteria for acquiring a campus chapter include number of Phi Beta Kappa faculty and proportion of degrees granted in the liberal arts, comprehensive colleges fail to qualify (and faculty taught in them fail to qualify the colleges where they teach). So an outside force that might encourage a more liberal mix of curricular offerings is absent exactly where it is most needed, and the prestige wars that favor universities (and highly selective four-year colleges) receive further fuel, little though it be.

The picture I have been painting shows economic concerns winning over the educative concerns or purposes of higher education at every turn, with consequences that are unfair, unethical, for students, faculty, and the community alike. It may be argued that the political-economic state of our society gives the academy no choice, and, moreover, that American culture is endemically anti-intellectual; certainly the academy is under great economic constraint, when it is not fighting for its very life (over the past few decades several hundred mostly small private colleges have disappeared). It is important to emphasize, however, that our bleak situation, insofar as it exists (and the reality is not uniformly dark), is the result of numberless particular decisions, usually made by well meaning people, without general campus review. Thus a dean or a president may decide to adopt a new program or to seize a rich donor's offer of funds for a new high-cost institute, an enrollment management committee may opt for merit scholarships or more luxurious dorms, a provost may "raise the bar" on publications and grants required for tenure, academic administrators may decide to close degree programs in languages, anthropology, classics, or philosophy that recruit few majors, and relatively few people on campus may even know. Still, the very fact that these are decisions of people, not forces of nature, is ground for believing that ethical choices do still exist, unless we also believe we are mere iron shavings in an econo-magnetic field. Where should we begin? If "Morality is...the enterprise of a community of interdependent individuals" (Rorty, 1993, p. 33), how can that community rouse itself?

It may help to realize that conflicts of values, the economic and Socratic, do not have to be settled by establishing universal priorities. By their very nature, resolutions will be local, contextual, and temporary. Yet they may still be far-reaching in their effects. The recent decision by several prestigious colleges to stop using SAT scores as admission criteria may ultimately destroy a practice unfair to lower-class and minority students, though beneficial to the wealthy Educational Testing Service. Over the past ten years, some research universities have strengthened their general undergraduate liberal arts requirements and some have sent senior professors to ignite freshman minds in small seminars. Apparently, they think the costs in specialized graduate instruction or strategic research are outweighed by the benefits to the general opening of views. The rights – and wrongs – of graduate assistants are beginning to be recognized. Support for the improvement of instruction has come from major foundations to campus projects and to programs of large professional organizations, and respected journals on college teaching have come into being. It should be perfectly possible for a consortium of competing colleges to weigh the values involved in merit scholarships and decide on a uniformly small quota for no-need offerings. It should also be possible for such a consortium to agree to stop escalating grant and publication requirements for junior faculty. Of course, decisions like these will not fund higher education and salve its economic woes. These woes will not vanish without major changes in our society's goals and expectations. Yet the academy is not without influence on those goals, as so many have argued. Surely our country's current support for environmental causes began on its campuses, as did its earlier white support for civil rights. And unfortunately, its present mainly economic ideas of the purpose of the academy also started, or were fed, by campus leaders who thought future employment of students a good bait for state legislatures.

The aims of higher education, then, result from ethical choices that are still being made. Colleges will always need to be viable financially, but they need not bend their every effort to increasing their wealth. We need much more than a log, but minds can meet around whatever replaces it, and generations of students can still be led from Plato's cave.

See also 1 THE SOCRATIC MOVEMENT; 5 HUMANISM; 6 ENLIGHTENMENT LIBERALISM; 9 ROMANTICISM; 11 CRITICAL THEORY; 40 UNIVERSITIES IN A FLUID AGE; 41 ACADEMIC FREEDOM; 42 THE ETHICS OF RESEARCH

References

Benjamin, E. (1995) A faculty response to the fiscal crisis. In M. Berube and C. Nelson (eds), *Higher Education under Fire: Politics, Economics, and the Crisis of the Humanities*. New York: Routledge, pp. 52–71.

Gamson, Z. A. (1993) The college experience: new data on how and why students change. *Change*, 25(3), 64–8.

Kean, P. (1994) Temps perdus: the woes of the part-time professoriate. *Lingua Franca*, 5(2), 49–53.

Lauter, P. (1995) Political correctness. In M. Berube and C. Nelson (eds), *Higher Education under Fire: Politics, Economics, and the Crisis of the Humanities*. New York: Routledge, pp. 73–90.

Rorty, A. O. (1993) Moral imperialism vs. moral conflict: conflicting aims of education. In B. D. Smith (ed.), *Education: Can Virtue Be Taught?* South Bend, In: Notre Dame University Press.

Slaughter, S. and Leslie, L. A. (1997) *Academic Capitalism: Policies, and the Entrepreneurial University*. Baltimore: Johns Hopkins University Press.

US National Commission on Excellence in Education (1983) *A Nation at Risk: The Imperative for Education Reform: A Report to the Nation and the Secretary of Education*. Washington, DC: US Department of Education.

Wright, B. (2001) The Syracuse transformation: on becoming a student-centered research university. *Change*, 33(4), 38–45.

Further reading

Astin, A. (1997) *What Matters in College? Four Critical Years Revisited*. San Francisco: Jossey-Bass.

Berube, M. and Nelson, C. (eds) (1995) Money, merit, and democracy at the university: an exchange. In M. Berube and C. Nelson (eds), *Higher Education under Fire: Politics, Economics, and the Crisis of the Humanities*. New York: Routledge, pp. 163–98.

Boyer, E. L. (1990) *Scholarship Reconsidered: Priorities of the Professoriate*. Princeton, NJ: Carnegie Foundation for the Advancement of Teaching.

Gaudiani, C. L. (2000) The hidden costs of merit aid. *Change*, 32(4), 19.

Gless, D. J. and Smith, B. H. (eds) (1992) *The Politics of Liberal Education*. Durham, NC: Duke University Press.

Hutchins, R. M. (1936) *The Higher Learning in America*. New Haven, CT: Yale University Press.

Kerr, C. (1994) Knowledge, ethics, and the new academic culture. *Change*, 26(1), 9–15.

Leslie, L. L. and Rhoades, G. (1995) Rising administrative costs: on seeking explanations. *Journal of Higher Education*, 66, 41–61.

Newman, F. (2000) Saving higher education's soul. *Change*, 32(5), 16–23.

Readings, B. (1996) *The University in Ruins*. Cambridge, MA: Harvard University Press.

Winston, G. C. and Zimmerman, D. J. (2000) Where is aggressive price competition taking higher education. *Change*, 32(4), 10–18.

40

Universities in a Fluid Age

Ronald Barnett

We live not just in times of uncertainty but also in an age of fluidity. These two conditions are caught up with each other: fluidity produces uncertainty and uncertainty increases fluidity. Universities are caught in these currents. Academics are called upon to be responsive to the wider society, to have even greater consideration for their students and to be accountable in their teaching practices. In shaping their programs of study, universities are asked to engage with constituencies outside the academy, especially the worlds of commerce and industry, and are asked to ensure that their research projects have impact in the wider society. The knowledge produced by universities is becoming part of the knowledge capacity in and for "the knowledge society."

In all this, the boundaries between universities and the wider world are becoming much weaker, if they have not actually dissolved. In turn, amid this fluidity, concepts of teaching, research, a course, the student, the academic, academic freedom, and even the "university" become fuzzy, contested, and open to multiple interpretations. These multiple interpretations are to be seen even within the academy itself. Disputes break out, for instance, over the proper relationship between teaching and research, the extent to which a university should be accepting funding from private donors and, even more fundamentally, the responsibilities of academics toward their students. In commenting on assignments, do professors have a responsibility to advise students on matters of linguistic expression, their "academic literacy," and even their spelling?

The disputes and the internal doubts are expressions of larger uncertainties as to the purposes and nature of universities. But these uncertainties over the nature of universities are themselves connected with the changing character of a world characterized by uncertainty.

In this chapter, I want to explore some of the implications of the state of uncertainty and fluidity facing universities. While I believe that the themes introduced should find a resonance in systems of higher education worldwide, the treatment I give them inevitably reflects a Western European perspective and specifically a view from the United Kingdom. While there are differences between European countries, in many ways the United Kingdom presents a special case in itself, because on many dimensions of contemporary academic life it constitutes a midway point between continental Europe and the USA.

The End of Universality

Today in the UK tenured members of staff can be heard expressing unease with the description of themselves as "academics." Presumably, for them, the term "academic" connotes a form of life around texts, the stewardship of a discipline, and the development of formal frames of understanding. In contrast, *their* callings and their responsibilities lie elsewhere, perhaps in the personal development of students, or in the development of a profession. Key concepts in their vocabulary might be "learning," "training," "mentorship," "action," and "problem-solving."

In other words, elemental categories, such as the idea of the "academic," have uncertainty written into them in the contemporary university. It is no longer clear, if it ever was clear, what is to count as a university or what the responsibilities of a university might be. At one time, universities could be held to have a universal mission to acquire knowledge and disseminate it. Now, that universal mission is itself in question from three directions.

First, there is increasing diversity in the mission of individual universities, with spaces and opportunities open for universities to engage with the wider society in new ways. Second, the fluidity and uncertainty of the wider world has caused the academic community to doubt its own central callings: "knowledge" and "truth" are being questioned as terms that have universal meanings. Postmodernism encourages such questioning, but can be seen as a symptom of larger societal and even global fluidities rather than a cause itself of the end of universal categories. Third, universities are less and less in charge of their own destinies, even if they retain substantial autonomy. The stakeholder society expresses its various expectations of universities. Students have become framed as consumers (of products) or customers (presumably expecting services with particular qualities delivered to certain kinds of standards). Amid these fluidities, universities may seem obliged to yield their stewardship of a collective universal mission. In a competitive market situation, it is each university for itself.

Against this background, how might we understand the contemporary university? Is an implication of these reflections that attempts to articulate "the idea of the university" are at an end (Rothblatt, 1997)? In the rest of this chapter, I pursue this question by focusing on some key topics concerning academic life, namely knowledge production, curriculum, and the idea of the "student." In concluding, I raise the issue of the responsibilities of universities.

Knowing about Knowledge

Universities are in the knowledge business; a belief in and a commitment to the pursuit and maintenance of knowledge has long been central to the modern university. Until recently, this commitment, which some have labelled a "dogma" (Nisbet, 1971), had an authority about it, since universities could fairly see themselves as the main if not the only producers of high-status knowledge. Now, that monopoly over the production of knowledge has broken down, in at least three senses.

First, in the "knowledge society," universities are no longer the only or even the dominant producers of knowledge. The knowledge society, after all, is characteristically a society in which knowledge production is distributed very widely, if not universally or evenly. Transnational corporations have their own "knowledge officers" who can orchestrate the knowledge production processes of their organizations and who can maximize the benefits to be gained from the resulting knowledge (Nonaka et al., 1999). In addition, professionals, management consultants, think tanks, government agencies, independent research institutes, and museums and galleries have joined the corporate sector as primary knowledge producers.

Second, what counts as knowledge or high-status knowledge is fluid and arguably owes much to the social, political, and even military climate that prevails at a given time (Toulmin, 2001). As knowledge producers proliferate outside the academy, so do the tacit criteria for what counts as knowledge. Variously, knowledge slides into information (Midgley, 1989), becomes experiential (Schon, 1987), is understood to have an essentially tacit character, takes on a performative orientation in the sense that it requires demonstrable effects in the world (Lyotard, 1984), or is a matter of problem-framing *and* problem-solving (Gibbons et al., 1984). What this adds up to is an assault on the implicit right of the academic community to legislate over knowledge as such. In the knowledge society, knowledge legislators are everywhere. Under these circumstances, the question has to be asked: what, if anything, is special about academic knowledge?

Third, with monopoly went universality. Implicit in the academics' self-understanding was a sense that the knowledge that they were producing had a universal character. The truths that they offered were not just their truths but universal truths with universal value, published in journals and readily available to world audiences. Such universality, however, can no longer be claimed with the same self-assurance. As bodies of knowledge proliferate, academic knowledge simply takes its place within the larger whole. More than that, as the academic tribes protect their territories (Becher and Trowler, 2001), it becomes apparent that academic knowledge itself is a conglomerate of epistemically diverse elements that are far from exhibiting coherent unity.

Reshaping the Curriculum

The idea of reshaping the curriculum, at least in the context of the UK in particular and Europe more widely, is actually misleading. The phrase could imply that there is to hand an explicit idea of the curriculum in higher education. Nothing could be further from the truth. Certainly, the term "curriculum" is hardly ever to be heard or seen in the context of debate over higher education, even in the specialist academic journals on higher education. These days, there is lots of talk about teaching and learning and, albeit to a lesser extent, such topics as student assessment. There is also a fast developing interest in the topic of academic professionalism and the relationship between research and teaching; and, taking its point of departure from Ernest Boyer's (1990) work, there is interest in "the scholarship of teaching." Curriculum, as such, however, barely receives a mention.

The 400–page report of the UK's National Inquiry into Higher Education (NCIHE, 1997) hardly uses the term "curriculum." What it does do, however, is to spend much effort in laying out its conception of the "skills" that it believes students should acquire, in addition to their "knowledge and understanding." The report offers a threefold classification of skills:

1 Key skills: communication, numeracy, the use of information technology, and learning how to learn.
2 Cognitive skills, such as an understanding of methodologies or ability in critical analysis.
3 Subject-specific skills, such as laboratory skills (Recommendation 21, p. 141).

There are two important things here. First, the attention that is paid to the matter of "skills" and the corresponding absence of any explicit attention to the matter of curriculum as such have to be put together as linked phenomena. What is going on here actually constitutes a national attempt to set out a view of curricula in higher education. Together with the student's knowledge and understanding, these skills *are* the curriculum, at least as seen by a national committee (appointed by and reporting to the government). Second, the attention given to the delineation of skills in the report is rather considerable: there is a section specifically devoted to "skills"; the matter of skills percolates the report; it is, as we see, a subject of one of the report's recommendations.

We can conclude, then, that among the many features of this report is an attempt not just to shape curricula in a certain direction but implicitly to shape the discourse on curricula. This report is implicitly saying that "skills" are the dominant element of curricula, and that curricula are only valuable insofar as they deliver "skills."

So far as those sections on skills are concerned, the Report of the Committee of Inquiry appears to have been successful in a particular sense. Since its publication, the discourse in the UK around curriculum matters has been framed almost entirely in a nuanced language of skills. A range of terms are now in general usage: "key skills," "generic skills," and "transferable skills" are perhaps the dominant terms and, from time to time, efforts can be seen being made to distinguish them (Bennett et al., 2000). Other terms also find their way into the curriculum discourse. On the one hand, yet other forms of "skill" are to be heard, such as "complexity skills"; on the other hand, yet other terms emerge, such as "outcomes," which turn out to refer largely to the skills that students are expected to have acquired on completing their course.

How do we understand what is going on here and what is its significance in philosophical terms? First, the concept of "curriculum" is being emptied of substance. A curriculum here becomes nothing other than its endpoints. Matters of educational process, of the character of the pedagogical transactions between tutor and student and between student and student, and of any general educational aims that the curriculum might serve are being airbrushed out of the picture. In short, in this discursive shift, in this reduction of curriculum to specifications largely of skills, we see a framing of the curriculum in instrumental terms. A curriculum is nothing but the production of a set of skills, and is only to be valued providing it delivers skills.

Second, the skills in question include to a significant degree ones that are assumed to be pertinent to the demands of both a global knowledge economy and a changing social order. For Newman, knowledge was its "own end." Now, knowledge appears to be valued for the particular ends it serves. Third, it is implicit that skills, such as communication skills, are all of a piece, that they can be developed in themselves, and that their character is uncontested. That communication "skills," if they could be said to exist at all, cannot be all of a piece and must be significantly context dependent seems not to have occurred to the writers of contemporary policy documents in the UK.

In a fluid age, universities are apparently content to go with the flow. In the shaping of curriculum, all the flows – discursive and material – are for a reshaping of higher education itself. Disciplines may already be losing their solidity as they become fuzzy and interdependent (Peters, 1999), but this performative shift in curriculum only aids that process of disciplinary dissolution.

The absence of a serious debate about curriculum, accompanied by a subtle reshaping of curriculum so as to generate personal competences for a fluid economy and society, ushers in a new performative universality. This universality, however, is only skin-deep. Its deep structure is one of difference, diversity, local "needs" (in the UK, regional agendas are now being played up), and flexibility associated with economic changes, as concepts and techniques take off that are likely to have economic value (Nowotny et al., 2001).

The Idea of the Student

In a fluid age, we can no longer assume that students share any qualities or intentions in common. A generation ago, in the so-called "elite" systems of higher education in Europe and especially the UK, students pursued higher education with mixed motives, but significant among those motives was an interest in becoming deeply immersed in a particular field of knowledge. The range of motives has hardly changed, but their balance has: much more prominent now is the determination to do well in examinations, and this largely due to the significantly higher earnings profiles that are available to college graduates (Reich, 2000).

There are several other dimensions of the changed student population. Especially in the UK, so-called mature students (formally, those over twenty-one but, in practice, often much older) form an increasingly large proportion of the student body. For some UK universities, the majority of their students are in this age range. Many have already experienced paid employment and have families. As such, they come into higher education with a range of learning orientations, hopes, and anxieties.

For those already in professional life, higher education may hold out the hope of a space for systematic reflection on the challenges of work in a professional situation. For such individuals, too, "problem-solving" may have much more to do with finding frameworks with which to tackle practical and operational challenges than theoretical problems within a discipline. In turn, the favored mode of argumentation of such individuals may itself be much more practical. For them, the test of a proposition may well be: "Does this help me to go forward in a professional situation?" Put crudely, "Does it work?"

In a market or quasi-market situation, in which universities must heed the voices of their students, these changes in the student body raise significant issues. There are the immediate challenges on faculty. How do I teach large classes? How do I engage a heterogeneous group of students? But larger questions also arise.

The key conceptual question is quite simple and intractable: what, in a fluid age, might we take the category of *student* to stand for? To tease this question out just a little further: are there particular responsibilities that attach to being a student that are at the same time universal across higher education? Or are student identity and responsibility simply to be specific to each course in each university? In the UK, for instance, it is not uncommon for course handbooks to give *both* a description of the responsibilities of faculty and the host institution to the students (including but going beyond institutional "student charters"), on the one hand, *and* a parallel description of the responsibilities of the students. The parallel statements reflect an explicit sense of a genuine educational transaction, to which the different parties are making their contributions. Still, the question arises, should a university have a common statement of its students' responsibilities? Can faculty entertain *any* prior expectations as to the kinds of human development that they might expect their students to undergo with their help? Can there be a general sense of the kinds of educational contribution that students should make to their own formation? To what extent is the pedagogical transaction to be a mutual exchange, with the student acquiring a due sense of turn taking, respect for others, a willingness to try out ideas, a determination to advance collectively the understandings in the conversation (that is itself historical and even global), a capacity to listen intently to others, a willingness to subscribe to the tacit rules of the conversation, and so forth?

It may be that, in a mass higher education, these and other essential ingredients of what it is to participate in an academic conversation will not easily be transmitted to students. In turn, they will not easily come to recognize their responsibilities. In the face of these obstacles, however, we must continue to recognize the significance of taking up the challenge.

Conclusion

Higher education has taken on fluidities and fragilities of the wider world. Key concepts in the practices of higher education – such as knowledge, student, curriculum, research, teaching – become fluid, their boundaries indistinct from adjacent concepts and practices. In the process, academic life becomes conceptually fragile: what was taken for granted evaporates. Questions arise that confirm the university's fragilities and the identities of its incumbents. Do "universities" require the presence of students? Do they need, *qua* "universities," to conduct research? Are there any limits on the sources or the conditions of funding that universities might attract? Do responsibilities attach to academics? Such questions are now literally infinite and testify to the significance of the problems that are associated with the idea of the university.

In short, the idea of the university has experienced dissolution. From Cardinal Henry Newman onwards, in the mid-nineteenth century, there was a literature that sought to identify and defend "the idea of the university"; indeed, books by Newman (1976), Jaspers (1965), Ortega (1946), and Minogue (1973) even carried titles more or less exactly using that phrase. In England, Henry VIII dissolved the monasteries by destroying them physically. Now the universities, also of medieval origin, are being dissolved in a different way.

The dissolution is *not* a dissolution in space. It is not that universities are now institutions that are distributed in virtual space (with the onward march of electronic communications), even though that is part of the picture. The dissolution in question that the universities are facing is conceptual. Universities no longer stand, it appears, for anything in particular. Nothing of substance attaches to their formerly core concepts. Their key practices run into those of the surrounding world. The private sector and university research units form private companies. Technology is "transferred." Individuals study in their own time and in their own place and can choose between private sector profit-making organizations or accredited "universities." Universities compete with and enter partnerships with management consultants in taking on consultancies, many of which have research dimensions. There is no fixity to any of the concepts or practices of the twenty-first-century university. Indeed, as if to underline the point, many private sector profit-making corporations now arrogate to themselves the term "university" (Jarvis, 2001). It appears that no practice, no idea, and no responsibility attaches to the term "university" any more.

Does any of this matter? I suggest that it matters profoundly. A situation of fluidity and fragility raises two interlinked questions: can we speak any longer of "the university"? And, if we cannot, can we any longer attach the notion of "responsibility" to universities? This latter question was raised explicitly by Jacques Derrida, but that he left it hanging, unanswered, is testimony to the problematic nature of both questions. After all, it only makes sense to talk of responsibility in virtue of there being a conception of universities *qua* universities at hand. If, though, there is nothing that can be taken to be common to universities in the contemporary age, then the idea that universities as such have responsibilities must fall. It might be tempting to say that a university has responsibilities in virtue of the mission that it has chosen for itself, but then, I would want to say, we are not really in the presence of responsibilities. Responsibilities come into view precisely when there is an acknowledged set of external principles or standards to which allegiance is given.

What is at issue here is nothing other than the nature of universities. The notion of a university came, over the past two hundred years or so, to stand for forms of universality: universal reason, universal knowledge, universal truth, universal forms of discourse that were in principle open equally to all. And it was those universal qualities that marked out universities *as* "Universities." In turn, it was through universities' allegiance to these universal norms that we could talk and write intelligibly of "the idea of the university." Now, however, in an age that has lost faith in such universals, the very idea that any kind of universality can attach to the notion of university appears passé. As such, the idea of the university also seems consigned to history.

We have here, surely, a major challenge in front of universities: how do we understand them in a fluid age? How might they understand themselves? If there is a new kind of universality at hand, perhaps it lies precisely in universities coming to understand that they have a responsibility to assist individuals and society more broadly to prosper in this age of fluidity, with all its uncertainties and turbulence (conceptual as well as technological). If something along those lines were to happen, then the idea of the university would be reborn and we could talk again of "the university" without embarrassment.

See also 5 HUMANISM; 6 ENLIGHTENMENT LIBERALISM; 9 ROMANTICISM; 14 POSTMODERN-ISM; 39 ETHICS AND THE AIMS OF AMERICAN HIGHER EDUCATION; 41 ACADEMIC FREEDOM; 44 THE PROFESSOR–STUDENT RELATIONSHIP AND THE REGULATION OF STUDENT LIFE

References

Baumann, Z. (1998) *Liquid Modernity*. Buckingham: Open University Press.

Becher, T. and Trowler, P. (2001) *Academic Tribes and Territories*. Buckingham: Open University Press.

Bennett, N., Carre, C., and Dunne, E. (2000) *Skills Development in Higher Education and Employment*. Buckingham: Open University Press.

Boyer, E. (1990) *Scholarship Reconsidered: Priorities of the Professoriate*. Princeton, NJ: Princeton University Press.

Derrida, J. (1991) Mochlos; or, the conflict of the faculties. In R. Rand (ed.), *Logomachia: The Conflict of the Faculties*. London: University of Nebraska.

Gibbons, M. et al. (1994) *The New Production of Knowledge*. London: Sage.

Jarvis, P. (2001) *Universities and Corporate Universities*. London: Kogan Page.

Jaspers, K. (1965) *The Idea of the University*. London: Peter Owen.

Lyotard, J.-F. (1984) *The Postmodern Condition: A Report on Knowledge*. Manchester: Manchester University Press.

Midgley, M. (1989) *Wisdom, Information and Wonder: What Is Knowledge For?* London: Routledge.

Minogue, K. (1973) *The Concept of a University*. London: Weidenfeld and Nicolson.

NCIHE (1997) *Higher Education in a Learning Society*. Report of the National Committee of Inquiry. London: HMSO.

Newman, J. H. (1976) *The Idea of a University*, ed. I. T. Ker. Oxford: Oxford University Press.

Nisbet, R. (1971) *The Degradation of the Academic Dogma*. London: Heinemann.

Nonaka, I., Umemoto, K., and Sasaki, K. (1998) Three tales of knowledge creating companies. In G. von Krogh, J. Roos, and D. Kleine (eds), *Knowing in Firms: Understanding, Managing and Measuring Knowledge*. London: Sage.

Nowotny, H., Scott, P., and Gibbons, M. (2001) *Re-thinking Science*. Cambridge: Polity Press.

Ortega y Gasset, J. (1946) *Mission of the University*. London: Kegan Paul, Trench, Trubner.

Peters, M. (ed.) (1999) *After the Disciplines: The Emergence of Culture Studies*. Westport, CT: Bergin & Garvey.

Reich, R. (2001) *The Future of Success: Work and Life in the New Economy*. London: Heinemann.

Rothblatt, S. (1997) *The Modern University and Its Discontents: The Fate of Newman's Legacies in Britain and America*. Cambridge: Cambridge University Press.

Schon, D. (1987) *Educating the Reflective Practitioner*. London: Sage.

Stehr, N. (2001) *The Fragility of Modern Societies: Knowledge and Risk in the Information Age*. London: Sage.

Toulmin, S. (2001) *Return to Reason*. Cambridge, MA: Harvard University Press.

41

Academic Freedom

Robert L. Simon

Colleges, universities, and many other educational institutions function as centers of debate and inquiry. Faculty at such institutions, and perhaps their students, often make claims to *academic freedom*. What is this academic freedom? Does academic freedom differ from the basic liberties of expression possessed by all citizens in liberal democratic states? Are there correlative responsibilities that fall on academics? What are the boundaries of academic freedom? Why is it important to protect it?

Consider the following examples.

1 A professor offends many of her students by arguing in a philosophy class that belief in God is irrational and that religion is a harmful social influence, stirring up hatreds and religious strife, and leading to persecution

2 A professor offends many of his students by arguing on the basis of statistical data that there are differences in intelligence between racial groups.

3 A professor uses as a text and endorses in class a notorious anti-Semitic tract that has no standing in his field of expertise.

4 A professor supports racist goals openly in public but he does nothing to express or indicate his political views in class or in his academic research.

5 A student argues in class that, based on the Bible, he regards homosexual behavior as sinful, and denies that homosexual unions should be recognized either by the state or private institutions.

6 A student, using vicious derogatory epithets, scrawls a hate message on the door of a gay student's dorm room.

Suppose that in each case, some members of the university community demand that the professor or student at issue be disciplined; perhaps even that the faculty members be fired. How are such demands to be assessed?

Each of these cases involves issues that differ in significant respects from issues involving basic civil liberties. For one thing, they all involve educational institutions, particularly institutions of higher education. Moreover, the first three cases involve the behavior of faculty in a classroom. Thus, in case 3, even if someone as a matter of basic civil liberties has the right to hold vicious anti-Semitic views, it is far less clear that a professor has the right to advocate those views to students in the classroom, especially since his position has no standing in his academic field. But if that is so, does the professor in case 1 have the right to present her anti-religious views in class, which also may be grossly offensive to some students?

To explore such issues, we need to examine the scope and nature of academic freedom. The idea of academic freedom was first formally advanced in German universities in the nineteenth century, although its origins go much further back, at least to disputes in the medieval universities when scholars challenged restrictions on inquiry laid down by the governing religious authorities. As it has developed, the doctrine of academic freedom has become quite complex and is not understood the same way by all commentators. Thus, how it may apply to contested cases often will be controversial. A good way to begin a discussion of academic freedom is by attempting to sort out different understandings of it and their implications for action.

Conceptions of Academic Freedom

In 1940, representatives of the American Association of University Professors and the Association of American Colleges (now called the Association of American Colleges and Universities) agreed on a statement that has become highly influential, in both courts of law and academic practice, that lays down basic principles of academic freedom. According to this *1940 Statement on Academic Freedom and Tenure*, colleges and universities exist to promote the common good rather than to further the interests of the individual teacher or institution. However, the statement asserts, "The common good depends upon the free search for truth and its free expression." But the free search for truth and its free expression cannot be carried on, it is further asserted, unless its practitioners are accorded protection from retaliation for the way they conduct inquiry or express their views of the research they have conducted, as either scholars or teachers in class.

This suggests that academic freedom belongs primarily to individuals, although educational institutions may claim academic freedom as well; for example, to set their own curricula without outside interference. Our discussion focuses on individual claims, however, since it is plausible to think institutional claims are derivable from the academic freedom of the individuals who engage in scholarship, teaching and research.

In any case, the *1940 Statement* breaks academic freedom down into different areas. The first involves freedom from interference or retaliation in conducting research, publishing the results, and teaching. However, the *Statement* maintains that while "Teachers are entitled to freedom in the classroom in discussing their subject ... they should be careful not to introduce into their teaching controversial matter which has no relation to their subject."

This aspect of academic freedom, which we can call the core conception, is clearly related to what we have identified as a major function of educational institutions, particularly colleges and universities. That function, broadly understood, is to engage in intellectual inquiry, seek deeper understanding and appreciation of important works, and engage in critical examination of ideas. Those engaged in inquiry must be at liberty to state and publish their thoughts without fear of retaliation by administrators, colleagues, or outside political forces. Otherwise, their ideas cannot receive a fair hearing and all of us are prevented from coming to a judicious, well informed evaluation of the merits of those ideas.

The core conception protects the freedom of academics that applies to their pursuit of their professional duties. Hence, it is distinct from the civil liberties of citizens, since it arises primarily from the professional responsibilities of scholar-teachers, and perhaps derivatively from the role of students in the intellectual process.

Thus, abridgement of academic freedom can have disastrous consequences. In science, if theories that might have been shown to be false are protected by silencing opponents, human lives can be placed at risk. Similarly, if a professor in a humanities class is prevented from expressing her interpretation of a text, her ideas cannot be evaluated on their merits. Perhaps even worse, the interpretation that is silenced might well be correct or especially insightful, and if widely accepted might lead us to revise our views of human relationships, or what is important in life. Academic inquiry is important, because without it errors and falsehoods may never be detected, new ideas or interpretations might never come to light, and our freedom to make up our own minds based on evidence would be limited in many crucial areas of thought. Thus, academic freedom not only has social utility; it is no less important as a protection of human liberty and autonomy as well.

While the core conception protects the rights of teachers and scholars to engage in inquiry both in their research and as teachers in the classroom, it also assigns them responsibilities not to misuse their freedom. In particular, teachers should not introduce controversial material into their classrooms *which has no relation to the subject being taught*. The point of this clause is to indicate that academic freedom does not entitle a professor to misuse the classroom to advocate controversial views unrelated to the material of the course. This does not mean a professor should never ever use class time to discuss world events or current campus controversies, but that professors should not distort the purpose of their classes by using them primarily as forums to proselytize in favor of their favorite political or moral perspectives.

Avoidance of abuse of power also implies that teachers and scholars should be fair and responsible in their presentation of the issues they discuss, both in their publications and as teachers in the classroom. At a minimum they should inform students when their own claims or those of others are controversial, and give a fair account of major alternative positions (or at the very least let students know what these positions are and where the views of their adherents can be found). Scholars who violate such requirements, particularly if the violations are extreme, would seem to be not engaging in inquiry but trying to use their position to get their favorite views adopted by their captive audience. It is doubtful, especially in extreme cases, that such practices are protected by academic freedom.

The core conception of academic freedom is relatively narrow, then. It protects the core activities of scholar-teachers but it does not exempt academics from normal institutional duties and requirements, such as the duty to meet classes on time or hold regular office hours, that do not conflict with their ability to teach or engage in scholarship.

However, the core conception may not encompass all that academic freedom should protect. According to the *1940 Statement*, academics "should be free of institutional censorship or discipline" when they engage in political activities but "their special position in the community imposes special obligations." In particular, they should strive to be accurate, fair, and reasonable in their presentation of their views. Thus, the second sense of academic freedom also carries responsibilities with it. Let us call this second sense of academic freedom the "extended" version, since it goes beyond the core version in covering political involvement of faculty and students that may have little if anything to do with their academic roles.

Is the extended version a legitimate extension of the core sense of academic freedom? In its favor, the extended theory recognizes that our society is committed to the idea of political freedom and insures that it is not restricted on campus. Moreover, the extended conception applies clearly to students. Under the core theory, which applies most clearly to scholar-teachers, students seem almost left out.

Nevertheless, the extended conception raises some serious problems. Before we turn to those, note that some activities engaged in by scholars and teachers, and perhaps sometimes by students, occupy an area intermediate between the core and extended conception. For example, scholars may be called upon to testify before government officials on areas relevant to their expertise, take part in public debates or discussions on issues relating to their research, or write letters to newspapers or participate in other public forums on areas pertinent to their scholarship. Thus, a professor who studies the theory of deterrence might write or speak out against the attempt to build a defense system against nuclear missiles, maintaining perhaps that it won't work or it will destabilize important arms control treaties. Such an activity is not purely teaching or research, but does constitute an expression of the writer's scholarly expertise and thus has a claim to the protection of academic freedom.

The extended conception is much more problematic. Law professor William Van Alstyne points out three major problems with regarding it as an aspect of academic freedom. First, he argues, the extended version provides a special protection for academics that is not provided for others, for activities unconnected to their work as scholars or teachers. The claim to extended protection, therefore, "implies a lack of equal protection for others that is false and a supererogation of elite status that is equally false, both inviting a general alienation and justified hostility by others" (Van Alstyne, 1972, p. 127). Second, the extended conception not only protects the liberty of academics but, as we have seen, asserts that there are correlative responsibilities. In particular, if academics are protected as scholars, they should function under stand-ards of reasoned discourse when enjoying that protection. However, as Van Alstyne argues, the result "is that the individual so situated is rendered less free in respect to his nonprofessional pursuits than others" (Van Alstyne, 1972, p. 127). Finally, he contends that the extended conception may cheapen academic freedom, just as constantly calling political opponents on the right "Nazis" trivializes the use of that term.

These points clearly have force, but may not be decisive. In particular, critics may argue that there is a real although indirect connection between protection of the core version and recognition of the extended version. Specifically, interference by their institutions with the political activities of professors is all too likely to have a chilling effect on free scholarly inquiry. Academics who see a colleague suffer institutional retaliation for political expression outside of campus may be far more reluctant than otherwise to expresses themselves freely in class and in their scholarship. Moreover, since the line between the academic and the political may be blurred, we may not want to cede to institutions the authority to draw that line, for they may be tempted to do so in highly partisan or even repressive ways. Hence, the extended version of academic freedom is needed as a check on the power of institutions, which is all too likely to be misused if left unrestricted.

It appears as if we are left with only two choices. First, we can accept the core conception of academic freedom but reject the extended conception. On this view, scholars would have the same civil liberties as others, but civil liberties are distinct from academic freedom, which must be grounded in the duties of academics as such. Alternatively, we can accept both the core and the extended conceptions, acknowledging that academics have intellectual responsibilities in both areas and hence have obligations when operating in the political sphere that others do not. The first alternative allows academics to be disciplined by their institution for political activity. The second either blurs the distinction between academic freedom and civil liberties or imposes special duties on academics who are politically engaged.

However, there is a third and more adequate conception of academic freedom that requires balancing and weighing a variety of factors. Consider the following cases. In the example that begins this chapter, philosophy professors are acting properly by bringing out logical difficulties with religious views, even if they conclude, after examination of the issues, that religious commitment is not rationally defensible, whether or not that view offends some students. Of course, the professors must rely on evidence, present opposing views, and insure that they have had a fair hearing. This case falls under the core conception.

Now, to consider a more difficult case, suppose a professor advocates in the public sphere a social or political view that is highly unpopular or even repugnant. Michael Levin, a tenured professor of philosophy at the City College of New York, asserted in a number of forums, including a letter in the 1990 *Proceedings of the American Philosophical Association*, that blacks were not as intelligent as whites. Levin appealed to alleged evidence in studies of intelligence in support of his claim. No evidence was brought forward suggesting that Levin promoted his views in class or that he treated his black students any differently than white students. Professor Levin was accused of being a racist by some students, faculty, and administrators. The President of City College, Barnard W. Harleston, created a new section of Professor Levin's required introductory course after the college dean had informed students enrolled in Levin's section that they could switch to the new section. Was Levin's speech covered by academic freedom? His views, however offensive, were not expressed in an inflammatory way, did not involve the use of epithets or slurs, and presupposed reference to what he regarded as a body of evidence supporting his views. The expression of his views seems to fall into the area, noted above, where academics speak out on public issues in areas where their skills as scholars bear on the analysis of the issue under consideration. If so, Levin's views are protected under either the core conception of academic freedom or its emanation covering participation in critical inquiry in the public realm.

This does not imply that Levin's views should go unchallenged. The correct form of challenge is through examination of the evidence and critical response to his arguments, not discipline by his institution for the mere expression of his views. While his views should be subjected to intense criticism (which I believe they would not withstand), he was speaking as a scholar and was within the arena of rational discourse where his position could itself be subjected to critical scrutiny. In fact, Levin's freedom of expression was protected by the courts and City College was enjoined from creating the alternate section of his required introductory course (*Levin* v. *Harleston*, 752 F. Supp. 620, SDNY, 1990; 770 F. Supp. 895, SDNY, 1991; affirmed in part and vacated in part 966 F. 2d 85, 2d Cir. 1992).

In a second case, Leonard Jeffries, a tenured professor and chair of the Black Studies department at City College, made an off-campus speech about bias in the public school curriculum. In his speech, he attacked individuals and made derogatory comments about Jews, claiming that they had a history of oppressing blacks, blamed rich Jews for financing the slave trade, and claimed that Jews and others developed a system of cultural oppression which consistently provided negative portrayals of blacks in the media. The speech aroused considerable criticism. As a result, the college administration attempted to remove Jeffries from his chairmanship of the Black Studies department.

In my view, the Jeffries case is more problematic than that of Levin (see also DeGeorge, 1997, pp. 102–3). It comes closer to a visceral expression of hate than Levin's, was not expressed in a forum where others could reply, included remarks directed against individuals, and made no attempt to deal with opposing evidence; for example, evidence showing Jews had no special role financing the slave trade. Moreover, it was alleged that Jeffries, unlike Levin, made racist remarks in class. Thus, it is less than clear that Jeffries was discharging his obligations as an academic. Although Jeffries's speech may have been protected under the civil liberties provided to all citizens by the Constitution, it is quite debatable whether his remarks, particularly the alleged comments in class, were covered by academic freedom (*Jeffries* v. *Harleston*, 828 F. Supp. 1066, SDNY, 1993; modified 21 F. 3d 1238, 2d Cir. 1994; cert. granted and judgment vacated by 115 S. Ct. 502, 1994). Indeed, if the allegations about classroom behavior were true, Professor Jeffries might well have violated obligations under the core conception not to violate his responsibilities as a teacher.

More extreme cases, in which speakers express pure hatred for minority racial or religious groups in an almost entirely emotive speech, using slurs and epithets, but virtually no reasoning or appeal to evidence, would not be covered by academic freedom (although they may be protected by general civil liberties), since no contribution to academic discourse would be involved.

Our discussion indicates, then, that judgment must be used in deciding what falls under the protection of academic freedom and what does not. Moreover, academic freedom is narrower in scope than fundamental civil liberties protecting freedom of expression. The core and extended conceptions supply guidelines for judgments about academic freedom, but it cannot be decided mechanically precisely where its boundaries fall. The alternative outlined here is to think not in terms of two opposed conceptions of academic freedom, but in terms of a sliding scale according to which the weight given to one factor relevant to academic freedom changes as the significance of other factors rises or falls. Thus, the less related expression is to academic duties, and the less it reflects critical inquiry or the less it is a form of rational discourse (as opposed, say, to epithets or slurs), the less likely it is to be protected by academic freedom. That is, the protection provided by academic freedom diminishes the less professional academic activity or critical inquiry is at stake.

Tenure and Institutional Neutrality

If there are rights to academic freedom, as well as obligations and duties that go with it, what responsibilities do educational institutions have to foster academic freedom? Two of the most important are preservation of institutional neutrality and support for a fair and impartial system of tenure. Because neutrality has raised some especially intricate issues, this section focuses on it, after some briefer comments on tenure.

A portion of the general public seems to view tenure as a form of job security for academics. However, the major reason for instituting a system of tenure in an educational institution "is its role in promoting and defending academic freedom" (DeGeorge, 1997, p. 29). Since tenured academics are free from retaliation for their opinions, they are in an excellent position to defend academic freedom for their colleagues, especially untenured faculty, and for students as well. Without a tenure system, faculty might be intimidated by fear of loss of their position or other forms of retaliation, placing the academic freedom of all at the institution in danger.

Tenure should not be granted lightly because there should be every assurance that students and colleagues will not be affected indefinitely by an incompetent individual. Standards for tenure should be demanding and the review process should be thorough and fair, considering potential for scholarship, evaluation of teaching, and commitment to service to the institution, weighted according to the particular institution's own goals. Tenure decisions should reflect a reasoned evaluation of the candidate's achievements and potential as a scholar-teacher.

Tenure is often criticized because it does not seem to allow for any control over faculty who have become unproductive scholars or poor teachers. However, that rests on a misunderstanding of tenure. Tenure provides protection from dismissal without due cause, but tenured faculty can be dismissed for incompetence, for financial exigency on the part of the institution, and for the all too vaguely defined flaw of moral turpitude. (Perhaps it would cover such extreme behavior as sexual harassment of students but should not be interpreted to cover private or merely unpopular behavior which does not violate fundamental moral obligations of the teacher-scholar.)

Thus, tenure is not incompatible with continuing review of the performance of faculty. However, what academic freedom demands is that such reviews be carried out by faculty peers with adequate procedures in place to prevent prejudicial findings based on the views the faculty member in question has professed.

Institutional neutrality requires that colleges and universities remain neutral on substantial issues that go beyond their educational mission. Historically, neutrality may have evolved as primarily a pragmatic compromise; if educational institutions were not political agents, they should be exempt from politically motivated interference. But as we will see, neutrality has tighter connections to academic freedom and critical inquiry than those of a mere bargain of convenience between opposing forces.

Neutrality does not require that individual teachers or scholars be neutral. Instead, it applies to the educational institution itself. However, skeptics claim that institutional neutrality is an impossibility that cannnot be achieved. Among the most common arguments for the impossibility of neutrality are that educational institutions necessarily are committed to such values as clarity of thought or the importance of education itself, that the decisions and policies that educational institutions make invariably have effects outside the academy, and that failure to oppose injustice is in effect to endorse the status quo (Wolff, 1969, p. 71). Thus, to many critics, particularly those on the political left, neutrality actually functions as a covert defense of keeping things the way they are, a radical conservatism dressed up in liberal clothing.

However, while some of these critical points have force, it is unclear that they are strong enough to undermine the case for neutrality. This is in part because there is more than one conception of neutrality. Accordingly, even if critical arguments undermine the claim that educational institutions can be neutral according to some conceptions of neutrality, it does not follow that all conceptions of neutrality thereby fail.

For example, the critics are quite right to point out that colleges and universities are not value-free. Surely, such institutions endorse the value of knowledge over ignorance and of critical analysis over uncritical acceptance of unquestioned dogma. However, as we will see, proponents of institutional neutrality do not mean to assert that academic institutions can or should be totally value-free, so the first critical argument simply misses the point of the neutrality thesis. Moreover, while it also is true that the decisions such institutions make have effects or consequences, proponents of the neutrality thesis may not mean to defend consequential neutrality either.

Consider the case of basketball referees. Clearly, the decisions the referees make during a game have consequences, and may even cost teams the contest. Moreover, the referees are not value-free in that they may act on various conceptions of what the game of basketball should be like: for example, how much body contact should be allowed. However, each may be neutral in that their decisions are based on their understanding of the rules of the game rather than a bias in favor of one team or the other. One might say that their justification for decision-making is neutral in that it concerns the common standards that apply to all teams rather than favoritism toward one team or another.

Similarly, the claim that academic institutions should be politically neutral is best interpreted to mean that their actions or policies should have a neutral *justification*. In particular, the justification should be in terms of the institution's role in protecting or promoting academic values, particularly critical inquiry understood to encompass both teaching and scholarship. Thus, if a university banned fraternities and sororities simply because the faculty disapproved of the values such societies encourage, that would be a non-neutral decision. But if the justification was that these societies harmed the academic mission of the college, perhaps by encouraging an anti-intellectual climate, such a decision would be neutral. Of course, whether the neutral justification would be a strong one or not is a separate issue, but because it would have been based on the academic mission of the school it would be neutral in the sense we are considering. Let us call this kind of neutrality institutional critical neutrality because its basis is the protection and promotion of critical inquiry (Simon, 1994, pp. 22–33).

It is far from clear that institutional critical neutrality is conservative, as the leftist critics charge. Whether or not critical inquiry will lead to support of existing arrangements, radical change, or moderate reform is an open question in each case. But even if such neutrality is possible, is it desirable, or even morally required?

Consider a college or university that announced it would be an active supporter of a particular position on a controversial issue. For example, University X announces it is a "pro-life" institution with regard to abortion. What are the implications? Does it simply announce its position? Does it denounce opponents as immoral? Does it make financial or other sorts of contributions to pro-life groups? Does it refuse to hire outspoken proponents of abortion? Does it allow full expression of opposing views? These questions suggest that there are degrees of partisanship and institutions that depart from neutrality may do so to more or less extreme levels.

Second, the consequences of partisanship are all too likely to be extremely harmful to critical inquiry, and to academic freedom. If, as seems likely, those who hold opposing views are less likely than others to want to work or study there, diversity of opinion among faculty and students will suffer. Moreover, if the college or university not only takes strong stands but also embarks on political action, it is likely to arouse opposition, not only on campus but from opposing external political organizations. Resources that may have been devoted to the support of academics will have to be shifted to political action, and perhaps significant outside support will be lost. Faculty and students may become reluctant to speak out against the institution's political positions for fear of retaliation and at best will have been relegated to official dissenters who are tolerated but whose views are deplored by their own institution. Perhaps worst of all, some issues may be placed off limits to inquiry, just as some religiously oriented institutions place fundamental articles of faith beyond the scope of critical examination. Finally, who decides what political stands the institution should take? Is it trustees, administrators, or politically active faculty? Do students or staff have a role? Clearly, few if any institutions have procedures in place to decide such issues, which suggests that decisions will at best be arrived at through struggles for power and at worst be forced upon dissenting minorities or those too involved in scholarly activity to enter the debate.

While none of this amounts to a proof, these considerations taken together make it reasonable to conclude that partisanship is a real threat to critical inquiry and to academic freedom. Academic inquiry and academic freedom are threatened by partisanship since it places the support of the institution in one direction, thereby chilling dialogue and limiting autonomy in the ways suggested above.

But even if the case for critical institutional neutrality is reasonable, it is not without difficulties. For example, colleges and universities make investments to promote their endowment. Doesn't this involve them not only in the broad economic system but in making investments that sometimes will be ethically controversial? Moreover, even within the academy, aren't educational issues inseparable from political ones? For instance, isn't the choice between the traditional curriculum and a more multicultural curriculum, emphasizing the work of women and non-white authors, basically political? More generally, isn't the line between the politically partisan and the academic sphere of critical inquiry presupposed by the proponents of neutrality either non-existent or too blurred to be of use?

Such criticisms are complex and cannot be pursued exhaustively here. However, it is important to note that proponents of neutrality do have lines of defense against such criticisms. For example, consider the dispute between proponents of traditional curricula and those who favor a more multicultural approach. If the whole dispute is political, in a sense that rules out rational adjudication of which curriculum is educationally best, the reformers themselves are deprived of one of their major arguments against traditionalists. That is, since on their own view curricular debates are matters of power rather than reason, they cannot consistently argue that their curricular proposals are actually more reasonable or educationally sound than the traditional view they oppose. On the other hand, if there are intellectual criteria that show one kind of curriculum is more defensible than the other, there is a neutral resolution of the dispute. The neutral decision would be to select the curriculum that is most justified educationally. Of course, such a choice is not value-free and might well have political consequences, but if it is justified by appeal to intellectual criteria, it is critically neutral in the sense that has been defended here. Similarly, if investment decisions are made with the justification of generating income in order to support critical inquiry and academic values, they arguably are neutral although, as we will see, not necessarily morally justified on that account alone.

Is the principle that academic institutions ought to be critically neutral absolute, overriding all other values? Clearly, the principle is supported by important moral considerations, including the relationship between neutrality, academic freedom, and critical inquiry. Thus, the principle has great weight against competing values, but this, I would suggest, does not make it always overriding.

For example, the defense of neutrality would not excuse the university for complicity in promoting a major injustice. Thus, if a university owned apartments and acted to exploit tenants by charging outrageous rents and not providing basic services, the excuse that it was only trying to maximize its profits in order to support academic values just would not wash. Likewise, if, during the struggle against apartheid in South Africa, critics were correct to argue that investments by colleges and universities directly contributed to the injustice of that system, they would have a strong case that divestment from such companies was morally required, even if such a policy was not neutral.

However, even if neutrality is not absolute, it nevertheless is very weighty and can only be outweighed by the most serious of considerations. It is doubtful if there is any uncontroversial or mechanical formula for doing the weighing, but as we have seen in our discussions of tenure and the different conceptions of academic freedom, some guidelines may be helpful. For example, there surely is a greater obligation on academic institutions to not act unjustly themselves than to prevent others from doing so. (When would they do so and where?)

In any case, there is no *a priori* method for determining just when neutrality may be overridden besides making clear just why neutrality is important and why only the weightiest considerations justify its violation. Perhaps it will help to clarify things further, however, if we explore an issue that bears quite directly on both academic freedom and the protection of critical inquiry.

Academic Freedom and Codes Prohibiting Hate Speech

In response to a disturbing number of on-campus incidents of racist, anti-Semitic, and homophobic speech and expression, some colleges and universities have formulated speech codes designed to define acts of hate speech and allow the institutions in question to punish those who engage in such behavior. For example, among the incidents which led to the promulgation of a code prohibiting hate speech at the University of Michigan were the distribution of a flyer declaring "open season" on blacks, whom it referred to as "saucer lips, porch monkeys, and jigaboos," and the telling of racist jokes on a campus radio station (*Doe* v. *University of Michigan*, 721 F. Supp. 852, ED Mich., 1989).

The principal arguments in favor of hate speech codes are that hate speech not only insults and degrades its victims, but also creates a hostile atmosphere which impedes the education of those who are its targets, and discourages them from participating fully as members of the academic community. The loss of their participation deprives everyone else of their contributions to dialogue, and undercuts critical inquiry. Nevertheless, it is highly controversial whether codes punishing speech or expression are a defensible response to acts of hate speech.

Consider, for example, the code developed at the University of Michigan. That code prohibited "Any behavior, verbal or physical, that stigmatizes or victimizes an individual on the basis of race, ethnicity, religion, sex, sexual orientation, creed, national origin, ancestry, age, martial status, handicap, or Vietnam-era veteran status." The code went on to encompass behavior or expression that creates "an intimidating, hostile, or demeaning environment for educational purposes" (*Doe* v. *Michigan*, 1989).

This code is striking for its vagueness. What counts as stigmatizing an individual or as creating a demeaning environment for educational purposes? This leads to a second objection. Not only is the code vague but it lends itself to interpretations that would either rule out of order presentation of controversial views on issues of race and gender or at least have a significant chilling effect on discussion. A potential contributor to the discussion might elect to remain silent, thereby impoverishing the debate, rather than risk being called to account for violation of the code. Third, the Michigan code favored some political views over others according to their content. Views regarded as racist and sexist fell under the code but other abhorrent views did not.

In fact, suit was brought against the university by a graduate student who feared that presentation of his research on alleged gender differences would be construed as "racist" or "sexist" and that the code would have a chilling effect on legitimate academic debate about such theories. His fears were not far-fetched, since the university published a guide to the code which listed as an example of punishable conduct a student who remarks in class that women aren't as good in a particular field as men.

Given that the Michigan code seemed to prohibit the expression of some ideas but not others, that it was vague, and that it would have a chilling effect on debate of controversial topics, it threatened critical neutrality and academic freedom alike. Perhaps not unsurprisingly, it was overturned in court (*Doe* v. *Michigan*, 1989).

However, while the Michigan code clearly suffered from a variety of defects, it also is true that expression of hate on a college campus can have a chilling effect on

579

speech, and harass, intimidate, or silence its victims (Matsuda, 1989). Moreover, even if some kinds of speech codes are indefensible, it does not follow that all hate speech codes are indefensible. For example, the chalking of hate messages on the doors of rooms of minority students surely is not protected by academic freedom and may be prohibited.

Perhaps what is needed is a code narrower in form than the broad type of standard promulgated at Michigan; one which targets abusive and intimidating behavior, but which does not affect general discussion of controversial issues. Perhaps codes prohibiting harassment of individual members of the academic community might provide a model.

On the narrower approach, which has been tried by such universities as Stanford and Duke, focus is placed not on the content of hate speech but on what the speaker does in employing it. In particular, the narrower approach focuses on the use of hate speech or expression to intimidate, harass, or degrade targeted individuals. Proponents of the narrower approach would claim that they are protecting the rights of members of the academic community, not limiting intellectual discourse to any significant extent. Thus, the narrower approach might represent a reasonable compromise between those who favor broad speech codes and those who reject any limitations on speech as a threat to academic freedom and civil liberties (Grey, 1991). Although no clear sharp line demarcates the boundary between substantive discourse and hate speech that harasses individuals, some narrowly drawn codes try to draw the line by distinguishing the highly emotive use of epithets and slurs from contributions to academic dialogue and discussion. Thus, for speech to fall under the Stanford code, it must be intended to insult or stigmatize identifiable individuals, must be directly addressed to the individuals it insults or stigmatizes, and must make use of insulting "fighting words" or non-verbal symbols that are commonly understood as expressions of hate (Grey, 1991, p. 104–7). Fairness demands that even such narrowly drawn codes be neutral in the sense of protecting not only members of designated minorities but all members of the academic community.

Perhaps narrowly drawn speech codes, sensitively formulated and applied, can be a reasonable response to hate speech and consistent with academic freedom. More broadly drawn codes are all too likely to limit the expression of ideas on controversial topics and so should be rejected. Normally, academic freedom itself provides perhaps the best means for countering most forms of hate speech: namely, open discussion and criticism according to the standards and canons of rigorous intellectual inquiry.

Critical Inquiry and Its Critics

Academic freedom, then, has been justified by its role in protecting critical inquiry and discussion. Critical inquiry is important because it allows ideas to be tested, allows us to examine our positions to see if they are justified, allows for the confirmation of old truths, the discovery of new ones, and the detection of falsehoods. However, have we been critical enough of such a conception of critical inquiry itself?

One line of criticism, influenced by some interpretations of postmodernist thinkers, questions whether there are any justified standards of critical inquiry at all. Some more radical critics may question whether there is any such thing as truth or justification, while more moderate ones tend to reduce such notions to agreement within a community such as the community of scholars (Rorty, 1994).

However, such a view, particularly in the extreme form, faces severe difficulties. For one thing, its proponents seem to believe that their critique of critical inquiry is more correct than defenses of it, and so that they are more justified than their critics. If so, they must acknowledge that their view satisfies certain standards of intellectual inquiry and justification better than alternatives. So the extreme postmodernist critics either embrace a form of critical inquiry themselves, or must admit that their own view lacks justification (since on their view there is no such thing) and is simply being asserted arbitrarily, and perhaps imposed through power.

More sophisticated critics may claim that they are not rejecting the ideas of truth or justification, but just rejecting the view that they reflect anything more than fundamental agreements within communities. This view deserves more attention than it can be given here. (For discussion see Searle, 1993; Rorty, 1994.) However, two brief comments are in order. First, it is not clear that even sophisticated proponents of this view can entirely abandon traditional notions of truth and justification, since they seem to be asserting that it is correct or true that community agreement is the ultimate standard. Moreover, even moderate postmodernists may want to distinguish between shallow versions of community agreement and those that arise from deeper reflection carried on by the most rigorous standards of intellectual discourse available (Morgan, 1994). Hence, they must acknowledge a distinction between community agreement that just happens to occur and agreement that is based upon intellectual standards of discourse. While those standards and canons of inquiry may themselves be rationally examined and revised in light of experience, they are not arbitrary and their examination is meaningless unless it is itself recognizably rational.

Concluding Comments

Without such independent academic centers of inquiry as colleges and universities, we would be deprived of critical insight into fundamental aspects of our lives, of new understandings and discoveries, and of expression of criticism and social analysis. Not only would our society be impoverished but our autonomy would be restricted as well, since our decisions would be based on a far narrower range of information and understanding than otherwise.

Academic freedom provides essential protection for intellectual inquiry and critical examination of ideas and forms of expression that is vital to education. As such, it should be placed among our most fundamental and cherished values.

See also 20 KNOWLEDGE, TRUTH, AND LEARNING; 21 CULTIVATING REASON; 39 ETHICS AND THE AIMS OF AMERICAN HIGHER EDUCATION; 40 UNIVERSITIES IN A FLUID AGE; 42 THE ETHICS OF RESEARCH; 43 AFFIRMATIVE ACTION IN HIGHER EDUCATION; 44 THE PROFESSOR–STUDENT RELATIONSHIP AND THE REGULATION OF STUDENT LIFE

References

AAUP (1995) 1940 Statement of Principles on Academic Freedom and Tenure with 1970 Interpretative Comments. In *AAUP Documents and Reports*. Washington, DC: AAUP.

DeGeorge, R. (1997) *Academic Freedom and Tenure: Ethical Issues*. Lanham, MD: Rowman and Littlefield.

Grey, T. C. (1991) Civil rights versus civil liberties: the case of discriminatory verbal harassment. *Social Philosophy and Policy*, 8, 81–107.

Matsuda, M. J. (1989) Legal storytelling: public response to racist speech: considering the victim's story. *Michigan Law Review*, 87, 3–68.

Morgan, W. J. (1994) *Leftist Theories of Sport: A Critique and Reconstruction*. Urbana: University of Illinois Press.

Rorty, R. (1994) Does academic freedom have philosophical presuppositions? *Academe*, 80, 52–63.

Searle, J. R. (1993) Rationality and realism. What is at stake? *Daedalus*, 122, 55–84.

Simon, R. L. (1994) *Neutrality and the Academic Ethic*. Lanham, MD: Rowman and Littlefield.

Van Alstyne, W. (1972) Reply to comments. In E. L. Pincoffs (ed.), *The Concept of Academic Freedom*. Austin: University of Texas Press, pp. 125–32.

Wolff, R. P. (1969) *The Ideal of the University*. Boston: Beacon Press.

Further reading

Gewirth, A. (1990) Human rights and academic freedom. In S. M. Cahn (ed.), *Morality, Responsibility, and the University*. Philadelphia: Temple University Press.

Golding, M. P. (2000) *Free Speech on Campus*. Lanham, MD: Rowman and Littlefield.

Hofstader, R. and Metzger, W. P. (1955) *The Development of Academic Freedom in the United States*. New York: Columbia University Press.

Van Alstyne, W. (1972) The specific theory of academic freedom and the general issue of civil liberty. In E. L. Pincoffs (ed.), *The Concept of Academic Freedom*. Austin: University of Texas Press, pp. 59–85.

42

The Ethics of Research

Michael Davis

For more than a century now, research has been integrated into higher education, distinguishing the modern university from its predecessors. Any philosophy of higher education should help us to understand the place of research in the university, especially the complex relation between teaching and research. This chapter attempts a small contribution to that understanding, an inquiry into the *ethics* of research (for a more detailed treatment, see Davis, 1999). It has four sections. The first defines the field. The second briefly describes the history of that field. The third summarizes what little we know about the apparent ethics crisis in research. The fourth outlines the practical responses to that crisis, ending with a suggestion for how philosophers might contribute.

Ethics and Research

Both "ethics" and "research" have enough different senses today to be dangerous if left undefined here. There are, for example, at least five senses "ethics" could carry in a discussion of "the ethics of research."

In one, "ethics" is a mere synonym for ordinary morality, those universal standards of conduct that apply to moral agents simply because they are moral agents (Don't lie, Keep your promises, and so on). Etymology fully justifies this first sense. The root for "ethics" (*ethos*) is the Greek word for custom, just as the root of "morality" (*mores*) is the Latin word for it. Etymologically, "ethics" and "morality" are twins (as are "ethic" and "morale"). In this sense of "ethics," research ethics has existed as long as research has (because research has always been the work of moral agents).

In four other senses, "ethics" is contrasted with "morality." In one, ethics consists of those standards of conduct that moral agents *should* follow (what is sometimes also called "critical morality"); morality, in contrast, consists of those standards that moral agents actually follow ("positive morality"). "Morality" in this sense is very close to its root *mores*; it can be unethical (in our first sense of "ethics"). "Morality" (in this sense) has a plural: each society or group can have its own moral code; indeed, even each individual can have her own. But even so, *ethics* remains a standard common to everyone (or, at least, may be such a standard, depending on how "critical morality" gets cashed out).

"Ethics" is sometimes contrasted with "morality" in another way. Morality then consists of those standards every moral agent *should* follow. Morality is a universal minimum, our standard of moral right and wrong. Ethics, in contrast, is concerned with moral good, with whatever is beyond the moral minimum. In this sense of "ethics," research ethics must consist entirely of aspirations. In fact, as we shall see, research ethics consists in large part of requirements.

The second (or "should") sense of ethics is closely related to the fourth, a field of philosophy. When philosophers offer a course in "ethics," its subject is various attempts to understand morality (all or part of morality in our first sense) as a rational undertaking. Philosophers do not teach morality (in our first, second, or third senses) – except perhaps by inadvertence. They also generally do not teach critical morality, though the attempt to understand morality as a rational undertaking should lead students to dismiss some parts of morality (in its second, descriptive, sense) as irrational or to feel more committed to morality (in its first or third sense) because they can now see the point of it.

"Ethics" can be used in yet another sense, to refer to those special, *morally permissible standards of conduct governing members of a group simply because they are members of that group.* In this sense, Hopi ethics are for Hopi, legal ethics for lawyers, and business ethics for people in business. Ethics – in this sense – is relative even though morality is not. But ethics (in this sense) is not therefore mere mores. Ethics must at least be morally permissible. So, for example, there can be no thieves' ethics, except with scare quotes around "ethics."

This fifth sense of "ethics" is, I think, the one that yields the most interesting interpretation of "research ethics." Given this sense of ethics, one might suppose that "the ethics of research" refers to standards of conduct that do, or at least should, govern those engaged in research. Unfortunately, that is not quite so. "Research," while a conveniently short term, is somewhat misleading. Lawyers, journalists, scholars, philosophers, theologians, and even astrologers engage in research. Yet their research lies beyond our subject. I must admit to having no explanation of why that is. Lawyering, journalism, philosophy, theology, and humane letters each have standards for conducting and reporting research, standards we might properly describe as their respective research ethics. And individual lawyers, journalists, and so on certainly violate those standards now and then. Yet, as far as I know, such researchers rarely appear in discussions of research ethics. Why? Are the present borders of research ethics determined merely by historical accident or, in part at least, by important practical or theoretical differences between research in the sciences and research in other disciplines? I raise this question only to put it aside.

My subject, then, might better be described as "the ethics of scientific research." But even that description has difficulties. What is "science" here? Does it include medicine, engineering, mathematics, and logic? What about "library science" or history?

Medical research has been at the center of discussions of research ethics from the beginning. Yet we might well wonder why. Much medical research is done by physicians (MDs), not people with a research degree (PhD). In this respect, medical research resembles legal research rather than scientific research. Medical research is also often highly practical, the purpose being to find cures for disease rather than to increase knowledge for its own sake. Medical research will seem to be scientific research only if we define scientific research by method rather than purpose. When engaged in research, physicians use methods common elsewhere in the life sciences.

If medical research is scientific research, then so is engineering research. Engineering research both resembles in method other research in the physical sciences and receives much of its funding from the same sources. Many engineers have a research degree. Engineering research is even occasionally explicitly mentioned in official documents concerned with the ethics of scientific research. Yet discussions of research ethics rarely include examples from engineering. Unlike physicians, engineers have had to carry on a separate discussion. What explains that? This is another question I raise only to put aside.

Here is a third. Like engineering research, much research in mathematics and logic is closely linked to scientific research generally. And like engineering research, research in logic and mathematics seems (more or less) to have been left out of discussions of research ethics. Of course, research in mathematics or logic is not generally laboratory research, but we have no reason to limit research in that way. The research of concern to us clearly includes more than laboratory research. For example, some recent scandals in research occurred during clinical trials.

Such considerations seem to provide reasons to include the ethics of mathematical and logical research within research ethics. There is, however, at least one good reason not to. Unlike engineering (and clinical research), research in mathematics or logic is rarely empirical; and discussion of research ethics has so far been limited to empirical research. Is non-empirical research of the sort mathematicians and logicians do therefore *not* scientific in the relevant sense? What then of the equally non-empirical work of computer scientists or theoretical physicists? Here is another question I raise only to put aside.

I have one more such question. There are several empirical disciplines that lie on the boundary between (what we call) science and (what we call) scholarship. I have in mind such diverse fields as lexicography, etymology, and history. Some of these disciplines have in fact had cases of alleged misconduct not too different from those in the sciences. For example, for much of the 1980s, historians debated whether a well known scholar had "fabricated data" by radically mistranslating archival material (Jacoby, 1987, p. 128). Such misconduct, though it clearly exists, is rarely mentioned in discussions of research ethics, never as an example of scientific misconduct. Apparently, disciplines like history are not sciences. Why not? Where does science end and scholarship begin?

Such questions are of practical as well as theoretical interest. The theoretical interest is obvious. Trying to define research ethics seems to reveal vast blanks in our conception of science. The practical interest may be less obvious. Consider then what a university committee appointed to hear cases of scientific misconduct should do when a complaint is brought concerning misconduct in historical, literary, or philosophical research.

That, I think, is enough about the boundaries of our subject. In this chapter, we talk only about the ethics of scientific research, with "science" having a relatively narrow interpretation. This, I think, is a wise strategy. Narrowing our field of study now does not preclude broadening it later. But it puts us in a better position to decide where the field's natural borders are. We are in less danger of being overwhelmed by the enormous diversity of research.

Topics

As a field of study, the ethics of scientific research has a relatively short history. Of course, we can identify certain precursors concerned with the "norms of science," especially the sociologists Max Weber, Talcott Parsons, and Robert Merton. We can also identify certain early essays by natural scientists complaining of "trimming," "cooking," "forging," or similar misconduct in research. The first such work seems to be Charles Babbage's *Reflections on the Decline of Science in England* (1830).

We can also identify more recent debates that, in retrospect, seem to be about the ethics of scientific research. Two deserve mention. One, begun just after the Second World War, primarily among physicists, concerned the responsibility of scientists for the use to which their discoveries are put. The other concerned the treatment of research subjects, both human and animal. In many countries, this latter debate quickly led to governmental regulation, to the establishment of review boards within research institutions, to substantial changes in the way research is conducted, and to a large literature.

While these discussions are, in retrospect, clearly relevant to research ethics, they are only now being integrated. The field itself is really much newer than such precursors suggest. Though saying when a new field of study began requires some arbitrariness, I think we may usefully date research ethics from 1982. Not much was written about the ethics of scientific research until a series of scandals in the 1970s aroused interest in the faking of research. Some of the scandals involved contemporary researchers. You may, for example, remember white mice with black spots painted on them where black fur should have been (Hixson, 1976). Some of the scandals involved older research; for example, in the 1970s, a famous pre-Second World War study of intelligence in identical twins was discovered to have been entirely faked (Hearnshaw, 1981). These scandals produced what (in retrospect) was a trickle of publications, popular as well as scholarly.

Then, two journalists, William Broad and Nicholas Wade, published *Betrayers of the Truth* (1982). *Betrayers* is a work of journalism, not scholarship, with most of the virtues and vices that that suggests. Let us begin with the vices.

Betrayers relies entirely on secondary sources for its stories of faked research. The book would have added nothing to the knowledge of anyone familiar with the history of science. Indeed, it would have subtracted a bit, since it relies on outdated sources for some of its stories. By 1982, for example, some scholars had begun to think that certain of Mendel's research practices, though they would now be improper, were at the time acceptable substitutes for statistical techniques not yet available (van der Waerden, 1968). Broad and Wade nonetheless list Mendel among those who betrayed the truth.

So much for vices. One virtue of *Betrayers* is its Watergate-style reporting, an excitement and indignation certain to get the attention of people till then unfamiliar with the history of science. Another virtue of *Betrayers* is that it combines this reporting with three theses certain to get the attention of people already familiar with the history of science: *first*, that fraud in science is common; *second*, that the belief of scientists that fraud is uncommon is the consequence of self-deception, not evidence; and *third*, that the much-vaunted guarantees of scientific probity – especially, quick replication of research – are myths. That there is a huge gap between these theses and the evidence *Betrayers* provides only enhanced the provocation.

Betrayers of the Truth provoked an enormous response, much of it from indignant scientists, but a surprising amount from scientists who had till then only worried privately about what they saw around them. *Betrayers* created a common vocabulary for scientists, scholars, and government officials interested in the problems *Betrayers* identified. Suddenly there was a field defined by those problems.

This way of defining the field was not without disadvantages. *Betrayers* was in fact almost entirely about empirical research in physics, biology, and medicine. While it managed to touch on a great many other problems, its focus was fraud. Early responses to *Betrayers* were also largely concerned with "fraud in science" (so called). Very soon, however, more general terms appeared, especially "misconduct in research" and "cheating in science." The positive terms "responsible research," "research integrity," "research ethics," and "ethics of scientific research" seem to have caught on only during the 1990s.

We may identify six topics central to research ethics, all related to fraud and all discussed extensively in *Betrayers*:

1 "Smoothing out" reported data; for example, quietly dropping certain experimental results because of unreported inferences concerning weaknesses in research design or implementation ("trimming").
2 Suppressing data clearly inconsistent with one's conclusions ("cooking").
3 The outright fabrication of data ("forging").
4 Plagiarizing the work of others; for example, by publishing as your own in one obscure journal work another published in another obscure journal. (*Betrayers* was concerned with plagiarism of this sort because it seemed to reveal a weakness of peer review. Neither the journal editors nor the journal readers knew the literature of their field well enough to recognize that what they were reading did not add to knowledge but merely repeated what had already been published. Was anyone reading those articles?)
5 Claiming credit for work you did not do; for example, by allowing yourself to be listed as co-author of a paper to which you contributed little or nothing. (*Betrayers* was particularly hard on senior researchers who took credit for the work of those under them but neither supervised it closely nor accepted responsibility when fraud was discovered.)
6 Turning "a blind eye" to the misconduct of others, whether from fear of reprisal, personal friendship, or concern for the welfare of the institution. (Why did researchers not put the truth first?)

Betrayers also touched on most of the following topics, which, in any case, soon became important because they seemed relevant to understanding what might lead scientists to commit fraud:

587

1   Keeping incomplete records of research, discarding records after research is complete, or denying others access to data on which published research relied.
2   An overemphasis by laboratory directors, academic institutions, and funding agencies on novelty; for example, by rewarding researchers for new work but not for checking the work of others.
3   Judging a researcher's productivity. Why the emphasis on *number* of publications? Why not more emphasis on *quality*? How is quality measured? How should it be measured?
4   Mistreatment of graduate students, postdoctoral fellows, and junior faculty. What happens, for example, if a postdoc expresses doubt about the research of another postdoc? What happens if she objects to giving the laboratory director credit for work he did not do? How can such underlings be protected if they become whistleblowers?
5   What journals demand of those who submit papers. Should each co-author be required to indicate what he is responsible for? Should journals check the research plan, records, or raw data? Should a journal try to replicate the research itself?
6   The competitiveness of contemporary science, especially such "research strategies" as reporting results in such a way as to mislead competing researchers, holding back research results long enough to make sure they will not be of use to competitors (or interfere with getting a patent), and denying competitors access to one's lab.
7   Unauthorized use of privileged information; for example, using information gained as a reviewer to redirect one's own research without receiving permission from the person whose work was reviewed and without giving credit.
8   Honest but reckless or negligent error in conducting or reporting research ("sloppy science"). What is science-as-usual and what is misconduct?

Once the discussion spread from fraud in science to questions such as these – many concerned with the general environment of research – research ethics might easily be thought to include other topics as well. The treatment of research subjects is an obvious example. The scientist's responsibility for the use to which her research is put is somewhat less so; sexual harassment of fellow researchers perhaps even less so. One topic that may not seem obvious at all deserves special mention, *conflict of interest*.

By "conflict of interest" I mean any factor that might tend to undermine a competent researcher's ability to make reliable judgments as researcher. Conflict of interest now seems to be a recognized part of research ethics. The concern is less possible fraud than the bad effect a large financial interest in the results of research can have on a researcher's judgment on anything from research strategy, evidence, and conclusions to treatment of graduate students, postdocs, and junior colleagues.

For more than a decade now, discussion of conflict of interest in research has focused on biomedical research in which university and industry have established various close relations (for example, allowing industry representatives to see research results well before publication) (Bowie, 1994). While some critics have called for an outright ban on such close relations, there are at least three reasons to adopt a more nuanced policy. First, the close relations do seem to benefit many researchers, providing them access both to techniques and to ideas that stimulate their research.

Second, graduate students, many of whom will end up in industry, get a chance to see industrial research up close earlier in their careers. And third, for many institutions of higher education (land-grant colleges, institutes of technology, and the like), close cooperation with industry is part of their traditional mission. The "pure science" of biology has simply become more like engineering, pharmacology, agriculture, and other traditionally applied fields (Davis, 1999).

That completes this incomplete survey of topics included under the rubric "the ethics of research." Now let us see what we know about them.

What We Know

Evidence of misconduct in scientific research is of at least six kinds.

First are the few spectacular cases widely discussed in print. Most of these concern biomedical research.

A second source of evidence is the reports on the basis of which governmental agencies such as the Food and Drug Administration may disqualify a particular researcher or undertake criminal prosecution. Most of these reports are about biomedical research (as is most of the research these agencies fund).

A third source of evidence is the retractions scientific journals seem to be printing with increasing frequency. These retractions seem to range well beyond biomedical research.

A fourth source of evidence is the new centralized procedures for handling charges of research misconduct that the large research universities installed during the 1990s. Though these procedures guarantee confidentiality, their centralization assures that a few people in each university will have a much better sense of the minimum extent of the local problem than anyone could have had before. Administrators responsible for receiving charges of research misconduct seem to have been surprised by the large number of charges received. While only a few of the charges turned out, upon investigation, to involve significant wrongdoing, even that few was more than they had expected (Davis, 1999).

A fifth source of evidence is the anecdotes scientists tell one another. Among scientists, journal editors form a special sub-category. Most editors have an informal blacklist, each name on it having its own story. Few disciplines seem to be without these.

The sixth source of evidence is the vague sense of many scientists that research misconduct is now common enough to threaten the well-being of science. This sense of trouble seems to vary considerably from field to field. Physicists, for example, seem much less likely to report it than biomedical researchers.

What can we conclude from this evidence? As in most other areas of human activity, *reported* misconduct is likely to be much less than *actual* misconduct, and not necessarily representative of its character. Whether it is worse than it used to be is less clear, however, and since none of the forms of misconduct seems new, our new interest in research ethics is itself in need of explanation. Why this interest now? One possible explanation is that *Betrayers* is all that is new. I find two other explanations more plausible, especially since they are consistent with each other. One is that the rate of research misconduct actually has increased recently; the other is that science

589

can no longer tolerate even the traditional rate of misconduct. What might be said in support of these two explanations?

Reasons for thinking that the rate of research misconduct might actually have increased include:

1   The greater cost of research today – and the greater dependence on outside (especially, governmental) sources to pay for it – creates pressures beyond those traditionally associated with the requirement to "publish or perish."
2   The greater cost of research today makes any unsatisfactory result a threat to the scientist's ability to continue research, reducing the relative importance of truth.
3   The increasing availability of research grants in certain fields (especially biomedical) tends to attract researchers with the "wrong motives"; that is, those more concerned to make money than to win the recognition of peers or discover something important.
4   The increasing number of university researchers without tenure or academic standing increases pressure to make a good showing on every project.
5   The increasing expense of particular sorts of research makes replication less likely (thereby weakening one check on a researcher's ability to deceive himself or others).
6   The increasing tendency to list as authors of an article all those in a particular laboratory rather than those who actually did the crucial work tends to dilute individual responsibility.
7   The increasing complexity of research, especially the need to cooperate with people from quite different disciplines, also tends to dilute individual responsibility for the project as a whole.
8   The increasing tendency to view the results of even "pure research" as "intellectual property" (the key to a valuable patent, copyright, or the like) leads to secrecy that is otherwise unacceptable, making concealment of wrongdoing easier.
9   Scientists increasingly feel that they are competitors in a rough business rather than cooperators in a noble enterprise and therefore feel less responsible for the misconduct of others in their field.

That is my list of possible reasons for thinking the rate of misconduct may have increased. I do not necessarily accept any of them. They are simply what I have heard others say at one time or another and not yet seen refuted.

Now for some reasons people might find research misconduct increasingly difficult to tolerate even at the traditional rate:

1   The increasing expense and difficulty of replication is making individual scientists more dependent than ever on the probity of others.
2   The increasing complexity of much research makes it harder than ever to identify where a certain experiment has gone wrong (or even that it has gone wrong), making each research project more vulnerable to misinformation in the literature.
3   The increasing tendency of journals to print less than a full description of research design makes informal cooperation among scientists more important (and denial of access to research notes or data more harmful).

4 The money involved in research is increasingly public money subject to unprecedented media scrutiny in an increasingly tight budget.

5 Conscientious researchers feel that as money for research becomes scarce, the misconduct of others puts them at a serious disadvantage in the competition for support.

6 The shortening of time between discovery and application increases the likelihood that third parties will be injured because of research misconduct.

7 The increasing centrality of statistically modest correlations, not results that "jump out of the data," makes small changes in what is reported as data increasingly important.

Responses

That brings me at last to practical responses to misconduct in research. There are at least five: (1) study, (2) regulation, (3) punishment, (4) education, and (5) environmental change.

I have, I think, already written enough about what there is to study. I should only add that the US federal government has been actively encouraging study. Federal agencies have supported individual research projects, research conferences, and even centers devoted to the study of research ethics.

By regulation, I mean adopting standards explicitly defining misconduct in research. The agency adopting the standard may be a professional society, a research institution, or a government. The funding agencies of most governments now have rules defining and forbidding misconduct in research. Most of the large scientific societies in the United States do as well. For example, the American Physical Society adopted a code of ethics in 1991. There is even an international effort to write a universal code of ethics for scientists. The problem today does not seem to be an absence of explicit standards so much as a failure to make those standards an explicit part of the research environment.

By punishment, I mean procedures enforcing the standards of research ethics, whatever the particular penalties might be and whatever the agency administering them. Most large universities now have procedures for soliciting, examining, and settling complaints and, when appropriate, imposing penalties. In the United States, the funding agencies have generally left punishment to the research institutions, stepping in only when they have clearly failed. How necessary punishment is to maintaining the integrity of research is an empirical question. But how necessary it will seem probably depends in part on whether one thinks of ethics on an analogy with other parts of morality (keeping promises) or on an analogy with law (enforcement of contracts).

By education, I mean changes in the way future researchers are taught. Until the 1990s very little was said about the ethics of research in most graduate programs. Graduate students caught on either from a few anecdotes professors or students told or from an occasional reprimand received, overheard, or rumored. Formal instruction in research ethics was virtually unknown. In this respect, graduate education in the sciences was almost two decades behind professional education in law and medicine.

591

But change has come. Most large graduate programs in the sciences now offer some instruction in research ethics. Textbooks (Shrader-Frechette, 1994; Resnik, 1998; Strike et al., 2002) are only now beginning to appear.

That brings me to the last practical response, changing the environment in which researchers actually work. Some of the other responses may change the environment as well. For example, explicitly teaching research ethics can make researchers more likely to notice and report misconduct. Insofar as researchers think about research ethics more often, and talk about it more openly, the working environment of researchers will discourage misconduct in a way it would not otherwise. Changing the standards of evaluation (for example, by reducing the importance of novelty or number) might have a similar effect.

Will any of these responses, indeed, even all of them, accomplish anything? That too is an empirical question. We do, however, have some evidence that they should accomplish something. These responses all tend to make the sciences resemble professions (like medicine or engineering). While every profession has ethics problems of its own, most professions seem to think they are better off with some combination of study, regulation, punishment, education, and environmental efforts than they would be without them.

What role is there for philosophers here? Their role is, I think, not so much to apply moral theory to the questions defining the field as to examine the arguments the practitioners themselves generate. To do a good job of examining those arguments, philosophers need to know a lot about the empirical background. But, as in philosophy of law or science, philosophers will probably find learning what they need to know about the practice in question easier than teaching busy practitioners to do philosophy.

See also 39 ETHICS AND THE AIMS OF AMERICAN HIGHER EDUCATION; 41 ACADEMIC FREEDOM; 45 THE ROLE OF ETHICS IN PROFESIONAL EDUCATION

References

Babbage, C. (1830) *Reflections on the Decline of Science in England.* Cambridge: Cambridge University Press.

Bowie, N. (1994) *University–Business Partnerships: An Assessment.* Lanham, MD: Rowman & Littlefield.

Broad, W. and Wade, N. (1982) *Betrayers of the Truth.* New York: Simon and Schuster.

Davis, M. (1999) *Ethics and the University.* London: Routledge.

Hearnshaw, L. S. (1981) *Cyril Burt – Psychologist.* New York: Random House/Vintage Books.

Hixson, J. (1976) *The Patchwork Mouse.* Garden City, NJ: Anchor/Doubleday.

Jacoby, R. (1987) *The Last Intellectuals.* New York: Basic Book.

Resnik, D. (1998) *The Ethics of Science: An Introduction.* London: Routledge.

Shrader-Frechette, K. (1994) *Ethics of Scientific Research.* Lanham, MD: Rowman & Littlefield.

Strike, K, Anderson, M., Curren, R., van Geel, T., Pritchard, I., and Robertson, E. (2002) *Ethical Standards of the American Educational Research Association: Cases and Commentary.* Washington, DC: AERA Publications.

van der Waerden, B. L. (1968) Mendel's experiments. *Centaurus,* 12, 275–88.

43

Affirmative Action in Higher Education

Bernard Boxill

The term "affirmative action" was at first used to refer to a court order that required a company found guilty of racial or sexual discrimination to make restitution to those it had wronged, and to alter its hiring and promotion practices to avoid such discrimination in the future. Nowadays it is used more generally to refer to race- or sex-sensitive policies designed to increase the number of racial minorities and women in universities and the workplace. Consequently it has come to be identified popularly with the preferential hiring and admission of women and racial minorities, although, as we shall see, many of its defenders maintain that the identification is seriously misleading.

Philosophers have used two main kinds of arguments to defend affirmative action, backward-looking arguments and forward-looking arguments. Backward-looking arguments support affirmative action on the ground that it is compensation for past injustices. Forward-looking arguments support affirmative action on the ground that it will have good consequences.

Although critics have sharply attacked both kinds of arguments, they aim their severest objections at the backward-looking arguments. Indeed, even the staunchest defenders of affirmative action now tend to look askance at such arguments. As Ronald Dworkin (1991) wrote in an op-ed piece in the *New York Times*, "Black applicants have no right to preferences now because other blacks suffered from injustice in the past. But affirmative action assumes no such right: It has a forward-looking justification. The policy promises a better educational environment and a less racially stratified society for everyone. It recognizes that prejudice has poisoned society for all of us, and that fostering opportunities for different races to study and work together is part of an effective even if slow-working antidote." Dworkin evidently believes that the case for affirmative action does not rely on any backward-looking considerations, but appeals only to the supposition that it will help bring about an integrated, perhaps prejudice-free, society in the future. I do not think that affirmative action should have to rely on this bold assumption, and in this essay I argue that it can be justified even if its consequences are somewhat less spectacular. I also argue that backward-looking arguments for affirmative action are not as easily dismissed as he seems to think and, indeed, that the case for affirmative action can be strengthened by a backward-looking consideration.

Affirmative Action and Prejudice

Dworkin believes that affirmative action has important good consequences. That is why he is so confident that forward-looking arguments support it. Among the good consequences of affirmative action that he cites is a "better educational environment." No doubt he is right. Affirmative action increases the diversity of the student bodies at elite universities, and other things being equal, a diverse student body is educationally superior to one in which everyone shares the same background. For one thing it aids the discovery and testing of the truth, and these are among the objects of a good education. Somewhat more controversially, Dworkin claims that affirmative action will have the good consequence of reducing racial prejudice by "fostering opportunities for different races to work and study together." This argument supports integrating schools and the workplace, but it need not necessarily support affirmative action. If fostering opportunities for different races to work and study together helps to reduce racial prejudice, we must integrate the workplace, integrate the primary and secondary schools, and integrate institutions of higher learning. Perhaps we can do this by encouraging black students attending mostly black colleges to attend mostly white colleges, and white students attending mostly white colleges to attend mostly black colleges. We may not need to preferentially admit black students to elite, and mostly white, colleges, universities, and professional schools. That is, we may not need affirmative action.

This suggests that Dworkin does not endorse affirmative action simply because it integrates universities but because it does so at the elite level. Given his view that affirmative action will reduce racial prejudice he therefore seems committed to the view that racial integration at the elite level will help reduce racial prejudice. This would explain why he numbers reducing racial stratification among the good consequences for society. Certainly, affirmative action will reduce the racial stratification of the society, but why is that a good thing? An egalitarian would applaud a less racially stratified society if such a society were also necessarily a less unequal society. But that need not be the case. A racially stratified society is one in which blacks are concentrated in the lower classes. A less racially stratified society is one in which blacks are not concentrated in the lower classes, but are represented proportionately in the middle and upper classes. But we can make a racially stratified society less racially stratified without making it more equal. We can do this by pushing some blacks up into the upper and middle classes while pushing some whites down into the middle and lower classes. Since this is arguably exactly what affirmative action does, it can make a society less racially stratified while failing to make the society more equal. But if reducing racial stratification means racial integration in universities at the elite level, then supposing that such integration does help reduce racial prejudice, we have an argument for affirmative action, even if it does not make the society more equal.

Undoubtedly affirmative action has integrated universities at the elite level. In this sense it has reduced racial stratification. But what reason is there to believe that integrating universities at the elite level will help reduce racial prejudice? One may hope that if the black and white students at elite universities become the society's main intellectual leaders, they will teach it the racial amity they learn at such universities, but we should not take it for granted that they will learn racial amity. Presumably Jews in Western Europe before the Second World War attended elite institutions. Certainly they were not concentrated in the lower class, and many held high positions, and enjoyed considerable standing among the intellectual elite. Obviously, however, this did not mean that the poison of anti-Semitism was disappearing. On the contrary, Jewish success may have helped to arouse the envy and hatred that made the holocaust possible. How can we be confident that a similar process might not occur if blacks become successful, and begin to hold top jobs and positions? Wouldn't it be almost natural for the descendants of slaveholders (or those who identify with them) to be outraged and angered when they are pushed from their high positions by the descendants of people their fathers enslaved?

I am not saying, or implying, that racial prejudice cannot be reduced, or even that racial prejudice cannot be reduced by racial integration at the elite level. I am saying that historical evidence suggests that mere racial integration at the elite level may not reduce, and may even exacerbate, racial prejudice. In other words we cannot endorse affirmative action on the ground that simply putting black and white students into the same elite universities will reduce their prejudices and encourage them to reduce the prejudices of society. History indicates that if elite integration is to have these effects it must be done in some special way, and involve some special measures.

The Talented Tenth

The argument that integration at the elite level reduces racial prejudice should not be confused with the argument that racial integration at the elite level gives the black elite an opportunity to learn how to deal with the white elite. The classic statement of the latter argument was given by Sir Arthur Lewis, a professor at Princeton and a Nobel Prize winner in economics.

Blacks in America are inevitably and perpetually a minority. This means that in all administrative and leadership positions we are going to be outnumbered by white folks, and we will have to compete with them not on our terms but on theirs. The only way to win this game is to know them so thoroughly that we can outpace them. For us to turn our backs on this opportunity, by insisting on mingling only with other black students in college, is folly of the highest order. (Lewis, 1973, p.145)

Lewis's argument stresses that it is not enough to put black students in elite white colleges and universities. While at such colleges and universities they must be sure not to mingle "only with other black students." This, Lewis claims, would be "folly of the highest order." But his point, it should be carefully noted, is not that mingling with whites will reduce racial prejudice. It is that mingling with whites will help blacks to "know" whites so thoroughly that they can "compete" with them and "outpace" them. Not only is this possible without any significant reduction in racial prejudice, it seems to anticipate a continuing racial rivalry.

But, of course, few would take affirmative action seriously if it simply helped a few elite blacks to learn to "compete" with and "outpace" whites. Surely it must do more than that, if it is to be justified. To see what more it can do we must take a look at the nature and function of higher education.

No one tries to make a case for institutions of higher learning solely in terms of the good it does to those who attend such institutions. Invariably the argument is that people who attend institutions of higher learning "give back" to their societies more than was given to them. There are two main versions of the argument. The first, older argument relies on the philanthropic motives of those attending institutions of higher learning. The second argument does not. I describe it briefly, and then set it aside, because the first argument is more relevant to our present concerns.

The second argument for higher learning probably came to the fore with the rise of science and it has become increasingly prominent with the increasing contributions science makes to human well-being. The argument is that investments in the institutions that conduct teaching and research in the basic sciences, as well as in those devoted to medicine, engineering, and agriculture, pay handsome dividends to the society as a whole. It does not assume that graduates of such institutions are motivated by the desire to act justly, and want to repay the society for making their education possible. Such a desire would usually be welcome, of course, but the argument can get along without it. All the argument needs is the plausible assumption that as graduates of institutions of higher learning pursue their enlightened self-interest, then almost inevitably they will make the inventions and applications in science that improve the lives of everyone.

The argument for higher education just sketched relies on the scientific creativity and the enlightened self-interest of an educated class, and stresses the material benefits society receives from such a class. The older argument for higher education, to which I now turn, stresses the moral and practical benefits society receives from the beneficiaries of higher education, and maintains that these individuals will be morally motivated to assist the society that paid for their education, at least when this education has been successful. Its classic exposition is, of course, Plato's *Republic*. In that book Plato argues that the ideal society will provide its future leaders with an extraordinarily deep and thorough education, and that these individuals will, in return, provide their city with the best protection and leadership it can get. Although the philosopher-kings get something for themselves from their education, for they are, Plato tells us, the happiest people in the society, he insists that their education is justified by the good it contributes to the city as a whole, and that they make their contribution from the desire to act justly. It is especially relevant to my argument that W. E. B. DuBois, the great black educator, appeared to endorse Plato's theory in his own theory of the Talented Tenth. "The Talented Tenth of the Negro race," DuBois wrote, "must be made leaders of thought and missionaries of culture among their people. No others can do this work and Negro colleges must train men for it" (DuBois, 1999, p. 533). More recently Glenn Loury has made a similar but somewhat more general point. It is "clear," Loury writes, that "black business, academic, and political elites must press for improvement in their own peoples' lives through the building of constructive internal institutions"(Loury, 1995, p. 49).

We should now begin to see, if only in outline, how a plausible argument for affirmative action in higher education can be constructed. It would go somewhat as follows. Affirmative action will not only help produce a class of educated blacks who will learn how to compete with and outpace their white counterparts. It will help produce a class of educated blacks who will become the Talented Tenth of the black society. That is, it will help produce a class of individuals who will be the intellectual leaders of the black community and who will use their learning and education to help solve its peculiar problems.

This argument does not rely on the assumption that affirmative action will significantly reduce racial prejudice. If affirmative action had this result it would be welcome, of course, but the present argument is that affirmative action has another good consequence that suffices to justify it. It provides the black community with a sorely needed Talented Tenth, and this is a good consequence because every society needs a Talented Tenth to flourish.

Objections

Perhaps the most familiar objection usually urged against affirmative action is that it violates the rights of young white males to a fair competition for places and positions. The key assumption of that objection is that color or race can never be a qualification for a job, position, or place in a university. Once this assumption is granted, affirmative action seems unfair because it gives preference to blacks on account of their color. The usual forward-looking response to this objection is to reject its key assumption and to argue that color can sometimes be a qualification for a job, position, or place in a university or professional school. This requires a reconsideration of what qualifications for a place in a university or professional school are. This begins with the fact, as I mentioned earlier, that the purpose of institutions of higher learning is to train people to serve the society, not to reward the highly intelligent. The purpose of medical schools, for example, is to train good doctors who will provide the society with good medical service. The qualifications for admission to medical school are understood with this purpose in mind. High grades and aptitude scores are normally among the qualifications for places in medical schools, because experience has taught us that people with them usually become better doctors than people without them. For similar reasons, a disposition to actually practice medicine, as far as such a disposition can be determined, is a qualification for admission to medical school, as is youth, for a medical education is very expensive, and it would be wasteful to train doctors who we know can only practice for a short time. Now suppose that the black community does not get good medical service, and that the government figures that it can get them such service by preferentially admitting black students into medical schools, supposing that black doctors are more likely to work in the black community than white doctors. In such cases, it seems that color can be among the qualifications for admission to medical school for the same reason that high grades and aptitude scores, and youth and a disposition to practice medicine are, and consequently that taking it into consideration for such admission is no more an injustice than taking high grades and aptitude scores into consideration. In particular, those who fail to be admitted into medical school as a result have no ground for complaint. Indeed, if this is correct, it seems seriously misleading to refer to affirmative action as preferential treatment since this suggests that blacks are being admitted on the basis of qualities that are not strictly qualifications.

It may be objected that color cannot be a qualification for admission to medical school because it is not an achievement; one is simply born that way. This objection persists in thinking of admission to medical school as a reward, because rewards are given for achievements. But as I have argued, admission to medical school is not a reward for high grades. Instead, it is based on an estimation that the person admitted will be a good doctor and will practice medicine. Thus although qualifications are often achievements they need not be. Youth and high aptitude, for example, are not achievements any more than color is, though they certainly can be among the qualifications for admission to medical school.

If these arguments are sound, color can be a qualification for admission to medical school, when taking it into account can help provide medical service for the black community which might not otherwise have it. For similar reasons, color can be a qualification for admission to institutions of higher learning in general, when taking it into consideration for admission to such institutions can help provide a Talented Tenth for the black community, which might not otherwise have the advantage of such a class. Further, it seems that in such cases, individuals disadvantaged by such a policy may have no legitimate grounds for complaint. To see this all we need to remember is that the reason for establishing institutions of higher learning is to provide the necessary conditions for the flourishing of all sections of the society. A very similar argument can be constructed to show that affirmative action in higher education for women may do no injustice to white males.

Unfortunately this argument is not altogether satisfactory as it stands. Suppose, for example, that certain pockets of people fail to get adequate medical service by engaging in behavior that is known to very likely have this effect; for example, by voluntarily segregating themselves from the rest of the society. Such people may deserve charity, but they do not have a right to affirmative action to assure them of adequate medical service because by their behavior they have forfeited, or at least waived, their right to it. No one can insist on following practices that are known to be harmful, and then justifiably claim a right to rescue from others who have acted more wisely. Such a right would result in the breakdown of society if it were taken seriously. It cannot be defended even if the harmful practices people engage in are a part of their culture. One of the advantages of living in a multicultural society is that no one is forced to follow the harmful practices of his culture, even if he grows up in it. Most Southern slave holders were born into the leisured, wasteful lifestyle that was a part of their culture. Was it just for them to enslave others to support it?

This consideration suggests that we may have to ask how people get into trouble before we can justify affirmative action to get them out of trouble. If they got into trouble through their own fault, then affirmative action may not be justified. Thus, if one is defending affirmative action in higher education along the lines I have suggested, it would seem necessary to appeal to the fact that the black community has not gotten into trouble through its own fault. In particular, its failure to have a Talented Tenth is not the result of unforeseeable misfortunes or self-indulgence. It did not insist on pursuing policies that would predictably deprive it of a Talented Tenth. For example, it did not voluntarily deny itself the benefits of fair interaction with the larger society. On the contrary it has yearned for full and equal membership in that society, and has made every self-respecting effort to achieve that end. Its segregation is the result of the injustice of the larger society. Even the so-called Black Nationalists called for black self-segregation only after whites savagely excluded them from the advantages of the larger society.

But comments like the one I cited from Dworkin above suggest that such backward-looking considerations cannot help justify affirmative action since blacks cannot have a right to preference because "other blacks suffered from injustice in the past." If that suggestion were true, it would be right to dismiss all versions of the backward-looking argument. Defending affirmative action for present day blacks on the ground that "other blacks suffered from injustice in the past" is a non-starter. Present day blacks cannot be compensated for the injustices suffered by "other" blacks in the past, or for that matter, other blacks in the present. This is a logical truth because to compensate someone is to compensate him for an injustice he himself has suffered. No one can be compensated for someone else's injury.

But there are versions of the backward-looking argument that cannot be so easily dismissed. Consider, for example, the argument that affirmative action compensates black people for the injuries they suffer because of the pervasive race prejudice of the society. This is certainly a backward-looking argument, for it appeals to past injust-ices, though, of course, these injustices did not occur as far back in the past as the argument Dworkin considers. But it is not obviously vulnerable to the objection that it proposes to compensate some people for the injuries of others. Its proposal is that affirmative action compensates present day blacks for the harms prejudice causes them, not that it compensates them for the harms prejudice caused other blacks. Or consider the argument that affirmative action compensates present day blacks for the injuries they suffer as a result of unjust injuries inflicted on other blacks in the past. This is obviously a backward-looking argument because it appeals to past unjust injuries. But it too cannot be dismissed on the ground that it proposes to compensate present day blacks for the harms done to other blacks. For example, it does not say that affirmative action compensates present day blacks for the enslavement of their ancestors. This would be ridiculous because only the slaves can be compensated for their enslavement. The argument says that affirmative action compensates present day blacks for injuries they themselves have endured, though it adds that these injuries were caused by the unjust enslavement of their ancestors.

These two arguments may provide the basis for a backward-looking argument for affirmative action. But I am concerned here only with using them to defend the case for affirmative action in higher education that I have suggested, namely that it can help create a Talented Tenth for the black community. Although slavery and its aftermath are among the potent causes of the fact that the black community lacks a Talented Tenth of adequate extent and distinction, the victims of social disasters normally pick themselves up and recover, often without notable help from anyone but themselves. Consequently it is important to add that persistent prejudice and discrimination has prevented the black community from overcoming the disabilities of a legacy of slavery and providing itself with a Talented Tenth. In other words, the black community is not in any way at fault for continuing to lack a Talented Tenth, and consequently has not waived any of its rights to be provided with such leadership by the society in general. In particular, if taking color into consideration for admission to institutions of higher learning will help create a Talented Tenth for the black community, then color can be a qualification for admission to such institutions and those disadvantaged by such policies have no legitimate grounds for complaint.

I assume that no reasonable person will deny that slavery imposed an enormous burden on the ancestors of the present black population, even after it was abolished. This should be especially clear when it is remembered that no serious effort was made to put the freed slaves on anything like an equal footing with the free white population. But it may be objected that blacks are still at fault for their predicament because for some time there has been no pervasive and harmful racial prejudice of the sort my argument relies on, or that if there is such prejudice it is matched by a similar prejudice against women and the white lower classes. Taking the second part of the objection first, I admit freely that racial prejudice is matched by a very similar prejudice directed against women. This would be an embarrassment for me if I denied that women deserve preferential admission to institutions of higher education. But I believe that women do deserve preferential admission to such institutions. I also do not oppose affirmative action in higher education for lower-class whites, but the case for it must be different from the corresponding case for affirmative action in higher education for blacks and women. That case is based on the idea that affirmative action will help create a black Talented Tenth, for blacks and women, but of course, the white lower classes already have a Talented Tenth; it is the Talented Tenth of white society. It will be objected that I ignore the extent of class prejudice in the USA. But I believe that it is far weaker than the prejudice against women and blacks. This is not necessarily true for all societies, of course. I understand that in many European countries it is a serious barrier to the advancement of the lower classes. Fortunately this is not the case in the USA. Many Europeans moved to the USA to escape class prejudice, and they have in general done a good job of keeping it at bay. Americans love to see the members of the lower classes rise – if they are white – for it confirms the idea of America as the land of opportunity, and the most successful Americans like to boast of their humble origins.

The complaint that there is no pervasive and harmful prejudice of the kind my argument depends on is not available to advocates of the forward-looking argument like Dworkin who claim that racial prejudice has "poisoned" society, and argue that affirmative action is justified in part because it reduces that prejudice. This argument would hardly be persuasive if they supposed that racial prejudice is merely offensive. If that were indeed the case, affirmative action would not be worth the trouble it causes even if it reduced racial prejudice. But, of course, many people reject all arguments for affirmative action, including the forward-looking argument that affirmative action helps to reduce racial prejudice. Such people, though perhaps mistaken, are involved in no inconsistency when they deny that racial prejudice is either pervasive or harmful.

We should not rely on the testimony of whites who claim that prejudice is not pervasive. They are affected by it only indirectly and are understandably apt to overlook it. Those who are directly affected by it rarely if ever deny that it is pervasive. No one claims that it is always salient. But it occurs often enough, and unpredictably enough, to work its evil effects. As DuBois put it, "but the terrible thing is – these things do happen – not all each day – but now and then...not everywhere, but anywhere.... Imagine spending your life looking for insults or for hiding places from them" (DuBois, 1970, p. 4). Further, many studies have demonstrated that the discrimination prejudice supports is also pervasive. In Thurgood Marshall's experienced observation, "It is unnecessary in the twentieth century in America to have individual Negroes demonstrate that they have been victims of racial discrimination. [It] has been so pervasive that none, regardless of wealth or position, has managed to escape its impact" (Marshall, 2001, p. 353).

This takes us to the objection that affirmative action distributes its benefits unfairly. The objection goes as follows. Part of the argument for affirmative action is that racial and sexual prejudice harms all blacks and all women. But affirmative action seems to compensate mainly middle-class and upper-class blacks. How can this be fair?

It must be conceded that most of the blacks and women admitted preferentially to colleges and universities, and to law schools and medical schools, come mainly from the middle classes and upper classes. This is not so by design. It is not as if colleges and universities, and law schools and medical schools, aim at recruiting only middle-class and upper-class blacks. They aim to recruit blacks who are academically prepared to handle the intellectual work they require of their students. But it happens, understandably, that most, though probably not all, of these students come from the middle classes and upper classes. But the objection is that this is hardly enough to justify the practice. Whatever its aim, the practice seems to compensate mainly the blacks in the middle classes and upper classes.

To answer this objection it is not enough to point out that lower-class blacks and women may not do well in higher education. This may only invite the retort that it still cannot be right to endorse a practice that compensates the less harmed before the more harmed. But this retort is based on several misconceptions. In the first place it is not absolutely clear that prejudice harms lower-class blacks and women more than blacks and women in the middle and upper classes. The generally poorer qualifications of the black lower classes compared to those of the black middle and upper classes do not necessarily imply that prejudice harms them more. These disabilities may be harms, but they could be caused by poorer educational opportunities and poorer home environments rather than by prejudice. Moreover, affirmative action in higher education does not attempt to compensate every black for all the harms he or she has suffered because of slavery and its aftermath of prejudice and discrimination. This would be impossible to do. We have no idea what individual blacks now living would have had if slavery had never existed. Indeed, had this tragedy never occurred, the African ancestors of present day blacks would probably never have left Africa, and never have had children with the people they in fact had children with, and consequently, since our identities depend on the identities of our parents, individual blacks now living would not exist. Supposing that prejudice and the legacy of slavery robbed the black community of a Talented Tenth, affirmative action in higher education is partial compensation to the black community as a whole for that harm only. Finally, the fact that we endorse affirmative action in higher education does not mean that we endorse it before other policies designed, for example, to improve the prospects of lower-class blacks. Affirmative action in higher education, as I have defended it, helps to create a Talented Tenth for the black community. It does not follow that this policy takes precedence over other policies for black advancement.

Perhaps the most obvious objection to my argument is that it is elitist. It is well taken if it means that I assume that better educated people can often invent and propose better solutions to the problems of their communities than the less enlightened. But in that case I do not see how it is a criticism. What is the point of education if it does not have this result? As far as I know, no serious theorist has questioned this advantage of education, and I include specifically radical egalitarians like Rousseau, Marx, and Lenin. On the other hand, nothing I have said suggests that the rights to political participation of the less educated are unequal and inferior to those of the Talented Tenth.

The elitist criticism aside, three further important objections to my view are as follows. First, even if, in a certain sense, every society must have a Talented Tenth to flourish, the black community is not a society in that sense. It is part of the larger American society, and that society has a Talented Tenth. Second, if the black community needs a Talented Tenth why does it need a Talented Tenth educated in elite universities? Third, is affirmative action likely to create a Talented Tenth, and not simply a privileged class?

It may seem that the first objection does not need a detailed or extended reply. The following seems sufficient. The black and white communities remain largely segregated. The black community faces problems that the white community does not face, and the educated classes of the white community are preoccupied with the problems of the community they are drawn from. Consequently, assuming that the peculiar problems of the black community can only be resolved by an educated class that is suitably related to and identified with it, it follows that the black community sorely needs its own Talented Tenth. But this short reply may beg the question. The black and white communities remain largely segregated, but this is a deplorable state of affairs we should strive to bring to an end. Indeed, it may be argued, one of the purposes of a Talented Tenth is to help to dissolve the animosities and suspicions that keep communities segregated, not to lead a segregated community. This objection could conceivably still support affirmative action in higher education, but its object would be to create an integrated Talented Tenth that will help to create an integrated community. In response I grant that one of the purposes of a Talented Tenth is to help dissolve the animosities and suspicions that keep communities segregated. It does not follow, however, that this done integration must follow. Groups may prefer to keep separate even if they do not hate each other. Pluralism is a viable and acceptable alternative to assimilation. Further, integration is unlikely between groups that are very unequal in educational and economic attainments. Even in the absence of racial animosity, people do not mix readily with their economic and educational inferiors. Consequently, even if assimilation is preferable to pluralism, it is likely to be preceded by a pluralism of roughly equal groups. But a black Talented Tenth may be necessary to help close the educational and economic gap between white and black groups.

Suppose that this argument is sound and that the black community must first have a Talented Tenth to help raise it to a respectable equality with other groups. Even so, it does not follow that we must have affirmative action in higher education. There was an educated black class before affirmative action. There would be a case for

602

affirmative action only if the black community's Talented Tenth must be schooled with the white elite. But why is that the case? Why can't the black Talented Tenth be schooled in the black colleges, as, indeed, DuBois seemed to suggest. The answer to this question is that the solutions to the problems of the black community are affected by decisions made at the highest levels in the white community. That is, blacks need to be represented among the top decision-makers if there is to be reasonable assurance that the interests of the black community will not be ignored. As Lewis recommends, the black elite must know the white elites so thoroughly that they can "outpace" them, not, I would add, for purely selfish reasons, but for the benefit of the black community.

The third and final problem is the most serious. Even if the black beneficiaries of affirmative action successfully fill positions of responsibility, are they likely to help the black community in the way that a Talented Tenth is supposed to help the society from which it is drawn? This objection is especially pertinent because of the anomalous position of the black community and the anomalous position of an educated class created by affirmative action. Educated classes do not necessarily benefit their communities. They have to be related to these communities in the right way, and educated in the right way. This is perfectly obvious if we think of the way Plato makes his case for a Talented Tenth. Not only are its members educated to appreciate their obligations to the community, they also think of the members of the other classes as their brothers and sisters. Are these conditions likely to be satisfied in a Talented Tenth created by affirmative action and educated in our elite universities? I doubt that such universities are likely to deliberately set about encouraging black students to identify themselves with the black community, and accept a responsibility to it. The waning of racial prejudice among the elite, itself a highly desirable development, may facilitate the black elite's identification with the white elite, and undermine its identification with the black community. The black elite may also find it difficult to identify with what has come to be known as the "black underclass." Its members may find it practically impossible to see things from the point of view of people so different from themselves in educational and economic attainments. On the other hand, the increasing availability of courses in black history and African-American philosophy at top universities may help persuade black students that racial identities are more persistent that they might otherwise think, and this might help kindle in them a feeling of identification with and responsibility for the black community. In any case, an extended empirical investigation of the results of affirmative action finds solid ground for hope. As William Bowen and Derek Bok conclude, the evidence suggests that many of the beneficiaries of affirmative action "are giving back and maintaining ties to their communities, while also forging links with the broader American society... social commitment and community concerns have not been thrown aside at the first sign of personal success" (Bowen and Bok, 1998, p. 171).

See also: 32 EDUCATION AND STANDARDS OF LIVING; 33 EDUCATIONAL EQUALITY AND JUSTICE; 34 MULTICULTURAL EDUCATION; 35 EDUCATION AND THE POLITICS OF IDENTITY; 41 ACADEMIC FREEDOM

References

Bowen, W. G. and Bok, D. (1998) *The Shape of the River*. Princeton, NJ: Princeton University Press

DuBois, W. E. B. (1970) On being black. In Philip S. Foner (ed.), *W. E. B. DuBois Speaks, volume 2*.

DuBois, W. E. B. (1999) The talented tenth. In H. Brotz (ed.), *African-American Political Thought 1850–1920*. New Brunswick, NJ: Transaction Publishers, pp. 518–33.

Dworkin, R. (1991) Race and the uses of law. *New York Times*, April 13, A17.

Lewis, W. A. (1973) The road to the top is through higher education – not black studies. In J. Blassigame (ed.), *New Perspectives on Black Studies*. Urbana: University of Illinois Press, pp. 133–48.

Loury, G. (1999) The moral quandary of the black community. In G. Loury (ed.), *One by One from the Inside Out*. New York: The Free Press, pp. 33–49.

Marshall, T. (1978) Regents of the University of California v. Bakke. In M. Tushnet (ed.), *Thurgood Marshall*. Chicago: Lawrence Hill Books, pp. 345–63.

Further reading

Boxill, B. (1972) The morality of reparation. *Social Theory and Practice*, 2, 113–22.

Boxill, B. (1992) *Blacks and Social Justice*. Lanham, MD: Rowman and Littlefield.

DuBois, W. E. B. (1995) The talented tenth: memorial address. In D. Lewis (ed.), *W. E. B. DuBois: A Reader*. New York: Henry Holt.

Dworkin, R. (1977) Reverse discrimination. In *Taking Rights Seriously*. Cambridge, MA: Harvard University Press, pp. 223–39.

Dworkin, R. (2000) *Sovereign Virtue*. Cambridge, MA: Harvard University Press.

Ezorsky, G. (1991) *Racism and Justice: The Case for Affirmative Action*. Ithaca, NY: Cornell University Press.

Fullinwider, R. (1980) *The Reverse Discrimination Controversy*. Lanham, MD: Rowman and Littlefield.

Gates, H. L. and West, C. (1996) *The Future of the Race*. New York: Knopf.

Hill, T. E. Jr (1991) The message of affirmative action. *Social Philosophy and Policy*, 8, 108–29.

McGary, H. (1999) Affirmative action: a review and commentary. In *Race and Social Justice*. Malden, MA: Blackwell.

Mosley, A. and Capaldi, N. (1996) *Affirmative Action: Social Justice or Unfair Preference*. Lanham, MD: Rowman and Littlefield.

Roberts, R. (2001) Why have the injustices perpetrated against blacks in America not been rectified? *Journal of Social Philosophy*, 32, 357–73.

Thomas, L. (1993) What good am I? In S. Cahn (ed.), *Affirmative Action and the University*, pp. 125–31. Philadelphia: Temple.

Thomson, J. (1973) Preferential hiring. *Philosophy and Public Affairs*, 2, 364–84.

Wasserstrom, R. (1976) The university and the case for preferential treatment. *American Philosophical Quarterly*, 13, 165–70.

44

The Professor–Student Relationship and the Regulation of Student Life

Peter J. Markie

Professors commonly regulate the academic aspects of students' lives, setting degree and course requirements, determining the subject matter of their studies, and defining and certifying their success. We exercise this power with extensive autonomy, and all of this seems quite right. Yet what is the basis for our authority and the autonomy with which we exercise it? What are the appropriate limits to its exercise? In this chapter I develop and defend a general answer to these questions, by first examining and discarding some inadequate accounts and then proposing one that succeeds where they fail.

Professors and Students' Academic Lives: Authority and Autonomy

Consider the extent of our authority over students' academic lives. In our own classes, we determine what they study and for how long. If we decide they need to cover a particular series of topics as presented in certain texts, we list the texts and readings on the syllabus as required. We decide whether they work collaboratively or independently. We set the standards for the evaluation of students' knowledge of the material and the process by which those standards are applied and certifications of achievement are made. We set the policies on attendance, make-up exams, and delayed grades. Beyond our individual classes, we join with our colleagues to define degree requirements, making some courses necessary and others optional, as well as department, college, and university policies on grades, attendance, academic standing, and so on. Generally, and quite properly, if a matter concerns students' academic activities, professors, individually or collectively, make the rules and so regulate students' lives.

Our power to regulate is a power to benefit or harm. When we use our power appropriately, we promote students' education, advancing both their intellectual and personal development. They confront new ideas, learn to think, gain knowledge, and mature intellectually. When we misuse it, we rob them of educational opportunities and, perhaps, harm them in other quite substantial ways. We may discourage them from beneficial areas of study, encourage them in misology, or destroy their self-confidence. Our self-interest can conflict with the proper use of our authority. We can, at times, gain various benefits for ourselves by setting inappropriate requirements for students. We can design a course to cover only the topics that interest us, rather than the ones students need and are prepared to learn. We can reduce our class preparation by teaching the same material over and over despite changes in the field. We can lessen our grading chores with an inappropriately small number of exams and other forms of evaluation. We can use our position of authority to pressure students into activities, from sexual relations to free assistance with our research, that they would ordinarily avoid.

Despite what is at stake in how well we use our authority to regulate students' academic lives and the potential conflict between the appropriate use of our authority and our own self-interest, we lay claim to, and are granted, a great deal of autonomy in its use. The institutional regulations that limit our ability to define our own expectations for our students are usually limited to technical aspects of teaching, such as the time period before a delayed grade becomes a failing grade, and, even then, they are established by the faculty collectively. Students who object to our regulations have little option beyond seeking their education elsewhere. Others associated with the university – deans, provosts, governing boards, alumni groups, and state legislators – seldom interfere. They assume that, lacking very strong justification, it is improper for them to regulate how we in turn regulate our students' academic lives. Various forms of teaching evaluation provide some monitoring of how well we teach, and, under that heading, how well we use our authority, but only in the most egregious cases do negative evaluations, and student complaints in general, trigger a restriction of our authority to design our courses and curricula as we will.

What, then, is the ultimate justification for both our power to regulate students' academic lives and the autonomy with which we are allowed to use it? Given that we can use this authority for better or worse, what are the appropriate limitations on its use and how are they defined? Why would it be improper for others to regulate our use of this authority in more substantial ways?

Let us consider two unsatisfactory answers as a way of clearing the ground for a successful one. A common answer is that professors are entitled to academic freedom. We define the academic expectations for our students as an expression of our own academic freedom to decide what and how to teach. Our autonomy in defining these expectations is based on the need for others, within and without the university, to respect that freedom. Yet this understanding of the basis for our authority and the autonomy with which we properly exercise it is as inadequate as it is common. To defend our power and autonomy by citing our academic freedom is simply to repeat ourselves and miss the basic issue: why should we be granted such academic freedom – such authority over students' academic lives and autonomy in its use – in the first place? Consider the fact that some instructors are subject to limitations on their autonomy that do not apply to others. Graduate teaching assistants with primary responsibility for their own classes may be properly subjected to requirements that they teach from certain texts, cover certain topics, or give certain sorts of exams. Professors teaching the same course are appropriately exempt from these restrictions.

Why is it appropriate to limit the graduate teaching assistants' autonomy and not the professors'? To say that the former have a lesser right to academic freedom than the latter is to beg the question. Why does the right exist in the first place and why do some instructors have more of it than others?

A second strategy is to appeal to a contract between professors and students. When we design a course, or an entire program of study, and students freely register to take it, mutual commitments are made. We agree to teach the course as we have designed and advertised it; they agree to the regulations that we impose. We, in effect, offer a product or service under certain terms; students wanting the service agree to the terms and provide us with our authority over that aspect of their lives. Our authority derives from their consent. They can end our authority by ending the relationship, withdrawing from the course, the program of study, or even the university. The appropriate limits of our authority are determined by our mutual agreement. Students agree to our being in charge of the course requirements and the like. They do not agree to provide sexual favors or help with our research.

This approach to understanding the basis and limits of our authority contains several instructive shortcomings. First, while the professor–student relationship is clearly consensual, it does not involve an explicit or implicit agreement, or even a shared understanding, that is detailed enough to appropriately define the limits of our authority. Most students, and many professors, simply do not have such a clear and detailed conception of their expectations for each other.

Second, the contract approach encourages us to make the mistake of thinking that the appropriate limits of our authority are simply determined by what students will accept. We misuse our authority if we devote an introductory undergraduate course to graduate level material on a single narrow topic of research interest to us. The fact that the students register for the course and stay in it, even when made aware of our plan, does not change that fact. So too, that the students consent to our plan to cancel half the class meetings or regularly end class early is not sufficient to make such behaviors legitimate exercises of our authority to regulate students' academic lives.

Third, the contract approach provides no explanation for why we should be granted extensive autonomy in the use of our authority. Why should not other parties intervene to regulate our agreements with students? What is the basis for our being allowed to set the terms of the agreement with so little institutional review? We are not after all independent contractors. We enter into our relationship with students as the employees of a college or university. Why should we be granted such authority to set up the relationship as we, individually, decide? If students are the consumers of a service we provide and so much of the power in the relationship rests with us, should not there be a student (consumer) protection agency? What is the basis for the fact that some instructors, e.g. graduate teaching assistants, quite properly have less autonomy in the exercise of their authority than others, e.g. full professors? The contract approach does not answer these questions.

Fourth, the contract approach fails to relate our authority and autonomy to our professional expertise. The reason why we have a right to set academic expectations and a right to students' compliance is not simply that students have agreed to the relationship. It is, in some way, because we know best. We are entitled to determine what students are required to study because, in part, we know what they should

607

study. The contract approach ignores this important basis for our authority and autonomy.

Finally, the contract approach reduces the professor–student relationship to one between a service provider and a customer. Two self-interested parties, students who seek a particular service (instruction) and a commodity (college credits, a degree), and professors who seek employment, enter into an agreement. The agreement assigns each certain rights and duties relative to the other. Appropriate behavior – including the appropriate regulation of the students' academic lives by the professors – is determined by the agreement. Some find this conception of the professor–student relationship attractive and urge us to think of our students as customers. We should, they suggest, focus on whether we are providing our student customers with a high-quality service and, in particular, one with which they are satisfied. Yet the professor–student relationship involves more than this. It involves, in particular, the professor's professional dedication to the end – students' education – beyond their self-interest and distinct from students' feelings of satisfaction. Just as the contract approach misses the important role that our expertise plays as a basis for our authority and autonomy, it ignores the important role of our commitment to our students' education.

So neither a simplistic appeal to our academic freedom nor the conception of the professor–student relationship as based on a mutual agreement provides adequate answers to our questions regarding the basis for and appropriate limitations on our authority to regulate students' academic lives. What, then, is the ultimate justification for both our power and the autonomy with which we exercise it? I now want to develop an answer to these questions. It is based in the assumption that university teaching is a profession in a very traditional sense similar to medicine and law. I present my answer in fairly broad terms but precisely enough to display how it represents an advance over the appeal to academic freedom and the contract approach. I then develop some features in more detail, laying out important implications of my approach.

The University Teaching Profession

The definite description, "The Professions," lacks a clear denotation. Does it cover all those activities at which someone may be properly described as being a professional? If so, the reference set has little apparent unity, for we use the adjective "professional" to modify a wide range of diverse activities. There are professional athletes and professional plumbers, professional pilots and professional race car drivers, professional dancers and professional fund raisers. For my purposes here, I shall adopt a more narrow perspective, conceiving of a profession in terms of four traditional traits. Each is exemplified by such paradigm professions as medicine and law.

The first trait is the possession of some expertise based in an advanced, highly specialized area of knowledge. Gaining entrance to the profession requires the certification of that knowledge; continuing in it carries the obligation to keep it current. Physicians have special expertise in treating and preventing human illness based in their knowledge of the science of medicine. Attorneys have special expertise in determining and promoting the legal interests of their clients based in their knowledge of the law.

The second trait of a profession is a commitment to use this defining expertise to promote an end beyond the professional's own self-interest. Physicians are expected to be dedicated to promoting the health of their patients. That is the goal to be served by their professional practice. Attorneys are expected to be dedicated to promoting the legal interests of their clients, and, as officers of the court, to promoting justice. That is the end to be served by their legal expertise. The relationship between professionals and those they serve is based on the former's commitment to use their expertise to meet the special needs of the latter. The combination of these first two characteristics – expert knowledge dedicated to a good beyond the professional's self-interest – is, in large measure, what makes professions so worthwhile. A good life is to be gained by dedicated service to an end greater than one's self-interest. It is also what earns professions a claim to special respect. Most important for our purposes, it is the basis for the next two characteristics traditionally associated with professions: authority and autonomy.

Professionals act with a great deal of authority within the practice of their profession. They have a right to have their professional judgments and prescriptions taken seriously by those they serve; they have a right to direct them in how to behave and how not to behave. They have a right of access to what would ordinarily be quite private areas of their lives. Physicians have authority over their patients with regard to all the areas related to their medical condition, from diet to exercise to general lifestyle. Patients may nullify the physician's authority by withdrawing from the relationship, but so long as they maintain it, they have a duty to follow the physician's prescriptions. So too, physicians have a right to private information about their patients that the patients would otherwise be under no obligation to share. The relation between attorneys and their clients is characterized by a similar investment of authority in the attorney.

The limits of a professional's authority are defined by two factors. One is the end to be served by the relationship. Physicians have a right to regulate their patients' lives only insofar as those regulations are intended to promote their health. They have no right to regulate aspects of their lives that are unrelated to that end. Physicians who prescribe unneeded tests and medications move beyond the limits of their authority. So too, they have a right to inquire into and gain knowledge about those aspects of a patient's otherwise private life that are relevant to the patient's medical care. They have no right to know other aspects of the patient's life, and the otherwise private information to which they properly have access must be kept confidential, except as required to serve the patients' medical well-being. The authority of attorneys over their clients is similarly limited by the goal of serving their clients' legal interests and justice.

The second factor limiting professionals' authority is the autonomy of those they serve. A physician's authority over patients begins and ends with the patients' freely entering into and departing from the relationship. So too for attorneys and their clients. Within the relationship, professionals have a duty not just to use their authority to promote the welfare of those they serve but to do so in a way that promotes their autonomy. Physicians have a duty to promote their patients' role as

609

fully informed participants in their own care. They must, for example, provide patients with reasons for medical decisions, obtain their informed consent, and avoid manipulating their decisions about their care. Attorneys have a duty to similarly involve their clients in the development of their case.

The fourth trait is the professional's autonomy. Professionals engage in their activity, regulating the lives of those they serve, with a great deal of independence. Professional associations play a primary role in setting the basic standards for appropriate professional conduct, determining sanctions for violations and determining the violations themselves. Within these standards, individuals are granted extensive latitude in their professional judgment. There are two bases for this autonomy. One is the fact that others are not appropriately situated to take on the regulator's role. Each profession is defined by a special expertise. Appropriate regulation requires that expertise; hence the need to turn to members of the profession itself. The regulation of particular cases requires both professional expertise and knowledge of the case; hence the presumption in favor of allowing individuals great latitude in determining their own conduct. Thus, we have the resistance of physicians to health maintenance organizations (HMOs) that attempt to intervene in the physician's judgments regarding appropriate treatment. The HMO representative is not, it is argued, appropriately knowledgeable of medicine and/or the particular case to limit the physician's professional practice. The other justification for the professional's autonomy is again the professional's basic dedication to the welfare of those to be served. That declared dedication warrants substantial trust.

Now, to what extent does university teaching possess the four characteristics just described? Certainly, university professors have certified expertise in an advanced area of knowledge. We are experts in particular subject areas and in teaching our subject to others at the different levels at which we offer courses. We are responsible for keeping our knowledge current.

We also have the second characteristic of being committed to using our special expertise to advance an end beyond our own self-interest. Professors and students are brought together by complementary needs, abilities, and commitments. The student brings to the relationship a self-acknowledged ignorance, combined, presumably, with a desire and an ability to learn and a commitment to follow the professor's lead in order to gain knowledge. Professors respond to the students' need with a commitment to guide them to the education they desire, given their continuing ability and desire.

The professor–student relationship is not a relationship between service providers and their customers. The acknowledged, ultimate goal of ordinary service providers is their own self-interest. They promote their own welfare in the form of profits by answering the perceived needs of their customers, having sometimes worked to create or enhance those felt needs in the first place, in whatever way will keep customers committed to their service. Insofar as they focus on the customers' good, they do so to promote their own self-interest. By contrast, the declared goal of professors is their students' education.

As already seen, the conjunction of the first two characteristics of professional practice, specialized knowledge in the service of others, is the basis for professionals' authority and autonomy. Professors' authority to regulate their students' lives is based on students freely consenting to a relationship in which our specialized knowledge is committed to advancing their education. We have a right to regulate those aspects of students' lives that are directly related to advancing our shared educational goal. Students have a duty to comply. Their obligation to accept our curricular and course requirements is comparable to patients' duty to follow their physician's prescriptions. Our authority and their duty stem not just from their consenting to our regulating their academic lives by accepting admission to the university and registering for our course, but from their freely entering into that relationship with the common understanding that our expertise would serve their educational interest.

The limits of our authority are determined by its defining goal and students' autonomy. We may, as professors, regulate only those aspects of students' lives that are directly relevant to achieving their education. We may require certain courses or programs of study. We may require certain texts or exercises within a particular course. We may not require sexual favors, assistance with our research projects, or help with our home chores. Our authority also begins and ends with students' freely entering into and departing from our relationship. Within our relationship with students, we have a duty to use our authority in a way that promotes their autonomy as fully informed participants in their own education. We must, for example, provide students with the reasons for our requirements and academic advice.

Our autonomy is similarly based on our expertise and commitment to students' education. Appropriate regulation of our teaching activity, determining what we require students to read, what assignments we demand that they complete, and so on, can only be done on the basis of an extensive knowledge of our subject matter. Those outside our fields do not have the requisite knowledge and so the regulation of our professional activity is quite appropriately turned over to us. The trust involved in the award of extensive autonomy is also supported by our commitment to use our knowledge to serve the students' educational well-being rather than our own self-interest or some other private agenda.

In all then, we have authority to regulate students' academic lives because we and our students have freely entered into a professional relationship in which we respond to their self-acknowledged ignorance and desire to learn with a commitment to use our knowledge to guide them to that goal. The limits of our authority are determined by the relationship's defining goal and the students' own autonomy. Our autonomy in exercising our authority is again based on our professional expertise and commitment to use it for our students' welfare.

One caveat is in order. Things are not, of course, quite so simple. Our professional relationship with our students exists within the university's overall educational enterprise. Students seek, and universities offer, not only education, but the institutional certification of that education in terms of grades, credit hours, and, ultimately, degrees. We thus take on additional roles in relation to students. We become public certifiers of student progress. We attest to our students and to the academic community the extent of their achievement. We may even take on the role of career advisors, counseling students on the relation between particular courses of study and various career objectives. We also teach our students as part of a collaborative effort with other faculty with whom we set curricular standards and degree requirements. In guiding our students to knowledge, we must focus on both our own view of what the students should know and the expectations of those colleagues who will inherit the task of guiding them to the next level of understanding and knowledge.

These additional elements add both various dimensions to our authority to regulate students' academic lives and restrictions on our autonomy. That our commitment is not just to guide students to knowledge but to certify their achievement adds additional justification to some of the ways we regulate their academic lives, such as requiring exams. That we pursue our commitment to our students' education within a cooperative venture further restricts our autonomy. We must design our course requirements to support the overall effort, within our department and college, to guide students to knowledge. In all, our professional relation with students is the core of our authority over their academic lives and our autonomy, but that core must be understood in the context of other cooperative relationships.

This account of our authority over students' academic lives, though still quite general, is clearly superior to a mere appeal to academic freedom, as it avoids begging the question. It also avoids the drawbacks of the contract approach. Recall that the contract approach assumes the existence of an at least implicit agreement or mutual understanding between professors and students on how and to what extent professors may regulate the students' academic lives. My proposal assumes no such common understanding. It begins instead with two much weaker assumptions: first, that professors have knowledge that students lack, know how to guide them to it, and are committed to doing so; second, that students freely enter into the professor–student relationship, aware of its declared goal to guide them to that knowledge. None of this is to assume that students have a clear set of expectations for their relationship with their professors or a developed sense of the ways and the extent to which professors may regulate their academic lives. It is not even to assume that students actually desire the education to which the professor–student relationship is devoted.

The contract approach also has the defect of encouraging us to think that the appropriate limits of our authority are simply determined by what students will accept. My proposal captures the fact that the limits are determined instead by what will actually promote the relationship's declared goal of advancing their education. We misuse our authority when we require students in an introductory course to study advanced topics beyond their ability. We do so, not because the students do not accept the requirement, but because the requirement does not advance the commitment from which our authority is derived, to advance the student's knowledge. My approach preserves an important relation between the students' consent and the limits of our authority, in the form of both their continuing consent to the relationship itself and our duty to promote their autonomy within the relationship.

The contract approach provides no explanation for our extensive autonomy in the exercise of our authority over students' academic lives. My approach does so. We can appreciate why some instructors may be granted less autonomy than others. Graduate teaching assistants with primary responsibility for their own course may be required to cover certain topics or use particular texts, where full professors face no such restrictions. The graduate teaching assistants do not yet have the expertise in the subject area and in how to teach it to justify more extensive autonomy in their teaching. Unlike the contract approach, my proposal thus relates our authority over students' academic lives and our autonomy in its exercise to our expertise.

Finally, my approach does not reduce the professor–student relationship to one between a service provider and a customer. It presents it as a relationship between professionals, in a traditional sense, and those whom they are committed to serve. The basic goals of the relationship determine what concerns are appropriate for students to adopt. They should be concerned with whether or not they are gaining the intended education, not with whether they are being entertained. The goal of the relationship also determines the appropriate standard for evaluating the professor's success. It is not a matter of customer satisfaction. It is a matter of student learning.

Implications and Extensions

My account of our authority over students' academic lives has some important implications. Our authority and autonomy are based on our ability and commitment to guide students to an education, and our ability depends on our knowing both our subject and how to teach it. Insofar as we lack the ability or the commitment, we lose our entitlement to regulate students' academic lives or at least our entitlement to do so with extensive autonomy. Some calls for increased faculty accountability, especially from those outside the university, are best appreciated in this context. As parents, legislators, business associations, and the like become skeptical about either our ability to teach well or our commitment to students' education, they quite reasonably question our authority to regulate our students' academic lives and the autonomy with which we exercise it. They propose ways of monitoring our ability and commitment through the educational success of our students, such as mandated assessment exams.

These challenges are not to be met by assertions of academic freedom, on the one hand, or by injunctions to treat students as customers to be satisfied, on the other. They are to be met head on by demonstrations of what is at question, our ability and commitment to our students' education. We can and should demonstrate our students' educational success. It is imperative that we retain control over how success is defined and measured, however. To cede control is in effect to ignore a basic premise of the authority and autonomy we seek to defend: that the authority to set educational standards properly resides with those with the requisite knowledge. To let others determine how our students are evaluated for the purposes of assessing our professional ability and commitment is to grant that we lack one or both at the start.

Developing my proposal further, we can also see some of its important implications for how we teach. Our authority is to regulate students' academic lives in support of their education. This education requires the attainment of knowledge, not just the acquistion of true beliefs (information). Students gain knowledge when they exercise their freedom to form true beliefs for which they have gained adequate justification. It is not enough that they form beliefs, even true ones. They must form true beliefs on the basis of adequate evidence. Evidence is gained through critical inquiry, including the examination of various competing positions. Our commitment is not, therefore, to get students to form a certain set of beliefs, their adoption of which can be appropriately measured on an assessment instrument to gauge success. Our commitment is to lead students through their own rational inquiry to the point where, as independent inquirers, they have arrived at true beliefs regarding the subject matter based on adequate evidence.

Students' education extends beyond their attainment of knowledge in a particular subject. It includes their development of good judgment, the ability to think and judge well and for themselves. References are often made today to the goal of developing students as "life-long learners." Properly understood, achieving this goal requires the development of basic intellectual skills, e.g. reading and thinking critically, the formation of such character traits as self-discipline and perseverance, and the adoption of values essential to learning, such as a commitment to the truth, objectivity, and the authority of rational argument. The goal is the students' development of their own intellectual autonomy, their ability to reason well and for themselves, and so the development of their two most distinctive traits as human beings: rationality and freedom.

We at worst misuse and at best waste our authority over students' academic lives when we design courses, requirements, and assignments that do not promote their education so conceived. Suppose we design our course with the goal of simply getting them to adopt certain beliefs or attitudes we would like them to have. I recently learned of one institution's plan for a course in "diversity," in which the course's success would be assessed by pre-and post-tests assessing changes in the students' attitudes. Assuming that the institution's goal is simply to change student's attitudes, what is the basis for the professor's exercise of power over the students in the course? It certainly is not the professional goal of advancing their education as autonomous and rational agents. Note that the problem here is not the course's subject matter, but its goal. The same issue is posed by science courses designed to get students to simply believe without understanding.

My position can also be extended to give us an important perspective on the issue of appropriate relations between professors and students beyond the academic realm. To what extent may professors enter into other sorts of relationships with students, e.g. friendships and romantic relationships? The answer is that such relationships are allowed only so long as they do not conflict with professors' ability to honor the commitments that define their primary professional relationship. I have argued elsewhere (Markie, 1990, 1994, chapter 4) that friendships and romantic relationships do not meet this standard.

Finally, and more speculatively, I suggest that my account of our authority over students' academic lives can be extended to help us at least partly understand the basis for other forms of regulation of students' lives. The life of a university student involves a good deal more than academics and his or her relationship with faculty, and when we think of the regulation of students' lives, we more often than not think of non-academic areas where faculty are notably, and sometimes intentionally, absent, e.g. life in the residence halls, and regulations are set by non-academic administrators and student life personnel. The principles that justify and define the appropriate range of regulation in these areas obviously include non-academic considerations, such as the need to maintain a safe community. Nonetheless, the goal of promoting students' education is also of central importance. The academic mission of a university is the ultimate justification for all its activities, including those of its office of student life, and how students' lives are structured outside of the classroom can promote or hinder their education. Here too, it is important that the appropriate conception of education be our guide. Just as our goal in the academic arena is not simply to get students to have certain beliefs, so too our goal here is not simply to get students to display "appropriate" behaviors manifesting "appropriate" attitudes. The educational goal is a community of autonomous rational agents who have learned good judgment. As David A. Hoekema has put it, "the aim of the college insofar as it continues to act in *loco parentis* should not be to induce moral behavior but rather *to foster moral maturity*" (Hoekema, 1990, p. 184). Here again, our authority is based on our commitment to students' enlightenment in the Kantian sense of the ability to use their intelligence to think for themselves.

Conclusion

Our relationship with our students is a power relationship in which most of the power, and a great deal of autonomy in its use, is ours. Like any such relationship, it requires justification. The justification does not stem from our academic freedom or simply from students' consent. It arises from a professional relationship defined by both the students' consent and our professional commitment to use our expertise to advance their education, to guide them from ignorance to knowledge, and, most importantly, to promote the development of their rational autonomy, their ability to think well and for themselves. If we would maintain our authority and our autonomy in its use, we must maintain our professional expertise and our commitment to use it in the service of this noble goal.

See also 36 THE ETHICS OF TEACHING; 39 ETHICS AND THE AIMS OF AMERICAN HIGHER EDUCATION; 40 UNIVERSITIES IN A FLUID AGE; 41 ACADEMIC FREEDOM

References

Hoekema, D. (1990) Beyond loco parentis? Parietal rules and moral maturity. In S. M. Cahn (ed.), *Morality, Responsibility and the University: Studies in Academic Ethics*. Philadelphia: Temple University Press, pp. 177–94.

Markie, P. J. (1990) Professors, students and friendships. In S. M. Cahn (ed.), *Morality, Responsibility and the University: Studies in Academic Ethics*. Philadelphia: Temple University Press, pp. 134–49.

Markie, P. J. (1994) *A Professor's Duties*. Lanham, MD: Rowman and Littlefield.

Future reading

Cahn, S. (1978) *Scholars Who Teach*. Chicago: Nelson-Hall.

Callahan, J. (1986) Academic paternalism. *International Journal of Applied Philosophy*, 3(1), 21–31.

Davis, M. (1999) *Ethics and the University*. London: Routledge.

Eble, K. (1983) *The Aims of College Teaching*. San Francisco: Jossey-Bass.

Hall, R. M. and Sandler, B. R. (1982) *The Classroom Climate: A Chilly One for Women?* Washington, DC: Association of American Colleges.

Hook, S. (1963) *Education for Modern Man*. New York: Alfred A. Knopf.

Shils, E. (1983) *The Academic Ethic*. Chicago: University of Chicago Press.

Strike, K. (1982) *Liberty and Learning*. New York: St Martin's Press.

45

The Role of Ethics in Professional Education

Norman E. Bowie

Why Ethics in the Professional Schools?

Courses in professional and business ethics are commonplace in professional schools and business schools. Philosophers hold endowed chairs in medical schools, business schools, and law schools in a number of important universities. Why would a professional school have ethics in its curriculum anyway? First, it should be noted that professions have codes of ethics; indeed, some of these codes such as the code of ethics of the American Bar Association are long detailed documents. A major part of ethics training in some professional schools is the teaching of the code.

Professions and the Public Good

A second answer might be found in the special purpose of the profession. A *profession* is defined not just by the expertise and specialized knowledge it requires, but by the public good it professes a commitment to promote. The quality of *professional judgment* is thus a function not only of technical expertise, but also of the extent to which that expertise is effectively brought to bear in promoting the public good. One of the tasks of teaching ethics in professional schools is consequently to assist professionals in determining what the phrase "practicing in the public good" means from the ethical point of view intrinsic to the profession.

For example, in the middle of the twentieth century, most professions had a ban on advertising; lawyers and doctors did not advertise on television, radio, or in the public press. Advertising was not considered professional. But critics of this practice pointed out that by keeping information out of the hands of the public, the cost of professional services was kept artificially high and out of the reach of some people. What passed as professional behavior, it was argued, was really greed in disguise. The courts finally struck down professional bans on advertising as a violation of free speech. In a similar vein, philosophers can serve as ethical critics of the professions by identifying practices that are ethically suspect or inconsistent with the public good upon which professionals stake their claim to the rewards of professional status.

The role of critic in the professional school is hard to play, however. On the one hand, a persistent critic is often considered a trouble maker and is usually marginalized or worse. The true gadfly just does not succeed in the professional school. On the other hand, there is always the danger that the teacher of professional ethics will err in the other direction. Far too often he or she will go along in order to get along. In that way the professional ethicist can be co-opted and become an apologist for the profession. The balance between being a critic and "selling out" is not easy to achieve, but is perhaps best captured by the notion of a *sympathetic critic*. The sympathetic critic understands the profession and the pressures and tensions the particular professional is under, so when criticism of the profession is necessary it is based on genuine knowledge and is only as harsh as the situation demands. For example, the critic of zealous client advocacy in law needs to understand the history of the practice and the arguments that can be made in favor of it. For example, in a famous murder case a lawyer knew that his client was guilty and he knew where the victim's body was. However, he did not inform the authorities or the parents of the young woman victim until after the trial was over. One could certainly criticize the attorney's conduct, but there were still many things that could be said in defense of it. An attorney is trained to protect his or her client, and indeed that is the expectation of a court when it must appoint an attorney. As a practical matter, whenever we seek legal advice, we expect our attorney to be our advocate. That must be kept in mind when we find an attorney acting on behalf of his or her client in ways that we may not approve.

Overcoming Information Asymmetry

Another consideration that bears on the value of teaching ethics in a professional school is the existence of information asymmetry in the profession. Information asymmetry occurs when the professional possesses specialized arcane knowledge that the client cannot obtain without significant difficulty. For example, doctors and lawyers have knowledge that clients need, but that clients cannot without great difficulty obtain for themselves. Managers possess asymmetrical information as well. The ethical problem arises with the separation of ownership and control. Managers have control and thus are tempted to make decisions in their own interests, rather than in the interests of the stockholders and thus *ipso facto* in the public interest. They can do this because of the existence of information asymmetry; since the stockholders cannot constantly monitor managers, the managers have information the stockholders do not have. Ethical issues arise concerning how that information may be used.

What prevents the professional from exploiting this information asymmetry? Nobel Prize winner in economics Kenneth Arrow has addressed this issue. If the profession is unable to convince the public that it will refrain from exploiting this information asymmetry, there will be a less than optimal use of professional services. The market in professional services will not be as large as it could be, and in that sense will not be optimally efficient, and thus not optimally conducive to the public good. Arrow's solution to the problem created by information asymmetry is ethics, and more specifically codes of ethics. By adopting a code of ethics – and possibly devoting

618

resources to instruction in the ramifications of that code – the profession indicates that its reputation is important and that it will not exploit information asymmetries. The need to overcome information asymmetry is a third reason to have ethics courses in professional schools, though one obviously related to the teaching of codes of ethics and the promotion of good judgment about what is consistent with the profession's commitment to serve the public interest. The concept of information asymmetry identifies a structural feature of professions that indicates the need for a counterweight to narrow self-interest, and the teaching of ethics might provide some of that counterweight.

This brings us, however, to the question of what one can reasonably expect to accomplish in teaching professional ethics.

What Are the Objectives of Professional Ethics Courses?

What should philosophers try to accomplish in these courses? What should the course objectives be? Some might argue that such courses should try to make professionals more moral or improve conduct within the professions. This attitude seems reflected in the groundswell of popular support for more ethics whenever there is a series of scandals. Even in universities, unethical behavior on the part of researchers elicits courses on research ethics. Many philosophers argue that improving professional conduct should not be the goal of these courses. They argue that the causes of professional misconduct are not well known and that a psychologist is in a better position to improve conduct than a philosopher is. This point is well taken, but I believe that improving professional conduct can be *a* goal or objective for professional ethics courses. Such courses can accomplish this goal in a number of ways.

First, philosophers can raise the sensitivity of students to ethical issues in the professions and business. Many students do not recognize the moral significance of things they do habitually in everyday life, let alone the ethical significance of choices they may have to make in contexts of professional practice they have never experienced. For instance, many students have never thought about the habit of eating meat as a moral issue, and by reading the work of Peter Singer on the treatment of animals their ethical sensitivity is raised. Similarly, research in business ethics has shown that many managers never see certain situations as ethically problematic, even when it seems obvious to those outside the business. This is often captured in the query, "What were they thinking?" Courses in professional ethics should raise the moral sensitivity of students to ethical issues within their chosen profession. To the extent that increased moral sensitivity results in more ethical behavior, philosophers can contribute to increased ethical behavior on the part of professionals.

Increased sensitivity works on the affective side, but philosophers can work on the cognitive side as well. The traditional philosophical skills – detailed analysis, the drawing of distinctions, careful argumentation rather than rhetoric, and the creation of counter-examples to claims and theories – are all useful in applied ethics, just as they are in other areas of philosophy. The use of these analytical skills is especially important in professional ethics because there are so many situations that appear to present moral dilemmas or genuinely ambiguous situations. Choosing well in these situations requires not only sensitivity to the ethically salient aspects of the situation, but also some sophistication in considering what principles apply to it. For instance, in medical ethics a principle that appears in many arguments and drives many decisions is the *doctrine of double effect*: roughly, that actions having both good and bad effects are permissible only if the bad effects are neither directly intended, nor directly the cause of the intended good effects, and the action is not wrong in itself. When and if that doctrine is appropriate is a question that calls for philosophical analysis, and training in such analysis can yield more carefully considered ethical decisions, thereby improving professional conduct.

The Application of Theory in Applied Ethics

Since one objective of professional ethics courses is the development of cognitive skills, one is led to wonder what the role is of traditional ethical theory, both metaethical theory and normative theory, in such courses. For the most part, the arcane disputes of contemporary metaethics are far removed from applied ethics, and of little interest to professionals. However, there are two metaethical issues that are of interest and immediate relevance. Professionals are usually concerned about what passes in philosophy as ethical relativism, although it sometimes has a particular twist in professional ethics. The concern in professional ethics centers on the question: is there some independent standard beyond the norms of the profession, practice, or culture that one can use to evaluate professional norms? Once the American Institute of Certified Public Accountants has made a ruling, is that the end of the matter or is their decision subject to a higher ethical norm? The other metaethical issue of interest is whether or not there are genuine moral dilemmas in professional ethics; that is, situations in which morality does not in principle have an answer. Traditional moral theorists are suspicious of dilemmas, but applied ethicists are usually more sympathetic and sometimes even teach professional ethics courses as a series of moral dilemmas.

Whether or not such dilemmas are genuine depends in part on how professional ethicists see the role of traditional normative ethical theory in applied ethics. Professional ethicists who are suspicious of genuine dilemmas and who think that standard theories such as utilitarianism or Kantianism can be applied directly to all issues in professional ethics will teach that way. But many in professional ethics think that such an approach is too simplistic. Between traditional normative theory and a specific issue is a set of intermediary concepts or principles, *bridge principles* as I shall call them, that take on even more importance than the "higher" theories. For example, in medical ethics *informed consent* is an important justificatory moral principle. Doctors are allowed to use certain invasive painful procedures on patients, and in certain cases are even allowed to withhold medical treatment and allow patients to die. What justifies that behavior? The fact that the patients gave informed consent. Another example from business ethics is found in the concept of a *fiduciary*. The nature of the fiduciary relationship justifies stricter obligations regarding conflicts of interest than apply to professionals in other roles. These concepts of informed consent and the fiduciary relationship are in turn justified by more abstract moral theories. The notion of informed consent can be justified both on utilitarian grounds and on the Kantian ground of respect for persons. But in professional ethics, much of the heavy lifting of justification is done by the bridge concepts themselves. The successful teaching of professional ethics requires that students learn the effective use of the profession's intermediary or bridge concepts, for the use of these bridge concepts is central to acquiring good professional judgment.

Another problem with the direct application of traditional normative theory is that it leads to simplistic answers to complex moral problems and as a result has the danger of turning students into ethical relativists of a kind. There are only a limited number of general ethical theories. If a student confronts an issue in business ethics that involves the treatment of the environment, the natural response is to open the ethical toolbox and apply utilitarianism. However, if the problem seems to be a lack of respect for human beings, as with death and dying examples from medical ethics, then the toolbox is opened and the Kantian respect for persons tool is used. But the direct application of these normative theories to problems in professional ethics is not very helpful. Consider the issue of welfare reform. Those who think state welfare programs make people dependent use the respect for persons principle to oppose them. Those who emphasize the importance of a list of primary goods as a condition for human action and independence use the respect for persons principle to defend guaranteed state welfare programs. Similarly, both the friends and the foes of affirmative action use the respect for persons principle to defend their respective positions. When students see that standard ethical theories can be used to defend either side of an argument, they adopt a kind of relativism. They conclude there is no right or wrong in ethical debate; that ethical debate is simply a matter of using one of the traditional normative principles to defend one's position, knowing full well that one's opponent can use the same principle.

Students need to know that issues in professional ethics are extraordinarily complex, and that ethical analysis usually requires a sorting out of empirical issues, conceptual issues, and the application of several normative concepts and principles. Should a physician participate in a patient's assisted suicide? Would such an action be wrong? To answer that question one needs to know the law in the jurisdiction in which the action would take place, and one would need to know what the various physicians' codes of ethics say about physician-assisted suicide. The principle of informed consent that is in turn justified by the respect for persons principle comes into play. So does the principle that one should relieve unnecessary pain and suffering. An empirical issue is whether it is reasonable to believe that morally permitting physician-assisted suicide will inevitably lead to euthanasia and wholesale violations of consent. A conceptual issue involves what is to count as informed consent. Is a person who is heavily medicated and in extreme pain and in a state of depression because of this terminal illness really capable of informed consent? And what about empirical evidence from those who wanted to die, but later in a clearer moment said that they were glad that physician-assisted suicide was considered immoral? How relevant is that evidence? Thus, whether or not a physician is morally permitted to assist in a suicide is a very complex issue. Simply applying utilitarianism or a principle of respect for persons would not help. And most issues in professional ethics are like that.

However, in pointing out the complexity of the situation, I do not wish to argue that there is not a correct answer, nor do I wish to contend that physician-assisted suicide presents us with a genuine moral dilemma. It may well be that when all things are considered, there would be something like a consensus among medical ethicists as to what is right, or more likely some consensus about when and under what conditions physician-assisted suicide might be right or even possibly morally required. Even in the absence of such consensus, one could expect agreement that *some* proposed "answers" are wrong. For example, an "answer" that ignored (did not take into account at all) the wishes of the patient would be wrong.

Thus the teaching of professional ethics requires more than knowledge of traditional ethical theory. It requires knowledge of the ethical norms of the profession, knowledge of the intermediary ethical concepts that guide ethical decision-making in that profession, and knowledge of the empirical and conceptual background to ethical decisions in a professional context.

The Professional Role

Another objective of professional ethics is to teach the student the special *role morality* that goes with the particular profession. There are special duties and obligations that attend the roles one has in life, and one cannot lead a complete ethical life unless one knows the special duties and obligations that are attached to these roles. There are special duties and obligations that are attached to being a friend, a spouse, and a parent, and there are duties and obligations that are attached to one's job and especially to the jobs that are classified as a profession.

This social fact is recognized in law in the United States. With respect to any job in which one acts on behalf of another (is an agent for another), one's conduct is governed by the law of agency, which stipulates that employees have duties of obedience, loyalty, and confidentiality to their employers. The duty of obedience requires that the agent obey all reasonable directions of the principal. The duty of loyalty requires that the employee act as a trustee toward his principal. And the duty of confidentiality, as the term implies, requires that the employee keep confidential any information that would interfere with the business of the principal. Thus, any American who works for another has these general duties that go with his or her role of employee. And although these duties are legal duties, most people would accept them as moral duties as well.

Those occupations commonly known as professions have additional role-related duties, as can be seen in the Hippocratic oath that physicians swear to honor, or in the codes of ethics found in law. That is why many persons who teach applied ethics argue that a philosopher ethicist must know something about the profession or practice to which she applies ethical theory. A legal ethicist must know a considerable amount about how lawyers work. A medical ethicist must know a great deal about the practice of medicine, and a business ethicist about the practice of business. Although a philosopher need not get a JD, MD, or MBA, she must be able to speak the language and converse with practitioners in her chosen field. As each of the applied fields has grown, applied ethicists have usually had to specialize in the ethics of only one profession.

The Problem of Dirty Hands

The existence of role morality has created an issue that cuts across many of the professions, and is known as the *problem of dirty hands*. Simply put, the issue is this: does the existence of a professional role permit professionals to do things that are not ordinarily morally permitted? An affirmative answer to that question raises the issue of dirty hands. The two most common examples are the so-called dirty hands problem in government or political ethics and the norm of the legal profession discussed above, that the attorney should be a zealous advocate for her client. The first arises when politicians violate the law, lie, or even permit or commit murder to protect national security. Can the police torture a suspected terrorist to save the lives of countless citizens? It should be noted that most professionals think that the professional rules that give professionals special moral license to do things that are ordinarily morally abhorrent are justified, but are the professionals right about this? Consider again the zealous advocacy rule in American law. Many have argued that the US adversary system, which requires zealous advocacy, allows many criminals to go free, and it is true that most other legal systems are far less adversarial than that of the USA and the advocacy of the defense team in those countries is far from zealous. Maybe it would be better (morally better) if the USA adopted a less adversarial system. But defenders of the current system argue that a less adversarial system would allow the state to imprison many who are not guilty, and that such a system might contribute to a more autocratic or even totalitarian state. Thus it is hard to know what ground rules for legal advocacy would be best, even if one has settled on a particular moral framework for evaluating institutions. The issue of when, if ever, professionals are morally permitted to do something that would be considered wrong if done by a non-professional remains a topic for research and discussion in professional ethics.

Techniques for Teaching Professional Ethics

Case studies

In traditional ethics courses, cases serve as counter-examples against which a theory is tested. Perhaps one of the most famous examples of a case that serves that function is the punishment of the innocent case that counted so forcefully against the theory of act utilitarianism. In professional and applied ethics, cases sometimes are used to test theory. However, the use of the case method in this context is much more complex, and the use of cases to test theory is a very small part of the pedagogy of case method teaching.

In professional and applied ethics, the cases are usually considered the basis from which the principles are derived. We get the principles from the cases rather than the other way around. In the law, one of the points of the use of cases is to extract legal principles from the case at hand. Although most ethicists have accepted the fact that cases provide an inductive grounding for principles, some have argued that the contribution of the case method is more than an inductive way to get to the principles. For example, Tom Beauchamp has argued that the extraction of principles from cases is not the function of the case method, but that its function "is to develop the capacity to grasp problems and find novel solutions" (Beauchamp and Bowie, 2001). This is a more particularist understanding of the case method. Kenneth Goodpaster (2002) has argued that the case method provides an opportunity for moral insight, and Patricia Werhane (1999) sees cases as opportunities to exercise moral imagination.

An advantage of the case method is that it engages students in the decision-making process. It is a kind of learning by doing. One might be tempted to think that the case method amounts to nothing more than a good bull session in which everyone gives his or her opinion but there is no objective reasoning or decision. But skilled case method teachers report that there is often a surprising amount of unanimity in reaching a decision, and even when unanimity is lacking certain views are seen as possible acceptable alternatives, while other proposed solutions are ruled out. What is significant pedagogically is that students become active participants in learning of a kind that encourages them to think like professionals, guided by professional aims, norms, and clear thinking. Case scenarios call upon them to put themselves in the shoes of professionals who must make ethically appropriate decisions, and thereby stimulate the development of a professional self-concept as well as the ethical imagination essential to anticipating consequences and sorting through alternatives.

Skilled case method teachers differ on the exact matrix for conducting a case discussion. However, nearly all case teachers would agree that a good case analysis must include: (1) a determination of the relevant facts of the case; (2) a determination of the relevant ethical issues; (3) a reciting of how the classical ethical theories bear on the issue; (4) a proposal for alternative courses of action that might provide ethically and professionally appropriate answers; and (5) an actual decision that can be defended on professional and ethical grounds.

Casuistry

Use of the case method can often be linked with a pedagogical commitment to casuistry. Casuistry has had a bad reputation and is often looked upon with suspicion in traditional ethics courses, but casuistry is far more accepted in professional and applied ethics. Perhaps that is because casuistry may be an acceptable method for dealing with the moral dilemmas that allegedly abound in professional ethics. Casuists do not believe that you can simply apply ethical theories to complex cases. To arrive at acceptable ethical solutions, casuists believe that you must pay detailed attention to the circumstances surrounding a case – a position that casuists hold in common with many feminists and communitarians. Casuistic thinking proceeds by analogy. A decision is made in one case and future cases are then tested to see how dissimilar or how similar they are to previously settled cases. If there is a close fit, then the decision in the previous case is accepted in the current case. Certainly some reasoning in professional ethics is casuistic, but not all is. Whether casuistry represents a superior form of ethical reasoning in professional ethics is a contentious and still unresolved issue. However, the value of casuistry is that it encourages special attention to the circumstances of a case and enhances one's ability to see the relevant similarities and differences among cases.

Socratic method

The Socratic method is the most appropriate technique to use with the case method. The Socratic method starts by asking questions with the aim of pointing out the inadequacies of early answers. As answers are rejected, the intention is to improve upon the answers until one gets closer and closer to a correct answer. Of course, one may never reach the correct answer, but hopefully one moves in the right direction. When the Socratic method is combined with the case method, a professional learns that certain answers are not ethically or professionally viable and that there is a limited range of "solutions" from which one must choose. In that way, ethical decision-making in the profession gradually improves.

Evolving Educational Strategies

One of the more controversial areas as we look to the future involves the integration of professional ethics across the professional curriculum. The dilemma is sometimes put as follows: should there be one course in medical ethics or business ethics or should ethical issues be raised in the context of discussion in all the regular courses? Ideally there should be a basic course and ethics issues should also be raised in the regular courses. A possible model might be mathematics in the economics curriculum. There is a separate course in calculus and calculus is also used in most of the economics courses. The danger of the single course is that ethics is likely to be perceived as owned by an individual in the professional school, rather than owned by the school itself – a perception that defeats interdisciplinary collaboration. The danger of not having a single course is that the ethics issues really do not get raised, or get raised in a perfunctory manner without any coherent reference points. Avoiding both these problems is why I favor both a single course and integration into the basic curriculum.

Such curricular integration demands interdisciplinary cooperation, and in this and other ways philosophers teaching ethics in professional schools must adapt to changing demands. The days when students passively sat at desks in classrooms taking down the truth from the professor are over. In the information age, the acquisition of knowledge is active and reactive. Our students are sophisticated users of the Internet, and they participate both in class and often outside of class via list servers. Those engaged in professional ethics have been forced to give up chalk and the blackboard for *Powerpoint* presentations, and they require a high level of competence if not mastery of the new technology. Philosophers are notoriously individualistic, but teamwork has become a focal point of professional education and we need to develop team projects that capture the synergies of group work. Professional education is interdisciplinary, given the array of empirical, conceptual, and ethical principles that apply, and philosophers engaged in professional education must keep abreast of the variety of developments that are relevant to the profession. The challenges here are different from those faced by philosophers teaching traditional ethics courses in philosophy departments, but the acceptance of these challenges by

625

many philosophers exemplifies the re-engagement with public life that has characterized so much of the field of philosophy in recent years.

See also 22 MORAL EDUCATION; 39 ETHICS AND THE AIMS OF AMERICAN HIGHER EDUCATION; 40 UNIVERSITIES IN A FLUID AGE

References

Beauchamp, T. L. and Bowie, N. E. (2001) *Ethical Theory and Business*, 6th edn. Saddle River, NJ: Prentice Hall.
Goodpaster, K. E. (2002) Teaching and learning ethics by the case method. In N. E. Bowie (ed.), *Guide to Business Ethics*. Malden, MA: Blackwell, pp. 117–41.
Werhane, P. (1999) *Moral Imagination and Management Decision Making*. New York: Oxford University Press.

Further reading

Applbaum, A. I. (1999) *Ethics for Adversaries*. Princeton, NJ: Princeton University Press.
Goldman, A. H. (1980) *The Moral Foundations of Professional Ethics*. Totowa, NJ: Rowman and Littlefield.
Jamal, K. and Bowie, N. E. (1995) Theoretical considerations for a professional code of ethics. *Journal of Business Ethics*, 14(9), 703–14.
Jonsen, A. R. and Toulmin, S. (1988) *The Abuse of Casuistry*. Berkeley and Los Angeles: University of California Press.
Luban, D. (1988) *Lawyers and Justice*. Princeton, NJ: Princeton University Press.
Walzer, M. (1973) Political action, the problem of dirty hands. *Philosophy and Public Affairs*, 2(2), 160–80.

Index